Henry Friendly, Greatest Judge of His Era

HENRY FRIENDLY

Greatest Judge of His Era

DAVID M. DORSEN

Foreword by
Judge Richard A. Posner

THE BELKNAP PRESS OF
HARVARD UNIVERSITY PRESS
Cambridge, Massachusetts
London, England
2012

Library of Congress Cataloging-in-Publication Data

Dorsen, David M., 1935–
Henry Friendly, greatest judge of his era / David M. Dorsen ;
foreword by Richard A. Posner.
p. cm.
Includes bibliographical references and index.
ISBN 978-0-674-06439-3
1. Friendly, Henry J.   2. Judges—United States—Biography.   I. Title.
KF8745.F75D67 2012
347.73'14092—dc23
[B]
2011031919

For Kenna

and

the Judges of the U.S. Courts of Appeals

Contents

Foreword by Judge Richard A. Posner   ix

Introduction   1

1   Early Years   5

2   Private Practice   34

3   Nomination and Confirmation   71

4   Getting Started   78

5   Judge Friendly   85

6   Law Clerks   103

7   Judges and Justices   114

8   Away from the Courthouse   127

9   First Amendment   139

10   Fifth Amendment   164

11   Other Bill of Rights Amendments   181

12   Other Constitutional Provisions   194

13   Habeas Corpus   210

14   Nonconstitutional Criminal Procedure   221

15   Specific Crimes   236

16   Business Law   249

17   Intellectual Property   272

18 Management and Labor   279

19 Railroad Reorganization   285

20 Administrative Law   294

21 Common Law and Federal Common Law   302

22 Federal Court Jurisdiction   318

23 Other Procedural Issues   326

24 At the End   339

25 Friendly's Legacy   346

Appendix A: Friendly's Clerks   361
Appendix B: Friendly's Published Nonjudicial Writings   367
Notes   371
Acknowledgments   487
Index   491

Foreword

Judge Richard A. Posner

I AM ON RECORD as having expressed skepticism about judicial biographies. In an article published some years ago I listed a variety of obstacles to successful judicial biography—such as that only lawyers and law professors were likely to be able or inclined to write judicial biographies but that nothing in their training equipped them to be biographers, that most judges live outwardly dull lives, that judges tend to be secretive about their work, and above all that as with other "intellectual workers" the connection between judges' accomplishments, on the one hand, and their upbringing, personal characteristics, psychology, and experiences—the natural focus of a biography—on the other hand, were difficult to tease out.[1] "Whenever a writer, artist, musician, any mode of imagination is made the subject of a biography, his light may be extinguished. . . . Life is simply a shell, the kernel of which is creative work. There is no real nourishment in biography. The words fly up, the lives remain below."[2] One wouldn't, in short, learn much of interest about a judge from a biography of him, I thought, and I therefore suggested "alternative genres" to judicial biography, such as the critical study, instancing—self-servingly—my little book on Cardozo.[3]

I was not entirely negative. I mentioned several fine judicial biographies; others have been published since I wrote my article. But I questioned the value of the genre, and had I been asked whether Henry Friendly was a promising subject for a biography, I would have said no. He had not had an exciting early life, like Oliver Wendell Holmes or Byron White; he was not a "character," like Learned Hand, or an enigma, like Cardozo; he had not been involved in great political events, like Brandeis, Frankfurter, and Robert Jackson. He had practiced law in New York (mainly administrative law, his principal client being Pan American World Airways, now defunct) for thirty-one years after clerking for Brandeis; had been appointed to the Second Circuit in 1959; had served there for nearly twenty-seven years with great distinction while also writing highly influential law review articles (some collected into books); had died, aged eighty-two; and that was it. A quarter of a century after his death, his judicial and scholarly work continued to command attention, but was receiving it—his favorite law clerk, himself a scholarly federal court of appeals judge, Michael Boudin, had embarked on a series of lectures on Friendly's achievements.[4] I would, in short, have thought a biography of Friendly an unpromising venture.

Was I wrong! For David Dorsen's biography is immensely illuminating. In addition to the impressive narrative and analytical skills that he has brought to the project, he has by dint of energy and application overcome the problem of delay that has plagued judicial biography and, a related point, has been able to exploit the unprecedented amount of material available to him about Friendly. Timing is critical. Inordinate delay in completion has been a grave problem for judicial biography. Holmes's scholarly biographer, Mark DeWolfe Howe, took so long that he died in medias res. (His successor, Grant Gilmore, abandoned the project because he hated Holmes.) The biographies of Hand and Cardozo took decades to complete, and by the time they were published everyone who had known those judges and so might have offered corrections of or supplements to the biographies was dead. A biography of Robert Jackson, who died more than a half century ago, was abandoned by successive designated biographers. William Brennan's biographer developed writer's block, which caused a twenty-five-year delay in the publication of the Brennan biography. It's as if the genre of judicial biography were under a malediction.

Which is not to say that a judge's biography should be begun the day he dies or while he lives, for if it is begun too soon, the biographer will lack perspective. Dorsen began his biography when Friendly had been dead for twenty years, and completed it in six. He interviewed every one of Friendly's fifty-one law clerks (all but one in person rather than by phone), along with Friendly's favorite secretary. He interviewed many of the lawyers who appeared before Friendly, and the judges, still living, who knew him. Friendly's elder daughter, a psychologist, talked at length to Dorsen about her father, with candor and insight, as did other close relatives. Dorsen had access to all of Friendly's case files—an enormous trove, which Friendly had donated to Harvard—and to Friendly's very extensive correspondence, and to two extensive oral histories. And Dorsen did what few judicial biographers have had the patience to do, and that was to read extensively in the briefs, and the tapes or transcripts of oral argument, in Friendly's cases, and read newspaper commentary on the cases—even to interview a number of the litigants.

But the assemblage of these materials of unprecedented richness was only the beginning of Dorsen's task. The materials had to be sifted and organized and analyzed; a narrative framework imposed; description of the life and of the work balanced; the relationship of background, family personality, education, and experience to Friendly's judicial and extrajudicial work explored; and the work itself characterized and evaluated. Dorsen had to explain what made Judge Friendly tick and in what lay the distinctiveness and distinction of Friendly's career.

He has done all that, and as a result we learn more about the American judiciary at its best than we can learn from any other biography—not only more, but an immense amount. I got to know Friendly quite well in the four and a half years during which our judicial careers (mine starting, his ending) overlapped. I not only find nothing in Dorsen's description and assessment of Friendly with which I disagree; I have learned much about Friendly that I did not know. Some of what I've learned has already induced me to make certain changes in my judicial practice; it will, I predict, have a similar effect on other judges; and by revealing what the best federal appellate judge of the past half century was really like as a judge it will help lawyers to understand judges, and thereby serve their clients, better.

I don't want to give the story of Henry Friendly away, in all its rich detail. But I do want to offer a few reflections that might otherwise escape the notice of some readers. A minor one perhaps is the remarkable ability of people, or at least of remarkable people, to rise above physical and mental ill health. Friendly suffered throughout his life from serious eye problems, yet he must have spent almost all his waking hours reading or writing (by hand). In addition, he suffered from depression—not quite "clinical depression," because he was missing some of the symptoms (notably, difficulty concentrating!), but serious enough that today someone as afflicted as he was would probably seek treatment. Yet neither the eye problems nor the depression slowed him down. He was immensely hard working and productive, and one cannot imagine his having worked harder or faster than he did had he been in tip-top health, except that the combination of vision problems and depression did shorten his life. He killed himself at a time when his mental acuity was unimpaired but his eyesight was going, and his spirit had been crushed by the death the previous year of his wife, whose high spirits had helped keep his depression in check. Because of depression he seems not to have obtained much pleasure from most of his work either as a practicing lawyer or as a judge, and while he knew that he was an outstanding judge he took only limited comfort from that realization because he considered judging a mere craft rather than an art or a science.

Another reflection that occurs to me, one supported by virtually every candid biography, is that people are not of a piece, or at least high achievers are not, or not often. There were five quite different Henry Friendlys: Friendly *en famille*—cold, taciturn, remote, and awkward; Friendly among his peers, mentors, clients, colleagues—tactful, personable, friendly, effective; Friendly in his dealings with his law clerks and with many of the lawyers who appeared before him—curt, grumpy, intimidating; Friendly in his judicial opinions and academic writings—formal, erudite, almost Teutonic; and finally Friendly in his correspondence—graceful, warm, generous, light— Bizet to the Wagner of his judicial opinions.

And something that may surprise some readers of the biography: brilliant people sometimes have great difficulty making productive use of other people. I am not speaking of delegation; there is too much of that among modern judges. It would have been a great waste of Friendly's time to have worked from opinion drafts of his law clerks, as most judges do nowadays, rather than writing his opinions himself, from scratch, as he did. But his clerks were very bright and energetic and could have helped more with research and even with critique of his drafts than they were allowed to do. He wasn't immodest, and he welcomed the occasional challenge from a clerk. But he didn't create an atmosphere conducive to eliciting criticisms and suggestions, or establish work protocols that would have maximized the clerks' contribution to his judicial decisions. He was so quick, so knowledgeable (having a photographic memory helped), and so experienced that he must have thought he could do everything himself faster and better than a law clerk could do anything—which may have been very close to the truth. The rapidity with which he wrote long opinions in near-final form astonished the clerks; it astonishes me.

Timing, I said, is important to biography; it is also important to a career. Friendly would have been a great judge in any era, but his contribution to the law would have been less in quieter times. His service as a judge coincided with a turbulent period in the history of the federal judiciary. The hammer blows of the Warren Court reached their crescendo in his first decade on the Second Circuit and were followed by the fractious and erratic jurisprudence of the Burger Court, all against a background of soaring caseloads in the lower federal courts. Friendly's opinions and academic writings, in field after field, proposed revisions and clarifications of doctrine that time after time the Supreme Court gratefully adopted.

My final reflection is, to me at least (I'm a judge, after all), the most important, because it concerns Friendly's essential qualities as a judge, which I think tend to be misunderstood—though not by Dorsen. Friendly was only sixteen when he entered Harvard College, and his academic performance as an undergraduate and then as a law student was sensational—probably the best in Harvard Law School's history. (Brandeis had had higher grades, but the grading system had later been reset to a lower level.) Friendly's photographic memory combined with his analytical power, energy, speed, and work ethic to make him the most powerful legal reasoner in American legal history. And so one might suppose that he was a formalist judge par excellence, deploying text and precedent to produce decisions that satisfied the legal profession's longing for formal correctness and objective validity. But that was not the kind of judge he was. He tempered academic brilliance with massive common sense. He was less mercurial, more matter-of-fact, than any of the other great judges. (The contrast in this respect between him and Learned Hand is particularly marked.) He saw cases not as intellectual puzzles to be solved but as practical disputes to be resolved sensibly and humanely. He bent his powerful legal intelligence to the service of shaping legal doctrine to the enablement of sensible results in individual cases. The aim was to improve the law—American law is in constant need of improvement, in fact is a mess to a degree that only insiders can appreciate—without unduly perturbing the doctrinal and institutional framework that provides necessary stability and continuity. Like all creative judges, Friendly did not feel himself bound by the issues as framed by the lawyers, and at times, we learn from this book, was surprisingly casual about waived or forfeited arguments. He didn't just decide interesting cases; he made interesting cases. He thus was something of a judicial buccaneer—a role not to be recommended, however, to the average judge. There are leaders and followers in adjudication as in other activities, and it is of a consummate leader that David Dorsen has produced a consummate biography.

Introduction

H ENRY FRIENDLY SUCCEEDED brilliantly at just about everything he did (athletics being an exception). Born in 1903 in Elmira, New York, he was the only child of a comfortably-off German-Jewish family. He went to public schools there before attending Harvard College and Law School; he graduated summa cum laude from both schools and was president of the *Harvard Law Review*. He had the highest numerical average at the law school since Louis Brandeis, Class of 1887.[1] He clerked for Brandeis in 1927–1928 and, turning down several offers to teach at Harvard Law School, became an associate, then a partner, at a Wall Street firm that is now Dewey & LeBoeuf (before 2007 it was Dewey Ballantine). In 1930 he married Sophie Pfaelzer Stern, the daughter of an esteemed Pennsylvania jurist and a prominent member of Philadelphia society. Their three children, one boy and two girls, all married and had children. In 1946 he helped form Cleary, Gottlieb, Friendly & Cox and also served as vice president and general counsel of Pan American Airways. He was appointed to the U.S. Court of Appeals for the Second Circuit in 1959. Under his patina of ordinariness was a complex person with an active inner life, not to mention a remarkable list of successes. In 1985 his wife succumbed to cancer; a year later, distraught over her death and burdened by concerns over his own health, he took his life.

Trials are mostly about facts, circumscribed to some extent by legal constraints, especially defining what a plaintiff must prove to prevail and what evidence he may properly present to the trier of fact to prove his case. By the time a case reaches the U.S. Supreme Court, which only a minuscule percentage do, all the facts are drained from it and the issues are almost abstract questions of constitutional or statutory law. In between in the federal system are the U.S. courts of appeals for twelve geographically defined circuits and one specialized court, to which a losing party can appeal as of right and present any issues he claims should require reversal. Those proceedings examine rulings made at trial (or earlier) to determine whether they were sufficiently in accord with the law to warrant affirmance of the result below or, alternatively, were so flawed as to require outright reversal or a new trial. Matters of fact are not reviewed except to place the legal issues in context or, on occasion, to determine whether the trier of fact resolved them so clearly erroneously as to constitute legal error. As a result, an argument in a court of appeals may bear little resemblance to the dominant concerns and disputes at the trial.

Since circuit judges almost always sit on panels of three and are subject to Supreme Court review, their power is fragmented and, in most areas of the law, greatly circumscribed by precedent. The role of a judge on the courts of appeals, unlike that of federal trial judges and Supreme Court Justices, is neither well understood nor appreciated, even though in the overwhelming run of cases they have what is tantamount to the last word. Compared to Supreme Court Justices, the job of circuit judges is unglamorous, though in many respects more difficult. Their caseloads are heavier, and they have to deal with every issue the parties raise on appeal. They decide cases on a far vaster range of subjects. Moreover, the help they receive from the parties' lawyers is frequently minimal compared to the far more thorough and careful product provided to the Justices. The discussion that follows demonstrates the extent to which Friendly and other circuit judges were required to supply, or at least considerably amplify and refine, the parties' arguments.

One scholar has noted, "The general public is, I suspect, unlikely to care very much about a court's reasoning process . . . ; the public concern is with results."[2] Because there are thirteen courts of appeals and the subject matter of the cases they hear tends to be mundane, the decisions of circuit judges are rarely evident to the public. Consequently, *how* Friendly decided cases may be more informative than *what* he decided. The influence of a circuit judge on the development of federal law depends largely on whether other federal judges view his work as worth emulating. On that criterion, as well as others, Friendly demands attention. He was productive, writing 1,056 published opinions (890 for the court, 88 dissents, 74 concurring, and 4 in the district court, not inclusive of *per curiam* opinions of which he was the author). This book portrays the life and work of an exceptional federal judge sitting on an important appellate court, the federal court that hears appeals from judgments of the U.S. district courts in New York, Connecticut, and Vermont.

Unusually, Friendly wrote virtually all his own opinions, and he did so almost always in a day or less. (Critics have had more time to analyze them.) He not only wrote opinions; he gave lectures and authored dozens of articles and shorter pieces printed in law reviews. Larry Kramer, a former law clerk and later the dean of Stanford Law School, describes as "amazing" Friendly's ability, after years of private practice, when he wrote little, to compose seminal articles in a number of fields.[3] A list of Friendly's law clerks appears in Appendix A, and a list of his nonjudicial writings is in Appendix B. Between his opinions and articles there was hardly an area of the law he did not influence.

I have organized Friendly's life through his years in private practice chronologically, and I have organized most of my discussion of his judicial years by subject matter to facilitate an understanding of his talents in the context in which they showed themselves. In researching his pre-judicial years I have benefited from six oral histories he provided, all of which centered on that period. As far as I can tell, no portion of four of the oral histories has ever been published, and the other two have been cited only in law review articles and then in a limited fashion. I also have been the grateful recipient of many lengthy interviews by Friendly's two daughters, Joan Friendly Goodman and Ellen Friendly Simon; his daughter-in-law, Irene Baer Friendly; and his son-in-law, Frank Goodman. I have also spoken to other members of his family.

For my discussion of Friendly's judicial years, I have examined all his judicial opinions and the dozens of extrajudicial writings, listed in Appendix B. Made available to me by the Second Circuit and the Special and Historical Collections Division of the Harvard Law School Library were his private papers, consisting of thousands of internal court memoranda and pieces of correspondence. With the help of the U.S. Archives and the Association of the Bar of the City of New York, I was able to review the parties' briefs filed in ninety-five cases in which Friendly wrote an opinion, and I listened to recordings of oral arguments (although many important ones are missing). I conducted more than 250 interviews, including those of fellow circuit judges, district judges whose work he reviewed, Supreme Court Justices, former colleagues from private practice, friends and acquaintances of his, all fifty-one of his law clerks (fifty in in-person interviews), three of his secretaries, knowledgeable academics, lawyers who appeared before him, and five parties in the cases in which he wrote opinions.

I met Judge Friendly before he was a judge. His daughter Joan, now ombudsman and professor of education at the University of Pennsylvania, was at Radcliffe when I was at Harvard College (both Class of '56), and she introduced me to her father. I saw him on a couple of social occasions. Joan married Professor Frank Goodman of the Pennsylvania Law School, a classmate of mine at Harvard Law School and a friend. Later, as an Assistant U.S. Attorney in the Southern District of New York (1964–1969), working in the same building as the U.S. Court of Appeals for the Second Circuit, I greeted the judge from time to time in the halls, argued several cases before him, and sat at counsel table several times while my colleagues argued before him. He was awesome on the bench and had a towering reputation, but at that time I knew only a small fraction of his accomplishments.

This biography is neither authorized nor underwritten by anyone, and I neither sought nor received exclusive rights to any material. Only after I had decided to write the book did I contact the Friendly family. I had seen Joan and Frank Goodman only a few times since 1959, and I had never met other members of the judge's family. Friendly's two surviving children, along with Frank Goodman and Irene Friendly, the widow of his son, David, offered information, discussion, disagreements, and arguments, all of which materially improved my book. I also interviewed Stephen Simon, the divorced spouse of Ellen Simon, and talked to ten of Friendly's eleven grandchildren. The children and their spouses wanted the work to portray Judge Friendly as faithfully as possible, and I have tried to do just that as my compliment to and respect for a remarkable judge.

CHAPTER ONE

Early Years

H ENRY JACOB FRIENDLY'S ancestors were dairy farmers in Wittel-shofen, Bavaria, in southern Germany, who, when Bavaria passed a law in the eighteenth century that required everyone to take a last name, adopted the name Freundlich (which translates to "Friendly"). While the extent of their religious devotion is unknown, the first Freundlichs in the nineteenth century had two seats at the local synagogue: one male seat and one female.[1] Friendly's great-grandfather, Josef Myer Freundlich, was born in 1803, married Lena Rosenfeld, also of Bavaria, in 1829, and died in 1880. According to a contemporary account, their estate burned down in 1831, apparently as the result of an accident. When their neighbors did nothing to extinguish the fire, because, the Freundlichs believed, they were Jewish, the couple sold their home and moved to the center of the village. Nevertheless, Josef remained a farmer and livestock dealer and prospered.

In 1852, to avoid serving in the German army, Josef's son Heinrich, Friendly's grandfather, and his brothers emigrated to the United States, changing their name to Friendly. A naturalized Henry Friendly (who changed his name from Heinrich) married Lena Hesslein, also from Bavaria, in New York City in 1860, and moved to the town of Cuba in upstate New York, where his parents joined him a decade later. Starting as a peddler, he soon owned a dry-goods store and then a carriage factory.[2] He had two sons, the first of whom, Myer Henry, the father of the future judge, was born in Cuba in 1862.[3] To work for his uncle Samson Friendly in the manufacturing and jobbing of shoes, Myer moved to Elmira, New York, at the age of eighteen.

At the turn of the century Elmira was a town of about forty thousand, as it is today. It was passionately Republican, from which there was no dissent within the Myer Friendly household. The family lived on the west side of town, which was primarily inhabited by Christians. The Jewish population, living mostly on the east side, was about four thousand. The German-Jewish community, of which the Friendly family was a prominent part, was quite small, with about a dozen families and few children. Grandfather Henry became active in civic affairs, serving as commissioner of parks and Jewish affairs and becoming president of a liberal temple, the Congregation B'nai Israel. A monograph on the first Jewish settlers in the area described him as "a man of stern and thrifty qualities" who was generous to Jewish congregations in the community. The same monograph credited him with innovative trimming of trees in one of the parks, a controversial move at the time, but one that experts from Cornell University validated. Another monograph, commemorating the centennial of B'nai Israel, referred to him as "generous" and "one of the leading men of Elmira in the late nineteenth century."[4]

In 1897, at the age of thirty-five, Myer married Leah Hallo of Meshoppen, Pennsylvania, the youngest of four daughters, whose father was a shopkeeper.[5] Named for his two grandfathers, Henry Friendly and Jacob Hallo, Henry Jacob Friendly was born on July 3, 1903. His parents were then forty-one and thirty-three, old in those days for a first child. In the early years of their marriage Leah had not been happy, once leaving and moving in with her sister Mattie and her husband, Max Heimerdinger, who lived in Chicago. Myer persuaded Leah to return; Friendly later commented, "I take it that I was the result of that persuasion." At three years, five months, precocious little Henry Jacob used the words "interrupt," "impatient," "depend," "consider," and "properly"; two months later he knew the letters of the alphabet; at four years and eight months he could point out on a map and spell the names of most foreign countries. At seven he could read almost any book written for adults.[6]

Although not a high school graduate, Leah was diligent and precise and had a superb memory, remembering not only what had happened but when it did. Later, she became an excellent bridge player. Seeking to improve herself, she joined and became the head of the local Shakespeare Club. She liked to read to her son when he was having eye trouble, which started at an early age. Leah poured all her attention on her son—"there was absolutely nothing she wouldn't have done for me," he remembered. She was serious, reserved, unemotional, undemanding, and undemonstrative.[7] When Henry was nine or ten she started taking him to local cultural events, which included a theater company that performed Gilbert and Sullivan and other, mostly musical, productions. The local streetcar company ran the theater, and for a time, if audience members came by streetcar, they would be allowed into the theater free rather than have to pay the twenty-five- or fifty-cent admission charge. When there was an evening performance, both his parents would take him.[8]

Somewhat dour and old-fashioned and without much fun in him, Myer was not intimately involved in his son's daily life. "Except for the fact that he had a rather low flashpoint, I didn't ever observe anything particularly objectionable about him," Friendly told an interviewer. Father and son never had a heart-to-heart talk, and Friendly acknowledged, "We didn't have a very close family."[9] As a child Friendly did some chores, but not an onerous number. "My father did require me to mow the lawn and, in the fall, rake the leaves, and since he was a bit of a perfectionist, he would survey my work with more acerbity than I thought was called for." Fallen leaves on the lawn were a special problem. "He seemed to think I should have it in a state of absolute perfection for his arrival. And that struck me as unjust."[10] Just or unjust, Friendly seemed to accept his father's standard for himself and in later years set high standards for the people who worked for him.

Although Friendly's red hair might suggest the opposite, he was docile and obedient as a child. The only "major" incident that Friendly remembered resulted from his going to school on a rainy day without galoshes or a raincoat. He knew his mother would likely punish him by locking him in a small lavatory on the first floor, so he hid a couple of books there before he left home that morning. When he came home dripping, his mother locked him in the bathroom, where he read peacefully. She grew worried when he made no demands to be let out, afraid that he had suffocated. She finally opened the door and found him reading contentedly. "That must have been very disappointing to them," Friendly recalled.[11]

Friendly's reputation as a well-behaved and earnest child did not necessarily endear him to his contemporaries. Morris E. Lasker, a federal district judge whose stepfather grew up in Elmira, related that in the late 1960s his stepfather's nephew, Dr. Ben Levy, visited him at the U.S. Courthouse in Manhattan. When Lasker told Levy that there was a judge from Elmira, Henry Friendly, and asked him whether he would like to pay him a visit, Levy replied, "Hell, no. When I was growing up, all I would hear from my mother was, 'that is not the way Henry Friendly would do it.' "[12]

The Friendlys lived comfortably in a large house. As Friendly recalled, they always had two maids and a part-time handyman to do the heavy work. In 1910 Myer acquired one of the early cars, an open Chalmers. Frequently in the summer they would set out on a Sunday afternoon with Friendly's grandmother and an aunt or two to visit Corning, Watkins Glen, Binghamton, or Ithaca for a picnic or other excursion.[13]

At about the same time, his parents started taking trips to the West during the summer, but, Friendly recalled, "for some reason they didn't take me along." They would park young Friendly in Chicago with his aunt Mattie and uncle Max, whose company he liked, as his mother did. One of Friendly's memories of the period was going to baseball games to see the Chicago White Sox or Chicago Cubs. Because he considered himself a "great baseball fan in those days," the annual visits to Chicago were no hardship. The Black Sox scandal shocked him.[14] Friendly was disdainful about another of his mother's sisters, telling an interviewer, "She led a rather useless existence [in her later years], so far as I could recall. . . . I never liked her very much."[15]

Friendly did not have a particularly glowing picture of family life among his parents' friends. He felt that "something must have gone terribly wrong with their family lives. . . . One could almost write a Buddenbrooks novel on what happened to the German Jewish families. . . . They certainly went in for zero population growth." Many German Jews never married, and many of those who did had no children. Friendly never resolved whether "this was something very ingrown, incestuous or whatnot." He once summed up his parents' relationship this way: "I didn't detect in my early youth that the marriage was any more unhappy than a great many others."[16]

When Samson, the uncle with whom Myer had gone into the shoe business, retired, he sold his interest to Myer, who became president of Friendly Boot & Shoes Co. Friendly helped his father now and then, preferring work in the office to stacking boxes of shoes, at which he was far from proficient. For a time the business did very well, but shoe manufacturers decided to abolish many middlemen like Myer, and he retired in 1917. When he turned to investing in mortgages, he prospered.[17] His success with mortgages, at which he appears to have had no formal training, suggests a good mind and financial acumen.

In the first decades of the twentieth century Elmira had two Orthodox synagogues and one Reform temple. Although Myer and Leah were not religiously observant, they joined the Reform temple with other German Jews, the same congregation that Myer's father had headed, and their son was bar mitzvahed. The Friendlys celebrated Christmas, albeit "in a mild way"; there was no tree, but they exchanged presents.[18]

Myer believed that anti-Semitism was widespread in Elmira, although the only manifestations that Friendly recalled were that the country club had only one Jewish member and that their Christian neighbors would say good morning and good evening, but otherwise wanted nothing to do with them. Friendly thought his father was as responsible as the neighbors for the lack of sociability, and that his parents might have joined the country club had they wished. Although he remembered feeling discomfort with some Christians, Friendly's friends were mostly Christian, which was uncharacteristic for most Jews at this time. Two of his friends, whom Friendly later described as "of the so-called superior group," the country club crowd, were Hubert Mandeville, the son of a prominent lawyer and president of the school board, and the son of a state judge.[19]

Myer was prejudiced against Jews who did not come from Germany; he "thought they were tricky and dishonest. All the stereotypes that are applied to Jews generally, he applied to [them]; well, he called them Kikes, in no uncertain terms." Myer did not prohibit his son from befriending them, but "he certainly did not encourage it." It was all right to go out with girls who were not German Jews, but that was not where he should look for a future wife. And interfaith marriage did not exist. On the emerging issue of Zionism, Friendly's father was very negative.[20]

About two thousand African-Americans lived in Elmira, Friendly remembered, most of them poor, except for a few who owned restaurants. There was no black ghetto, but all but a few lived in poorer integrated neighborhoods. Friendly played catch with some black children with whom he went to school. He later said, "Nobody thought anything about it. On the other hand, I don't think there were any real social relations between the whites and the blacks. As far as school was concerned, nobody gave it a second thought."[21]

While Friendly liked playing baseball in his large backyard, everything suggests that he was not a natural athlete. He was overweight in his teen years—at eighteen he was five feet eight inches tall and weighed 185 pounds—before he slimmed down in adulthood. Myer was a sportsman and fisherman, but after a few forays Friendly wanted no part of those activities, which disappointed his father.[22] Throughout his life Friendly lacked manual dexterity and had difficulty with gadgets of all sorts, including a Sony Walkman, and doing anything much more challenging than turning doorknobs. "I couldn't drive a nail in straight if my life depended on it," he conceded.[23]

Fittingly, the one serious injury that Friendly suffered as a child was not incurred in sports, but when he punctured his hand with a lead pencil and got a life-threatening case of blood poisoning, which left him without the use of the pinky on his left hand.[24] His eye problems, which began early, led in 1936 to detached retinas in both eyes, a condition that plagued him the rest of his life. As an adult his perennial vision problems required several operations, with accompanying periods of hospitalization. It may have been because of his poor eyesight or his lack of coordination, or perhaps for some other reason, but Friendly never drove an automobile.[25]

At thirteen Friendly wrote a letter to his mother on Mother's Day, when she was at a hotel in Atlantic City. In clear script it began, "I am writing you specially today because tomorrow is 'Mother's Day' and I feel it my sacred duty to tell you how often I think of you and to tell you how, every day, I appreciate you more. I can never be as good as you would wish me to be but I will bend my greatest efforts towards that goal and if I do succeed in even partially fulfilling your wish I know that I shall owe it all to you and Papa, for Lincoln said, 'Whatever I am I owe to my mother.' "[26]

Notwithstanding the fact that he spent portions of three winters with his family in Florida, missing a lot of school, Friendly skipped several grades. His prime interests were American history and English literature, including the work of George Eliot and William Makepeace Thackeray, as well as historical novels; he liked mathematics, but he had no interest in science.[27] In addition to his schoolwork and extracurricular reading, he occasionally visited a great-aunt who was a talented musician and played piano scores from Wagner's operas for him.[28] He also enjoyed walking about the hills that surrounded Elmira, usually alone. A favorite destination required taking a streetcar to near East Hill and then walking up the dirt roads to the home of Mark Twain. The Hannibal, Missouri, native had married "Livy" Langdon, the daughter of one of the leading citizens of Elmira, in 1870. In his octagonal study Twain had worked on portions of some of his best-known novels, including *Tom Sawyer* and *Huckleberry Finn*. (Livy died in 1904, a year after Friendly's birth, and the Elmira house was no longer occupied by the famous writer, who died in 1910.)[29]

Friendly praised the Elmira school system, including his high school, which had "the somewhat quaint name of the Elmira Free Academy." A member of the graduating class of 1919, Friendly had fond memories of the academy, and not only because he did so spectacularly well there. He recalled that "some history teachers were excellent.... The whole school was good. Very devoted and dedicated teachers who worked for a pittance." Aside from being first in his class, he was editor in chief of the school paper and was on the student council, the debating team, and something called the Class Song and Motto Committee. When he graduated, he had the highest score of any student in the fifty-five-year history of New York State Regents examinations.[30] His standing among his peers is reflected in the yearbook of Elmira Free Academy for 1919: "Henry's wisdom so over-whelms the rest of us that we can only sit amazed and speechless. Can any of us ever forget that memorable day when Henry was giving a very elo-quent explanation on Virgil? . . . When he had finished, we were even more firmly convinced of our ignorance. . . . But Henry is as true a friend as he is a fine student and he has greatly helped to make this last year a successful one."[31]

As a young teenager Friendly was very eager for war, remarking later, "Of course, I was very moved by the outbreak of World War I." For a time pro-German, a position engendered by his older relations, Friendly switched sides decisively when the United States entered the war. "I got maps, and stuck pins in, in all these oddly named places." While in high school he made speeches in little towns near Elmira to sell war bonds. During sum-mers he stayed home, relaxing and reading: "[I was] really just wast[ing] the summers, except for the reading I did." Preferring solitary and intel-lectual pursuits, he embraced reading and long walks for the rest of his life.[32]

Friendly's first serious encounter with the law occurred while in high school, when he was a witness in a lawsuit his father brought for breach of warranty over a new furnace acquired for their home. The furnace was fed not by piling coals on top of the fire, but from underneath. To Myer's com-plaints, the furnace salesman kept saying that there was not enough draft, so the company cut holes in the Friendlys' "beautiful hardwood floor." But still there was insufficient heat from the furnace. At the trial young Friendly "was the expert witness on the size of these holes that [they had] cut in the floor." Fifty-seven years later, Friendly still had vivid memories of the trial:

> The star witness was a very nice black man who took care of the furnace. The lawyer in Binghamton had made a big mistake by asking him the question, he said, "Mr. Brent, have you ever had any experience in taking care of an under-feeding furnace before?" And this fellow was the soul of honor, you know—he looked at him and said: "UNDERFEEDING . . . that ain't no underfeeding furnace—that's an UNDERHEATING furnace." And then he was off to the races, you know, he was telling how he'd have to remove the ash, most of which was unburned coal, and he was going on and on, and the judge, who lived about a half a block away, and knew this fellow, knew he was the most truthful man in the world, just sort of tickled the bench with his gavel—because he was enjoying every moment of it—that was the end of the case, I think.[33]

Cornell University in nearby Ithaca would have been a natural choice, but Friendly wanted to be farther from home. He had always wanted to go to Harvard, and he remembered having "that big Crimson catalogue, and looking with fascination at the names of all these wonderful courses." He added, "How I got the catalogue I don't know."[34] His eye problems almost delayed his starting college by a year. At the last minute, however, the doctor gave consent for him to start in the fall of 1919.[35] By the time Friendly left for college two months after his sixteenth birthday, he had seriously begun to chafe at Elmira, feeling cramped by a small city that offered too few opportunities.

During his early years in Elmira, Friendly developed his curiosity, self-awareness, self-confidence, and independence. He learned to value culture, especially through his voracious reading, to appreciate the importance of self-improvement, and to take responsibility for his actions. He knew his mind and knew that it was a good one, and he was prepared to make decisions for himself. While he had a variety of what he would call friends, they were more like close acquaintances that boys of that age made. The absence of sisters, little contact with girls his own age, and a mother who did not communicate with him candidly or intimately no doubt helped create emotional problems that existed throughout his life. He never learned what it meant really to talk to others, especially to a woman. Although he was reflective, he was not introspective. From his association with the lawyer father of a friend, Hubert Mandeville, he developed a respect for law and the laws of the society in which he lived, as well as the imperative of honesty. In his first sixteen years he also absorbed some Bavarian characteristics from his parents and other relatives: respect for order, structure, and obedience and a certain degree of formality. Harvard had accepted him based on merit, and he was confident he could succeed.

When the time came, Friendly's father took him by train to Boston. After spending the night in a hotel in the shoe district, where his father had often stayed on business trips, they traveled to Cambridge. There they rented one of the last available rooms in the freshman dormitory, a suite for one that he described as rather nice, although a little expensive. No other freshman at Harvard came from Elmira, and he knew none of his classmates. By nature not gregarious and two years younger than most students, he set out on his own to absorb what Harvard had to offer. Acknowledging his lack of camaraderie in his years at Harvard, he explained later, "It would be easy to blame that on my having been younger, but I really don't think it would have made any difference if I'd been a year or two older."[36]

AT HARVARD, Friendly realized the high quality of his Elmira education: "I looked at the elementary course in English, and [it] didn't seem to me I'd learn very much from it that I hadn't already learned." He found he could take an "anticipatory examination," which if he passed would obviate the need to take the course, and if he failed would not count against him. "I was told there was absolutely no chance, that that was only for boys who had gone to Exeter and Andover, and places like that, and very few of them got excused. Well, I took it, and I got excused. So apparently the English instruction [in Elmira] had been pretty good."[37]

As a freshman Friendly took government with Harvard's President, A. Lawrence Lowell, as well as history, mathematics, physics, elementary French, and physical training. He did well. Very well. He received A's in everything but physical training, where he received a B. In his sophomore year he took history of French literature, economics, philosophy, psychology, and three history courses, and his grades were all A's. The grades in his junior year did not deviate; he earned A's in German, advanced courses in economics, and government and in two history courses. He was elected to Phi Beta Kappa at the end of his junior year, signaling that he was one of the top eight students in the Harvard Class of '23. When he could, he audited courses in other disciplines, especially in the fine arts. He "avoided science courses because of a lack of real comprehension." He graduated summa cum laude, with his B in a physical training course the only deviation from his straight A's.[38]

Fellow students noted Friendly's academic accomplishments. In 2008 Albert Gordon, one of Friendly's classmates, at the time only weeks away from his 107th birthday, reminisced about meeting Friendly his freshman year and seeing him in class. Gordon, later the head of Kidder, Peabody & Co., remembered Friendly's being universally respected: "we thought of him not only as the smartest in the class but the smartest at Harvard College." Gordon further recalled that they were seated near each other for the final examination in a history course, one part of which consisted of a choice between two essay questions. Everyone was writing his answer when the professor entered the classroom, walked over to Friendly's desk, and asked him which question he was answering. When Friendly responded, the professor expressed disappointment and said that he had written the other question just for him. Friendly tore up his exam book and answered the other question.[39]

Joining the debating team as a freshman, he traveled to Bates College, a small school in Lewiston, Maine, which had one of the best debating teams in the country. The temperature in the small town was ten degrees below zero, and Friendly had the unattractive affirmative of the proposition that the coal mines should be nationalized. He lost. He quit the team in his sophomore year because he felt he could make better use of his time. He chose not to try to join the literary magazine, *The Advocate*; although invited by his classmate John Mason Brown, later a prominent author and columnist, he decided that he did not write well enough, and, besides, his forte was nonfiction rather than "imaginative writing."[40]

Campus social life was segregated along class and religious lines in the early 1920s. Elite scions of the best Christian families who had gone to the top preparatory schools, perhaps 10 percent of the class, kept to themselves after their freshman year, mostly in their elaborate and highly exclusive "final" clubs. For example, Gordon, a member of Delta Kappa Epsilon, never saw Friendly socially, although Friendly had a large number of Christian friends.[41]

The intellectual level of the campus was not particularly high. "Those were the days of the Gentleman's C," Friendly explained later. Among the students he met in his freshman year was Marshall Stone, who was in his mathematics class. Friendly had done well in mathematics in high school, scoring 100 in both algebra and plane geometry, and while he had no thought of being a mathematician, he planned on taking several courses in the subject. He changed his mind when he compared his performance in one course with Stone's. "I always told him later I was glad that he'd become such an eminent professor of mathematics, because that made me feel better," Friendly recalled.[42]

Friendly spent his spare time soaking up the cultural activities of Boston rather than congregating with fellow students. He bought a Saturday night subscription to the Boston Symphony Orchestra, saw theater productions, frequented the Boston Museum, attended the opera during its short season, and engaged in anything else of interest he could manage. He dated "in a very modest way." "I'd not seen much of girls during college or law school," he conceded.[43]

Friendly relished the challenges of understanding history, whether it was modern American or medieval European history. He was stimulated by the new approach, in which Harvard was in the forefront, that emphasized intellectual history as much as political history. Because he had studied American history in high school, he gravitated to European history at Harvard, which had an all-star professorial lineup. He took a course on the intellectual history of medieval Europe from Professor Charles Homer Haskins, a prominent medievalist, who, along with Charles Howard McIlwain, he called "the real giants of the Department." Other prominent members of the faculty were Archibald Carey Coolidge, an authority on nineteenth- and twentieth-century European history, and the renowned Frederick Jackson Turner, whom Friendly found exceedingly dull. Many courses were very large, which hampered familiarity with the senior professors, so

Friendly sought out Samuel Elliot Morrison and Frederick Merck, rising professors of American history.[44]

In his junior year Friendly won second prize in the prestigious Bowdoin competition with a history paper entitled "The Fall of Naples: An Episode in the Risorgimento."[45] The 7,500-word essay covered the busy year of 1860 and conveyed the excitement of the events. The paper was not like an undergraduate effort, but like the work of a seasoned scholar, not like a circumscribed monograph, but like a chapter in a venturesome book. As with his other papers, Friendly was not content to summarize existing scholarship, but sought to stamp his own mark on the subject. Adhering to his (and McIlwain's)[46] precept for primary sources to draw on documents in French and Italian, he provided sophisticated reasoning and nuanced evaluations. The major theme of the paper was the jockeying of Camillo Cavour and Giuseppe Garibaldi. Friendly portrayed Cavour as "a master opportunist" of great ability, who tried to give Garibaldi just enough rope to achieve the goal of acquiring Sicily and Naples for Sardinia while restraining Garibaldi when his actions threatened Sardinia's relationship with the major powers. Friendly's portrait of Garibaldi is worth quoting:

> He had the patriotism of Schiller and the young Germans, the sickly petulancy of Rousseau, and the *mal du siècle* of Chateaubriand; he gathered into his make-up the tremendous self-admiration of a Hugo, the love of display of a Gautier, and the courage of a Byron. It is to the latter of course that he has been most often compared; but much more than Byron he was the Poet in action. He was more of a poet than the martyr of Missolonghi, and he was unquestionably more of a man of action. He took two continents for the scene of his activities, while Byron confined his to a narrow corner of the world; and his transcendent military genius veiled many of the more unlovely elements in his character.[47]

Friendly's older daughter, Joan Friendly Goodman, saved five of his undergraduate papers. All reflect a command of the facts, bold thinking, and incisive analysis. One effort was a mammoth work of 140 double-spaced typewritten pages, exclusive of an introduction, a table of contents, three genealogical charts, a four-page bibliography, and a note added at the last minute to include a reference to a just-published book. Its title was "Palmerston, Russell, and Queen Victoria, 1846–51," and it provided a detailed analysis of the inner workings of the British government and monarchy during a series of international crises in the middle of the nineteenth century. The issue for Friendly was the very integrity of the British Constitution: "While Palmerston erred by his failure to show due respect for his sovereign, the Queen showed a much more dangerous disrespect for the constitutional limitations hedging in her position and actually attempted to determine the foreign policy of the government." Although Palmerston and Russell undeniably were at fault, Friendly concluded, the Crown was "guilty of overstepping its constitutional bounds and of attempting to direct foreign policy."[48]

Friendly also wrote a 6,000-word composition entitled "Disputed Points in the Life of Columbus to August 3, 1492," which evaluated recent research of a French historian, Henry Vignaud, who sought to deconstruct Columbus's largely self-created myth that he was a man of great scientific sophistication and vision. After explaining that Columbus, unlike Napoleon, had to wait for almost four centuries for a disapproving biographer, Friendly observed, "But if Columbus waited many years for a critical account of his life, he ought now to be fully content." His professor wrote on the paper, "A complete, well-balanced, critically sound discussion, an excellent report."[49]

Friendly's insight into the character and complex motivations of those he wrote about was powerful, especially for a young man from a small city remote from centers of European culture. Stylistically the papers showed signs of some later proclivities. He employed vivid and pungent phrasing, as he later would as an attorney and judge. To an argument that Charles V wanted the surrender, not the sacking, of Rome, he retorted, "The merest tyro would have known that for unpaid troops surrender and a sack were equivalent. Charles pointed a cannon at the Holy City; he is not freed from the consequences of the explosion because another struck the spark."[50] While his sentences were not unduly long,[51] a practice he developed later, some paragraphs were. One Faulknerian paragraph contained more than eight hundred words, one third of the entire paper in which it appeared. He employed inverted sentences, sometimes to excess: "After the flight from Lisbon are placed by many historians the overtures to Genoa and Venice."[52]

By his senior year Friendly had settled on modern European history as his specialty. Nevertheless, he enrolled in a course taught by McIlwain called History of England through the Accession of Henry VII. The texts for the early part of the course were in Latin, except for a few Anglo-Saxon pages. McIlwain had said nothing about this in the course catalogue; he just assumed that an educated man would be able to read Latin. Within a few weeks Friendly had expanded his high school Latin to a level that allowed him to read the old documents. He attributed his quick absorption of Latin to McIlwain's conclusion that it was not hard to learn— "one found that Mac was right"—rather than to his own intellect. McIlwain's emphasis was on documents—reading the original documents and interpreting them correctly. Always try to understand the words in the way they were understood by the people of the time, McIlwain urged his students, a creed Friendly repeated after he ascended to the bench thirty-five years later. Friendly said, "[I] found this course by all odds the greatest educational experience I had at Harvard College."[53]

For his paper in McIlwain's course, Friendly addressed "church and state in England under William the Conqueror."[54] William, whom Pope Gregory VII had blessed, challenged the hegemony of the Church of Rome and emphasized less religiously focused nationalism. He cast the issue in terms of a battle of wills between the Pope and William, both reformers. As long as William lived, Friendly concluded, "The relations of Church and State were clearly those of Normandy, not the 'caesaropapism' of Anglo-Saxon times."[55] By using his powers judiciously, Friendly found, William gently rebuffed Pope Gregory's demand for an oath of fealty and separated the ecclesiastical cases from the secular courts, a major move that weakened the Church.[56] "The unique feature of William's ecclesiastical policy is that in the character of its author were blended in almost equal proportions the will to power and sincere devotion to the Christian Church," he concluded, noting that the formula did not disintegrate until a century later, over the contest between Thomas à Becket and King John.[57] The paper earned Friendly an A and the $250 first prize in the Bowdoin competition. The history faculty was so impressed with the paper that they told him that with a relatively modest amount of work it would be accepted as a Ph.D. dissertation.[58] McIlwain wrote to Friendly, "I have no hesitation in saying to you that of all the students I have come in contact with in my whole teaching experience of some twenty years, you are the best fitted for this work."[59]

Despite his success, Friendly was realistic about Harvard, writing to his daughter Joan upon her transferring from Swarthmore to Radcliffe College, in effect a part of Harvard at the time, in September 1954, "I can freely say— how much it means to me to have a child, and particularly you, at Harvard. It isn't just sentiment, for my own years were a mixture of great pleasure in the intellectual and a fair amount of unhappiness on the social side—I'm speaking of the undergraduate years."[60] Twenty years later he told a member of the history department, "I owe everything to Harvard."[61] That same year, however, he rejected the idea that his college years coincided with any sort of golden age. "I think [the undergraduate experience at Harvard has] gotten much, much better. . . . The whole attitude toward intellectual matters and the learning process, social responsibility, has improved. . . . I didn't make many enduring friends, and I don't suppose I really had a very good time, except for my studying."[62]

Friendly was shocked when, at the end of his junior year, President Lowell, who had strongly opposed the nomination of Louis Brandeis to the Supreme Court in 1916, proposed that the college institute a *numerus clausus* that would limit the admission of Jews.[63] Decades afterward Friendly recalled Lowell's rationale: "there had been a gradual increase in the number of Jewish students, . . . that was as high as it should get, . . . [so] why not be honest about it? . . . It wasn't going to be good for the Christian students and wasn't going to be good for the Jewish students. . . . President Lowell . . . proposed to the Corporation and the Board of Overseers that there be this limit, I think it was 15 percent, on Jewish students."[64] Actually, Lowell's proposal was more complicated and less onerous than generally remembered, even by Friendly. Only Jewish transfer students who had not qualified for admission as freshmen were subjected to the quota, mostly day students who lived in the Boston area.[65]

"All hell broke loose," Friendly remembered. Lowell finally appointed a faculty committee on admissions to review the proposal, confident it would support him. It might have done so had Lowell's predecessor, eighty-nine-year-old Charles W. Eliot, not put his considerable influence on the side of defeating the proposal.[66] In the end the committee recommended against a quota and urged that more students be admitted from areas of the country other than the Northeast in an effort to create a truly national university. According to a Harvard publication at the time, "regional balance" would mean "that the proportion of Jewish students would be reduced," since it would "bring to Harvard more students from the high schools of towns and smaller cities, especially of the West and South."[67]

Friendly's reaction to Lowell's proposal was stronger than might be expected, given that he was not religious and had many Christian friends: "that did have a very traumatic effect—in fact, I made up my mind that if that passed, I wasn't going to go back to Harvard my senior year, in spite of all the losses that I would suffer from doing that. I just thought one couldn't tolerate it."[68] He seemed to be rebelling against the injustice rather than identifying with the excluded Jews. In either event, he apparently was prepared to make a huge personal sacrifice for a matter of principle.

In later years Friendly expressed some tolerance for Lowell's proposal: "That [proposal] was quite liberal since the Jews were only about three percent of the population and no one wanted Harvard to become a predominantly Jewish college." Friendly also accepted the fact that Harvard had been more liberal in admitting Jewish students than many other colleges.[69] Still, the incident continued to gnaw at Friendly. In a letter to the

Harvard Alumni Bulletin in 1967, he referred to "President A. Lawrence Lowell's proposal to emulate Czarist Russia and anticipate Hitler Germany by establishing a *numerus clausus* for Jews at Harvard College."[70] At a luncheon with the Harvard Law professor Paul Freund in the summer of 1985, Friendly remarked that in the mid-1930s Hitler could have pointed to Harvard's setting a quota on Jews to try to justify his own horrific actions.[71]

Surviving from Friendly's college years are eight letters he wrote to his mother, all dated around her birthday or Mother's Day. They are similar in tone and opening paragraphs before they turn to discussing aspects of life as a college student, such as cultural activities and schoolwork. The letters recite Friendly's undying love for his mother, but his concept of love, as expressed in the letters, is distant, idealized, and without true intimacy; the portions of his letters that praise his mother could have been copied from a book of Victorian love letters, as a sampling of his first college letter shows:

> At last my stationery has arrived and it seems fitting that my first letter should be a congratulatory one to you. I shall not go into spasms of panegyric love for you know of my love far better than I can express it. You must also know of my wishes for your health and happiness during the coming year as well as in many future ones. . . . Sometimes when I have heard in lectures about the difficulty of regulating life according to the standards of pleasure, of happiness, or even of duty, I have almost despaired of being able to lead a truly successful life. But when your picture looks over me as I go to sleep, I can say that there is a standard and model, in following which no difficulty, philosophical or ethical, appears, one which I may safely take as a guide to life.[72]

The final extant college letter on Mother's Day in 1922 includes a reference to his powerful mood swings even before he reached twenty: "Just as Dante was enabled by his love for Beatrice to climb from deepest Hell to highest Heaven, I have been accustomed when things looked blacker than is their wont, to think of you, of your courage, of your energy, of your unselfishness. And I find that, as years go on and as we are separated more and more, that thought grows ever stronger both in its intrinsic beauty and in its pragmatic effects."[73] He continued to write similar letters for at least six more years.[74]

Three letters that Friendly's mother wrote him between 1916 and 1921 survive, and their tone is realistic and practical. In addition to telling her son to be truthful, honorable, diplomatic, and not extravagant, she wrote him during his first days at Harvard:

I feel that what you have desired and worked for is now being realized, and while I know you will have some lonely hours (in fact I would be disappointed if you didn't, for it would be a reflection on your parents or indifference on your part) yet you fully realize that to attain anything really worth while brings some hardships, and these very trials only help to form our character. All that loving hearts and willing hands can do, has been done for you. You have been blessed beyond the average and both your father and myself have full confidence in you. I know you may have limitations, but I know you will overcome these, having good and pure thoughts, aim for the high things in life so that those who love you will always be as proud of you as they are today.[75]

Friendly applied for and won a prestigious Shaw traveling fellowship that paid for him to spend a year in Europe following graduation. But exposure to McIlwain had shattered Friendly's plans and also shattered his parents' expectation that upon his return he would head for Harvard Law School. In the spring of his senior year he told his parents that after the year in Europe he would return to Harvard to seek a Ph.D. in medieval English history with McIlwain. "Well, they didn't take that as the finest piece of news they'd ever heard," Friendly conceded, acknowledging his father's tendency to measure success in terms of financial security. His parents took preemptive action.

Through her sister Mattie, Friendly's mother had met U.S. Court of Appeals Judge Julian Mack when he practiced law and was a state court judge in Chicago. Leah wrote to him "about this dreadful thing that was about to occur" respecting her son. Mack tried to calm the waters. It may not be a catastrophic choice, he said, but it was an important one, and he suggested that Friendly see the one man whose advice would be valuable above all others. The man was Harvard Law School professor Felix Frankfurter. Friendly met with Frankfurter, who handled things just right, Friendly recalled. At their lunch he sympathized with Friendly's infatuation with McIlwain. Taking advantage of the subject of the paper Friendly wrote for McIlwain, Frankfurter explained, "[In] the field in which you're interested, the development of political and legal institutions in medieval England, it wouldn't hurt you to know a little law. So, why don't you take a year in Europe and come back to the Harvard Law School for a year. You might like it and decide to continue. If you don't like it, it will have done you good." Friendly acquiesced; the undergraduate had met the master.[76]

Friendly spent the 1923–1924 academic year in Europe. In Germany he saw the catastrophic inflation, strikes, and other signs of distress, so after only ten days he moved on to Amsterdam and then to Paris. He spent five or six months in Paris, attending the L'École Practique, including a seminar taught by a friend of McIlwain's, where he delivered a paper in French on a parliament held in France in 1305. The few lectures on law Friendly attended he found dull, and confessed, "Between the two, I much preferred history. . . . If anything could give one a distaste for law that was it." He spent most of his time reading, attending theater and opera, and walking. From Paris he went to Italy and then to England and Oxford, where he attended lectures on English history given by eminent but tedious professors. On a visit to Cambridge he reported, "I slept in . . . my great god . . . Maitland's bed!"[77]

Friendly's parents joined him in Europe in the spring, and they traveled to Germany, where the situation had improved greatly. Their longest stop, one week, was in Nuremberg, where Friendly celebrated his twenty-first birthday with his parents and German relatives, for he "spoke enough German that [he] could get along perfectly well." From there his parents went to Italy while Friendly visited France to explore places he had missed, returned to England for a cathedral tour, and took a ship back to the United States, arriving before his parents. He thought the year abroad was only moderately successful, leaving him somewhat dissatisfied with his progress in learning foreign languages as well as with the lack of direction in terms of his career.[78] But it was time to start law school.

FRIENDLY WENT DIRECTLY to Cambridge from the ship that brought him home from Europe. Harvard Law School was then large and growing, from 945 students in 1920 to 1,440 in 1925. Because law school was a new challenge, he could not be certain that he would do well. After all, roughly one-third of Harvard's first-year law students did not return for their second year, and there were "gruesome tales of disaster" and "staggering stories of astonishing hours of work." "I was laboring under this atmosphere of fear," Friendly confessed. One night a week, occasionally two, was all he dared devote to a social life. Even those who could deal with the pressure "would have been better off if [they] hadn't had quite so heavy a dosage."[79]

Friendly established himself with the law school's faculty and fellow students in an incident on the first day of classes in the course on Torts. Professor Manley O. Hudson asked the class in what language *I.D.S. & Wife v. W.D.S.*, a very early English case well-known to generations of law students, had been originally published. After students guessed English, Latin, and Anglo-Saxon, the professor called on Friendly, who responded that it was Law French. Hudson looked skeptical, and pressed Friendly on how he could prove it was Law French. He couldn't, Friendly replied, but he knew it was and could explain why. Hudson then produced the original of the case from the old yearbook that he had obtained from the stacks, and Friendly repeated that it was written in Law French. Manley then instructed Friendly to read it.

> By this time I was getting a little annoyed, and so I said: "Do you want me to read it, or do you want me to translate it?" Well, he said, "First read it and then translate it." Well, I said, "I don't know what the accent was at that time. The best I can do is read it as if it were modern French." So after a little while he got tired of that. And he said: "Now translate it." Well, you see, this is where the work I'd done in Paris stood me in good stead. So I started to translate it. As soon as he found I could, of course, he didn't care about prolonging that agony. So that really made my reputation at the Harvard Law School, on the first day.[80]

Many years later, when Friendly was in private practice, his firm hired one of Professor Hudson's sons, who knew the story. When Friendly said that he had always wondered how Professor Hudson ever had that idea, his son said, "Well, don't you think that perhaps Felix [Frankfurter] put him up to it?" A bit crestfallen, Friendly explained, "Oh, that took a lot of the joy out of it. That could very well have been the case."[81]

Under the early method of teaching in American law schools, a practice still in use in Europe, professors lectured to the students about the law, presenting, in effect, an oral treatise in the classroom. Some professors on occasion called on a student to recite material, such as, "State the exceptions to the hearsay rule that require the unavailability of the declarant." Responding required rote memorization, not thinking, yet thinking is what makes good lawyers. Harvard's method during Friendly's years in law school, and to a considerable extent today, began with Christopher Columbus Langdell, who, while dean of the Harvard Law School in the 1870s, created the "case method" of teaching. The professor engaged students in a Socratic dialogue on appellate opinions and their meaning, changing the facts until the governing principle underlying the law emerged. Instead of memorizing answers, the case method provoked arguing by analogy, making discriminating distinctions, and employing reasoning. In 1964 Friendly described this process to entering students at the University of Chicago Law School:

> What we were to learn was not the law, but how to "do law"—as today's philosophers say they "do philosophy". . . . Your efforts thus will be primarily directed not at learning "law" but acquiring a "legal mind." . . . The legal mind is an inquiring mind. It does not accept; it asks. Its favorite word is

"why." . . . It is analytical; it picks a problem apart so that the components can be seen and judged. It is selective; it rejects characteristics that are not significant and focuses on those that are. . . . It is a classifying mind; it finds significant differences between cases that superficially seem similar and significant similarities between cases that at first seem different. It is a discriminating mind; it has a profound disbelief in what Professor Frankfurter used to call "the democracy of ideas."[82]

Within two months of Friendly's entering law school, Professor Frankfurter invited him to his house. Although he was not in any of the professor's classes, they had met in circumstances that suggested a student with a bright future in the law, and other law professors had praised his ability. Frankfurter made Friendly one of his favorites, along with James Landis (later dean of Harvard Law School) and Thomas Corcoran (later active in the New Deal), which meant that he would summon him from the library for discussions whenever he wanted on whatever topic interested him at the time, even if it was in the middle of examinations. Largely because of Frankfurter, Friendly developed an interest in federal jurisdiction and the new subject of administrative law, which dealt with public law rather than private law. Friendly took every course on public law that Harvard taught, although for reasons he could not explain he did not take Frankfurter's seminar on federal jurisdiction.[83] He learned to read statutes very carefully and quoted Frankfurter: "'Though we may not end with the words in construing a disputed statute,' he said in his lecture, paraphrasing one of his opinions, 'one certainly begins there.' It was to enforce this 'hoary platitude' that as a teacher, he had developed his threefold imperative to law students: (1) read the statute; (2) read the statute; (3) read the statute!"[84]

Grades were based exclusively on examinations that the first-year students took in the spring. The examinations were essay questions that posed a hypothetical factual situation, often grotesquely complex, followed by a question such as "Who wins and why?" More points were awarded for demonstrating able analysis and, to a lesser extent, judgment, than knowledge of the law, although all such skills helped. Quick thinking and quick writing also benefited a student, and so did a knack for organization and a good imagination.

Among the other courses Friendly took in his first year was Contracts with Professor Calvert Magruder, later a U.S. Circuit Judge for the First Circuit and a friend. Not only did he give Friendly an excellent grade, but Magruder sent him a congratulatory note, in which he said, "[I have] never run across as beautiful [an exam] book as yours in Contracts, . . . [nor one with your] sense of values and emphasis, the logical construction of your answers, your compactness & facility of expression."[85] Friendly replied with grace, "May I extend to you my most sincere thanks for your very kind note regarding the Contracts exam. No one, I suppose, can honestly say that he dislikes praise, and when one is entering a new field with a very considerable doubt as to one's aptitude of it, commendation is doubly sweet. I cannot, therefore, sufficiently express my gratitude either for your letter or for the stimulating lectures which, if I may venture to use the term, were the 'proximate' cause of it."[86]

Finishing first in his class in his first year, Friendly became a member, along with a dozen or so other top students, of the *Harvard Law Review*, which was the premier legal journal in the country. It was the equivalent of more than a full-time job. The *Law Review* published leading articles on the law, generally by professors, which the students edited and for which they checked the citations, along with shorter pieces written by the students. David Riesman, who served as a law clerk for Justice Louis Brandeis before becoming a prominent sociologist, wrote that the "most remarkable institution of the law school world [was] the law review. So far as I know, there is nothing in any other professional group which remotely resembles this guild of students."[87] When Friendly became president of the *Law Review* in the spring of his second year, he wrote to his parents, "It is certainly the greatest honor in the Law School, except for the Fay Diploma—which is awarded at the end of three years, and I am particularly gratified in that very few Jews have ever held the office."[88] Friendly later won the Fay Diploma. As his letter implied, the post of president did not automatically go to the student who was first in the class. Rather, there was an elaborate election in the spring of his second year, a process that continues today.

In addition to his work on the *Law Review* during his second year, Friendly was active in the Ames Competition, a highly competitive Harvard Law School moot court tournament. All the cases took place in the hypothetical, imaginary, and enlightened State of Ames. Along with a teammate, he won the Marshall Prize for the best brief in the competition. Conventional wisdom had it that law students were expected to spend half their time on classes and half their time on the moot court. Not factored in were the considerable time demands of the *Law Review*, which made his Marshall Prize all the more impressive. Although Friendly worked less on his courses in his second year than in his first, he again was first in his class.[89]

During his first summer while at the law school, 1925, Friendly went back to Elmira and "did nothing, just as [he]'d done before," which probably meant an active program of reading and long walks and paying an occasional visit to a leading citizen of Elmira.[90] The next summer he went to New York City at the invitation of Frankfurter, who was teaching at Columbia Summer Law School and living with Emory Buckner, the U.S. Attorney for the Southern District of New York, whose wife had gone away for the summer. Frankfurter did not think that teaching would keep him sufficiently busy, so he asked Landis, Corcoran, and Friendly to join him and commandeered for them a large apartment on West Seventy-Second Street. The three students met some remarkable men, who, like Frankfurter and Buckner, were summer bachelors: Judge Learned Hand, Judge Augustus Hand, Judge Julian Mack, and C. C. Burlingham, a leader of the New York bar. The men had dinner together several nights a week, and Frankfurter often arranged for the three students to attend.[91] Because Frankfurter taught during the day, Friendly occupied himself by researching diversity-of-citizenship jurisdiction.

Events then took an unexpected turn. Buckner was preparing to prosecute the former Attorney General Harry Dougherty for fraud in connection with the Alien Property Custodian's office (before the unrelated Teapot Dome scandal), and he asked Frankfurter if he knew where he could get hold of a couple of bright young men in a hurry to work with him on the case. Frankfurter responded that he thought he could produce two the next morning. Corcoran and Friendly immediately went to work for Buckner, who paid them out of his own pocket.[92]

In the position of president of the *Harvard Law Review* in 1926—Friendly persisted in calling himself "Editor in Chief"—he never worked harder, before or after.[93] He went to the *Law Review* office at 9 A.M. and worked until 10 or 11 P.M., taking time only to eat and to attend an occasional class. He studied for his classes on weekends. In a letter to his mother that autumn, he described his education in dealing with subordinates: "Things are running quite smoothly on the Review. Fritz [F. A. O. Schwartz] is a treasure. I admire tremendously the way in which he handles the new men; he knows just how aloof to hold himself without becoming haughty or difficult to approach. I think I err on the side of being too familiar when things are going well and then becoming too severe when anything goes wrong."[94]

As president of the *Law Review*, Friendly got to know people who became prominent in later years. The editor in chief of the *Yale Law Journal* was Herbert Brownell, who, as Attorney General under President Dwight Eisenhower, became involved thirty years later in Friendly's judicial nomination. Erwin Griswold, who went on to become dean of Harvard Law School and Solicitor General of the United States, succeeded Friendly.

Friendly does not appear to have assisted Frankfurter when he represented Nicola Sacco and Bartolomeo Vanzetti. In an atmosphere of near hysteria over anarchist activity, the two had been convicted and sentenced to death for a homicide committed during a robbery. In 1927 Governor Alvin T. Fuller of Massachusetts appointed a commission headed by Harvard's President Lowell and two other distinguished citizens to review Judge Webster Thayer's much derided conduct of the trial. When the commission supported Thayer, Friendly wrote Frankfurter, "The whole thing is perfectly incredible. One simply cannot believe that a fair minded and intelligent man could spend three months on a case and then come out with an opinion which reads in parts like a movie scenario and in others like the assertions of a bigot."[95]

In the middle of Friendly's second year, Frankfurter told him that he was going to appoint him law clerk to Justice Louis Brandeis the year after he graduated. A year later, however, Frankfurter proposed a change, namely, that Friendly delay taking his clerkship with Brandeis for one year and remain for a fourth year at Harvard studying, teaching, and doing research for Frankfurter.[96] After speaking with his family and others, Friendly, who was tired of law school, turned Frankfurter down.[97] But before he told Frankfurter, his parents visited Brandeis in Washington, apparently without telling their son. Brandeis wrote to Frankfurter about the meeting: "The only definite advice I gave them was to leave their son alone; to let him make up his own mind & not merely to say so, but let him see & know that they will be happy in whatever decision he makes. I put this as strongly as I could; & think they understood me." Brandeis did not want to get involved in a family issue or, for that matter, in a dispute with Frankfurter. "I definitely refused to transmit through them any advice as to the son." Friendly decided to start the clerkship with Brandeis in the fall of 1927.[98]

Friendly graduated Harvard Law School with an 86 average. If this number does not sound especially high, a student who scored 75 received an A, which was enough to earn a degree magna cum laude, and an average of 80, six points below Friendly's, was sufficient to graduate summa cum laude and usually be first in his class. Friendly received, in effect, an A++ average. Frankfurter later described Friendly as "by long odds one of the ablest lawyers who came out of the Harvard Law School in my time."[99]

Friendly later contrasted Langdell's case method of teaching with the teaching he encountered in Europe the year after graduation. The case approach he called "a delight": "I thought it was great. I'd never seen anything like it."[100] Reminiscing in a letter to his daughter Joan when she was transferring to Radcliffe College, he described his years at Harvard Law School as "pure gold."[101] He rated his experience high, largely because of his work with fellow students on the *Law Review*. When it came to the law school faculty, however, he was consistently negative, and wrote to Frankfurter a few months after he graduated, "After a few thrilling months with Williston and Hudson at the beginning of the first year, everything seemed to slide. . . . In fact, when I came to sum up the reasons why I got more out of Law School than I did out of college, the method of instruction would be about the last thing I'd think of. . . . I think the School at present is pretty bad."[102] Decades later Friendly said that "the H.L.S. faculty of our day was over-rated," and he told a *Harvard Law Review* dinner, "Bad as some of the older professors were, the younger ones were worse." To a friend he wrote, "I had [Roscoe Pound] in Criminal Law and he was even more boring than [Joseph H.] Beale, which is saying a lot."[103] A major concern of his course in Corporations was with the question of whether a corporation could marry. "We concluded," he would say, "that in general a corporation could not marry—but there might be *circumstances*."[104]

Friendly spent the summer between law school and his clerkship with Brandeis completing his research and writing an article, "The Historic Basis of Diversity Jurisdiction," published, with Frankfurter's consent, under his own name in the *Harvard Law Review* in 1928 (discussed in Chapter 22).[105]

FRIENDLY HAD a potentially awkward start with Justice Brandeis. The day he arrived in Washington a newspaper published a front-page story with pictures of Friendly and Brandeis and the caption "The two highest Harvard Law men to work together."[106] Friendly recalled, "I was debating what to do, whether I should just take the train [back] to New York or not, and I thought at least I'd better say goodbye to the Justice." It turned out that Brandeis had not seen the article. Actually he never read newspapers; he thought it was a waste of time. Friendly "apologized all over the place, and [Brandeis] just thought it was the biggest joke."[107] Even though Brandeis's average at the Harvard Law School had been around 95, there has been some controversy over whether Friendly or Brandeis had the highest average in the history of the law school, because between the time Brandeis went to Harvard Law School in the Class of 1877 and the time Friendly attended fifty years later the school had changed its grading system.[108]

At the time the Supreme Court heard cases in the basement of the U.S. Capitol Building and the Justices did their work at home. Brandeis lived on the fourth floor of an apartment building, with his office, or chambers, consisting of two small rooms, just enough room for him and his clerk, on the floor above. The only member of the Court to have no secretary, Brandeis wrote all his opinions and correspondence in longhand with a fountain pen. The Supreme Court's printer acted, in effect, as his secretary when he wrote opinions. Rather than attempt to write an opinion from beginning to end, he wrote a short version and repeatedly corrected, refined, and expanded the printed drafts until he was satisfied.[109]

By the time Friendly arrived at his office between 8 and 8:30 A.M., Brandeis already had been there some three hours and returned to his apartment for breakfast, leaving considerable work for Friendly to do. Brandeis would return around 9 A.M. and stay for a couple of hours. On days when the Court was not sitting, Brandeis would go for a walk or drive with his wife, have lunch, take a nap, and return around 3 P.M. As a result Friendly spent relatively little time with the Justice, seeing him twice a day for twenty to thirty minutes and rarely attending oral arguments.[110]

Brandeis did nearly all the drafting of a text, relying on his clerk to draft footnotes. He also made up his own mind, Friendly recounted, and "didn't particularly care what the clerk thought. . . . He spoke with certainty about everything. The pale cast of doubt did not enter very much into his mind. . . . Neither bitter personal attack nor temporary defeat could shake Brandeis' faith in the future, provided men would continue to fight."[111] Brandeis's thoroughness and discipline in doing his own work contributed to Friendly's education. Brandeis was, Friendly said, "an absolutely superb technician: really the best in cases like complicated Interstate Commerce Commission cases." He added, "When I say the best, of course these aren't opinions that he'll go down in history for, but his ability to take one of these cases and get at the facts, organize the material . . . I think he was perfectly tremendous in the way in which he organized things." Friendly played an important role in these efforts, which assisted him in his later years in private practice and as a judge.[112]

When it came to construing statutes, Brandeis was a leader in judicial restraint (or judicial modesty), deferring to the legislative and executive branches. In matters of social legislation, Friendly said that Brandeis "wanted to give great leeway to the legislature," which he viewed as the people's branch of government.[113] It was a popular position among liberals and moderates in the post-*Lochner* era, a 1905 case in which the Supreme Court had held unconstitutional a New York statute that for health reasons limited the hours that bakers could work.[114]

Friendly greatly enjoyed hearing Brandeis share his experiences, writing Frankfurter, "My hero worship is beginning. When the Justice begins to discourse on shoe manufacture in the '80's, or on the difference between corn prices in 1925 and 1926, it seems incredible that this is the man who knows more law than almost the rest of the Court together." Friendly had the greatest respect for Brandeis's intellect, and much later rated him higher than both Learned Hand and Frankfurter, who were his numbers two and three, respectively.[115] The feeling of esteem evidently was mutual. An oft-repeated story is that during Friendly's clerkship, Frankfurter telephoned Brandeis and asked how Friendly was doing. The Justice responded, "Don't you ever send me another such man as Friendly." The professor, taken aback, asked why he felt that way. The Justice responded, "If I had another man like Friendly, I would not have to do a lick of work myself."[116] Remarkably, in addition to serving his Justice well, during the year's clerkship Friendly appears to have read most of the decisions ever rendered by the Supreme Court.[117]

When Brandeis arrived back in the office one Saturday afternoon after the Justices had voted on a case in which they had invested considerable time and effort, Friendly asked him how the case had come out. Brandeis replied that it was the usual; they had lost. Friendly got upset and said so, adding that, of course, the country would survive the decision, but "what awful precedents the Court is setting up." Brandeis replied prophetically, "Don't worry. A future Court won't pay any more attention to this case than the majority is paying to those we cited. The important thing is to keep fighting."[118]

The most noteworthy case of the 1927–1928 term was *Olmstead v. United States*,[119] which challenged the government's wiretapping of a suspected criminal's conversations. Writing for the Court, Chief Justice Howard William H. Taft held that actual physical invasion of one's house was required for a violation of the law and that the wiretaps had been affixed outside the premises. As originally drafted, Brandeis's dissent relied on the ground that wiretapping violated state law, although Friendly tried to convince him that his opinion could be strengthened by asserting that wiretapping was a search and seizure within the ambit of the Fourth Amendment. Friendly persisted and eventually prevailed.[120] Brandeis's landmark dissent stated that it was "immaterial" where the connection with the person's telephone was made and analogized the situation to the opening of a letter mailed to someone else. The dissent argued that the Fourth Amendment should not be construed literally, relying heavily on the 1886 Supreme Court decision in *Boyd v. United States*,[121] which found a constitutional violation when a person subpoenaed was required to produce his incriminating records, a case Friendly later criticized. Brandeis's dissent was very broad: "every unjustifiable intrusion by the Government upon the privacy of the individual, whatever the means employed, must be deemed a violation of the Fourth Amendment."[122] The Supreme Court overruled *Olmstead* in 1967.[123]

Friendly described the background of one passage deleted from the dissent. "There [was] a very eloquent passage in the [draft] opinion," he explained, "in which Brandeis depicts how, with the growth of technology, invasions of privacy would get worse and worse. . . . He worked up to a crescendo where he said: 'And now, with the advent of television, unless this Court prevents, it will be possible to peer into the inmost recesses of the home.' " Friendly's memorandum explained to Brandeis that that was not how television worked: "you can't just beam a television set out of somebody's home and see what they're doing." The two argued for a while until Friendly offered to go to the Library of Congress and get articles on television, a solution Brandeis welcomed because he was sure he was right. As Friendly observed later, "Unhappily, I was right."[124] The Harvard professor and Supreme Court authority Paul Freund has noted that but for the efforts of one overzealous law clerk the *Olmstead* case would have been the first reference to television in a judicial opinion.[125]

Unlike some of Brandeis's clerks, Friendly found him relatively easy to communicate and get on with. Writing in 1980 to Lewis J. Paper, a biographer of Brandeis, Friendly said, "I have thought a bit more about your request that I characterize LDB as 'aloof' or 'warm' and my inability to do either. I have come up with 'benign.' He was kindly but always kept the appropriate distance."[126] Because many of Brandeis's other clerks considered him aloof and remote,[127] Friendly's reaction may tell us as much about him as about Brandeis. When Paper published his biography of Brandeis in 1983, Friendly commented, "I like the way in which Paper shows the whole man, warts and all, and there were warts."[128]

During Friendly's clerkship the Court was badly polarized, and, except for Harlan Fiske Stone and Oliver Wendell Holmes, Brandeis did not have friendly feelings for his colleagues, although he had a high regard for Willis Van Devanter's ability.[129] The venerable Holmes, however, annoyed Friendly. Brandeis hated to talk on the telephone, so his clerk would answer it when it rang. Holmes would call at noon, when he knew that Brandeis and his wife were having lunch, because he really wanted to talk to Friendly. Holmes would ask him if his boss was up to date on a case, and Friendly would invariably say he was. He would then tell Friendly that in that case he himself did not have to do anything on the case. Friendly resented Holmes's relying on Brandeis to do his work.[130]

Brandeis would have been pleased if Friendly had shared his interest in Zionism and other Jewish issues, but the clerk was not so inclined. The

Justice did not try to force it,[131] but he repeatedly mentioned his hatred of the present leadership of the Zionist movement, including Louis Lipsky, with whom he disagreed on key issues. Other subjects were the anti-Semite Justice James McReynolds, who refused to talk to or shake hands with Brandeis, and some of the people who had opposed his confirmation to the Supreme Court. Friendly described Brandeis as "a good hater; oh, he could hate very well."[132]

Friendly was not fond of Alice Goldmark Brandeis, the Justice's wife: "She was a pain in the neck, in my view . . . she was just too good for this world, or thought she was." He acknowledged that she *did* come from a distinguished family, the Goldmarks, "and she never let you forget that." Mrs. Brandeis "was one of these plain livers and high thinkers. She did better at the first than at the second," Friendly ventured. Their furniture was threadbare and unattractive, and he so disliked the "atrocious food" she served that he always preferred to come *after* dinner to engage in the sparkling conversation there among the important guests.[133]

Mrs. Brandeis tried to get clerks to work for her on her projects, Friendly remarked. For example, she was writing a book on a relative, Karl Goldmark, whom Friendly described, possibly out of distaste for her, as a "minor Austrian composer." (He was a Hungarian of some stature.) He recounted with a chuckle, "I really had to try to let her know that I was sufficiently occupied with the Justice." Friendly complained that Mrs. Brandeis made everyone feel that Brandeis was very old. "I often wondered why she made him seem so decrepit. He seemed to be in perfect health."[134]

During his clerkship, Friendly received an offer from Harvard Law School for an assistant professorship, which Brandeis, who liked his clerks to enter the public or academic life,[135] urged him to accept. Brandeis also strongly urged him not to practice in New York because it was too big and the people too remote. In fact, Brandeis made the bizarre suggestion that Friendly move to Omaha, Nebraska,[136] although he never seriously considered working in any city other than New York. After spending a year clerking he was ready for the real world; he wanted to be a grown-up. He also wanted to make a good living. While he had been willing to make financial sacrifices to become a professor of history, he was not willing to do the same to become a professor of law. He liked the law, but he loved history.

Teaching at Harvard Law School was not the only alternative to private practice that Friendly considered. He also explored working for the Interstate Commerce Commission. On April 7, 1928, he wrote James Landis that he was going to join the prestigious law firm of Root, Clark, Buckner,

Howland & Ballantine rather than the faculty of Harvard Law, adding, "I've thought seriously about the ICC. I've met one or two of the better examiners, and they seem to be highly competent men who have the joy of making important decisions. Of course, the pay is small, but if one gets up with it, a Railroad will generally pay more. However, I am dutifully going to Root, Clark."[137]

The divide between Jewish and Christian firms and lawyers in the 1920s in New York City was a real wall, as it had been and would remain for decades, especially among the elite firms. Writing in the late 1970s, Milton S. Gould, a prominent trial lawyer in New York whom Friendly respected, described the nature of legal practice at the time Friendly and he were entering private practice: "[T]he really great gulf that divided the New York bar was the prevailing ethnic and religious bigotry and prejudice. I emphasize this because it was a pervasive fact of life, and its diurnal presence permeated our thoughts and our lives. . . . [T]hose of us who came to the New York bar a half-century ago found ourselves in a microcosm in which racial and religious bigotry, xenophobia, anti-Semitism, and every other form of 'elitism' were openly practiced and generally accepted as immutable facts of life."[138]

Friendly knew Emory Buckner from his work on the prosecution of Dougherty as well as the dinners he attended with Frankfurter. Another senior partner in the firm was Grenville Clark, a classmate of Franklin Delano Roosevelt who was active in the American Civil Liberties Union as well as being a very good corporate lawyer. Elihu Root Jr., the son of a Senator and then Secretary of State during World War I, although not a legal heavyweight, was a delightful and popular companion. Younger partners included Leo Gottlieb, who, along with Buckner, was largely responsible for Friendly's joining the firm. Gottlieb, of the Harvard Law Class of 1920, the same as Clark, had been first in his class all three years there (like Friendly) but then (unlike Friendly) declined to clerk for Justice Brandeis in order to go to Root, Clark, where he became a partner in 1925.[139] At the time a few of the better firms were hiring a few Jewish associates, but Root, Clark was one of only two Wall Street firms with a Jewish partner, which was important to Friendly.[140]

The other firm was Sullivan & Cromwell, which had a greater Jewish presence than Root, Clark. Alfred Jaretzky Sr., who died in 1925, had been the firm's managing partner between 1910 and 1914. At the time Friendly was clerking for Brandeis, the firm had three Jewish partners: Eustace Seligman, Alfred Jaretzky Jr., and Edward H. Green.[141] At the suggestion of a friend, Friendly interviewed at the firm. He later told Stephen Grant, a law clerk who went to Sullivan & Cromwell after his clerkship, about his experience there. After a series of interviews, Green, who was the hiring partner, told Friendly the firm was offering him a job, but that they needed to know his answer by 5 P.M. the following day. Friendly's reaction was, "I'm a Jewish boy from Elmira; they don't want me but have to make an offer because I was Editor-in-Chief of the Harvard Law Review." He turned down the offer. When he was at Sullivan & Cromwell, Grant asked Judge David W. Peck, the firm's senior litigating partner and a close friend of Friendly's, about the incident. Peck responded that the firm had always had Jewish partners and that he couldn't believe there was anti-Semitism. Moreover, Grant learned, in those days the firm demanded a prompt response to every job offer.[142]

CHAPTER TWO

Private Practice

IN SEPTEMBER 1928 Friendly entered private practice, where he remained for thirty-one years. The firm planned for him to work exclusively for Grenville Clark, who had suffered a nervous breakdown and was constitutionally unable to delegate work. The partners felt that Clark might find it easier if one top-notch assistant was assigned to him, thinking that Friendly's superb record at Harvard would break down Clark's resistance. They were wrong. After Friendly spent a few months mostly reading the *New York Times* and engaging in other non-income-producing activities, Buckner released him from Clark. Nevertheless, over the years Friendly did considerable work with Clark, including assisting him with cases involving insurance companies, savings banks, and bankrupt railroads.[1] Friendly even placed Clark with Brandeis and Frankfurter as the men who most influenced him.[2]

In late 1928, when Elihu Root Jr. learned that a senior associate, John Marshall Harlan, was not available for an assignment, he assigned Friendly to assist another associate on a simple routine matter for two of Root's new clients, Pan American Airways, which had been founded in 1927, and Pan American Grace Airways (or Panagra), a company jointly owned by Pan American and W. R. Grace & Co. Friendly soon tackled a more serious matter for Pan American and Panagra, when another carrier challenged the award to them of an important mail route in Chile.[3] At the time revenue from U.S. Post Office business was essential to the survival of air routes and airlines. Friendly met the client's president, Juan Terry Trippe, whom he described as a swarthy young man (albeit Friendly's senior by a few years), who wanted answers before he finished asking his questions. Trippe was the son of a well-known New York banker; contrary to the implications of his name, he had no Spanish or Latin American blood or connection and did not know Spanish. He went to Yale in 1916, then left to enlist in the Naval Reserve Flying Corps, qualifying as a bomber pilot but seeing no action. After the war he returned to Yale, where he organized the first college flying club and found his career.

Because Root, Friendly later recounted, "had a fine mind, but had difficulty making it up," Trippe started going directly to Friendly for quick answers. Friendly initially cleared his answers with Root, later informed Root only after the fact, and eventually bypassed Root entirely. Root, something of a dilettante, was happy to have Friendly take responsibility for Pan American's legal matters. Within a few years Friendly was handling Trippe's important problems largely on his own.[4]

In time Friendly developed considerable, albeit qualified, respect for Trippe, whom he described as "a man of tremendous imagination, great courage, [and] a terrible administrator. . . . His idea of the proper time to commence a meeting would be about 5:00 or 5:30 in the afternoon," when he would summon Friendly to his apartment and keep him waiting, sometimes for hours. Friendly was upset at being ignored, but as an associate was helpless to do anything about it.[5] It certainly did not make his difficult job any easier. Trippe acted the same with just about everyone who met him, whether they were competitors, supposed allies, or government officials. Unmindful of the needs or desires of others, he drove his employees mercilessly and treated them shabbily. He ran the company as though it were his private fiefdom, for example, by simultaneously rationing key information to and overwhelming the directors with a flood of details. Sometimes he simply lied to the board. Amazingly, he got some very able people to work for him, including Charles Lindbergh;[6] Evan Young, a veteran State Department official; Andre Priester, a Dutch engineer; and Friendly.

A 1929 amendment to the Foreign Mail Act of 1928 allowed payment to airlines for the miles traveled for delivery of foreign mail to a foreign country, but not for the return trips to the United States. After an amendment provided for the retroactive payment for return trips and other services, Trippe sent Friendly to Washington to address the problems in earlier contracts and draft new contracts to extend routes from Puerto Rico to Trinidad and Dutch Guiana as well as from Mexico City to Guatemala and the Canal Zone, all important extensions of Pan American routes at the time. What was envisaged to take a week or so instead occupied Friendly for almost a year and a half.

Trippe was a man on a mission, and Pan American was now the world's largest international airline. By the end of 1929 it had grown from a company capitalized at $534,000 to one capitalized at $6 million, with twelve hundred employees, forty-four multiengine transport planes, seventy-one terminals, and landing rights over almost all of South America.[7] Needless to say, there was plenty of legal work. Although Friendly did not handle liability matters, aircraft purchases, or tax or corporate matters for Pan American, he was deeply involved in intergovernmental relations and drafting contracts, including those with the Post Office. He was a forerunner of a new era of regulatory lawyers ushered in by the New Deal. For other clients he assisted partners who gave corporate advice, wrote appellate briefs in commercial litigation, and, as the Depression deepened, assisted in bankruptcy work, including matters involving railroads.

When the stock market crash occurred in October 1929, followed by the Great Depression, Friendly was in an enviable situation, with a secure job in a growing firm. Working for a fast-growing client was another plus. As he said, "I personally felt no pain during the Depression." In August 1929 he took a trip with a friend to the White Mountains in northern New Hampshire. He explained, "I somehow owned some pretty bad stocks, and I thought, well, if anything happens to me on this trip, we were going to do some mountain climbing, I wouldn't want anybody to know I'd ever owned stocks like that! So I sold this large investment [$7,000 or $8,000, about $100,000 in today's dollars] in early August."[8]

Friendly's desultory social life began to improve. In winter and spring of 1929 his relationship with an art student collapsed and he started going out with Sophie Stern. After a short courtship, which was interrupted by a trip she took to Europe with her family, they were engaged. On September 4, 1930, at the age of twenty-seven, he married her. Or, to be more accurate, she married him, for it was on her initiative. Sophie was attractive, vivacious, intelligent, and poised. With her intuitive empathy she was quick to make close friends. An only child of a prominent Philadelphia Jewish family, her father, Judge Horace Stern, later Chief Justice of the Supreme Court of Pennsylvania, was widely respected, even revered. Her mother, Henrietta Pfaelzer Stern, was more socially prominent, coming, unlike her husband, from an established and wealthy Philadelphia family.[9] For Friendly the marriage was a major step up socially, but it is unlikely that he thought of Sophie in such terms; he was hopelessly captivated by her charms and beauty. He wrote to his mother, "And then one morning I awoke, and found that the world seemed very different from what it had before, and I knew that I was in love," an uncharacteristically bright and optimistic statement. Continuing, he wrote, "She reminds me of you in many ways. She's sweet, and gentle, and thinks of other people and their feelings before herself and her own." Friendly's mother, however, lacked Sophie's exuberance and self-confidence and tended to be retiring and remote, if not intimidated, especially in the presence of the Stern family.[10]

Sophie also was in love. Friendly seemed to represent everything she wanted in a husband; he was intelligent, well educated, motivated, successful, dependable, attentive, and devoted to her. She greatly valued her freedom, and Friendly gave her that unstintingly. His inhibitions and emotional constraints never impeded his wife's free spirit. Whether or not she recognized that her new husband's emotions were far less developed than his intellect, she embarked on the marriage with her typical enthusiasm. She devoted herself to becoming an exemplary wife, running the household, arranging their social life, and, after a few years, raising three children. Her pursuing her interests permitted him likewise to pursue what interested him most—and his three children were not his passion. Sophie had other interests as well as the family, including, after World War II, earning a master's degree in social work from Fordham in addition to her B.A. from Swarthmore. She was the perfect professional's wife, and if she was outspoken at times—she voted for the Socialist Norman Thomas—it bothered no one, clearly not her husband. Everyone loved her.[11]

After a six-week honeymoon in Italy and Paris, the couple lived in Greenwich Village for two years before moving into a luxury apartment building at 1088 Park Avenue, at the corner of Eighty-Ninth Street. It was a particularly impressive move during the Depression, and the financially comfortable Friendlys employed help—a cook and a maid, who doubled as the server at dinner. The building into which they moved had banks of elevators and one apartment on each floor. The absence of next-door neighbors reduced to nearly none any casual interaction among families living in the building. When the Friendlys socialized, it was with other Jewish couples living on the Upper East Side.[12]

Friendly had told Brandeis and Frankfurter that he wanted to spend at least three years at the firm before entertaining other job opportunities. Accordingly, on May 22, 1931, Brandeis wrote to Frankfurter, "Re Friendly. I had been thinking last night of Friendly and that his 3 year trial period would be up soon. I hope he will conclude to go to Harvard now." Dean Roscoe Pound and Professors Calvert Magruder and Edward Morgan also were urging Friendly to accept a position at the law school. Friendly turned them all down, but it was not an easy decision. He wrote to Frankfurter, "I have never come to a decision that has caused me more genuine regret."[13] That same day he wrote to his friend James Landis, "I've had a terrible week. I don't think I've ever had a problem that caused me such real anguish. . . . I'm by no means sure that I decided right." He explained his decision: "My life, as you know, has always been a pretty soft and easy one. It's only since my coming to New York that I've had to battle people, to fight, sometimes to win and sometimes to lose. I think the experience has been a developing one and that I should be doing myself an injustice if I cut it too short. . . . I have enjoyed practice well enough that I'd like to explore it a little farther."[14]

Brandeis and Frankfurter made other efforts to pry Friendly loose from his lucrative private practice. In 1932 they tried to convince him to join the Reconstruction Finance Corporation, which President Herbert Hoover created in the last year of his administration. Within a week of the request Friendly told them that he had met with Eugene Meyer—who later bought and became publisher of the *Washington Post*—and was "eager to come," an early indication that Friendly had mixed feelings about staying at Root, Clark. He would have been Assistant General Counsel. Brandeis told Frankfurter that Friendly "show[ed] more emotion than he ever disclosed to me." Friendly wrote to Frankfurter, "You may be interested to know that when my father-in-law sounded out Judge Cardozo on the subject of my going to Washington, his quick reaction was against it." Friendly "deeply disappointed" Frankfurter when he decided not to take the RFC position.[15] A year later Brandeis contacted Frankfurter "as to [the] possibility of wrenching Henry Friendly loose now. Friendly must have regretted many times his decision not to come here [Washington]." But he was a married man and starting a family, and he felt an obligation to support them in a comfortable style. Although Friendly lost interest in working in Washington, Harvard Law School periodically sought to pry Friendly away from his law practice, but it never succeeded.[16] These were Friendly's decisions, because Sophie was not interested in money or in the things that money could buy.

ONE LEGAL MATTER in which Friendly assisted John Harlan was in a class by itself. A cause célèbre that lasted from 1931 to 1933, a titillating estate case, was the most pleasurable matter on which Friendly worked while in private practice. It involved the considerable wealth of Ella Virginia von Echtzel Wendel, a renowned, even spectacular eccentric recluse who was living in a Fifth Avenue mansion when she died in 1931.[17] Ms. Wendel, the sole survivor of a family with nary a child or first cousin in sight, had an estate at the time of her death estimated by newspapers at $40 to $50 million (about $550 million in today's dollars), almost entirely in real estate, probably because her father was an associate and in-law of John Jacob Astor. Her will gave 80 percent of the estate to five charities and the balance to unidentified next of kin. Root, Clark was retained to represent the estate and carry out her wishes.[18]

Two groups soon emerged: one consisted of the five charities whose principal aims were to uphold the will and resolve the issues as quickly as possible so they could obtain the money; the other group consisted of various "next of kin" claimants. The prospect of inheriting a fortune attracted a number of purported, if dubious, beneficiaries. Given the vast amount of money involved, 2,303 would-be cousins had filed claims, some demonstrating extraordinary imagination.[19] Remarkably, more than two hundred lawyers soon represented claimants, with the largest group of 291 represented by Arthur Garfield Hays and Samuel Untermeyer, two New York lawyers. These claimants all wanted to overturn the will, for if the will was declared void, the charities would take nothing under New York law. Of course, the claimants first had to establish that they were the closest kin.[20]

With the consent of Surrogate James Foley, a State Judge in the court that heard matters involving wills and estates, Harlan and Friendly submitted to the claimants a questionnaire that required them to detail the bases of their alleged consanguinity. "By making these people state their own claims we would ultimately be able to get rid of most of them, who in their own story were more remotely related."[21] Eight hundred questionnaires were returned, one claiming a relationship in the third degree, three claiming a relationship in the fourth degree, and thirty-three claiming a relationship in the fifth degree. Because the last group included nine claimants who clearly established they were claimants in the fifth decree, Foley dismissed those claiming a sixth-degree relationship or higher, plus the fifteen hundred who did not respond. He set the remaining twenty-four claimants for trial.

First to be tried was the claim of Thomas Patrick Morris, born and raised in Scotland, who alleged that he was the son of John D. Wendel, the brother of the deceased, and the nephew of Ella Wendel and therefore a relative in the third degree. If he prevailed, Morris would win a fifth of the estate and, if he could invalidate the will, the entire estate. Harlan went to Scotland to depose people who knew John Wendel and others with potential information about Morris's claim, while Friendly stayed in New York going through the documents. Harlan had given Friendly twenty-three points of possible inconsistency in Morris's account to explore. When Harlan returned, Friendly announced that he had demolished twenty-one of the points on which Morris relied. "I was really looking for a little praise at that time and John says, 'What about these two other points!' And I think that was the only time in my life I ever got angry at John. I said, 'For God's sake, here we've been laboring like beavers while you've been playing golf in Scotland. . . . Why worry if you've gotten this fellow proved a liar in about 30 or 40 instances, isn't that enough?' 'No,' he said, 'I think we should investigate these two other points."[22] Friendly had finally encountered someone more thorough than himself.

Convinced that Morris was a fraud, Harlan and Friendly set about to demonstrate that virtually everything he said was false. To show he was genuine, Morris related in his deposition incident after incident, including meetings with John Wendel in a number of locations over a period of many years. Harlan's questions were framed in such a sympathetic manner that Morris got the impression that he was being afforded an opportunity to strengthen his case. "John's technique was to get Morris to be very, very specific about each of these dates," Friendly explained.[23] Indeed, when Morris later told his detailed story on the stand, he was quite credible. An attorney who represented claimants other than Morris wrote, "At the time the story was not much shaken on cross-examination." When Morris rested his case, the lawyer said, "It had been most impressive. The [other parties'] lawyers had lost their air of amused indifference."[24]

"The Wendels never threw anything away," Friendly said later. "We had John Wendel's checkbooks for 40 or 50 years." There were also thousands of checks and other documents that the lawyers meticulously converted into a daily time line covering 1879 to 1902.[25] Harlan recalled Morris as a witness and confronted him with the documents. Thus, on the day Morris claimed he was visiting John Wendel, his alleged father, in Arizona, the lawyers had documents showing that Wendel had stayed at a hotel on Long Island and had written checks there. There were countless such conflicts. Morris had produced a marriage certificate, not the official certificate but "the kind that were with family Bibles with honeysuckles and wedding rings," which attested to the marriage of John Wendel and Mary Ellen Devine on June 11, 1876. Using expert testimony, Harlan and Friendly proved that the paper on which John G. Wendel's will and marriage certificate was printed was not produced until after 1913 and that all signatures on the certificate were forged (although they never found any of the alleged signatories). Eventually, the two lawyers located fourteen Bibles printed by the company over a period of years that had the same form of marriage certificate. After the estate introduced all its evidence, even Morris's attorney conceded that the certificate was a forgery. The Surrogate ordered the testimony and exhibits forwarded to the district attorney for possible prosecution.[26]

As a result of the digging by Harlan and Friendly, the other contested claimants either withdrew or, in the case of six sisters, watched as their claims dissolved into puddles of demonstrated perjury and forgery. Among the sisters' other problems, Harlan's cross-examination of their key witness, a real estate salesman who supposedly discovered probative documents previously overlooked by professional investigators, established that they had promised him an outlandish 50 percent of their recovery.[27] Harlan and Friendly had eliminated all but the nine whose claims had been accepted.

Remaining was the issue of whether Ms. Wendel's will was valid. Because her competence was hardly a foregone conclusion and the stakes were enormous, the parties entered into settlement negotiations that led to an agreement in 1933. Five of the fifth-degree relatives had settled precipitously for only $25,000 each. The four remaining successful claimants, represented by Hays and Untermeyer, received a total of $2,125,000 (of which their lawyers received one-third), another sixty of the residuary legatees "received something," and the charities received the rest. Root, Clark's fee for its services was $400,000, a considerable fee at the time but below what the successful claimants' lawyers pocketed for far less work.[28] Friendly's final write-up in *The Bull,* the firm's internal newsletter, concluded, "It is [an] interesting coincidence that on the same day that the settlement was approved by Surrogate Foley, Thomas Patrick Morris was given an indeterminate sentence of from one to three years."

Almost five decades later Friendly spoke glowingly of his experience in the *Wendel* case. "Reminiscing in later years, John Harlan and I often remarked to each other that the *Wendel Estate* litigation was the most enjoyable forensic experience of our lives. It combined the elements of drama with—what is not always available—the financial resources needed to do a thoroughly professional job."[29] For Friendly and Harlan, the public interest considerations in the case were minor, if they existed at all. "Our pleasure came from the *gaudium certaminis,* the joy of battle, and from pride in a task well done."[30] Friendly could never say enough good things about Harlan: "He was awfully nice to work with. I frankly didn't have any idea that he had the intellectual grandeur that he had displayed. I enjoyed every minute that I spent with him and I knew he was a wonderfully able lawyer, but I never realized that, in addition, he was a deep thinker." The two, Friendly added, became close friends.[31] It was a friendship that lasted to the day Harlan died.

An important railroad case on which Friendly worked as an associate involved an attempt by a committee consisting of holders of railroad bonds, mainly insurance companies and savings institutions, to protect their investment from a disastrous decline in the fortunes of the railroads.[32] The members of the committee, who held $3.250 billion in railroad bonds—nearly one-third of the outstanding bonds in the country—asked the Interstate Commerce Commission (ICC) to dispense with tariff requirements and raise freight rates by 15 percent, which they said would enable them to earn a fair return and stay in business. Not unexpectedly, shippers opposed the rate increase. Six hundred lawyers participated. The desperate tone the hearing sometimes took is indicated by Friendly's account in *The Bull*: "The real high point of the case, however, will be reached today when a representative of the Methodist Church of the south will argue for five minutes on the theme that the present plight of the railroads is due to the fact that they run trains on Sunday." When the ICC decided the case, the firm's clients lost the battle but won the war: the ICC denied the request for an immediate 15 percent increase but sanctioned pooling arrangements and other progressive proposals that aided the railroads.[33]

Friendly was involved in a variety of bankruptcy matters; the most important was the bankruptcy of Paramount Pictures, but he also dealt with less prominent clients and claimants.[34] His experiences were turning him into a sophisticated, if not somewhat cynical, business lawyer. During a 1933 trip to Tallahassee, Florida, he observed the Florida legislature and saw the considerable power wielded by the drug store industry in opposing a law that taxed chain drugstores. Afterward he stopped off to see Brandeis in Washington, arriving shortly after the Supreme Court had decided *Louis K. Liggett Co. v. Lee,* which involved a Florida statute designed to protect independently owned retail stores from competition from chain stores.[35] The Court majority struck down a portion of the statute, with Brandeis writing a learned dissent that echoed his anti-big-business sentiments. Friendly told Brandeis, "I was watching the Florida legislature, and I don't think they had any of those social benefits in mind that you discussed. I think they were influenced by the drug lobby." Brandeis, Friendly said, did not crack a smile or say anything but rather changed the subject.[36]

Friendly's work for Pan American included representing the company's interests before Congress. In 1933 Senator Hugo Black commenced an investigation into alleged manipulation of contracts to the airlines by the U.S. Post Office without competitive bidding. In connection with his representation of Pan American, Friendly had taken the night train to Washington to get a contract signed before a competitor could negotiate. "[T]hat was one of the things that later became a big item in the Black Committee and the Post Office investigations—that we had done this to suppress bidding and we certainly had!"[37]

Friendly did his part in stalling Black's investigation by telling him that they couldn't get the information from such remote locations as Buenos Aires. With the statutory deadline for concluding all hearings approaching, Black set a date for Pan American to appear. As Friendly described it, "I was sitting in my office one day and looking at the statute and it occurred to me that the way the statute read, the contractor had a right to a hearing. It was a right of the contractor." He finally had "read the statute!" He "couldn't see any good coming out of a hearing," so they informed the Post Office that they were waiving a hearing. The only people whom Pan American hadn't told was the staff conducting the investigation, who were "madder than hell," Friendly related. "[It was] one of the best services that I rendered to Pan American."[38]

Friendly found time to write two law review articles in the mid-1930s. One was "Some Comments on the Corporate Reorganization Act," which appeared in the *Harvard Law Review.*[39] He had encountered the new law while assisting partner Leo Gottlieb with the reorganization of a subsidiary of Paramount Pictures. His second article, which was in the *Columbia Law Review*, was entitled "Amendment of the Railway Reorganization Act."[40]

Friendly's career at Root, Clark was nearly derailed before he became a partner. When five lawyers founded the firm in 1910, they agreed that all would receive identical financial shares in the partnership. They hired six or seven excellent young lawyers, including Leo Gottlieb and Wilkie Bushby, who in turn became partners at the same level as each other, albeit below the level of the founding partners. The process was repeated with a smaller group some years later. An assumption of what Friendly called "the layer cake theory of partnership" was that considerable space between the groups was required. The assumption was tested when Robert Page came up for partnership. Page graduated two years ahead of Friendly from Harvard Law School and had also been president of the *Harvard Law Review*. Friendly said of him, "He had absolutely everything. . . . He was an extraordinarily fine lawyer." In 1935 Page "was turned down, for no reason except that he was too close in age to the two or three that had been taken in the last take-in," and he had no choice but to leave. Form was clearly dictating substance.[41]

Seeing the implications for himself, Friendly went to Emory Buckner, who, validating his fears, told him that he was too close in age to the youngest partners and that it made sense for him to look elsewhere. So Friendly proceeded to talk to the principals of Debevoise & Plimpton, who, however, in 1936 chose Page over Friendly and William O. Douglas, then Chairman of the Securities and Exchange Commission.[42] When Clark learned of Buckner's response to Friendly, however, he exploded. Clark liked Friendly but also had a better argument: "This firm has gotten where it has largely by getting the best people out of the Harvard Law School. How do you think it's going to affect our recruiting if we turn down two editors-in-chief? Not one, but two!"[43]

FRIENDLY BECAME A PARTNER on January 2, 1937. It was an impressive achievement during the Depression: competition for positions, much less partnerships, was furious in firms like Root, Clark, not to mention that Friendly was a Jew in a prominent Wall Street firm. Although it was Root who brought in Pan American, Friendly had created an important niche with Juan Trippe. Friendly's personal clients were not a significant part of the firm's income, but luckily for him firms gave little weight to the size and number of potential partners' personal clients at the time.[44] He was set in private practice.

By January 1937 Friendly and Sophie had two children, David (four) and Joan (two); their last child, Ellen, was a year away. They were very well-off and living comfortably, but not ostentatiously. Friendly's parents had retired and moved to St. Petersburg, Florida, where Friendly dutifully called his mother weekly. Myer Friendly died of a massive blood clot in 1938 at the age of seventy-six. He left a considerable estate valued at approximately $500,000 (about $7.6 million in today's dollars), which he gave almost entirely to Leah and Henry, while making several bequests to local charities. Leah moved to Philadelphia, where she found a place near one of her friends, which was just one block from Sophie's parents. Myer's death accelerated Friendly's concern for end-of-life issues, including a fear that a stroke would incapacitate him, a fear that he retained throughout his life.[45] During the summers in the late 1930s, when work permitted, Friendly would visit his family at the summer house they had rented on Cape Cod. "There would be weeks when I would be [working] from Monday until Friday afternoon. . . . I didn't really see too much of [the children], except in the summers," and, he added, not always so very much even then. World War II required him to spend time in Washington and to send the children to summer camp, which meant that he saw his family even less.[46]

Prolongation of the Great Depression and the rise of Hitler seemed to confirm Friendly's pessimism and gloom about the future of the world. When the plight of the Jews in Germany reached crisis proportions in the mid- and late 1930s, he advanced money and brought over a number of his German relatives, including his German cousin, Max Wildberg, whom he loaned $1,500, a considerable sum in the Depression. He also assisted in the paperwork required for his relatives' immigration and helped them settle in the United States and elsewhere.[47]

A month after Friendly became partner, Roosevelt sent shock waves through the legal profession and the country when he announced his plan to enlarge the Supreme Court by adding one new Justice for each Justice over seventy who did not retire. The genesis of the "Court-packing" plan was in the extraordinary number of New Deal statutes that the Supreme Court, often called the "Nine Old Men," declared unconstitutional. The plan, which Friendly opposed, affected his relationship with Frankfurter, who, until then, had opposed mechanical changes in the Supreme Court as a way of changing its decisions. During the five months of debate, Frankfurter conspicuously remained silent out of loyalty to Roosevelt, if not to his ambition of becoming a Supreme Court Justice. "At the time," Friendly said later, "I was pained by his silence—indeed, this led to a temporary cooling off of the exceedingly warm relations we have had since 1923." They reestablished their relationship after Frankfurter joined the Supreme Court in 1939.[48]

Early in 1937 Friendly found himself in Hartford, Connecticut, substituting for his senior partner, Arthur A. Ballantine, in a debate over Roosevelt's plan with Charles E. Clark, Dean of Yale Law School, who later would be Friendly's colleague on the Second Circuit. Friendly, who argued against the plan, was introduced as a former clerk for Justice Brandeis. When he returned to New York City he found he had made a front-page headline that he remembered as "BRANDEIS LAW CLERK DENOUNCES COURT PACKING PLAN." He immediately wrote a contrite letter of apology to Brandeis, to which Brandeis replied that he should not be concerned. Brandeis meanwhile had joined with Chief Justice Hughes and Justice Van Devanter in their famous letter to Roosevelt and the Senate, saying that, despite Roosevelt's expressed concerns, the Court was well up to date with its work and did not need the help of extra Justices.[49]

Reflecting the respect in which the new partner was held, Grenville Clark gave Friendly a major role in an important railroad reorganization matter, another assignment that contributed to Friendly's expertise in railroad problems. Friendly made the overall financial presentation for the country's railroads in a matter called *Ex parte* No. 128, "The Fifteen Percent Case, 1937–38."[50]

In 1937 Friendly took on another important project. The antiquated laws dealing with air travel needed revision. The established United States airlines, both domestic and international (Pan American), realized that they were vulnerable because airmail contracts were due to expire in the summer of 1938. A fledgling airline could put in a low bid for a route against them, win the bid, and then hold up Pan American or another carrier for a large payment to get the route back.[51] As Friendly explained, "This was industry asking for regulation rather than the government imposing regulation . . . the whole industry was [behind the legislation]." Under the statute that emerged, any company that had an airmail contract would get a "certificate of public convenience and necessity" under a "grandfather" clause. Although the assignment of drafting a law was given to an interdepartmental commission appointed by President Roosevelt, there is little doubt that Friendly, along with other industry representatives, was the moving force in drafting the Civil Aeronautics Act. Commercial aviation became a regulated industry by choice.[52] The Civil Aeronautics Board (CAB) quickly became the body that declared life or death for airlines.[53]

From the passage of the Civil Aeronautics Act of 1938 until the entry of the United States into the war on December 8, 1941, Friendly appeared frequently before the CAB, although in 1941 a detached retina in his right eye slowed him down temporarily. During this period the CAB decided eighteen cases in which Friendly appeared on behalf of Pan American or one of its subsidiaries.[54] Almost all the proceedings involved extensions of Pan American routes in Latin America or the setting of mail rates, which provided a large measure of Pan American's revenue. Because the issues, such as the demand for service and the costs involved in transporting mail between two terminals, were overwhelmingly factual and required great attention to detail, they were arduous, and, almost invariably, dull.

Trippe had become wedded to the idea that Pan American, which had instituted transatlantic passenger service,[55] should be the only American international air carrier, much like those of individual European and later Asian countries, that is, "the Chosen Instrument." Nevertheless, in 1938 American Export Airlines, Inc. (AEA), a wholly owned subsidiary of American Export Lines, a steamship company, threatened Pan American's international hegemony, provoking a battle of lawyers and lobbyists before the CAB as well as the Post Office and Congress. AEA sought certificates of public convenience and necessity to fly from American cities to locations in western Europe. The key issues were the nature and extent of competition envisaged by the Civil Aeronautics Act of 1938 and the degree to which AEA was qualified to perform the services for which it sought a certificate. Friendly argued that AEA was "a company without experience in aviation, with a nominal investment and with very slender personnel," "financial vicissitudes," and an "unsavory past reputation."[56] Moreover, foreign carriers provided competition. AEA emphasized that *American* competition was essential and that it was traditional for an airline to be granted routes when it was not ready to fly the next day, and that it would catch up. The Act, drafted by Friendly and others, was ambiguous for international carriers on whether American competition was required to satisfy the statute.

Missing or ignoring Friendly's arguments, the CAB sided with AEA, perhaps expressing American distaste for monopolies, especially by the unpopular Pan American. Indeed, acknowledging Pan American's competence, the CAB found "that it does not appear that the quality of service by [Pan American] is inadequate in any respect."[57] Because the President had the final word on applications for international routes under section 801 of the Civil Aeronautics Act, the CAB presented its order to Roosevelt, who approved it on July 15, 1940. The decision was a stinging defeat. It was becoming evident that Trippe could count on neither the CAB nor the President.

The courts were Trippe's next refuge, and the forum shifted there when Pan American filed a petition in the U.S. Court of Appeals for the Second Circuit to review the CAB's orders. Rejecting Friendly's arguments, the court held that the President's "necessary approval or disapproval makes him, and not the Board, the ultimate arbiter." Because the President could rely on material outside the record and had complete discretion, the decision was unreviewable by the courts.[58] For all intents and purposes the decisions of the CAB, rarely disturbed by the White House in any event, had become virtually immune from judicial review. The court never reached the merits of Friendly's principal arguments,[59] but it did accept his contention that the statute prohibited a steamship company from owning AEA.[60] So while AEA was still going to fly the Atlantic, it would do so not as a subsidiary of American Export Lines, but of American Airlines, which bought AEA and renamed the company American Overseas Airways (AOA).[61]

PAN AMERICAN MADE two major contributions to the war effort in which Friendly participated as a negotiator, solver of legal problems, and drafter of the key contracts; he also "sat at Trippe's side during the conferences."[62] First, starting in the summer of 1940, under the guise of expanding its land-based service, Pan American built landing fields in the portion of Brazil that jutted out into the Atlantic Ocean. Neither the United States nor Pan American, which was then flying mostly seaplanes, had land bases in Brazil, and the project provided important bases from which to fight German submarines and to ferry airplanes to North Africa.[63] As Friendly recalled, "A direct approach by the Government to those South American countries for the right to establish bases would not be well received at that time. So a plan was devised, I believe by President Roosevelt himself, that it would be nice if Pan American decided it needed more [land] bases and larger ones."[64] The landing fields also would serve as bases for fighters if Germany sought to invade the Western Hemisphere by landing in Brazil from Dakar, in western Africa. The government agreed to pay the cost out of a discretionary fund that Congress had provided the President. "Drafting the contract with the judge advocate general of the army, working out the financial details in a manner best designed to preserve the secrecy desired by President Roosevelt, and obtaining the necessary clearances from various departments proved to be a laborious task."[65]

After Trippe met with Secretary of War Henry L. Stimson, a fellow Yale graduate, to discuss the plan, Stimson presided over a meeting on October 30, 1940, attended by Trippe, Friendly, Pan American's lawyer John Cooper, senior military officers, and others. In his diary Stimson complimented Trippe's attitude at the meeting: "The negotiations went off very well and very briefly considering the importance of the matter. . . . I thought Trippe took very fairly the three propositions that I put up myself."[66] The Secretary of War may have been impressed by Trippe's cooperation, but no one else was. Once the meeting in Stimson's office ended, so did Pan American's congeniality. Acting on instructions from Trippe, Friendly and Cooper pressed for every conceivable advantage, prompting a State Department advisor, Lawrence Duggan, to write, "The necessity for a situation where this company that literally exists only because of Government subsidy dictates to the Government under what terms it will undertake certain improvements for our national security is too fantastic for my credulity."[67] Friendly and Cooper had taken the War Department to the cleaners. A subsequent Senate investigation headed by Senator Harry S. Truman found no evidence of wrongdoing on the part of Pan American but criticized its tactics.[68] Trippe and Friendly and his colleagues made no distinction between representing a client in an ordinary commercial context and in a matter involving national defense.

The other Pan American wartime program ferried aircraft across the Atlantic from South America to Gambia in western Africa. After the United States, Britain, and Pan American signed a series of complex agreements, the War Department's contract with Pan American had to be amended ten times in four years to cover fifty-two projects in sixteen countries. Once again Friendly spent months in Washington negotiating and drafting contracts and amendments.[69] An academic study concluded, "It is . . . no exaggeration to say that commissioning Pan American Airways in June, 1941, to reinforce the trans-African route probably saved Egypt and markedly changed the course of the war in Russia, China, and the Pacific."[70] Trippe's war efforts notwithstanding, his reputation for unprincipled aggressiveness spread wide and deep. Franklin Delano Roosevelt called Trippe "the most fascinating Yale gangster I ever met."[71]

With the end of World War II in sight, Trippe renewed his effort to become the sole international carrier of the United States. But after a hard-fought proceeding, on June 1, 1945, the CAB certified for international travel Transworld Airlines and American Airline's AOA, cutting the pie, moreover, in a manner that disfavored Pan American.[72] The CAB forwarded its decision to the President, who had the final word on the award of international routes. No fan of Pan American, President Truman promptly approved CAB's action.

With administrative, judicial, and executive relief all but out of the question, Pan American turned to Congress. Trippe's goal was to secure by legislation his dream of running the sole U.S. carrier flying international routes, although why he thought he could win, much less overcome an all but certain Truman veto, is not clear. Through his network of relationships, Trippe was able to secure in the spring of 1945 a hearing before the U.S. Senate Subcommittee on Aviation of the Committee on Interstate and Foreign Commerce. Following the so-called Chosen Instrument hearings, the Senate committee rejected the bill by a vote of seven to two.[73]

In early 1944, through the good offices of Elihu Root Jr., Friendly represented the New York Telephone Company in the district court in a case involving a technical question of "original cost" accounting. Simplified, the issue was whether the Federal Communications Commission (FCC) could order New York Telephone to remove from its surplus account (and hence from the capital investment on which its rates would be based) the value of certain used property that it had received years earlier from AT&T pursuant to what amounted to a bookkeeping entry. This case was the first time Friendly represented any of the components of the Bell system, and, while his nominal client was New York Telephone, he in substance was representing the entire Bell system. He told his wife that evening about the "great new case" he had. When she asked whether the case had "any human interest in it," he replied, "Not an iota, but what a great case."[74]

Despite the untenable arguments his predecessors had made before the FCC, Friendly nevertheless managed to win in the district court, which barred the FCC from enforcing its order.[75] His victory was so sweeping that he urged the client to settle before the case reached the Supreme Court, where he feared the result would not hold. Settlement talks progressed nicely until the Federal Power Commission convinced the FCC to go to the Supreme Court rather than leave the "terrible" district court ruling on the books.[76] Friendly proceeded to argue the case before the Supreme Court, which decided the case in 1946 (described later in the chapter).

During the war years Friendly made his only other argument before the Supreme Court when he was assigned to represent a hapless convict who was trying to set aside his conviction for robbing a federally insured bank.[77] Selvie Winfeld Wells, who had pled guilty to four counts of bank robbery and faced forty-five years in prison, filed a petition for a writ of habeas corpus to set aside his conviction on the ground that his guilty plea had been coerced by threats. The district court concluded that "in the opinion of the court such an appeal is not taken in good faith," and the Fifth Circuit affirmed the denial of Wells's appeal. The Supreme Court accepted the case and assigned Friendly to represent Wells. It developed that nowhere in the lower courts had Wells challenged the district court's certification that the appeal was taken in bad faith. Moreover, Wells previously had filed two unsuccessful petitions in California for postconviction relief, including one that resulted in an evidentiary hearing at which he testified. Finally, Wells had filed his appeal to the Fifth Circuit under the wrong statutory section. Although Friendly believed that he had a good case on the merits, not even he had answers to these arguments, and he was not surprised that a unanimous vote kept Wells in prison.[78]

FRIENDLY AND GOTTLIEB had started talking about forming a firm in the late 1930s, although both were reluctant to give up the security of Root, Clark.[79] Encouraging the move was George Murmane, an investment banker and an important international client of Root, Clark and, equally important, a principal of American Bosch, a major international manufacturer of automobile equipment. This development coincided with events that changed Gottlieb's attitude toward Root, Clark and accelerated his interest in leaving. By 1940 Buckner, one of the senior partners, was ill and played a limited role in the firm's decisions. (He died in 1941.) Wilkie Bushby, described by contemporaries as "a man not so fondly remembered by almost all who worked under him as 'a mean son-of-a-bitch,'" decided to abolish equal compensation for partners of the same generation. For support Bushby first approached Gottlieb, who turned him down, telling him that he was not prepared to participate in the appraisal of his partners, all of whom were good lawyers making important contributions to the firm. Also, both Gottlieb and Friendly had concluded that Bushby was an anti-Semite.[80] Disappointing the two, Harlan supported Bushby. But with the advent of the war Gottlieb and Friendly decided to do nothing for the duration.

In 1945 it was time to take action. Friendly left Root, Clark with a group of other midlevel partners to form Cleary, Gottlieb, Friendly & Cox, thereby fracturing one of New York City's best law firms, for reasons that were not clear at the time.[81] Gottlieb later revealed the role that Friendly played in founding Cleary, Gottlieb: "Since I knew by then that

Henry was by nature cautious, and even inclined to be pessimistic, his confidence in, and enthusiasm for, the new venture was most persuasive." In actuality Friendly was very perplexed about what to do, but he finally concluded that he had no alternative, if staying meant being the only Jewish partner with Bushby and the others.[82] Gottlieb had a number of important clients, including Nathan W. Levin, who handled the investment and business affairs generally of the family of Julius Rosenwald, the dominant shareholder and head of Sears Roebuck & Co.; the investment and banking firm Salomon Brothers; Royal Typewriter Company; and the Guggenheim family, which had extensive mining interests. For his part, Friendly, who had become general counsel to Pan American during the war years, could be confident in bringing the airline with him to the new firm. He also was hopeful of receiving some of the considerable accounting and rate business of American Telephone & Telegraph Company and New York Telephone, along with work from his smaller clients.

Gottlieb and Friendly agreed that they needed a good taxman, and there was no doubt that the Root, Clark partner George Cleary was the one they wanted, and he agreed. The expanded group next approached Hugh Cox, whom they liked and respected. When the war started Cox was appointed deputy to the Attorney General for war-related matters and then Assistant Solicitor General. He was receptive and also recommended two of his Justice Department colleagues, who joined the group. One was Fowler Hamilton, who became a name partner in the 1950s. Like Friendly, Cox and Hamilton had declined faculty positions at Harvard Law School. The other person from the Justice Department was George W. Ball, who had worked in the New Deal, then the law firm of Sidley & Austin in Chicago, and returned to the government when the war started. Jean Monnet (later the founder of the Common Market, which became a client of Cleary, Gottlieb) had appointed Ball General Counsel of the French Supply Council. Melvin Steen, who had just become a Root, Clark partner, also joined the group. Cox came in as an equal partner; Hamilton, Ball, and Steen joined one level down. The departure of Cleary, Gottlieb, Friendly, and Steen from Root, Clark at the end of 1945 was amicable. Not only did the senior firm graciously announce in *The Bull* that it was wishing the new firm well, but on a more substantive level it sent them legal business, a tangible indication of fellowship in the world of private practice. Still, the split was a terrible blow to Root, Clark.[83]

Starting a new law firm as the war economy was ending was not without difficulties. As Ball said later, the founders of the firm were "those intrepid men, who had the vision and audacity—or foolhardiness, as some then thought—to launch a frail ship in such turbulent waters."[84] In fact,

Friendly told his family that they might have to economize. By this time his children were thirteen, eleven, and seven. They were in expensive private schools, with expectations of going to private colleges, and perhaps graduate school. As things turned out, the new firm succeeded from the start, and the Friendlys continued to live well on Park Avenue. But although they were financially secure, Sophie and the children were not in the best shape emotionally.[85]

Joan described her father's "dragging spirit" and the absence of a strong attachment to life. Friendly, it seems, was comfortable sharing his emotions with Sophie (and others) only in writing, and he sent her many love letters, especially on their anniversary. Only two such letters survive. In 1967 he wrote, "Your 'infinite variety,' your youthful looks and spirit, your willingness to care for others when care is needed without becoming weighed down, your optimism and enthusiasm make life with you an unending joy."[86] A letter written in 1965 was reflective:

> Surely we were immature and knew little of each other on September 4, 1930; in a sense we still seem a bit like children. Yet we have managed to shoulder a fair share of responsibilities and meet the ups and downs which must come to all people in so many years, and perhaps it is the very childlike quality that enhances our enjoyment of many things which others would find dull or even disagreeable. Great capacity for happiness was not one of the gifts with which I was most generously endowed. Such as I have had I owe mainly to you, and to the children for whom you are almost solely responsible, with the grandchildren affording further promise.[87]

Friendly's use of the word "promise" to describe his grandchildren reflected his detachment, although he later recognized their personal qualities, as when he called his eldest grandchild, Lisa Goodman, "beguiling."[88] Recognizing his difficulty in engaging people on a personal basis, he told a grandson, "Lohengrin, *c'est moi*."[89]

Friendly's dejection and pessimism, which continued throughout his life, led him to focus on the "worst" possibilities, such as his mistaken concern that his daughters would not get married. (It was during the last year of his life that he actually confronted the worst, when Sophie died.) He frequently felt that the world was falling apart and that he was helpless to do anything about it, but it is impossible to know whether he would have been professionally diagnosed as depressed. Given the course of Friendly's life, the insights of a victim and student of the illness are worth considering:

> When [serious and clinical depression] comes, it degrades one's self and ultimately eclipses the capacity to give or receive affection. It is the aloneness

within us made manifest, and it destroys not only connection to others but also the ability to be peacefully alone with oneself. . . . In good spirits, some love themselves and some love each other and some love work and some love God: any of these passions can furnish that vital sense of purpose that is the opposite of depression. . . . In depression, the meaninglessness of every enterprise and every emotion, the meaninglessness of life itself, becomes self-evident. The only feeling left in this loveless state is insignificance. . . . Grief is depression in proportion to circumstances; depression is grief out of proportion to circumstances.[90]

The American Psychiatric Association requires the presence of at least six of nine listed criteria for a diagnosis of major depressive disorder. Friendly displayed few of these, but he assuredly had some symptoms and episodes consistent with depression, such as intense sadness, gloominess, and pessimism throughout much of his life. On the other hand, he suffered no weight loss, had no sleeping or eating disorder,[91] did not suffer from fatigue, took pleasure in certain activities, and, most conspicuously, had no diminished ability to think or concentrate. He had pleasures, and traveling was high among them. In 1931, for example, Sophie's parents went to a Zionist meeting in Zurich and the Friendlys joined them after the meeting. Forty-three years later Friendly commented that they stopped at Salzburg, "where [he] saw a great performance of the Rosenkavalier." He could also remember where and what they ate when traveling in Europe. He savored those memories.[92] Nevertheless, to some laypeople who knew him he seemed depressed, and they described him as depressed. His manifold attributes will speak for themselves.[93] Whatever label one affixes on Friendly's personal nature, the debilitating pressures of his consistently dispirited attitude made his achievements all the more impressive.

Friendly was neither physically nor emotionally close to David and Ellen, his oldest and youngest children, who felt that they were not high on his list of interests. He was very awkward physically and appeared uncomfortable when he held hands with or put his arm around one of his children. The girls slept in the same bedroom, and their father would wake them in the morning just before their alarm went off, close the windows, and open the shades. While he was far from unkind, he did not kiss them, hold them, or say he loved them. His daughter Joan explained her father's unsuccessful efforts at closeness: "What he experienced he had difficulty expressing and because he expressed so little the feelings never were shaped, modulated, refined. . . . I knew what he wanted, but couldn't express himself. His coming into the bedroom to wake us was a failed gesture. He was slightly gruff, too loud, used his voice rather than a caress to wake me, but I knew it was his way of saying I want to care for you. I saw the intent behind the deed when the gesture failed. He was always on the verge of giving vent to tenderness but, except in his letters, rarely able to do so."[94]

As the children grew older, new patterns in their family life emerged, such as when the girls were allowed to leave the kitchen and join their parents and older brother in the dining room for dinner, which was after their father had one or two scotches or martinis. At first the daughters welcomed the change, but Ellen quickly became disenchanted. Dinner was uncomfortably formal, structured, and slow. When the family was seated, the maid would take the service plates to the kitchen one at a time and re-place each, one at a time, with the first-course plates. When the first course was finished, Sophie would ring a little bell and the maid would return, again removing one plate at a time to the kitchen and reemerging five times, bearing one warm plate for the next course on each trip. Then the maid would bring around a platter and each person would serve himself. If any-one wanted seconds, the maid would return with the platter. Each person had a finger bowl to be used and removed, again one at a time. After the war, serving wine further added to the length of the meal. Joan and Ellen also remember that although they had a cook and their father had a good palate and appreciated good food, the food at home was austere and not very tasty. There was a set meal for each night of the week. Friendly appar-ently believed that it was not important to dine well at home, although he occasionally complained about the food. As adults, his children were not interested in fine dining.

From the standpoint of the children, dinner conversation left much to be desired. Sophie often would start with a question to her husband about some development in the news or a cultural event. While the conversation could be lively, Friendly's views were almost invariably pessimistic, at times bordering on despair—the world was going to hell in a handbasket. Sometimes the conversation was contentious, yet Friendly could be toler-ant of radical views, at least with his wife and the young. He repeated the familiar saying that if you were not a radical before twenty you had no heart, and if you were a radical after twenty you had no head.

Joan and Ellen were disappointed that conversations seemed never to have anything to do with them. Sitting in the dining room, Ellen faced a large mirror and would stare at herself during the meal, feeling that she had nothing better to do. While their mother would regularly talk to the children about school and their friends, that was not true of their father, who showed little interest in such things. He seemed to be always holding court.[95] He seemed neither to understand nor to welcome the company of children. After dinner he would retire alone to his study and for hours read and listen to his collection of phonograph records, many of which were monaural that he resisted replacing with stereophonic records, a subject about which he thought and talked a lot.[96] On occasion he would listen in the dark, which disconcerted his children and later his grandchildren.[97] His daughters also remember feeling that their father, who had a limited capacity for alcohol, sometimes had had one drink too many, which made him irritable.

With Sophie in charge of their social life, the couple often entertained or went out in the evenings. Their social friends were initially parents of their children's friends—mostly doctors, businessmen, and lawyers—which, Friendly explained, got them "into a kind of rut," as they exchanged invitations with them for years and long after their interests had diverged. Friendly did not socialize with his clients or partners, so he saw neither Juan Trippe nor John Harlan socially.[98] From time to time the Friendlys hosted large parties, and while Sophie may not have loved them, she did her part. At family gatherings Friendly talked almost exclusively to his father-in-law, Judge Horace Stern.[99] When the children invited their friends to the house, Sophie was in the middle of the mix, but Friendly would quickly retire to his study or bedroom. When the youngsters generated noise that interfered with his reading or sleep, he would forcefully inform them of their transgression.

In 1949 Friendly and Sophie, who both enjoyed traveling, started taking ambitious vacations in the summer and less elaborate ones in the winter; because of Sophie's strong preference, these were all outside of the United States.[100] On their European vacations Sophie went by ship—she refused to fly—and Friendly followed by air, flying first class on his Pan American pass. The children would first go to camp, and then join their parents, also flying first class courtesy of their father's client or, after 1959, former client, a perquisite to which Joan, as a liberal and populist, objected. Starting in 1960 Friendly arranged to arrive several days before Sophie so he could hike in the Alps with Ernst Steefel, a German-born lawyer who had been a contemporary at Cleary, Gottlieb.

Friendly enjoyed the work of the world's leading artists, and he admired artistic thinking, bestowing the highest praise on the creation of a great work of art or an original theory.[101] His reverence for great accomplishments on the part of others was part of his modesty and pessimism. A student of the Middle Ages and the Renaissance, he particularly loved old cathedrals and could sit in them for hours.[102] When his children were present, he would assume the role of guide, explaining to them why the sights were interesting and important and providing vivid historical vignettes, which they often found enjoyable, although sometimes his encyclopedic knowledge overwhelmed them. In contrast to true artistic accomplishments, he considered craftsmen and interpreters relatively minor figures. Seeing himself as a craftsman, albeit a talented one, he did not regard himself as someone truly special.

When Sophie and the children traveled without Friendly, which they usually did for a portion of their trip, they got on simply and with few inhibitions. Sophie's frugality, exuberance, and warmth affected just about everything she did, from buying clothes to traveling. Joan remembered her mother's concern with expenses, including her instructing the children to ride on the Madison Avenue bus rather than the Fifth Avenue bus because it was a nickel cheaper. Not stingy, she was building character. She talked to and listened to her children, and they talked frequently and frankly about all subjects, including sex. Years later her daughters described their relationships with their mother as that of "friends."

Not in love with ideas or the world of ideas like her husband, Sophie was a romantic who enjoyed reading romantic novels. Buoyant and vivacious, but never giddy, she loved to dance and was attractive to men, although she was no flirt. Her friends included both men and women. She was to the political left and always sympathetic to the underdog, those people who had gotten a bad deal in life. Although poles apart from Friendly both intellectually and emotionally, Sophie nevertheless liked being Mrs. Henry Friendly, for she greatly admired and loved her husband, even though he did not reach her soul and did not satisfy her emotionally. Their complicated marriage was not a close and intimate one, and not one that was mutually supportive, as Sophie would have liked. Friendly got more from Sophie than she did from him, but she never complained. Although he must have realized that he was far from an ideal husband, he was uncritically in love and grateful for all that she provided, including their children. As their daughter Joan saw it, her father was a spectator, watching and wondering how it was that someone miraculously had put together this wonderful family of which he was a part.

The children assimilated many positive traits and learned world-wise lessons from their father. Honesty in dealing with others was a given, as was taking responsibility for one's actions. Friendly did not want his children to think that he was anything special, partly because he did not feel that way himself. Honors were not important to him and, by extension, should not be for his children. He imposed no pressure on them to get good grades and never looked at their report cards, but instead emphasized the importance of good character. Later, when the children began dating, the character of their dates mattered most. He passed on to his children his strong and broad ethical sensitivity; for example, he taught them to honor an accepted invitation, no matter how much more attractive a second one might be; he was conscientious and reliable, always prompt for appointments and responded to letters and messages right away, and he expected the same of his children. Friendly's loyalty to his mother for nearly three decades after his father died was another example for his children. No hint of male supremacy clouded his outlook.

David, the oldest of the children, was a disappointment to his father, not so much because he lacked ability or interests, but because his interests were so different from his father's. When Friendly had nothing to talk about with his son, he acted as if this was David's fault. Moreover, Friendly was incapable of small talk, and he received most of his information about David and Ellen from Sophie and Joan. As a child, David required attention for his learning problems and had a hard time at highly competitive Horace Mann, a top private school in New York City. Occasionally, Friendly would sit down with him and conscientiously help him with his math homework, but he regretted that David was not more assertive. At Carleton College in Minnesota, David did very well. He excelled in subjects like physics that left Friendly cold, and it is doubtful Friendly understood his cutting-edge work in computer programming. David became a highly respected clinical pediatric ophthalmologist, and though Friendly was disappointed that he had made no outstanding discoveries and seemed to lack drive, he became an active member of a board of directors of a foundation in which David was involved. But all in all, David had almost no rapport with his father.

Although Ellen was appreciative of what he had done for her, including instilling values and recognizing that she had an obligation to help people in need, her relationship with her father can best be described as estranged. Friendly made her feel all but extraneous to his life, even though she was interested in music, which he loved, and studied voice and the piano. Unlike her brother, she did not even have the dubious experience of feeling that she disappointed her father. Ellen felt slighted by the apparent agreement between her parents that she, unlike her sister, could not succeed in a field of scholarship. She did not consider herself an intellectual or seek parity with Joan, but being bright, accomplished, and a graduate of Vassar, she did want respect. Also, more than Joan, she was conscious of her father's generally latent temper.

Joan, the second oldest and a Phi Beta Kappa graduate from Radcliffe with a Ph.D. in education as well as extensive training in psychology, was unique in making an enormous effort to try to develop a relationship with her father. Unlike her siblings, she would not accept defeat when her father did not respond, and would struggle to engage him. For example, she would give him her school papers to read and let him know that she expected him to read them. It worked, for they developed a rapport and then an intimacy. While most of their talk was intellectual and impersonal, it developed into more than that and created a strong bond between them. Joan became more and more radical as she progressed from high school to college and then to graduate school, so their political disagreements sometimes led to heated exchanges in which Friendly's face would turn red. However, they would quickly reconcile, and their discussions about current events, politics, and more personal subjects would proceed.[103]

Because Friendly could be more expressive in writing, he sent Joan letters full of compliments and fatherly love. When at Swarthmore in 1953 she told her father that she was not making friends and was unhappy there, he wrote, "I refuse to believe there is any difficulty with *you*. I do feel for you, for I know what it is to feel alone and to find it difficult to relate to people. Perhaps you are too much like me." He wrote in 1955 on her twenty-first birthday:

> From the moment that I saw my round pink cheeked daughter, I knew that I would love her dearly; but I could have no inkling of the delights that were in store. How could I realize that within that small head were such a thirst for knowledge, such an appreciation of scholarship, such love for her fellow beings—and such understanding of that peculiar old fellow who had the luck to be her father. You need hardly be told of all the good things that I wish for you on this birthday, when I would so much like to be with you. You have all the qualities for enormous happiness. I can only wish that you get your ideas and desires well sorted out, and that you may have the health, and the good fortune, required for their realization.[104]

Twenty-three years after her father's death, Joan, who knew him well, shared her sense of him:

> [There was] pathos in my father's makeup. . . . In human relations there was a gulf between what he observed, understood, felt and what he could express. . . . The gruffness and remoteness resulted from his lack of expressive modulation; they were a default position. But occasionally one saw breakthroughs, or attempts at them: When he would awkwardly offer me money at the moment of a departure, the look in his eyes when I greeted him after an absence, when he opened the blinds to wake me (he thought gently) in the morning. . . . He was far from being a mean person. He was more somber than angry, more solitary and introverted than ambitious, more cut-off than cutting-down. He meant no man harm though he was often indifferent.[105]

Joan's summary is charitable to the extent that she absolves her father from responsibility for many of his actions, but she appears to hit very close to the mark. Brilliant with ideas and knowledge, Friendly missed or ignored the extent to which he was conspicuously favoring Joan over her siblings with intimacy, and oblivious to the corrosive effect his unequal attention was having on his other children.

Friendly's attitude toward religion was as complex as the rest of his life. He identified as a Jew, his social friends were mostly Jewish, and he strongly opposed discrimination against Jews. Yet he was not a believer, and the idea of an active deity sent a shiver down his spine. In fact, he was strongly opposed to religious schools and organized religion. While his Judaism was totally secular, for the sake of the children he joined a Reform temple, bought seats, and attended some services with his family on High Holy days and did not object to having the children confirmed. Later, he reluctantly attended the bar and bas mitzvahs of his grandchildren.[106] But he was willing to go only so far. Months after Joan's marriage to Frank Goodman, the couple attended a Seder at the Friendlys' apartment. When most others drank Manischewitz kosher wine, he poured good French wine for himself and others who shared his taste.[107] Joan was surprised when she learned two decades after her father's death that he had not severed his connections with the temple after his children grew up, but did so only when Sophie died in 1985. It was then he wrote to the temple, "Mrs. Friendly's death brings up the question of my continued membership in the Synagogue. . . . Unfortunately I have no religious faith and I continued the membership in deference to the desires of my wife."[108]

Friendly's major philanthropic activity was with the Federation of Jewish Philanthropies, along with a few other Jewish-based organizations, in which he participated at the suggestion of his father-in-law, who had been president of the Philadelphia Federation. For many years he attended meetings two or three times a week after dining at home. The Federation's work included modernizing hospitals and building community centers.[109] Friendly was chairman of the budget committee, and when the influx of Jewish refugees from Germany exploded in the mid-1930s, he helped solve life-and-death problems by personally soliciting desperately needed funds from prominent Jewish financiers, starting with Felix Warburg of Kuhn Loeb & Company, the chairman of the Jewish Agency. Their meeting was a success; Warburg, with his friends, agreed to provide the substantial sums needed to rescue countless European Jews.[110] Between the end of World War II and when he became a judge, Friendly served for many years as chairman of the Federation's building fund committee, as vice president and chairman of a special committee to develop a comprehensive program of medical and social services for the entire Federation, and as a member of Mayor Robert Wagner's committee to survey New York City hospitals. He preferred fundraising because he didn't like the internal politics of organizations and had little empathy for the disadvantaged as individuals. Shortly before his death he said that he wished he could profess great satisfaction in his Federation activities, but admitted, "In retrospect I think the effort was not worth the sacrifice."[111]

Friendly's public service activities were not confined to Jewish charities. Throughout his years in private practice, he was active in bar associations on the county, city, state, and national levels, serving on committees on bankruptcy, aeronautics, public utility law, insurance law, loyalty and security, judiciary, court reform, and admissions as well as on the executive committee of the city bar. These were time-consuming activities that rarely challenged his intellect, but they satisfied his sense of obligation and contributed to an impressive public service résumé. He continued his support of Harvard, which included serving, at the request of President James Conant, on an important law school committee starting in 1943 to recruit members of the faculty, which had been depleted by the war.[112]

WHEN THE DOORS OPENED at Cleary, Gottlieb, Friendly & Cox in January 1946, just seven lawyers were operating offices in New York and, exceptionally, in Washington, D.C. Soon the firm hired nine associates in New York, three of whom had been with Root, Clark, including two women. For Friendly, along with being the third name in the new firm came a new title, Vice President and General Counsel of Pan American. His new status, however, did not improve his working relationship with Trippe or his reservations about the man. Holding, in effect, two full-time jobs, he maintained offices at both Cleary, Gottlieb at 5 Wall Street and at Pan American's offices on the upper floors of the Chrysler Building a few miles to the north.[113] While most of his efforts on behalf of Pan American involved regulation and litigation, he also devised an innovative technique that made it possible to finance the development of air transportation while sending planes all over the world without the risk of seizure by creditors.[114]

Four weeks after Cleary, Gottlieb opened for business, the Supreme Court reversed Friendly's victory in the original-cost accounting case, referred to earlier, which he had won in the district court for the New York Telephone Company when he was at Root, Clark.[115] Although Friendly lost the case in the Supreme Court, he had analyzed it correctly and had done everything he could to salvage the favorable lower court decision. More important, he had made a good impression, and, as he hoped, New York Telephone soon sent him more business, matters that required huge amounts of work, some of it, to his displeasure, in Albany.[116] Proceedings to justify a rate increase for New York Telephone, on which he worked

well into the 1950s, required proving that the current rate failed to constitute just and reasonable compensation. These were long and onerous proceedings necessitating meticulous attention to detail, but with few challenging legal issues.[117]

The rate cases, however uninspiring, had direct relevance to Friendly's
later work as a judge. In 1979 he wrote an opinion upholding an application of the New York Port Authority for an increase in tolls for cars using
tunnels and bridges (discussed in Chapter 15).[118] More significantly, his
rate work provided important tools that he utilized when he undertook to
act as chief judge of a court whose mission was to provide compensation
to freight railroads in the Northeast for surrendering their assets as part of
a multibillion-dollar reorganization (the subject of Chapter 14).

Another disappointment for Friendly occurred on May 17, 1946, when
the Civil Aeronautics Board rejected Pan American's effort to remain the
only U.S. carrier permitted to fly to countries in Latin America.[119] Whether
because of antipathy to Juan Trippe or a philosophy inconsistent with Pan
American's aspirations, the CAB usually ruled against the company. President Truman, no friend of Trippe, promptly approved the CAB's orders.[120]

In contrast, events in 1948 suggested success in the future. After the post-
war reshuffling of routes in the North Atlantic, discussed earlier, American
Airlines' American Overseas Airways, TWA, and Pan American became
competitors over the Atlantic. AOA tired of the relentless competition and
agreed to its sale to Pan American, subject to approval by the CAB. TWA
and others, however, promptly challenged Pan American's acquisition of
AOA in what was the most important and interesting of the numerous,
mostly routine matters Friendly handled for Pan American.[121]

Before the CAB the principal issue was whether the three transatlantic
competitors—Pan American, TWA, and AOA—should be reduced to two
by Pan American's acquisition of AOA in what the CAB labeled the *North
Atlantic Transfer Case*. The main adversaries were Juan Trippe's Pan
American and Howard Hughes's TWA. The CAB's Public Counsel, whom
the Civil Aeronautics Act charged with representing the "public interest,"
supported TWA. As in all proceedings in which airlines fought to obtain
contested routes, the parties presented the examiner with a library of facts,
including the number, characteristics, and age of each airline's fleet; the
number and qualifications of operating personnel; the capacity and load
factors of each plane on each route; myriad projections of future activity
under a variety of hypotheses; and much more. Friendly was superb at
managing numbers, although he lacked his mentor Brandeis's passion for
them. No longer finding many regulatory matters to be "great cases," he
performed his duties methodically and without joy.

While almost all of the direct evidence of the parties was submitted in the form of affidavits, which included seemingly endless statistics, lawyers cross-examined opposing airline officials and experts. Friendly was very good at cross-examination. From his early years on the *Wendel* case, he made sure that he was the best-informed person in the room. Several times in the battle with TWA he demolished the testimony of high corporate executives, who were not accustomed to having their pronouncements questioned, much less being forced to defend themselves against an aggressive interrogator. One such executive was Thomas F. Braniff, the president of Braniff Airlines, who on direct examination railed against Pan American's dominating the Mexican market and throwing its weight around, thereby causing a Mexican official to cancel Braniff Airlines' landing rights.

On cross-examination Friendly got Thomas Braniff to concede that all Braniff Airlines had were emergency permits that Mexico could revoke; that a number of airlines other than Pan American opposed the granting of the permits; that Braniff Airlines had failed to use five of the seven routes that the Mexican government permitted it to use and that it had promised to use; that Braniff did not know the names of many of the domestic Mexican airlines; and that Braniff Airlines had appealed the cancellation of its routes to a higher government agency and to a Mexican lower court and then to the Mexican Supreme Court, losing each time. Friendly also showed that Braniff Airlines had defied the Mexican government in refusing to pay a seventy-peso landing fee; that although Braniff disputed the applicability of the fee, it had been in force for nearly a decade; and that when confronted with the problem, Braniff Airlines tried to bargain its way out of its difficulty.[122]

Friendly had similar success with E. O. Cocke, Vice President for Traffic and a director of TWA. Friendly challenged two statements that Cocke made on direct examination: first, that Pan American had a competitive advantage and dominated the route from the United States to northern Europe, and second, that consolidation of AOA and Pan American would divert 10 percent of TWA's transatlantic traffic to the enlarged Pan American. On the first issue, Friendly showed that Cocke's statement simply lacked factual support. On many routes served by both, TWA's service was more convenient and faster; travel agents had no reason to prefer Pan American to TWA and there was no evidence they did; and in recent weeks TWA had outsold Pan American on the critical route from New York to Shannon, Ireland. After getting Cocke to testify that he could not "recall any period in which . . . TWA out-carried Pan American," Friendly presented Cocke with a flood of data that showed many such periods. Even though traffic was Cocke's responsibility at TWA, he testified that he had not read, and in some cases was not even aware of, government reports that showed that his direct testimony was false.[123]

With respect to the second point, the 10 percent diversion, Friendly pressed Cocke on how that number was prepared and what facts he had to support it. On cross-examination Friendly got him to demonstrate that the figure was little more than a guess. In one time period, for example, TWA flew 1,099 passengers on a route on which Pan American did not compete. After intense questioning on the number of passengers that would be diverted to a merged Pan American and AOA, Cocke was reduced to saying, "[P]erhaps it is only one; it is still just a diversion."[124] As with Thomas Braniff, Friendly demonstrated that the highly placed witness did not know what he was talking about.

The hearing had its lighter moments, although they were very few indeed. To a question posed to Trippe by Public Counsel William F. Kennedy, Friendly interrupted, "Wasn't that just answered?" Examiner Wrenn agreed: "I think he has answered it. I think he has gone over it, Mr. Kennedy." Kennedy did not give up:

> *Mr. Kennedy:* Mr. Examiner, I think we ought to be clear as to the importance of this particular issue. I cannot imagine the President of the United States not being interested in such an arrangement between Pan American and BOAC [British Overseas Airways], and it is the President of the United States who will decide this case.
> *Mr. Friendly:* But he does not need to read it three times. He is probably pretty busy.[125]

Friendly's quip was typical of his humor—understated, dry, intellectual, and, in this case, joined with a razor-sharp and devastating disdain for empty-headedness and pomposity. On another occasion he employed the rapier with less levity:

> *Mr. Kennedy:* Mr. [Adolph A.] Berle testified that he was advised by officials of the British Government that there were conversations on this subject between Mr. Trippe and Mr. Critchley.
> *Mr. Friendly:* He didn't say anything of the sort.
> *Mr. Highsaw [also a Public Counsel]:* He did so, pages 3694 and 3695.
> *Mr. Friendly:* That is [a] question. Public Counsel often make the mistake of failing to distinguish between questions and answers.[126]

Friendly did not always act with equanimity, but he imposed constraints on his conduct. His hard questioning of Sydney B. Smith, who testified as Public Counsel's witness and presented the underlying data that formed the basis for their position, provoked Public Counsel to object to his shouting at the witness. Friendly responded, "It is the most dishonest exhibit in the hearing." An hour later, at the close of the day's testimony, Friendly, not quite apologizing, explained that he was not accusing the witness of personal dishonesty.[127]

The North Atlantic Transfer Case had another dimension for Friendly; it marked the demise of his friendship with James Landis, who was president of the *Harvard Law Review* the year before him and who had become dean of Harvard Law School after clerking for Brandeis and then held important posts in administrative agencies. In 1974 Friendly described his relationship with Landis: "Well, that was very bad. See, we'd been great friends, and . . . you know his history at Harvard—he was kicked out as Dean [of Harvard Law School] because he was having this affair with a gal who'd been his secretary during his service during the War. And keeping her up in the North End of Boston, while avowedly living with his wife. That was a little too much for the Harvard faculty to take, so he was eased out of that job and became chairman of the Civil Aeronautics Board."[128]

Friendly continued, "I was perfectly delighted [with Landis's appointment to the CAB in 1946], because, not that I thought I was going to get any favors from Jim, but I thought it would be a great thing to have a man of such ability and character in that job." Later, however, when Truman failed to reappoint him as chairman of the Securities and Exchange Commission, Landis blamed Trippe and Friendly. Friendly explained what he thought was the real reason for Landis's nonappointment: "It was during those years his addiction to the bottle was increasing. . . . I expect the real reason was that President Truman knew that he was drunk from about 3 o'clock in the afternoon."[129]

Landis had entered the case as counsel for a group of pilots and other TWA employees who asserted that they were interested in purchasing the company. Despising Pan American and Juan Trippe and considering them unfit to operate the AOA route, Landis may have taken the case without a fee.[130] He charged that Pan American's annual report to its stockholders deceptively gave the impression that the airline was better off than it was, singling out Pan American's overstating assets by listing the full cost of its equipment and property as an asset and listing the reserves for depreciation as a liability, rather than providing a net figure. Friendly pointed out that the result was a wash—it did not matter if $10 million was listed as assets and $5 million in depreciation was listed as a liability, or $5 million was listed as assets. Landis fought back. Eventually, Friendly pulled out of his briefcase the annual reports of the American Telephone and Telegraph Company and the United Gas Corporation, which took the same approach to depreciation as Pan American. Friendly observed that they were pre-pared by two major accounting firms.[131] He asked Landis whether he was pitting his "judgment against these eminent accounting firms," to which Landis replied, "No I am simply pitting the judgment of the agencies of the Government of the United States."

Friendly was ready for Landis. He quoted the SEC rule applicable to annual financial reports accompanying proxy statements: "Such annual report including financial statements may be in any form deemed suitable by the management."[132] He continued pressing Landis: "Is there any other governmental requirement known to you in regard to annual reports to stockholders?" To this Landis could only reply, "No. There is none that I know of in regard to annual reports to stockholders." A few minutes later, Friendly pressed again: "There was no violation of the regulations of the SEC?" Landis could say only, "No, not here."[133]

Friendly's presentation convinced the examiner, who upheld Pan Ameri-can's acquisition of AOA in a 189-page typewritten opinion that tracked the arguments made in Friendly's brief. The matter then passed to the CAB and the President. When the White House released the opinion of the Board, dated July 10, 1950, and an order of President Truman that approved it, their content surprised almost everyone. Not only did Truman's order permit the acquisition to proceed, but it awarded Pan American routes to Paris and Rome that it had not requested.[134] Howard Hughes was apoplectic; Trippe was ecstatic, but not surprised.

In 1948, when Pan American and AOA signed their contract, Trippe and his senior aides had engaged in high-level machinations and lobbying, which included a meeting between Trippe and President Truman, in which the latter gave a commitment to approve the acquisition. These events led Trippe to expect Truman would ratify the transaction. When, on May 17, 1950, the CAB forwarded to the White House without public announce-ment its decision *reversing* the examiner's approval, Truman, apparently distracted by the start of the Korean War on June 25, 1950, signed an order on June 29 endorsing the disapproval and returned it to the CAB. When a leak alerted Trippe to his problem, he called a highly placed White House aide who spoke to the President. The White House told the CAB that the President had changed his mind, and not only was he approving Pan Amer-ican's acquisition of AOA, but he also was adding some routes. The CAB should rewrite its opinion and order to conform to the President's new position. The CAB's May 17 decision was buried.[135]

As far as TWA was concerned, once the President affixed his signature in accordance with the law and released the order, he had completed his statutory duty and the matter was over. After getting no satisfaction from the CAB, TWA appealed to the Second Circuit, where Friendly relied on the 1941 *American Export* case that he had lost and a subsequent Supreme Court case that took the same position.[136] Agreeing with Friendly, the Second Circuit held that the President's action was unreviewable.[137] Presumably, Friendly now felt better about his earlier defeat, although he must have had questions, if not qualms, about how the proceeding managed to turn around in his favor so decisively.

Having been rebuffed on all fronts in his effort to bar competition in the international market, Trippe thought it only fair that Pan American fly domestically. Why, he asked reasonably, if domestic airlines were allowed to fly willy-nilly from the United States around the globe, shouldn't the internationally oriented Pan American be allowed to fly between points within the United States?[138] Rejecting the advice of Friendly "to get some domestic routes when [he] could still get them," Trippe set a dangerous strategy, namely, that Pan American would accept no limitation on its domestic routes.[139] Because he feared that accepting any domestic route would destroy the company's chance to become America's "Chosen Instrument" for international air travel, Trippe insisted that his airline be allowed to carry domestic as well as international through-passengers and refused to articulate priorities among the routes he sought.[140] The CAB rejected all of Trippe's arguments in what was known as the *Domestic Route Case*.[141] It saw no need to increase the supply of planes and routes for international passengers because, it had concluded, demand would level off rather than increase. The defeat, while not seen as catastrophic at the time, created insurmountable problems for Pan American flowing from the fact that passengers who took connecting flights to their international flights would choose to remain with the airline on which they started their trip.

CLEARY, GOTTLIEB CONTINUED to thrive. At the end of 1950 the firm had twenty-seven lawyers and forty-one nonlegal personnel. More impressive, since its first year the firm's fees per lawyer increased from $115,000 to $310,000 (the latter $2.76 million in today's dollars), reflecting both the growth of existing clients and the acquisition of new ones. For example, the firm added Bing Crosby for matters arising in the eastern United States, the French government and several of its wholly owned entities, Sherman Fairchild (who invented a camera and was involved in airplane manufacturing), *Newsday*, and Federated Department Stores.[142] Meanwhile, however, two of the three lawyers originally recruited from the Justice Department left the firm. After several years in a desultory search for a place to live in New York City while commuting from Washington, Hugh Cox and his wife decided that they did not want to move to New

York, and Cox joined the Washington firm of Covington & Burling as a partner.[143] George W. Ball left the firm to work in the government, where he served as Undersecretary of State and U.S. Ambassador to the United Nations. The firm attracted two old friends: Elihu Root Jr. and Grenville Clark resigned from Dewey, Ballantine, the firm they helped found, to join Cleary, Gottlieb as "Of Counsel." Clark worked part time, while Root spent virtually all of his time engaged in public service activities.[144]

One case in the mid-1950s involving railroads generated favorable reports about Friendly in the *New York Times*, although it later created discomfort for him as a judge. In 1954 Robert R. Young, a maverick entrepreneur and president of the Chesapeake and Ohio Railroad, launched a takeover of the New York Central Railroad in a riveting proxy battle. Young and Allan P. Kirby, an extremely wealthy businessman, controlled the Alleghany Corporation, which owned a large block of New York Central shares. Many considered Young a populist battling the entrenched bankers and financiers, led by the Vanderbilts, the Whitneys, and the Morgans, along with Chase Bank, Kuhn Loeb, and Metropolitan Life Insurance Company. Young charged them with causing New York Central to shortchange passenger service in favor of the more profitable freight service.

To challenge the Wall Street board, Young nominated a diverse group, including a former railroad engineer, a physician, a woman, a Jew, a Texas oil man, along with other, more traditional businessmen and lawyers. Young's slate owned more than one million shares of New York Central, 18 percent of the total, while the incumbent board owned seventy-three thousand shares, or less than 2 percent. Among Young's claims was that the current board lacked a stake in the railroad. Each side also accused the other of ethical violations. Press, radio, and television coverage was pervasive throughout, along with flurries of full-page newspaper advertisements. It was more like a political contest than a proxy fight.[145]

Friendly sought to secure immediate depositions of Young and Kirby and succeeded in taking Young's deposition. The following day's headline in the *New York Times* was "Young Hadn't Met 7 of His Nominees," and the subhead was "At Pre-Trial Hearing He Also Admits Aides Wrote Many of His Letters to White [president of Central]."[146] Friendly's name led the third paragraph. He had succeeded in converting into a liability Young's attempt to produce a diverse board of directors with a measure of independence. That Young's staff wrote some of his letters was hardly worth a mention, much less a headline. Kirby, claiming a heart ailment and proffering a doctor's note, succeeded in delaying his deposition until after Central's annual meeting, a few days later.[147] When the proxy votes were counted, Young and Kirby won.[148]

Friendly continued to argue appellate cases. While most of his work was for Pan American,[149] he won an important case for the New York Telephone Company in 1955–1956. First the intermediate appellate court and then the New York Court of Appeals sustained the company's position against the Public Service Commission and held that the latter acted improperly in refusing to "receive proof of reproduction cost less depreciation as some evidence of present value in the case of utility property which, due to the unique restrictions placed upon it by law, cannot readily be valued by other usual methods, such as so-called 'market,' 'sales' or 'exchange' value."[150]

Friendly represented other clients, although it is unknown who brought them to the firm. He won a complex case in the First Circuit under the Public Utility Holding Company Act before Judge Calvert Magruder, a former Brandeis clerk and the same man who had congratulated him on his law school examination paper.[151] Margruder's law clerk noticed that the judge and Friendly exchanged almost imperceptible nods before Friendly gave the best argument the clerk heard all year.[152] Involved was a dispute among holders of different classes of a registered investment company as to the power of the courts to modify a decree entered in 1942 that ordered the liquidation of the company in order to permit it to continue in business without giving the minority the right to withdraw. One high-profile client who sought Friendly out was Albert Einstein, who retained him on a small personal matter.[153]

In the spring of 1959 Trippe called Friendly to his office and asked, "How would you like it if we could buy, I think, six of Howard Hughes's Boeing jets, including some in the best delivery positions, for cost?" Friendly replied, "I think that would be just fine. And I'd also like to buy the Crown Jewels at cost." But Trippe was serious. "Don't be so flip about it. I just talked with [Hughes] and that's what we're going to do. And his lawyer's coming over to see you about 3 o'clock." As Friendly explained, "I never drew a contract involving so much money so rapidly, but I thought it was better to get something done. If there were some bugs in it, we'd get them out later."[154] Hughes's lawyer, Ray Cook, arrived, looked at the contract, and had no major changes. They retyped the document, and Cook started pulling out his pen, but Friendly stopped him:

> I said, "well now, don't do anything of the sort." And he said, "Why not? I've shown you my power of attorney. Anything wrong with it?" I said, "No, looks all right to me, but I'm not going to let you do this without calling Mr. Hughes

and reading it to him over the phone." "Oh," he said. "Why?" "Well," I said, "I'll tell ya. There are just two reasons—first, I like you, and I don't want you to get into trouble. And second, I have some doubts about Mr. Hughes's liability, and I would like to do anything I could to remove them." "Well," he says, "you know, it may take hours to get Mr. Hughes." "Well," I said, "Ray, it's a 40 million dollar deal; I guess we can invest a few hours in this."[155]

A few hours later Hughes called back, and he and Cook talked privately, after which Cook said all was fine and they signed the contract. Friendly explained what followed:

[Cook] came in about noon the next day looking very crestfallen. He said, "Well, I have some bad news for you." I said, "What's that, Ray?" He said, "I just had a call from Mr. Hughes. The deal is off." "Well," I said, "I have some bad news for you, too." He said, "What's that?" I said, "Well, we have a bond issue in registration before the SEC, and after the contract was signed last night, that was taken down and filed at 9 o'clock this morning. It was a post-effective amendment, and much as we'd like to accommodate you, there's just nothing we can do about it."[156]

At that point in his narrative Friendly chuckled. He had succeeded in pushing Cook to clear the contract explicitly with Hughes before filing it the first thing the following morning, thereby making sure that the agreement would survive any effort to set it aside. That was one of Friendly's last actions in private practice before he became a judge.

Throughout his years in private practice Friendly benefited from colleagues of remarkable ability. To a man—there were few women at Cleary, Gottlieb and fewer at many other firms—they considered Friendly one of the best lawyers they ever encountered. His rigorous, demanding, and unempathic approach to his subordinates, however, made it certain that anyone who did not do first-rate work would have many sleepless nights. A Cleary, Gottlieb associate in the 1950s said that Friendly was terribly demanding and not very nice about it.[157] Former associates at Cleary, Gottlieb related that Friendly wrote on a memorandum that an associate gave to him, "This is good and original. But what is good is not original and what is original is not good."[158] Quite a few associates were simply scared of him, which may have made them perform ineffectively. While some did not want to work for him,[159] those who did and measured up to his high standards benefited from the experience. Lyman M. Tondel Jr., an associate at Root, Clark and after 1951 a partner at Cleary, Gottlieb, stated, "He was a great chief—welcoming suggestions, appreciative of aid, considerate of other aspects of one's life, loyal in the last degree, putting his junior forward at every opportunity. . . . I cannot overemphasize Henry Friend-ly's ability to marshal, exhaustively, complex facts, to isolate legal issues, to fix sensible priorities, and to sum up his conclusions or arguments in his ever-increasingly clear, pungent, literate style."[160] Professor Gerald Gunther said, "[Friendly] was my first boss in practice. . . . I was fresh out of law school and guys said, 'Don't go near that red-headed s.o.b. because he'll really make you work.' . . . And he did, and he was the greatest lawyer I ever saw."[161]

Friendly's renowned efficiency included his dictating briefs to two secre-taries working in tandem. After he made whatever few changes he con-cluded were necessary, the product of the day's work would be given to associates to check and improve. Richard W. Hulbert, a former associate and later longtime partner of Friendly's, gave his evaluation of the process: "In truth, there was little for us to do. The dictated product reflected a finely organized hierarchical structure of topics and subtopics, supported by impressive facts . . . and an almost encyclopedic recall of federal court, particularly Supreme Court, decisions."[162] Friendly's extraordinary speed created another problem. When galley proofs of a brief came back from the printer, Friendly called the associates who worked on the brief into his of-fice, where each would read his own copy. When they were halfway through reading the galleys, Friendly had finished reading and editing his copy and would ask if anyone had any corrections or changes. "None of the rest of us had finished the draft. Of course, no one called that to his attention."[163]

CHAPTER THREE

Nomination and Confirmation

T HE YEARS 1952 AND 1953 were milestones for Friendly, the first marking the twenty-fifth anniversary of his graduation from Harvard Law School, and the second his fiftieth birthday. More important, Dwight D. Eisenhower was elected President of the United States, the first Republican in the White House in two decades. As Friendly later explained, it was time to think about the future, since the present was unsatisfying: "I was getting quite sick of what I was doing—I was leading this double life, being Vice President and General Counsel of Pan Am, and also a member of my firm. I think that would have been a difficult wicket even without a client so difficult as Mr. Trippe. . . . It was a terrible strain. . . ."[1] His cases gave him little pleasure. "I was getting sick of trying cases before the Civil Aeronautics Board, where it seemed to me the result bore little or no relationship to the effort that was put into [the] trial of the merits of the case." Eisenhower's presidency offered hope: "It became known on Wall Street that the Attorney General Brownell, whom I had known ever since law school—he was Editor-in-Chief of the Yale Law Journal the year I was at the Harvard Law Review and he and I and two others were the authors of the first edition of the Bluebook. . . . And rumors abounded that he was interested in getting good people for the Circuit bench." Friendly admitted, "I was ripe for the idea."[2]

Friendly understood how judges were selected and that contacts and political activity played a major part, but he hoped that merit might control at least some of the appointments to the Second Circuit. He had no interest in the district court, which had been suggested to him as a stepping stone to the appellate bench. In fact, he quietly visited a federal district court as a spectator for a week, and that experience reinforced his strong preference for the appellate judgeship, which he conveyed to Brownell.[3] Years later he confessed to a district judge that he could not understand how they managed to do their job.[4] Nevertheless, he continued to worry that his rejection of a district judgeship could imperil his chances for a seat on the Second Circuit.[5]

The U.S. Court of Appeals for the Second Circuit, based in Manhattan, supervised the judicial output of the U.S. district courts in New York, Connecticut, and Vermont. While the organization chart of the federal courts places the Supreme Court squarely above circuit courts, by the 1950s the High Court was hearing fewer than one hundred cases a year, almost all of them involving constitutional questions or cases in which circuits disagreed on matters of federal law. Friendly observed, "[W]e don't have the final say—but on lots of types of cases we really do—admiralty, for example. I am now working on a case involving an owner's lien problem. There is no great Supreme Court interest in that one!"[6] Moreover, unlike the Supreme Court, circuit courts must decide all issues raised by the parties. They play a critical but unheralded role in the federal court system.

Friendly's reputation for brilliance was his greatest strength in seeking a judicial appointment. Yet it is worth noting the extent to which his reputation seemed to flow not from the prior thirty years but from his outstanding record at Harvard Law School and clerkship for Brandeis. Though he was a name partner in a respected Wall Street firm and active in bar association activities, these did not particularly distinguish him from many of his contemporaries. Moreover, most of his work had been in specialized segments of administrative law, and the quality of his performance at Root, Clark and Cleary, Gottlieb was personally known to only a handful of his colleagues and adversaries. In actuality his record on paper was less than impressive. He had lost his two biggest court cases,[7] and his overall record before appellate courts was twelve wins and sixteen losses (including two losses before the Supreme Court); even worse was his record before the CAB in contested cases. While a won-loss record is not an accurate reflection of a lawyer's ability, it is nonetheless an objective criterion of sorts (and always important to clients). Only two cases received noteworthy coverage in the *New York Times:* his skirmishes with James L. Landis in the *North Atlantic Route Transfer* case and his battle over taking the depositions of Robert R. Young and Allan P. Kirby in their New York Central takeover attempt.[8] Neither report emphasized his legal acumen and ability.

His published articles were from decades earlier, and he did not have a professorial appointment with any law school. Nevertheless, Friendly's reputation was deservedly stellar.

Among the first to promote Friendly for a judgeship was Justice Felix Frankfurter, who was indefatigable but not always effective, partly because of the intensity of his approaches to people. While most of Frankfurter's efforts have been made public,[9] Friendly's personal endeavors, gleaned mostly from his unpublished papers and from interviews by the author, have not been. Also, an important meeting between Frankfurter and Senate Majority Leader Lyndon Baines Johnson has been insufficiently described.

In 1953 and 1954, while Friendly was still mulling his future, Eisenhower appointed Carroll C. Hincks, a federal district judge from Connecticut, and John Marshall Harlan, Friendly's former law partner, to replace Judges Harrie Bingham Chase and Thomas Walter Swan. It was after the death of Justice Robert Jackson and the elevation of Harlan to the Supreme Court in 1954 that Frankfurter began his effort to assist Friendly by forwarding to Senator Irving W. Ives, a New York Republican, a letter written by Learned Hand, who while generally favoring the promotion of district judges to the courts of appeals, praised Friendly highly as a candidate. The appointment to fill Harlan's seat, however, went to J. Edward Lumbard, to whom Brownell had promised the position in exchange for Lumbard's agreement to serve as U.S. Attorney for the Southern District of New York.[10] Soon thereafter, in anticipation of another vacancy, Friendly asked many of his friends and acquaintances to write letters to members of the executive and legislative branches of the government. These supporters included the financier Louis M. Loeb and State Senator Thomas Desmond of New York as well as many prominent lawyers around the country whom Friendly had met mostly in bar association activities.

Prospects, however, were not good. On July 10, 1955, Learned Hand, who knew Friendly largely from the summer of 1926, wrote him, "I am afraid that, as you say, you will not get the job [as Harlan's replacement] . . . but I have the satisfaction of having tried to give the court as good a standing as any court can have, if it gets you among its members."[11] Before the next vacancy occurred, Friendly suffered what he called "the real blow," when he developed a cataract in his left eye. Happily, the operation on his eye was successful and played no role in the judicial selection process.[12]

With the death of Judge Jerome Frank on January 13, 1957, Frankfurter immediately wrote to Attorney General Brownell urging the appointment of Friendly, but the real battle was between District Judge Irving R. Kaufman and Leonard P. Moore, whom Brownell had persuaded to become U.S. Attorney for the Eastern District of New York based on a commitment similar to Lumbard's. Frankfurter, it seems, was as ardently against Kaufman's appointment as he was in favor of Friendly's. Frankfurter and Hand, along with others, wanted no part of the claim of Kaufman supporters that his promotion would signal approval of the death sentences for Julius and Ethel Rosenberg following their conviction for espionage.[13] The nomination went to Moore. Shortly thereafter Brownell resigned and was replaced by Deputy Attorney General William P. Rogers, but not before, it appears, Brownell made a commitment to Kaufman that he would get the next nomination.[14]

When Judge Medina announced on January 28, 1958, that he was retiring from active duty on the Second Circuit, Frankfurter wrote Rogers to endorse Friendly. The Association of the Bar of the City of New York recommended Friendly and the American Bar Association reported him "exceptionally well qualified."[15] Nevertheless, Friendly reconciled himself to the fact that "District Judge Kaufman ha[d] a lien" on the vacancy.[16] Friendly's candidacy was impeded by the New York State Republican Party's lukewarm support. Kaufman, a Democrat, had strong bipartisan support from the State Republican Party; Senator Styles Bridges, the leader of the conservative Republicans; Senator Jacob Javits, a New York Republican; the powerful Democratic House Judiciary Committee chairman Emanuel Cellar; and even Medina.[17] Taking no chances, Kaufman continued to seek support from persons with influence. He made an appointment to see Learned Hand, who, concerned that Kaufman was there to seek his endorsement, maneuvered to prevent him from asking. He told his clerk, Ronald Dworkin, to remain in the room, introducing him to Kaufman, "Here's Judge Ron," to signify that Dworkin was going to remain. Kaufman was unable to solicit Hand to support his candidacy.[18]

Despite Kaufman's front-runner status, before starting his 1958 summer vacation Friendly wrote to a prominent former state judge, David W. Peck, "I have asked my partner Leonard Sheriff to act as a coordinator and press the button if he thinks my return from Europe is indicated."[19] Meanwhile, a bill to increase the number of federal judges was complicating negotiations, and a deadlock developed that lasted through 1958.

When sentiment developed in early 1959 to provide the Second Circuit with a much needed judge, Friendly, not the controversial Kaufman, emerged as a consensus compromise candidate. On January 15 Friendly wrote to Harlan, "So far as I can gather, everything is in good shape—save only for the lack of a formal 'yes' from the senior Senator from New York [Javits]."[20] District Judge Charles Wyzanski, who knew both Javits and Friendly, sought to convince Javits not to block Friendly's appointment. Resisting, Javits told Wyzanski that Friendly "had done nothing for the [Republican] party."[21] Friendly had made moderate monetary contributions to New York Republicans (who were not far from Democrats on social issues in those days), but had done little else.[22] A year later Friendly told his first law clerk, Milton Grossman, that he voted Republican unless there was a very good reason not to, which Grossman interpreted as meaning that he was going to vote for Kennedy over Nixon.[23] Friendly later kept a bust of Kennedy in his chambers.[24]

Friendly suffered a setback when the *New York World Telegram* endorsed the elevation of District Judge Archie O. Dawson to the Second Circuit,[25] but this was more than offset by the almost simultaneous publication by the *New York Times* of a letter that Learned Hand had written to Eisenhower strongly endorsing Friendly: "I think there have been not more than two occasions during the long period I have served as a judge when I have felt it permissible to write a letter in favor of anyone for judicial appointment."[26]

During this imbroglio, when Friendly and Kaufman communicated by emissaries, Kaufman suggested the following compromise: Kaufman would get the next slot, and in turn he would support Friendly for Hincks's spot. Friendly's reaction was that a "retarded five-year-old" would see through the ruse, since Hincks's successor obviously would be from Connecticut. Friendly nonetheless passed along the proposition to Deputy Attorney General Lawrence E. Walsh, a friend and former district judge in the Southern District of New York, who burst into laughter when he heard the story.[27] Walsh's support for Friendly and his reservations about Kaufman are evident from his autobiography, which never mentioned Kaufman by name. After extolling Friendly, Walsh wrote, "[A]n ambitious and able district judge, a favorite of the president of the Schenley Distillery Company, also coveted the position. The company lobbyist persuaded Senator Styles Bridges . . . to block Friendly's nomination. . . . Rogers and I would not yield. Notwithstanding the senator's personal request, the president backed us and refused to withdraw the nomination."[28]

On March 10, 1959, Eisenhower sent Friendly's name to the Senate for confirmation. Friendly immediately wrote Hand, "I can't let the day go by without voicing again my very deep appreciation for your having written to the President. Ed Walsh tells me this was of decisive importance. The amateurs can't win this kind of victory over the professionals without a *deus ex machina*—and I've always regarded you as a kind of *deus*. There you were Zeus with the thunderbolt—sometimes perhaps we can see you in the Dionysus character which I think you prefer."[29] Welcoming the nomination, a *New York Times* editorial proclaimed, "Seldom has a selection been met with more unqualified and bipartisan approval." The *Washington*

Post also applauded Friendly's nomination: "Department of Justice officials surveyed the most outstanding lawyers in the New York area and found Mr. Friendly's name coming repeatedly to the top."[30]

Violating the protocols of senatorial courtesy, however, those in charge had failed to clear the nomination with Javits. As the senior U.S. Senator from a state within the judicial circuit's jurisdiction and a member of the President's party, Javits had an informal veto. Two weeks after the nomination he said that he would not oppose Friendly, but he did little to advance the process.[31] The crucial person had become Senator Thomas Dodd of Connecticut, the Democratic chairman of a subcommittee on the appointment. Friendly spoke to Dodd but made no progress,[32] which was not surprising since Dodd had publicly rebuked Trippe. After Hincks retired on May 16, adding another vacancy to be filled,[33] a *New York Times* editorial condemned delays in confirming judges.[34]

Friendly again mobilized his friends around the country to write to senators, telling a lawyer friend in Tennessee, "What is needed is for someone to stir the Subcommittee into action. However, I assume that it would be asking too much of your Senator to assume that role."[35] He was referring to Estes Kefauver, a Democrat from Tennessee and a powerful member of the Judiciary Committee. Friendly replied to a letter from a friend in Chicago, "Indeed, I do not 'mind' your having written Senator Dirkson. In fact, with time marching on as it was, I was just on the point of asking some friend in Chicago to do this."[36] There were more than a dozen similar letters, but none from a member of Harvard Law School's faculty.

On June 5 Friendly's former law partner George W. Ball sent him a memorandum: "I talked to Bob Eastabrook, who is the editor of the editorial page of *The Washington Post*. I asked him if he wouldn't begin to needle the Judiciary Committee on their failure to move on judicial appointments. He said that he had your case very much in mind and he thought the situation was a 'crying scandal,' and that the *Post* would certainly start writing about it."[37] Friendly replied the next day: "Thank you for your memorandum of June 5 in regard to the Judiciary Committee."[38] The *Post* editorial that appeared on June 9, however, was almost disastrous. After pointing out that the nomination was three months old and no hearing had been scheduled, it continued:

> The delay apparently is a result only of political considerations. Although Mr. Friendly has the recommendation of such respected judges as Learned Hand, as well as the endorsement of lawyers in the New York area, he does not have the support of Sen. Jacob K. Javits (R-N.Y.) and other New York Republican leaders. It will be a sad commentary on these New York GOP politicians if

they cannot rise above purely party considerations and back Mr. Friendly, whose qualifications for the bench are of the highest order.[39]

Friendly was chagrined and quickly moved to mitigate damages. To Attorney General Rogers he wrote, "I was shocked to learn of the editorial concerning me which appeared in yesterday's Washington Post." To Senators Javits and Keating, New York's junior senator and a Republican, he telegraphed, "Have just seen editorial concerning me in yesterday's Washington Post. Am utterly dumbfounded at this. Cannot understand how anyone could attribute delay to you or any other Republican. While I knew nothing about this editorial, as I am sure you realize, nevertheless wish to express my deep regret at this wholly unfair criticism of you and your colleagues." There is no evidence that Friendly wanted to accuse the Senate Republicans of causing the delay, but he was too involved and knowledgeable to claim that he "knew nothing about this editorial," unless he was giving the word "knew" or "this" a strikingly narrow construction.

"Out of the blue," in late August or early September 1959 Friendly received notice that his confirmation hearing would be held in a few days. When he went to Washington to be briefed at the Department of Justice, he discovered that Frankfurter had left him a note asking him to stop at the Supreme Court after the hearing. His session with the Senate committee passed without incident, and he proceeded to the Supreme Court, where Frankfurter greeted him with a smile and the question, "Well, do you want to hear the story of why they finally held your hearing?"

Frankfurter told Friendly that only Senate Majority Leader Lyndon Johnson could handle Senator Dodd, whose approval seemed essential to his appointment. Frankfurter had spoken to Learned Hand, and the two had decided that Frankfurter should deal with this. Accordingly, he arranged to meet with Johnson in the latter's office. When Frankfurter started to explain to Johnson how important it was to get Friendly on the bench, Johnson cut him off: "Felix, are you telling me that this Jewish boy should be on the Second Circuit? That's enough for me." Johnson then called out to his secretary to get Dodd on the phone. She came back a few minutes later and said that she was terribly sorry but that Senator Dodd was at that moment in the Senate barbershop getting his hair cut. Johnson said, "I don't care where Dodd is; I thought I told you I wanted to speak with him on the telephone." The call was immediately put through to Dodd, seated in the barber's chair. Johnson told him in no uncertain terms that he expected the notice for Friendly's hearing to go out in fifteen minutes.[40] The September 7 hearing, which was followed two days later by Senate confirmation, was the result.

CHAPTER FOUR

Getting Started

AFTER FRIENDLY'S NAME surfaced in early 1959 as the likely nominee for a seat on the Second Circuit, his clients assumed that his nomination would sail through without difficulty and they began consulting other lawyers, leaving him with almost nothing to do for weeks and then months. Uncertain of confirmation, he nevertheless decided to prepare for the day when he might be Judge Friendly. We know for certain only that he read the legendary casebook *The Federal Courts and the Federal System* by Henry M. Hart Jr., a Harvard professor, and Herbert Wechsler, a Columbia professor, which first appeared in 1953. The 1,500-page book included edited texts of important cases, accompanied by discussions (described as "notes") that contained numerous hypothetical questions on almost every serious problem concerning the jurisdiction of the federal courts or the source of applicable law (constitutional, federal, or state) applied by the federal courts. Friendly later said, "The book, while not exactly summer reading, proved to be the most stimulating and exciting law book I had encountered since Wigmore's *Evidence*."[1] In 1975 Friendly wrote to Professor Gerald Gunther that he was placing Gunther's casebook on constitutional law "on the very small shelf behind my desk devoted to the books that I use most often, notably Hart and Wechsler."[2] During his years on the bench Friendly cited Hart and Wechsler a total of twenty-seven times.

A second 1,500-page tome Friendly appears to have read in anticipation of confirmation was *The Legal Process: Basic Problems in the Making and*

Application of Law, also by Hart along with a fellow Harvard professor, Albert M. Sacks. Friendly later praised it as a "great book."[3] Professor Morton J. Horwitz of Harvard called the book "[t]he most influential and widely used text in American law schools during the 1950s."[4] Another scholar called it "the most influential book not produced in movable type since Gutenberg."[5]

The Legal Process had evolved from a series of mimeographed handouts and appeared in 1958 as a "tentative edition" in mimeographed form, which was used at Harvard and many other law schools.[6] It built on the writings of the Harvard Law professors Thomas Reed Powell, Felix Frankfurter, and Lon L. Fuller and spawned a new school of jurisprudence, or legal philosophy,[7] called, appropriately, the "Legal Process School." The volume consisted of fifty-five provocative legal problems with lengthy commentaries that addressed questions relating to matters like statutory construction, the proper use of legislative history, and the overruling of a judicial precedent. It focused on identifying the best forum or entity to decide a dispute, whether public or private, and the importance of following sound procedures. It also favored taking a flexible, purposivist, and largely nontextualist approach to reading statutes.[8] A judge should first identify the purpose of the statute and what policy or principle it embodied, and then should reason toward the interpretation most consistent with that policy or principle.[9]

A professor who taught *The Legal Process* as a course some twenty times has described the thrust of the volume: "The moderate philosophy embodied in these materials . . . emphasized the central role that procedure plays in assuring judicial and legislative objectivity and the corollary 'principle of institutional settlement,' which holds that judgments properly arrived at by institutions operating within their appropriate sphere or authority should be accepted as binding on the entire society until changed."[10]

The implicit premise of *The Legal Process*, both the book and the school, was that the country was on the right track and that if the size of the pie grew, everyone would end up with a larger piece, thus reflecting an overall complacency with the legal, economic, and political system; there was no need for radical surgery. The book considered problems as they came up in common law and statutory law, not constitutional law (the book does not mention the 1954 decision in *Brown v. Board of Education*),[11] and in that context took a moderate to moderate-to-liberal approach.[12] For example, the book criticized the Supreme Court for applying stare decisis when a change in the law was needed,[13] and it criticized an old New York case (1902) for not creating a right to privacy.[14] Like most observers, Hart and Sacks failed to foresee the extent to which the following decade would

fracture their assumptions. They also did not see that improving procedures carried a legal system only so far. Starting a decade later, along with
the huge changes instituted by the Warren Court in the 1960s, the Legal
Process School came under criticism from the left-leaning critical legal
studies movement and the right-leaning law-and-economics movement. Its
influence waned but did not disappear.[15]

As a judge, Friendly would frequently find himself in agreement with *The
Legal Process,* although that did not mean he did not put his own cast on
the materials. Followers of Hart and Sacks, most notably Alexander Bickel,
a professor at Yale Law School,[16] and Herbert Wechsler,[17] extended their
teaching to encompass constitutional issues, emphasizing judicial restraint
on matters they believed were better left to the legislature, such as reapportionment, aspects of criminal justice, and in the case of Wechsler, desegregation, generally taking the conservative position. Like Bickel and Wechsler,
Friendly favored following the legal-process approach on constitutional issues, although less uniformly. Friendly never lost his interest in process.

Friendly crammed on substantive areas that he would soon, he hoped,
need to be familiar. In 1975 he wrote to Dean Grant Gilmore of Yale Law
School that he had acquired the second edition of his book on admiralty
to replace the copy he "bought in 1959, while awaiting confirmation." He
also undoubtedly read many opinions decided by the Second Circuit over
the previous several years to inform himself of the precedents that he
would have to apply as well as to educate himself about the individual
judges. After he read the first dozen of Learned Hand's opinions, he concluded that none was particularly distinguished, and that gave him confidence. Then he read the next one and it was a gem, which depressed him.[18]

Friendly's personal papers contain an unpaginated seventy-seven-page
loose-leaf commonplace book, or copybook, mostly in his handwriting but
also containing some photocopies from books and articles. In it he had assembled hundreds of quotations under subject headings, starting with "Arguments" and ending with "[Ludwig] Wittgenstein."[19] The English, German,
French, and Latin entries cited sources as old as Aristotle and Tacitus. Many
quotations were from writings in the 1950s and 1960s, sandwiched between much earlier writings. The latest entry was published in 1975. The
sources were varied and learned. Most often noted was Oliver Wendell
Holmes Jr., with Learned Hand, Felix Frankfurter, Paul Freund, Samuel
Johnson, Frederic William Maitland, and the professor and later judge Jerome Frank frequently reproduced. Also represented were Montaigne and
Jeremy Bentham. The entries range from the cynical ("The jurors usually
are as unlikely to get the meaning of those words [the charge] as if they
were spoken in Chinese, Sanskrit, or Choctaw")[20] to the quirky ("If you

can think about something which is attached to something else without thinking about what it is attached to, then you have what is called a legal mind").[21] Some entries were deflationary: "A metaphysician who had written on the secret of Hegel was congratulated upon his success in keeping the secret."[22] Among those relating to history or legal history was "No single fault has been the source of so much bad history as the reading back of later and sharper distinctions into earlier periods where they have no place."[23] His favorite may have been "Many questions are solved by walking; *Beati omnes qui ambulant.*"[24]

The most popular topic was the interpretation of statutes, which he dispersed under the headings "Interpretation," "Judges," and "Statutes." Many entries said that judges should use their good sense and pay attention to the purpose of the statute. Friendly quoted jurists: "[O]ne of the surest indexes of a mature and developed jurisprudence [is] not to make a fortress out of the dictionary; but to remember that statutes always have some purpose or object to accomplish, whose sympathetic and imaginative discovery is the surest guide to their meaning";[25] "Statutes . . . are not to be deemed self-enclosed instances[;] they are to be regarded as starting points of reasoning, as means for securing coherence and for effectuating purpose";[26] and "When we take our seats on the bench we are not struck with blindness, and forbidden to know as judges what we see as men."[27] Surprisingly there was almost nothing on American constitutional law.

In an important respect Friendly was poised to do his job. A judge on the court of appeals reviews the actions of the district courts or federal agencies to decide whether the proceedings in the district court were so flawed as to require reversal. Friendly had written numerous briefs and presented oral arguments in courts of appeals and had read and analyzed many thousands of judicial opinions. But because he neither had participated in a jury trial nor had argued an appeal from a jury verdict, his approach to the review of jury verdicts and judges' charges to juries was theoretical, not practical; for example, he had no conception born of experience of harmless error in the context of a jury trial.

How much had Friendly's thirty-one years of private practice prepared him for the *kinds* of cases he would be deciding? The answer, it turns out, is not very much. For example, of the first one hundred cases in which he wrote an opinion, twenty-five were criminal (including five habeas corpus cases); twelve were labor; eleven were admiralty, including injuries to seamen; seven were on income tax or tax collection; and seven were on personal injury and other torts. Nevertheless, he welcomed the variety of cases, believing the judge "is none the worse—indeed, he is much the better—for sharpening his skills on a variety of grindstones."[28]

Friendly entertained doubts about his ability to do a first-rate job. He had confidence in his intellect and writing ability, but he had never had to write an opinion that decided that one argument was better than another, so he wasn't sure how good a judge he would be. When notified of his first sitting dates, he wrote to Frankfurter, "I can tell you I am mighty scared. It's one thing to contemplate this from afar and quite another to think of sitting in four weeks hence with experienced judges."[29] Soon after he started he told Learned Hand that he was having a hard time making up his mind about a case. Hand slammed his fist on a table and said, "Damn it, Henry, make up your mind. That's what they're paying you to do!"[30]

Friendly's first day on the bench, October 6, 1959, taught him a valuable lesson. Following a flood, a railroad sold preferred stock to bolster its economic situation. The government filed suit in *United States v. New York, New Haven & Hartford R.R.*[31] to stop the sale, claiming that a carrier subject to the Interstate Commerce Act could not lawfully change the rights of holders of a large portion of its preferred stock without authorization from the Interstate Commerce Commission. On the appeal, Friendly found for the government. After the judgment had become final, the government brought to the court's attention the Expediting Act of 1903,[32] which required appeals in ICC cases to go from the district court straight to the Supreme Court, bypassing the court of appeals. Following additional briefing, Friendly agreed and vacated his earlier opinion. The event was particularly embarrassing because it directly implicated the Supreme Court. Frankfurter sent Friendly a comforting note. After saying that he told his students, "I thought it was invigorating for a lawyer to lose his first case," he added, "After coming down here I decided that it was a healthy experience for a judge very early in his career to stub his toe by reasonably enough relying on a solid assumption without subjecting it to critical examination." Friendly thanked him for his "note of consolation."[33] Thereafter, he independently examined the jurisdictional bases for reaching his court and dismissed many cases on his own initiative (*sua sponte*).[34]

To assist him as an appellate judge, Friendly sat on the district bench several times in his first year, including on an admiralty case where each of the sailors told stories favorable to his ship. Upset at the evident perjury, Friendly went to Learned Hand, who told him that he wouldn't think much of a sailor who wouldn't lie for his ship.[35] Another opinion Friendly wrote as a district judge has become something of a cult classic. *Frigaliment Importing Co. v. B.N.S. Int'l Sales Corp.* (discussed in Chapter 22),[36] raised the tantalizing issue "What is chicken?"

Perhaps because he initially was insecure about making judicial decisions, aggravated by his experience with the Expediting Act of 1903,

Friendly started out with a rather structured approach that relied on literal and constricted readings of statutes and precedent. He disregarded many of the lessons of private practice, including his pragmatic and common-sense approach to solving legislative and other legal problems. At first he seemed almost to have emulated the Civil Aeronautics Board's failure to understand the needs of lawyers and parties to litigation and to consider the importance of examining the consequences of its decisions.

December 8, 1959, was a special day for Friendly. A judge for just ten weeks, he was to sit on a panel with Learned Hand, a jurist he revered like no other, and Chief Judge J. Edward Lumbard, another judge he greatly respected. As it turned out, in two of the three cases they heard that day Friendly disagreed with both men. *Peter Pan Fabrics, Inc. v. Martin Weiner Corp.* was a technical case under the Copyright Act of 1905, involving the sufficiency of the statutory notice, when a fabricator discarded the edge of the bolts of cloth that contained the notice when he made garments from plaintiff's fabric.[37] Friendly said that if there was no statutory notice, then there was no copyright. The second case, *United States v. Mayhury*,[38] was a challenging case under the Double Jeopardy Clause of the Fifth Amendment, which arose from a bench (nonjury) trial where the district judge rendered inconsistent judgments on the two counts. Friendly gave little weight to the purposes of the laws in both cases. He opted for a similar approach in the third that he heard that day, *Cargill, Inc. v. Commodity Credit Corp.*,[39] where the issue was whether the CCC was entitled to a jury trial on its counterclaim under its charter, which provided, "All suits against the Corporation shall be tried by the court without a jury." Friendly held that a counterclaim was not a suit against the CCC. (The three cases are discussed in Chapters 10, 11, and 17.)

Friendly's appointment to the Second Circuit pleased the faculty and students of Harvard Law School, especially members of the *Harvard Law Review*, who might now hope to become his law clerks. Yet the *Law Review*, which published a disproportionate number of comments on his opinions—six of his first-year opinions, including the three heard on December 8, but only two other Second Circuit cases where he did not write an opinion—gave Friendly a decidedly negative reception. Years later, Friendly observed, "[T]he students who run the law reviews . . . regard our opinions as presumptively erroneous."[40] Four of the *Law Review*'s six comments on Friendly's early cases concluded that he had reached the wrong result, in one case describing his opinion as "theoretically incorrect" and deficient "practically speaking."[41] Regarding *Nolan v. Transocean Air Lines*,[42] the fifth case, while the student editors found the issues close, they were not kind to Friendly: "But whether or not the lines of cases can be reconciled, the court's [Friendly's] brusque language indicates a perhaps unfortunate reluctance to fulfill the important role that a federal court might play in the creative development of state law."[43] As to *Peter Pan Fabrics*, the sixth case, the editors agreed that Friendly had the better technical argument, that the absence of a copyright notice on each garment doomed the plaintiff's case for copyright infringement, but suggested that his analysis was incomplete: "If protection is now to be afforded objects to which notice is not so easily attached, the price of such protection seems to be a partial abandonment of the requirement of strict compliance with the notice provisions,"[44] which was Hand's position.

Friendly set a constructive tone early in his dealings with his colleagues. He was sensitive to their feelings, generous with his compliments when appropriate, and expressive of his difficulties in deciding cases. In *Peter Pan Fabrics* he wrote to his colleagues, "I have become very troubled about this case. In fact, I have become so troubled that the instinct for reversal which I had on reading the briefs but lost at the argument has taken over."[45] In a labor case he wrote, "Although my heart goes out to LPM's [Judge Moore's] noble efforts, my head remains unconvinced. Since I see no reason for prolonging the agony, I attach a proposed dissent which I have made as short, as incomprehensible and as innocuous as possible."[46] Also, whenever he could, he accepted changes to his drafts suggested by other judges.[47]

On March 26, 1960, six months after Friendly started, Hand wrote Frankfurter, "Friendly is realizing all our hopes,"[48] an arguably overgenerous evaluation since Friendly had written opinions in only nineteen cases, including the appellate cases just discussed. His other opinions involved mostly routine issues of income tax and labor law, federal contract disputes under the Miller Act, a patent case (involving latex girdles), an unfair competition case, and a possible conflict between state law and the Federal Rules of Civil Procedure. Hand wrote his letter before Friendly wrote any opinions on securities laws, administrative law, federal court jurisdiction, grand jury procedure, and others areas on which he left an indelible mark. It was also before Friendly had given any lectures or published any law review article as a judge.

However one views his initial opinions, what is conspicuous about Friendly is how quickly he developed into a superb judge. By no later than the spring of his first year on the bench, he had settled comfortably on a judicial philosophy and judicial style, while providing bold revisions and refinements in many areas of the law.

CHAPTER FIVE

Judge Friendly

AFTER JUSTICE John Marshall Harlan swore in Friendly as a circuit judge in the U.S. Courthouse in Lower Manhattan on September 29, 1959, Friendly went to work. An appellate judge does most of his work in his chambers, and Friendly's was on the twenty-third floor of the courthouse. He had a private office in the chambers, and there he worked with the door closed, bent over a desk or a long table, depending on what he was doing. Whether because of frugalness or indifference to his surroundings, his office contained government-issue furniture along with some favored books and mementos.[1] His indifference to his surroundings mirrored his indifference to his clothes[2] and honors. He was concerned with achievement rather than show, and he was not building character, as his wife was. Furniture simply was not important.

Other than on days when there were oral arguments, which occupied about one week a month except during the summer, a Second Circuit judge could go through an entire day without seeing anyone but his secretary and law clerk. Judges rarely dropped in on each other. For the first seven years of his service, Friendly had but one clerk, which then became two, and then three when he served as Chief Judge in 1971–1973 or was writing opinions about the reorganization of the northeast railroads in 1980–1981 and 1982–1983. Except for his two years as Chief Judge, he had one secretary.

Friendly wrote more than opinions in his chambers; he also wrote speeches (many of which were published), articles, and shorter items, such as book reviews and tributes, for inclusion in law reviews.[3] His productivity in this area would have been prodigious for an academic who made research and writing his primary activity, but for a new appellate judge who carried a full-time judicial load it was extraordinary. Friendly exploded with speeches and articles. By the end of 1962 he had produced an analysis of administrative agencies,[4] a book on administrative law that reprinted three comprehensive lectures at Harvard,[5] a talk on what it meant to switch from being a practitioner to being a judge,[6] a tribute to Brandeis that contained considerable analysis,[7] the same respecting Learned Hand,[8] and a book review of the role and practice of an appellate judge.[9] This added up to 255 book pages in three years, with the vast majority yet to come. Between 1960 and 1965 he wrote no fewer than fourteen deeply reflective, scholarly articles.[10] In 1967 sixteen of his articles and tributes were published by the University of Chicago Press as *Benchmarks*.

His former law clerk and now Stanford Law School dean Larry Kramer explained, "You cannot fully appreciate how amazing it was for Friendly to practice law for thirty years writing almost nothing. He becomes a judge and suddenly writes seminal articles in a number of fields. It doesn't happen that way. Amazing."[11] Professor Akhil Reed Amar of Yale similarly lauded Friendly's articles.[12] Judge Richard Posner has predicted that Friendly would become better known for his articles than for his judicial opinions.[13] A flaw in some of Friendly's earlier lectures, especially his lecture series on administrative law at Harvard, was that they were so arcane and dense as to prevent assimilation by any but the cleverest listeners; they needed to be read, and reread. Friendly, moreover, was not a lively speaker.

Despite an increasing number of fellow judges and scholars who applauded his work, Friendly, due to his innate modesty, undervalued his own accomplishments. He sounded discouraged in a letter to his daughter Joan in July 1967:

> Just for fun I have thumbed through this year's opinions. I would say only a dozen at most displayed any originality, and only three could be regarded as occupying some new ground. Of course the other cases have to be decided, it is better that they be decided well. It is fun sometimes to write a well constructed opinion even if the ideas are banal, and occasionally there's a chance to tidy things up a bit. However, we kid ourselves into thinking we're much more important than we really are, since on issues of state law we can always be overturned by the state courts, which doubtless take some delight in doing precisely that, and on issues of federal law by the novem sancti [Supreme Court].[14]

Friendly's days in his chambers followed a pattern. When he arrived, he would say hello, take his coat off, enter his inner office, and shut the door, which would stay shut for long periods at a time while he worked. Some judges engaged in banter, but Friendly was all business from his arrival around 9:30 A.M. until his departure between 4:30 and 5:30 P.M.[15] When it was time to quit, he got up even if he was in midsentence in the opinion he was writing, said good-bye, and left.[16] Once in a great while he would stop to have a brief conversation with his clerks, which usually consisted of his reminiscing about his career. He almost never discussed anything personal.[17] One clerk observed, "It was so difficult for him."[18]

Assignment of cases to the three-judge panels was random, although judges had some say about when they would sit and a limited say about with whom they sat. Friendly, followed by the law clerk assigned to a case, would read the printed briefs and appendices.[19] (An appendix consists of relevant portions of the record selected by the parties, and ranges in length from a few dozen to thousands of pages.) Unlike the clerks in other chambers, Friendly's clerks did not write bench memos to assist the judge at oral argument, a point of pride with the judge.[20] He understood and remembered what he read. He was insistent that no case was unimportant, whatever its subject matter or dollar value, and he chastised any clerk who did not give a case his full attention.[21]

Unique among the circuits, no formal conferences about cases took place in the Second Circuit either before or after oral argument; moreover, there was almost no informal discussion. Rather some time between the same day and a week later, in about half the cases that were deemed sufficiently important, each judge would produce for the other two judges on the panel a "voting memorandum," as short as one page or longer than a dozen, in which he gave his intended vote, sometimes noted as tentative, and the reasons.[22] These documents constitute a remarkable record; they record the thoughts of the judge contemporaneously and are revealing and reliable, since they represent a step in the reasoned effort to resolve a case.

Friendly's internal memoranda to his colleagues were replete with criticism of the lawyers, stating, "[A]s usual the really interesting question is one the parties have scarcely discussed,"[23] or "One is rather tempted to reverse on the basis of the ineptitude of counsel."[24] In other memoranda to his colleagues he called briefs "wretched,"[25] "miserably drawn,"[26] displaying "abysmal ignorance,"[27] "unintelligibl[e],"[28] and "well below the level of tolerance."[29] About one case he said, "Reading the briefs here is like reading Alice in Wonderland."[30] He would express sympathy with defendants who were the victims of their incompetent counsel.[31] "While one sympathizes with anyone who was represented by the late Archibald Palmer . . . , that is scarcely a ground for reversing the conviction of an undeniably guilty defendant."[32] Other counsel were "stupid,"[33] "incompetent,"[34] or "ludicrous."[35] In one case he reversed a conviction on a ground that defense counsel never argued: that the indictment failed to charge a crime.[36] Occasionally, he would include humor, such as "If the John Birch Society conducts all its affairs as incompetently as these lawsuits, the republic hasn't much to fear,"[37] and "[T]he judge was favored by such ineptitude on the part of defense counsel that I fear the result is unassailable."[38]

The advocacy of the U.S. Attorneys, especially from the Southern District of New York, was good, and he rarely had occasion to question their competence.[39] However, lawyers for the states fared no better than their private counterparts in Friendly's internal memoranda, in which he noted "the utterly inadequate briefs and arguments [they] receiv[ed] from the [State Attorney General] in habeas corpus cases": "[T]he [State] Attorney General's briefs and arguments by the unprepared youngsters he sends to the court have been simply beyond belief."[40]

Friendly did not spare prominent attorneys from his attacks. In one case he sent this memorandum to the panel: "[T]he case has been shockingly ill presented, especially when we consider that one firm contains the admitted (by himself) greatest lawyer in the United States, if not the world, and the other is commonly considered a first rate office in the field of litigation."[41] When a lawyer advanced a frivolous argument, Friendly told his colleagues, "I vote to affirm from the bench without hearing the appellee and to impose double costs and a $5,000 attorney's fee. . . . The fact that he is a respected member of the bar makes action even more necessary."[42] On another occasion he contented himself with recomputing and correcting erroneous elaborate calculations contained in briefs prepared by lawyers from elite law firms.[43]

Curiously, what seemed to upset Friendly as much as the incompetence of counsel in writing briefs was their failure to follow technical rules of the court regarding the form of briefs and appendices. He lost his temper when a lawyer submitted an appendix with no index.[44] He threw an almost illegible appendix at the court clerk with instructions never to accept any filings of such poor quality again.[45]

Despite his experiences with inept counsel before the Second Circuit, he opposed major changes in the system: "As you know, I think the problem of incompetence of counsel, at least in the appellate courts, has been greatly exaggerated and that the proposed cure is probably worse than the disease."[46] Friendly maintained confidence in the workings of the lightly regulated adversary system but recognized that his stance imposed an additional burden on judges to root out overreaching, to assist parties ineptly represented, and to insist that the adversary system be truly adversarial.[47]

Friendly wanted briefs to tell him something he did not know and reasons for why he should vote for a party. Providing an accurate and intelligible statement of the facts was important, but it helped more for a lawyer to present the facts in a manner that aided his client. It was also important to provide the relevant precedents, especially from the Supreme Court. But that alone also was not sufficient. Friendly said that he could distinguish just about every decision,[48] but sometimes he could use help. If the statement of facts should tell him why he should vote for a party, the argument section of a brief should tell him how he could vote for a party. At oral argument he sought from the lawyers new information or a new approach that would help him decide the case. A former clerk stated, "His oft-made suggestion that counsel should skip the preliminaries and address the central issue surely caught counsel (and perhaps other members of the panel) by surprise."[49] When he asked a question and the lawyer responded that he would get to that later, Friendly would lose interest and not engage the lawyer with questions.[50] He also could be dismissive of a lawyer who had a hopeless task through no fault of his own, in one case asking a criminal defense lawyer, "Why are you wasting our time?"[51] He did not suffer fools gladly, although he gave everyone a chance to prove he was not a fool—not a big chance, but a chance.[52]

Friendly appreciated not only superior traditional arguments, but untraditional ones that taught him something. Thus, he enjoyed hearing Eleanor Jackson Piel, the widow of Gerald Piel, a former client of his at Cleary, Gottlieb, who simply went up to the bench and chatted with the judges during argument on a criminal case.[53] In a case involving a patent for a baby stroller, a lawyer brought to the argument the stroller that was the focus of the case (it was an exhibit at the trial), which intrigued Friendly.[54] In another case he preferred a brief by a lawyer for a member of the mob that consisted of run-on sentences to a very proper brief in the case prepared by a leading law firm; the former taught him something he did not know.[55] What Friendly did not like was extreme advocacy,[56] probably because he considered resolving cases an intellectual exercise among gentlemen and gentlewomen.

Friendly could get excited when lawyers did a first-class job. His opinions and memoranda bestowed praise on special legal performances, although only once did he describe a lawyer's performance as "superb."[57] On the other hand, in reading briefs and records Friendly was conscious of the identity and reputation of the lawyer as well as of the district judge, and he would express disappointment when someone whom he respected performed poorly.[58]

Friendly's memoranda to his colleagues demonstrated the importance of lawyers' providing him with good reasons for finding for their clients. He did not vote contrary to the law, but that did not prevent him from struggling to arrive at the result he preferred. While he often dealt with this situation silently, he sometimes told his colleagues about his dilemma:

> If there were any way in which we could sustain the result here without making what I consider an unfortunate precedent, I would welcome it.[59]

> This is a nauseating case in more ways than one. I don't think we should let the conviction stand if there is any way to reverse it.[60]

> I must say that . . . reversal is most distasteful to me. I hope that one or the other of you will be more inventive in devising a theory for affirmance.[61]

> I literally beat my clerk's brains to see if we could not find some tenable ground for reversal. . . . But the results were negative.[62]

> I vote to affirm. I do this with reluctance and with the hope that the writer of the opinion may find a basis for reversal, since the result seems to me to defy the probable intention of the parties and thus to be quite unjust.[63]

> If either of you can see a way to affirm, that will be fine with me.[64]

Friendly had few rules for himself, but he did mention one: "While I do not particularly like this disposition, I am proposing it on the basis of a principle I have long followed as a judge, namely, when in doubt take the course that involves the least pain."[65]

Friendly's intracourt memoranda did not spare district judges:

> This trial is a fine example of what can be accomplished by two incompetent lawyers and a judge who, with all respect, seem unlikely to rival Cardozo.[66]

> [T]he two judges in the Eastern District who have been concerned here have no conception how a bankruptcy proceeding ought to be conducted.[67]

> This is a beautiful example of how an application for a temporary injunction should not be handled.[68]

> It takes a real genius to create as many problems in a simple case as Judge Constantino did here.[69]

> Judge Burke has done a job of messing up this case which is extraordinary even for him.[70]

> This is Vermont justice as administered by Gibson, J.[71]

Friendly liked to get his voting memoranda out first to influence the votes of the others; he told a clerk that he didn't want his fellow judges to think something stupid.[72] While other judges ate lunch following oral argument, Friendly brought his law clerk into his office to discuss each case and then, in the clerk's presence, dictate to his secretary his voting memos for the cases argued that day.[73] His memos tended to be longer and more sophisticated than other judges', containing discussions that were impressive, given that, with few exceptions,[74] he and his clerks had conducted no independent research. Almost always he dictated memoranda in nearly final form in well-crafted paragraphs that his published opinions frequently mirrored, with Judge Jon Newman calling his voting memoranda "draft opinions."[75] In some difficult cases, the voting memoranda provoked more rounds of memoranda.[76] Although voting memoranda long antedated Friendly, they became closely identified with him, but as the workload increased in the 1970s and early 1980s the judges wrote them in fewer and fewer cases, and after Friendly died they soon disappeared.[77]

Friendly rarely changed his mind between writing his voting memorandum and sending his completed opinion to his colleagues on the panel, which is noteworthy given the usually poor quality of the parties' briefs and oral arguments. At least in his early years he did struggle and vacillate once in a while in difficult cases, such as in *United States v. Maybury*,[78] a double-jeopardy case, and *Commissioner of Internal Revenue v. Ferrer*,[79] a tax case. In *Roginsky v. Richardson-Merrell Co.*[80] he sent a follow-up memorandum to his colleagues four days after his voting memorandum: "I have been worrying over my memo in the above. I can't dispel the feeling voiced therein that, because of my horror at the result reached, I have applied a different standard as to the jury's power to draw inferences than I otherwise would. I am not sure this is justified—still less that the Supreme Court would tolerate it."[81] In another matter, *Kerner v. Flemming*, it took Friendly a few days to recognize that a claimant for Social Security disability payments had been wrongfully deprived of his rights.[82] (These cases are discussed in later chapters.)

While he usually adhered to his initial reaction, in a few instances he changed his mind when his original position "would not write."[83] Likewise, on rare occasions he would change his mind after he reviewed the proposed opinion of a colleague.[84] Friendly drew on one resource unavailable to many of his colleagues—he could pick up the telephone and speak to a distinguished professor about a legal problem, usually, but not always, in the form of a hypothetical question. When his clerk Donald Board asked him whether that was ethical, Friendly replied succinctly, "I do it."[85]

Friendly discussed problems that he had to face before setting words on paper: "The first job . . . is to decide—that's not always easy. Beyond that, all kinds of questions open up. After the result, is it a case in which we should say as little as possible? Is it a case in which we should try to elaborate the more important reasons? Let your mind roam, is it useful to say more than necessary because of the problems before the lower courts? . . . Sometimes there is no choice. The case is obviously important."[86]

To a far greater extent than a Supreme Court Justice, who was making LAW, Friendly was deciding cases in the context of more or less established legal principles. Throughout his tenure Friendly paid close attention to the facts, a product of his study of history, his clerkship with Brandeis, and his years of private practice, including the *Wendel* will case with John Harlan and the Pan American route cases.[87] Since the parties' lawyers often did not give him the information or documents he needed, he would obtain the full record of the case from the clerk of the court, once noting in an opinion, "Study of the transcripts shows that the Government's case was far stronger than indicated in the briefs."[88] One by-product of Friendly's interest in the facts and his desire to state them forcefully was that his most elegant writing appears in the recitation of the facts. Foreign to Friendly was Cardozo's statement, "There is an accuracy that defeats itself by the over-emphasis of details. I often say that one must permit oneself, and that quite advisedly and deliberately, a certain margin of misstatement."[89] When the Supreme Court created a vast and detailed body of constitutional law regarding the interrogation of suspects, Friendly lamented, "What haunts this whole subject is that so many say so much while knowing so little."[90]

WHEN IT CAME TIME for him to write an opinion, Friendly would take two letter-sized lined white pads—one for the text of the opinion, the other for the footnotes—and start writing longhand at his desk without having prepared a written outline. In front of him were the parties' briefs and, more important for him, the bound appendix. He would start with "Friendly, J.," the way the opinion would appear in the printed reports, and keep writing until he finished. The facts came first. His knowledge of the facts, which sometimes exceeded that of the parties' lawyers, gave him ideas for arguments that the lawyers missed, a common event repeatedly noted below. The large number of times that Friendly decided on the basis of arguments that he originated suggests that he was scrutinizing the facts as a step in fashioning an opinion that best resolved the issues.[91] He could organize his vast knowledge of the law and other disciplines in his mind and match them with the operative facts.[92] District Judge Jack Weinstein, who sat with Friendly on a few cases, put a different cast on his approach: "He wanted to write a law-review article; I wanted to decide a case."[93]

Friendly was an extraordinarily fast and relentless worker. For example, unless a case was unusually complex, he routinely completed the opinion in less than a day. One clerk said, "During my year of clerking I never saw the judge spend more than a day writing an opinion (and write them all he did)."[94] Friendly would compose the opinion at the same speed as he did when copying something; in fact, he was copying something, something that was in his head.[95] His speed makes the high quality of his opinions all the more remarkable since, unlike Brandeis and just about every other judge, he rarely revised or edited an opinion after he edited the initial draft. When a lapse seems to appear in one of his opinions, the reader senses that it was not ignorance or an oversight, but rather a calculated determination.[96] Possibly because of the speed at which he thought and wrote, his opinions tended to radiate competence and clarity rather than scintillating prose, although many elegant excerpts from his opinion are quoted below.

Bestowed on Friendly was not only a fabulous memory, but one enhanced by a well-developed visual sense. To absorb, comprehend, and recall the legal ruling he apparently created a visual image of the occurrence.[97] For example, when Friendly asked the government attorney arguing *United States v. Re*,[98] why certain prosecution evidence was admissible, he replied, "*United States v. Annunziato*,"[99] referring to the earlier Friendly opinion. Friendly leaned back, smiled, and said, "I was just thinking of Harry Terker handing over his envelope," which was the transaction underlying the helpful ruling in *Annunziato*.[100]

For writing, Friendly's weapon of choice was a pen, first a fountain pen, later a ballpoint pen.[101] When his ballpoint pen ran out of ink, he would buzz a clerk and hold up the pen in his left hand while he continued to write with a backup instrument. The law clerk would enter, take the pen, replace the cartridge, and return the pen to him. When his clerks gave him a cluster of inexpensive disposable ballpoint pens, he was thrilled.[102]

Why did he write his opinions by hand rather than dictate, as he did in private practice? He did it to slow himself down. If he dictated, he would have quickly overwhelmed his only secretary; she could not type and take dictation at the same time.[103] Had the government provided Friendly with a second secretary, as did Cleary, Gottlieb, his output would have been considerably greater, or at least faster.[104] As it was, he produced more opinions than his colleagues; between 1961 and 1977 he produced over 20 percent more opinions than the average judge on the Second Circuit who sat regularly.[105]

Friendly's prodigious powers of concentration translated into a requirement that he be allowed to work in peace and without distractions. A clerk who needed a book in the judge's office would silently enter the office, take the book off the shelf, and leave quickly and quietly. One clerk said his heart was in his throat whenever he needed a book there. Usually it turned out all right, but Friendly would bark when a clerk made noise or took too long.[106] He had a desk and a long table in his office, and it was a rule that he was *never* to be disturbed when he was working at the desk.[107] His private office was a very quiet place. There were some interruptions that Friendly readily accepted, such as when his doctor, his stock broker, a former clerk, a member of the American Law Institute, or another judge would telephone him. His daughter Joan recounted, "Once I screwed up my courage and called him at work, full of apologies for bothering him, and he responded so earnestly: 'Joan, you can bother me any time you want because it is never a bother,' or words to that effect." But she still felt uncomfortable calling him.[108]

Friendly often decided the case on the basis of what parties should have argued, whether or not they did so. He recognized the problems associated with such a course of action, including missing a counterargument, but considered them less serious than the alternative of choosing the least odious argument.[109] Moreover, even good briefs rarely cited law review articles, an authority Friendly respected. Thus, in one case in which the successful party's competent brief cited no law review articles on the central issues, Friendly's opinion cited six.[110] Also parties rarely considered history important enough to include in their briefs, yet many of his opinions contained historical discussions.

As the years went by, Friendly saw that the increase in workload threatened to affect the quality of the court's product. To Judge Shirley Hufstedler of the Ninth Circuit, he wrote, "I find myself tending to state conclusions without articulating the reasons as fully as I used to do,"[111] a change to which his aging may have contributed. In his last years he worked somewhat shorter hours and took naps in the afternoon. Also, instead of reading the parties' briefs when they came in, he waited until shortly before argument and then made notes in the margins.[112]

Friendly edited his handwritten drafts, usually moderately, although sometimes extensively, before he gave the two pads, to which he sometimes stapled inserts, to his secretary to type triple spaced on legal-sized paper and give directly to a clerk to check.[113] Whereupon he turned to his next opinion. Except when prompted by his clerks' suggestions or when a case was unusually difficult, the final texts of his opinions were his first drafts as typed, with minor changes.[114] The opinions were logical, clearly written, and economical yet elegant in structure and reasoning. Friendly had a few stylistic quirks, including writing long sentences, using "which" when "that" was more appropriate,[115] often using "indeed" and "in fact," and tending to eschew commas and hyphens. (Clerks were of two minds regarding long sentences. Stephen Barnett: "I felt that I was spending half my time breaking up his sentences."[116] David Engel: Friendly's long sentences "could seem fairly often a rather efficient and, on occasion, even a graceful, vehicle for fully conveying his complex view of the relationships among a set of ideas or considerations."[117])

Friendly was critical and often caustic in opinions as well as in his memoranda. A comparatively mild comment was that he found the case more difficult than did the district judge, his fellow judges,[118] or the Supreme Court,[119] or, less often, that he found it less difficult.[120] In *Bergman v. Lefkowitz*,[121] Friendly's draft opinion read, "Despite the vehemence of the attack on the trial judge's decision, we find the case considerably less difficult than he did and consequently affirm."[122] Judge Waterman objected to the second clause: "It does seem to me that since your own opinion covers 17 pages, plus 11 pages of footnotes, it is unnecessary to imply that the trial judge found unnecessary difficulty in the case."[123] Friendly changed the second clause to simply "we affirm."[124] His comments about the degree of difficulty of a case were unusual, since judges rarely express doubt or difficulty in an opinion.[125] At times he was almost conversational in tone.

A common refrain in opinions was that the parties failed to cite or understand critical items of authority:

We cannot understand how the government can misread these cases so egregiously.[126]

Since the briefs cite none of the relevant decisions of this court, it may be educational, particularly for the Government whose default in this regard is truly incredible, for us to deal with the subject at greater length than would otherwise be justified.[127]

Somewhat incredibly, neither the [State] Attorney General nor counsel for Mrs. Gras raised the issue.[128]

To even things up, the Government likewise has not cited the case most helpful to it.[129]

[The issue] cannot be determined on the simplistic all-or-nothing basis urged by the two parties.[130]

[A]lthough the assistant district counsel thus gave away a large part of the IRS' case, he did not succeed in giving away all.[131]

In a major criminal case, *United States v. Borelli*,[132] Friendly concluded that the U.S. Attorney had wrongfully and foolishly withheld from the defense a piece of impeachment material: "We add our wonder at the Government's willingness, not unique to this case, to imperil convictions hoped to be obtained after immense effort, by caviling [*sic*] over the delivery of such a paper, whose admission would not add appreciably to the strength of the defense but whose erroneous exclusion might lie just beyond an appellate court's power of rescue under the harmless error rule."

Friendly's opinions frequently criticized the lawyers' presentations. Sometimes a seemingly innocuous sentence could send shivers down the spine of a lawyer. For example, in *Roginsky v. Richardson-Merrell, Inc.*,[133] a diversity-of-citizenship case, the plaintiff prevailed at the trial in a suit for compensatory and punitive damages for an injury allegedly caused by a drug promoted and sold to lower cholesterol levels, but Friendly reversed the award of punitive damages. The applicable law was clear that to recover punitive damages the plaintiff had to demonstrate culpability on the part of management. Friendly's opinion observed, "Because defendant asserts, and plaintiff does not dispute, that for purposes of applying this rule to the case at bar 'management' includes only the presidents and vice-presidents of Richardson-Merrell and its Wm. S. Merrell Division, we need not decide whether, under New York law, the acts of inferior supervisory employees would otherwise be deemed the acts of the corporation for purposes of assessing punitive damages." So far, so good. But to that sentence Friendly appended, mercilessly, citations to New York cases that, it could be argued, showed that the defendant had conceded away what was a winning position, namely, that the acts and knowledge of lower-level supervisory employees could sustain an award of punitive damages.[134]

Friendly also published a few harsh criticisms of judges. In *Painton & Co. v. Bourns, Inc.*,[135] District Judge Constance Baker Motley badly misread the Supreme Court decision in *Lear, Inc. v. Adkins*.[136] In granting summary judgment to Painton, Motley, citing *Lear*, ruled that federal patent law preempted state unfair competition law, a contention so strained that Painton had not even argued it before Motley and did not defend it on appeal.[137] Motley also had provided an alternative ground for summary judgment based on breach of contract, which prompted Friendly to publish his cruelest comment about a district judge: "If anyone other than the parties has had the patience to read so far in this portion of the opinion, he will long since have asked himself how this controversy over the interpretation of the contract could have been thought appropriate for summary judgment. We cannot give a satisfactory answer."[138]

Such harsh criticism of a trial judge was so atypical of Friendly that one wonders why he allowed it to remain in his opinion.[139] The year before he had written to Judge Arlin M. Adams of the Third Circuit, "When I reverse, particularly in a matter like this, I usually try to refrain from much mention of the judge's name. Since this is in the headnote, phrases such as

'the judge' or 'the court' will usually suffice. While Cannella is no Cardozo, he has the saving grace of being well aware of this and is a fine human being, as you indeed indicate on p. 5. Although this is simply a matter
of taste, you might want to consider some reduction in 'Cannella's.' "[140]
Motley, moreover, was far down on the list of people he seemed to want to
embarrass publicly. Friendly was very impressed with her courageous role
in the civil rights struggle before she became a judge and, aware of her
disadvantage because of the narrowness of her legal experience, wanted
her to succeed. One clerk said, "Judge Friendly respected her, but not as a
judge."[141]

When the judge writing the majority opinion was satisfied with his effort, he sent his draft to the other two members of the panel for comment.
Aside from correcting typographical errors and making minor language
changes, sometimes including advice to his colleagues on proper gram-
mar,[142] judges made substantive suggestions, some very important. Friendly's case folders at the Harvard Law School library contain hundreds of
his comments on draft opinions by other judges and vice versa, which show
that his lists of suggested changes, sometimes running five double-spaced
legal-sized typewritten pages, were generally longer and more probative
than those he received. He never criticized without suggesting an alternative[143] and sometimes, apparently for reasons of tact, preferred to give his
comments orally.[144] He cared greatly about the written opinions of other
judges; after all, he usually was affixing his name to them.[145] After sitting
by designation, Supreme Court Justice Tom Clark wrote Friendly a handwritten note: "Here is the final on *Mele*. I have incorporated all of your
suggestions—and they have been so helpful. You were so kind in your appraisal of the opinion. I hope it is helpful. It has been great sitting with
you—and I shall always cherish the memory. My best always. Tom."[146]

Newly appointed Judge James L. Oakes responded with a twinkle to
Friendly's harsh comments on his proposed opinion: "I feel a little like a
young and somewhat over-eager pugilist who has been given a good lesson
by a more experienced pro. Duly chastened for his pugnaciousness, with
nose a little bloody and left eye slightly swollen, his genuine attitude is
respect for the ability of the pro. With this attitude of respect I have attempted to edit and modify the concurrence per the attached, retaining
most of the substance but avoiding the pugnacity and correcting some
defects aptly pointed out by H.J.F."[147] On another occasion, when he received a critical memorandum from Friendly, Oakes sent back a one-word
memorandum: "UNCLE."[148]

Friendly filed his opinions well before the time they would be listed as
delinquent by the clerk's office, which was sixty days after argument, and

he was horrified on the rare occasions that he discovered one of his cases on the delinquent list. In one instance he found that he had circulated his draft promptly, but one of the judges had not responded by returning a slip of paper to show he concurred. He stormed out of chambers; when he returned he was holding up the concurrence slip like a trophy.[149]

Once completed and filed, opinions were printed individually in booklet form and given to the parties; West Publishing Company, which published the reports in consecutive volumes; and other interested people. Usually this was the end of the Second Circuit's involvement in the case, except in the rare instance when a party prevailed on its petition for rehearing, either before the same three judges or before the entire complement of active judges (*en banc*). In a sense, however, Friendly was never finished with his opinions. He was willing to acknowledge, even years later, that his opinions may have been wrong. For example, he wrote to an academic, "As one who had some responsibility for the *Silver Chrysler* decision I have come to believe that it was a mistake and your persuasive Note reinforces that view."[150] He said pretty much the same thing to his colleagues when he referred to "the ill-advised *United States v. Fox,* 403 F.2d 97, 100 (1968), for which I admit partial responsibility."[151] Moreover, he acknowledged in print a possible error in his well-known opinion in *Frigaliment Importing Co. v. B.N.S. International Sales Corp.*[152]

Friendly absented himself from chambers twice a year for vacations with his wife, taking the longer one in the summer.[153] Since briefs did not stop arriving, he told his clerks to send him two copies of everything he should read. One copy would go to the place where he was supposed to be when the package was due to arrive, the other to the next place on the itinerary.[154] Friendly often wrote to his colleagues about cases while he was abroad.[155] But he waited until he was in chambers to write opinions. Significant and troubling, eye surgery for a detached retina and related problems kept him out of chambers several times during his judicial career, and he was hospitalized for five weeks in 1979 with subacute bacterial endocarditis.[156] When he was incapacitated his clerks came to his home, where they assisted him, sometimes reading to him briefs, draft opinions, and recently issued decisions.

The fact that he wrote his opinions without having prepared outlines, started from the beginning, and did not go through drafts meant that, more than with most judges, his opinions reflected his actual thinking process and are important independent of their subject matter. (A detailed consideration of Friendly's opinions begins in Chapter 5.) Justice John Paul Stevens noted that Friendly revealed his judging process far more than most judges.[157] When Friendly wrote *dicta,*[158] he gave the impression that he chose at the last minute not to decide the case on that ground, with statements like "but we don't have to decide that issue." As a result, he seems to have taken the task of writing *dicta* more seriously than many judges.[159]

Judge Richard A. Posner has observed that the impact of authorship by law clerks affects not outcomes—judges rarely delegate the decision making—but the structure and arguments of the opinions. Clerks, Posner said, were more legalistic and less pragmatic; "experience has yet to rub off the legalistic undercoat applied to [clerks] by their law school education,"[160] which included a premium on strict legal analysis and adherence to precedent as the main ingredients in arriving at a decision. Partly as a result of writing their own opinions, the opinions of Friendly and other judicial authors do not "remain on the semantic surface of issues" but explore "the consequences of adopting one meaning over another."[161]

Friendly did not like those people who did not do their own work, and he was stunned when he found upon starting his judicial career that his fellow judges, including Judge Lumbard, did not write their own opinions.[162] Alone among the judges on his court, he rather than the clerks wrote the initial drafts of his opinions, except for the more complex patent cases (which he hated because he was not technically trained or proficient in patent law)[163] and portions of the enormously complex railroad-reorganization cases (discussed in Chapter 19).[164] Sometimes he gave a clerk the opportunity to draft an opinion or two near the end of the term. When a clerk asked him why he didn't let him draft opinions, he answered, "Because they pay me to do that."[165] He told another clerk, "Every time I let a clerk draft an opinion I get into trouble."[166]

Few lawyers tangled with Friendly when his opinion criticized them. An exception was a lawyer who sent Friendly a three-page letter complaining about a footnote that read, "The [district] court was undoubtedly handicapped by the practice of plaintiffs' counsel, repeated on appeal, of assembling a mass of accusations, liberally larded with references to Vesco, without analysis of their legal significance."[167] In his letter the attorney wrote, "I have never until now lost my sense of awe and respect for you and the great judges with whom you share the Bench." He admitted making mistakes, but he asserted that Friendly was "wrong and unfair" to District Judge Charles E. Stewart Jr. and him, and he "most respectfully insist[ed]" that Friendly correct his opinion. The lawyer concluded by quoting from Gilbert and Sullivan's *Iolanthe* the Lord Chancellor's recollection of his early days at the Bar: "I'll never throw dust in a jury-man's eyes, or hoodwink a judge who is not overwise," hardly the smartest choice of quotations to employ regarding a judicial colleague of Friendly's. The writer sent copies of his letter to four other judges and three lawyers in the case.[168] Friendly responded promptly: "I have your letter of October 16 concerning footnote 17 of the opinion in the above. I enjoyed reading the familiar quotation from 'Iolanthe' and the remarks by my one-time preceptor, Mr. Justice Brandeis. However, I have no disposition to make any change in the footnote, which was written after detailed examination of the proceedings in both courts." He sent copies to the same seven as did the lawyer.[169]

In another case the initial release of Friendly's opinion said that a government lawyer had made "a statement manifestly and knowingly wrong." When the lawyer, Harry T. Dolan, Special Assistant to the Attorney General, sent Friendly a letter hotly disputing the accusation, Friendly sent the other panel members a memorandum: "I am chagrined to have to report that Mr. Dolan's criticism is justified to some extent." Friendly wrote Dolan a letter admitting, "Further examination of the record indicates that the statement was in error in certain respects and we are glad that you have called this to our attention. An order modifying the opinion is being entered; a copy of this is enclosed for your information."[170]

Friendly interrupted his work for lunches, which tended to follow a pattern. In the first couple of years he ate in the judges' dining room because of the opportunity to lunch with Learned Hand. Later, he usually ate alone at the long table in his office, partly because he did not feel comfortable talking when district judges were within earshot. While he might change his reading from law to history during lunch, he always ate pretty much the same thing: a glass of College Inn tomato juice, cottage cheese, a slice of pumpernickel, and herring from a jar. Some clerks had the quotidian assignment of shopping for the ingredients for these lunches. One clerk recalled having trouble finding College Inn tomato juice at the nearby store. Learning that the company was discontinuing the brand, he went to twenty other stores and bought all the tomato juice he could find. Finally, he could locate no more. Nervously he went into the judge's private office and told him that he was unable to find any more College Inn tomato juice. Friendly looked up and said, "It doesn't matter. I didn't like that brand much anyway."[171]

Fortnightly, as well as on their birthdays, Friendly went out to lunch at the Merchants Club, not far from the courthouse, with District Judge Edward Weinfeld. More rarely he went with his former partners Leo Gottlieb and Lyman Tondel; another Wall Street compatriot; another judge, usually a younger one from the district court, such as Marvin Frankel; or a former clerk.[172] Friendly cherished his lunches with Weinfeld, where the topics ranged "from mere gossip to recent rulings by the Supreme Court to matters of transcendent national or international significance," and included the doings of their children and grandchildren.[173] Occasionally, Friendly ventured into restaurants in Chinatown and Little Italy, located near the courthouse, where he delighted in discovering new gems with his luncheon partners.[174]

Friendly was an inveterate letter writer, corresponding often with judges and professors about legal matters. The lengthy list of his correspondents included Professors Herbert Wechsler, Henry Hart, Louis Henkin, Kenneth Culp Davis, Charles Alan Wright, Albert A. Ehrensweig, Walter Gelhorn, John Maguire, Arthur Corbin, Richard W. Jennings, Gerald Gunther, Frank Easterbrook, Charles Fried, Brainerd Currie, Stephen Burbank, and Grant Gilmore; Judges Richard A. Posner, Ben C. Duniway, Shirley M. Hufstedler, Jack Weinstein, Charles Wyzanski, and Harry T. Edwards; numerous lawyers around the country;[175] and others, including Frederick Merck and Anthony Lewis. He often initiated correspondence with academics by providing them with his unsolicited detailed comments, generally but not universally favorable, on their law review publications.[176] On occasion academics would send their articles to him, and he would give them his detailed comments. Once, after reading a thick book of Indian poems, Friendly sent the author a long letter of appreciation.[177]

Friendly also released his frustrations by writing letters. In 1961 he wrote to his former partner George Ball, who was then Undersecretary of State, criticizing the government's policy concerning Berlin, which Friendly felt was "being tailored to meet the views of the West Germans."[178] He wrote to Senators Robert Kennedy and Javits and others in support of the bill to create a public television corporation as the "only hope for obtaining high quality programs . . . that will meet the demands of whatever segment of the public [that] does not like the current diet of soap operas, westerns, sports events, and vapid news programs all liberally laced with commercials."[179] He wrote to Mayor Robert Wagner of New York City to oppose a bill that would prohibit meters in cars belonging to private car services.[180] He complained in a letter to the *New York Times* that airports gave priority to "private planes carrying three or four privileged passengers," noting candidly that he wrote "as one who has benefited and still occasionally benefits from travel in private planes."[181]

Perhaps the most arresting of Friendly's letters is one, almost populist in tone, that he wrote in September 1974 to President Gerald Ford with a copy to Congressman Wilber Mills complaining about the recently enacted "50% ceiling on the taxation of 'earned' income," which allowed recipients to keep half their excessive earnings. His letter was a plea to have the ceiling repealed: "The recent announcement of a contract whereby a high school basketball player will receive $600,000 a year in salary for five years prompts me to write about a serious inequity in the tax laws." The letter also targeted the salary of the chairman of General Motors, who was "rewarded for his failure to foresee the need of switching to small cars." Moreover, the "outrageous salaries," particularly the latter, were providing "a trump card to union leaders in wage negotiations." He added, almost parenthetically, that the salaries dwarfed those of federal judges.[182]

One other aspect of Friendly's career in the Second Circuit warrants mention: his two-year tenure as chief judge in 1971–1973, between the chief-judgeships of J. Edward Lumbard and Irving R. Kaufman. The post went to the senior active judge under seventy, who had to relinquish the post when he reached seventy. Unlike judges who relished holding the position, such as Irving Kaufman, Friendly would have been happy to do without the honor. His interest was in resolving intellectual, not personnel or administrative, problems. In one instance lawyers telephoned to complain that a district judge was bringing his dogs into the courtroom when he was trying cases. Friendly looked up at the ceiling and muttered, "Jesus Christ."[183] For an indifferent and uninterested administrator, the administrative tasks associated with being chief judge were considerable and to Friendly annoying and unproductive.[184] His position also required him to spend time responding to inquiries by Congress and testifying before congressional committees.[185] He was delighted to extricate himself from the position.

Administrative problems were not confined to the chief judge. Several years earlier Friendly had had an encounter with the government bureaucracy about telephones, when he wanted a fourth telephone installed in his chambers. The position of the General Services Administration was simple and can be restated as follows: Three people—the judge, his secretary, and his law clerk—however talented and industrious, do not require four telephones. To challenge the GSA's hardly frivolous position, Friendly had to resort to writing a three-page letter, which started, "The strange thing is that I should have to be writing this letter at all."[186]

CHAPTER SIX

Law Clerks

THIRD-YEAR LAW STUDENTS competed intensely for a clerkship with Friendly. Aside from clerking for a Supreme Court Justice (and not all of them), no other clerkship was so attractive, at least in the Northeast, and the student with the highest average in his class at Harvard Law School could not count on being selected. Friendly hired his clerks after interviewing them. At first, Harvard Law School professor David Cavers screened candidates and sent him a few each year, from whom he would choose one.[1] Until his eighth year all the clerks came from Harvard, but then he started taking clerks from Yale, Columbia, Chicago, and occasionally other schools, relying largely on recommendations by professors who taught there. Friendly was interested in ability, and nothing else; for example, political leanings and politics never came up in his interviews.[2] When an applicant for a clerkship told Friendly that he received an A in Administrative Law from Professor Antonin Scalia, a scholar Friendly admired,[3] he subjected the applicant to a withering cross-examination on the subject. Friendly not only turned him down, but wrote a letter to his sponsor, the highly regarded Professor Edward Levi of the University of Chicago Law School, to complain about the applicant's deficiencies.[4]

For Friendly's clerks it was an unusual opportunity to work with a brilliant jurist, and almost all were positive about their experience, some exuberantly so.[5] While the clerks recognized that Friendly rarely went out of his way to provide instruction to them,[6] the opportunity to see him in action and to participate in the creation of excellent opinions in itself was educational. Several former clerks volunteered that Friendly's was one of the best minds they had ever encountered, and many praised his sweeping intellectual curiosity. One clerk compared the experience with "sitting next to Garry Kasparov while he explained each [chess] move."[7] Another likened Friendly to Pelé, the soccer star, though in Friendly the electrons or synapses moved faster.[8] An academic called his clerkship "by far the single most significant year in [his] understanding and development in the law."[9] Another said that Friendly taught "entirely by example. He did his work; you did yours; then you worked together . . . in the craft of the law."[10] A third academic said that "he was a joy to work with."[11] A judge said simply, "To have been his clerk was the greatest privilege I have known."[12] While Friendly inspired a number of his clerks to become judges,[13] he discouraged at least one. Professor Philip Bobbitt, a distinguished scholar, concluded after working for Friendly that he could not be as good a judge as Friendly and therefore he would not become a judge.[14]

After Friendly's secretary typed his handwritten draft of an opinion triple-spaced, she would send it directly to a clerk to cite-check what the judge had written as well as supply omitted case names or citations and, when the clerk rose to the occasion, to suggest substantive changes. Friendly apparently considered this mode of input by his clerks the most efficient way to involve them in preparing his opinions. Their responsibility was summarized in a manual for clerks that David Currie, Friendly's clerk in his second year on the bench, first drafted.[15] The 1978 manual, which had grown to forty-nine double-spaced pages, included this injunction: "The Judge welcomes criticism; challenge the draft in every reasonable way you can. *Assume, at the start, that everything said, by way of fact or law, may be wrong (or incomplete) and make sure it becomes right. . . . This is your most important single function.*"[16] But the quality of Friendly's work often left little productive work for the clerk. Professor David Currie said that the clerkship was a "modest position."[17] Compared to other clerkships there was so little to do that some clerks couldn't understand why they were there.[18]

In addition to reviewing Friendly's opinions, the clerks wrote detailed memoranda, some running dozens of pages, on intricate subjects that came up in cases, such as a history of jury trials in England before the adoption of the Bill of Rights, or the legislative history of a statute, to assist Friendly in writing an opinion. While he usually assigned the topics to clerks, some clerks read the parties' briefs and tried to predict what might help the judge.[19] To anticipate what he might need, one pair of clerks looked on the judge's desk after he left for the day.[20] It was not always easy trying to figure out what he wanted.

When clerks made significant contributions in the process, Friendly was delighted. "He was never happier than when a law clerk confronted him with interesting disagreement," and when a clerk really delivered, he would light up with joy.[21] A law clerk who exercised initiative made him beam with pleasure. He frequently gave them credit in memoranda to his fellow judges: "My law clerk's examination of the law and the facts has led me to conclude, contrary to my first impression, that we should reverse."[22] In another case: "I am indebted to my law clerk for pointing out what now seems to me the error in the way in which this matter was handled by the judge and by counsel on both sides."[23] After the panel unanimously signed off on an opinion affirming the district court, the clerk Mark Wolinsky wrote a fourteen-page memorandum on his own initiative that showed why the judges were wrong. Friendly circulated the memorandum to the other two judges, and the panel unanimously reversed the district judge.[24] Decades later many former clerks mentioned as high points in their legal careers getting Friendly to change his mind, which he was willing to do when presented with cogent reasons. Some kept notes from Friendly that praised their work.[25]

One clerk described what happened when he challenged Friendly after receiving a 227-page draft, which Friendly had written in four days:

> I read the opinion. Pages 137 to 193 are completely wrong. I walk in and tell him so: "Take a few days, Bruce, and write a new draft. . . ." [I] tend to wake up at 4 a.m., staring into darkness, tossing and turning, composing and recomposing.
>
> Three weeks later my draft is done: there's still a lot of Henry Friendly there, but not a trace between pages 137 and 193. . . . We review the new draft, line by line. The Judge has made countless changes, large and small. . . . Every time I object to a new modification, he tries to answer each of my questions, and almost always revises the revision yet again—in ways neither of us had clearly anticipated.
>
> Four hours later, we reach page 136. I wait for him to turn the page: "I think you've made a good point in the second full paragraph of 137." From then on, the draft takes an entirely new turn. My revision has convinced the Judge to drop his old fifty-five pages and to begin writing on a clean slate. The result is an opinion far stronger and deeper than either of the earlier drafts.[26]

Another clerk expressed a similar viewpoint:

> Once the law and the facts were understood, I usually found myself in agreement with the Judge about a decision. But when disagreement remained, the real fun began, because there is nothing the Judge enjoys more than a good debate. Most often these debates provided the vehicle for the Judge to refine

his initial views, and as this occurred, his arguments would become even more persuasive, which usually moved me to alter my own views. But when disagreement continued, the Judge always listened carefully and could be persuaded by a well-reasoned argument which appealed to his profound sense of justice.[27]

Friendly called these interchanges with his clerks "fun,"[28] exceptions to his generally somber and burdened attitude. One clerk called them "open season."[29] He told clerks not to worry about his feelings, and it was absolutely fair combat.[30] He was delighted when a clerk found he had made a mistake.[31] He had no vested interest in his ideas or expression; if the clerk had a better idea, he'd accept it, although he could grow impatient as he quickly saw the implications of a clerk's point.[32] One of his few requirements was that any clerk who raised a problem had to propose a solution, and he would use the clerk's version when their relative merits were close.[33] Judge Pierre Leval described a rejection: "His expression of displeasure sounded more like 'ngngngrrrrrnggguessI'llstickwithwhatI'vegot.' "[34]

Nevertheless, errors, sometimes embarrassing ones, found their way into opinions, which upset Friendly. If a clerk made a mistake that crept into a published opinion, the judge would never let him or her forget it.[35] An undiscovered example appeared in his discussion of the sufficiency of a complaint. Friendly's published opinion reads, "For example, if a limited partner had an investment of $100,000 and was paid off with 1000 shares of stock taken at $10 per share but known to have real value of only $5, he would have been defrauded of $50,000."[36] Friendly would have been mortified.

When Friendly wanted to see a clerk, he would press a buzzer and the clerk would enter without knocking. The number of buzzes, which were loud, would inform whether he wanted his secretary or a clerk and, when he had more than one clerk, which clerk. One problem was that when they opened his door, Friendly was already speaking. He often mumbled. Clerks generally were too intimidated to ask for clarification and would proceed on the basis of what they thought he said. Sometimes a clerk would ask the secretary to translate, trying to imitate the unintelligible mumblings and grunts. One clerk remembers Friendly greeting him with, "Why do you think the plaintiff has any right to recover on Point 2?"[37] When he entered Friendly's domain, one of the more intrepid clerks was greeted with, "How much do they get?" Pausing, the clerk asked, "What is the sentence before that one?" Friendly had not realized that the clerk had no idea which case he was talking about or who "they" were.[38] Some clerks found the sound of the buzzer scary. In fact, one clerk recounted that when he bought a house, he had the doorbell changed because it reminded him of Friendly's buzzer.[39] Occasionally a clerk would stand up to Friendly, reacting to pointed criticism by telling him, "I'm going to make mistakes; I'm not you."[40] Friendly did not seem to understand what it meant to have merely a very good mind. Judge Michael Boudin said that after clerking for Friendly it was impossible to be intellectually intimidated by anyone.[41]

Many former clerks explained that others—although rarely directly admitting it was themselves—were intimidated by Friendly. Whether or not Friendly intended it, intimidation was certainly present in varying degrees. One clerk stated that the common denominator of all visits to Friendly's office was fear coupled with anxiety.[42] Deadpan, Chief Justice John G. Roberts Jr. gave a specific example of this phenomenon. After explaining that he was not among those intimidated by Friendly, he shared that one time after Friendly buzzed him into his office he complained that everything was darker than usual and that some of the lights must have been out. Roberts could not bring himself to tell the judge that he was still wearing his clip-on sunglasses. He told Friendly's secretary after he left his office.[43]

When he was displeased, such as when a clerk was progressing too slowly, Friendly often showed his displeasure with sarcasm. Fast in turning out work, Friendly could be intolerant of clerks who were slower. On more than one occasion he walked over to a clerk and asked, "Have you given birth yet?"[44] His repugnance at seeing time squandered can be illustrated by his response to Roberts's getting stuck in the elevator: Friendly had someone take him briefs so he wouldn't be wasting time.[45]

How hard clerks worked varied widely.[46] The record for the longest hours probably went to co-clerks Gregory Palm and James Smoot, who, without telling the judge, each slept two nights a week in the chambers, showering in the judge's private bathroom before he arrived.[47] Smoot started keeping track of his "billable" hours, but discontinued the practice because it was masochistic and, besides, "who had time for it?"[48]

Among Friendly's least successful clerks were those who simply accepted what he wrote as gospel.[49] To encourage thoughtful answers, he made a practice of asking clerks for their views before he spoke.[50] When a clerk hemmed and hawed, Friendly said through a clenched jaw, "You're not helping me any."[51] He demanded the same level of competence and care from his clerks as he did from himself and generally had little patience for people who did not meet that standard. Thus, when a clerk misspelled the name of one of the lawyers in a case, Friendly told him, "If I cannot trust you to get the name of a lawyer right, how can I trust you to do anything else?"[52] One clerk started a memorandum with, "At the risk of incurring your wrath once again. . . ."[53] He had little sympathy for those clerks who could not perform.[54] Exacerbating the problem was Friendly's tendency to make early judgments about his clerks. He communicated his disappointment to them, making turnabouts difficult: "The judge was not good if something went wrong," one clerk concluded.[55] He would write terrible evaluations of clerks who did not perform up to his standards.[56]

Because of Friendly's extreme penchant for orderliness, or perhaps because of his eye problems, he wanted to be sure where everything was when he took the bench to hear an appeal. Clerks drafted a map to show the placement of the parties' briefs and appendix (with all rubber bands removed), a pad of lined paper, three sharpened No. 2 pencils with their points facing to the courtroom and their erasers lined up, two pens, the Federal Rules of Appellate Procedure, and so on. It was like a map of place settings for a formal presidential dinner. There was a routine for everything.[57] With a few exceptions the clerks accepted their place-setting assignment with the seriousness with which it was made and were worried lest they misplace an item. But a few clerks thought it peculiar.[58]

On one occasion Friendly found mail in his papers when he was sitting on an oral argument; he shouted at his clerk when he returned to chambers, but soon regained his equanimity.[59] On another occasion on the bench Friendly was provided with the parties' briefs but not an appendix. He berated a lawyer in the case from the bench until she said she had filed one, and he then berated the clerk of the court for not delivering an appendix to his chambers until the clerk said he had. Learning of the problem, Friendly's law clerk, A. Raymond Randolph, found the appendix on the floor of the chambers and had to march down the aisle of the courtroom to hand it to the judge. Randolph awaited the judge's return with dread. When Friendly arrived he stared at Randolph. "I don't know why," Randolph related, "but I started to laugh. The judge joined in. That was the end of it."[60]

Friendly's relentless adherence to routine and, to a somewhat lesser extent, to hierarchy, struck all. Clerks, even some of the ones who were most satisfied with their experiences, were disappointed by his remoteness and his lack of rapport, along with his obsessive attention to detail and form. Friendly was an old-fashioned boss. Not unkindly, one clerk said that at times he felt like a private secretary to an official in the Austro-Hungarian Empire.[61] Friendly had come from an era that was much more stratified, and his interest in history took him back even further. He tended not to see his clerks as individuals. One clerk said that Friendly tended to assume that a current clerk would know what he had told a prior year's clerk.[62]

Friendly apparently did not find many things funny. However, he could display a good, and highly intellectual, sense of humor.[63] One clerk known for his wit explained, "He had a good sense of the ridiculous."[64] A district judge who heard Friendly as master of ceremonies at the circuit's Judicial Conference in Lake Placid, New York, and later became a friend, described Friendly's humor as appealing to an intellectual audience.[65] However, he had a tendency to repeat his jokes.[66]

Friendly was not always considerate in accommodating employees' personal needs. He kept his secretary Elizabeth Flynn working the afternoon of Good Friday.[67] That a clerk took the day off to attend his graduation from Harvard Law School—"There was no way my Polish father and Scottish mother were not going to attend my graduation"—seemed to annoy Friendly.[68] Another clerk had to return to the office after his bachelor party and barely made it to the wedding.[69] The wife of a clerk was due to give birth, and he did not know what to do about taking time off. He spoke to his wife, then called a couple of former clerks, "who wouldn't touch the issue." Finally, he left a note in the judge's inbox explaining the imminent birth along with the fact that he was to play an integral part in the delivery process, so that his role was almost as important as his wife's. That evening, when Friendly walked by the clerk's desk on his way home, he said, "Your role is not almost as important as your wife's." The clerk took a half day off.[70] When another clerk called Friendly to tell him his wife had given birth that morning and he would not be in that day, Friendly's sole comment was, "See you tomorrow." The clerk thought it was funny.[71]

Friendly's chambers were a meritocracy. He had his favorite clerks, and he did not keep their names secret from his former clerks, members of law school faculties, and a number of judges and Justices.[72] In fact, if asked, he probably could have ranked his clerks from his favorite down, and the list would have correlated almost perfectly with his estimation of their ability.[73] Topping his mental list of fifty-one clerks was Michael Boudin,[74] with Pierre Leval a close second, both of whom served as sole clerks.[75] Others he rated very high included the early clerks David Currie and Bruce Ackerman and the later clerks Raymond Randolph, Frederick Davis, William Bryson, Ruth Wedgwood, Merrick Garland, John Roberts, and David Seipp. Roberts had received a summa cum laude in history and won the Bowdoin Essay Prize, like his boss.[76] Of the eleven just mentioned, six became appellate judges and four became professors.

Friendly also categorized his most influential clerks, among whom he placed Richard Daynard, who, he said at a clerks' reunion dinner, got him to change his mind more than any other clerk.[77] He told one former clerk that the clerk who had come up with the most ideas was Bruce Ackerman, but asserted, "I didn't use a single one of them."[78] He did, of course, but he may have made this remark because of Ackerman's unusual number of ideas and his unquenchable enthusiasm for them.[79]

Only one clerk left early for not satisfactorily performing required duties, and even then Friendly made certain that the departing clerk received a good position.[80] When Friendly recommended someone, whether as an applicant to a law school or for a job, and the person performed unsatisfactorily, he blamed himself, which made the chambers an unhappy place.[81] Just as he freely told friends and acquaintances who his best clerks were, he could unthinkingly identify a less successful clerk to a person who had no reason to know, telling one person who knew him professionally, "Boy, did I make a mistake that year," identifying a particular clerk by name.[82]

In his last years Friendly had a clerk go to Foley Square and track down a taxi for him and bring it to the courthouse steps, where he waited. Some clerks thought this task was inappropriate for former law students who were hired as law clerks, while others welcomed it because it gave them an opportunity to speak with the judge.[83] Friendly dismissed their performance of tasks such as these to a fellow judge with the quip, "That's all they're good for."[84] His sarcasm and denigrations were not characteristics that would endear him to everyone, but they may have been products of his difficulty in expressing affection.[85] One person to whom Friendly could bring himself to speak candidly about his clerks, Judge Edward Weinfeld, assessed Friendly's views in a 1984 letter: "I assume you saw the profile in today's NY Times on William C. Bryson. With Pierre's [Leval] picture in the same paper two days ago, I suggest our Friendly, J., is swelling with pride—and justly so."[86]

Whether Friendly's remoteness was more an intellectual decision as to the proper form of the judge-clerk relationship than the result of his inability to engage in a personal relationship is unclear, although occasional deviations from the norm suggest that it may have been the latter. For example, he took a few clerks to the theater.[87] And when one of the later clerks told the judge in the spring that he was going to Italy and Greece with his girlfriend after the clerkship ended, Friendly prepared a ten-page handwritten program, including highlights of each hill town.[88] Friendly may have been motivated by his passion for European culture, which he wanted others to share, but these actions were also one way he related to people.

With rare exceptions Friendly would see little of his clerks socially. Generally, a clerk had just one lunch with him, which took place on the last day and was known as "the Deficiency Lunch." It was ordinarily at Schrafft's, an upscale chain, and not at a club, where Friendly went with his equals.[89] Along with presenting clerks with his autographed photograph, the evident purpose of the lunches was to provide evaluations, which made some clerks wonder why he had not disclosed his criticisms earlier in their tenure.[90] Friendly and his wife had most clerks to their apartment for one dinner during the year, to which the clerk's spouse was invited, if one existed. Friendly did not see as part of his job description making the dinners particularly relaxing to the clerks, although Sophie made efforts to make them comfortable. Exceptions to the pattern were his monthly invitations to dine at his home to Peter Edelman, who was married to a federal judge's daughter;[91] occasional dinner or theater invitations to Philip Bobbitt;[92] a couple of dinners with Gregory Palm;[93] and nearly monthly lunches with Todd Rakoff and Bobbitt.[94]

Friendly generally was supportive in assisting clerks to obtain Supreme Court clerkships and positions in the government and academia,[95] although he told one clerk at the start of the court term that he should not expect any assistance, and he would provide negative letters about people he felt were wanting.[96] Former clerks asked Friendly to recommend them for membership in the American Law Institute, the Council on Foreign Relations, and the Harvard Club, and his files are replete with copies of his recommendations.[97]

Once a clerk finished the year, the relationship with Friendly could become more congenial, open, and personal, a process that took many years for some and was never achieved by others.[98] One clerk described the change as one from a distant relationship to Friendly's taking a "fatherly interest,"[99] and another clerk said that Friendly felt he had an alternative family.[100] When they visited New York, many out-of-town former clerks would ask him to lunch, which he welcomed, although some felt uncomfortable doing so.[101] After a few years on the bench Friendly began inviting his past and present clerks to an annual dinner at the Merchants Club, where former clerks, some uncomfortably, recited what they had accomplished in the preceding year. Sometimes a comment provoked Friendly, such as support for airline deregulation or a comparison of Brandeis with Ralph Nader, both of which he sternly rejected.[102] Reunion dinners continued after Friendly's death, although no longer on an annual basis. One of Friendly's clerks described the first reunion after he died: "We told each other nightmare stories, how he made you feel like crap. There was no feeling of hatred. It was like basic training—you come out the other end brutalized but the better for it."[103]

No former clerk quite attained the position of Michael Boudin, who accompanied the Friendlys on a trip to Scotland, serving as their driver. Boudin recalled that when he got lost, Friendly would mumble under his breath, "Mumble, mumble, cannot even figure out how to get there." Sophie would chirp, "Now, dear, he's doing his best."[104] In the early 1980s the Friendlys were accompanied on a tour of the Cotswolds, near Oxford, by Boudin; Pierre Leval; Leval's wife, Susana (who totally captivated Friendly); Susana's mother; and the Levals' daughter, India, age five. Friendly got along wonderfully with India, but when the group arrived for lunch at an elegant restaurant and were told that children were not welcomed, Friendly let it be known that that was the Levals' problem. The Friendlys lunched with Boudin while the Levals went elsewhere.[105]

Perhaps the most intriguing progression involved Philip Bobbitt, a Friendly clerk in 1975–1976 and now a distinguished international constitutional scholar with appointments to three law schools on two continents. According to Bobbitt, he may have been the worst clerk Friendly ever had. "Like many great men, he was impatient. While he was a wonderful leader, I was not a good follower," Bobbitt has admitted. His acknowledged deficits included failure to accommodate Friendly's demands for following office procedure on myriad little things. He had Friendly saying to himself, "I just don't know; I just don't know." Bobbitt was so unhappy that he asked the judge if he could leave early, something no one did. Friendly raised no objection.[106]

For reasons Bobbitt cannot fathom, he telephoned Friendly in 1979 to announce that he was working for Lloyd Cutler in the Carter White House. Friendly was delighted, in part because he regarded Cutler as perhaps the nation's best lawyer and in part because he liked his clerks to go into public service.[107] The two saw each other often after that, mostly for lunch, and Friendly would talk to Bobbitt about politics, the legal academy, and his early professional life. Friendly told him that although he had failed as a law clerk, he was hurt by his decision to leave early, a statement that shocked Bobbitt, mostly because he had trouble believing that anything he did could hurt the judge.[108]

The quality and personality of Friendly's secretaries were critically important. In addition to ordinary office work, Friendly's secretaries handled his financial and other personal matters, such as summarizing his bank statements and preparing deposit slips and checks for his signature.[109] He had four principal secretaries. First was Elizabeth Flynn, who accompanied him from Cleary, Gottlieb and with whom he was very comfortable; she stayed with him until she retired in 1972. She was followed by Sydney Schwartz, a young woman who left in 1977 to go to law school, the recipient of a strong letter of recommendation from Friendly.[110] Next was Pat Hall, another young woman, who remained until 1983, when she left to marry the former Friendly clerk Paul Mogin. Friendly hired his last secretary, Charlotte A. Kimbrough, after her previous boss, Judge Murray Gurfein, died.[111] The last three arrived fully aware of Friendly's towering reputation and were apprehensive about working for him. Schwartz said that starting to work there was "terrifying"; Hall also was a "nervous wreck" when she started.[112] Kimbrough, who was no less in awe, found Friendly reserved in manner, all business, unwilling to waste a minute, and not one for small talk: "I learned never to say to him, 'How are you?'"[113]

Hall undoubtedly was his favorite; indeed, clerks said he adored her. She worshipped him, and he appreciated her for, among other things, making him more relaxed. Not only was her personality and manner full of sunshine and optimism, but she was an excellent secretary. What Hall describes as her breakthrough with Friendly occurred in October 1978, her second year. She and a clerk, Warren Stern, were chatting about the World Series, and she told him that she was going to talk to the judge about it. Although Stern fearfully cautioned her not to, she asked the judge what he thought of the Series when he came in. He replied, "That guy Guidrey is very good." Hall had lunch with the clerks and got along well with them.[114]

Friendly was more able to talk to Pat Hall than to his clerks or many of his friends, and he could be quite open with her. Moreover, he was interested in her development. "Once he buzzed me in and asked if I had read Proust. I said that I had read some of *Swann's Way*. He said, read it and we'll talk about it. We did. . . . I was really, really fortunate to see the other side of him, his warmth and sweetness. . . . The Judge loved *The Jewel in the Crown* [a public television series] and wanted to talk about it—the personalities, what was going to happen next. These are things that the clerks never saw." More notably, he talked to her about members of his family and other personal things. She was a very rare breakthrough in his cloistered emotional life. In 1983, her last year, Friendly would give her a hug and say, "Ho, ho, ho, to be seventy again."[115] When Hall married Mogin, Friendly, with a special dispensation from New Jersey, performed the ceremony in that state.[116]

CHAPTER SEVEN

Judges and Justices

WHEN FRIENDLY BECAME Judge Friendly in 1959, the Second Circuit had only four active judges: Chief Judge Charles E. Clark and Circuit Judges J. Edward Lumbard, Sterry R. Waterman, and Leonard P. Moore.[1] Near the end of 1959 Lumbard replaced Clark as Chief Judge, and the court became more congenial and efficient. Although it was a competent court, it no longer received the same plaudits as a decade earlier, when the Second Circuit consisted of Chief Judge Learned Hand and Circuit Judges Thomas W. Swan, Augustus N. Hand, Harrie Brigham Chase, Charles E. Clark, and Jerome Frank.[2]

The active judges as 1960 opened were of the same generation and most had similar professional experience. A Republican from the prominent New York City law firm of Donovan & Leisure who became the U.S. Attorney for the Southern District of New York, Lumbard was conservative, especially in criminal matters. Sterry R. Waterman, a Republican who took office one day after Lumbard, was a Vermont practitioner who served for a decade as the executive director of the Vermont Unemployment Compensation Commission. Waterman was one of the most liberal members of the court.[3] The career of Eisenhower's next appointee, Leonard P. Moore, was similar to Lumbard's, including a lengthy association with a Wall Street firm and service as U.S. Attorney for the Eastern District of New York.[4] An active Republican, on assuming the bench in 1957 Moore was conservative, generally to the right of Lumbard. In 1960 Eisenhower made his final appointment, J. Joseph Smith, from Connecticut, a former Democratic congressman and district judge. His judicial philosophy was closer to Waterman's than to Lumbard's or Moore's.[5]

For Friendly the court of appeals was neither a collegial experience nor one of much intellectual exchange, in part because the panels never met to discuss the cases.[6] While his colleagues were not his equals intellectually, Friendly treated them with respect, and he and his wife traveled abroad with Moore and his wife. He regarded Harold Medina, who had taken senior status shortly before Friendly's appointment, as a character and accepted that Medina would be Medina, a man with considerable knowledge of languages and history who sometimes brought his exuberance into Friendly's chambers.[7] Medina, who often gave Friendly rides home in his chauffeur-driven car, had run a highly successful bar review course and taught at Columbia before becoming a judge. Charles Clark was irascible.[8] Just before Friendly was sworn in, Frankfurter sent him a handwritten note: "I can give you the infallible test for ascertaining when you may deem yourself a survivor [?] in the Second Circuit: when Charles Clark dissents from an opinion of yours in an ill-mannered opinion of his."[9] Clark had written the Federal Rules of Civil Procedure, a project Friendly, who had more faith in the judicial development of procedural rules, criticized.[10] Finally, Friendly accepted that the formidable Learned Hand, who sat periodically before he died in 1961, was past his prime in 1959.[11]

Following Smith, twenty judges were appointed to the Second Circuit during Friendly's tenure. The first Kennedy appointment was Irving R. Kaufman, whom Kennedy nominated after Congress created three new judgeships in 1961. Kaufman, who quickly became known for his liberal opinions on civil rights, prisoners' rights, and the First Amendment, served as Chief Judge from 1973 to 1980. Next was Paul R. Hays, a professor at Columbia Law School, with whom the Friendlys spent some time socially and became friends.[12] Thurgood Marshall, the head of the NAACP Legal Defense Fund who argued successfully *Brown v. Board of Education*,[13] had a relatively short tenure of four years on the Second Circuit before President Johnson appointed him to the Supreme Court.[14] Friendly admired Marshall for his great accomplishments as a civil rights lawyer.[15] In Friendly's mind Marshall had *mattered*, and he went out of his way to assist Marshall, who was unfamiliar with many subjects of the court's work. A biography of Marshall states, "For advice when he was over his head, [Marshall] walked over to the chambers of J. Henry Friendly [*sic*], a politically conservative judge who became Marshall's mentor."[16] Then, five years after Kennedy had appointed him to the district court in Manhattan, Lyndon Johnson appointed Wilfred Feinberg to the court of appeals in 1966. Formerly editor in chief of the *Columbia Law Review* as well as one of the best district judges, Feinberg assumed the post of Chief Judge when Kaufman turned seventy in 1980 and continued to serve as Chief Judge after Friendly's death.[17]

The appointments that followed were of a generation different from Friendly's. James L. Oakes, one of four judges appointed by Richard Nixon in 1971,[18] was as liberal as any member of the court. A former officer of the *Harvard Law Review*, law clerk to Judge Harrie B. Chase, and Attorney General of Vermont,[19] Oakes frequently sat, and disagreed, with Friendly on the disposition of criminal cases, although they got along very well. As the years went on, Friendly became more of an icon to his colleagues. Thomas Meskill, previously governor of Connecticut, said that when he was appointed to the Second Circuit in 1975, he and his friends called it "Friendly's Court."[20] Jon O. Newman, a 1979 appointee who had clerked for Chief Justice Earl Warren and served on the district court in Connecticut, could not bring himself to call Friendly by his first name for a year.[21] Friendly had high opinions of his younger colleagues Oakes, Newman, and Amalya Kearse, an African-American woman who was a champion bridge player as well as an able lawyer and judge.[22] He also praised the work of Ralph Winter, a former Yale professor, and Meskill, who Friendly found made the transition from governor to judge successfully.[23] By 1984 the court had thirteen active judges.[24]

Feinberg, who sat with Friendly on more than five hundred appeals, called him "an ideal colleague," noting Friendly's enthusiasm, eagerness to take on complex cases, and willingness to listen to the parties and his colleagues before making up his mind.[25] Friendly's fellow judges did not feel any hint of condescension on his part. Judge Richard J. Cardamone stated, "He was more interested in learning how we thought than announcing what he thought."[26] Meskill echoed the sentiment: "What struck me most was what a great listener he was."[27] From Newman: "Judge Friendly was not arrogant and knew that he may not know something." Newman added that it wasn't that other judges did not disagree with Friendly, but that they were careful before they disagreed.[28]

One happy experience for Friendly at the hands of his colleagues was their party celebrating his eightieth birthday, an intimate affair attended only by the circuit judges and their spouses and replete with entertainment.[29] Judge Walter Mansfield knew many people in the theater world and "was the producer, director, and master of ceremonies," while various judges wrote songs and skits and took turns playing Friendly. Among the skits was one in which Friendly—ever the perfectionist—went to heaven and started correcting Gibbon and other great historians about errors in their work.[30] The chorus wore white robes with wings while "Friendly" wore a red wig. The central song was sung by a Friendly stand-in to the Gershwins' "It Ain't Necessarily So," with one verse:

> Herodotus garbled the facts
> Of many historical acts,
> His books have distortions
> Of major proportions
> On pillages, pogroms and sacks!

Another Friendly stand-in sang to Gilbert and Sullivan's "I Am the Very Model of a Modern Major General" and covered the range of Friendly's life. Two of the verses were:

> When I was very young athletic sports could not be taught to me
> My physical coordination wasn't what it ought to be,
> But still in all veracity, I say without mendacity,
> I am the very model of a student of capacity.

> I keep a very watchful eye upon exchanges for securities
> I'm rarely very tolerant of food and drug impurities.
> I'm surely not a bleeding heart for those whose crimes are national
> And felons seeking habeas will find me barely rational.

> CHORUS:
> And all of us who serve with you are always proud to yell it, judge
> You are the very model of a very wise appellate judge.[31]

Three judges from other circuits were closer to Friendly than those on the Second Circuit. One of them, John Minor Wisdom of the Fifth Circuit, one of the judicial heroes of southern school desegregation, followed Carl McGowan of the District of Columbia Circuit on the special court that oversaw the liquidation of the freight railroads in the Northeast starting in the mid-1970s. While he thought highly of McGowan, Friendly especially admired Wisdom, whom he considered a kindred spirit in his approach to the law.[32] Richard Posner, whom Friendly got to know after Posner was appointed to the Seventh Circuit in 1981, invigorated him at a time when he was losing interest in his work. During the four years of their friendship, they wrote some sixty-five letters to one another. In 1984 Friendly wrote to Posner, "Every [opinion] is a masterpiece of analysis, scholarship, and style. About a year ago I said that you were already the best judge in the country; having uttered that superlative, I am baffled on how to better it."[33] Posner reciprocated the sentiment.

In correspondence Friendly would single out for commendation younger circuit judges in other circuits. With a good nose for talent, he listed Richard Arnold, Robert Bork, Stephen Breyer, Frank Easterbrook, Ruth Ginsburg, and Antonin Scalia.[34] An early encounter with Professor Ginsburg at a conference, however, did not amuse him. After they broke for lunch, Friendly was standing next to her near the table and pulled out a chair for her. She turned to him and stated, "The time has long since passed when a man can tell a woman where to sit." Friendly was shocked by her retort.[35]

Friendly was close to several district judges from the Southern District of New York who were housed in the same building. The foremost by far was Edward Weinfeld, who was a mature judge when Friendly arrived and who outlived him by several years. Practically from the day Friendly became a judge, they became fast friends. Weinfeld wrote of their relationship in a 1978 tribute: "I regard as one of my life's most meaningful experiences the deep and warm friendship we share. . . . Though we had not met until he came to the Court of Appeals, our first conversation reminded me of Woodrow Wilson's comments on his first meeting with Colonel Edward M. House. When the Colonel observed that soon after their meeting they shared confidences which men usually exchange after years of friendship, the President-to-be remarked, 'My dear friend, we have known one another always.' I had the same feeling after meeting Judge Friendly, and our friendship has grown with the years."[36]

Friendly echoed the characterization.[37] For him the relationship appears to have been unique. While he had intellectual companions like Herbert Wechsler and Paul Freund, he could not relate to them as he did with Weinfeld. Friendly accepted the fact that he had trouble making friends.[38] Indeed in 1983, responding to a warm letter from Weinfeld, he wrote, "You know how warmly I reciprocate your remarks. Our friendship has been one of the great joys of my life; the years here would have been barren without it." Friendly would send Weinfeld reprints of his articles accompanied by glowing compliments to him on the title page. Weinfeld would acknowledge them with notes describing Friendly as one "of this century's 'giants' in American jurisprudence" or a similar accolade.[39]

The law professor William Nelson of New York University, Weinfeld's former law clerk, friend, and biographer, sees the differences between Friendly and Weinfeld as greater than their similarities. Both, of course, were brilliant, conscientious, and overflowing with integrity. But Weinfeld was a traditional liberal New York City Democrat. Somewhat surprisingly, he was more old-fashioned and apparently less communicative on personal matters than Friendly. Weinfeld was reticent about his daughters and concealed his eight-year bout with cancer. While Friendly discussed with Weinfeld his planned suicide, Nelson is convinced that Weinfeld never talked to Friendly about his long-festering cancer.[40]

In 1965 Friendly, who strongly wanted Weinfeld to join him on the Second Circuit, called Peter Edelman, his former law clerk who at the time was an important aide to Senator Robert F. Kennedy, to see what could be done. Kennedy told Edelman he would try, but to tell Friendly that the President and not he was responsible for choosing circuit judges. Kennedy added that Wilfred Feinberg had considerable support, including support generated by his brother Abe, who was a big contributor to the President, and that Weinfeld should get people to put pressure on the President for his candidacy. Friendly called Edelman a couple more times, with similar results. When the President appointed Feinberg, Friendly was furious. Ignoring Edelman's protestations that Robert Kennedy had not made the decision, Friendly accused Kennedy of not trying. Several years passed before Edelman and Friendly spoke again.[41]

Friendly's respect and affection for Weinfeld did not color his review of his friend's work, although it pained him to reverse him.[42] In twenty cases in which he wrote an opinion, a more personal act than signing onto someone else's, he acted to affirm Weinfeld twelve times, to reverse him outright three times, and to give a mixed outcome five times. Friendly thus affirmed Weinfeld 60 percent of the time and did not affirm him 40 percent of the time, figures only slightly better than his average for all judges (a 52.5 percent affirmance rate). The 60 percent affirmance rate contrasts with Weinfeld's 89.2 percent affirmance rate by all Second Circuit judges during the three court terms starting in the fall of 1965 and ending in the fall of 1968,[43] a period when both Weinfeld and Friendly were in their primes. The two sat together on three-judge panels six times, and they agreed fully in only half of them. Their intellectual disagreements had no adverse affect on their close relationship.

District judges that Friendly liked, respected, and saw socially were William C. Conner (the only district judge who had been a patent lawyer),[44] Marvin Frankel,[45] Murray Gurfein,[46] Morris Lasker,[47] Abraham Sofaer,[48] and his former clerk Pierre Leval, whose wife, Susana, was an art historian and whose relationship with Friendly blossomed after Leval became a district judge in 1977. Friendly also singled out District Judges M. Joseph Blumenfeld,[49] Charles Metzner,[50] Jacob Mishler,[51] and Charles T. Sifton[52] for their fine work. District Judge Jack Weinstein from the Eastern District in Brooklyn was a law professor at Columbia and the author of a major treatise on procedure and evidence. From Friendly's standpoint, Weinstein was brilliant, perhaps too brilliant, and liberal, perhaps too liberal, with the result that Friendly frequently found himself voting to reverse him. While Weinstein's ingenuity unquestionably exasperated Friendly and worse—Friendly once told a clerk, "Jack Weinstein, he drives me crazy"[53]—Friendly greatly respected his intelligence and professionalism. He wrote to Weinstein, "F. Frankfurter used to say that he wrote his dissents for the cognoscenti, and when I was working on the concurring opinion in *Rubin* I thought many times that I was really writing it for you and hoping that you would agree, as I believed you would."[54]

Judge Irving R. Kaufman presented a unique case. When asked about Friendly's relationships with judges, almost every clerk singled out Kaufman as someone Friendly could not tolerate, someone he considered a showboat flush with self-importance. Friendly was outraged by Kaufman's having announced that he had gone to a synagogue to pray over whether to impose the death penalty on Julius and Ethel Rosenberg following their convictions for espionage, and then, apparently with divine guidance, ordered the executions.[55] He also was appalled by Kaufman's blatant campaigning for the seat on the court of appeals and later for other positions. Friendly wrote to his daughter Joan in 1967, "There is gossip of Paul Freund for SG [Solicitor General of the United States], but I'll believe that when it happens. A bad little bird has been whispering that my ambitious colleague, so well initialed as IRK, has designs on that office also, but I wonder if he'll take the risk."[56] Friendly's clerks generally referred to Kaufman as "Irk."

Friendly may have suspected that Kaufman often called reporters at the *New York Times* to urge them to write articles on his opinions. Craig Whitney and Martin Tolchin, who each covered the court of appeals for the *Times* when Kaufman was a circuit judge, received such calls. When Kaufman telephoned, Whitney started his mental stopwatch to see how long it would take Kaufman to mention that he was a friend of the *Times*' publisher, "Punch" Sulzberger, in connection with his efforts to get his name in the paper.[57]

Kaufman was tyrannical to subordinates. He regularly screamed at his clerks and often fired them, without giving them a warning or another chance. He then had to call a law firm, often Cahill Gordon, to find a replacement.[58] Annoyed by the fact that Friendly's opinions contained references to scholars of antiquity and to the giants of the early centuries of English law, Kaufman berated his clerks for not putting in their drafts of his opinions what Friendly's clerks had put in his, evidently ignorant that it was Friendly who was responsible.[59] Kaufman also had his clerks scour advance sheets and prep him on interesting cases in other circuits so that when he gave Friendly a ride home he would be able to keep up with Friendly, who had read the cases.[60] In answer to the question why

Friendly would accept a ride home from Kaufman, at least part of the explanation was that he did so because he preferred a car ride to the subway and was unhappy with paying the taxi fare. Friendly could be stingy on occasion.[61]

When he succeeded Friendly as Chief Judge, Kaufman plunged with relish into the administrative aspects of the position, at which he excelled. He was wedded to efficiency and liked to affirm cases from the bench to remove them from the docket and improve the court's (his) statistical record. On several occasions he looked at the other judges to see if they would affirm a criminal case from the bench, but sometimes Friendly objected, and the case was assigned to a judge to write an opinion. When, after further research and analysis, the opinion came out later, more than once the conviction was reversed.[62] Friendly had total disdain for Kaufman's conduct and tried to avoid sitting with him on the same panel.[63]

IN 1962 FRIENDLY wrote that "when the history of American law in the first half of this century comes to be written, four judges . . . will tower above the rest—Holmes, Brandeis, Cardozo, and Learned Hand."[64] In his last years, however, Friendly soured somewhat on Holmes. "As the years go on, I wonder how much of a poseur Holmes was and whether my generation was not overly impressed by him."[65] In another letter he said, "I hope I am not being snide, but when one looks back at the great man's opinions in cases about which he did not care very much, there are plenty of bad ones."[66] Friendly had an eye for style. After reading a Black dissent, Friendly told his clerk, "Either Hugo is writing his own opinions or he has a very old and crotchety law clerk."[67]

Friendly observed in the spring of 1972, "During the current term, the Court has lost its two intellectual leaders, Mr. Justice Black and Mr. Justice Harlan, and none of the nine justices approaches them in stature. . . . For the first time since I have been a lawyer, the Court does not contain a single member who would deserve the over-used adjective 'great.' "[68] A few years later he repeated, "I doubt that we have ever had a higher level of competence on the Court, certainly there are no McReynolds, Sanfords or Mintons. What is lacking is a single Justice to whom one could apply the adjective 'great.' "[69] From the perspective of 1985 he had some complimentary words for Brennan: "I would rate Brennan as both a lawyer and a politico, and extremely skillful in both roles. In time, we will be talking about the Brennan Court rather than the Warren Court. Perhaps his use of Warren to promote his own ideas shows what a good politico he was."[70]

Friendly noted the momentous decisions in torts, contracts, fiduciaries, and federal courts in the first four decades of the century before stating,

"Against the galaxy of these and many other decisions, what of like importance have recent years of Supreme Court decision offered, with the solitary exception of *Brown v. Board of Education?*"[71] He respected the Court as an institution, but he frequently was critical of its opinions as well as some of its members, including Chief Justice Warren Burger.[72] His correspondence, even with strangers or near-strangers, was replete with criticisms of individual opinions and sometimes of Justices.[73] Nevertheless, it bothered him when he was reversed.[74]

In addition to Holmes, Brandeis, Cardozo, and Hand, over the years Friendly also identified as "great" Justices Harlan Fiske Stone, Frankfurter, Robert Jackson, and Hugo Black, and Judge Roger Traynor, a progressive and activist from California whom Friendly called the "ablest judge of his generation."[75] Traynor, who was born in 1900 and sat between 1940 and 1970, was the only contemporary of Friendly's on his list.

The backgrounds of members of his list varied. Four of the nine (Holmes, Stone, Frankfurter, and Traynor) had been law professors. Six (Holmes, Brandeis, Cardozo, Black, Jackson, and Hand) had substantial experience in private practice, although only Brandeis had a sophisticated commercial practice, and Holmes and Hand were not successful as practicing lawyers. Two of the seven who served on the Supreme Court (Holmes and Cardozo) had prior judicial experience, while five (Brandeis, Stone, Frankfurter, Black, and Jackson) did not. Only one (Hand) was not on a court of last resort. One (Black) had held elective office, and five (Brandeis, Stone, Frankfurter, Jackson, and Traynor) had extensive experience within the executive branch. Several published major outside academic articles while sitting as a judge,[76] but two did not (Brandeis and Stone), and two others (Holmes and Black) wrote little.[77] All stopped serving as a judge in 1971 or earlier, although Richard Posner almost certainly would have made the grade if Friendly had lived long enough to make another list. Perhaps most extraordinary was the range of judicial philosophies, encompassing, for example, judicial activists (or innovators) (e.g., Traynor);[78] judges exercising judicial restraint (e.g., Brandeis and Frankfurter); and judges with other philosophies (e.g., Black and Cardozo). In sum, no single trait was essential to earn the epithet "great," as further evidenced by Friendly's comments on the judges:

> [W]e may suspect that if [Cardozo] had been invited by Brandeis to devote a part of the summer to reading reports on the textile industries, as Holmes once was, he would have echoed Holmes's response: "I hate facts. I always say the chief end of man is to form general propositions—adding that no general proposition is worth a damn." Indeed, only his deep respect for Brandeis would have prevented an ever tarter reply.[79]

There were other reasons why Judge Hand could never find in Brandeis the comfort and delight he did in Holmes. Brandeis possessed a certainty about everything that Hand had about nothing. . . . Hand lacked any such joy of battle [as Brandeis].[80]

Decision came quickly to [Brandeis]—he knew nothing of Cardozo's anguish or "wrestling with the angel." But the personal decision, which was the end of the judicial process for Holmes, was only the beginning of it for Brandeis. For him the path of duty was not merely to arrive at the truth but to make it prevail.[81]

Brandeis' approach in most constitutional and other cases seems to me to have been essentially pragmatic, Holmes' to have rested on more general concepts.[82]

[Hand] came slightly to mistrust Cardozo's pre-Raphaelite beauty of expression. . . . [H]e seemed to fear that in Cardozo the love of phrase had occasionally outrun the quest for accurate thought, so that language, instead of being the servant of decision, may in some degree have become its master.[83]

In response to a letter from Frankfurter in 1963 commenting on Friendly's review of a book on Justice Holmes,[84] Friendly stated his position "in the matter of Cardozo," which, while positive, was not effusively so:

To start out with areas of agreement, I wholly concur in your observations, and in the much more pungent ones of LH [Learned Hand], concerning Cardozo's style which, as Judge Hand use to say, reeked mightily of the boudoir— strangely enough since I doubt if Cardozo was even in one. Secondly, I agree Cardozo's books are not works of original scholarship, such as The Common Law [by Holmes] assuredly was, even though many of the details would probably not have been approved by historical scholars at the time. Where I do part company is in your low estimate of the utility of Cardozo's books. It seems to me that he performed signal service by working a great many ideas, including Holmes', into a synthesis on which judges and lawyers have been drawing ever since.[85]

Friendly's favorite judge was Learned Hand, the only one who served as a federal circuit judge and not on a court of last resort, and he expressed his admiration for Hand in words that could equally be applied to himself:

Judge Hand's continued membership on lower federal courts had a significance that my earlier discussion neglected. His stature as a judge stemmed not so much from the few great cases that inevitably came to him over the years, even on what he delighted to call an "inferior" court, as from the great way in which he dealt with a multitude of little cases, covering almost every subject in the legal lexicon. Repeatedly he would make the tiniest glowworm illumine a whole field.[86]

Friendly listed the characteristics that made Hand a great judge, which included intellectual ones he himself possessed and personal ones that he did not:

> Superb as Judge Hand's achievements were, they are not strange in the light of the capacities he brought to the job. Some of these lay in his genes, others were acquired characteristics. A catalogue, necessarily incomplete, would list among them a strong and inquiring mind; a warm and vivid nature; intense concentration and sharp analysis; education in philosophy under James, Royce, and Santayana, and in law under Ames, Thayer, and Gray; a knowledge, both wide and deep, of the world's great books from the Greeks' day to our own; the few warm friendships that are all any man can have, and wide acquaintanceships with seniors, contemporaries, and juniors of many sorts and in varied disciplines; a gift of style or, more accurately, of styles, for his could vary as was appropriate from the simplest to the most sublime; a rare insight into the nature of his fellow men; and, finally, and not least important, a sense of humor, even—indeed especially—about himself.[87]

Friendly wrote a scathing review and gave a negative interview of a history of the Second Circuit by the political scientist Marvin Schick entitled *Learned Hand's Court*, which covered the years 1941–1951, when Hand was Chief Judge. Friendly told an interviewer in 1970, the same year as the book's publication, "I'm continually struck by how totally inadequate the analysis of political scientists is about judicial opinions. For example, this guy Schick. That article struck me as just a travesty, and his book seemed to be a major disaster." His review criticized Schick's concentration on the animosity between Clark and Frank, the two most liberal judges; on the liberal-conservative division within the court; and on the failure to discuss the content of Hand's great opinions on copyright, tax, commercial law, and negligence.[88] Probably displeasing Friendly was that the book dealt with the judges' personalities and emotions and publicly aired the court's dirty linen, which detracted from Hand's commanding presence.[89]

While Friendly continued to admire Frankfurter, the darling of Harvard Law School, Friendly's later years coincided with his distancing himself from some of his mentor's dogmas. Frankfurter emphasized judicial restraint, which included refraining from deciding "political questions," which Henry Hart and Herbert Wechsler defined thus: "Every question about official action which is not a judicial question is a political question in the sense that it is a question to be decided by one or the other of the political departments of government, or by the electorate."[90] As Justice Frankfurter wrote for a plurality of the Court in *Colegrove v. Green*,[91] the apportionment of legislatures was long considered a "political question," and for decades the Court refused to interfere with the states' apportioning, malapportioning, or nonapportioning seats in legislatures. In 1962 a liberal majority of the Supreme Court discarded this restraint in *Baker v. Carr*,[92] with Frankfurter filing a vociferous dissent. Friendly wrote him, praising his "magnificent dissent in *Baker v. Carr*": "This is one of your truly wise and great opinions."[93] Only five years later, however, Friendly acknowledged that he may have been mistaken and that *Baker v. Carr* was correctly decided. Friendly spoke in 1967 at the 150th anniversary celebration of the founding of Harvard Law School. "At least some of us who shook our heads over *Baker v. Carr* are now prepared to admit that it has not been futile. It has not impaired, it has rather enhanced the prestige of the Court. Indeed, the Chief Justice has characterized this as the most fundamental and important opinion of our speaker's [Justice Brennan] first decade."[94] For Friendly, unlike Frankfurter, the analysis was primarily pragmatic. When Friendly saw that something worked, his objections tended to disappear.

Fifteen years later Friendly distanced himself from Frankfurter's position on the *Flag Salute* cases, where the Supreme Court first upheld the power of a state to compel pupils to salute the flag despite their religious convictions to the contrary,[95] but then reversed itself to uphold pupils' right to refuse to salute on the basis of the right to freedom of speech.[96] Deeply patriotic, Frankfurter voted for the state and against the freedom-of-religion claim on both occasions. In 1982, speaking at the Frankfurter centennial, Friendly confessed error for having supported Frankfurter both in those cases and in *Baker v. Carr*.[97]

When it came to Hugo Black, Friendly's admiration was not universally shared at Harvard. In 1967 the Harvard University Board of Overseers, which included Friendly, enthusiastically agreed to award an honorary degree to Professor Herbert Wechsler of Columbia Law School.[98] Friendly advocated awarding an honorary degree to Justice Black as well:

> Although I had started my career with an intense dislike of Senator Black arising from his investigation of airmail contracts and this had continued, with some stimulation from Justice Frankfurter, for years after his elevation to the Supreme Court, by 1967 I recognized that he was indeed a great figure. I thought Harvard should honor him in his own right and in an endeavor to heal the wounds of the Frankfurter-Black bitterness. There was a fairly lively discussion of this in the Board of Overseers, many of whom still regarded Black as a dangerous radical, but my view finally prevailed—only to result in

a letter from the Justice declining the nomination. Characteristically he wrote that, while he would be delighted to receive an honorary degree from Harvard, he did not see how he could properly do this without having to accept all similar invitations.[99]

What sets Friendly apart from the checkerboard of backgrounds of the judges he most respected was the remarkable ordinariness of his physical stature, personality, and life. Of average dimensions and unexceptional features, he grew up in a small city the son of a middle-class merchant father and a housekeeping mother. He moved to New York City and lived a quiet life for three decades as a lawyer in a traditional Wall Street firm representing traditional Wall Street clients. Married to the same woman for fifty-five years, with three normal children and eleven grandchildren, he had none of the experiences of many on his list. For example, Stone and Jackson were both Attorneys General; Stone was dean of the Columbia Law School and Jackson the chief prosecutor at Nuremburg as well. Holmes saw military action as a soldier in the Civil War. More outgoing as well as possessing a well-known contemplative countenance, Learned Hand lived much of his life as part of a triangle involving his wife and a French professor, Louis Dow.[100] Brandeis had been a presidential advisor and a conspicuous crusader for the underdog. Cardozo was single and something of a recluse, and also bore the cross of his corrupt father, a judge before him. Traynor, by far the least known of Friendly's selections, was the son of impoverished Irish immigrants, who became an academic and then served as Deputy Attorney General of California under Earl Warren, where he created much of California's modern tax regime.

CHAPTER EIGHT

Away from the Courthouse

THE YEAR 1959 was busy for Friendly in respects other than his change in career. Two of his children married, and the third got engaged. Joan, his older daughter, married Frank Goodman, a lawyer who had been graduated from Harvard Law School, where he was an editor of the *Harvard Law Review*. He later became a professor at the University of Pennsylvania Law School. Ellen married Stephen Simon, a symphony orchestra conductor who was the nephew of Walter Annenberg, the wealthy publisher, diplomat, and philanthropist. David became engaged to Irene Baer in November, and they married a year later. Friendly played a role only in the courtship of David and Irene.

David and Irene met at Bellevue Hospital in Manhattan when David, an ophthalmologist, was on duty in the Navy and Irene was training to become a nurse. Bearing few material goods, Irene's parents and sister had fled Germany from the Nazis before the war. Irene was born in the United States in 1939. She and David started dating in early 1959. During the summer of 1959, when David's tour of duty took him to California and Sophie traveled in the Soviet Union, Friendly, who strongly favored his son's marriage to Irene, took Irene out on what she describes as weekly "dates," which both thoroughly enjoyed. They would go out to dinner and sometimes to the movies, often ending the evening with a call to David. Irene remembers Friendly being cheerful and having a good time, enjoying his funny quips as much as she. When David got hepatitis at Camp Pendleton in

California, Friendly arranged for Irene to fly there, refusing to take her stash of small bills which she ingenuously tendered in a paper bag. Later, Friendly financed the rest of her education at New York University and nursing school.[1] Irene was the kind of person and spouse Friendly (and Sophie) favored; she had character.

Friendly communicated with David, in part because of his serious eye condition, which included a treatable corneal ulcer that required surgery every half-dozen years. By September 1977 he had undergone seven eye surgeries.[2] Although David would not treat his father, he would recommend ophthalmologists. A difficulty emerged periodically because Friendly was convinced that his eye condition was more perilous than did his doctors, who did not believe that his condition threatened to make him functionally blind. Differences in opinion made him believe that his son was underestimating his condition and was insufficiently sympathetic.[3] In addition, he blamed David when he did not get better as quickly as he wanted to. For David it was a no-win situation. During one of David and Irene's visits to New York City, they chose to stay in a hotel rather than with his parents because the atmosphere had become so strained.[4] Friendly confided to his secretary Pat Hall that he was disappointed with his relationship with his son, with whom he had almost no interests in common and no rapport, and he called Michael Boudin the son he never had.[5] David died of cancer in 1993.

Stephen and Ellen Simon would occasionally have Sunday dinner at her parents' home, where Simon and Friendly would talk about music. Friendly especially enjoyed seventeenth- and eighteenth-century music, and he had a good collection of records of music from that period, to which he loved to listen; music relaxed him.[6] He had almost no interest in music after Beethoven, a lack of interest that carried over to art of all forms from the previous hundred years or so. Simon pointed out that the music Friendly liked reflected and contributed to his sense of order; he did not like dissonance in music as well as in other fields, and had no interest in modern art.[7] Friendly's shared musical interest with Simon drew him no closer to Ellen on an emotional level, however. Ellen and Simon were divorced in 1976 in a hotly contested proceeding in which Friendly provided active assistance to the lawyers from Cleary, Gottlieb who represented Ellen. Friendly fought to make sure that Ellen, who was an elementary school teacher, and her children were well provided for and was otherwise very supportive of her. He hoped that his efforts would provide an entrée to become closer to her, but their relationship did not improve. Over the following decades Ellen and Simon stayed on good terms, and he played the organ at Friendly's funeral service.[8]

While they disagreed on politics, Friendly and Joan were absorbed by the same things and he treated her as a serious adult.[9] Joan was also the child about whom Friendly would talk to friends and colleagues. Richard Posner did not know that Friendly had another daughter until after Friendly's death.[10] After their marriage Frank and Joan moved to the West Coast, where Frank practiced and then taught law before they moved to Philadelphia. Friendly's relationship to Joan became closer and his correspondence with her became even more effusive as time went on, such as his letter sent in December 1979: "Each passing year makes me more keenly aware how profoundly I love you. Along with Mom you are the truly bright spots in my life; nothing else matters anywhere near as deeply. Your mixture of gaiety, spontaneity, invincibility, understanding, brainpower,—I am running out of words—but I shall end with love, is a source of never ending wonder and delight. . . . I never cease to marvel how we can spend hours together and scarcely get started on all we want to discuss."[11]

The relationship between Friendly and his wife also continued largely as before on both personal and social levels. Sophie Friendly remained her exuberant self. In a letter to his former clerk Philip Bobbitt, Friendly agreed with Bobbitt's description of "Sophie's combination of vivaciousness and guilelessness."[12] Whatever the context, Sophie scintillated; Friendly usually didn't. When the Friendlys held large parties, Frank and Joan would attend if they were nearby. At one party in 1960 or 1961, there was a gap in the conversation, which Friendly promptly filled by turning to his law clerk, David Currie, and stating, "Speaking of admiralty. . . ." Joan immediately cut in curtly, "No one was speaking of admiralty, Dad, and no one wants to speak of admiralty."[13] What happened at family parties duplicated what had happened a generation before, although this time Friendly huddled with his professor son-in-law Frank rather than his judge father-in-law Horace, while ignoring other guests.[14]

When the children started having children, Sophie dove into her role as grandmother. In addition to visits with individual children and their families, in the late 1960s Sophie started organizing annual parties for their children and their increasing number of grandchildren. She was the proverbial life of the party, such as when she did cartwheels to attract their attention. When the grandchildren got a little older, she would take groups of three with her to Europe. When they got older still, she would talk to them about serious matters, including sex.[15]

Friendly's grandchildren have limited recollections of their grandfather. To most he was an occasional brooding presence; Sophie was the attraction. Returning from a family reunion, Friendly told his secretary that he had talked to a thirteen-year-old grandchild and found her "shallow."[16] His grandchildren had normal interests and led normal lives with some intellectual content, but to Friendly they lacked drive and discipline.[17] Even when he enjoyed seeing them, he failed to convey his pleasure to them. There was a consensus among the children and grandchildren that he thought the grandchildren as a group were undistinguished and that he had little interest in them, although he later developed a relationship with several who excelled academically and wrote a glowing letter of recommendation to a trustee of Colgate in support of one grandchild.[18] Daniel Simon shared with Friendly a love of music but noted, "[He] never forgave me for not liking Mozart."[19] Just months before his death, Friendly sent a long letter to his granddaughter Ellen Goodman, who had written him about her junior year at Harvard: "What strikes me . . . is that your courses seem to require—or inspire—so much more in the way of deep reflection. That, after all, is the important thing. One forgets the facts." Of course, Friendly remembered many of the facts he had learned in college, as his knowledge of Russian history demonstrated. But he understood—and took the time to impart to his granddaughter—wisdom about the purpose of a college education.[20]

Friendly and Sophie frequently spent time with the Columbia law professor Herbert Wechsler and his wife, Doris, including on New Year's Eve.[21] They also saw another Columbia law professor and his wife, Louis and Alice Henkin.[22] Friendly preferred dining with friends in bibulous groups of eight or ten to almost any other activity. At home-and-home dinners with professors and judges, including Marvin Frankel, William Conner, and Abraham Sofaer, Friendly was genial, witty, and scintillating.[23] He grew closer to some Harvard Law School professors, especially Louis Loss, Louis Jaffe, and Paul Freund, and saw them socially when circumstances permitted. One thing that did not change from a generation earlier, when Sophie was in charge of choosing their friends, was that the group remained almost entirely Jewish.

Friendly was not close to his more remote relatives, with the exception of Reuben Oppenheimer, a Maryland judge whose wife and Sophie were cousins. Friendly had uncommon respect for and much in common with Oppenheimer, and the couples traveled abroad together.[24] Friendly was related to two prominent newspapermen: Alfred Friendly, who was managing editor of the *Washington Post*, and Edwin S. Friendly, who was general manager of the *New York Sun*.[25] Fred W. Friendly, who served as president of CBS News, was a very distant relation, and the two barely knew each other.[26]

Friendly did a considerable amount of work at home, although he did not write opinions or articles there. He read (and remembered) the initial paperback editions of Supreme Court, the Second Circuit, and, in his early years, courts of appeals decisions from all the circuits (known as "advance sheets"). In 1981 he said, "During all the time when I was an active judge and for a considerable period thereafter, I did at least 60% of my brief reading at home, during evenings or on weekends. I still do a considerable amount of this." He read the *Harvard Law Review* cover to cover as well as selected pieces in other law reviews.[27] He also read many books, including more than 2,400 pages in two volumes of the *History of the Supreme Court of the United States*, which he reviewed.[28]

When he was involved as a judge in the railroad reorganization in the mid- and late 1970s, Friendly would dine in New York City with Judge John Minor Wisdom, sometimes joined by Wisdom's grown daughter, Kathleen (Kit) Wisdom, who found Friendly easy to talk to and not at all condescending.[29] In fact he was almost never condescending to audiences in whatever context, partly because he was not focused on his audience. His daughter-in-law, Irene, who drove him from New York to Cape Cod one summer, said that Friendly seemed to assume that she would understand everything he said on the law and other subjects.[30]

He continued his habit of reading a broad range of mostly contemporary books and articles, including ones by legal philosophers like H. L. A. Hart and Ronald Dworkin.[31] He ordered scholarly volumes that he could not readily find in local bookstores, such as a four volume set by F. Geny, *Science et Technique en Droit Prive Positif*, from Paris; Nikolaus Pevsner's *An Outline of European Architecture*; and *Oldenbourg's The Crusades* from London. From the Harvard Co-op he obtained Beadle, *Introduction to Biology*; Perry, *The Spanish Seabourne Empire*; and *American History, Recent Interpretations,* edited by Eisenstat.[32] Friendly was less interested in literature, starting but not finishing *Ulysses* by James Joyce.[33] He and his wife subscribed to a concert series at Carnegie Hall and attended other cultural events, including plays. While he would sometimes say that he had just seen a great play, he thought that the level of the theater was declining.[34]

Friendly's philanthropic and professional activities changed after 1959, when he resigned from most charitable boards and became less active in local bar associations. At the time of his appointment as a judge he was serving as the head of a Federation of Jewish Philanthropies committee on local hospitals and as a director of the Greater New York Fund. His involvement in the former ended in a messy dispute with a number of prominent Jewish leaders over the etiquette of distributing drafts of reports.[35]

From 1960 Friendly worked on Harvard-related activities; the American Law Institute (ALI; he was appointed to the Council in 1961, having been a member since 1939); the American Bar Association; the Council on Foreign Relations (he became a member in 1946, but attended more meetings after he became a judge); the American Academy of Arts and Sciences (he was a Fellow); the Center for Administrative Justice; a project funded by the American Bar Association whose purpose was to reform administrative procedure; and occasionally other projects. Harvard and the ALI took the most time.[36] He also contributed many thousands of dollars to Harvard and to other charities.[37]

The ALI, founded in 1923 by Brandeis, Cardozo, Learned Hand, George Wharton Pepper, and others, is an elite organization made up of professors, judges, and private practitioners. Its Council, a group of about fifty members, determines matters of Institute policy and reviews drafts of ALI "Restatements" of the law in many fields (including contracts, torts, and conflict of laws), a generally conservative, nonpartisan, and nontheoretical enterprise.[38] The work of Council members is technical and hard and requires a considerable amount of time studying drafts. Friendly also served as a member of the ALI's Executive Committee and was a principal consultant or advisor on the jurisdiction of federal and state courts, administrative law, conflicts of laws, corporate responsibility and ethics, codification of the basic securities statutes, international jurisdiction, and a pre-arraignment code for prisoners.[39] As described by Geoffrey Hazard, a former ALI director, Friendly was a consummate realist who listened well and made penetrating comments.[40] Professor Yale Kamisar, who disagreed with Friendly on the scope of rights for persons arrested, said that Friendly's statements commanded respect like no one else's and that the participants in the project, including the ALI director Herbert Wechsler, would accept Friendly's word on the content of the law.[41] "In Council meetings Henry's gentle tones carried enormous weight."[42] However, as with his work on Jewish charities, Friendly did not consider his many hours attending meetings of the ALI Council a good use of his time.[43] The pace of discussions on issues that he rapidly understood and resolved in his own mind must have exasperated him much of the time, although he apparently never complained or reduced his commitment.

With Harvard, Friendly served as president of its alumni association, a member of the university's Board of Overseers, chairman of the Special Overseers Committee on restructuring the university, a member of the law school's ad hoc committee reviewing faculty appointments, and chairman of visiting committees to the law school and the university.[44] These posts were not honorary, and Friendly traveled to Cambridge and elsewhere to attend meetings and engage in correspondence and telephone calls. He wrote to Harvard President Nathan M. Pusey in 1964 that he might resign from the committee on law school faculty appointments: "A year or so ago the Committee approved the promotion of an assistant professor despite the almost unanimous student view that he was a poor teacher, because the faculty said he had other fine qualities and that they thought his teaching would improve, which, so far as I can ascertain, has not yet occurred. . . . What I do not like is what seems to me an utterly false impression that the Committee amounts to something and that it shares responsibility for poor appointments."[45]

When he found himself in a field that was outside his expertise, such as the visiting committee for the philosophy department, he studied not only the department but the substance of its teaching.[46] He concluded that there was a "malaise," which related more to the state of philosophy in general than the Harvard department in particular.[47] One of his major accomplishments was heading the fund drive to raise millions of dollars to build an international studies building at Harvard Law School, an important expansion. Probably his stickiest assignment was serving on a committee to regulate outside work by members of the law school faculty.[48] Friendly accepted these substantial assignments despite his distaste for administrative and personnel matters.

In accordance with the low value he placed on honors, Friendly hung honorary degrees and plaques in his study at home, where few people would see them; some he simply stashed away at the bottom of a hall closet.[49] Though he repeatedly declined many invitations to give lectures, he accepted a few when he felt he had something to say, which included Columbia's James S. Carpentier lecture, the Oliver Wendell Holmes devise lecture at Dartmouth College, the Oliver Wendell Holmes lectures at Harvard Law School, and the Benjamin N. Cardozo lecture at the Association of the Bar of the City of New York.

Friendly also judged moot court competitions at law schools. The 1982 final of Harvard Law School's Ames Competition, in which he had participated as a student, concluded on a sour note. Appellants had failed to address a jurisdictional issue until their reply brief, and Friendly, acting as chief justice, chastised Michael Poindexter, the student representing the appellants, for not raising it in the principal brief. Many felt he was too harsh. Shortly after the argument Friendly wrote to Harvard Law School Dean James Vorenberg, "In retrospect, I was a bit sorry I was so hard on Mr. Poindexter. However, as someone said to me, that is the way it happens in court and the contestants might as well get use[d] to it." His clerk at the time agreed: "Friendly behaved like he was in the real world. He had only one way of practicing law."[50]

Friendly was serving on Harvard University's Board of Overseers in April 1969, when students engaged in a strike that caught the university unprepared. Later, he largely blamed Harvard Law School Professor Archibald Cox, who was the counsel to the Board of Overseers (and subsequently the Watergate Special Prosecutor), for the university's unsatisfactory performance. "[A]fter the Columbia Affair in the spring of '68, we were very worried as to what was going to happen at Harvard. And our counsel was a gentleman by the name of Archibald Cox. And he came to about every other meeting of the Board of Overseers, and assured us that everything was in complete order and he had all kinds of contingency plans, both of which turned out not to be so. So, the University was caught completely unprepared."[51]

After the strike the Board of Overseers appointed Friendly chairman of its long-range study committee, "one of these things you can't say no to." The report of Friendly's committee, which received considerable publicity, accepted many of the students' criticisms, including the charge that their instruction lacked relevance and did not cope with problems of "institutional racism, the Vietnam war or the arms race."[52]

An integral part of Friendly's social life was membership in the Harvard Club and in the Harmonie Club on Manhattan's Fifth Avenue, the latter a bastion of the German-Jewish elite in New York City, of which he became president.[53] He used the downtown Merchants Club largely for his occasional out-of-chambers lunches and judicially related functions. Another part of his life was participating in a Saturday luncheon group, which consisted mostly of judges, some lawyers, and an occasional nonlawyer, almost all of whom were Jewish and either reform-minded Democrats or moderate Republicans, and known in Friendly's chambers as the "Jewish Judges Club."[54] Attending were the federal judges Wilfred Feinberg, Milton Pollack, Marvin Frankel, and Jack Weinstein; the state judges Stanley Fuld, Samuel Silberman, Millard Midonick, and Allan Murray Meyers; and Bernard Newman, a former Republican County leader who sat on the U.S. Court of International Trade. Nonjudges included a former district judge, Simon Rifkind; New York Attorney General Louis Lefkowitz; Max Freund, the managing partner of Rosenman & Colin; Milton Handler, a senior partner in Kaye Scholer; Ernst Steefel, Friendly's hiking companion; and Arthur B. Krim, an entertainment lawyer and executive as well as a Democratic fundraiser. Occasionally attending was Mike Stern, a journalist based in Rome. Conversation ranged from current events to the arts to interesting or humorous cases.[55]

A student of English law and, to a lesser extent, French law, Friendly traveled abroad to converse with leading practitioners and judges in Europe.[56] The Friendlys continued to travel extensively during the summers, following the same pattern as during the pre-judiciary years, with Friendly flying and Sophie taking a ship. Sophie's reluctance to fly was so well established that, appearing in a skit at Friendly's eightieth birthday party, she told the Friendly stand-in, "Remember your motto, 'One if by land, and two if by sea, and if it's by air, you don't go with me.' "[57] With the help of his secretary, Friendly did most of the planning and arranging for the vacations, which were peripatetic. For example, on their 1970 summer vacation Sophie spent two weeks traveling and Friendly visited the Alps before they joined up in France, where they stayed at a total of fourteen hotels in five weeks.[58] While many of the summer trips were to France and England, they also traveled throughout Western Europe,[59] as well as to South Africa, North Africa, Egypt, Turkey, Iran, Israel, China, Hong Kong, and India. In 1977 the couple took an around-the-world trip.[60]

With travel as with law, he kept an open mind, reflected, for example, in his comments about his three days in China. While complaining about the prevalence of the revolutionary party line, he wrote to Joan, "The fascination is in the people. There are swarms of them, and they look happy, well if drably clothed, and properly fed. Even on the strength of such scant observation I have no doubt they are vastly better off than they have been for centuries, and certainly far better off than people in India. Mao and his colleagues must have been remarkable leaders to accomplish this in some twenty-five years."[61]

Living well while traveling remained one of Friendly's few extravagances. When he visited the law courts in London and Paris, he and Sophie stayed at the Ritz and Vendome, and he enjoyed dining at the best restaurants.[62] He wrote a partner in the Paris office of Cleary, Gottlieb, "La Pyramide still deserves its three stars."[63] For her part, Sophie enjoyed the daring and personal rather than the luxurious. On a few occasions she boldly took long trips by herself, including a train trip across the Soviet Union, something that was uncommon for women forty or fifty years ago.[64] During the winter the two took shorter trips to warmer climates, such as Haiti, Martinique, Mexico, and Cairo, often with Judge and Mrs. Moore.[65] In March 1970 the Friendlys took a cruise on an Italian ship, and he confessed to his clerks and secretary, "[The] Italian food is all too good—I'll have to confine myself to cheese made of skimmed milk when I return. The only rub concerns our fellow-passengers. About two-thirds of them are Californians, and if I were in Ray's [clerk A. Raymond Randolph] place, I'd think twice before settling there. Most of them regard New York as a foreign city and their political views are somewhere to the right of Reagan. Yet they are well supplied with money—many of them having taken the cruise both ways, a rather evident lack of imagination."[66]

A DECADE AFTER HIS APPOINTMENT to the Second Circuit, the prospect of a promotion to the Supreme Court injected itself into Friendly's life. That the prospect was slim was partly a matter of bad timing. The 1960 presidential election came barely a year after his appointment to the Second Circuit, and whatever chance he had in the near term evaporated when Democrat Kennedy beat Republican Nixon. Unbeknownst to Friendly, he was not totally ignored when the first vacancy occurred fourteen months into Kennedy's presidency; Theodore Sorensen prepared a list of nineteen candidates, which included Friendly and two other Republicans.[67] The appointment went to a Democrat and a friend of Kennedy's, Byron R. White. A similar light brush with the High Court occurred in the Johnson administration when Attorney General Nicholas Katzenbach prepared a list of a dozen candidates for the "Jewish seat" vacated by Arthur Goldberg. Friendly, the Harvard Law professor Paul Freund, and University of Chicago President Edward Levi were on the list, but then so was the reluctant Abe Fortas, who finally succumbed to Johnson's persuasion.[68]

It took the election of Richard Nixon in 1968 for Friendly to have a chance for a Supreme Court appointment, just as it took Eisenhower's election to place him in contention for the circuit court. The first vacancy was created by the resignation of Chief Justice Earl Warren. By the time of Nixon's inauguration in 1969, however, Friendly was sixty-five years old and, if appointed, would have been the oldest appointee ever to the High Court. Nixon seems to have publicly mentioned Friendly twice, once during the presidential campaign, when he referred to Friendly as a possible Chief Justice, and once on the notorious Nixon White House tapes, where Nixon referred to him as a "regional candidate."[69] The September 23, 1968, issue of *Newsweek* reported, "Nixon himself has even started to pass the word on his idea of an ideal successor to Warren: Henry Friendly, a senior judge on the Second Circuit Court of Appeals (in New York)." After the presidential election, the *Baltimore Sun* named Warren Burger and Friendly as two contenders, and *Time* magazine referred to Friendly "as one of Richard Nixon's leading candidates for Chief Justice of the Supreme Court."[70] When Nixon appointed Warren Burger as Chief Justice, James Reston wrote in the *New York Times* that "the liberals and intellectuals would clearly have preferred Paul Freund of Harvard or Judge Friendly, who is probably the most admired judge in the lower courts."[71]

Although he relished the challenge that promotion would bring, he had reservations about aspects of the Chief Justiceship. Fifteen years later

Friendly wrote to District Judge Charles Wyzanski, "Fortunately I never allowed myself to take seriously Mr. Nixon's mention of me as a candidate for the Chief Justiceship. Believe it or not I would not have wished to be Chief Justice. I am sure I would have been a very bad one and I would have absolutely hated to do all of the things the present incumbent [Burger] so enjoys."[72] He did say, however, that he would not have turned down the job.[73]

That Friendly thought that appointment as Chief Justice was possible and welcome can be inferred from a letter he sent to Walter Annenberg. In early November 1968 Friendly gave a lecture entitled "The Fifth Amendment Tomorrow: The Case for Constitutional Change," in which he advocated a constitutional amendment to narrow the Fifth Amendment's privilege against self-incrimination.[74] In his letter to Annenberg he wrote, "While I prepared these lectures many months ago, without the slightest idea that a Republican administration might come into office, I would not want to be disqualified simply for having stood up and said that the Court, for the best of motives, has gone too far and is likely to go further still."[75]

The resignation of Abe Fortas from the Court in May 1969 led Friendly to think that he might be tapped. On the eve of the appointment of Harry Blackmun to the Court, the *New York Daily News* pictured three people as the leading contenders: Blackmun, Friendly, and Bernard Segal, a Philadelphia lawyer.[76] Although the story had little, if any, factual basis as far as Friendly and Segal were concerned, for many northerners Friendly was an ideal candidate—a nonsouthern, nonracist, nonliberal—but he was not what Nixon wanted. As soon as Fortas resigned, Nixon told Attorney General John N. Mitchell to find a southerner who was a "strict constructionist."[77] Nixon nominated Judges Clement Haynsworth and then Harold Carswell, both southern judges, and, when the Senate rejected both, he ended up appointing a Minnesotan, Blackmun. According to a published account based on rather thin evidence, Attorney General Mitchell "had consulted with some unknown Republicans about the possibility of substituting Judge Henry Friendly of the Second Circuit for Judge Haynsworth,"[78] but obviously nothing came of it. Friendly was never considered when two vacancies developed in 1971. After a confusing process that considered thirty-six prospects, Nixon appointed Lewis F. Powell Jr. and William H. Rehnquist.[79]

Friendly fixed much of the responsibility for denying him the Supreme Court appointment on Attorney General Mitchell. He described an occurrence in 1971: "Mitchell attended our Second Circuit Conference and this was put to him rather strongly by Ed Weinfeld, whom he had known when Ed was in private practice, and by John Harlan. However, Mitchell turned both of them off quite sharply with the age argument. Of course, this, as it soon became apparent, had nothing to do with my case since Nixon was determined to appoint a Southerner."[80] Actually, age was potentially significant. Powell's age, which was sixty-four (two years younger than Friendly's), was the "only factor" against his nomination in 1971, according to John W. Dean, the White House counsel, who was deeply involved in the process.[81] Another problem confronting Friendly was his religion. In recorded conversations Nixon said that he had no interest in perpetuating a "Jewish seat" on the High Court and that he did not want anyone to give him "a Jew's name," adding, "I don't want a liberal Jew on the Supreme Court."[82]

CHAPTER NINE

First Amendment

FRIENDLY WAS GIVEN virtually no instruction at Harvard Law School regarding the constitutional-law issues prominent in the past half century. Instead, the focus was on the Constitution's Commerce Clause, which is reflected in his only surviving Harvard Law School examination.[1] During his year with Brandeis, he worked on a few important Bill of Rights cases, including wiretapping in *Olmstead v. United States*. His private practice was virtually bereft of constitutional questions.

Although he wrote a number of opinions, most of Friendly's contribution to constitutional law was in his extrajudicial writings. His guide on what to write about was simple: "It was because I got annoyed with something."[2] Whether it was a lecture or an opinion, he paid careful attention to the language and history of the Bill of Rights and the Civil War Amendments, infused with McIlwain's lesson to read documents as did the people at the time they were written. His approach was highly textual, at times exhibiting strains of originalism,[3] although also demonstrating concern for individuals' fundamental rights. While he employed the Constitution cautiously, he was prepared to recognize a private area in both civil and criminal cases, albeit at times narrow, from which the government was barred. If pressed to affix a label, one would say he was most of all a conservative in the traditional mold, judicially restrained and reserved, but not always agreeing with either the judicial or political right. Indeed, the number of times he eschewed the conservative position will surprise those who have based their appraisals on his meticulous reading of the Fifth Amendment and his parsimonious view of the scope of habeas corpus. In today's parlance he would be a moderate or centrist on most constitutional issues, identified with John Marshall Harlan, Lewis Powell, Sandra Day O'Connor, and Anthony Kennedy rather than William Rehnquist, John G. Roberts Jr., Antonin Scalia, and Clarence Thomas.

Friendly was less interested in the First Amendment[4] than in several other constitutional provisions. He gave one lecture on the First Amendment sponsored by the *Connecticut Law Review* on April 18, 1969,[5] three months after President Richard Nixon had taken office. Despite possible harm to his prospects for nomination to the Supreme Court, Friendly boldly chastised those who claimed that it was inappropriate to criticize the Court's decisions, even sharply.[6] His judicial opinions revealed that he was willing to let important institutions, such as the government, a university, or the bar, make judgments in areas duly assigned to them by the Constitution, statutes, or policy.[7] Pornography and libel cases did not involve the same institutional interests, and here he tended to favor freer expression of ideas. His view of the Establishment of Religion Clause of the First Amendment was cut from a different cloth, and he opposed most governmental attempts to accommodate religious observance. In fact, he had nothing good to say about organized religion.

During the tumultuous time of protests against the Vietnam War, prospective lawyers, relying on the First Amendment's guaranty of freedom of speech, challenged in *Law Students Civil Rights Research Council, Inc. v. Wadmond* a number of questions New York State asked applicants to the bar that were designed to ensure that they possessed the knowledge, skill, and character to become lawyers.[8] A decade earlier the Supreme Court had limited the qualifications a state could require of bar applicants to those having a rational connection with the applicant's fitness and capacity to practice law.[9] Civil liberties organizations sought to limit further the scope of the inquiry. Although the decision by a lower federal court was not important to them when the Supreme Court was governed by a liberal majority, during the course of the case Chief Justice Warren Burger was substituted for Earl Warren and then-conservative Harry Blackmun for Abe Fortas.[10] Plaintiffs' chances of prevailing dropped, and a victory before Friendly became important.

Plaintiffs objected especially to two written questions that sought information about whether the applicant had participated in any organizations that taught or advocated the overthrow of state or federal governments by force or violence and whether the applicant believed in the principles underlying the U.S. government.[11] Friendly ruled that, with minor changes made to clarify, for example, that the applicant's membership had to coincide with the organization's unlawful advocacy, the questions were appropriate to ask future lawyers. As for plaintiffs' challenge to personal interviews, Friendly recast the objection as a challenge not to personal interviews as such, but rather on their scope, and resolved the issue with a reassuring statement: "We have no reason to assume that as the scope of the committees' written inquiry is contracted, there will not be a similar adjustment in the focus of their spoken questions."[12] District Judge Motley dissented. To her the procedure was "clearly a political test for determining admission to the bar in violation of rights secured by the First and Fourteenth Amendment to the federal constitution."[13] The new Supreme Court majority affirmed, referring to Friendly's decision as "a thorough opinion."[14] Justices Black, Douglas, Marshall, and Brennan dissented on grounds similar to Judge Motley's.[15]

Friendly's most intellectually challenging freedom-of-speech case was *Cortright v. Resor*,[16] which dealt with the First Amendment rights of the military, a troubling problem in the best of times. David Cortright, a college graduate and a musician, enlisted in the Army in 1969 for three years under an agreement that he would be assigned to the 26th Army Band, Fort Wadsworth, New York, for at least one year. Soon he was signing antiwar newspaper advertisements and circulating antiwar petitions (collectively referred to as his "petition activities"). Then, during a parade on Staten Island on July 4, 1970, five women—Cortright's fiancée and the wives of four band members—walked behind the band, carrying signs with such slogans as "Military Wives for Peace" and "Nix-on War." Spectators threw objects at the women, one hitting Cortright's fiancée, and a veteran hit another woman, which the local press duly reported. Two weeks later the military ordered Cortright transferred to Fort Bliss, Texas.[17]

To block his transfer Cortright both brought a complaint against his superior officers under Article 138 of the Uniform Code of Military Justice[18] and filed a civil suit in federal court. The two principal factual issues in the proceedings were whether Cortright had played a significant role in disrupting the July 4 parade and whether the military had transferred him because of his petition activities as opposed to activities relating to the parade, the latter being a far more defensible position. The Army's investigation, which afforded Cortright limited rights, concluded that his military complaint was without merit.[19] In the civil suit, however, District Judge Jack Weinstein, sitting without a jury, held a two-day trial and rescinded Cortright's transfer to Fort Bliss.[20] Weinstein found that Cortright was not involved in disrupting the parade: "Neither the [military's] Article

138 Proceeding nor the trial revealed that [the five women] were acting otherwise than on their own behalf. . . . Nor was there any evidence that anyone in the Band acknowledged their presence or participated in any way in their activity." Likewise, he found that Cortright's petition activities played the major role in his transfer.[21] The Army appealed.

On appeal Friendly reversed on the ground that Weinstein's factual findings could not be supported: "What triggered the difficulties here was the prearranged participation of Cortright's fiancée and the four wives in the July 4 parade. While these ladies had every right to engage in a protest march of their own and carry such signs as they wished, it does not follow that the Band members were entitled to arrange for or to sanction their accompanying the Band when it was performing its mission of leading a Fourth of July parade. . . . [The First Amendment] did not entitle [Cortright] to arrange to have his fiancée march by his side and carry such a sign."[22]

Friendly, who tended to choose his words carefully, was uncharacteristically vague as to what Cortright had done: "the prearranged participation of Cortright's fiancée and the four wives in the July 4 parade" and his proceeding "to arrange for *or* to sanction their accompanying the Band."[23] Friendly also decided that Cortright's parade activities were the principal cause of his transfer, observing, "[I]f Cortright and his like-minded friends had limited themselves to signing peace petitions or engaging in protest marches while on leave, the Army command would [not] have interfered in any way." A footnote asserted, "Insofar as the district court may be taken to have found . . . that the Army's actions were directed at Cortright's having signed the November 1969 and circulated the spring of 1970 petition [rather than at the July 4 parade incident], we would be obliged to regard any such findings as clearly erroneous."[24]

Friendly's opinion observed that civilian review of the military's decisions was very limited, citing *Orloff v. Willoughby*,[25] where the Supreme Court stated that it had "found no case where this Court has assumed to revise duty orders as to one lawfully in the [armed service]. . . . The military constitutes a specialized community governed by a separate discipline from that of the civilian. Orderly government requires that the judiciary be as scrupulous not to interfere with legitimate Army matters as the Army be scrupulous not to interfere in judicial matters."[26] Friendly noted that the military had an important mission in which good order and discipline were important, and that "members of the armed forces, at least when operating in that capacity, can be restricted in their right to open discussion."[27] In view of the commander's "good faith belief that he was acting for the good of the Army, the matter should have been ended so far as the civilian courts are concerned,"[28] which seemed to all but eliminate First Amendment rights for members of the armed services. Friendly closed his opinion thus:

> [W]e are far from holding that under no circumstances could a civilian court interfere with a transfer order or prescribe other relief if that were needed to prevent abridgment of a soldier's First Amendment rights. We hold only that the Army has a large scope in striking a proper balance between servicemen's assertions of the right of protest and the maintenance of the effectiveness of military units to perform their assigned tasks—even such a relatively unimportant one as a military band's leading a Fourth of July parade, and that its actions here did not overstep these bounds.[29]

Dissenting, Judge Oakes criticized Friendly for "substitut[ing] our judgment [when] conflicting inferences may be drawn from the established facts by reasonable men, and the inferences drawn by the trial court are those which could have been drawn by reasonable men." Oakes also identified a problem in Friendly's analysis: Friendly argued that courts could not get involved in matters such as assignments, yet he specifically left open the possibility that he would intervene if the facts were stronger: "A war unpopular with many people, including soldiers, presents the courts with complicated new problems. This difficulty seems evident to me in the majority opinion which relies heavily upon *Orloff v. Willoughby* for the proposition that the courts shouldn't interfere with internal military matters on the one hand, while suggesting that if appellee had made 'a stronger showing' or had 'a stronger case than this one' we might interfere."[30]

Since authors of majority opinions see dissenting opinions before they file their opinions, Friendly was willing to permit Oakes to credibly accuse his opinion of containing a contradiction, a serious criticism. Oakes insisted that the military *demonstrate* that a legitimate military interest was impaired or threatened, as opposed to simply opining that the offending conduct was weakening morale, discipline, or effectiveness, which they could readily do, adding that the military, while possessing expertise in the field of discipline, lacked expertise in the application of the First Amendment and may value discipline more than the First Amendment permitted.[31] Unlike Friendly, Oakes had a passion for the free speech guarantees of the First Amendment.

The trial record supported Weinstein and Oakes. Cortright had testified that the sum of his participation in the women's activities on July 4 was that one of the band members told him to tell his fiancée to call one of the wives about a planned demonstration, which he did, without knowing what was involved and without offering her any advice on the subject.[32] The signs the women carried on July 4 did not associate them with the band, the women did not try to interfere with the parade, and their demonstration did not affect the performance of the band. Cortright's action hardly *required* a finding that he "arrange[d] for or sanction[ed]" his fiancée's participation in the march. In addition, Brigadier General Ciccolella, Chief of Staff of the First U.S. Army, provided the Army's self-impeaching evidence on this issue on cross-examination: "Q. What evidence did you have that the band members invited the women to participate [in the July 4 parade]? A. That was an *assumption* on our part."[33]

The evidence equally supported Weinstein's finding that Cortright's petition activities precipitated his transfer. When asked if the participation by the women in the march "enter[ed] into your decision on those transfers," Ciccolella answered, "To a small degree,"[34] indicating that the major reason for the transfer was Cortright's petition activities. In addition, several days after the parade Chief Warrant Officer Patrick Flores, the commander of the band, told a meeting of the band that the band's privileges were being eliminated "as the result not only of just the recent July 4th parade, but a whole series of events, and he specifically named the first petition and the second petition."[35]

Probably the most damaging evidence for the Army was provided by Major General Walter H. Higgins Jr., Commanding General of Fort Hamilton, who had written a four-page letter on July 17, 1970, to his superior, Lieutenant General Jonathan O. Seaman, that Weinstein found so embarrassing to the Army that he promptly placed it under seal. To Weinstein the letter was "a smoking gun."[36] The letter, which Weinstein unsealed in 2007 on the application of the author, stated that Higgins's first reaction on taking command in mid-1969 was to transfer Cortright, "the individual most evident in dissident activities," but decided "to play it cool" while maintaining surveillance on him. Higgins's letter acknowledged that the command had ordered Cortright's transfer to Fort Bliss "after Colonel Merrick's discussion with your headquarters. . . . Others should be moved in conjunction with the dissidents so that the criticism cannot be made that only those who are involved in one of the incidents are being reassigned." In other words, the general would keep Cortright on the base until after the military investigation was completed, and then he would get rid of him. The military was running a kangaroo court.

How can Friendly's uncharacteristic imprecision be explained? When he received Oakes's proposed dissent, Friendly wrote a bland memorandum to his colleagues on the panel: "We are not in disagreement on basic principles. JLO [Oakes] thinks Weinstein made findings of fact by which we are bound. I think rather that we have paid attention to evidence which he simply brushed aside,"[37] although he did not—and could not—identify particular evidence that Weinstein supposedly ignored or misread. Friendly, ordinarily a strong advocate of deferring to findings by district judges,[38] seems to have permitted himself an unduly free hand with Weinstein's factual findings.[39]

There was another serious difficulty with Friendly's opinion. He was writing to reverse the district court, yet he was basing his decision on grounds that the losing party had not argued there or, in fact, in the court of appeals. The government began its brief's argument section: "In this brief, we focus principally upon the questions relating to the correctness of the district court's determination that the military orders here involved were invalid."[40] The brief never argued that Weinstein's findings, discussed above, were "clearly erroneous,"[41] the requirement for reversal on factual grounds. While it is standard practice to affirm a district court on grounds not argued, it is extremely rare to reverse on grounds not properly raised at trial, other than jurisdiction. As a matter of fact, Friendly wrote to his colleagues in another case, "The only difficulty I see with disposing of the case on this ground is that the point seems never to have been raised in the district court or even here, and I suppose that a few thousand cases say that we therefore cannot consider it."[42] Friendly had engaged in a form of nonideological judicial activism (or salutary creativity) that commentators rarely consider. Perhaps more than any of his opinions, *Cortright* would have benefited from another draft.[43]

Friendly's contribution to the law of libel and slander consisted of only three opinions, yet each of them was a precursor to a significant decision by the Supreme Court. Four months after the Supreme Court constitutionalized defamation law in the 1964 landmark ruling in *New York Times Co. v. Sullivan*,[44] which extended First Amendment protections to media defendants sued for libel by public officials, Friendly drafted the Second Circuit's opinion in a libel case brought by the well-known activist scientist Linus Pauling. The *New York Daily News*, which had linked Pauling with Communist positions and causes, prevailed in the district court. After rejecting Pauling's various claims of error on appeal, Friendly observed, "If we took a different view on the matters here reviewed, it might be necessary to consider whether the judgment would have to be affirmed in any event in the light of *New York Times Co. v. Sullivan*."

Apparently the first judge to discuss public figures in a post-*Sullivan* opinion, Friendly presciently saw that the same principles *Sullivan* applied to press criticism of "public officials" should be applied to press criticism of public *figures* like Pauling, a pro-press position:

Although the public official is the strongest case for the constitutional compulsion of such a privilege, it is questionable whether in principle the decision can be so limited. A candidate for public office would seem an inevitable candidate for extension; if a newspaper cannot constitutionally be held for defamation when it states without malice, but cannot prove, that an incumbent seeking election has accepted a bribe, it seems hard to justify holding it liable for further stating that the bribe was offered by his opponent. Once that extension was made, the participant in public debate on an issue of grave public concern would be next in line.[45]

Friendly entered this constitutional territory gratuitously, since the issue was not raised by the parties and was extraneous to the outcome.[46] Not long after, the Supreme Court held in *Curtis Publishing Co. v. Butts*[47] that *Sullivan* was applicable to public figures as well as public officials.

Friendly's second defamation case involved the conservative columnist William F. Buckley, who sued the *New York Post* in Connecticut for libel; the *Post* successfully moved in the district court to dismiss the case on the ground that requiring it to defend outside of New York City would violate its constitutional rights. According to the *Post*, the First and Fourteenth Amendments directed courts to require more contacts between it and Connecticut than if the alleged harm had been caused by a nonmedia entity, such as an insurance company. Friendly reversed on the basis that *Sullivan* provided sufficient protection to the media:

> Newspapers, magazines, and broadcasting companies are large businesses conducted for profit and often make very large ones. Like other enterprises that inflict damage in the course of performing a service highly useful to the public, such as providers of food or shelter or manufacturers of drugs designed to ease or prolong life, they must pay the freight; and injured persons should not be relegated to forums so distant as to make collection of their claims difficult or impossible unless strong policy considerations demand. . . . Hazards to publishers from libel actions have recently been much mitigated by the development of substantive principles under the First Amendment, notably in *New York Times v. Sullivan.* . . . It is a legitimate question whether this will not sufficiently protect communications media without superimposing a necessarily vague First Amendment standard upon the application of long-arm statutes and thereby possibly creating undue hardship for a plaintiff like our traduced educator or clergyman.[48]

Seventeen years later, agreeing with Friendly, the Supreme Court in *Calder v. Jones*[49] held that the First Amendment should not be considered on choice of forum.

Buckley provided Friendly with the setting for one of his most cynical comments in a published opinion, when he questioned whether the identities of the parties in *Sullivan* may have affected the result: "We cannot but wonder whether the [Supreme Court in *Sullivan*] would have felt the same way if the *dramatis personae,* instead of being 'Bull' Connor and a newspaper internationally known for its high standards, had been an esteemed local educator or clergyman and an out-of-state journal with a taste for scandal which had circulated 395 copies of a libel stating he had corrupted the morals of the young."[50]

Friendly's final libel opinion, *Cianci v. New Times Publishing Co.,*[51] grew out of an article in a magazine called *New Times* about Vincent A. Cianci Jr., the mayor of Providence, Rhode Island, who was running for reelection. The lengthy article recounted that twelve years earlier Cianci, a law student at the time, raped a young woman at gunpoint and using a drugged drink, and then paid her $3,000 to drop her charges during a criminal investigation. The article claimed that Cianci failed three lie-detector tests, while his accuser, given the pseudonym "Gayle Redick," passed. According to the article, a state crime lab expert said it was one of the most clear-cut cases of rape he had ever processed, but that Cianci was not prosecuted because lie-detector tests were not admissible in court, corroborating evidence was limited, and Redick had accepted payment from Cianci and was unwilling to testify. Cianci sued the magazine for libel.

Cianci testified in a deposition that he had met Redick, who went with him to his room, but denied all the pejorative elements of the story, including drugging her and having sexual intercourse with her. He admitted he paid her $3,000, but said that was to settle a threatened civil suit and had nothing to do with any criminal charges. District Judge Constance Motley nevertheless granted *New Times'* motion for summary judgment with the statement that the article was not defamatory since it "carefully refrains from saying that Cianci was indicted, officially charged, or guilty of the crime of rape as claimed by Redick. Nor does the article ever state that Cianci paid Redick $3,000 as part of an agreement to drop criminal charges," at best a remarkably narrow reading of the article. But Motley chose to decide the case on a ground that defendants had not argued, finding decisive "not [only] the mere absence of a defamatory connotation in the article," but that "to whatever extent the article implies that Cianci was guilty of rape or improper payoffs, such implications are constitutionally protected as expressions of opinion."[52]

Like the briefs, the oral arguments displayed an all too common lack of insight. Strangely, Cianci's lawyer did not challenge the magazine's lawyer's statement: "I don't think really anyone could argue that Judge Motley did not properly apply the law of opinion." Since Motley's statement that the article was not false was an alternative holding in her dismissing the complaint, Cianci was, in effect, conceding the case. In other words, even if he won everything he argued, he'd still lose. When it was his turn, the magazine's lawyer drowned out the judges' questions with stentorian interruptions in a condescending tone. Friendly quietly told him, "You're not making any headway with me by shouting," but to no avail. The magazine's lawyer then pulled out that day's *New York Times* and started discussing articles on the first page that involved alleged misconduct by someone or other, explaining that he was demonstrating that the *New York Times* also printed allegations, which left the judges bewildered. Annoyed, Friendly asked under his breath why the lawyer did not discuss his own case, again to no avail. Although told his time was up, the magazine's lawyer repeatedly and loudly directed the judges to consider the First Amendment ("it's important," he urged), despite Friendly's angry admonition, "Don't repeat that; I realize that."[53]

Friendly found indefensible Motley's ruling as a matter of law that the magazine article was opinion, and ruled broadly for appellant Cianci, even though he had failed to make the winning argument, namely, that the article was not opinion:[54]

> In support of this conclusion the judge [Motley] quoted a passage from Justice Powell's opinion for the Court in *Gertz v. Robert Welch, Inc.*, 418 U.S. 323, 339–40 (1974), which has become the opening salvo in all arguments for protection from defamation actions on the ground of opinion, even though the case did not remotely concern the question:
>
> > Under the First Amendment there is no such thing as a false idea. However pernicious an opinion may seem, we depend for its correction not on the conscience of judges and juries but on the competition of other ideas.
>
> Justice Powell's very next sentence, however, was that "there is no constitutional value in false statements of fact." The alleged libels in *Gertz*, which were deemed sufficiently "factual" to support an action for defamation, included an "implication that petitioner had a criminal record" and charges that he was a "Leninist" or "Communist-fronter." The sort of idea which can never be false was illustrated by reference to Thomas Jefferson's Inaugural Address, where the President argued for freedom for those "who would wish to dissolve this Union or change its republican form." A statement that Cianci raped Redick at gunpoint twelve years ago and then paid her in an effort to obstruct justice falls within the Court's explication of false statements of fact rather than its illustration of false ideas where public debate is the best solvent.[55]

Friendly continued: "Almost any charge of a crime, unless made by an observer and sometimes even by him is by necessity a statement of opinion. It would be destructive of the law of libel if a writer could escape liability for accusations of crime simply by using, explicitly or implicitly, the words 'I think.' . . . To call such charges merely an expression of 'opinion' would be to indulge in Humpty-Dumpty's use of language." Friendly reversed the dismissal of the complaint and permitted Cianci to proceed.[56]

The article turned out to be far from the most serious of Cianci's problems. In 1984 he pleaded guilty to felony assault for torturing with a lighted cigarette and a burning log a man he suspected of sleeping with his estranged wife, and was forced to resign as mayor. After staging a comeback and again being elected mayor in 1990, he was convicted in 2002 of racketeering in connection with his activities as mayor and was sentenced to a five-year prison term, resigned as mayor, and served the sentence. The subtitle of a biography of Cianci called him "America's Most Notorious Mayor."[57]

It took the Supreme Court twenty-five years to adopt Friendly's decision in *Cianci*. *Milkovich v. Loraine Publishing Co.*[58] held that factual statements could not be protected by adding "in my opinion" or "I think," noting, "As Judge Friendly aptly stated: '[I]t would be destructive of the law of libel if a writer could escape liability for accusations of [defamatory conduct] simply by using, explicitly or implicitly, the words "I think."'"[59]

FRIENDLY'S SINGLE OPINION on pornography was the 1968 holding in *United States v. A Motion Picture Entitled "I Am Curious-Yellow."*[60] District Judge Thomas F. Murphy sustained the confiscation of the Swedish movie under the Tariff Act of 1930[61] on the ground it was "obscene or immoral." It was undisputed that the number and variety of sexually explicit scenes was considerable for a movie made for general distribution.

After noting that the experts disagreed over what the movie was "about," Judge Hays, who wrote the Second Circuit's lead opinion reversing Murphy, described it as "the search of identity" by a young girl considering her relationship to a variety of political, social, and economic problems. He held that the trial judge committed error in submitting the issue of obscenity to the jury: "[T]he question whether a particular work is [obscene] involves not really an issue of fact but a question of constitutional judgment of the most sensitive and delicate kind." Hays found the film was not obscene both because the dominant theme was not sex and because it was not utterly without redeeming social value.[62] Judge Lumbard dissented and voted to sustain the forfeiture, stating, "[T]he verdict of a jury of twelve men and women is a far better and more accurate reflection of community standards and social value." To him the plot was nonexistent and the sexual scenes "[bore] no conceivable relevance to any social value, except box-office appeal."[63]

Concurring in the reversal, Friendly concluded that he could not join Lumbard's decision because, as an "inferior federal court," the panel was bound by Supreme Court decisions, however difficult that might be to ascertain "in light of the divergent views within the Court and the consequent multiplicity of opinions." If the test were the one in the 1957 seminal decision *Roth v. United States*,[64] "'whether to the average person, applying contemporary community standards, the dominant theme of the material taken as a whole appeals to prurient interests,' I might well join Chief Judge Lumbard for affirmance. But," Friendly stated, "quite clearly, it is not." The standard later established in *Memoirs of a Woman of Pleasure* was "much more permissive."[65] Neither party's brief had argued that Supreme Court decisions after *Roth* had altered in any way the applicable standard. The government's brief argued simply that the movie was pornographic and without redeeming value of any sort, and petitioners argued that the movie was a serious artistic endeavor, a position supported by testimony from an impressive slate of critics and commentators, but which evoked no judicial acknowledgment. Friendly also rejected the possible argument that there was

> no sufficient nexus in this film between the scenes of nudity and the sexual activity and the problems of the girl—one could hardly call her the heroine—in trying to work out her relationship with life. Although *Memoirs* did not in terms require such a nexus, I would agree that the presence of "redeeming social value" should not save the day if the sexual episodes were simply lugged in and bore no relationship whatever to the theme; a truly pornographic film would not be rescued by inclusion of a few verses from the Psalms. While this case may come somewhat close to the line, I cannot conscientiously say that a connection between the serious purpose and the sexual episodes and displays of nudity is wholly wanting.[66]

Friendly concluded:

> When all this has been said, I am no happier than Chief Judge Lumbard about allowing Grove Press to bring this film into the United States. But our individual happiness or unhappiness is unimportant, and that result is dictated by Supreme Court decisions. . . . What we ought to make plain, however, and not at all in a "'tongue-in-cheek" fashion, is that our ruling [would change if minors were not excluded from the film or if advertising for the film focused on its sexual aspects.][67] . . . With these reservations and with no little distaste, I concur for reversal.[68]

While Friendly expressed the requisite unhappiness at reversing the confiscation of the movie, it is not clear how he would have voted were he writing on a clean slate. His voting memorandum stated, "Somewhat to my surprise I vote to reverse. . . . I did not find the film so offensive as I expected. . . . I cannot believe any catastrophic result will ensue from the film being seen by anyone foolish enough to go."[69] Earlier, he had expressed his view that very limited antisocial conduct flowed from pornography: "It should have been completely obvious that among the motivations behind legislation against obscenity the idea of preventing action considered to be anti-social is almost the least important, and that in consequence the Supreme Court is way off the beam when it applies to dreary pornography the same test that it does to communist propaganda."[70]

JUDGE FRIENDLY PLAYED a role in one of the most significant First Amendment cases in the country's history, the *Pentagon Papers* case, on which the country was transfixed and bitterly divided. Not only was the case important in its own right, but circumstances surrounding it, including the impact it had on President Nixon, led to the cover-up of the Watergate burglary and to the unprecedented resignation of Nixon on August 9, 1974.[71] The first installment of the so-called Pentagon Papers appeared at the top of page 1 of the Sunday, June 13, 1971, *New York Times*. The leaked documents came from a forty-seven-volume, seven-thousand-page "Top Secret" study authorized by Secretary of Defense Robert McNamara during the administration of Lyndon Johnson. The man who leaked the documents, Daniel Ellsberg, had worked on the project years earlier. Ending with the election of Nixon, the study covered the U.S. involvement in Vietnam between 1945 and 1968 and included facsimiles of many original cables and other documents. Only fifteen copies were made of the study. After switching from a hawk to a dove on the Vietnam War, Ellsberg obtained a copy of the Pentagon Papers and gave it to the *New York Times* after having made unsuccessful attempts to convince members of Congress and others to publish the material.

Arguing that nothing short of barring further publication could adequately protect national security, the Nixon administration filed suit on Tuesday, June 15, 1971, in the District Court in Manhattan against the *Times* and others to enjoin further publication of the classified information.[72] The legal battle between the Nixon administration and the *Times* rivaled the contents of the Papers for the public's attention. Pursuant to a random-assignment system the case went to Judge Murray I. Gurfein, a Nixon appointee who was so new on the job that this was his first case. In his initial ruling Gurfein, who had been an intelligence officer in World War II, entered a restraining order barring publication of the fourth and subsequent installments until he could hold an evidentiary hearing.

At the hearing held on Friday, June 18, part of which was public and part *in camera* (closed to the public), the government, represented by U.S. Attorney Whitney North Seymour Jr. and his assistant, Michael Hess, called three witnesses who testified to the classification process and the significance of the "Top Secret" classification. Although the witnesses opined that the publication would cause enormous harm to the security and diplomatic relations of the United States, they were remarkably light on specifics, even when Gurfein pressed them to identify which parts of the documents hurt the United States and how. As Hess later explained, "We didn't have much to work with, so we emphasized something we had, that the Pentagon Papers were stolen merchandise."[73] The *Times*' lead lawyer was Alexander Bickel, a Yale Law School professor and distinguished constitutional scholar, but neither a First Amendment expert nor an experienced litigator. Based on the evidence, Gurfein's excellent opinion found the government's case unpersuasive—publication would not "seriously breach the national security" or "vitally [affect] the interests of the Nation"—and denied an injunction but continued the restraining order to allow the government an opportunity to appeal without further publication of the Papers.[74]

Meanwhile, the *Washington Post*, which by then had acquired substantial portions of the study from Ellsberg, published its first installment on Friday morning, June 18. The government immediately sued to enjoin further publication, along the lines of its suit against the *Times*. After granting a temporary restraining order, the district judge in Washington, D.C., held a hearing and denied the government's motion primarily on the ground that it had failed to provide specifics of how publication of the material could harm the country.[75] The case was now before two courts of appeals, barely a week after the initial publication.

Prepared over the weekend, the government's submission to the Second Circuit consisted of a public legal brief, a sealed brief, and an appendix (the last two discussing classified data). The government relied on the President's inherent power; the Espionage Act,[76] a criminal statute; and *Near v. Minnesota*.[77] That forty-year-old Supreme Court case, which had refused by a five-to-four vote to enjoin a newspaper from publishing libelous and racist remarks, said, "No one would question but that a government might prevent actual obstruction to its recruiting service or the publication of the sailing dates of transports or the number and location of troops."[78] The government's appendix summarized the *in camera* testimony of its witnesses and provided references and analyses that, it claimed, demonstrated that the Papers contained information highly damaging to the security and diplomatic relations of the United States and to the stability and safety of South Vietnam. For the first time in the case, the government claimed that it had not had a full opportunity to present all the facts to Gurfein.

The *Times* likewise submitted a public legal brief and a sealed factual brief. The legal brief argued both that the First Amendment barred the prior restraint and that the Espionage Act did not encompass the Pentagon Papers, pointing out that without an enabling statute the government was powerless to enjoin its publication, notwithstanding its top-secret classification. The *Times*' sealed brief characterized the government's evidence during the *in camera* hearing as vague and the contents of the Papers as stale and pointed to the many instances when supposedly top-secret information was published without dire consequences.

When the lawyers appeared in the Second Circuit courtroom on Monday morning, June 21, 1971, Friendly announced that all eight of the active judges of the court would hear argument the following afternoon. The court's initial hearing of the case *en banc*, which appears to have been unprecedented, further emphasized its importance.[79] U.S. Attorney Seymour argued first, stressing the stolen nature of the documents, although, when questioned, conceded that how the *Times* obtained the documents was not dispositive of the case. Judge Walter Mansfield observed that many of the documents marked "Top Secret" were almost thirty years old or had been made public, so the fact of classification was not persuasive. But when he said that Seymour conceded that some documents marked "Top Secret" were not top secret, Friendly intervened to help Seymour: "I don't know that you had conceded that." Mansfield pressed Seymour: "Do you say that each and every one of those documents today is actually of a nature that should be classified top secret?" Seymour was unresponsive, stating that there was a declassification system to which the *Times* had not submitted.[80]

Mansfield asked another question: "Mr. Seymour, doesn't this just boil down to an issue of fact that was decided by Judge Gurfein, and isn't our position simply to determine whether his finding was clearly erroneous or not supported by substantial evidence?" Seymour had no satisfactory answer. He said, "I don't think it is as simple as that, your Honor," and went on to talk about a presumption of regularity of the classification system.[81] (He could have said that the answer was no, either because the issue was a constitutional question of law or that Gurfein had applied the wrong legal standard, analogous to the issues in prosecutions for pornography.)[82] When Friendly pressed Seymour on why he had agreed to the procedure and timetable that Gurfein had followed, Seymour tried to pass the responsibility onto Gurfein and the *Times*—Gurfein had set the

schedule and the *Times* had not sought to have the documents declassi-
fied. But Seymour had failed to object to the schedule in the district
court.

With Bickel, Friendly became more active and aggressive. In fact, the
judge embarrassed Bickel, a scholar whom he respected and with whom he
had corresponded.[83] It was telling what Friendly could do in two minutes
to a professor of Bickel's stature:

> *Mr. Bickel:* May it please the Court, Mr. Seymour, your Honors, we hear a
> great deal about stolen documents. The word has been in this case from
> the very beginning. Just very briefly I would like to point out that there
> is no evidence anywhere in the record, certainly not, that the Times stole
> these documents or that anyone stole them.
>
> *Judge Friendly:* You know that someone gave them to the Times when he
> had no authority to do it, though?
>
> *Mr. Bickel:* That is the allegation, your Honor. But how he got them—
>
> *Judge Friendly:* Is there the slightest doubt about that?
>
> *Judge Kaufman:* You have not denied that, have you?
>
> *Mr. Bickel:* We have not denied that the Times did not get the documents
> from a government source authorized—
>
> *Judge Friendly:* Why not just say the answer is the Times got them without
> authorization? Then we need not waste time quibbling about that.

Judge Friendly had just given Bickel an opportunity to end his discomfort,
but Bickel could not bring himself to accept it, even though Seymour had
conceded that the source of the documents was not dispositive.

> *Mr. Bickel:* That, it seems to me, begs a certain question. I am not arguing
> that. I am only very briefly trying to get the word "stolen" out of this
> discourse.
>
> *Judge Friendly:* They received them from someone who had no authority
> to give it to them, and they knew perfectly well that was the fact, and
> according to Mr. Seymour they had known about it for three months, is
> that right?
>
> *Mr. Bickel:* I don't know who they received them from. They received it from
> somebody. I don't for a moment suggest it, but it could, for example, on
> this record be Mr. Clifford or Mr. McNamara, for all we know.
>
> *Judge Friendly:* You aren't serious. Why don't you face the facts?
>
> *Mr. Bickel:* I am not a bit serious about that, of course. But I don't know
> where they were gotten and I am simply resisting the word "stolen."
>
> *Judge Friendly:* Nobody says the Times went into the Department of Defense
> with a chisel. It is equally clear that someone gave it to the Times when he
> had no authority to do so. We are all agreed on that. Why not go on from
> there?
>
> *Mr. Bickel:* I am simply resisting the word "stolen," which it does seem to me
> is a highly colored word.

Judge Friendly: Let's say they received the goods in the process of embezzlement, then, if you prefer.

Mr. Bickel: Without dwelling further on the point, may I say I resist that as well?

Judge Friendly: You may resist it.[84]

With Friendly's line about embezzlement, the overflowing courtroom exploded with laughter.[85] He had turned Bickel into a quibbler about the obvious, not the best spot for someone trying to uphold the majesty of the First Amendment in the face of the government's attempt to impose prior restraint on the press for the first time in the history of the Republic. The *Times'* attorney Floyd Abrams later reported, "Bickel was pounded mercilessly by Chief Judge Friendly from the moment he rose to respond. The printed page cannot fully reflect the anger with which Friendly spoke. . . . He was disparaging and then some. . . . [H]e was angry and sarcastic from start to finish and nothing he said conveyed anything but disdain for the position (or the conduct) of the *Times*."[86] When Friendly pressed Bickel to articulate a constitutional standard, Bickel failed, stating that "neither this Court nor the Executive has any discretion to tell the *Times* not to publish it if as a matter of law it is entitled to publish it."[87] Judge Mansfield picked up the questioning at this point, and Bickel never managed to assert a strong First Amendment position. It was left for the American Civil Liberties Union as amicus curiae to make those arguments.[88]

Most of the hour of *in camera* hearings was devoted to procedural matters, such as whether the court should accept the government's last-minute appendix containing new affidavits and how long it would take to declassify documents that were not secret. Some judges, including Friendly, pressed Seymour on how years-old documents could harm the war effort in view of the extensive prior publication of the facts they contained. The most significant development in the *in camera* hearing followed this statement by Seymour: "[T]hat this is a coverup of political embarrassment is so plainly poppycock in terms of this administration trying to protect a prior administration of a different political party—that makes no sense at all. I have no doubt your Honor, getting back to your question about why it took a couple of days to get the wheels going here, that there was great agonizing over Scylla and Charybdis of having a great time, sitting back and watching the other fellows sweat it out and protecting the national security."[89]

Arguing *in camera* for the *Times* was William E. Hegarty, a partner in the Cahill, Gordon law firm, who, in response to questions posed by Friendly, said that the *Times* had initiated meetings with the government in other situations and on occasion chose not to publish on its own initiative, but the *Times* saw nothing in the Pentagon Papers that required either of those actions. Fifteen minutes later Hegarty had an epiphany: "[I]f you think back to Mr. Seymour's remark, should they take advantage of the political embarrassment of the preceding administration or should they look out for national security, if that is an accurate summary of what was going on in Washington, I am unpersuaded as to what National security is involved."[90] In other words, since no President would sacrifice a true national security threat for party politics, the disclosure of the material could not constitute a mortal threat. It was a telling point.

Unwilling to leave the response to Seymour, Friendly provided an answer, but it failed to advance the government's position: "I think what Mr. Seymour meant was that even if these precise documents might not deal a mortal blow to the nation, that the administration—that you can't let this thing go every time an employee steals some documents and delivers them to a newspaper." Hegarty immediately saw that Friendly's statement all but acknowledged that the publication of the study was not a threat to the nation, and asserted, "[T]here is no case at law or in equity in this Court on that factual assumption." Friendly resisted: "No, I take it Mr. Seymour says this is in a kind of gray area. If we add something that is purely historical, we are in that gray area, but that the Government has an obligation to protect the secrecy of the documents. That is his position. Some of us will agree with him and some of us won't."[91] But gray areas are not national security crises of the sort warranting prior restraint of the press. After a brief recess, Friendly announced that the court would render a decision within the next few days, continuing the stay meanwhile.

For the next twenty-four hours the judges and their clerks worked feverishly on the case, plowing through mounds of materials. The pressure, the rush, and the publicity were enormous.[92] Law clerks wrote memoranda, provided to all judges, analyzing the government's factual contentions. After the argument, five of the judges composed and shared with their colleagues their voting memoranda: Kaufman, Lumbard, Mansfield, Oakes, and Smith; Friendly, Feinberg, and Hays did not circulate memoranda. Identical sets of the voting memoranda, not previously made public, obtained from Judge Feinberg and from Friendly's papers at Harvard Law School, provide an unusually reliable insight into the thinking of a circuit court in an extraordinarily important case.[93] Every memorandum was serious, measured, and undogmatic; no judge took an extreme position. Those voting for the *Times* accepted that there were circumstances when the government could enjoin publication to protect a serious threat to national security, and those voting for the government accepted that the burden was on the government to demonstrate specifically serious risk to national security. The major point in the memoranda of Kaufman and Oakes, who voted to uphold Gurfein, was the failure of the government to have "met its extraordinary burden of showing that publication of any specific portions of the Vietnam papers . . . would so gravely damage the security of this nation that their suppression is justified."[94] The three memoranda favoring reversal accepted that the *New York Times* should be allowed to publish the Papers if a thorough examination demonstrated that there was no risk to the war effort, further agreeing, "So far the Government has failed to meet its burden."[95] They primarily argued that the government had insufficient time to review the mass of papers, which dealt with important matters of national security, and that a short delay would not harm the public.

As recalled by Judge Feinberg, there were discussions among the judges about the importance of resolving the case quickly, although he did "not recall whether there was *any* discussion on the subject of writing an opinion," whether for the court, concurring, or dissenting.[96] On Wednesday, June 23, the day following argument, the Second Circuit issued its decision. Consistent with their memoranda, the judges voted five to three to remand the case to Gurfein for a further hearing, a victory for the government. There were no opinions, just the court's one-sentence *per curiam* (unsigned) decision and order that read in its entirety:

> Upon consideration by the court in banc, it is ordered that the case be remanded to the District Court for further in camera proceedings to determine, on or before July 3, 1971, whether disclosure of any of those items specified in the Special Appendix filed with this Court on June 21, 1971, or any of such additional items as may be specified by the plaintiff with particularity on or before June 25, 1971, pose such grave and immediate danger to the security of the United States as to warrant their publication being enjoined, and to act accordingly, subject to the condition that the stay heretofore issued by this court, shall continue in effect until June 25, 1971, at which time it shall be vacated except as to those items which have been specified in the Special Appendix as supplemented and shall continue in effect as to such items until disposition by the District Court.[97]

While seemingly bereft of legal determinations, the order implied decisions on some important issues, most of them in favor of the *Times*. Thus, the order ignored the argument that classification ipso facto can support suppression and did not require the *Times* to go through a declassification procedure. In fact, it seems to have rejected any analysis that gave deference to the government's position or procedures, rejected giving any weight to the fact that the *Times*' source was tainted, and ignored the Espionage Act as a source for relief. And in remanding to Gurfein, the order did not require or even suggest that he should read the entire study. In the other column, no mention was made of the government's failure to object to Gurfein's demanding schedule. In retrospect that was a futile argument; the court was not going to imperil national security because the government had neglected to make an objection regarding scheduling.

The substance of the order was unusual for two related reasons. First, it identified no error committed by Gurfein and it provided no reason or basis for remanding the case to him.[98] Second, it neither stated what issues the appeals court decided nor discussed what approach the district court should take on remand. The suggested legal standard—whether disclosures "pose such grave and immediate danger to the security of the United States as to warrant their publication being enjoined"—was not inconsistent with what Gurfein had said. The court simply informed Gurfein that what he had done did not warrant affirmance, gave the government a few more days to come up with something, and told Gurfein to take another look at whatever material the government might present.

As noted, Friendly wrote no voting memorandum. However, he did write a twenty-one-page double-spaced document (including eight pages of footnotes) that strongly supported the government and was far more sophisticated than any brief or opinion in the case, including the three pro-government opinions in the Supreme Court.[99] Friendly's document (really a draft)[100] made four principal points.

First, the case "should be decided without reaching the grave constitutional issues" for the reason that the *Times* had acquired the papers unlawfully and "deliberately failed to avail itself of any of the [available] remedies."

Second, the President was paramount in foreign and military affairs. Friendly emphasized, "Statesmen who were much closer to the origins of the Constitution than we are, were eloquent in their assertion of the powers of the President in foreign relations and the necessity for imposing such secrecy with respect to their conduct as they determined to be required," quoting John Marshall and Thomas Jefferson.

Third, after meticulously parsing the Espionage Act to determine whether it covered the *Times*' conduct, Friendly concluded that it was unnecessary to decide the issue because whether an injunction was justified did not turn on whether the *Times* violated that act, but rather on the seriousness of the potential harm to national security. For the United States to prevail in a civil action for an injunction against the *Times* did not require it to prove criminal behavior.

Fourth, because of the expertise of the responsible government officials and the lack of institutional expertise on matters of national security on the part of federal judges, "a Top Secret classification must at least create some inference in [the government's favor]."[101] Friendly saw the government's initial burden of proof satisfied by its demonstrating a serious risk to national security, which the testimony of its experts accomplished. He recommended remanding the case to Gurfein for twenty days for negotiations or, failing agreement, a decision. Significantly, by relying on the embezzlement of the Papers, by explicitly rejecting a requirement that a violation of a federal statute was necessary for an injunction, and by giving deference to the classification system, Friendly's memorandum was more favorable to the government than the Second Circuit's order.[102]

Why Friendly wrote the draft and what he did with it cannot be ascertained with certainty. Unlike an opinion, it did not start with "Friendly, J." Unlike a voting or similar memorandum, it was not addressed to his colleagues (or anyone else), had no heading, was undated, and left the author unidentified. Friendly's handwritten notation on the first page of his edited *handwritten* draft instructed his secretary to make only three copies; his handwritten note on the typed memorandum said, "File in U.S. v. New York Times." Friendly's clerk at the time, Walter Hellerstein, worked on an earlier nine-page draft of the twenty-two page document. He has described the longer version as possibly an opinion that Friendly did not publish.[103] Neither Judge Feinberg nor his clerk assigned to the case remembers seeing such a document, and no copy of a Friendly-authored document was found in his case file.[104] Two of the presumably three copies are in Friendly's case file.

The diction of the twenty-one-page document alternates between that of a memorandum and that of a judicial opinion. To the extent it reads like the latter, it is not clear for which judge on which court it was intended; thus, it alternates between "we" and "I" as the speaker. It reads, "Since this view has not persuaded a majority of the Court, I go on to state other reasons for disagreement with my brothers. . . . A large portion of the able opinion below deals with the question whether the publication of Top Secret documents by the Times violates the Espionage Act."[105] The first quoted sentence, which is informal for a judicial opinion, is inconsistent with a draft opinion to be issued by Friendly, who was in the *majority* in the Second Circuit. Moreover, if it was a draft opinion for Friendly, it is difficult to understand why he did not publish it, or at least circulate it. An alternative is that it was a draft opinion for someone else, possibly a Supreme Court Justice, but that does not follow since the Second Circuit wrote no opinion (although the district court did).

Hellerstein distinctly remembers that Friendly was unusually agitated about the case, was visibly irritated by the *New York Times,* and exhibited a sense of urgency surrounding the preparation and dispatch of the document.[106] In fact, the twenty-one-page document contained two typographical errors, as well as retaining instructions to his secretary to insert a quotation rather than the quotation itself and leaving a blank for the insertion of authority.[107] At about the time the Second Circuit entered its order, Hellerstein relates, Friendly inserted the document into a manila envelope addressed to Justice John Marshall Harlan, his friend and former law partner, a highly unusual and arguably unethical action.[108]

The Supreme Court agreed to hear the two cases and set argument for Saturday, June 26, just three days after the Second Circuit's order. On June 30 the Supreme Court affirmed the District of Columbia Circuit and reversed the Second Circuit by a vote of six to three. In a brief *per curiam* opinion the Court held that a prior restraint comes to the Court "bearing a heavy presumption against its constitutional validity" and that "the Government has not met that burden."[109] Later, each Justice published his own opinion, with no opinion gathering more than three Justices.

Justice Harlan's dissenting opinion said, "This frenzied train of events took place in the name of the presumption against prior restraints created by the First Amendment," before listing seven difficult questions that the litigation had not answered. The seven included four addressed at far greater length by Friendly: the significance of the *Times'* unlawful possession of the Papers, the President's primary role in foreign affairs and the corresponding narrow role given to the courts, the existence of the Espionage Act, and the expertise of government officials. Other questions Harlan raised related to the power of the Attorney General to sue in the name of the United States and whether the First Amendment precluded courts from issuing an injunction. Harlan concluded, "It is a sufficient basis for affirming the Court of Appeals for the Second Circuit in the *Times* litigation to observe that its order must rest on the conclusion that because of the time elements the Government had not been given an adequate opportunity to present its case to the District Court. At the least this conclusion was not an abuse of discretion."[110] The other two dissenting opinions did not discuss substantive issues, just the accelerated schedule.

Harlan's law clerks at the time do not remember seeing Friendly's composition, and no copy appears in Harlan's files relating either to Friendly or to the case.[111] While Harlan's dissent overlaps Friendly's draft to some extent, none of the language in the dissent or in its numerous drafts, dated as early as June 25, suggests that Harlan or his law clerks saw Friendly's memorandum.[112] The most likely conclusion is that Friendly wrote the document and probably dispatched it to Harlan, but the Justice either did not receive it or chose to ignore it. There is no credible alternative reason why Friendly would have written it.

FRIENDLY, WHO REJECTED organized religion, wrote nothing extrajudicially and no opinion until 1984 on the meaning of the clause of the First Amendment that reads, "Congress shall make no law respecting an establishment of religion or prohibiting the free exercise thereof." In 1965, in the immediate aftermath of the Supreme Court's decision in *Engel v. Vitale*,[113] which held that the First and Fourteenth Amendments barred the nondenominational "Regents' Prayer" from public schools,[114] school officials in New York ordered the cessation of all prayers in public schools, including barring kindergarten children from reciting "God is Great, God is Good, and We Thank Him for our Food, Amen." Parents of children sued to require the school officials to permit that prayer, on the ground that the Constitution did not prohibit student-initiated prayers of that sort. Agreeing, the district judge found for the parents. On appeal the parties argued whether the prayer violated the First Amendment, but Friendly saw the case in a different light: "Neither provision [of the Constitution] requires a state to permit persons to engage in public prayer in state-owned facilities wherever and whenever they desire. . . . Determination of what is to go on in public schools is primarily for the school authorities. . . . The authorities acted well within their powers in concluding that plaintiffs must content themselves with having their children say these prayers before nine and after three."[115]

No one involved in the case had seen the crucial difference between a school board's decision to *permit* a prayer and its decision to *prohibit* a prayer. No principle interfered with the decision *not* to have prayers recited during the school day. Friendly reversed.

Friendly's next brush with the clause was in *Curran v. Lee*,[116] when New Haven, Connecticut, subsidized a Polish Roman Catholic parade. After the district court entered summary judgment in favor of the city, permitting the parade to proceed, Friendly's voting memorandum registered his objections to the parade:

> I think that subsidizing such a parade would be a violation of the establishment clause. . . . It seems hard for me to say that a parade honoring a Roman Catholic saint on his birthday, with a Catholic bishop in the reviewing stand and a priest (perhaps the bishop) and a member of the Knights of Columbus among the grand marshals, has "only a remote and incidental effect advantageous to religious institutions." Furthermore it seems that subsidization of such a parade could well lead to a violation of the entanglement test. If the cardinal and the bishop wanted to walk in the St. Patrick's Day parade as

they did in the Polish parade, wouldn't the City have to tell them that if they did so the subsidy would be withdrawn?[117]

The panel ducked the difficult issue. In a bland and politic *per curiam* opinion, not written by Friendly, the court unanimously affirmed in favor of New Haven: "The record in this case fails to give a description of the parade. . . . On this record we cannot tell what is the purpose of granting aid to the parade, what is the effect of granting such aid, and whether granting such aid fosters excessive governmental entanglement with religion."[118]

Finally, in 1984, a time of doctrinal uncertainty and confusing precedents, Friendly wrote the Second Circuit's opinion in *Felton v. Secretary, Dept. of Education*,[119] where, when other programs had proven ineffectual, New York City sent public school teachers into nonpublic schools, including religious schools, to provide remedial instruction to educationally deprived children. State law prohibited public school teachers and their supervisors, who were entirely in charge of the program, from involving themselves in religious activities or content. In a suit by taxpayers Friendly said that while he accepted the good faith of the city and the value of the program, the program was unconstitutional: "[T]he Establishment Clause, as it has been interpreted by the Supreme Court, constitutes an insurmountable barrier to the use of federal funds to send public school teachers and other professionals into religious schools to carry on instruction, remedial or otherwise, or to provide clinical and guidance services of the sort at issue here."[120] His analysis of the Court's cases

> leads inescapably to the conclusion that public funds can be used to afford remedial instruction or related counseling services to students in religious elementary and secondary schools only if such instruction or services are afforded at a neutral site off the premises of the religious school. . . . To be sufficiently certain that public employees, in a program like the present one, will maintain strict religious neutrality, they and the institutions in which they work must be subjected to "comprehensive, discriminating and continuing state surveillance." This itself is a constitutionally excessive entanglement of church and state.[121]

Precedent did not require a search of the record to find entanglement; the mere possibility was sufficient to reject the program.

The decision was one in which Friendly's strong support for the separation of church and state coincided with Supreme Court case law as it then stood. In a heated discussion with his son-in-law, Professor Frank Goodman, Friendly answered Goodman's argument that *Felton* was philosophically wrong with the statement, "I was just following the Supreme Court.

What was I supposed to do?"[122] Nevertheless, Friendly structured the opinion in a manner that increased the likelihood that the Supreme Court would affirm him. He placed heavy reliance on *Meek v. Pittenger*,[123] virtually the same as *Felton,* including on the problem of entanglement, which held unconstitutional a secular textbook program for private schools. He later explained that in writing the opinion as he did his object "was to make the [Supreme] Court face up to the fact that it could not sustain the New York program without overruling, in contrast to distinguishing, *Meek v. Pittenger.* I thought that this, as well as some of the other considerations developed in the opinion, might give a little pause to Blackmun and Powell about the constant erosion of the establishment clause."[124]

In an opinion bearing the caption *Aguilar v. Felton* the four liberal Justices plus Justice Powell in a philosophically split Supreme Court affirmed Friendly by a five-to-four vote, relying heavily on *Meek* while endorsing Friendly's opinion: "[T]he picture that emerges is of a system in which religious considerations play a key role in the selection of students and teachers, and which has as its substantial purpose the inculcation of religious values."[125] In a companion case decided the same day,[126] the Court struck down a Michigan program similar to New York's on the ground that the school system had made *no* provision for monitoring the program. Dissenting, Justice Rehnquist noted with some justification, "In this case the Court takes advantage of the 'Catch-22' paradox of its own creation, whereby aid must be supervised to ensure no entanglement but the supervision itself is held to cause an entanglement."[127]

A dozen years later a differently constituted Supreme Court took a narrower view of the Establishment Clause and overruled its earlier decision, again voting five to four, with Justice O'Connor writing, "[O]ur Establishment Clause law has 'significant[ly] change[d]' since we decided *Aguilar.*"[128] The opinion also addressed the Court's prior reliance on the entanglement between the state and the religious schools. "Since we have abandoned the assumption that properly instructed public employees will fail to discharge their duties faithfully, we must also discard the assumption that *pervasive* monitoring of Title I teachers is required."[129] The Establishment Clause was the most notable constitutional-law area in which Friendly sided with the Supreme Court's liberal wing.

CHAPTER TEN

Fifth Amendment

T HE FIFTH AMENDMENT established important procedural rights:

> No person shall be held to answer for a capital or otherwise infamous crime, unless on a presentment or indictment of a Grand Jury . . . ; nor shall any person be subject for the same offence to be twice put in jeopardy of life or limb; nor shall be compelled in any criminal case to be a witness against himself, nor be deprived of life, liberty, or property, without due process of law; nor shall private property be taken for public use, without just compensation.

From a perspective of nearly five decades it is hard to appreciate the tumult caused by the Supreme Court's series of opinions in the 1960s protecting suspects and defendants from questioning by the authorities on the basis of the Fourth, Fifth, and Sixth Amendments, which Friendly characterized as "a 'Great Debate' on criminal procedure."[1] Starting with the 1963 term, the Supreme Court in *Massiah v. United States*[2] reversed a conviction under the Sixth Amendment's Right to Counsel Clause when, after indictment, federal agents recorded a conversation between Massiah and his codefendant; ruled in *Escobedo v. Illinois*[3] that the constitutional right to counsel attached as soon as the police focused upon an individual; and mandated in *Miranda v. Arizona*[4] that arresting officers detail to suspects in custody their rights before questioning them.

Friendly saw little support in the language of the Constitution for some of the positions taken by the Supreme Court, especially those that concerned self-incrimination.[5] For example, he wrote, "What is important is that on any view the Fifth Amendment does not forbid the taking of statements from a suspect; it forbids compelling them." The world and the Constitution were more nuanced, and many interests existed, such as convicting the guilty, protecting those in danger, maintaining vital institutions, and efficiency. "[T]he true picture is not the solid sheet of black depicted in the *Miranda* opinion but a spectrum."[6] Friendly's attitude coincided with and possibly explained another view of his, namely, that the task of judging required making judgments, sometimes difficult judgments, a responsibility he embraced. It also required judges' having good reasons for a position and explaining them in opinions, something he said the Supreme Court often failed to do.[7]

For Friendly, the Court's opinions were often unsatisfactory more for their reasoning than the results in particular cases. In 1969 he said, "The Court is the appointed defender of the Constitution. On the whole it has performed that role gloriously well, and never more so than in recent years."[8] He probably understated the extent of his disagreement with the Court's results, however, when he said, "[T]he fingers of one hand would outnumber the instances where I disagree with the decisions, as distinguished from opinions."[9] Friendly was more critical of the Court in a letter he wrote in March 1970 to Professor Alexander Bickel of Yale: "[W]ith the best of motives, the Warren Court's lack of analysis and restraint has created a jerry-built structure that is bound to collapse. I once called this the domino method of constitutional adjudication. How to preserve the good that the Warren Court did and prune out the excesses will truly require statesmanship."[10] Professor Yale Kamisar of the University of Michigan called Friendly "probably the nation's most eminent critic of *Miranda* (and the Warren Court's criminal procedure cases generally)."[11]

Major issues in the battle over the Warren Court's changes in the law concerned the rights of suspects, especially people found at the scene of a crime or escorted to a police station, whom the police sought to question. For Friendly it was critical whether their rights should be protected under the Constitution and, if so, whether under the Sixth Amendment's right to counsel or the Fifth Amendment's Due Process Clause. Friendly saw reliance on the Sixth Amendment as incorrect both as a matter of constitutional text and policy. On May 28, 1964, ten days after the Supreme Court's decision in *Massiah*, he wrote to retired Justice Frankfurter:

I am really burned up at the opinion of your Court in United States v. Massiah. . . . [T]o spell all of this out of the words of the Sixth Amendment that guarantees an accused the right "to have the assistance of counsel for his defense" seems to me as wooden and unwarranted an interpretation of the Constitution as the economic decisions under the due process and equal protection clauses during the time when you had given me the privilege of serving Mr. Justice Brandeis. Doesn't the Court realize that placing such decisions on constitutional grounds projects it into details as to which it has no real competence and also precipitates a flood of habeas corpus applications from prisoners who will suddenly discover that not merely convictions after trial but pleas of guilty were procured by someone talking to them after they had been indicted and been assigned counsel?[12]

At the bottom of his letter Friendly wrote a handwritten addendum: "Apparently the guiding principle now is 'Don't decide on anything *but* constitutional grounds if such a ground exists.' " It was imperative to allow room "for reasonable difference of judgment or play at the joints."[13] In a letter to an academic he described the Supreme Court's opinions in *Massiah* and *Escobedo* as "astounding."[14]

Friendly's 1965 lecture entitled "The Bill of Rights as a Code of Criminal Procedure"[15] urged the Supreme Court to rely on the Fifth Amendment, which provided flexibility for evaluating pre-indictment police interrogation, rather than on the more rigid Sixth Amendment. The Fifth Amendment permitted giving weight to a variety of important goals, such as recovering kidnap victims or stolen property as well as identifying and apprehending confederates.[16] He emphasized the text of the Sixth Amendment: "Extension of the assistance of counsel clause to the point of arrest or even to the moment of arrival at the police station would require . . . radical textual surgery. The Sixth Amendment concerns 'criminal prosecutions' and guarantees an 'accused' the assistance of counsel 'for his defense.' Since every other clause in the amendment speaks to the trial stage, strong evidence would be needed to overcome this language and show that the framers intended the counsel clause alone to come into play long before any prosecution was launched and thus to preclude interrogation whose very purpose is to determine whether to prosecute."[17]

For Friendly, literal meaning was entitled to a presumption of validity, which could be rebutted only by a strong showing that another meaning was required, whether one in accord with the intensions of the founders or otherwise. Addressing the Supreme Court's creation of a constitutional rule governing police interrogation of suspects, he stated, "We have no basis for thinking that the founders would have wanted a single absolute to rule this congeries; since we do not know what they would have done and there is nothing like a consensus as to what should now be done, we had best stick fairly closely to what they said and, in the democratic tradition, afford opportunity for reasonable solutions by legislation, rule or decision, and empirical demonstrations of their merit. In many instances these could well accord a degree of protection considerably beyond what the Constitution requires; but, unlike constitutional absolutes, they could be subject to exceptions and qualifications necessary for a fair balance of the interests at stake."[18]

In letters to friends and colleagues he pointed out that at a trial, where ignorance of its arcane rules could mean conviction of the innocent, an uninformed defendant needed counsel. He wrote to Abraham Sofaer, a young professor who later became a district judge and a friend, that "once the protections of the self-incrimination clause and the right to assistance of counsel are moved back beyond the beginning of the criminal prosecution, we enter an area where things are not black and white and there is need for reasonable compromise—unless the interests of criminal defendants are to be put beyond those of society. To my mind, of course, that is the truly liberal point of view. I resent appropriation of that term by admirers of absolutes."[19]

Friendly lambasted the Court's other arguments, including the proposition that "all in-custody interrogation is inherently coercive," as lacking in evidentiary foundation. "To say that such answers are 'compelled' is to indulge in Humpty Dumpty's free wheeling use of words."[20] But in one important respect he was not far from the Warren Court: "I believe that police or prosecutorial interrogation for the sole purpose of extracting a confession from an arrested person . . . should be prohibited in the absence of counsel or of a warning making it unmistakably clear that the arrested person is entitled to have counsel before making up his mind whether to talk or not."[21] Friendly sought to balance the needs of law enforcement and the interest of society in apprehending a criminal with the essential dignity of the individual.[22] "[T]he whole business involves a weighing of the interests of society against those of the individual, and the scales register differently when society's interest is in detecting a murderer rather than putting a prostitute away."[23] For him, a policeman's questioning a suspect found at the scene of a crime without giving him a *Miranda* warning was likely to produce reliable information and was nowhere near the affront to the "dignity and integrity of its citizens" and the individual's "right to a private enclave where he may lead a private life" that accompanied pumping out someone's stomach or even taking a blood sample without his permission.[24]

Friendly's 1965 lecture may have played a role in the Supreme Court's important switch from reliance on the Sixth Amendment in *Escobedo v.*

Illinois (1964) to the Fifth Amendment in *Miranda v. Arizona* (1965). As he later wrote with tongue in cheek, "[M]ost people then [1964] considered [the Sixth Amendment] to have been the primary basis of the [*Escobedo*] opinion. We were mistaken. *Miranda v. Arizona* teaches that *Escobedo* was essentially a self-incrimination decision."[25]

If Friendly could not overrule *Miranda,* he proposed narrowing its reach to permit the admission of physical evidence discovered as a result of non-*Mirandized* confessions, perhaps the first person to have done so.[26] "Thus, there is good reason to impose a higher standard on the police before allowing them to use a confession of murder than a weapon bearing the confessor's fingerprints to which his confession has led." So long as interrogation did not violate due process, at least the reliable fruits of a confession should be admissible.[27] For Friendly, a violation of *Miranda* was of a different species than a traditional coerced confession, so the rules could differ. He argued that use of a suspect's answers to questions designed "merely to find other evidence establishing his connection with the crime differs only by a shade from the permitted use for that purpose of his body or his blood."[28] The privilege against self-incrimination does not extend to "identification and the reasonable examination of [the person's] body, furnishing specimens of its fluids, providing examples of his handwriting, and exercising his voice. . . . None of these matters comes within the language, the history or any valid policy of the fifth amendment. . . . What is so difficult to reconcile from the standpoint of an ordered society is the uncompromising rigidity concerning what can be taken from a man's mouth in the form of speech with this commonsensible view concerning what can be taken from it in the form of saliva." Since prosecutors can use a person's blood to find real evidence of criminal activity, he asked rhetorically, why shouldn't they be able to use a person's words to find real evidence, such as a gun or counterfeit bond, of criminal activity?[29]

Friendly's rhetorical question did not satisfy liberal scholars. Thus, Professor Yale Kamisar, who met Friendly when they worked together on an ALI criminal law project, questioned Friendly's equating taking blood from a suspect and use of the fruits of an interrogation that violated *Miranda.*[30] In the case of real evidence obtained in violation of *Miranda,* Kamisar argued, there was an antecedent constitutional violation, one that did not exist when blood was extracted from a suspect. Kamisar also asked pointedly, "Why would a police officer bent on obtaining a weapon or drugs or valuable documents care if a failure to give the *Miranda* warnings produces unusable answers if the answers yield usable fruits?"[31] Friendly, who was greatly concerned with deterring unlawful conduct, considered the possible reaction by police, but evidently did not regard it as serious in the *Miranda* context.[32] In view of the fact that confessions received in violation of *Miranda* and traditional coerced confessions were prohibited by the same constitutional provisions, Kamisar considered Friendly inconsistent in advocating the admissibility of the fruits of a confession in a violation of *Miranda* but not in a traditional coerced-confession case. Perhaps Friendly, who knew the value to police of real evidence obtained as a result of questioning and recognized the arguable inconsistency described by Kamisar, concluded that he would nevertheless create an exception for fruits as a way of significantly disarming the *Miranda* rule.[33] But, atypically, he did not discuss these problems in his writings.

IN A 1968 ADDRESS, "The Fifth Amendment Tomorrow," Friendly proposed a constitutional amendment to replace the gloss implanted on the Fifth Amendment's Self-incrimination Clause by the Supreme Court.[34] Contrasting the situation in the early 1950s, when Senator Joseph McCarthy and others were trampling constitutional rights, Friendly wrote, "At the end of the 1960's it is necessary to vindicate the rights of society against what in my view has become a kind of obsession which has stretched the privilege beyond not only its language and history but any justification in policy, and threatens to go further still."[35] He contrasted the policy behind the Self-incrimination Clause of the Fifth Amendment with the salutary nature of many other privileges that preserved relationships possessing social value and encouraging acceptable conduct:

> In contrast [to other privileges], the fifth amendment privilege extends, by hypothesis, only to persons who have been breakers of the criminal law or believe they may be charged as such. Again, while the other privileges accord with notions of decent conduct generally accepted in life outside the court room, the privilege against self-incrimination defies them.... Finally, the privilege, at least in its pre-trial application, seriously impedes the state in the most basic of all tasks, "to provide for the security of the individual and his property." ...
>
> One would suppose that such a collection of detriments would have led the Supreme Court to expound the basis for the privilege thoughtfully and carefully before asking the country to accept extensions in no way called for by the fifth amendment's words or history. It thus is strange how rarely one encounters in the Court's opinions on the privilege the careful weight of *pros* and *cons,* the objective investigation of how rules of law actually work, and, above all, the consideration whether a less extreme position might not adequately meet the needs of the accused without jeopardizing other important interests, which ought to characterize constitutional adjudication before the Court goes beyond the ordinary meaning of the language.[36]

Friendly reviewed the policies asserted for the privilege against self-incrimination and found almost all of them wanting. For example, the protection of the innocent, fear of inhumane treatment and abuses, and maintaining a fair state-individual balance had no relevance to the great majority of cases. With respect to the argument that the privilege ensures privacy, he observed that, "as privacy proponents concede, it is 'not easy to square the privacy interest as a prime purpose of the privilege with immunity statutes that require surrender of privacy.' "[37] He noted the justification the Supreme Court gave in 1886 in *Boyd v. United States*[38] for denying the government the right to compel a person to produce incriminating preexisting commercial documents; the production constitutes the witness's assurance that the articles produced are the ones demanded. To allow the government to compel production, the *Boyd* Court said, would be "contrary to the principles of a free government. It is abhorrent to the instinct of an Englishman; it is abhorrent to the instinct of an American. It may suit the purposes of despotic power, but it cannot abide the pure atmosphere of political liberty and personal freedom." Friendly's comment? "This tells us almost anything, except why." He rejected the reasoning in *Boyd* and found subsequent explanations no more enlightening, adding that the argument "reeks of the oil lamp."[39]

Friendly's proposed constitutional amendment permitted "[c]ompulsory production, in response to a reasonable subpoena or similar process, of any goods or chattels, including books, papers and other writings."[40] Relying on facts foreign to the Amendment's drafters, he noted that most of us are used to turning over documents at the request of the IRS and that none of the reasons for the privilege appeared to apply. "The writings typically sought to be produced are not the outpourings of an individual's soul, for which first amendment protection against subpoenas may be in order, but rather the books and records of an enterprise that is criminal or has been unlawfully conducted."[41] Friendly recognized that there had to be "a shelter against government snooping and oppression concerning political and religious beliefs," but that should be the province of the First Amendment rather than force someone "to make a claim, often farfetched and possibly beyond what he can conscientiously do, that an answer would tend to incriminate him."[42]

Friendly's amendment went further and proposed eliminating the warning mandated in *Miranda,* requiring individuals to make themselves available for certain tests (such as blood tests and providing handwriting exemplars), permitting judicially supervised interrogation of suspects, permitting judges to explain in a neutral way the defendant's failure to have testified in the grand jury after having acquired counsel, eliminating bars to the discharge of government employees or the revocation of licenses after the individual refused to answer questions in a disciplinary hearing, and other revisions. It was a comprehensive reordering of the privilege, an effort that received considerable comment, much of it negative.[43]

Years later one of Friendly's opinions in a self-incrimination case presaged an important Supreme Court decision regarding the ordered production of records. The IRS served a summons on John L. Beattie Jr., the subject of a criminal income tax investigation, to produce the original work papers of his accountant. When he learned about the investigation, Beattie instructed his accountant to deliver the work papers to him. On Beattie's appeal from an order to comply with the summons, Friendly relied on the Fifth Amendment's language: "[I]n order to bring a case of compelled production of papers within the privilege, the process must elicit not simply 'responses which are also communications' but communicative responses tending to incriminate." His point was that production of the papers by Beattie established nothing, since he had no personal knowledge of the circumstances of their preparation and could not represent they were authentic. If Beattie's accountant was under investigation, the production by the accountant of his work papers might invade his private enclave, Friendly observed, but "the accountant's workpapers could not be brought within the taxpayer's 'private inner sanctum.' By their very nature private inner sanctums are not transferable."[44] In the process Friendly rewrote and expanded the government's argument, which had conceded that "the client may have a Fifth Amendment privilege to refuse to authenticate the workpapers."[45]

Both sides sought *certiorari*. While their petitions were pending, the Supreme Court held in *Fisher v. United States*[46] that the Fifth Amendment privilege did not excuse an attorney from producing a client's records that his client sent him, even if the client sent them for the purpose of seeking legal advice: "[E]nforcement against a taxpayer's lawyer does not 'compel' the taxpayer to do anything—and certainly would not compel him to be a 'witness' against himself." Employing language similar to what Friendly used in *Beattie* (and giving him credit),[47] the *Fisher* Court held that "the act of producing—the only thing which the taxpayer is compelled to do—does not itself involve testimonial self-incrimination." The Supreme Court vacated the judgment in *Beattie* and remanded the case to the Second Circuit "for further consideration in light of *Fisher.*"[48]

Years later the Supreme Court moved in Friendly's direction in *New York v. Quarles*,[49] where an in-custody defendant had directed the police to a gun without having received a *Miranda* warning. Writing for the majority, Justice Rehnquist created a "public safety" exception to *Miranda*, which, like Friendly's proposal, considered interests other than the defendant's. Justice O'Connor, concurring, relied on Friendly to conclude that real evidence discovered in violation of *Miranda* should be admitted.[50] The following year, in *Oregon v. Elstad,*[51] the Court substantially adopted that position. Friendly not only contributed to the development of the law, but he helped frame the terms of the academic debate for many years.

Friendly also wrote an opinion in an effort to narrow the "required records" exception to the Fifth Amendment, which allows the government to subpoena records that a government statute or regulation requires someone to maintain and that have a "public aspect." The panel majority in *In re Doe*[52] affirmed an order of contempt entered against the pseudonymous Dr. John Doe for his failure to produce his financial and medical records, including patient records, in an investigation into the criminal distribution of tens of thousands of "Quaaludes," a regulated drug. Friendly dissented with respect to the order to Doe to produce patient records. While a physician had to produce his patient records in connection with a state's disciplinary investigation, he explained, there was insufficient relationship between the purpose of the regulations making the record available in physician disciplinary proceedings and a criminal investigation by a federal grand jury into the unlawful distribution of narcotics (a distinction not made in the briefs), once again looking to the purpose of a statute or regulation. Instead, Friendly believed the right to privacy applied. "Patients' files would seem, almost by description, to be the antithesis of a record with 'public aspects.'"[53] He questioned the whole premise of the required-records exception to the Fifth Amendment, noting that if carried to its full logic, it was capable of destroying the privilege.[54] This was a liberal position. Friendly wanted a narrowed, but coherent, privilege against self-incrimination.

THE YEAR 1970 set off what Friendly called "a due process explosion" in the number and scope of administrative hearings after the Supreme Court decided *Goldberg v. Kelly,*[55] which expanded the rights of welfare recipients whose payments had been suspended. The Court said, "By hypothesis, a welfare recipient is destitute, without funds or assets. . . . Suffice it to say that to cut off a welfare recipient in the face of the brutal need without a prior hearing of some sort is unconscionable, unless overwhelming considerations justify it. . . . The fundamental requisite of due process of law is the opportunity to be heard . . . and a pre-termination hearing for welfare recipients must include the right to present oral testimony and the right to cross-examine witnesses, both of which had been denied to welfare recipients."[56]

Friendly's major scholarly contribution on the subject was his 1975 lecture entitled "Some Kind of Hearing."[57] Along with a historical analysis of administrative-law hearings, Friendly's lecture supplied a creative blueprint for evaluating the hearing rights of persons subject to administrative action, which had been minimally defined in *Goldberg* (although the opinion stated that cross-examination was required in almost all administrative hearings).[58] Friendly supported *Goldberg*'s discarding the old teaching that required a determination "whether the issue was one of adjudicative or of legislative fact. If the former, a full trial-type hearing was demanded; if the latter, something substantially less would do"—and substituting a balancing-of-interests standard for the old bipolar distinction.[59] While Friendly was not the first to recognize that the nature of hearings could vary with the circumstances,[60] he may have been the first to analyze the problem systematically. "For starters I would draw a distinction between cases in which the government is seeking to take action against the citizen from those in which it is simply denying a citizen's request. . . . Even a beginner in mathematics knows that the distance between two points on a vertical access is the same whether one measures down or up. . . . [But] whatever the mathematics, there is a human difference between losing what one has and not getting what one wants."[61]

To ascertain the best counterpoise between the rights of individuals and to obtain the effective functioning of the agencies whose task it was to provide those rights, Friendly balanced the need for various procedural protections, such as an unbiased tribunal, the right to call witnesses, the right to counsel, and the right of cross-examination, with the nature and importance to the individual of the various governmental actions, such as revocation of parole, reduction of welfare payments, and eviction from subsidized housing. For Friendly, "the vital thing is to emphasize that as one goes down the scale, less and less is constitutionally required"; the more serious the governmental action, the greater the protections that should be afforded.[62] His analysis recognized the problem of making hearings too much like a civil trial, with attendant delay and the wasteful expenditure of the government's limited resources, which could undermine the very reforms desired.[63] In this spirit, he left room for hearings on papers without an oral presentation or even eliminating the adversarial system in some cases. While Friendly's lecture could be viewed as abstract, or even mechanical, it rested on a firm empirical base.[64]

One year after Friendly's lecture the Supreme Court in *Matthews v. Eldridge*[65] substantially accepted his analysis to permit the termination of Social Security benefits on the basis of written answers to a questionnaire. Kenneth Culp Davis, a leader in administrative law, wrote Friendly, "On the *Goldberg* problem the federal courts have four levels: Going up the scale, they were the district courts, courts of appeals, the Supreme Court, and Judge Friendly in a law review. The highest authority effectively reversed the Supreme Court even before *Eldridge.*[66] Nevertheless, Friendly's academic lecture is less arresting than some of the right-to-hearing cases he decided, whose subject matter was half a world away from his experience as general counsel to Pan American.

Sixty-one years old and suffering from a serious heart condition and diabetes, Philip Kerner, a one-time carpenter and furniture upholsterer, brought an action to set aside the denial of Social Security disability benefits, which were payable for "inability to engage in any substantial gainful activity by reason of any medically determinable physical or mental impairment which can be expected to result in death or to be of long-continued and indefinite duration."[67] The Social Security Administration (SSA) conceded that Kerner could not engage in his former occupations, but concluded that he could perform some "kind of substantial gainful activity, including some form of light or part-time sedentary work." It explained that the fact that "work within his capacity to perform may not be readily attainable" did not absolve him from meeting the "strict standard set forth in the Act," namely, an inability to engage in any substantial gainful activity.[68] The district court granted the Secretary's motion for summary judgment and Kerner appealed.

After oral argument Friendly told his colleagues, whose voting memoranda indicated their votes to affirm, "My initial reaction was that there was nothing to this appeal. Perhaps I should have followed that impulse. However, the more I dig into this case, the more I become convinced that the appellant has not yet had the full consideration of his claim which Congress must have intended."[69] While noting that "it is impracticable to treat even the relatively small proportion that go to hearing with the elaboration of the trial of a personal injury case," Friendly's opinion in *Kerner v. Flemming* spoke for a unanimous court in remanding the case to the Secretary to take more evidence. The crucial issue for Friendly was whether Kerner's impairment had resulted in "inability to engage in any substantial gainful activity," and here the evidence "was exceedingly unsatisfactory"; "[n]one of the doctors testified and few of the medical reports deal in any illuminating fashion with [Kerner's] ability to work." Friendly elaborated:

> Such a determination requires resolution of two issues—what can applicant do, and what employment opportunities are there for a man who can do only what applicant can do? Mere theoretical ability to engage in substantial gainful activity is not enough if no reasonable opportunity for this is available. . . .

[T]here was basically only a catalog of the names of Kerner's various complaints and contradictory conclusions of the vaguest sort.... Unsatisfactory as all this was, the evidence as to employment opportunities was even less.... [T]he evidence affords no sufficient basis for the Secretary's negative answer.[70]

In letters he wrote in the following weeks Friendly supported *Kerner* even more adamantly. He wrote Professor Louis Jaffe of Harvard Law School, "If the secretary does not have this [information] on tap, then he damn well ought to."[71] He wrote to another friend, "The way Kerner got polished off was utterly disgraceful."[72] Friendly then did something extraordinary, setting out, unsuccessfully it developed, to assist Kerner with his medical problems by contacting a personal acquaintance associated with Jewish charities.[73] He explained in a letter to a judge in another circuit who had a similar case, "I had been concerned from the outset lest we were handing somewhat of a Pyrrhic victory to Kerner and had talked to a cardiac rehabilitation center with which I had some contact when at the bar; they agreed that they would take Kerner on. After the petition for rehearing threat disappeared, I communicated with his lawyer suggesting that this would be perhaps a more advantageous solution than pursuing the further hearing which we had ordered. He agreed but said that Kerner was rather a litigious sort and despaired of accomplishing anything. Recently I had a letter from Kerner, who somehow is existing in an apartment in Brooklyn, which in effect asked me to order the Government to pay his pension without a hearing."[74] Kerner's refusal to engage in rehabilitation was no surprise to Harold Tompkins, his conscientious lawyer on the second appeal, who called Kerner "a very strange client." *Kerner v. Flemming* remained one of Friendly's favorite cases.[75]

Four years later Friendly learned that he was not done with Philip Kerner. Following remand in late 1960, the SSA held a new five-day hearing on Kerner's condition and work prospects, which included new medical testimony. The SSA's Appeals Council composed a fifty-two-page opinion, finding against Kerner, who again filed suit in the district court. On a new appeal denominated *Kerner v. Celebrezze*,[76] Friendly expressed confusion as to why the SSA had engaged in so much additional work on the rather minor case: "[W]e had not supposed there would be a second round of evidence as to the degree of Kerner's heart involvement as distinguished from medical and other testimony as to the activities suitable for a person with the history described in the previous record and the corresponding employment opportunities."[77] Although disappointed, and perhaps dismayed, Friendly could do nothing but affirm.[78] After the case was finally over, Kerner sued Tompkins in the small claims court for $150, the filing fee in the Second Circuit. At the hearing Kerner called Tompkins a Communist. Kerner lost that case, too.[79]

One collateral issue remains. Friendly had not told the lawyers on the second appeal that after the first appeal he had communicated with Kerner and his attorney and had tried to assist Kerner to obtain physical rehabilitation.[80] The nagging question remains why Friendly did not recuse himself or, more realistically, obtain everyone's consent for him to sit on the second appeal. Friendly did nothing wrong on the first appeal; the case was no longer pending before him. The issue was bias—or the appearance of bias—in favor of Kerner on the *second* appeal, and the nature of the earlier contacts suggests that Friendly should have disclosed what he had done. That his efforts on behalf of Kerner had nothing to do with the merits of the case was not dispositive; the mere fact that he sought to help Kerner might be thought to create an appearance of bias. But if it was an ethical violation, it was surely not a serious one.[81]

Friendly's sliding scale of procedural protections can be seen in operation in *Frost v. Weinberger,*[82] where because of a ceiling on payments, the SSA reduced the $159.30 monthly benefits a widow and her children received to $95.70 when it discovered that the deceased had fathered two illegitimate children. Ignoring Mrs. Frost's lawsuit to bar reduction without a hearing, the SSA conducted a hearing *after* the reduction, ruling against her. The district court reversed the SSA on the ground that Mrs. Frost was constitutionally entitled to a *pre-reduction* evidentiary hearing.

On the SSA's appeal Friendly observed that, while *Goldberg v. Kelley* barred termination of benefits without a hearing for New York's welfare recipients, the decision recognized "'that some governmental benefits could be administratively terminated without affording the recipient a pre-termination evidentiary hearing.'" Weighing arguments on both sides, he emphasized that benefits were not based on need, that the evidentiary hearing probably would be long and complex, and that "the SSA has no financial stake and is totally disinterested as between the two sets of claimants [which] should help to insure a correct pre-reduction decision." He continued:

> The crucial factor [in *Goldberg*] was that such aid was given to persons on the very margin of subsistence; in such instances "termination of aid pending resolution of a controversy over eligibility may deprive an *eligible* recipient of the very means by which to live while he waits." . . . The [Supreme] Court's decisions can be fairly summarized as holding that the required degree of procedural safeguards varies directly with the importance of the private interest affected and the need for and usefulness of the particular safeguard in the given circumstances and inversely with the burden and any other adverse consequences of affording it.[83]

Friendly's "summary" of the Supreme Court's decisions was an instance where he created a salutary rule by reformulating less than clear Supreme Court precedents, while at the same time attributing the result to those precedents. In effect, he created a rule and anointed the Supreme Court as its originator.

THE FIFTH AMENDMENT guarantees that a person shall not "be subject for the same offence to be twice put in jeopardy of life or limb," which is designed to protect people from repeated prosecutions for the same crime. The application of the Amendment is clear when a prosecutor attempts to retry someone after a jury acquitted (or convicted) him for the identical crime. But most cases are not that simple. Suppose the evidence shows that Bob and Ray were standing next to each other when Jones took out a revolver and fired two shots, one hitting Bob and the other Ray. Nevertheless, the jury convicts Jones of shooting Bob but acquits him of shooting Ray. In 1932 the Supreme Court upheld the conviction of Jones by a *jury* for shooting Bob even though it was inconsistent in acquitting him for shooting Ray.[84]

The question that confronted the panel of Learned Hand, J. Edward Lumbard, and Friendly on December 8, 1959, in *United States v. Maybury*[85] was whether a conviction should be reversed when a *judge*, as opposed to a jury, renders an inconsistent verdict. A grand jury indicted Joseph Maybury on two counts relating to a single stolen $68 U.S. Treasury check payable to Abraham Kohl. The first count charged Maybury with forging Kohl's name on the reverse of the check, and the second count charged him with uttering (passing) the check knowing it to have been forged. The Treasury check had been mailed to Kohl, and Kohl never received, signed, or endorsed it or authorized endorsement. On the reverse side were the signed names "Abraham Kohl," "Joseph Maybury," and "William Kozin." Trial by jury was waived and the case was tried before District Judge Matthew T. Abruzzo Jr., long regarded as one of the least endowed district judges from both a mental and a temperamental viewpoint. (In 1945 Judge Charles E. Clark sent his colleagues a memorandum that said, "We found that Abruzzo could not read.")[86]

Maybury's story was that he and a man known to him as Barney were drinking on and off for three days in a tavern in Brooklyn; Barney ran short of cash and asked William Kozin, the bartender, to cash the Treasury check for him; and Barney, who "could not write too good," asked Maybury to sign his name. Maybury testified that he believed that Barney was the rightful payee and he signed the check for Barney and then, at Kozin's request, his own name. The government, however, called Kozin to testify that Maybury was alone when he cashed the check and that he did not know of any habitué of the tavern by the name of Barney. Abruzzo acquitted Maybury of forgery under Count 1 of the indictment on the ground "There is no evidence that he forged Kohl's name," but found him guilty of uttering the check under Count 2 on the ground that "the defendant . . . signed the name Abraham Kohl without any right to sign it."[87] Maybury argued that the acquittal of the forgery charge was inconsistent with the conviction of the uttering charge, that the acquittal should control, and that Count 2 should be dismissed,[88] while the government argued that the uttering count should stand because the trial judge found Maybury guilty.

Lumbard voted to bar retrial of Maybury on both counts, while Hand voted to sustain both the acquittal for forgery and the conviction for uttering. Hand said that the uttering conviction should be reversed *if* "there was some inconsistency in the finding upon one of the facts constituting the crime charged in Count 1 [forgery] and upon the same fact constituting the crime charged in Count 2 [uttering]." He added, "I should not agree that the conviction cannot stand, unless it appeared that [Abruzzo] relied upon Maybury's endorsement as a necessary fact in determining to convict."[89] Since such reliance by Abruzzo was plain, Hand seemed headed for reversal for uttering, but he inexplicably voted to affirm the conviction on that count.

Friendly rejected the government's reliance on cases that upheld inconsistent *jury* verdicts: "special considerations relating to the role of a jury," the substitution of a jury for a trial by ordeal, and the requirement of a unanimous verdict made the jury the "voice of the country" and distinguished a jury from a judge in a criminal case, an originalist approach.[90] Friendly described why acquittal for forgery did not require reversing the conviction for uttering: "[N]o case has been found where the doctrine [res judicata] has been applied to acquittal on one count of a multiple count indictment when the defendant has successfully appealed conviction on another count of the same indictment, and certainly not where the very ground of appeal was that the acquittal and conviction cannot stand together. If this were the law of judgments, it would have to apply to acquittals resulting from the verdict of a jury as much as to those stemming from the judgment of a judge."[91]

Concluding that Maybury "made use of" the acquittal on the uttering count in order to obtain a reversal on the forgery count, Friendly voted to retry Maybury on both counts: "To say that Maybury has not brought his acquittal before us seems to me right in form and wrong in substance." But Friendly did not explain where his concept "made use of" came from or why it should be dispositive. He wanted to retry both counts, Lumbard wanted to dismiss both counts, and Hand wanted to affirm (sustaining the acquittal on Count 1 and the conviction on Count 2). Hand resolved the impasse by sustaining the acquittal on Count 1 and joining Friendly in ordering a new trial on Count 2.

Friendly seems to have been wrong. A Supreme Court case on which he relied for a different point stated, "The verdict of acquittal was final, and could not be reviewed without putting him twice in jeopardy, and thereby violating the Constitution."[92] Also, retrying a person found not guilty seems repugnant to the spirit behind the Constitution and, it seems, the framers' intent.[93] Another, albeit technical, argument also suggests that Friendly was wrong. The government wanted to retry Maybury on Count 1, which it had lost. Friendly's proposed outcome would have improved the government's position, but the government had filed no cross-appeal, so the court lacked the power to grant affirmative relief.[94] There was another problem: the Constitution prohibited the government from appealing an acquittal.[95]

In *Graham v. Smith*[96] the state had persisted in trying Graham for crimes for which sufficient evidence of guilt was lacking or on which he had been acquitted. The outcome depended on the import of two cases, *Price v. Georgia* in the Supreme Court[97] and *United States ex rel. Hetenyi v. Wilkins* in the Second Circuit.[98] Friendly wrote:

> While there is language in *Hetenyi* and *Price* that might suggest that the State must be deprived of any conviction on a trial that had included a charge barred by double jeopardy, we do not believe that the courts *intended* to go so far. *A sufficient basis* for the *Hetenyi* and *Price* decisions was that the presence of the barred more serious charge created a serious risk that the jury in *Hetenyi* might have been led to compromise on a more rather than a less serious unbarred charge, e.g. second degree murder rather than first degree manslaughter, or in *Price,* to have convicted on a lesser included offense, voluntary manslaughter, rather than to have acquitted or hung. On that view Graham's case is distinguishable; the jury convicted on the more serious charge and there is thus no indication that the verdict was a compromise resulting from the inclusion of the barred charge.[99]

In effect, Friendly rewrote *Hetenyi* and *Price* to say what he "believe[d] the courts intended," and narrowed their holdings to what he concluded was a "sufficient basis" for the two decisions. All in all it was a creative, if not cavalier, treatment of precedent, whatever one may think of the result. Friendly seems to have forgotten his earlier statement, that "[a] court's stated and, on its view, necessary basis for deciding does not become dictum because a critic would have decided on another basis."[100]

In ten other double-jeopardy cases Friendly was less formalistic than in *Maybury* and, when the issue was open to dispute, more sympathetic to defendants than in *Maybury* and *Graham*. For example, he held that dismissal of the charge of selling counterfeit stamps barred trial on the charge of possession of the stamps with the intent to sell them;[101] that the "dismissal of the indictment" based on the facts following a trial constituted an acquittal;[102] and that an acquittal of the theft of postal money orders barred trial on any charge that required defendant to have been involved in the theft (but not on the charge that he received stolen goods).[103] In *United States v. Coke*[104] the defendant objected to his receiving a longer sentence following his appeal and a retrial. Rejecting the broad ground urged by Coke, Friendly constructed a more modulated rule that discriminated on the basis of the facts underlying the increased sentence: "Our belief that the Constitution does not mandate a universal prohibition of higher sentences after a retrial for the same offense obtained at the defendant's instance does not mean that the subject should be left completely at large." While the fact that the first judge sentenced Coke without ordering a presentence report while the retrial judge obtained one was an insufficient basis for increasing his sentence after retrial,[105] new evidence about the crime introduced at the retrial could sustain a longer sentence, so long as the judge on the retrial explained his reasons for the increase. Friendly's early effort in *Maybury* seems rather rigid in this company.

CHAPTER ELEVEN

Other Bill of Rights
Amendments

FRIENDLY DID NOT HESITATE to criticize Supreme Court decisions that he found unduly handcuffed law enforcement and imposed excessive burdens on attempts to convict the guilty. The latter, after all, was an important goal of the criminal justice system. His position on the Fourth Amendment included hostility to the rule announced in *Mapp v. Ohio*,[1] which suppressed reliable evidence of a defendant's guilt even when there was no violation of his fundamental rights. He rejected imposition of the drastic remedy of excluding crucial and reliable evidence when, years after a crime, a narrow majority of an appellate court concluded that a search, albeit conducted in good faith, was unlawful. He told members of the California Bar in 1965 that the balance was out of kilter:

> The beneficent aim of the exclusionary rule to deter police misconduct can be sufficiently accomplished by a practice, such as that in Scotland, outlawing evidence obtained by flagrant or deliberate violation of rights. It is no sufficient objection that such a rule would require courts to make still another determination; rather, the recognition of a penumbral zone where mistake will not call for the drastic remedy of exclusion would relieve them of exceedingly difficult decisions whether an officer overstepped the sometimes almost imperceptible line between a valid arrest or search and an invalid one. Even if there were an added burden, most judges would prefer to discharge it than have to perform the distasteful duty of allowing a dangerous criminal to go free because of a slight and unintentional miscalculation by the police.[2]

Friendly made his only judicial statement on the exclusionary rule in a case in which a judicial officer approved a search warrant supported by deficient affidavits: "The exclusionary rule, as applied in Fourth Amendment cases, is a blunt instrument, conferring an altogether disproportionate reward not so much in the interest of the defendant as in the interest of society at large. If a choice must be made between a rule requiring a hearing on the truth of the affidavit in every case even though no ground for suspicion has been suggested and another which takes care of the overwhelming bulk of the cases, the policies of the Fourth Amendment will be adequately served by the latter even though a rare false affidavit may occasionally slip by."[3] Friendly saw little chance for abuse when the police obtained a warrant from a judicial official. His decision arguably was usurping the prerogative of the Supreme Court. Fifteen years later the Supreme Court took essentially the same position for essentially the same reasons in *United States v. Leon.*[4]

Friendly's Fourth Amendment opinions show concern over invading fundamental, although not necessarily less important, rights of individuals. During an investigation into possible mail and wire fraud, an Assistant U.S. Attorney instructed Cynthia B. Schwartz to furnish the grand jury with samples of her handwriting. When she refused, citing the Fourth Amendment, District Judge Morris E. Lasker directed her to comply, and when she again refused, he held her in civil contempt. She appealed and, writing for a unanimous court, Friendly affirmed. Rejecting as unsound decisions of the Seventh and Eighth Circuits on which Schwartz relied as well as the extreme positions taken by both parties,[5] he said that while people have a "reasonable expectation of privacy," an inquiry by a grand jury was different from questioning after arrest: "The test must be whether the requirement invades a 'reasonable expectation of privacy.' . . . Handwriting and voice exemplars fall on the side of the line where no reasonable expectation of privacy exists."

In *United States v. Bennett,* where federal agents seized from the defendant's pocketbook a letter that was in furtherance of a narcotics conspiracy, Friendly scrutinized the evil at which the Fourth Amendment was directed:

[A]n approach geared to the objective of the Fourth Amendment to secure privacy would seem more promising than one based on the testimonial character of what is seized. . . . [T]he Fourth Amendment does not protect broadly against the seizure of the things whose compulsory production would be forbidden by the Fifth. . . . [T]he vice [restricted by the Fourth Amendment] lies in the unlimited search. The reason why we shrink from allowing a personal diary to be the object of a search is that the entire diary must be read to discover whether there are incriminating entries; most of us would feel rather differently with respect to a "diary" whose cover page bore the title "Robberies I Have Performed." Similarly the abhorrence generally felt with respect to "rummaging" through the contents of a desk to find an incriminating letter would not exist in the same measure if the letter were lying in plain view.[6]

In an exchange of letters on *Bennett* with Professor Telford Taylor of Columbia, Friendly expressed concern over an expansive concept of a lawful search into private enclaves: "[W]e don't want law enforcement officers to riffle through masses of correspondence . . . in the hope of turning something up, even when there was probable cause to search for weapons, narcotics, etc. I insist that this is an important distinction." His solution was to prohibit warrants from authorizing searches (and to prohibit searches incident to lawful arrests) for documents "in the absence of a showing of probable cause that the premises contain material of this sort which, in [Justice] Brennan's phrase, 'will aid in the particular apprehension or conviction.'" Friendly was concerned with the subject matter searched, rather than geographical boundaries, which he considered artificial.[7]

On July 7, 1967, Webster Bivens filed in the district court a handwritten complaint that alleged he was the victim of a warrantless and illegal search and seizure by federal agents and sought $15,000 damages from each defendant agent.[8] He claimed that, without any basis and in the presence of his wife and children, federal agents forcibly handcuffed him and placed him under arrest for violation of the federal narcotics laws. Ruling that "federal officials acting in the performance of duty are not liable in actions such as this one," the district judge dismissed the complaint and also denied Bivens's application for leave to appeal *in forma pauperis* and for assigned counsel, stating that the appeal was "frivolous" and not taken "in good faith."[9] The Civil Rights Act of 1871, 42 U.S.C. § 1983, created a cause of action against a *state* officer who, acting under color of state law, violated someone's civil rights. No comparable statute applied to a federal officer, only the stark language of the Fourth Amendment itself.[10]

Nearly eight months later Friendly was sitting as the motions judge, assigned to decide mostly routine motions, when by chance Bivens's motion for leave to appeal *in forma pauperis* came to him. Friendly saw the unfairness—despite protections against the federal government provided to citizens by the Bill of Rights, a state prisoner had greater rights than a federal prisoner—so he telephoned Stephen Grant, a recent clerk, and asked him if he would be willing to take on a pro bono criminal appeal.

Grant, who was with a prominent Wall Street firm, told Friendly that he was not a litigator. After a brief discussion with his former clerk, Friendly entered an order that reversed the district court's denial of leave to appeal *in forma pauperis* and assigned Grant to represent Bivens.[11]

Grant's brief cited sixteen treatises and law review articles and student comments, explaining that scholarly opinion favored the existence of the damage claim. The government's brief in opposition relied solely on case law. Judges Lumbard, Medina, and Waterman ruled unanimously in favor of the government.[12] Although they found that the agents' alleged action may have violated the Fourth Amendment, they refused to imply a damage remedy absent a statute.

Grant was considering giving up the fight when he received a short note from Friendly: "The opinions in the *Bivens* case demonstrated that you made the best possible try." Friendly's next sentence was of a very different sort: "I hope that you will seek to take the matter further." Friendly was encouraging Grant to go to the Supreme Court to reverse his colleagues on the Second Circuit. This was quite extraordinary. Grant took heart and filed a petition for *certiorari,* which the Supreme Court granted. Friendly gave Grant advice in a note to him:

> (1) How silly can you get? It is absurd that Bivens could have recovered if the search had been by a state officer but could not recover when the search was by federal officers, to whom alone the Fourth Amendment was originally directed.
>
> (2) The award of damages in a case like this was the implementation of a common law remedy, an action for trespass, going back to English precedents, including the famous *Entick v. Carrington,* which was well known to the founders.
>
> (3) In light of (2), by reversing the Second Circuit the Court would not have to say that *any* violation of constitutional right would lead to a federal suit for damages.[13]

When Grant argued the case for Bivens before the Supreme Court, he faced Assistant Solicitor General A. Raymond Randolph, also a former Friendly clerk. In *Bivens v. Six Unknown Agents of the Federal Bureau of Narcotics*[14] the Court ruled six to three in favor of Bivens, finding a cause of action for damages under the Fourth and Fifth Amendments. The division among the Justices was unusual. Joining Brennan's majority opinion were Douglas, Marshall, Stewart, and White, a liberal to moderate-conservative alignment. Harlan, a moderate-to-conservative Justice, filed a concurring opinion. In dissent were Burger and the newly appointed

Blackmun, but also Black, who stated, "[I]t seems to me to be a matter of common understanding that the business of the judiciary is to interpret the laws and not to make them."[15] Friendly's name appears nowhere in the opinions in the landmark search-and-seizure case where, in the face of adverse decisions by lower courts in earlier cases, including one by Learned Hand,[16] the Supreme Court created a cause of action for damages directly under the Fourth Amendment. This was the second time Friendly nonjudicially sought to influence the Supreme Court to find a constitutional right. The first was when he prevailed upon Justice Brandeis to include in his dissenting opinion in *Olmstead* that wiretapping violated the Fourth Amendment.[17]

With the case back in the district court for trial, a skirmish ensued over Grant's attempt to subpoena a sizable number of documents from the government. The upshot was they settled the case. Each defendant paid Bivens the sum of $100, not a large amount, but symbolizing an important victory.[18] Friendly soon came to deplore the broad reach of *Bivens*. When reversing the district court in the context of a particularly unattractive application of *Bivens*, Friendly wrote, "[U]nless and until the Supreme Court chooses to place some limits on *Bivens* and its progeny, we have no alternative to reversing the judgment."[19] After 1980 the High Court narrowed the scope afforded to *Bivens* actions, based primarily on the existence of alternative remedies provided by Congress.[20] In 2001 the Court limited *Bivens* to cases where the plaintiff had no other remedy.[21]

FRIENDLY ENDORSED the Supreme Court's enlightened *Gideon v. Wainwright,* which gave a defendant facing jail the right to be represented by a lawyer once he got into court even when he was too poor to afford one. Nevertheless, he criticized the decision's lack of precision, especially its failure to say whether the right rested on the Fifth or Six Amendment.[22] He wanted so important and necessary an opinion to be doctrinally sound. When applying the Sixth Amendment, which begins, "In all criminal prosecutions" and continues to speak of trials, he was a textualist. He defined counsel as a member of the bar in good standing based on the history of the constitutional protection when he sustained the right to be represented by counsel at trial in *Solina v. United States*.[23] (The case arose on habeas corpus and is discussed in Chapter 13.) Moreover, to ensure the exercise of that right, he rejected the argument that a defendant's conviction could not stand because the denial of counsel constituted "harmless error." He sought an elevated role for what he considered a properly construed Sixth Amendment. His dissent in *United States v. Massimo* emphasized the importance he attached to the right to counsel:

Since Massimo's "criminal prosecution" had begun, the Sixth Amendment entitled him to counsel at any "critical stage," which interrogation to elicit his guilt surely was, unless the protection was waived. Warnings by law enforcement officials and subsequent action by the accused might suffice to comply with the Fifth Amendment strictures against testimonial compulsion would not necessarily meet what I regard as the higher standard with respect to waiver of the right to counsel that applies when the Sixth Amendment has attached. Indeed, in the case of a federal trial there would seem to be much ground for outlawing all statements resulting from post-arraignment or indictment interrogation (as distinguished from volunteered statements) in the absence of counsel when the questioning has no objective other than to establish the guilt of the accused, even if the Sixth Amendment does not require so much.[24]

Friendly was similarly solicitous of claims made under the Confrontation Clause of the Sixth Amendment, which provides that "[i]n all criminal prosecutions, the accused shall enjoy the right . . . to be confronted by the witnesses against him." In the grand jury, where the accused has no opportunity to cross-examine witnesses, courts faced the question whether at the defendant's trial a witness's grand jury testimony could be used to prove the facts in issue. Friendly reversed a conviction when the trial judge admitted grand jury testimony of a witness who neither would take an oath that he would tell the truth nor answer responsively to the prosecutor's questions—in other words, was unavailable for cross-examination.[25] He opposed the introduction of untested evidence in a criminal trial even in narrowly defined contexts: "Now the *Proposed Federal Rules of Evidence* would go far beyond our decision, dangerously and wrongly so, and allow such use by any prior utterance by a witness, even an oral one which he denies having made."[26] Friendly, who was adamant that the right to confront witnesses, like the right to counsel at trial, should not be compromised, was decades ahead of the Supreme Court.[27]

IF ANY PART of the Constitution requires (and defies) an originalist reading, it is the Seventh Amendment, which states that jury trials shall be held by the standards applicable when the Amendment was ratified: "In Suits at common law, where the value in controversy shall exceed twenty dollars, the right of trial by jury shall be preserved." Application of these words has precipitated thousands of decisions, particularly since many procedures employed today had no direct counterpart in 1791.[28]

In *Cargill, Inc. v. Commodity Credit Corp.*,[29] one of the three cases on which Friendly sat with Learned Hand and Lumbard on December 8, 1959, the issue was whether the CCC was entitled to a jury trial on its counterclaim after Cargill sued it. The CCC's charter provided that "[a]ll suits against the Corporation shall be tried by the court without a jury." Friendly read the statute literally without regard to the congressional purpose and found that the CCC had no right to a jury trial because the suit had been brought "against" the Corporation. "The statute speaks in terms of 'suits,' not of claims.' " That "Cargill would have been entitled to a jury trial if [CCC] had sued it affords no basis for a contrary inference; for Congress lacked constitutional power to provide otherwise."[30]

Twenty-three years later Friendly rejected literalism and formalism (which gives a minor, or no, role to the facts of social life)[31] and heeded Learned Hand's remark that he was fond of quoting: "There is no surer way to misread any document than to read it literally."[32] The later case, which was a near legal replica of *Cargill*, was *Ministry of Supply, Cairo v. Universe Tankships, Inc.*,[33] where the Ministry, an instrumentality of Egypt entitled to sovereign immunity, sued Universe Tankships. Babanaft International Co. intervened as a plaintiff and cross-claimed against the Ministry, relying on a statute that withdrew sovereign immunity with respect to any "counterclaim" arising out of the same transaction as the original claim. The district court ruled against Babanaft on the ground that the statute said "counterclaim" and not "cross-claim." Reversing, Friendly held that the language did not bar application to cross-claims and that "we can think of no good reason why Congress should have wished" to distinguish between the two. The same could have been said about *Cargill*. More likely Congress wanted to provide for a jury trial when a claim was asserted against a private party, rather than the CCC. Moreover, Friendly's decision in *Cargill* seems doubly questionable in view of the preferred status the Seventh Amendment gives to jury trials.[34] December 8, 1959, turned out not to have been one of Friendly's best days.

WHILE THE EIGHTH AMENDMENT, barring "cruel and unusual punishments," is the only constitutional provision that explicitly relates to prisoners, it far from occupies that large field. Friendly's one statement on the serious problem under the Eighth Amendment of disproportionate sentences occurred in a draft-card-burning case, where he wrote to his colleagues on a panel in response to a proposed *per curiam* opinion, "The proposed p.c. conforms to the memos. But I have since read and been considerably impressed by an article of Dean Alfange, Jr., 'Free Speech and Symbolic Conduct: The Draft-Card Burning Case,' 1968 *Sup. Ct. Rev.* 1, 49–51. Insofar as the opinion rests on the permissibility of a five-year sentence for mutilating a draft card, I could not agree with it."[35] While Friendly seems never to have addressed his views on the question of capital punishment, he described sympathetically Frankfurter's antipathy to it: "There was his detestation of capital punishment, a needless destroyer of life. There was his sense not merely of outrage as a lawyer but of affliction as a man when he thought life was being unfairly taken, as in the great case of Sacco and Vanzetti. No one ever heeded more poignantly than Felix and Marion Frankfurter, in the summer of 1927, the lesson that 'any man's death diminishes me, because I am involved in Mankinde.' "[36]

Friendly's decisions on the rights of prisoners and detainees centered on questions of status, in particular, persons detained before trial versus those who have been convicted; those entitled to be free versus those who have escaped prison; and those who have never been convicted of a felony versus those who have served their sentences. (Efforts of those in prison after conviction to obtain their release are the subject of Chapter 13 on habeas corpus.) Friendly sought to balance the rights of society against those of the individual in the particular circumstances. In general he seemed primarily concerned with the demands of law enforcement, although he insisted that prisoners be treated fairly and be afforded what human dignity required. Three cases are discussed.

1. For Friendly, a person who was awaiting trial was more sympathetic than one who had been duly convicted. In *Johnson v. Glick*[37] he considered an appeal by Australia Johnson, a state prisoner awaiting trial in the Manhattan House of Detention (the "Toombs"), who alleged that a guard, without provocation, struck him twice on the head with something enclosed in his fist and then denied him medical care. Friendly reversed the district judge who had dismissed the complaint. To find the source of Johnson's rights he went far beyond the parties' briefs[38] and reached back nearly three centuries to locate the origins of the "cruel and unusual punishments" language in the tenth clause of the Bill of Rights of William and Mary as well as in the constitutional debates. Not only did the Eighth Amendment not apply until after conviction, Friendly concluded,[39] but he doubted whether a prison guard's spontaneous attack constituted "punishment." "The thread common to all these cases is that 'punishment' has been deliberately administered for a penal or disciplinary purpose, with the apparent authorization of high prison officials charged by the state with responsibility for care, control, and discipline of prisoners. . . . We have considerable doubt that the cruel and unusual punishment clause is properly applicable at all until after conviction and sentence."[40]

Friendly located Johnson's right in the Due Process Clause, relying heavily on *Rochin v. California*,[41] where the Supreme Court found a constitutional violation when police officers pumped the stomach of a detainee to recover narcotics he had swallowed. Not every common-law assault or battery could give rise to a constitutional claim, he said: "The management by a few guards of large numbers of prisoners, not usually the most gentle or tractable of men and women, may require and justify the occasional use of a degree of intentional force. Not every push or shove, even if it may later seem unnecessary in the peace of a judge's chambers, violates a prisoner's constitutional rights." His was a generally liberal opinion, which also showed concern for the difficult job of prison guard.[42] Years later the Supreme Court applied the reasonableness standard that Friendly articulated in *Johnson v. Glick* to arrests or investigatory stops involving "free citizens."[43]

2. What are the rights of an escaped felon? The police recaptured Michael Roy in a shopping-center parking lot and seized firearms from his car.[44] The panel majority called Roy "a trespasser on society . . . [who] should have the same privacy expectations in property in his possession inside and out- side the prison," that is, virtually none, but decided alternatively that the arresting officers had probable cause to arrest him. While Friendly agreed that the arresting officers had probable cause to arrest Roy and to search him and his car, he rejected a doctrine "whereby certain classes of persons could be denied Fourth Amendment protections that would otherwise ex- tend to them." He called the majority's metaphor branding Roy a trespasser on society a "novel" and "frightening" prospect that suggested that Roy was totally at the mercy of the police. Friendly wrote, "Although the pic- ture of an escapee reembarking on a career of crime is not attractive, soci- ety should be equal to apprehending him without violating the guarantees of the Fourth Amendment."[45]

3. After he completed his substantial sentence, Gilbert Green, who had been convicted and sent to prison in *United States v. Dennis*[46] for having conspired to organize the Communist Party to advocate the overthrow of the government by force and violence, sued to regain the voting franchise. Not only was Green convicted of conspiring to destroy the system in which he sought to participate as a voter, but he further defied the system by remaining a fugitive for over four years, for which he was found in contempt of court and sentenced for that. Friendly decided the case on the basis of a general legal principle rather than on the unusual facts and found Green's Eighth Amendment claim insubstantial. "Depriving con- victed felons of the franchise is not a punishment but rather is a 'nonpenal exercise of the power to regulate the franchise.' . . . And if it were a pun- ishment, the framers of the Bill of Rights would not have regarded it as cruel and unusual."[47] He wryly explained why he did not refer to English experience at the time the Constitution was adopted: "It is true that with nearly all felonies punishable by death in 18th century England, the voting rights of convicted felons had not been a live issue there."[48]

While Friendly's comment referring to the attitude of the framers contains the language of originalism, it is impossible to accept him as an originalist in the context of punishment under the Eighth Amendment, which included flogging at the time of its adoption. In fact, he wrote that the "plainest example" in the Bill of Rights "invit[ing] the courts to develop and then to apply notions of social policy" was the Cruel and Unusual Punishment Clause. "Nearly everyone agrees with Chief Justice Warren's statement that the concept of cruelty is not static but must continually be reexamined in the light of 'the evolving standards of decency that mark the progress of a maturing society.' "[49]

IN HIS LIFETIME Friendly published no judicial opinion on the right to abortion, perhaps the transcendent right-to-privacy issue. Just shy of twenty years after Friendly's death, however, Judge A. Raymond Randolph, a former Friendly clerk, disclosed for the first time that in 1970—three years before *Roe v. Wade*[50]—Friendly had written a draft of an opinion in a case that challenged New York's strict antiabortion statute, *Hall v. Lefkowitz*.[51] Immediately after the oral argument Friendly told Randolph, "I'm going to write something that might goose the New York legislature into doing something."[52] Years later he wrote to a friend that he had "tentatively" decided to sustain New York's abortion statute "despite my own intense dislike of it." His letter candidly explained his strategy: "Contrary to the prediction of one of my colleagues, who was much more politically knowledgeable than I, that there was simply no chance of repeal, I thought there might be—or at least that nothing would be lost by acting on that premise for a while. Hence we exercised great liberality of time to complete discovery, etc. I proved right—by the margin of the vote of that courageous assemblyman from Auburn who lost his seat as a result."[53]

Friendly began the draft—he later wrote to a professor that he "had set down some notes of an opinion"[54]—by challenging reliance on *Griswold v. Connecticut*,[55] which concerned a state statute that criminalized the use of contraceptives even by married couples, as a basis for finding a constitutional right of abortion. While the ideas that Friendly expressed on abortion cannot claim originality,[56] his expression was particularly forceful in rejecting the claim that the New York law violated a right to privacy:

A holding that the privacy of sexual intercourse is protected against governmental intrusion scarcely carries as a corollary that when this has resulted in conception, government may not forbid destruction of the fetus. The type of abortion the plaintiff particularly wishes to protect against governmental sanction is the antithesis of privacy. The woman consents to intervention in the uterus by a physician, with his usual retinue of assistants, nurses, and other paramedical personnel.... While *Griswold* may well mean that the state cannot compel a woman to submit to an abortion, it is exceedingly hard to read it as supporting a conclusion that the state may not prohibit other persons from committing one or even her doing so herself.... While we are a long way from saying that [prior] decisions compel the legislature to extend to the fetus the same protection against destruction that it does after birth, it would be incongruous in their face for us to hold that a legislature went beyond constitutional bounds in protecting the fetus, as New York has done, save when its continued existence endangered the life of the mother.... However we might feel as legislators, we simply cannot find in the vague contours of the Fourteenth Amendment anything to prohibit New York from doing what it has done here.[57]

To the plaintiff's argument that Friendly was reading *Griswold* too narrowly and that the case established "the principle that a person has a constitutionally protected right to do as he pleases with his—in this instance, her—own body so long as no harm is done to others," Friendly rejoined, "Apart from our inability to find all this in *Griswold*, the principle would have a disturbing sweep." It would seemingly invalidate laws against suicide, bestiality, drunkenness unaccompanied by a breach of the peace, and some laws against drug use, laws that existed at the time the Fourteenth Amendment was adopted. Friendly poignantly reviewed circumstances that could "transform a hardship into austere tragedy" for a woman with an unwanted pregnancy,[58] before continuing: "Yet, even if we were to take plaintiffs' legal position that the legislature cannot constitutionally interfere with a woman's right to do as she will with her own body so long as no harm is done to others, the argument does not support the conclusion plaintiffs would have us draw from it. For we cannot say the New York legislature lacked a rational basis for considering that abortion causes such harm,"[59] in particular, to the fetus.

In a very real sense, Friendly had completed his opinion. But he had not forgotten what he had told his law clerk, and continued. "We would not wish our refusal to declare New York's abortion law unconstitutional as in any way approving or 'legitimating' it. The arguments for repeal are strong; those for substantial modification are stronger still.... But the decision what to do about abortion is for the elected representatives of the people, not for three, or even nine, appointed judges." Recognizing arguments on both sides of the debate, Friendly proposed a balancing of interests depending on the facts, quite different from the rigid and overly detailed majority opinion in *Roe v. Wade*. Friendly's draft proceeded to suggest, along the lines of his "Some Kind of Hearing" article, various "policy" choices to define the right to an abortion, such as whether there was rape or incest, whether the health of the mother was threatened, and whether the mother was below a certain age. So too, "[o]ne can also envision a more liberal regime in the early months of pregnancy and a more severe one in later months." Variations in procedures should be considered, such as requiring second opinions and involving social workers.[60]

In a law review article published in 1978, Friendly considered abortion in the broader context of courts' tackling problems involving social policy, such as invalidating contracts in violation of public policy and remedying race discrimination. Although he had difficulty locating the right to abortion in the Constitution, he stated that he personally favored some right, especially in the early months of pregnancy: "The considerations of social policy militating against both the strict Texas statute considered in *Roe* and the more modern Georgia statute considered in *Doe* were strong indeed. . . . I would like to believe that in their core—forbidding prohibition of abortion in the early months of pregnancy—they [the Justices] were right."[61]

Friendly reiterated that nothing in Brandeis's right to privacy supported a constitutional right to an abortion; a finding that wiretapping constituted a search under the Fourth Amendment in *Olmstead* did not lead to the conclusion that a state could not regulate abortions to some degree.[62] Since terminating a pregnancy, unlike using a contraceptive, was not private, a label and rationale were required other than a constitutional right to privacy. He was very critical of just about every aspect of the majority opinion in *Roe v. Wade*:

> A detailed presentation of these considerations of social policy would, to my mind, have furnished a much more persuasive basis for judicial intervention than the opinion's lengthy discussion of the Hippocratic Oath and the abortion practices of the ancient world or debate concerning the precise moment when a fetus becomes a person. . . . I think that the Court's abortion opinions should have dealt more with the evils of today and less with history. . . . Finally, however unprincipled this may sound, I would have welcomed some language indicating that the decisions were limited to a social problem of the greatest moment and were not to be taken as announcing a set of rights to a liberty that had not been previously known.[63]

Friendly was cautious when it came to expanding constitutional rights to invalidate prohibitions on pregnant women's working and laws against homosexual conduct, as well as laws prohibiting abortions, and he was not prepared to do so in the absence of a principled ground. He asked, "[W]here do the courts get the power to decide this?"[64] He saw no basis for rejecting the argument that "the state's interest in preserving the fetus was alone a sufficient justification for drastic limitation of abortions." He added the proviso that courts could prevent restriction on abortions on the basis "of evidence that the cost would result in unfair discrimination."[65] Thus, he recognized that the anti-abortion laws were an intrusion on women[66] and raised the possibility of sustaining some abortion laws on grounds of equal protection based on economic status, but he was not prepared to decide on that ground.

Friendly carried his approach of "Some Kind of Hearing" into new territories in a talk, "The New Liberty," which he gave at the University of Virginia on Founder's Day, April 13, 1978. His expansive address, which identified rights that were in need of substantial protection against government interference, equated the right to die with the right to marry: "A restriction on the right to marry, or to die without pain and in dignity, would demand more justification than a requirement to wear a motorcycle helmet or a seat belt."[67]

CHAPTER TWELVE

Other Constitutional Provisions

THIS CHAPTER DEALS with four other constitutional provisions. First is the Fourteenth Amendment's elusive concept of state action: "No State shall make or enforce any law which shall abridge the privileges or immunities of citizens of the United States; nor shall any State deprive any person of life, liberty, or property, without due process of law; nor deny to any person within its jurisdiction the equal protection of the law." Second is the Equal Protection Clause of the Fourteenth Amendment. Third is the relatively dormant provision that protects the "privileges and immunities of United States citizens." That language appears in Article IV, Section 2, of the Constitution, and a parallel provision applicable to the states appears in the Fourteenth Amendment. Fourth is the rarely litigated Thirteenth Amendment's prohibition against involuntary servitude. Some of Friendly's most lucid writing appears in this chapter, whose subjects are less dominated by ideology and less contentious than some constitutional issues previously discussed.

The Fourteenth Amendment prohibits states from depriving any person "of life, liberty, or property, without due process of law" and from denying to any person the "equal protection of the laws." In 1883 the Supreme Court held in the *Civil Rights Cases*[1] that the Fourteenth Amendment applies only to a relatively narrow band of "state action" and not to acts of private persons. While the Civil Rights Act of 1964 and later statutes placed private persons in virtually the same position as state entities insofar as race discrimination was concerned, other, nonracial issues remained, such as the rights of student demonstrators subjected to university disciplinary actions.

Friendly's 1968 lecture on state action, "The Dartmouth College Case and the Public-Private Penumbra," is both one of the best and yet least known of his scholarly writings. Funded by a devise from the estate of Oliver Wendell Holmes Jr., the lecture celebrated the sesquicentennial of Daniel Webster's famous argument before the Supreme Court in the *Dartmouth College Case*,[2] where the Court held that New Hampshire could not "pack" Dartmouth College's board of trustees by legislation increasing the size of the board, because the 1769 royal charter of the college had given the trustees the right to fill all vacancies on the board. Professor Gerald Gunther, a leading American constitutional scholar of the last third of the twentieth century, called Friendly's lecture "one of the most thoughtful and lucid analyses we have had of this fascinating mess."[3] Judge Michael Boudin observed that Friendly's "skeptical view . . . toward expansion of the state action doctrine has largely prevailed."[4] The published version of the lecture was not included in a law review but appeared as a supplement to the *Texas Quarterly*,[5] and, though encased in attractive packaging, it received limited circulation.

To provide a theoretical rationale for making difficult decisions as to what constitutes state action, Friendly offered a thesis: "[T]he constitutional problems in this area are not susceptible of black and white solutions; much depends on the extent of government involvement, on the seriousness of the particular social and political values at stake, and on the precise guarantee invoked."[6] He offered some difficult hypothetical cases to his audience, reminiscent of his days as a student at Harvard Law School. Suppose, for example, Dartmouth declined to accept Jewish students and the students brought an action to eliminate Dartmouth's tax exemption. What should the Supreme Court do? Clearly, the Court should hold for the students, he said. But what about Dartmouth's applying a secret quota regarding the number of Jewish students? Friendly continued with a series of tough questions:

> Granted that reasonable latitude should be accorded on my view, do we want the admission policies of "private" colleges to be subject to judicial scrutiny and revision at all? Moreover, if the equal protection clause of the Fourteenth Amendment is applicable to Dartmouth, must the due process clause likewise be? What would this imply with reference to such matters as the expulsion of students without a trial-type hearing or for engaging in protests—a lively issue today—, the discharge of officers of instruction without a similar hearing or because of alleged antipathy of the college administration to their political

views, required attendance of the students at religious services, or the barring of speakers for unpopular causes from the campus?[7]

The result might transfer university administration from the trustees and faculty to the courts, Friendly suggested. Even if the courts could be trusted to handle the sensitive problems, the burden on the universities (and the courts) to respond to such challenges would be considerable. Friendly raised a counterargument: "It may be answered that this would only be placing private universities where public ones already are." Does it make sense, he asked, for two nearly identical institutions to be treated under very different standards? Perhaps drawing on his experiences with the Federation of Jewish Philanthropies, he answered with a resounding, "Yes." He explained: "[O]ne of the great contributions of the *Dartmouth College* decision was the impetus it gave to voluntary associations as a factor in American life. May we not in the long run make a greater contribution to liberty by preserving independence for such associations, subject to corrective legislative action, than by imposing on them a rigid and uniform constitutional absolutism—even if in some instances what seems a wrong goes unrighted?"[8]

Emphasizing deficiencies in the reasoning of the Justices and the scholars—indeed he called the situation a "jurisprudential vacuum"— Friendly presented a scholarly and historical commentary on the Supreme Court's decisions:

> Working with the materials we now have, I find in the decisions two lines of thought relevant to the application of the Fourteenth Amendment in the area of "eleemosynary" institutions such as schools, colleges, libraries, and hospitals. One is that if private action has resulted in a general and serious denial of values the Amendment was meant to protect, an answer that the state has merely failed to prevent this will not suffice. The other is that when the state has acted, it may be required to act in an exemplary fashion, particularly with respect to discrimination, even when it has acted ever so gently and the practical effect of its default is small.[9]

Friendly once again proposed relying on a complex balancing approach that took into account incremental differences in the involvement of the state, the nature of the right that is circumscribed, the extent of the circumscription, whether the policy was exclusionary or inclusionary, whether there was action or inaction by the state, whether the conduct was isolated or whether the state allowed a whole class of institutions to practice discrimination, and the impact of the challenged conduct.[10] Thus, "the farther the state is from the center of the stage, the less should be the Court's concern." A discriminatory provision that appears in the instrument creating a charity is more likely to be a violation than actions by an administrator when the instrument is silent. A nonprofit hospital could least of all be allowed to discriminate in providing services. A charity created for the benefit of immigrants from County Clare would be less offensive than one that excluded Jews or blacks, where there would be little tolerance for discrimination. "The serious question in all these cases is whether the state's permitting the trustees to observe the settlor's restriction is a matter of constitutional magnitude. . . . My preference would be to apply to all these cases the same test—has the disposition produced results so contrary to the grand design of the equal protection clause that the state cannot in good conscience allow them to continue?"[11]

Friendly recognized that his formulation was not going to be easy for the courts to apply, but he was not sympathetic. Along with more work came more responsibility (power). His position would, he said, take "judges into the business of judging by requiring them to base decisions on differences of degree," pointing out that Holmes said, "The whole law does so as soon as it is civilized."[12] Countering the argument that the Fourteenth Amendment should apply generally to charitable institutions because the state had exercised its power to regulate them in some degree, he maintained that "what is always vital to remember is that it is the *state's* conduct, whether action or inaction, not the *private* conduct, that gives rise to the constitutional claims. . . . [T]he essential point [is] that the state must be involved not simply with some activity of the institution but with the activity that caused the injury."[13] Careful analysis was required.

The last major point Friendly made in his lecture was that "cases where the state has not merely stood aside and granted tax exemption and the services customarily furnished to all citizens, but has supplied pecuniary aid afford much stronger grounds for applying constitutional guarantees." Once again his answer was not a simple one: "I venture to think that the Constitution does not condition this fruitful partnership on bringing private institutions into conformity with all standards applicable to the state, and that there is room for distinction according to the nature and amount of state aid and the particular grievance asserted."[14]

Friendly ended his speech with a plea for greater tolerance for diversity among philanthropic institutions. He rejected the claim that philanthropy operating with government help and performing governmental functions should be treated identically with the government. The result would be "to turn our lively pluralistic society into a deadly uniformity ruled often by constitutional absolutes. . . . If the private agency must be a replica of the public one, why should private citizens give it their money or their time?"

He coupled this point with an argument against the Supreme Court's moving too quickly to fill a possible void. In fact, he praised "[t]oday's activist court . . . for treading rather cautiously in the area we have been discussing. . . . [O]n the whole it may be better that the Court should plot a few reference points even on what may be largely an intuitive basis, which can be readily erased if they prove unwise, before it attempts to project a curve to which all future determinations must conform."[15] He may have sought to discourage the Supreme Court from expressing a flawed theory and to increase the chances that his own vision would prevail.[16]

Amazingly, within a few months of his speech Friendly found on his desk *Powe v. Miles*,[17] a case precisely like a hypothetical he had discussed. Alfred University in upstate New York had four colleges, including the Liberal Arts College and the New York State College of Ceramics (CC). While the Liberal Arts College was private, CC was part of the New York State University by virtue of a detailed statutory scheme, with the state's annual appropriation accounting for about 20 percent of Alfred's budget.[18] Student demonstrators obstructed Alfred University's annual Army ROTC ceremony, and seven of them persisted after the Dean of Students announced they were violating university guidelines and instructed them to leave. When Alfred's President temporarily suspended the seven, four at the Liberal Arts College and three at the CC, they filed suit for reinstatement in the federal court. Following a hearing, District Judge John T. Curtin dismissed the complaint on the ground that they had failed to show state action.[19]

Writing for a unanimous court, Friendly first considered the status of the liberal arts students, who claimed that Alfred University performed a "public function." Unlike a mall or park, Friendly observed, the university grounds were not open to the public, and education traditionally had been a private as well as a public undertaking. He rejected as unpersuasive the argument that New York's Education Law and its regulating educational standards in private universities made their discipline of students the acts of the state. At this point Friendly repeated a statement that appeared in his *Dartmouth College Case* speech that has been widely quoted as a requisite for finding state action: "[T]he state must be involved not simply with some activity of the institution alleged to have inflicted injury upon a plaintiff but with the activity that caused the injury. Putting the point another way, the state action, not the private action, must be the subject of complaint."[20] The difference was between New York's setting the policy for control of demonstrations at private universities (state action) and its exercising some regulatory powers over the standard of education offered by private universities (not state action relevant to demonstrations).

Friendly pointed out that New York's aid to Alfred outside the CC was small, well under 1 percent of its budget. Moreover, "there is no reason why the liberal arts students should regard the President and the Dean of Students as arms of the State in conduct concerning them."[21] Unless the state was directly involved in the allegedly offending activity, the law that governed the private activities of citizens would control. "To be sure, on a strictly literal basis, whatever Alfred University does is 'under color of' the New York statute incorporating it. But this is also true of every corporation chartered under a special or even a general incorporation statute, and not even those taking the most extreme view of the concept have ever asserted that state action goes that far."[22]

The issue with respect to the CC, however, was "a rather close one." While acknowledging that the state funded the CC and its equipment belonged to the state, the defendants argued that the university could not resist tort-liability claims on the basis of the state's sovereign immunity and that the state was not liable for its breaches of contract. But, according to Friendly, those circumstances were "of little value" in resolving the dispute because the concerns and considerations were different. Labels applied in one area of the law have little value in other contexts that involve different considerations, and unthinking reasoning by analogy is no solution: "If New York chooses not to consider itself liable in tort or contract for the acts of its contract colleges, that is its affair. The question whether it has so far involved itself in the operation of the New York State College of Ceramics that acts of its delegates constitute action 'under color of any State law, statute, ordinance, regulation, custom or usage' is a different one, whose resolution depends upon federal law."[23]

In the end his principal reason for holding that the actions of the CC constituted state action was deceptively simple: "We hold that regulation of demonstrations by and discipline of the students at the New York State College of Ceramics at Alfred University by the President and the Dean of Students constitutes state action, for the seemingly simple but entirely sufficient reason that the State has willed it that way."[24] For Friendly the name of the institution and the governing statutory provisions were persuasive. "The statutory provisions are not mere verbiage; they reflect the Legislature's belief that the citizens of New York would demand retention of State control over an educational institution wholly supported by State money." The state furnished the land, building, and equipment and met, if necessary, its entire budget; "the students of the New York State College of Ceramics can properly regard themselves as receiving a public education. . . . [I]n the last analysis [the State] can tell Alfred not simply what to do but how to do it" regarding the CC. Thus, both the superficial aspects of the relationship, including the name of the institution, and the substantive aspects, including the role of the state in the statutory scheme, were significant in Friendly's finding state action, even though he did not find that the state "was the subject of the complaint."[25]

The result of Friendly's reasoning was troubling. For all practical purposes the situations of the seven students were identical. It almost certainly appeared that way to the students. Yet their rights were quite different. Friendly was philosophical: "[I]f we should hold there was state action with respect to the CC students, it would be impractical to have different rules for the two groups. Perhaps so, but that would be Alfred's problem."[26]

Friendly's conclusion did not mean that the judgment for defendants would be reversed as to the CC students, only that the court of appeals would have to decide an issue not reached by Judge Curtin, namely, whether plaintiffs were deprived of "any rights, privileges, or immunities secured by the Constitution and laws."[27] In other words, was the state action *unconstitutional* state action? Friendly reviewed Alfred University's guidelines on demonstrations and concluded that they were not constitutionally wanting. Not every denial of free speech is unconstitutional. "Even with respect to a public park the principles of the First Amendment are not to be treated as a promise that everyone with opinions or beliefs to express may gather around him at any public place and at any time a group for discussion or instruction." Friendly concluded that Alfred's rule requiring forty-eight hours' advance notice of student demonstration was not unreasonable when advance notice was feasible, as it was in this case. There was no unconstitutional state action taken against the CC students, so, for different reasons, Alfred prevailed against both groups of students.[28] In a footnote to the published version of his *Dartmouth College* lecture, Friendly added, "While ending up with the conclusion here expressed, I found the problem considerably more difficult than I had imagined—a fine example of the virtue of the common law system which requires decision to be made on the basis of the particular facts."[29]

Two years later Friendly encountered another difficult state action case after New York State passed legislation directing all colleges to adopt rules and regulations for the maintenance of public order on campuses. In *Coleman v. Wagner College* Friendly concluded that the act was sufficient to establish state action, since the college was exercising a power "emanating from the legislature." He explained, "Henceforth it can thus be forcefully argued, a private college in promulgating rules and regulations for the maintenance of order on the campus is exercising a power emanating from the legislature even though it could have acted on its own, as many in fact have done."[30] His formula required a finding of no state action when a college promulgated a sufficient regulation before the passage of the statute; that would not involve the enforcement of the state's regulation. But the timing of the legislation seems too fine a distinction to distinguish otherwise identically situated colleges, because once the statute is enacted, a college would not be free to rescind its requirement or cease to enforce it, and so from then it would be acting under compulsion of the statute.[31]

Six years after *Powe*, *Jackson v. Statler Foundation*[32] presented another major theme from his *Dartmouth College Case* lecture, the right of private foundations to engage in certain types of discrimination. Alleging race discrimination by virtue of the foundations' refusing to hire him as a director, to give scholarships to his children, and to grant money to his foundation, all for reasons of race, Reverend Donald L. Jackson brought suit for damages, an injunction, and the revocation of the foundations' tax-exempt status under the Internal Revenue Code against thirteen charitable foundations located in the Buffalo, New York, area. Judge Curtin dismissed the complaint.

The case was one of the very few that upset Friendly's equanimity toward his colleagues. Reversing the district court, the original panel (without Friendly), found for Jackson in a short *per curiam* opinion. But after several judges on the circuit, including Friendly, suggested rehearing the case *en banc,* the panel substituted a longer opinion in which Judge Smith noted, "This appears to be the first case in which the issue of the tax status of tax-exempt 'private foundations' has been raised," then proceeded to review the many legal restrictions on foundations, including a requirement that they file detailed annual reports, a prohibition against various types of self-dealing, a requirement that they make their grants in an objective and nondiscriminatory manner, and limitations upon the purposes and recipients of their payments. Also mentioned was that foundations performed many public functions and received substantial tax benefits. Reversal was required to develop the relevant facts, the panel held.[33]

The foundations filed a petition for rehearing *en banc*, which the court denied on a four-to-four vote. Dissenting from the denial, Friendly attacked the panel's opinion vigorously, even intemperately. "Somewhat incredibly," he wrote, the panel thought the decision was "so obvious as to deserve only a single paragraph of a per curiam opinion"—a gratuitous revelation to the public—before it substituted a revised and signed opinion: "[I]n my view it is analytically unsound, dangerously open-ended, and at war with controlling precedent both in the Supreme Court and in this circuit. Indeed, with all deference, it seems to me the most ill-advised decision with respect to 'state action' yet rendered by any court and unless corrected will be the source of enormous damage to the great edifice of private philanthropy which has been one of this country's most distinctive and admirable features."[34]

For Friendly the legal fallacy of the panel's decision was its failure to distinguish between two types of cases. When the government grants a tax exemption, that clearly is state action, and a suit to revoke the exemption is clearly directed at state action. But that does not mean that discrimination by the foundation in hiring was state action; the foundation was the *recipient* of the tax exemption. Moreover, in the former class of cases the courts "have struck down tax exemptions for institutions practicing the crudest form of racial discrimination—the exclusion of blacks from attendance in schools or membership in clubs of a public nature." Under the panel's extension of the concept of state action to many foundation actions, "[t]he foundation might be exposed to damage claims for prior discriminatory conduct and could be required by a court to make decisions not only as to the disposition of charitable donations but in the selection of its employees in accordance with the restrictions imposed on governmental agencies."[35]

Friendly again believed that the panel lost sight of his principle "that the state must be involved . . . with the activity that caused the injury. . . . [C]ourts should pay heed, in testing for government action, to the 'value of preserving a private sector free from constitutional requirements applicable to government institutions.' . . . I see nothing offensive, either constitutionally or morally, in a foundation's choosing to give preferentially or even exclusively to Jesuit seminaries, to Yeshivas, to black colleges or to the NAACP."[36] Diversity was one of the triumphs of private foundations, Friendly believed. Their auctions did not threaten to undermine "the grand design of the equal protection clause." He concluded with an unusual plea to the foundations to seek *certiorari* and to the Supreme Court to grant it. "It is to be hoped, in any event, that other circuits will not follow this disastrous course." While the foundations took Friendly's advice, the Supreme Court did not,[37] but no court has followed the majority opinion. Foundations held a very special place for Friendly.

The case returned to Judge Curtin, where it died with a whisper. Although he entered an order permitting Jackson to file an amended complaint and to add new defendants, including the Commissioner of Internal Revenue, a necessary party to consider tax issues, Jackson filed a new and nearly identical action in the U.S. District Court for the District of Columbia, which perforce transferred the new case to Curtin. Defendants served interrogatories, but Jackson steadfastly ignored Curtin's orders to answer properly. When defendants moved to dismiss, Jackson failed to file opposing affidavits. On July 18, 1975, Curtin dismissed both cases. Years later

Curtin lamented that the case was "a great waste of everyone's time." He described Jackson as a person concerned with the welfare of his children and himself rather than a civil rights advocate, adding, "[T]o appreciate the case you had to know Mr. Jackson. He was a true American character."[38]

In 1982 Friendly presented a coda to his views on state action in remarks at a conference sponsored by the *University of Pennsylvania Law Review.* After having waited fourteen years for the Supreme Court to explain the concept of state action, which he felt was overdue, he chastised the Justices: "Although we now have a dozen more Supreme Court decisions, which seem less ready to find state action than did those of earlier years, most of the opinions have been perfunctory and conclusory. If we now know more about the location of the border between public and private action, this is rather because the Court has pricked out more reference points than because it has elaborated any satisfying theory."[39]

FRIENDLY CONSIDERED the Equal Protection Clause of the Fourteenth Amendment in connection with abortion and state action, discussed earlier. He made his views known on another momentous issue, race relations, not in opinions, but in lectures and letters, where he praised the outcome of *Brown v. Board of Education*[40] but stated that "the decision was not, for whatever reasons, embodied in a good opinion.... [T]he Court and the country would have been better off if the Court had placed the *Brown* decision on jural considerations which were clearly within its province as the interpreter of the Constitution and which would have yielded readier and more acceptable answers in future controversies rather than on unestablished facts concerning segregation's psychological effects on public education."[41] He could not understand why the opinion did not simply overrule the "separate but equal" formula of *Plessy v. Ferguson,*[42] instead of disingenuously focusing solely on education. Indeed, the Supreme Court took the former approach the same day as *Brown* in *Bolling v. Sharpe,*[43] which invalidated school segregation in the District of Columbia on the ground that separate but equal violated due process.

Friendly made no public comment on affirmative action or reverse discrimination. One year before the Supreme Court's landmark decision in *Regents of the University of California v. Bakke*[44] in 1978, which constituted a challenge to a medical school's setting aside certain places for minority members, along with many conservatives Friendly came down on the side of traditional concepts of academic merit in a letter to a friend:

> I have read a good many articles on the subject but cannot get away from my gut reaction that reverse discrimination is just as unconstitutional as the other

kind. Of course, what sometimes is called reverse discrimination is not really so but simply inadequacies in testing procedures. My criticism is addressed to the kind of discrimination where applicants known by everyone to be inferior are being selected over those better qualified. From what I have heard, the reverse discrimination in admissions procedures generally has to be accompanied by a continuation of this discrimination in grading, with the result that the institution is putting its imprimatur on people who have not really met its standards.[45]

After the Court decided *Bakke*, Friendly wrote to Justice Lewis F. Powell Jr., whose opinion took a central position between four Justices who broadly favored affirmative action and four others who broadly condemned it. While Powell's opinion was weak on theory, it was pragmatic and extremely popular.[46] Quotas were bad, he said, but giving consideration to race was permissible. Powell cited Harvard's admissions policy as a good example of the kind of policy he favored; it obtained diversity but did no (overt) quantification.[47] Friendly, who viewed Powell's solution as akin to the resolution of the *numerus clausus* issue when he was in college, wrote him to express his appreciation "for the great service you have rendered the nation. This case had the potential of being another *Dred Scott* case. . . . Your moderation and statesmanship saved us from that. . . . It reminds one of Mark Twain's remark that God protects children, drunkards, and the United States of America."[48]

Friendly's judicial output on the subject of equal protection (under the umbrella of the Due Process Clause) was a concurring opinion. Relying on *Terry v. Ohio*,[49] which sustained a "reasonable" "stop and frisk," the Second Circuit in *United States v. Bell*[50] found a search reasonable under the Fourth Amendment when a ticketed airline passenger acted suspiciously and guards searched him and found narcotics. The case raised no issue of racial profiling or discrimination. Friendly's concurrence took a broad view of governmental power:

When the risk is the jeopardy to hundreds of human lives and millions of dollars of property inherent in the pirating or blowing up of a large airplane, the danger *alone* meets the test of reasonableness, so long as the search is conducted in good faith for the purpose of preventing hijacking or like damage and with reasonable scope and the passenger has been given advance notice of his liability to such a search so that he can avoid it by choosing not to travel by air. Since all air passengers and their baggage can thus be searched, there is no legal objection to searching only some, thereby lessening inconvenience and delay, providing that there is no national or racial discrimination without a rational basis (such as the destination of a particular flight).[51]

Friendly's voting memorandum in the case was more explicit: "Surely there would be nothing wrong in TWA asking for a search of all Arab passengers on a flight stopping at Lydda. . . . For that matter, under present circumstances I would see nothing wrong in any international airline requiring a search of all Arab passengers."[52]

In the economic arena Friendly welcomed experiment[53] but was prepared to hold a state statute unconstitutional if it engaged in unfair discriminatory treatment. In *Latham v. Tynan*[54] the panel majority upheld a state statute that suspended the license of any driver or owner of an uninsured motor vehicle that became involved in an accident "unless the operator or owner or both deposit security" in a sum determined by the state Commissioner of Motor Vehicles. The panel explained that Connecticut, had it chosen, "could have conditioned the licensing to operate and the registration of motor vehicles only upon compliance with some compulsory insurance requirement." In a pithy dissent Friendly pointed out that the majority's hypothetical statute, unlike the actual Connecticut statute, would have treated all drivers the same:

> However valid the axiom 'the greater includes the lesser' may be in mathematics, [Supreme Court decisions] have demonstrated it to be an exceedingly unsure guide in constitutional law. . . . The Connecticut statute requires security to be posted by an uninsured careful driver who has been the unfortunate victim of another's fault or of an unavoidable accident, whereas the uninsured careless driver is placed under no such burden so long as his luck holds. The discrimination can hardly be justified in terms of keeping uninsured careless drivers off the roads since by hypothesis the second driver is more likely to cause a liability-producing accident than the first.

PROFESSOR PHILLIP KURLAND wrote in 1972, "Perhaps the only certain content of the privileges or immunities of national citizenship is what has come to be known as the right to travel, between states and within them."[55] Article IV, Clause 2 of the Constitution states, "The Citizens of each State shall be entitled to all Privileges and Immunities of Citizens in the several states." Neither this clause nor its slightly different counterpart in the Fourteenth Amendment has made much of a mark on constitutional law; most of their potential has been assumed by other constitutional provisions, such as the Due Process Clause.[56]

Spanos v. Skouras Theatres Corp.[57] was Friendly's forum for interpreting the clause in Article IV. In 1953 the Skouras Theatres Corp. and related corporations (Skouras) retained Nick C. Spanos, a California attorney prominent in the application of the antitrust law to the movie business, to do legal work in a federal court case in New York City. When Spanos asked for the final portion of his fee, Skouras discharged him and Spanos sued. Skouras's defense was that Spanos was not admitted to practice by New York State, was therefore engaged illegally in the unauthorized practice of law, and should not recover his fee because courts do not enforce illegal contracts. The district court disagreed and awarded Spanos $89,606.29, on the ground that New York could not prevent the compensation of an attorney on a matter that dealt solely with federal law in a federal court.

On Skouras's appeal both sides again argued statutory construction and public policy. Accepting Skouras's argument that "virtually no legal services may be rendered in New York by a person not admitted to the state bar," the panel reversed, with Judge Lumbard writing for himself and Judge Smith, and with Friendly dissenting. Because the federal government had the power to determine who could practice in its courts, Lumbard said, Spanos's problem was not that he ran afoul of a state rule, but that he failed to conform to a federal rule. New York lawyers could appear in the federal courts; the local rules of the federal district court provided for a motion for temporary admissions (*pro hac vice*) to members of the bar of any other state. But Spanos had not done that, and the district court could not retroactively correct the deficiency. Friendly's dissent was short and caustic: "[The] palpably unjust result reminds me of Chief Justice Erle's observation as to the occasional predilection of the best of judges for a 'strong decision,' to wit, one 'opposed to common-sense and to common convenience.'"[58]

The court granted Spanos's motion for a rehearing *en banc,* and this time several bar associations weighed in as *amici curiae* on the side of lawyer Spanos. After the parties had filed their allotted briefs, the Association of the Bar of the City of New York for the first time raised Article IV's Privileges and Immunities Clause. No further briefs were filed, no oral argument was held in the *en banc* proceeding, and no one responded to the Association's argument.[59] With Friendly writing for a seven-to-two majority, the full court reversed the panel.[60] Since the contract engaging Spanos contemplated court appearances on his part, Friendly wrote, the defendants "impliedly assumed the obligation of having their New York lawyers in the action make any motion that was necessary to render such appearances lawful. There is not the slightest reason to suppose that if by their lawyers defendants had sought admission *pro hac vice* for the colleague whose services they had been at such pains to secure, the motion would have been denied."[61]

Examination of Spanos's briefs shows Friendly's contribution to this argument. Spanos argued that the New York law did not apply in federal courts, but also said that "it was easily within the power of the attorney of record to arrange for that admission."[62] Friendly took Spanos's soft argument and converted it to the point that it was Skouras's *obligation* to have Spanos admitted and their failure to do so meant that Skouras could not benefit from that failure. Moreover, Friendly added, Skouras could not capitalize on Spanos's failure to file a motion *nunc pro tunc* (retroactively), because Skouras fired him and thereby prevented him from curing the deficiency.[63]

While he had thus decided the case in favor of Spanos on statutory and policy grounds, Friendly chose to violate the well-established rule that courts should make every effort to avoid deciding constitutional claims. He proceeded to consider the constitutional ground not addressed by the parties, because of "the importance of the problem and the desirability of furnishing guidance to the bar. . . . [W]e hold that under the privileges and immunities clause of the Constitution no state can prohibit a citizen with a federal claim or defense from engaging an out-of-state lawyer to collaborate with an in-state lawyer and give legal advice concerning it within the state. . . . Having exercised their constitutional right to obtain the expert legal assistance on their antitrust claim which they desired, defendants cannot be heard to object to paying the bill."[64]

Friendly's deciding the constitutional issue, particularly an unprecedented application of a constitutional provision,[65] seems inconsistent with his earlier review of Alexander Bickel's book on Brandeis's unpublished opinions. Citing Brandeis's willingness for a court to entertain a constitutional issue "only when it is absolutely unable otherwise to dispose of a case properly before it," Friendly stated, "Of course, the Court should not decide the constitutionality of a statute without fully hearing those interested in sustaining it."[66] In a later article Friendly explained that while Brandeis decided *Erie R.R. v. Tompkins*[67] on a constitutional ground that was neither briefed nor argued by the parties, the parties were on notice that the Court was considering a constitutional decision in view of the many questions from the Court to counsel on the issue. "There was thus no unfairness to the parties [in *Erie*], who could have sought permission to submit further briefs on this point if they had desired."[68] Likewise, after the bar association filed its brief and Skouras was on notice that the Second Circuit was considering a constitutional issue, Skouras could have but made no effort to seek leave to file an additional brief on the constitutional issue.[69]

Friendly's opinion on the constitutional issue lacked his customary historical narrative and analysis, which, in fact, the bar association's brief had provided.[70] His opinion also contained a possible error. He said that it was the clients' (Skouras's) privileges and immunities that were implicated ("Having exercised their constitutional right to obtain the expert legal assistance"). However, the defendants were all corporations, and it has been settled law that corporations are not citizens for purposes of the Privileges and Immunities Clause, and therefore could not receive its protection.[71] Furthermore, Spanos could not assert the claim because someone cannot ordinarily obtain the benefit of a constitutional right of another person.[72] For unexplained reasons Friendly settled for a partially inaccurate as well as a less than thorough opinion.

INCIDENTS OF SLAVERY or involuntary servitude occasionally surface. When an employer, David Shackney, kept a Mexican family working on a Connecticut chicken farm principally by using threats of deportation if they strayed, he was indicted and convicted under a federal criminal statute that punishes "[w]hoever knowingly and willfully holds to involuntary servitude," a statute based on the Thirteenth Amendment.[73] On Shackney's appeal Friendly's opinion observed that the government expansively construed the language "Whoever knowingly and willfully holds to involuntary servitude," as equivalent to "Whoever knowingly and willfully holds to service by duress." He continued, "To test the consequences of such a reading, appellant's brief put a series of cases, starting with that of a man chained to his work bench and kept under restraint at all times, and ranging through the instant case to others where an employer threatens an employee who wishes to leave his service with blackballing in the industry, revealing a crime to the police, or preventing the employee's son from achieving a much desired admission to Yale."[74]

On oral argument Friendly took the federal prosecutor through appellant's hypotheticals one by one, and when the prosecutor responded that all violated the statute, Friendly leaned back and smiled.[75] His opinion evaluated the government's responses: "The Government manfully answered that all these cases constitute a holding to involuntary servitude, although also denying 'that the outer limits of that statute need be explored in this case.' With the most profound respect for the illustrious university at New Haven, we cannot believe that retention of an employee by a threat to prevent his son's admission there was quite what Congress had in mind when, in the great words of the 13th Amendment, it forbade a holding in involuntary servitude."[76] Friendly held that the use or the threatened use of physical coercion, such as beatings and physical barriers to leaving, was essential for involuntary servitude.

Years later the Ninth Circuit rejected Friendly's approach and held that involuntary servitude exists "when an individual coerces another into his service by improper or wrongful conduct that is intended to cause, and does cause, the other person to believe that he or she has no alternative but to perform the labor."[77] The Supreme Court resolved the split in the circuits in *United States v. Kozminski.*[78] Writing for the majority, Justice O'Connor held that involuntary servitude existed only when a victim was compelled to work based upon the defendant's use or threat of physical or legal coercion, and not psychological coercion. She added, "In short, we agree with Judge Friendly's observation that '[t]he most ardent believer in civil rights legislation might not think that cause would be advanced by permitting the awful machinery of the criminal law to be brought into play whenever an employee asserts that his will to quit has been subdued by a threat which seriously affects his future welfare but as to which he still has a choice, however painful.' "[79]

CHAPTER THIRTEEN

Habeas Corpus

WHILE THE RIGHT to habeas corpus is established in Article I of the Constitution,[1] its content and application have been left to Congress and the courts. Until 1953 habeas corpus provided little relief, especially to state prisoners who sought postconviction relief in federal court for constitutional violations. "[F]or purposes of habeas corpus a detention was not to be deemed 'unlawful' if based upon the judgment of a competent state court which had afforded full corrective process for the litigation of questions touching on federal rights."[2] With very few exceptions federal habeas corpus relief was circumscribed by a raft of technical rules requiring the prisoner to have pressed his constitutional claim at every stage of the proceeding, including, for state prisoners, in prior state habeas corpus petitions. In the ten-year period 1945–1955, fewer than 2 percent of petitioning state prisoners found relief in the federal courts.[3]

In 1953 the Supreme Court commenced what was seen as a revolution in *Brown v. Allen*,[4] where "eight of nine Justices assumed on habeas corpus that federal district courts must provide review of the merits of constitutional claims fully litigated in the state-court systems."[5] Ten years later, in *Fay v. Noia*,[6] the Court held that the existence of an "independent" state ground to support a state conviction, such as failure to appeal a conviction to a higher state court, no longer barred federal court remedies. The pair of decisions immensely expanded the rights of state prisoners to a federal forum. Friendly observed that from 1950 to 1969 the number of state prisoners seeking relief in the federal courts grew from 541 to 7,359, which constituted 10 percent of the entire civil caseload,[7] and the number was increasing. Between 1961 and 1979 habeas petitions by state prisoners increased 1,682 percent.[8] Friendly appeared to view his role as moderating between the restrictive views that prevailed before *Brown v. Allen* and the huge expansion fired by the Warren Court that not only struck down procedural restrictions on the assertion of federal constitutional rights, but greatly expanded the number and scope of those rights.

Writing in the *Harvard Law Review* in January 1963, Harvard Law professor Paul Bator criticized *Brown v. Allen* for its weak history, weak reasoning, and inadequate accommodation of federalism, including the strains it would place on the federal system. For Bator, habeas corpus provided a forum for a convicted defendant who had not been given a full and fair opportunity to litigate constitutional claims.[9] Bator's thesis was that it was impossible to be certain that a federal judge was more accurate than a state judge, so for institutional reasons there should be no review when the state judge adhered to proper procedures. Friendly told Bator that he considered his article "full of brilliant and suggestive insight."[10]

Friendly's concern for habeas corpus process first showed itself in 1962, when he *expanded* the scope of the federal writ. Many defendants who found their sentences increased under recidivist statutes claimed that there were serious defects in the *earlier* conviction used to increase the current sentence. There was no dispute over who should decide the validity of the prior conviction when the same state that imposed the recent sentence had entered the previous conviction, but who should determine the validity of the prior conviction when it was from a different state? Traditionally, federal courts routinely told the defendant to challenge his allegedly unconstitutional prior conviction in the court that convicted him in that case, despite the hardship if not impossibility of doing so effectively. For one thing, the state of the prior conviction had no interest in reviewing it. Friendly changed the practice in *United States ex rel. LaNear v. LaVallee.*[11]

In 1950 Franklin LaNear received a longer sentence in a New York court because he had pleaded guilty to burglary in the state courts of Missouri in 1938. In his federal habeas proceeding LaNear claimed the Missouri conviction was void because he pleaded guilty when he was seventeen years old, barely literate, not advised of the precise nature of the charge against him, and without counsel. When a federal district court in New York denied the petition on the ground that LaNear had not sought relief in the Missouri courts and thus had failed to exhaust state judicial remedies, he appealed. The applicable federal statute read, "An application for a writ of habeas corpus in behalf of a person in custody pursuant to the judgment of a State court shall not be granted unless it appears that the applicant has exhausted the remedies available in the courts of the State, or that there is either an absence of available State corrective process or the existence of circumstances rendering such process ineffective to protect the rights of the prisoner."[12]

Contrary to earlier decisions, Friendly decided that the term "the courts of the State" and "State corrective process" referred to the state whose courts were holding the petitioner in custody, which in the present case was New York:

> Only in form is LaNear's complaint over what Missouri allegedly did; in every practical sense his grievance is over what New York is doing with what Missouri did. Missouri's allegedly unconstitutional action against him had spent its force until New York made it a legal basis for increased sanctions of its own. . . . [The writ] includes a claim that New York is disregarding a prisoner's constitutional rights if it takes into account a conviction, obtained in violation of fundamental requirements. . . . The alleged violation of constitutional right thus being New York's and New York having provided no method for questioning an out-of-state conviction used as a basis for a multiple-offender sentence, a New York prisoner challenging the validity of such a conviction on constitutional grounds may proceed directly in a Federal court.[13]

Friendly fashioned a federal remedy, which, it is worth emphasizing, increased the burdens on the federal district and circuit courts. In order to avoid overruling Second Circuit precedent, which would have required having LaNear's case heard *en banc,* Friendly struggled to distinguish cases that endorsed the prior interpretation. He went to extreme, possibly excessive, lengths. For example, he circumvented *United States ex rel. Atkins v. Martin*[14] with the statement, "[W]e did rely on failure to exhaust Florida remedies; but this was only an alternative ground and the meager *pro se* brief filed by the relator [petitioner] did not contend that exhaustion was not required."[15] While a court's *dicta* need not be followed, Friendly pointed to nothing that would permit ignoring an alternative holding. "Holding and dictum are generally thought of as mutually exclusive categories."[16] Friendly was engaging in creative readings of precedent to provide fundamental rights to incarcerated individuals. In fact, when it suited his purpose Friendly defined "dicta" very broadly to include a statement that "was unnecessary to the decision there" and ones that "were not essential to the holding."[17]

In *Collins v. Beto,*[18] a case in the Fifth Circuit, where he sat by designation, Friendly wrote to Chief Judge Elbert P. Tuttle about his opinion concurring in reversal because of a coerced confession based on all the circumstances, but not on denial of the right to counsel, which he considered an unwarranted constitutional absolute. Without informing him of his rights, police had kept Clarence Collins, who had limited capacity, incommunicado for thirty-six hours while moving him from place to place. "Although this may be pressing slightly beyond any case yet decided by the Court, I am quite prepared to do a bit of anticipating in this area in a case where the police's behavior so thoroughly deserves condemnation."[19] Friendly was prepared to push the envelope when police violated basic rights.

More often Friendly decried the breadth and inefficiency of federal habeas corpus, as when a Second Circuit panel on which he sat permitted a state defendant who had allegedly pleaded guilty on the advice of counsel to challenge his guilty plea on the ground that his confession, allegedly the reason why he had pleaded guilty, had been coerced.[20] Friendly dissented: "Men who first confess and then, on the advice of counsel, plead guilty to serious crimes, do so because they are"; people who receive proper process, including advice of counsel, should not be permitted to complain after conviction. He condemned the "thousands of tedious journeys which we here inflict on state and federal judges" without "any real prospect that a few innocent defendants may be found at the end of the tunnel."[21] His reference to the guilt of the petitioner provoked Judge Kaufman to chide him for the reason that guilt or innocence was irrelevant.[22] Siding with Friendly on the merits, the Supreme Court reversed the Second Circuit, although without mentioning guilt or innocence.[23]

One year later, with the Second Circuit sitting *en banc*, Friendly informed his colleagues that he would vote to deny state prisoners' habeas corpus petitions that claimed that they were unconstitutionally deprived of good-behavior time credit, for the reason that the petitioners had not exhausted their state administrative remedies.[24] When, however, the Supreme Court in a summary reversal without briefs or argument came to the opposite conclusion in *Wilwording v. Swenson*,[25] Friendly felt compelled to reverse course. His caustic concurring opinion explained, "I do not understand how a state prisoner ... can opt out ... of exhaustion of state remedies when these are available simply by styling his petition as one under the Civil Rights Act. But *Wilwording* seems to indicate that he can. For that reason I am constrained to concur in affirming the orders of the district court."[26] Faced with Friendly's rebuke, the Supreme Court retreated from *Wilwording* and reversed the Second Circuit's pro-prisoner ruling. While the state's brief devoted two pages to Friendly's opinion, the Court's majority opinion did not cite it.[27]

In 1970 Friendly gave an important speech on habeas corpus entitled "Is Innocence Irrelevant? Collateral Attack on Criminal Judgments."[28]

Someone who had violated the law, Friendly argued, should "swiftly and certainly become subject to punishment, just punishment." Because collateral attack may be delayed until evidence is lost and witnesses are no longer available, the guilty prisoner may win on a retrial, which almost always was the remedy granted. Friendly was concerned with finality, a subject to which he gave increasing attention as the years passed. Moreover, collateral attack was a drain upon the finite resources of the community, and the flood of worthless applications was likely to prejudice the occasional meritorious one.[29]

History was largely on Friendly's side: "It has now been shown with as close to certainty as can ever be expected in such matters that . . . the assertion that habeas as known at common law permitted going behind a conviction by a court of general jurisdiction is simply wrong." He labeled as incorrect the Supreme Court's statement in *Fay v. Noia*, that at the time of the founding of the nation "there was respectable common-law authority for the proposition that habeas was available to remedy any kind of governmental restraint contrary to fundamental law."[30] Friendly had little confidence in the Supreme Court's ability to rationalize habeas corpus, telling an English friend, "[T]he Supreme Court has twisted the English cases to its own ends."[31]

Friendly began his speech by quoting from Justice Black's dissent in *Kaufman v. United States*, to which Black alone subscribed, that pressed for including guilt or innocence as one factor in deciding whether to grant habeas corpus: "[T]he defendant's guilt or innocence is at least one of the vital considerations in determining whether collateral relief should be available to a convicted defendant. . . . In collateral attacks . . . I would always require that the convicted defendant raise the kind of constitutional claim that casts some shadow of a doubt on his guilt."[32] Friendly called "incredibl[e]" both that Black's statement was made in dissent and that the other dissenting Justices separated themselves from it.[33] Unmeritorious petitions filed by guilty defendants who had litigated their claims at trial were threatening to undermine the criminal justice system and deprive potentially meritorious claims of judicial attention. Friendly criticized the position that mandated "a second round of attacks simply because the alleged error is a 'constitutional' one."[34]

Friendly's thesis, which was even more restrictive (conservative) than Black's, was that on habeas corpus, as opposed to direct appeal, a petitioner ordinarily should have to make a colorable showing of innocence before his claim would be considered, a position for which there is little, if any, historical support.[35] He went further than Black's excluding from grounds for relief *claims* unrelated to the issue of whether the defendant was innocent. Friendly required a petitioner to show *both* that the challenged testimony was unreliable *and* that he may be innocent. For him, violations of a defendant's rights that did not create a likelihood of convicting the innocent did not warrant federal post-appeal relief.[36] On alleged violations of *Miranda v. Arizona*[37] he said, "The mere failure to administer *Miranda* warnings before on-the-scene questioning creates little risk of unreliability, and the [minimal] deterrent value of permitting collateral attack goes beyond the point of diminishing returns." Still, Friendly rejected some of the more extreme conservative positions proposed by Republican administrations.[38] He also argued, "The policy against incarcerating or executing an innocent man . . . should far outweigh the desired termination of litigation," a liberal position that the Supreme Court has rejected and scholars find to be without historical support.[39] Even as qualified, Friendly's proposal was strong medicine, and he knew it. During his entire career on the bench he expressly found a colorable issue of innocence in only three of the hundreds of criminal or habeas corpus appeals in which he wrote an opinion.[40] A sniff of innocence would get his attention.[41]

While Friendly made cogent arguments based on history and practical considerations, he did not attempt to develop a theoretical foundation for his position, such as Bator's focus on the questionable role of redundant relief when proper procedures had been followed in the first proceeding. For example, Friendly did not discuss that since the writ of habeas corpus was designed to determine whether or not the petitioner was being "unjustly detained," that meant that the petitioner should be required to present evidence that he was innocent.[42]

The other main prong of Friendly's article was that violations of certain fundamental rights could create a basis for collateral relief even without a credible claim of innocence. The clearest case was a defendant who was without counsel at trial. Similarly, relief should be granted when the facts supporting the claim were outside the record and were not available for review on appeal;[43] when the state failed to provide proper procedures for making a defense at trial and on appeal; and when new constitutional developments relating to criminal procedure favored the defendant.[44]

The same year as the article appeared Friendly sat on a habeas case that involved the right to counsel. After a trial by jury for bank robbery at which Paul Peter Solina Jr., represented by Walter T. Coleman, was convicted, District Judge Jacob Mishler imposed the maximum sentence of twenty-five years, stating, "I can't recall a case so heavily weighted against the defendant as this one was." The court of appeals affirmed the conviction.[45] When, more than a decade later, Solina learned that Coleman had not been a lawyer admitted to practice, he filed a petition for a writ of habeas corpus. Coleman had been graduated from an accredited law school, taken courses in criminal law, participated in numerous hearings, and consulted regularly at the trial with experienced counsel representing other defendants, but was not admitted to the bar.[46] After holding a hearing, Mishler denied Solina's petition, finding the error "harmless beyond a reasonable doubt."[47]

To determine what "counsel" meant in the Sixth Amendment, Friendly excavated two-hundred-year-old history and concluded that Coleman did not qualify, which was sufficient to grant relief on habeas.[48] This was a case where Friendly followed his mentor Charles McIlwain's prescription to read words the way they were understood at the time they were written. He rewarded Solina even though "[t]here is simply nothing to suggest that a licensed lawyer for Solina could have arrived at a plea bargain, provided a single juror with a rational basis for having a reasonable doubt, induced the judge to impose a lesser sentence, or prevailed upon appeal, and everything to indicate he would not."[49] Rejecting the argument that the failure to provide a licensed attorney was an error that could be deemed harmless, Friendly held that the "problem of representation by a person like Coleman is not simply one of competence . . . but that he was engaging in a crime. Such a person cannot be wholly free from fear of what might happen if a vigorous defense should lead the prosecutor or the trial judge to inquire into his background and discover his lack of credentials."[50] The result gave Friendly little satisfaction: "The conclusion that we must reverse the denial of the motion to vacate Solina's conviction is one that we have reached without enthusiasm on the facts here. It may well be impracticable for the Government to retry Solina 13 years after the event. . . . Perhaps . . . something is to be said for an automatic rule that relieves the courts of the difficult task of making harmless error determinations in lack of counsel cases where the representation is more nearly suggestive of prejudice or the evidence of guilt less overwhelming. Be all this as it may, the question is no longer open to debate in any court save one."[51]

Despite Friendly's statement that he was required to reverse, no Supreme Court case had held that harmless error was inapposite in a case like Solina's. In *Holloway v. Arkansas*,[52] the Supreme Court decision on which Friendly relied, the trial court insisted that an attorney represent defendants with conflicting interests. Chief Justice Warren Burger's opinion granted the petition: "[W]henever a trial court improperly requires joint representation over timely objection reversal is automatic." Key for Burger was that with joint representation it was impossible to ascertain the nature and prejudice of the constitutional deprivation. "[I]n a case of joint representation of conflicting interests the evil—it bears repeating—it is what the advocate finds himself compelled to *refrain* from doing, not only at trial but also as to possible pretrial negotiations and in the sentencing process. . . . [A]n inquiry into a claim of harmless error here would require, unlike most cases, unguided speculation."[53]

While *Holloway* held that improperly mandated joint representation was unique because prejudice was indeterminable, that was not Solina's claim. Thus, the *holding* in *Holloway* provided Solina with no grounds for relief. But Burger had added a broad (and confusing) *dictum*: "[T]his Court has concluded that the assistance of counsel is among those 'constitutional rights so basic to a fair trial that their infraction can never be treated as harmless error.' Accordingly, when a defendant is deprived of the presence and assistance of his attorney . . . in, at least, the prosecution of a capital offense, reversal is automatic."[54] Departing from his customary practices of eliding *dicta* and regarding the factual setting as the essence of the holding, Friendly chose in *Solina* to rely on the *dictum* and, in fact, to apply the *dictum* expansively to a noncapital case in the very situation the Court had distinguished.

Another pro-defendant opinion by Friendly evolved into a Supreme Court decision that expanded an important right of defendants. Based on evidence found at the crime scene, the police arrested Theodore R. Stovall for the murder of Dr. Paul Behrendt and the grievous wounding of his wife, Dr. Frances Behrendt. Although Stovall told the magistrate that he intended to get an attorney, the police nevertheless took him to Frances's hospital room, where she identified him as her assailant. At his trial the state introduced both the hospital identification and the identification Frances made in the courtroom. Stovall was convicted and sentenced to death, and the state appellate courts affirmed.

Stovall's federal petition for a writ of habeas corpus claimed that the police violated his Fifth and Sixth Amendment rights. Missing the major point, Judge Moore's opinion for the Second Circuit sitting *en banc* in *United States ex rel. Stovall v. Denno*[55] said that the magistrate followed the statute "punctiliously" in advising Stovall of his right to counsel. Friendly dissented on the basis of the Sixth Amendment: "I fail to understand why, in the interval between preliminary hearing and trial, a defendant is not entitled to the assistance of counsel when the state wishes to make use of him to obtain evidence that will have independent testimonial value." Disagreeing with Moore, Friendly said there was plenty that counsel could have done for Stovall, including convincing the magistrate not to permit the confrontation. He scoffed at the state's suggestion that Stovall's visit to the hospital room gave him the chance to be exonerated: "[I]f the state official were motivated by such solicitude, the natural course would have been to ask Stovall whether he wanted to go."[56] Friendly was concerned that the suggestive nature of some out-of-court identifications could precipitate the conviction of innocent defendants.

While Friendly concluded that Stovall had the better legal argument, this did not mean that he wanted him to go free. With the evidence overwhelmingly against Stovall, retrial was almost certain to produce a conviction. However, it became evident during the appellate process that Stovall intended to raise an insanity defense for the first time at a new trial. This tactic concerned Friendly, who had been on the original panel (before the case was considered *en banc*). At the end of his opinion for the panel he asked the question, almost certainly for the benefit of the state prosecutor, whether under New York law Stovall could raise an insanity defense not argued in the first trial.[57]

The Supreme Court heard Stovall's habeas appeal along with two direct appeals, one from a conviction in another circuit and one from a state court. In *United States v. Wade*[58] and *Gilbert v. California*,[59] the Court agreed with Friendly's analysis and held that the defendants' constitutional rights had been violated. In *Stovall v. Denno*,[60] however, it denied habeas corpus on the ground that its ruling should not apply retroactively to habeas corpus cases, but only prospectively. Thus, Stovall, whose constitutional rights had been violated, and Friendly, who made an accurate assessment of the law seventeen months before the Supreme Court did, were both losers, albeit Stovall's loss was the more serious.

More typical for Friendly was *Nelson v. Scully*,[61] where he reversed the grant of a writ that challenged a specific jury instruction. Rejecting Judge Oakes's dissent, Friendly found the instruction when read in context to have been sufficient. To Oakes's argument as to how the jury might have been misled, he replied that a juror was not "a trained lawyer possessing the analytical skill of our dissenting brother. . . . [T]his is attributing altogether too much legal acumen to the ordinary juror—who had not imbibed Wigmore's Evidence with his mother's milk."

Friendly's "Innocence" article soon influenced the Supreme Court. In 1976, in *Stone v. Powell*,[62] the Court, citing Friendly's article, reversed *Kaufman v. United States*[63] and held that habeas corpus did not provide a remedy for a conviction based on illegally seized evidence, which was, as Friendly had emphasized, no less reliable than legally seized evidence. A decade later *Kuhlmann v. Wilson* relied on Friendly's writings to limit successive applications for relief under habeas corpus. Justice Powell wrote in his concurring opinion, "[T]he 'ends of justice' require federal courts to entertain such petitions only where the prisoner supplements his constitutional claim with a colorable showing of factual innocence. This standard was proposed by Judge Friendly more than a decade ago as a prerequisite for federal habeas corpus generally. As Judge Friendly persuasively argued then, a requirement that the prisoner come forward with a colorable showing of innocence identifies those habeas corpus petitioners who are justified in again seeking relief from their incarceration. We adopt this standard."[64]

Herrera v. Collins, decided by the Supreme Court in 1993, stated that a claim of innocence is "a gateway through which a habeas petitioner must pass to have his otherwise barred constitutional claim considered on the merits."[65] As one academic wrote, "As if in answer to Judge Friendly's original query, 'Is Innocence Irrelevant?,' the Court shift[ed] the pith of the habeas inquiry from procedural demands for fairness to substantive claims of innocence."[66] In 1996, however, Congress, confronting a rapidly deteriorating situation, hastily passed the Antiterrorism and Effective Death Penalty Act of 1996,[67] which enacted provisions aimed at limiting and restructuring the habeas corpus process, but went in a different direction from Friendly. The *Harvard Law Review* observed, "Clearly the AEDPA rejects Friendly's 'guilt matters' theory."[68] Nevertheless, Congress left standing a number of Supreme Court decisions that relied on Friendly's article.

ANOTHER HABEAS CORPUS OPINION by Friendly was important for its political, not legal, implications. In 1951 Morton Sobell was convicted along with Julius and Ethel Rosenberg of providing secrets to the USSR in time of war. District Judge Irving R. Kaufman sentenced the Rosenbergs to death and Sobell to thirty years in prison. The case and executions rivaled *Sacco and Vanzetti* for the intensity of public interest and reaction. Friendly sat on Sobell's fifth petition for habeas corpus, which argued that Kaufman had committed an error of constitutional magnitude when he permitted the prosecutor to cross-examine Ethel Rosenberg about her having pleaded the Fifth Amendment before the grand jury.[69] Sobell based his habeas petition on the Supreme Court's 1957 decision in *Grunewald v. United States*,[70] which on direct appeal unanimously reversed a conviction because the prosecutor cross-examined the defendant concerning his plea of the Fifth Amendment in the grand jury as bearing on his credibility in testifying at trial that he was innocent. Sobell's arguments implicated the highly charged question of whether a constitutionally flawed trial precipitated the controversial death sentences imposed on the Rosenbergs and whether if they had been alive they would get a new trial. Friendly's voting memorandum read, "[W]e must admit that on a direct appeal today we would reverse not only as to Ethel but almost certainly as to Julius and very likely as to Sobell as well."[71]

Analyzing *Grunewald,* Friendly's opinion observed that five of the nine Justices reversed on *non*constitutional grounds, namely, that the probative value of the cross-examination was small compared to its impermissible prejudice to Grunewald. In other words, there was little inconsistency between Grunewald's plea of the Fifth Amendment and his later testimony at trial, while the likelihood of the jury's finding Grunewald guilty because he had pleaded the Fifth Amendment was considerable. This was an evidentiary, not constitutional, ruling. Friendly assumed without deciding that Sobell would have prevailed on direct appeal because the Second Circuit had reversed convictions of defendants when substantial errors affected a codefendant.[72]

Turning to Sobell's status on habeas corpus, Friendly assumed "in all likelihood too favorably for [Sobell]" that he would prevail if he had been denied a constitutional right or a serious nonconstitutional right "if it was not correctible on appeal or there were 'exceptional circumstances' excusing the failure to appeal." The first ground was not available to Sobell: "[E]ven if the Supreme Court would now deem *Grunewald* to be constitutionally grounded, a sufficient answer here would be that any constitutional relief must be limited to the person whose claim of privilege was later used against him. 'The privilege is that of the witness himself, and not of the party on trial.'" On the second ground, Friendly, after a careful examination of the precedents, found no valid reason why Sobell (and implicitly the Rosenbergs) did not raise the issue on direct appeal.[73] After all, Grunewald did just that a few years later.

CHAPTER FOURTEEN

Nonconstitutional Criminal Procedure

FRIENDLY SHOWED CONSIDERABLE CONCERN for a defendant's rights on direct appeal. In *United States v. Panico*[1] he dissented from his colleagues' affirming a conviction for criminal contempt, arguing that the defendant's capacity was in doubt and that the trial judge, who ruled without a hearing, relied on facts not within his personal knowledge. Friendly observed that "procedural safeguards in the administration of criminal justice do not exist for the sole benefit of nice people."[2]

Friendly challenged a variety of pro-prosecution procedures, including some long-standing ones: "I am no friend of the rule allowing the credibility of a defendant who takes the stand to be impeached by proof of a criminal record."[3] He opposed permitting hearsay to substitute for in-court identifications[4] and advocated taking steps to reduce inaccurate eyewitness identifications, which he called "the greatest single factor in leading to the conviction of innocent people."[5] In a case in which a defendant made no claim that he was entrapped, the *prosecutor* introduced evidence that suggested that he was entrapped and then presented evidence of his other crimes to rebut entrapment. Friendly wrote to Judge Learned Hand, "The government ought not be able to utilize the dirty business of entrapment to damage the defendant still further unless he raises the issue."[6] Two years before the Supreme Court addressed the practice in *Bruton v. United States*,[7] Friendly reversed a conviction in *United States v. Bozza*[8] when prosecutors introduced one defendant's confession with the names of the codefendants he implicated blacked out. In *United States v. Kramer,*[9] he wrote "one of the first opinions employing collateral estoppel against [the] Government in a criminal case."[10] Friendly also endorsed the right to plead of inconsistent defenses: "I was correct in saying that the question of pleading both innocence and entrapment has long been a matter of controversy in this circuit but apparently was wrong in thinking that it had been settled. . . . I think the time has come to settle this in favor of the idea that inconsistent defenses can be pleaded. It has always seemed to me to be absurd to allow this in civil cases but to cavil about it in criminal ones."[11]

Friendly resisted change, however, in two circumstances. He opposed appellate review of sentences on the ground that it would generate an enormous amount of work and that appellate judges were not trained in the disciplines needed to do a good job.[12] He opposed televising court sessions because of "the effect of television on witnesses, jurors and, I regret to say, even judges."[13]

This chapter includes cases involving important matters of procedure. Unusually, the three principal ones received considerable press coverage.

Bronx congressman Mario Biaggi, a candidate for the Democratic Party nomination as well as the Conservative Party candidate for mayor of New York City in 1973, was ahead in the polls to succeed John V. Lindsay, who was not running for reelection.[14] On the front page of the April 18, 1973, *New York Times,* the reporter Nicholas Gage asserted that "authoritative sources" had revealed that Biaggi had "refused to answer at least 30 questions when he appeared before a Federal grand jury more than a year ago" and that he "invoked the Fifth Amendment on questions mostly on his finances, but that he answered many other questions."[15] The disclosures evidently were an unauthorized and illegal leak about Biaggi's grand jury testimony. Biaggi repeatedly and publicly denied that he had pleaded the Fifth Amendment privilege against self-incrimination. The story captivated the public.

To try to repair the considerable political damage the disclosures caused,[16] Biaggi bought five minutes of prime time on the three television networks on April 25, where he announced that he would file a motion the next day in the district court seeking the appointment of an unusual court consisting of three district judges to examine the grand jury transcript and make a public report whether he had claimed a constitutional privilege about his "personal finances and assets."[17] The next morning, however, U.S. Attorney Whitney North Seymour Jr. moved first, seeking the release to the public of the verbatim *transcript* of Biaggi's grand jury testimony, but redacted so as to eliminate the names of persons other than Biaggi in order to protect their privacy. Biaggi countermoved for full disclosure of all of his testimony on the ground that the redacted testimony would lead to speculation about the redacted names. District Judge Edmund Palmieri, ordinarily a studious and conservative judge, granted Seymour's motion and denied Biaggi's, saying, "[T]his court can only conclude that this [Biaggi's] blatantly unsanctioned petition was made with an expectation of its denial by the court, and for the purpose of publicly exploiting the court's denial of the motion. . . . A rigid application of the rule of secrecy under the unusual circumstances of this case would permit this salutary rule to be subverted for a use for which it was never intended."[18] Biaggi appealed.

For many centuries in England, the grand jury stood between the Crown and the people to protect them against its excesses. The grand jury is engraved in our Constitution. The Fifth Amendment reads, "No person shall be held to answer for a capital, or otherwise infamous crime, unless on a presentment or indictment of a Grand Jury." Among the protections is strict secrecy of grand jury proceedings, which originated in seventeenth-century England as a method of preventing abuses.[19] Federal grand jury secrecy is governed by Rule 6(e) of the Federal Rules of Criminal Procedure, which provides for disclosure in only three situations. Disclosure "may be made to the attorneys for the government for use in the performance of their duties," for the purpose of a motion to dismiss the indictment, and "in connection with a judicial proceeding." (The last does not include a judicial proceeding instituted for the purpose of obtaining disclosure.)[20] Unauthorized disclosures have led to prosecutions for obstruction of justice or punishment as contempt of court.[21]

Argument was one week later before Friendly, Hays, and William J. Jameson, a respected district judge from Montana and a friend of Friendly's.[22] From the start Friendly believed that Palmieri's decision was wrong and that the grand jury transcript should not be released, asking his clerk, Frederick Davis, rhetorically, "What does Rule 6(e) mean if it allows judges to release this kind of thing whenever they want to?" But when Friendly started writing his opinion, he concluded that he should have a copy of the transcript, and he told Davis to get it from the U.S. Attorney. At the end of the day, as he was walking toward the chambers' door, Friendly remarked to Davis, "Have you read the transcript? No? Well you better read it right away because we're changing the opinion and we're going to affirm."[23] But Friendly still had the problem of getting another judge to agree with him. Hays refused to budge from the position—previously Friendly's—that Rule 6(e) simply meant what it said and there were no exceptions. Jamison, however, would vote with Friendly.

Two days after argument Friendly filed his opinion in *In re Biaggi*,[24] which stated, "It is a tradition of our law that proceedings before a grand jury shall generally remain secret," a weaker statement of the principle than usual.[25] He listed the interests protected by the tradition:

> the interest of the government against disclosure of its investigation of crime which may forewarn the intended objects of its inquiry or inhibit future witnesses from speaking freely; the interest of a witness against the disclosure of testimony of others which he has had no opportunity to cross-examine or rebut, or of his own testimony on matters which may be irrelevant or where he may have been subjected to prosecutorial brow-beating without the protection of counsel; the similar interests of other persons who may have been unfavorably mentioned by grand jury witnesses or in questions of the prosecutor; protection of witnesses against reprisal; and the interests and protection of the grand jurors themselves.[26]

The secrecy of grand jury testimony was not absolute, Friendly observed, and while no disclosure could be made upon the application of the government alone, it could be made when the interested parties agreed, since no one would be harmed. Moreover, "[h]aving sought disclosure, Mr. Biaggi could not condition his demand upon this being done only in a manner harmful to others. Our reading of the grand jury testimony in redacted form indicates that there is little chance that the questions asked and answers given will provide a context for meaningful inference about the identities of the deleted names."[27] Friendly, relying on the "public interest," a term frequently used by his friend from California, Judge Roger Traynor, and other activist judges,[28] filed an opinion with only a limited amount of analysis and virtually no citation of authority or historical background. He cited one old district court decision in support of his argument: "Insofar as the rule of secrecy 'was designed for the protection of the witnesses who appear,' *In re Grand Jury Proceeding*, 4 F. Supp. 283, 284–285 (E.D. Pa. 1933), Mr. Biaggi waived this protection."[29] There was no failure of scholarship on the part of Friendly's chambers. No case had released grand jury minutes unconnected with a pending or anticipated judicial proceeding. No case had released grand jury minutes to the general public.[30] *Biaggi* did both.

Hays dissented. None of the exceptions in Rule 6(e) applied, he said, and the Rule did not permit a court to graft a new exception. Specifically, there was no "public interest" exception to the rule: "I do not believe that we have the power to legislate this additional exception and I therefore respectfully dissent."[31] Hays cited no cases. Unusually, the *New York Times* printed both opinions of the court and pictures of the three judges.[32]

Unmentioned by both opinions was powerful authority against Friendly's position. In *Doe v. Rosenberry*,[33] Learned Hand wrote, "We find it unnecessary to consider whether the common law would have authorized the [disclosure] order, because Rule 6(e) . . . is the measure of the plaintiff's privilege." Friendly cited *Rosenberry* in a footnote on a different point[34] but did not mention Hand's statement that Rule 6(e) was the extent of the privilege. The opinions simply ignored *United States v. Weinstein*,[35] an opinion Friendly wrote eighteen months earlier for a unanimous court. District Judge Jack Weinstein had dismissed an indictment after he had entered a judgment of conviction. Reversing on the ground that what Weinstein had done was impermissible under the Federal Rules of Criminal Procedure, Friendly stated that judges could not supplement the rules:

> [N]o Rule gives the judge an overriding power to terminate a criminal prosecution in which the Government's evidence has passed the test of legal sufficiency simply because he thinks that course would be most consonant with the interests of justice We believe the failure of the Rules to bestow such a power precludes its exercise. The Federal Rules of Criminal Procedure were designed to provide a uniform set of procedures to govern criminal cases within the federal courts consistent with the requirements of justice and sound administration. Where previously recognized powers were thought appropriate for inclusion in the rules, this was expressly done.[36]

Friendly ordered disclosure of the minutes, explaining that in the event that the transcript was publicly released, "we may wish to supplement this opinion so that the grounds for and the limits of our decision may be even more clearly understood." After the transcript's release, which showed that Biaggi had relied on the Fifth Amendment on numerous occasions in the grand jury, Friendly wrote that the issue Biaggi presented to the district judges "was framed, whether wittingly or not, in such a manner as to create a false impression in light of the publicity that had given rise to it."[37] Friendly made it rather clear that he thought the framing was witting. Biaggi had filed a carefully crafted statement with the district court: "These headlines are false in that at no time in my appearance before the Grand Jury on or about October 29, 1971 and November 26, 1971, was I ever asked a question about my personal finances and assets to which I claimed my constitutional privilege against self-incrimination under the Fifth Amendment to the Constitution of the United States, or any other constitutional privilege."[38]

In the contemporaneous Watergate scandal, that kind of carefully hedged statement was termed "a nondenial denial." The denial was not categorical and left a loophole that Biaggi pleaded the Fifth Amendment on another occasion or on another subject. The precise question that Biaggi framed in all likelihood would have required a negative answer, despite the substantial truth of the *New York Times'* accusation. Friendly concluded his supplementary opinion, "Our decision should therefore not be taken as demanding, or even authorizing, public disclosure of a witness' grand jury testimony in every case where he seeks this and the Government consents. It rests on the exercise of a sound discretion under the special circumstances of this case."[39] Friendly did not describe the special circumstances. While ordinarily studious in separating the principles of law from the identity and nature of the parties, he evidently concluded that Biaggi was unconscionably attempting to manipulate the judicial system with his lies. More than any of Friendly's other one-thousand-plus opinions, *Biaggi* eschewed theory and scholarship, even consistency, for rough, in fact very rough, justice. Many conscientious judges would have done the same thing.[40]

Biaggi lost the primary to Abraham Beame, who became mayor of New York City. Biaggi disappeared as a political force. In 1987 he was convicted for receiving bribes and for obstruction of justice and was sentenced to two and a half years in prison. In 1988 he was convicted again, this time for extortion, and received a sentence of eight years in prison.[41] Former New York City mayor Edward I. Koch has said that Biaggi's unsavory reputation would have made his election bad for New York City, adding that the disclosure of Biaggi's pleading the Fifth Amendment probably was the turning point in the election.[42] With Friendly and Hays voting for different outcomes, a district judge from Montana, who agreed with Friendly in every one of the thirty-six cases on which the two sat together, may have cast the deciding vote on the next mayor of New York City.

FRIENDLY FAVORED RIGHTS for targets of grand jury investigations. Unlike at a trial, targets of federal grand jury investigations have had no right to be present, no right to have counsel present, and, not surprisingly, no right to cross-examine witnesses. Targets also could not prevent the grand jury from relying on hearsay, even solely on hearsay, largely for the reason that allowing defendants to challenge their indictments would impose major delays. The Supreme Court announced that rule in *Costello v. United States*,[43] a case that required the use of 141 prosecution witnesses at trial. Dissenting a decade after *Costello*, in *United States v. Payton*,[44] Friendly found the limitation on the rights of defendants unacceptable when the case was a straightforward one and "the grand jury had no way of knowing that the testimony it heard was hearsay." He suggested, with some justification, the main reason the government persisted in using hearsay testimony by a surveilling agent was to avoid having the participating agent testify in the grand jury, which could allow the defendant to use that testimony to impeach his trial testimony.[45]

After writing several decisions that threatened to, but did not, dismiss an indictment in these circumstances,[46] Friendly, acting upon his belief that the only word Assistant U.S. Attorneys understand was "reversed,"[47] wrote an opinion for a unanimous court dismissing the indictment in *United States v. Estepa*,[48] a case similar to *Payton*. "[T]he prosecutor [cannot] deceive the grand jurors as to the shoddy merchandise they are getting so they can seek something better if they wish."[49] While the Second Circuit has maintained its vigil over activity in federal grand juries, no other circuit has dismissed an indictment on the grounds articulated in *Estepa*.[50]

A NEW YORK STATE COMMISSION appointed in the early 1970s to probe a major scandal in the nursing-home industry published devastating criticism of most of the industry and its regulators, both state and municipal. The commission's report led to the appointment of a Special New York State Prosecutor, Charles J. Hynes. A state grand jury empanelled by Hynes and a federal grand jury empanelled by the U.S. Attorney for the Southern District of New York filed indictments against a number of nursing-home owners and operators, including Bernard Bergman, a prominent figure in the industry, along with his son. Newspapers and television gave extensive coverage to the scandal, investigation, and indictments.

The federal charge against Bergman and his son focused on filing false tax returns and false Medicaid claims, while the state charges included larceny and bribing a state assemblyman. Extended negotiations with the two prosecutors led to two nearly identical and nearly simultaneous plea agreements. Bergman, who had provided important information and evidence to the prosecutors, alone would plead guilty in the federal proceeding to financial crimes and in the state proceeding to bribing a state legislator, and he would be sentenced first on the federal charges. Also, Hynes "will recommend to the Judge of the New York State Supreme Court who will sentence Bernard Bergman . . . [that] no sentence additional to that imposed by the United States District Judge on the federal indictment be imposed here." The explanation was that Bergman voluntarily disclosed the facts of his crimes and that the federal judge would know the relevant facts when he sentenced Bergman. Paragraph 8 of the plea agreement read, "Bernard Bergman will pay to the State of New York, voluntarily, without any civil action or litigation of any kind, whatever sums of money are owing to the State of New York from the Towers Nursing Home and any other nursing home in which he has an interest arising out of Medicaid payments. This amount shall be determined after consultation and examination of all financial and business records and documents by and between accountants representing the United States, the State of New York, and Bernard Bergman."[51]

Bergman subsequently pleaded guilty to both indictments on the same day. State Supreme Court Justice Aloysius J. Melia, who took Bergman's guilty plea, explained to him that though he could sentence Bergman up to the maximum of four years on the state charge, he ordinarily accepted a prosecutor's recommendation and saw no reason why he would not do so in Bergman's case. In fact, he had never failed to accept the District Attorney's recommendation, as Bergman's lawyers knew.[52]

A dispute promptly arose between Bergman and Hynes concerning paragraph 8, both with respect to the amount owed and the timing of the payments. Hynes claimed that Bergman owed at least $2.5 million, while Bergman refused to present a number. When criticized by federal District Judge Marvin E. Frankel for failing to do so, Bergman came up with the number $363,877, which caused Hynes to tell Melia that he considered the plea bargain to be breached. Regarding the timing of the payments, which was not mentioned in the plea agreement, Hynes wanted payment before sentencing; Bergman wanted sentencing first. Melia informed the parties that payment came first.

When Frankel sentenced Bergman to four months' imprisonment, the media erupted with criticism of the short sentence. Hynes issued a statement: "I am extraordinarily disappointed by the sentence that Dr. Bergman received today. One wonders whether essential justice has been accomplished when a man such as Bernard Bergman is given this kind of sentence."[53] When Bergman appeared before Melia soon after the federal sentencing, the amount Bergman conceded that he owed had inexplicably quadrupled, from $363,000 to $1.4 million, and he again asked for immediate sentencing. Hynes remained firm both on his demand for $2.5 million and that payment precede sentencing. When Hynes obtained the appointment of an accounting firm to arbitrate the disagreement, Bergman quickly accepted the state's figure and agreed to sign a confession of judgment.

At the sentencing in state court, two months after the federal sentencing, Hynes stated, "Since both items of the agreement have been satisfied, I have the obligation to fulfill my commitment under the March 4th agreement and, your Honor, would recommend that whatever sentence you impose be a concurrent one with the Federal sentence imposed on June 17, 1976. . . . [I]t is in recognition that the agreement was complied with by the defendant [in] both areas, cooperation and restitution, I made the recommendation I was required to make."[54]

Bergman's trial attorney, Gustave Newman, said he wanted to be sure that Hynes was recommending no prison time in addition to what Frankel had imposed. Hynes stated that that was his recommendation, and Newman said "I think [*sic*] you."[55] But Melia was not convinced. Citing Bergman's "shilly shally on the amount owed to the People of the State" and his absence of remorse, to Bergman's chagrin Melia sentenced him to a term of one year in prison to follow the federal sentence.

After serving his federal sentence, Bergman hired a new attorney, Nathan Lewin, who had clerked for Justice Harlan, and appealed the additional prison term to the Appellate Division of the State Supreme Court, which affirmed the sentence without opinion and denied him leave to appeal to the New York Court of Appeals. When Bergman filed a petition for a writ of habeas corpus in the federal district court, he replaced Lewin with Professor Alan M. Dershowitz, a colorful and controversial member of the Harvard Law School faculty. Bergman was allowed to remain at large pending consideration of his petition.

Following an evidentiary hearing in the federal district court and its denial of the petition in *Bergman v. Lefkowitz*, Bergman appealed on the ground that Hynes violated his plea bargain. He argued that Hynes's public statement criticizing the briefness of the federal sentence destroyed his ability to comply with his obligation to recommend no additional prison time and that his statement to Melia was woefully inadequate in the circumstances. Dershowitz argued in his brief and more cogently at oral argument (where he showed more clearly how his two claims reinforced each other) that Bergman was concerned that Melia, an elected state judge subject to political pressures from his constituents, would be inclined to punish Bergman harshly. So Bergman and his lawyers had bargained for and obtained an arrangement for a federal judge with lifetime tenure (Frankel) and then the prosecutor (Hynes) to commit themselves to a fair (short) sentence, which would give Melia political cover when he imposed no additional prison time on the state charges. Responding to Dershowitz, the state Assistant Attorney General argued in effect that contentions about the content of Hynes's statement constituted a charade, since Melia obviously knew exactly what happened and why, and what Hynes said before Melia did not really matter. But that response ignored Dershowitz's argument that the relevant audience was not Melia, but his constituency. For Friendly it was a distinction without a difference and he did not mention it in his opinion.

Friendly read the agreement with Portia's eyes: "Admittedly the plea bargain did not expressly prohibit the Special Prosecutor from commenting on the federal sentence. Still it is not unreasonable to read into the agreement an implied term that the Special Prosecutor would not comment on the federal sentence in a manner that would constitute a reneging on his obligation to recommend that the state judge impose no additional sentence or make it practically impossible for the state judge to accept such a recommendation. He did neither."[56] Moreover, Friendly said, Hynes's statement to the press did not suggest that he would not adhere to the plea bargain if Bergman performed his obligation to make restitution.

Friendly also rejected Bergman's claim that Hynes spoke "grudgingly or, as Judge Goettel stated, 'tepidly.'" Relying primarily on an argument that Hynes did not make, Friendly concluded that Hynes made the recommendation he had promised:

> In almost all cases where a prosecutor agrees in a plea bargain to make a sentence recommendation, he is recommending not what he wants but something less, which the agreement requires. This is the very essence of the bargain and the sentencing judge is well aware of it. We thus see nothing sinister in Hynes' stating that he was acting in pursuance of the plea agreement unless something in his facial expression or his tone indicated to the judge that he would prefer not to have his recommendation accepted. There is no evidence to that effect. . . . We would not regard a rule permitting a plea bargain to be avoided as a denial of due process because of lack of adequate gusto in a prosecutor's recommendation, particularly when this is discerned by defense counsel only after a disappointing sentence, as promoting the sound administration of criminal justice.[57]

After concluding that "admittedly Hynes made the recommendation he had promised to make," Friendly ordered the immediate issuance of the mandate denying the writ, asking Judge Mansfield to "ride herd on this and make sure that this instruction is carried out and that the mandate does in fact issue immediately." But Friendly was not sanguine about ending the case soon. He added, "None of this, of course, will deter Mr. Dershowitz from making a motion to recall the mandate and to grant a further stay pending petition for certiorari under [Federal Rule of Civil Procedure] 41(b)."[58]

Dershowitz's 1982 book, *The Best Defense*, reargued his petition, while haranguing Friendly for concluding "inexplicably and without support in the record" that "*admittedly* Hynes made the recommendation he had promised to make."[59] Thirty years after the case ended, Dershowitz, still smarting, explained that the defense "absolutely, categorically disputed [the point]" and that Friendly's statement "was the worst thing you can say about a lawyer."[60] Dershowitz, however, missed Friendly's thrust. Friendly was not talking about Dershowitz when he used the word "admittedly"; he undoubtedly was referring to Gustave Newman's "thank you" after his request for an emendation was rewarded.[61] People do not ordinarily say "thank you" when they receive less than they feel they are entitled to.

FRIENDLY DID NOT LIKE bullies. He preferred winners to have the stronger facts and arguments. His view made him antagonistic to over-reaching by a frequent—and powerful—party in his court, the United States of America. While ordinarily an admirer of the U.S. Attorney's offices, he did not like it when the prosecutors piled on or shaved corners. Thus, he chastised a prosecutor whose summation to the jury falsely suggested that the government "is carefully monitoring the testimony of the cooperating witness to make sure that the latter is not stretching the facts—something the prosecutor usually is quite unable to do."[62] Friendly dissented and voted to reverse when a prosecutor withheld exculpatory evidence from the grand jury when responding to a question that called for its disclosure.[63] He was inclined to give the government some slack, but not when he saw reasons to question its integrity.

As part of its investigation of the Queens County District Attorney's Office that led to *United States v. Archer*,[64] the government, as it sometimes did, created a sting, under which Sante A. Bario, an agent of the U.S. Bureau of Narcotics and Dangerous Drugs, posed as Sam Barone, a "hit man" from Las Vegas. After he was "arrested" by Vincent Murano, a New York City policeman who was part of the sting, for possession of two loaded pistols, a felony, Bario let it be known that he was willing to pay money to have the case dismissed. After posting bail, Bario met the defendant Leon Wasserberger, an associate of a bail bondsman, who introduced him to the defendant Frank Klein, a Queens attorney. Klein told Bario that the only feasible course of action was to have the grand jury return no indictment, which would cost at least $10,000, with some of it going to a Queens Assistant District Attorney. After Bario agreed, Klein told him that he had spoken to the Queens Assistant District Attorney in charge of the grand jury, who turned out to be the defendant Norman Archer, the highest ranking black prosecutor in the office. In response to a request by Klein for a telephone number where he could be reached in Las Vegas, Bario said he would be out of the country. (Friendly's opinion remarked that in telling Klein that he was going to be out of the country, "Bario responded, truthfully for once.")[65] Later, Bario told Wasserman to have him paged at the Sahara Hotel or leave a message there; in fact Bario had no contacts with the hotel. The final price was $15,000, to be shared among the trio of conspirators. A week later Archer questioned Bario before the grand jury, where Bario told a fictitious story invented by Archer, who examined him sympathetically and added a few more fictions.[66] The Queens County grand jury did not indict Bario.

A federal grand jury, however, indicted and a petit jury convicted Archer, Klein, and Wasserberger for violation of the Travel Act, section 1952 of Title 18, the federal criminal code. The provision—formally entitled "Interstate and Foreign Travel or Transportation in Aid of Racketeering Enterprises"—made it a federal crime when someone "travels in interstate or foreign commerce or uses any facility in interstate or foreign commerce, including the mail, with intent to . . . promote, manage, establish, carry on, or facilitate the promotion, management, or carrying on, of any unlawful activity." The defendants appealed.

Friendly began his opinion not by admonishing the defendants, who included a state prosecutor and a defense lawyer who had displayed an all-too-eager willingness to fix a state criminal case for cash, but with criticism of the method the government employed to root out corruption within the criminal justice system: "We do not at all share the Government's pride in its achievement of causing the bribery of a state assistant district attorney by a scheme which involved lying to New York City police officers and perjury before New York judges and grand jurors; to our minds the participants' attempt to set up a federal crime for which these defendants stand convicted went beyond any proper prosecutorial role and needlessly injected the Federal Government into a matter of state concern."[67]

Considering whether to dismiss the case on the ground of prosecutorial misconduct, Friendly quoted the celebrated passage in Brandeis's dissent in *Olmstead v. United States*:[68] "If the government becomes a law-breaker, it breeds contempt for the law; it invites every man to become a law unto himself; it invites anarchy." Friendly's view of law enforcement efforts against official corruption was quite puritanical: "We are not sure how we would decide this question if decision were required. Our intuition inclines us to the belief that this case would call for the application of Mr. Justice Brandeis' dissent in *Olmstead*. . . . [T]he Government agents displayed an arrogant disregard for the sanctity of the state judicial and police process. . . . Since we conclude reversal to be required on another ground, we leave the resolution of this difficult question for another day. We hope, however, that the lesson of this case may obviate the necessity for such a decision on our part."[69]

Friendly turned to "the question whether the prosecution should be dismissed because the initiation of the investigation was founded on a grossly inflated conception of the role of the federal criminal law." The bribery was a violation of only state law, and there was no indication, Friendly said, that the Queens District Attorney's Office was violating any federal law. Taking a narrow view of the Travel Act, one of many federal statutes that, to his displeasure, federalized essentially local crimes,[70] he dissected the three groups of interstate telephone calls on which the government relied to prove a violation of the Travel Act and reversed the convictions "for insufficiency of the evidence to show a violation of, or a conspiracy to violate, the Travel Act, with instructions to dismiss the indictment."[71] Friendly opposed converting state crimes into federal crimes through an expansive construction of the Commerce Clause (although he accepted federal jurisdiction when federalism considerations were less pronounced).[72]

Supported by *amicus curiae* briefs filed by the District Attorneys of New York and Queens counties and the New York Attorney General, the government petitioned for rehearing, which prompted a *per curiam* opinion written by Friendly quite different from his initial one. Friendly acknowledged the prosecutors' desirable effort to "clean these Aegean stables of the State," and that dismissal of Archer from his post as a result of the investigation "is indeed a 'good' result, as the petition repeatedly emphasizes." What seems to have changed his attitude, but not his mind, were facts (mostly not in the court record, his *per curiam* opinion noted).[73] He also mentioned "the copious citation of cases, including many not included in [the government's] original brief, not one of [which] supports application of the Travel Act where the sole 'federal' elements were telephone calls from or to an undercover agent."[74] Characteristically, he examined and distinguished cases on the basis of their facts. Friendly denied the petition.

Friendly was not through with Archer, whose case was turned over to a special prosecutor appointed by Governor Rockefeller. After being indicted and convicted in state courts, Archer and his codefendants filed a petition for a writ of habeas corpus. Affirming the federal district judge who had denied the writ, Friendly rejected Archer's argument based on prosecutorial misconduct with the statement that there was no shocking conduct directed at the defendants, and that the discussion in the previous opinion, as well as in *Olmstead*, was "concerned with a proper principle of federal criminal procedure, not with a question of due process applicable to the states."[75]

FRIENDLY WROTE the court's opinion in what appears to be the first recorded case involving a prosecutor's hypnotizing a government witness before trial in an effort to obtain additional facts and testimony.[76] Largely on identification testimony by Joseph Michael Caron, a District of Connecticut jury convicted James Miller for conspiracy to import heroin, and the Second Circuit affirmed.[77] One of Miller's posttrial motions for a new trial claimed that the government failed to disclose to the defense its pretrial hypnosis of Caron.

The disclosure to defense counsel of Caron's hypnosis was serendipitous. A year after the Second Circuit affirmed Miller's conviction, Steven Duke, his dogged and creative counsel, sought the consent of U.S. Attorney (and later Judge) Jon Newman to place Caron under hypnosis in the presence of counsel for both sides to try to obtain evidence to upset Miller's conviction. Because the case was hardly overwhelming and he wanted to make sure Miller was guilty, Newman gave his consent. Just before being placed under hypnosis, Caron asked, "Is this going to be like the one Butler gave me in Texas?" This question astonished everyone. Caron had been arrested in Texas along with Miller and others for several crimes, including the sale of eighty-six kilograms of drugs. To help him recollect details regarding Miller's case, an Assistant U.S. Attorney in Texas, William B. Butler, enlisted a hypnotist. Soon after the hypnosis, Miller's case was severed and transferred for trial to the District of Connecticut, and Butler traveled there and interrogated Caron further. While Newman conducted most of the trial, Butler examined Caron. Since Caron was uncertain about new details he had disclosed while under hypnosis, Butler neither asked him about any refreshed recollection at the trial nor mentioned the hypnosis to Newman.[78]

Friendly reversed "with some reluctance" and ordered a new trial:

> [T]he defense already possessed an abundance of impeaching material, the hypnosis incident seems without much force apart from the elaboration of the defense's psychiatric experts, and we have our own view how seriously a jury of Connecticut Yankees would have been likely to regard that. Still, as the record stands, the hypnosis had arguably placed at least some obstacle in the way of one of the most valuable protections accorded Miller by way of the Sixth Amendment—the possibility that the sanctity of the oath and effective cross examination might lead Caron to recant his identification and at least to admit doubt. . . . If the price of our decision should be the ultimate escape of a guilty man rather than the vindication of an innocent one, this is the kind of case where that price is worth paying.[79]

Friendly, concerned about creating false memory, accepted that "repeating what had been said when previously the man had some doubts, under the hypnosis, will at least lessen if not remove these."[80] While he rejected Miller's argument that the prosecutor's participation in Caron's hypnosis should bar Caron from appearing as a witness in any retrial,[81] he allowed a significant role to the volatile discipline of hypnosis by reversing the conviction on the ground that the defendant was denied cross-examination of

Caron on the hypnosis.[82] This was a practical solution that was respectful of defendants' constitutional rights, although Miller's plausible claim of innocence may have made reversal more palatable for Friendly.[83] When Miller was retried, a jury acquitted him.[84] A later study of hypnosis states that although it does not increase the accuracy of a witness's testimony, "particularly troubling for courts, hypnosis leads to increased, but misplaced, confidence on the part of subjects regarding their memory of events."[85] This was a case in which the U.S. Attorney, the defense counsel, and the judges did their jobs and more.

CHAPTER FIFTEEN

Specific Crimes

FRIENDLY USUALLY READ statutes creating crimes narrowly and with common sense so as not to unduly expand their reach, which is evident in his opinions on international narcotics conspiracies and prosecutions of young men for evading the draft during the Vietnam War, discussed in this chapter. Two other cases demonstrated his concern that statutes creating crimes be read precisely. In *United States v. Cioffi*,[1] a prosecution for the unlawful "use" of counterfeit stamps, the trial judge defined "use" to include employing the stamps to induce the purchase of similar stamps. Friendly reversed the conviction: "Both the context and the history of the statute indicate that 'use' in § 501 means use for a postal purpose, not 'use' in a broader, colloquial sense," a point, incidentally, that Cioffi's brief neglected to make. (The Supreme Court reached a contrary result twenty years later in *Smith v. United States*, upholding conviction for a case in which a gun was "used" in a narcotics transaction—it was exchanged for narcotics.)[2] In *United States v. Ivic*, Friendly scrutinized the law's language and legislative history to find that the Racketeer Influenced and Corrupt Organizations Act (RICO)[3] applied only to criminal conduct that had an economic motivation and not to terrorist activity, a dispositive point missed by the defendants.[4]

When Friendly became a judge, it was very unusual to find a lawyer or an accountant prosecuted for stock fraud. Robert M. Morgenthau changed that in 1961 when he became U.S. Attorney for the Southern District of New York, the federal judicial district of the New York Stock Exchange and the headquarters of many financial institutions. If fact, before Morgenthau took office, it was the policy of that office not to prosecute lawyers for many financial crimes.[5] Friendly was sympathetic to Morgenthau's efforts, as demonstrated by his opinions in two early Morgenthau prosecutions. In *United States v. Benjamin*[6] a stock promoter, his lawyer, and a certified public accountant appealed their convictions for stock fraud. Friendly wrote, "This appeal concerns another of those sickening financial frauds which so sadly memorialize the rapacity of the perpetrators and the gullibility, and perhaps the cupidity, of the victims. It is unusual in that the vehicle, American Equities Corporation, owned nothing at all—and, in a happier sense, in that the SEC was able to nip the fraud quite early in the bud."[7]

To the accountant's claim that he was not guilty of fraud because his false audit reports, which depicted the corporate vehicle for the fraud as the owner of properties and companies it neither owned nor had any firm arrangement to acquire, were labeled "pro forma," Friendly answered that the argument "involves a complete misconception of the duties of an accountant in issuing a report thus entitled. . . . It would be insulting an honorable profession to suppose that a certified public accountant may take the misrepresentations of a corporate official as to companies it proposes to acquire, combine their balance sheets without any investigation as to the arrangements for their acquisition or suitable provision reflecting payment of the purchase price, and justify the meaningless result simply by an appliqué of two Latin words."[8]

Friendly resoundingly indicted white-collar crime by professionals:

> In our complex society the accountant's certificate and the lawyer's opinion can be instruments for inflicting pecuniary loss more potent than the chisel or the crowbar. Of course, Congress did not mean that any mistake of law or misstatement of fact should subject an attorney or an accountant to criminal liability simply because more skillful practitioners would not have made them. But Congress equally could not have intended that men holding themselves out as members of these ancient professions should be able to escape criminal liability on a plea of ignorance when they have shut their eyes to what was plainly to be seen or have represented a knowledge that knew they did not possess.[9]

If *Benjamin* was a relatively easy case in the sense that the evidence was strong and the defendants far from leaders in their professions, the circumstances were very different in *United States v. Simon.*[10] Defendants were a senior partner, a junior partner, and a senior associate in the internationally known accounting firm of Lybrand, Ross Bros. & Montgomery. Friendly wrote, "While every criminal conviction is important to the defendant, there is a special poignancy and a corresponding responsibility on reviewing judges when, as here, the defendants have been men of blameless lives and respected members of a learned profession." He added, "This is no less true because the trial judge, wisely in our view, imposed no prison sentences."[11] Defendants called on a pillar of the bar, David W. Peck, the former presiding judge of New York's First Appellate Division, to argue their appeal. While most of the oral argument dealt in deathly seriousness with the legal and factual issues, Friendly was responsible for one moment of levity, which Peck did not welcome. Peck argued that the government had stopped at nothing to convict his clients, noting that prosecutor Peter Fleming had actually shed tears in his summation. Friendly leaned forward and asked Peck, "Where is that in the record?"[12]

The charged offense was based on a single footnote in the financial statement of Continental Vending Machine Corporation, headed by Harold Roth, which failed to disclose that Continental's loans to its subsidiary Valley Commercial Corp. were not for a proper business purpose, but to assist Roth in his personal financial problems.[13] In Morgenthau's words, "It was a thin case," but "I prosecuted them because they were guilty."[14] The first trial ended with a hung jury. The second jury convicted the defendants only after it reported itself deadlocked and the judge sent the jurors back for further deliberations. District Judge Walter R. Mansfield announced that he would have acquitted the defendants.[15]

What made the case particularly difficult was that the defendants argued that their actions were consistent with generally accepted accounting procedures (GAAP)—and the prosecution did not seriously disagree. As described by Friendly, "The defendants called eight expert independent accountants, an impressive array of leaders of the profession. . . . With due respect to the Government's accounting witnesses, an SEC staff accountant, and, in rebuttal, its chief accountant, who took a contrary view, we are bound to say that they hardly compared with defendants' witnesses in aggregate auditing experience or professional eminence." In fact, the SEC's chief accountant had declined to testify in the prosecution's direct case.[16] The court accepted the prosecutor's position that conformance with GAAP was evidence, but not conclusive proof, of legality. Friendly paraphrased the defendants' argument and then answered it:

> We join defendants' counsel in assuming that the mere fact that a company has made advances to an affiliate does not ordinarily impose a duty on an accountant to investigate what the affiliate has done with them or even to disclose that the affiliate has made a loan to a common officer if this has come to his attention. But it simply cannot be true that an accountant is under no duty to disclose what he knows when he has reason to believe that, to a mate-

rial extent, a corporation is being operated not to carry out its business in the interest of all the stockholders but for the private business of its president. . . . If certification does not at least imply that the corporation has not been looted by insiders so far as the accountants know, or, if it has been, that the diversion has been made good beyond peradventure (or adequately reserved against) and effective steps taken to prevent a recurrence, it would mean nothing, and the reliance placed on it by the public would be a snare and a delusion.[17]

Like the eighteenth-century Lord Mansfield (William Murray), Lord Chief Justice of the King's Bench and the second highest judicial officer in England, Friendly saw that it was not enough for people in the securities industries to follow the standards of the marketplace. The commercial world needed just, predicable, and enforced rules to gain the confidence of the public.[18] The leaders of "learned professions" served the public, not vice versa. "This was a trial bitterly but honorably fought, by exceedingly capable and well-prepared counsel, before an able judge experienced in complicated litigation and a highly intelligent jury. Finding that the evidence was sufficient for submission to the jury and that no legal errors were committed, we must let the verdict stand."[19]

Four years after the case ended a professor wrote an article about it that complained that the opinion was hard to understand.[20] Friendly responded with a letter that "describe[d] the mental process through which [he] went in preparing the opinion," including the proper role of industry standards. The judge's unusual account is quoted in full:

I began by considering how we would view this if it were a civil case. It seemed to me perfectly evident that accountants can no more be permitted to establish generally accepted principles which will protect them from a charge of negligence than any other profession. To say that proper auditing procedures under no circumstances require investigation of advances to a company owned by a principal stockholder would be like a rule of a medical association that a surgeon is under no obligation to make inquiry whether someone about to undergo an operation has had any coronary difficulties, or a rule of a bar association that a lawyer advising on the purchase of real estate need look only at the contract and has no obligation to cause a title search to be made.

Our problem, however, was that we were dealing with a criminal case, and the difficulty was enhanced by the apparent lack of motive on the part of the defendants. The solution I found was that the generally accepted principles could not fairly be construed to cover a case where an accountant has come upon evidence clearly putting him on notice of actual fraud. In such cases all generally accepted principles must be considered as yielding to the overall duty of an accountant to ferret this out.[21]

Friendly rejected the idea that one team could set the rules to its advantage.

FRIENDLY INTRODUCED his opinion in *United States v. Borelli,* his most important conspiracy opinion, in the following way: "[T]he instant case gives point to Mr. Justice Jackson's description of conspiracy as 'that elastic, sprawling and pervasive offense,' whose development exemplifies, in Judge Cardozo's phrase, the 'tendency of a principle to expand itself to the limit of its logic'—and perhaps beyond."[22] He next capsulized his difficulty with the government's evidence:

> The [narcotics] conspiracy is alleged to have begun in 1950 and to have lasted until 1959. The only acts of participation proved as to one appellant were in 1951. As to others there was no evidence of participation later than 1955. Two who first appear in 1958 were found to have been in "partnership in crime" with those who, so far as the proof shows, left the stage seven and three years before. Tacitly recognizing inclusion of all the appellants in a single conspiracy to be something of a *tour de force,* the Government contends in its able brief and argument that the convictions are buttressed by impressive authority and impeccable logic.[23]

Involved were exporters, importers, wholesalers, and runners. New participants replaced those who were imprisoned or otherwise taken totally or partially out of action. A new source of supply was found in the spring of 1958, resulting in a "second phase" of the conspiracy. A cooperating member of the conspiracy, Salvatore Rinaldo, bore the burden of presenting the government's case. Two other conspirators supplemented or corroborated parts of his story, while narcotics agents confirmed various comings and goings.[24]

The principal issue on appeal was whether the government's evidence, which the court of appeals was required to accept on the defendants' appeal, demonstrated the existence of one conspiracy or several distinct conspiracies. (This is a typical instance of the major issue on appeal having little or nothing to do with the issues fought in front of the jury.) The issue was "extraordinarily significant," Friendly asserted. Not only would a finding of several conspiracies result in reversal and a retrial, actually several smaller retrials, but it also would affect rulings on "the admission of declarations that are often presented" and "bore importantly on the problem of the statute of limitations."[25] Under the rules of evidence, a statement made by one conspirator during and in furtherance of a conspiracy is admissible against all members of that conspiracy. Similarly, a conspirator is responsible for actions of others who are members of the same conspiracy. Dividing the single charged conspiracy into several conspiracies would weaken the evidence and lose all defendants who and whose co-conspirators in a narrowed conspiracy did nothing after mid-1957. This is one example of Friendly's seeing the law as a complex organism and not a set of isolated rules.[26]

To make sense of the problem, Friendly evaluated the venerable concept of conspiracy in its contemporary context (which no defendant argued):

> The basic difficulty arises in applying the seventeenth century notion of conspiracy, where the gravamen of the offense was the making of an *agreement* to commit a readily identifiable crime or series of crimes, such as murder or robbery to what in substance is the conduct of an illegal business over a period of years. There has been a tendency in such cases to "deal with the crime of conspiracy as though it were a group [of men] rather than an act" of agreement. Although it is usual and often necessary in conspiracy cases for the agreement to be proved by inference from acts, the gist of the offense remains the agreement, and it is therefore essential to determine what kind of agreement or understanding existed as to each defendant.[27]

It was difficult, Friendly continued, to tell how broad an agreement can be inferred from the purchase of narcotics in bulk. The purchaser knows there are others involved in supplying and distributing the narcotics over an uncertain period of time, but there must be limits. Friendly recognized that the scope, purpose, and nature of a conspiracy may be different from the point of view of each member, a concept that had been ignored in thousands of cases.[28] He rejected the broad language in some opinions as attributable "to extravagant claims of prosecutors that a few acts of assistance by persons on the periphery warrant a jury's finding an agreement to participate forever in the activities of the central core."[29] Friendly both clarified and rejuvenated the concept of conspiracy, which had become muddled through slipshod application.

Friendly decided that even though there was sufficient evidence to permit a finding of a single conspiracy, the convictions could not stand because the instructions to the jury were inadequate. He concluded that the jury had to decide the extent of each defendant's agreement based on the trial judge's summary of the evidence applicable to him. The defendants' lawyers had not objected to the jury instructions at the trial, so Friendly imposed a greater burden on the defendants to prevail, namely, proof of "plain error." In fact, the defendants' claim on appeal was that the evidence demonstrated multiple conspiracies, not that the instructions were deficient, a quite different argument. *Borelli* was the rare opinion in which Friendly reversed despite the defendants' failure to give the district judge a fair opportunity to correct an error.[30] He seemed to have been unwilling to allow a large number of disparately situated defendants to be convicted by an almost certainly confused jury when the government was in a position to provide sensible trials and to give the jury the opportunity to sift the evidence properly.[31] Courts have cited his opinion well over three hundred times for a variety of legal points.[32]

THE LATE 1960S and early 1970s were for many a time of passionate opposition to the Vietnam War. Rabid demonstrators and rabid police triggered riots in the streets, and disapproving students closed down universities in protest over the war. Hundreds of thousands of people marched on Washington. Friendly's children and their spouses recall no discussion with him about the morality of the war, perhaps because none of them lived in New York City at the time, and his views on the war remain unknown.[33] What they remember are discussions with him about their desire to demonstrate against the war. A Republican white male professional in his sixties, he was hardly enthusiastic at the prospect, but, perhaps surprisingly, he did not try to stop his offspring from participating. After national guardsmen shot students at Kent State University, Ellen told her father that she wanted to participate in demonstrations. His reply was that, although he didn't agree with her, she was free to do so.[34] When the judge's daughter-in-law, Irene Friendly, went to a potentially violent demonstration in Washington, D.C., with one of her small children in tow, they ended up having to duck into a building in order to avoid inhaling tear gas. But even that experience did not cause Friendly to issue a rebuke.[35] He was tolerant of dissent, at least when it had an intellectual basis.

As both the Vietnam War and opposition to it heated up, more and more young men sought to avoid the draft, many by claiming that they were conscientious objectors. Few if any areas of the law precipitated as large a proportion of dissents within the Second Circuit as Selective Service Act cases. Between 1963 and 1973 Friendly sat on appeals from twelve convictions for violations of the Act or denials of petitions for writs of habeas corpus filed by inductees who challenged their induction. Of the twelve, six prompted a dissent. Of the cases in which the court divided, Friendly voted for the government in three and for the defendant in three; between mid-1965 and mid-1968 the dissent rate in the Second Circuit overall was 3.2 percent.[36] His memorandum to his colleagues in 1969 reflected his ambivalence: "Although I am not a great enthusiast over c.o. claims, particularly those stimulated by a notice to report for induction, we have here the case of a young man whose up-bringing and long-held views are exactly of the sort that Congress meant to protect."[37] His Selective Service opinions demonstrate evenhandedness with defendants whose conduct many considered unpatriotic and worse.

A local Selective Service Board rejected the claim of Vincent Francis McGee, a divinity student, for conscientious objector status. His indictment in *United States v. McGee*[38] charged him with failure to report for induction (Count 1) and failure to submit to a physical examination and other violations (Counts 2 through 4). After McGee's conviction by a jury, District Judge Thomas Murphy, a walrus of a man who had been New York City Police Commissioner, sentenced him to two years in prison on each of the four counts, to be served concurrently. When the case got to Friendly in early 1970, he told his clerk A. Raymond Randolph that he was considering dismissing McGee's appeal under the doctrine of exhaustion of administrative remedies because of McGee's failure to have appealed his classification within the Selective Service System before going to court. Randolph described what happened: "'What do you think?' Friendly asked. I began by saying that application of the exhaustion doctrine in this criminal prosecution struck me as exceedingly harsh. 'Harsh!' he exclaimed, 'don't tell me about harsh. You're here to give me your legal analysis, not your feelings.'"[39]

After the argument the panel preliminarily voted unanimously to affirm McGee's conviction. Months went by before Wilfred Feinberg, the judge to whom writing the opinion had been assigned, announced that he had changed his vote from affirmance to reversal because he believed that applying the exhaustion doctrine would be "too harsh."[40] With Feinberg dissenting, Friendly (with Judge Smith joining his opinion) decided against McGee on the basis of his failure to exhaust administrative remedies, without disputing that McGee was deeply devoted to becoming a Catholic priest and morally opposed to the war.

McGee sought and received review in the Supreme Court. In an exceptional telephone call and note to Randolph, by then an assistant to the Solicitor General, the office that represented the government in the Supreme Court, Friendly implored Randolph to try to do something to reduce McGee's sentence. The sentence was too harsh, Friendly said.[41] But there was nothing Randolph could do. The Supreme Court affirmed the conviction, eight to one, leaving McGee with the prospect of serving two years in prison.[42]

McGee enlisted the New York Civil Liberties Union in his cause and moved before Judge Murphy to vacate his conviction or, alternatively, to reduce his sentence. Murphy denied the motion and McGee appealed. Friendly set aside as marred by error the conviction on Count 1 and then, over a strong dissent by Judge William Timbers, vacated McGee's sentence on the other counts and sent the case back to Murphy for resentencing. In the majority opinion for himself and Montana District Judge Jameson, Friendly wrote that since Count 1 of McGee's indictment was the most serious, Murphy's sentencing might have been influenced by the conviction on Count 1, and he should either reduce the sentence on the other counts or explain why he wouldn't.[43] Dissenting, Timbers said that Murphy had acted well within his discretion in imposing the two-year sentence on Counts 2 through 4 and that Friendly was improperly interfering with the sentencing process.[44]

Rarely does a district judge have a chance to give measure for measure to a judge on the circuit court, and Murphy made the most of his opportunity, both substantively and stylistically. Thus, he wrote, "We must first digress to call attention to some inadvertent statements in the majority opinion of the court, since they cast a shadow on our judgment where none exists." He continued, "Whether Count 1 was 'most serious' or 'far more serious,' as the majority opinion repeated three times—the undeniable fact remains that the Congress has determined that all are equally serious, since it affixed a five-year sentence and a $10,000 fine for the maximum punishment as to each. Again, the court characterized the two-year concurrent sentence we imposed as *severe* in the opinion of the Government (see fn. 6). This, too, must be inadvertent error, since nowhere in the Government's brief is there such a characterization. Obviously the sentence is mathematically lenient if it is mensurative by what Congress has authorized."[45]

Murphy expressed annoyance at "the direction to share in the appellate court's belief that the sentence should be reduced or, as a minimum standard, to give at least a summary explanation of our reasons for declining to do so. . . . [W]e would not reduce the sentence by one day no matter what the 'belief' of the Court of Appeals is. The sentence is within the statutory limit and, as Judge Timbers said so cogently, 'It is none of our appellate business.' All of this aside, herewith is our *apologia* for declining to homologate the court's belief (direction?) that we should reduce the sentences on Counts 2 through 4."[46]

Murphy produced a fusillade of reasons for his sentence, including McGee's lack of candor, the seriousness of the crimes charged in the indictment, the fact that the crimes were committed at different times, McGee's "stiff-neckedness" (quoting the court of appeals opinion), his misguided sense of martyrdom (his attorney likened him to Martin Luther), and "Mr. Justice Marshall's analysis in affirming the conviction." Noting McGee's reluctant testimony that he lacked sponsorship by a bishop to become a priest, Murphy slashed, "During the trial we always had a serious doubt about McGee's intention to become an ordained Catholic priest." He added that he often sentenced people who enjoyed good reputations— "doctors, lawyers, accountants, and a host of others"—"In fact, I remember a district judge sentencing a judge of the Court of Appeals to jail for two years," a reference to the mortifying conviction for bribery of Second Circuit Judge Martin T. Manton in 1939.[47] Murphy closed, "As a famous Irishman said in concluding his allocution before he was condemned to death, 'I have done.' "[48]

Friendly again wrote Randolph, "Can't you get someone in the Criminal Division to show a little sense. McGee has really been imprisoned long enough." A month later he wrote again to Randolph: "Unfortunately, Judge Murphy did become quite obstinate on the remand of *McGee*. Whether he would have done so but for the hint of Judge Timbers, we will never know." Friendly continued, "McGee has appealed again, and I have granted a motion for a preference, but I must say I do not see what we can do for him. I do wish you could get the Criminal Division either to relent or, if that is not possible, to intervene with the parole board. This man has already been in prison for ten months, and I certainly would not want to have any longer imprisonment on my conscience."[49]

The Parole Board turned down McGee's application for parole. Two weeks later, however, Friendly gave Randolph good news: "We received word yesterday from the American Civil Liberties Union that the parole board had reconsidered its action and had granted McGee parole effective today. This contributes greatly to my peace of mind."[50] McGee returned to court on June 7, 1972. Thirty-five years later he remembered Friendly sitting on the bench smiling "ear-to-ear" as the court bailiff called his case. Friendly leaned forward and told McGee that he could go home now, his case was over.[51]

United States v. Jakobson[52] raised the intricate question of which religious beliefs qualify for exemption on conscientious objector grounds. The Universal Military Training and Service Act exempted from military service anyone "who, by reason of religious training and belief, is conscientiously opposed to participation in war in any form. Religious training and belief in this connection means an individual's belief in a relation to a Supreme Being involving duties superior to those arising from any human relation, but does not include essentially political, sociological, or philosophical views or a merely personal moral code."[53]

Arno Sascha Jakobson, a son of immigrants who, in Friendly's words, "became estranged from the Jewish faith,"[54] refused to be inducted and was prosecuted after the draft appeal board denied his application for status as a conscientious objector. To determine the validity of Jakobson's claim, Friendly sought guidance in the legislative history and evolving court interpretations of the conscientious objector provision, starting in 1917. The concern was the First Amendment and its bar to requiring a person to profess a belief or disbelief in any religion.[55]

"To summarize Jakobson's religious views," Friendly wrote, "is not altogether easy. . . . He recognizes an ultimate cause or creator of all existence which he terms 'Godness.' In theory an individual's relationship to Godness can take one or the other of two forms, a 'vertical' relationship in which man relates directly to Godness, or a 'horizontal' one in which man relates to Godness indirectly by binding himself to the qualities of Godness that exist in every creation in Mankind and throughout the world." Jakobson had adopted the latter, Friendly concluded: "The way to arrive closer to Godness is by approaching the universals inherent in existence."[56] The answer for Friendly lay in the theology of Dr. Paul Tillich, the eminent Protestant theologian, whose views he summarized in a lengthy footnote before declaring, "Jakobson's definition of religion as 'the sum and essence of one's basic attitude to the fundamental problems of human existence' and his insistence that man can know nothing of God and that Godness can be approached only through psychic involvement in reality parallel the views of this eminent theologian rather strikingly. We cannot believe that Congress, aware of the constitutional problem, meant to exclude views of this character from its definition of religion, or to require lay draft boards and personnel of the Department of Justice to pass on nice theological distinctions between vertical and horizontal transcendence."[57]

Friendly's statements about Tillich and Congress's intentions would probably have surprised the members of the Armed Services Committees who drafted the Universal Military Training and Service Act. They certainly surprised Jakobson. His able brief cited the Bible and a number of sources, including *Religious Philosophy* by Harry A. Wolfson, but it did not cite Tillich.[58] The point is not that Jakobson missed Tillich, but rather that Friendly exerted himself on behalf of a conscientious objector.[59] In fact, Jakobson had never read anything by Tillich and regarded himself as quite unsophisticated: "Judge Friendly was being very kind when he stated that my often awkwardly expressed views paralleled the views of this eminent theologian rather strikingly."[60]

The draft board had not stated on which of two grounds it relied—that Jakobson was not sincere or that his conscientious objection did not meet the requirements of the statute. Friendly found that the former would require affirmance, but not the latter, so Jakobson's conviction could not stand. But rather than simply reverse and remand for a new trial, Friendly took the bolder and more generous step of dismissing the indictment; because the Appeal Board had acted five years earlier, he considered his action "more just under the circumstances."[61] Affirming the Second Circuit, the Supreme Court followed Friendly's teaching: "The Court of Appeals stated in No. 51 that Jakobson's views 'parallel [those of] this eminent theologian [Dr. Paul Tillich] rather strikingly'" and proceeded to quote portions of Tillich's writings that Friendly had assembled in his opinion.[62]

FRIENDLY'S ARTICLES were generally philosophically conservative on criminal law constitutional issues. It makes sense to ask whether his judicial opinions were conservative as well. Some of his more liberal colleagues thought so,[63] and a study placed him within a conservative "bloc" of judges on his court.[64] Most lawyers who appeared before Friendly believed that he was pro-government, not radically so, but with a definite leaning in that direction. The story is told that an Assistant U.S. Attorney approached the lectern to argue for the government in the Second Circuit when the fire alarm went off. While everyone headed to the doors, the attorney remained fixed. Finally a U.S. Marshal approached him and told him that he had to leave. Turning to the Marshal, the attorney said in an excited voice, "Look, I have a panel of Friendly, Lumbard, and Hays. I'm not going *anywhere*."[65] While some defense lawyers considered Friendly to be reliably in favor of the prosecution,[66] a Legal Aid lawyer who subsequently became a state judge wanted Friendly on the panel when she thought she had a good case.[67] Eleanor Jackson Piel, a criminal defense lawyer who appeared before Friendly, said, "There was something in him that reacted to injustice."[68] But the question remains whether his votes and opinions in criminal law cases were conservative.

Classifying Friendly's opinions is not simple. Circuit judges, unlike Supreme Court Justices, do not all sit on the same cases. Also, during a substantial portion of Friendly's tenure on the court, panels affirmed some convictions from the bench, and collecting and analyzing those decisions is both difficult and unreliable. Thus, any overall scorecard of votes on criminal appeals becomes a very blunt assessment. A more promising approach examines whether Friendly more often sided with the government or the defense when he wrote an opinion when the court was not unanimous, closer cases where the judges were alerted to their controversial nature.[69] Although not a perfect measure, a significant deviation from his colleagues might be meaningful.

Friendly wrote an opinion a total of fifty-four times, including *en banc* and habeas corpus cases, when he sat on a divided court in criminal matters in the Second Circuit. In those matters the court favored the *prosecution* by a margin of 60 percent to 40 percent. However, in 65 percent of those cases, Friendly voted for the *defendant*. Thus, on divided panels in criminal cases on which Friendly sat, the other judges voted for the defendant only 28 percent of the time. This measure contradicts Friendly's reputation as a conservative judge.

Probably explaining part of the difference was Friendly's creativity in finding grounds to decide the case not appearing in the district courts' opinions or appellate briefs, many of which resulted in reversals. In the period from mid-1965 to mid-1968, for example, Friendly's opinions were 39 percent for reversal, at least in part, and the great majority of those favored defendants, who tended to be appellees only in some habeas corpus petition cases. Comparable figures for other judges have not been found,[70] but the large number and the likely reason for it tends to suggest that his reversal rate was higher than the average for all judges.

Friendly's overall reversal rate, however, does not account for much of the enormous discrepancy between him and his colleagues. Moreover, it does not explain the temporal pattern of his voting. Of the first twenty of the cases, he voted for the defense seventeen times, or 85 percent. Thereafter his vote leaned toward the defendants by only 17–16. The first phase ended in the summer of 1971, at the time Nixon replaced Warren, Black, Fortas, and Harlan with Burger, Blackmun, Powell, and Rehnquist. This produced more conservative Supreme Court decisions. While at first blush it makes sense that a lower-court judge would vote more conservatively once the Warren Court became the Burger Court, it is not so simple. If all judges' votes became more conservative, that would not alter the position of a single judge in comparison with his colleagues. Likewise, changes in the composition of the Second Circuit do not appear to account for the discrepancy, since there were liberal and conservative circuit judges throughout Friendly's judicial tenure. Also the voting patterns of the other judges do not really explain much without a detailed analysis of all their decisions, which is impractical to perform and unlikely to be very enlightening.

Most important seems to have been the changes in the nature of the issues during Friendly's tenure. Friendly was receptive to claims that defendants' fundamental rights were denied, but less responsive to what he regarded as technical violations that did not interfere with the search for truth, more typical of the issues he faced later in his judicial career.[71] Moreover, starting in the late 1960s Friendly was more disturbed than most judges by the boldest strokes of the late years of the Warren Court and was prepared to restrict its decisions, often by making creative distinctions that some other judges would not accept.[72] Nevertheless, the evidence contradicts the conclusion that Friendly was a conservative judge in criminal cases.

CHAPTER SIXTEEN

Business Law

llewellyn? p. 368

FRIENDLY'S THREE DECADES practicing law were instructive, and what he said about Brandeis largely also applied to himself: "To have said that Brandeis was not afraid of a balance sheet was a considerable understatement; he positively reveled in them, and in statistics of all sorts."[1] For his part, Friendly understood, and understood the importance of, balance sheets, but he did not revel in them. His experience had taught him the importance of providing decisions that were rational, consistent, clear, and workable; he did not want others to endure the irrationality and unpredictability that he experienced before the Civil Aeronautics Board. His efforts led him to probe beyond the narrow problem before him, as when he noted that "much of the seeming confusion in this field of law [government contracts] stems from the failure to make necessary distinctions as to who is suing whom for what."[2]

This chapter contains some surprises. Friendly vigorously enforced securities laws in favor of inexperienced and duped investors. He steadfastly administered the tax laws to require taxpayers to pay the taxes they owed. In these two important areas his opinions demonstrate initiative, sympathy to government regulation, and some elements of economic liberalism. While his contribution to other areas of business law were less directed, he helped rationalize, modernize, and promote fairness in admiralty, antitrust, and bankruptcy laws and the law relating to punitive damages.

Despite the fact that he was a Republican who had spent most of his professional life with business executives, Friendly believed that the securities laws should be enforced more vigorously. He was a lifelong investor in the stock market who frequently telephoned his broker from his judicial chambers,[3] and he understood the industry and the imbalance in information and power possessed by the individual investor in dealing with a stockbroker or corporation. His votes to reverse the district court, which he did fifteen times, were *always* in favor of a plaintiff who was an unsophisticated investor bereft of complicity or gamesmanship. When two corporations were fighting or when the SEC sought to enjoin misconduct involving securities, however, his record was more balanced. For example, in SEC actions for injunctions, he frequently affirmed the issuing of injunctions against companies but narrowed them substantially to take into account mitigating circumstances.[4]

Friendly's commanding sense of duty carried over from criminal prosecutions to civil suits against fiduciaries that used their offices for personal gain. When Lazard Frères decided to terminate its role as advisor to a mutual fund that it had organized nine years earlier, its handpicked successor, Moody Investors, paid it a substantial fee for the privilege of succeeding it as advisor. In *Rosenfeld v. Black*[5] shareholders of the fund filed suit to recover the portion of the fee unrelated to continuing to perform the services Lazard had agreed to provide. Friendly identified the evil in permitting Lazard to retain the fee: "If lured by the possibility of profit, the retiring adviser might recommend a successor who was less qualified or more expensive than other candidates, and who might be on the lookout for ways to recoup his 'succession fee' at the expense of the Fund." It did not matter to him that succession fees were acceptable "under the morals of the marketplace" (indeed a "succession fee" was standard practice in the industry),[6] any more than it did in *United States v. Simon*, the criminal case charging an accounting firm with failing to disclose the misuse of corporate assets.[7] Bringing the principles of equity into the common law applicable to federal securities, he announced in *Rosenfeld*, "Equity imposes a higher standard": "A fiduciary endeavoring to influence the selection of a successor must do so with an eye single to the best interests of the beneficiaries. Experience has taught that, no matter how high-minded a particular fiduciary may be, the only certain way to insure full compliance with that duty is to eliminate any possibility of personal gain."[8]

Lazard settled the suit for $1 million. In the wake of the case, at least fifteen more similar suits were filed against mutual fund managers. The case, according to the industry, operated "to undercut the economic base of the mutual-fund business." The *New York Times* agreed: the industry was "facing a new and fundamental crisis."[9]

Who could enforce the securities law was a major issue. Important securities statutes provide for enforcement by the SEC or the Department of Justice, but not expressly by victims in a private suit. Starting around 1946, lower federal courts found an "implied" private cause of action in the antifraud provisions of the Securities Exchange Act of 1934.[10] In 1975, however, the Supreme Court identified specific, and strict, requirements for finding implied remedies,[11] "and, by the end of the decade, decisions like *Touche Ross & Co. v. Redington*[12] and *Transamerica Mortgage Advisors, Inc. v. Lewis*,[13] adopted a presumption against them, rebuttable only by affirmative evidence of congressional intent."[14] Reversing the district court at least in part in four cases, Friendly found an implied private cause of action in the securities laws in the twilight, if not the deep dusk, of the era during which the Supreme Court welcomed implied claims.[15] In 1980, while one of the cases was pending, Friendly's clerk, John G. Roberts Jr., now the Chief Justice of the United States, told his boss that the Supreme Court was not finding implied causes of action any more. Friendly replied, "They didn't say that to me."[16] In finding implied causes of action, he was taking a position hostile to conservatives, who opposed the expansion of federal remedies for plaintiffs.[17]

Friendly engaged in a bold and creative reading of precedent when, reversing the district court, he upheld an alleged federal claim in the face of a Supreme Court case that seemed to require dismissal of the claim. In *Goldberg v. Meridor*[18] minority stockholders of a corporate subsidiary sued the corporate parent and its individual shareholders for undervaluing their shares in the subsidiary in a stock-for-stock exchange. Confronting plaintiffs was the one-month-old Supreme Court decision in *Santa Fe Industries, Inc. v. Green*, which held that "a breach of a fiduciary duty by majority shareholders, without any deception, misrepresentation, or nondisclosure," did not violate the federal securities laws.[19] Friendly focused on two misleading press releases that failed to disclose facts relevant to the exchange of stock as well as conflicts of interest by the controlling shareholders. But it was also necessary to find that the misleading press releases were material to plaintiffs' claims. Friendly fixed on a statement in *Green* that "under Delaware law [minority stockholders] could not have enjoined the merger." That was not the case in *Goldberg v. Meridor,* and he upheld suit in the federal courts.

Friendly reached this result, moreover, even though the injunction issue did not seem to be particularly significant to the Supreme Court's analysis,[20] and the plaintiff had failed to make that argument. *Santa Fe v. Green* was designed to limit federalizing a substantial portion of *state* corporate law, a goal with which Friendly ordinarily sympathized in other contexts. He thought, however, that Justice Byron White's opinion in the case bordered on the incoherent. He later called the opinion "alarming," adding that he didn't know what the case meant. The reason was that the opinion said that Rule 10b-5 "may be held inapplicable when the cause of action was 'one traditionally relegated to the state courts.' " But, Friendly said, that described virtually the entire ambit of Rule 10b-5.[21] Friendly also had serious problems with the Court's concept of federalism: "[A] parent's looting of a subsidiary with securities outstanding in the hands of the public in a securities transaction is a different matter; in such cases disclosure or at least the absence of misleading disclosure is required. It would be incongruous if Rule 10b-5 created liability for a casual 'tip' in a bar of a country club . . . but would not cover a parent's undisclosed or misleadingly disclosed sale of its overvalued assets for stock of a controlled subsidiary with securities in the hands of the public."[22] This was a classic case of Friendly's construing as narrowly as possible Supreme Court cases with which he disagreed.

Dishonest press releases agitated Friendly; he understood that that was how many less sophisticated investors obtained information, but he could see management's bind in *SEC v. Texas Gulf Sulfur Corp.* (TGS), where the SEC claimed that TGS had issued a press release that was misleadingly pessimistic. Finding the record inadequate, the majority of the Second Circuit, sitting *en banc,* remanded the case to the district court to decide if the release was misleading, as a prelude to deciding whether to issue an injunction regarding future press releases.[23] In a more nuanced concurrence Friendly opined that the issue involving the press release "transcend[s] in public importance all others in this important case." It was undisputed, he said, that TGS's purpose in issuing the release was good, namely, to try to correct erroneous ebullient newspaper articles and that the erroneous press release could not have benefited the persons responsible for issuing it.

Friendly acknowledged that the press release "was a wholly insufficient statement of what TGS knew," and it was possibly issued negligently. But, his opinion cautioned, "The consequences of holding that negligence in the drafting of a press release such as that of April 12, 1964, may impose civil liability on the corporation are frightening." Discouraging the investment community and others from informing the public of important business and financial development would be counterproductive. "If the only choices open to a corporation are either to remain silent and let false rumors do their work, or to make a communication, not legally required, at the risk that a slip of the pen or failure properly to amass or weigh the facts—all judged in the bright gleam of hindsight—will lead to large judgments, payable in the last analysis by innocent investors, for the benefit of speculators and their lawyers, most corporations would opt for the former."[24]

Four months later, in *SEC v. Great American Industries, Inc.*,[25] however, Friendly penalized a company that issued a false press release without mitigating circumstances. Among one defendant's failures was its neglect to disclose the startling fact that two-thirds of its purchase price for properties was to be paid to third parties as a finder's fee.[26]

In *Gerstle v. Gamble-Skogmo, Inc.*,[27] Friendly held that a proxy statement was misleading, although for a different reason than the district court. He took a basket of plaintiffs' confusing contentions and countercontentions and created an orderly narrative and legal analysis, placing points in their proper perspective and making distinctions and arguments plaintiffs missed. He decided that the defendant, a company that was merging with an outdoor-advertising company (GOA), misled plaintiffs (GOA shareholders) into thinking that after the merger of the companies GOA would continue to engage in the unprofitable outdoor-advertising business; the defendant's unstated actual intention was to sell off GOA's assets at a substantial profit. It was unnecessary for the plaintiff to establish fraud or manipulation, Friendly said, although they had to show some fault on the part of the defendants, an issue that neither party had briefed.[28] Louis Loss, a Harvard Law professor, noted, "I have heard it said that [it was] his favorite [case], quite understandably."[29]

Friendly was concerned with the extraterritorial reach of federal securities laws, a difficult and important problem. He recognized that while international law permitted the United States to legislate with respect to acts either committed or producing effects within its territory, "it would be . . . erroneous to assume that the legislature always means to go to the full extent permitted. . . . [Courts must] determine whether Congress would have wished the precious resources of United States courts and law enforcement agencies to be devoted to them rather than leave the problem to foreign countries,"[30] another example of his focus on legislative purpose. Stocks registered on a U.S. exchange presented little difficulty for the courts.[31] More challenging was when stocks were not.

Friendly stated the issue in *Leasco Data Processing Equip. Corp. v. Maxwell*:[32] "Still we must ask ourselves whether, if Congress had thought about the point, it would not have wished to protect an American investor if a foreigner comes to the United States and fraudulently induces him to purchase foreign securities abroad," and answered in the affirmative. In *Bersch v. Drexel Firestone, Inc.*[33] and *IIT v. Vencap, Ltd.*,[34] both of which involved a Canadian corporation, Friendly decided that it would be too extreme to permit American jurisdiction when there was no more than "an adverse effect on the country's economic interest or on American securities prices," noting, "Moderation is all."[35] While acknowledging in *Bersch*, "[I]f we were asked to point to language in the statutes, or even in the legislative history, that compelled these conclusions, we would be unable to respond," Friendly ventured a comprehensive standard. He concluded that the anti-fraud provisions of the federal securities laws applied to losses by Americans resident in the United States, to losses to Americans living abroad if material fraudulent acts in the United States contributed significantly to the losses, and to losses to foreigners directly caused by acts within the United States.[36] A leading casebook summed up part of Friendly's contribution: "A surprising number of similar cases were brought in U.S. courts in the ensuing years. . . . Typically, the parties try to position themselves on one side or the other of the *Leasco, Bersch, Vencap* trilogy." Every court of appeals followed Friendly's opinions on the international reach of federal securities law, and his decisions can be found in casebooks forty years after he rendered them.[37]

Friendly's hegemony lasted until 2010, when the five most conservative members of the Supreme Court explicitly rejected his analysis, a rare instance when the majority and dissent basically fought about a circuit judge's jurisprudence. Taking a highly textual approach and relying on the absence of language in section 10b indicating its applicability to extraterritorial events as well as the principle or presumption against the extraterritorial reach of federal legislation, *Morrison v. National Australia Bank* held the section applicable only to stock fraud relating to stocks listed on American exchanges.[38] Concurring in the result, but disagreeing with the change in the standard, Justice Stevens saw insufficient reason to depart from the long-accepted test created by "[o]ne of our greatest jurists."[39] Gary Born, a former Friendly clerk and an authority on international securities transactions, reacted: "*Morrison* was the territorial presumption reincarnated in its most unthinking form."[40]

JUST AS FRIENDLY had no sympathy for misbehaving corporations, he had none for conniving investors who had no real cause for complaint. His principal concern was for people like the plaintiff in *Katz v. Amos Treat & Co.*, who was "a dentist by profession and an operator of securities by avocation,"[41] or his apocryphal "Auntie Mame."[42] In *Pearlstein v. Scudder & German*,[43] he separated himself from his colleagues on the panel over whether a sophisticated speculator should be allowed to recover damages against a broker for violation of provisions of the federal securities laws that required the customer to make full payment within seven business days of purchase, on pain of having the securities liqui-dated.[44] Stanley S. Pearlstein, a nonpracticing lawyer and professional in-vestor, sued a brokerage firm that at his insistence extended him credit in violation of the provision. Acting against the advice of his broker, Pearlstein purchased approximately $200,000 in convertible bonds, ignored the bro-ker's many demands for payment of the balance, and refused to permit the bonds to be sold. Finally, months later, the broker sold the bonds and Pearl-stein sued to recover his claimed losses, approximately $85,000.[45]

The panel's majority concluded that the broker violated the law when it failed to sell the bonds after seven business days had expired without payment. Congress, it said, decided to place the responsibility for observ-ing margins on the broker, and the customer's knowledge did not matter. Writing for the majority, Judge Waterman stated, "In our view the dan-ger of permitting a windfall to an unscrupulous investor is outweighed by the salutary policing effect which the threat of private suits for com-pensatory damages can have upon brokers and dealers above and be-yond the threats of governmental action by the Securities and Exchange Commission."[46]

Friendly filed a vigorous dissent that demonstrated the importance to him of the facts: "Although the opinion's statement of facts is accurate as far as it goes, a somewhat fuller narrative is needed to place the matter in proper setting." Friendly dwelt on Pearlman's sophistication, shady deal-ings, and machinations. "Equity and justice are qualities that Pearlstein's claim conspicuously lacks. He bought the bonds against defendant's ad-vice, refused to sell them on its urging, remained silent when defendant was pressing for payment, and settled his liability after having had legal advice. Equity would leave the loss where it lies."[47] "[S]peculators will be in a position to place all the risk of market fluctuations on their brokers, if only the customer's persuasion or the broker's negligence causes the latter to fail in carrying out [the regulation] to the letter." Furthermore, he pointed out, the purpose of the statute was not to protect lenders or speculators but to regulate monetary policy.[48]

While Friendly treated dishonest corporate defendants harshly, he was loath to penalize defendants, such as Scudder & German, who acted in good faith and whose conduct could not lead to speculative abuse. "This case illustrates the need for putting some brakes on the onrush of civil liti-gation for violation of the securities laws if that doctrine is to be an instru-ment of justice rather than the opposite. With all respect, the scholarly opinion of my brother Waterman seems to me to reach a conclusion that shocks the conscience and wars with common sense. Apart from unfairness of the result on the facts of this case, press reports of 'backroom troubles' of many brokerage houses and the sharp decline in security prices could give the decision far-reaching consequences."[49]

In *Chasins v. Smith, Barney & Co.* Friendly dissented when the court failed to grant a rehearing *en banc* after a panel held Smith, Barney liable under federal securities laws for failing to disclose to Abram Chasins, a noted musicologist, that it was making a market in the securities it recommended and sold to him in the over-the-counter market.[50] Friendly explained that Smith, Barney's having made a market could not possibly have harmed and might have helped Chasins, noting that the conclusions respecting market making "are predicated on an essential misconception of the role of a market maker in over-the-counter transactions."[51] Although Friendly could not change the minds of the judges in the majority, they finally agreed to add a paragraph that virtually eliminated the case as a precedent: "We here go so far only to hold that under the particular circumstances proved in this case the court was correct in holding that the failure to disclose was the omission of a material fact."[52]

Friendly also had little use for the plaintiffs in *Denny v. Barber*,[53] whose only real complaint was that they lost money and who were objecting that companies in which they invested did not have, in Friendly's words, "greater clairvoyance." "In sum, the complaint is an example of alleging fraud by hindsight. For the most part, plaintiff has simply seized upon disclosures made in later annual reports and alleged that they should have been made in earlier ones." Years later Judge Frank Easterbrook of the Seventh Circuit incorporated the first sentence into his opinion in *DiLeo v. Ernst & Young*: "There is no 'fraud by hindsight' in Judge Friendly's felicitous phrase, and hindsight is all the DiLeos offer."[54] Friendly's language, bolstered by Easterbrook, attracted enough interest for it to have served as the subject of an entire law review article, entitled "Fraud by Hindsight," that traced the evolution and use by judges of the term and the doctrine.[55]

Friendly also worked for the reform of the securities laws by serving for many years on the American Bar Association's Committee on Federal Regulation of Securities and on an advisory group appointed by the American Law Institute on the same subject. He also assisted with the ALI's controversial project on corporate governance, whose purpose was to establish rules or standards for corporate officers and directors on conflicts of interest and similar issues.

At the time of the ALI project corporations were exerting pressure on their lawyers to try to defeat certain proposals for reform, including one to create greater transparency and to require a certain number of independent directors on boards of publicly held corporations. Some New York firms sent their lawyers to Philadelphia to vote against them. While many in ALI leadership positions were avoiding taking sides, Friendly supported numerous reforms, including a stringent requirement that a majority of directors on public companies be independent. He saw other conflicts of interest, writing to Professor Melvin Eisenberg, the ALI reporter (drafter and coordinator) for the governance project, "I read recently that the big eight accounting firms were developing a head-hunting business as a sideline. How can an accountant be really independent if he has successfully recommended the chief executive or financial officer? Should not something be said about this?"[56] The academics who led the reform effort praised Friendly's courage and judgment.[57] ALI's director said simply, "Friendly was not personally assertive. He didn't have to be."[58] Loss said about Friendly that he, "without a doubt, did more to shape the law of securities regulation than any judge in the country."[59]

In one respect, however, Friendly seems to have taken a philosophically conservative position with respect to corporations, namely, the right or obligation of corporations to engage in socially desirable activities. He wrote to Harvard's president Derek C. Bok:

> Last spring I gave some attention to a related subject in connection with a talk on the governance of corporations. I found it amusing to apply the social contract theory which [Harvard] Professor [John] Rawls has revived. I thought it evident that when a business corporation was formed there was a contract among the original investors that the corporation should be operated so as to maximize profits by any means that were legitimate . . . and that new stockholders adopted this contract. It would follow that stockholders who objected to a corporation's operating in South Africa, not because the operation involved undue risk as it very well may, but because of dislike of the policies of the South African government, were acting in breach of the contract. If they did not like what the corporation was doing, their remedy was to sell their stock. If this is correct, then it would be morally wrong for Harvard to vote in favor of stockholder proposals that a corporation should withdraw from South Africa simply because of disapproval of that country's racial policies.[60]

FRIENDLY DID NOT ENJOY deciding tax cases. He believed, moreover, that on appeal tax cases should be decided by a special court of appeals, which consisted of experts and was devoted to the arcane subject.[61] Despite this fact and although Friendly never practiced tax law and did not consider himself an expert on tax law,[62] he wrote fifty-seven tax opinions, a number of which were significant and continue to appear in tax treatises and casebooks.[63]

For Friendly it was beyond debate that the Code had to accord equal treatment to identically situated taxpayers who were litigating their tax liability in different forums. While reasonable minds might differ as to the meaning of some Code provisions, he had no patience for a system that treated litigants differently based on their economic resources. When he found that the law differed between the district court (where taxpayers go when they pay the tax and sue for a refund) and the Tax Court (where the IRS sues to collect the tax), he balked: "We cannot believe the Supreme Court intended that . . . the result should depend on whether a widow could afford to pay the tax and sue for a refund rather than avail herself of the salutary remedy Congress intended to afford in establishing the Tax Court and permitting determination before payment."[64]

During the 1963 term of the Second Circuit, Friendly told his clerk Pierre Leval[65] that it made sense for judges to read tax statutes "literally," exactly the way they were written, because it was one area of the law that Congress revisited frequently; it had the will and the ability to change the law if it felt that the courts reached a result contrary to its intention. Friendly also recognized that the specificity of the tax code and the interrelation of its sections made deviating from the text hazardous,[66] although a judge should also give appropriate weight to context, legislative history, legislative reenactment, and even legislative silence in tax cases.[67] Supporting Friendly's literal approach was his knowledge that statutes sometimes were the result of compromise and that failure to respect the stated compromise would encourage improper interpretation. Thus, in *Divine v. Commissioner of Internal Revenue* he observed that "[i]n substance § 421 represented a trade-off," and the court "should carry out the evident purpose of Congress."[68] Perhaps contributing to his literal approach to tax cases was the fact that the Supreme Court reversed his 1961 purposive opinion in *Gourelli v. Internal Revenue Commissioner* by a vote of nine to zero.[69] Significantly both Friendly's literalism and his deviations from literalism tended to assist the Commissioner.

The opinion that best reflected Friendly's position on the importance of a literal reading of the Code was his dissent in *Commissioner of Internal Revenue v. Gordon*,[70] where he found himself alone and frustrated by the majority's result. Although the taxpayer had not complied with section 355 of the 1954 Code relating to corporate distributions of stock in a controlled corporation, which required events to be completed within one tax year, the majority allowed him favored tax treatment. The case implicated tax-related events that spilled over to a second year and Friendly chided his colleagues "for the magic whereby two distributions of 57% and 43% in different years become one of 100%." Referring to section 355 as "the section held by my brothers to afford a tax shelter," he asked whether the result would be different in the first year if the taxpayer did not go through with distributing the balance of 43 percent of the stock in the second year—a thorn in the side of the majority in view of the requirement that tax liability for the first year must be decided at the end of the first year. "When Congress has meant the events of one year to affect the tax for another, it has said so in language all can understand. See, e.g., §§ 172(b), 381, 382, 1301, 1302, 1303."[71] Unanimously reversing the Second Circuit majority, the Supreme Court held, in words reminiscent of Friendly, that "[t]he requirements of the section are detailed and specific, and must be applied with precision. . . . [A] court is not free to disregard requirements simply because it considers them redundant or unsuited to achieving the general purpose in a particular case."[72]

Probably Friendly's most famous tax opinion was *Commissioner of Internal Revenue v. Ferrer,*[73] where he struggled over whether the Code mandated that the proceeds of the sale of certain rights should be taxed as ordinary income or capital gains. The taxpayer was Jose Ferrer, the star and director of the movie *Moulin Rouge,* the 1952 film about Toulouse-Lautrec based on a book with the same name. Friendly began his opinion delightfully: "The difficulties Mr. Ferrer must have had in fitting himself into the shape of the artist can hardly have been greater than ours in determining whether the transaction here at issue fits into the rubric 'gain from the sale or exchange of a capital asset held for more than 6 months.' "[74] Friendly struggled to find a comprehensive solution to the tax problem within the text of the statute but ultimately surrendered after spending several weeks "sweat[ing] over it."[75] He ended up treating separately under the applicable Code provision each of the transferred rights, such as the surrender of the right to perform the play in exchange for the right to create a motion picture and the right to a royalty percentage from the motion picture. Nearly a half century later the opinion is still cited by the courts[76] and included in casebooks used to teach income tax law.[77]

Friendly read the Code literally in *Estate of Rockefeller v. Commissioner of Internal Revenue,*[78] his last tax case. The Estate, which continued the case when Nelson A. Rockefeller died, claimed a deduction for over $500,000 in expenses he incurred in connection with his confirmation by the Senate and House of Representatives as Vice President in 1974 pursuant to the Twenty-fifth Amendment.[79] Friendly rejected Rockefeller's argument that the sum was deductible as "ordinary and necessary expenses paid or incurred . . . in carrying on any trade or business."[80] The language of the Code, reinforced by case law, the judge said, appeared to limit the deduction "to cases where the taxpayer was seeking employment in the *same* trade or business . . . [with] a high degree of identity in deciding the issue of sameness."[81] He readily found that Governor of the State of New York did not qualify as the same trade or business as Vice President of the

United States, giving the word "same" its "everyday meaning." The Governor enforced the laws of the state, supervised many departments and agencies, made appointments to lesser offices, and lobbied with the federal government, while the Vice President presided over the Senate and readied himself for the possibility of assuming the presidency on a moment's notice.[82] To Friendly, "same," the word in the statue, meant "same" and not "similar." He gave as an alternative ground—not argued by the Commissioner—that there was a gap between Rockefeller's service as governor and his consideration for Vice President (during which he headed two government commissions), so he did not move directly from Governor to Vice President.[83]

Friendly also took a literal view of the Code in *Rosenspan v. United States*,[84] where the taxpayer, a traveling salesman who traveled three hundred days a year and had no permanent abode, took a deduction for unreimbursed meals and lodging incurred, in the words of the Code, "while away from home in the pursuit of a trade or business." Friendly wrote, "It is enough to decide this case that 'home' means 'home' and Rosenspan had none,"[85] although he also supported his conclusion with legislative history and other grounds. As recently as 2005 one article stated, "The leading authority on the plight of the truly homeless taxpayer is Judge Friendly's well reasoned opinion in *Rosenspan v. United States*," adding that "[t]he court's decision in *Rosenspan* seems appropriate but harsh."[86]

Friendly's tax opinions also had a less literal component. Offsetting the rigid construction of statutes has been a venerable doctrine adopted by the great majority of judges and commentators, who have agreed that the literal meaning of an unambiguous statute should not be followed when it would lead to an absurd result.[87] Over the years a small number of Supreme Court decisions applied the concept, especially *Church of the Holy Trinity v. United States*,[88] where the Court refused to apply a statute that prohibited the importation of "labor or services of any kind" to an imported clergyman. The most expansive view of the absurdity doctrine was *United States v. American Trucking Associations*, a nontax case decided by the Supreme Court in 1940, which stated, "[E]ven when the plain meaning did not produce absurd results but merely an unreasonable one plainly at variance with the policy of the legislation as a whole this Court has followed the purpose, rather than the literal words."[89]

Despite his claim as a literalist in tax cases, Friendly actively relied on the absurdity doctrine, employing it several times in favor of the United States in an effort to avoid undesirable results.[90] He chose the accommodating *American Trucking* in four tax opinions, in contrast to his colleagues on the Second Circuit, who relied on the case in only one during his tenure as a judge.[91] Language that produced an unintended result, Friendly concluded, did not deserve full recognition as the will of Congress. On occasion he would effectively rewrite a provision of the Code to prevent giving business taxpayers a windfall unintended by Congress. He could be pragmatic while maintaining that he was a literalist.

J.C. Penney Co. v. Commissioner of Internal Revenue[92] presented Friendly with "the rare case in which it is as clear as anything ever can be that Congress did not mean what in strict letter it said." Involved was the meaning of a complex Code provision relating to the liquidation of certain wholly owned subsidiaries. By its terms the Code imposed a tax only on liquidations that took place "following the adoption of a plan of complete liquidation,"[93] and J.C. Penney's liquidation occurred *before* the adoption of a plan. Citing, in Friendly's words, "a cross-reference in a section inserted in the Internal Revenue Code of 1954 during a late stage of its passage," J.C. Penney argued that its sale or liquidation was not covered by the statute and was not taxable. Friendly disagreed:

> With commendable candor taxpayer's counsel acknowledged, in answering a question at argument, that he could conceive of no reason why Congress should have wished to confer benefits with so lavish and discriminatory a hand. The legislative history suggests none. Congress is free, within constitutional limitations, to legislate eccentrically if it should wish, but courts should not lightly assume that it has done so. When the "plain meaning" of statutory language "has led to absurd or futile results," the Supreme Court "has looked beyond the words to the purpose of the act"; "even when the plain meaning did not produce absurd results but merely an unreasonable one plainly at variance with the policy of the legislation as a whole" the Court "has followed that purpose rather than the literal words."[94]

United States v. American Trucking Associations was the sole citation for this statement.

Despite his bow to literalism, Friendly refused to allow a congressional drafting gaffe to distort the tax law, simply stating in one case, "The argument stresses the form at the neglect of substance; the letter of § 1201(b) must yield when it would lead to an unfair and unintended result."[95]

ADMIRALTY WAS ANOTHER field in which Friendly wrote extensively, with fifty-seven opinions to his credit, not including suits by seamen for personal injuries. Some of his cases were examples of long-standing federal nonstatutory, or common, law, while others considered the application of old federal statutes to more modern conditions. *Hellenic Lines, Ltd. v. United States*, one of the former, began, "This Odyssey concerns a large government shipment of bagged flour from various Gulf [of Mexico] ports to United Nations Relief and Works Agency (UNRWA), on plaintiff's vessel, MV Italia, intended to arrive at Aqaba, Jordan, around May 20, 1967. After various delays and peregrinations hereafter described, the shipment finally reached Ashdod, Israel, on July 17, 1967. However tortuous was the voyage, the course of this suit in admiralty to determine the rights of shipowner and cargo has equaled it."[96]

Early in 1967 the U.S. Department of Agriculture awarded a contract to transport a substantial quantity of bagged flour from Gulf of Mexico ports to Aqaba for distribution to Palestinian refugees. A series of mishaps followed—described in the opinion as "rift[s] in the lute"—that required a number of ship substitutions prompting departure delays, as well as detours to pick up additional cargo on the East Coast, before the *Italia,* the ship finally employed, sailed for Aqaba via Piraeus, Greece. "None of the above facts would have been seriously consequential," Friendly wrote, "save for an occurrence that no one anticipated. On June 5, 1967, shortly after the Italia passed Gibraltar, the Six Day War broke out between Israel and a number of Arab nations. The Suez Canal was immediately closed to traffic. On June 10 major hostilities ceased, pursuant to a resolution of the United Nations Security Council."[97]

After misrepresenting its location to the U.S. government, the *Italia* unilaterally unloaded its cargo at Piraeus and demanded additional money because shipments to Piraeus, even though closer to the United States, were on a higher conference rate than the negotiated rate to Aqaba. For reasons Friendly acknowledged he could not begin to comprehend, Hellenic Lines, rather than keep the prepaid freight to Aqaba of $114,301.51 and hope that the government would absorb the extra expenses, filed suit in admiralty to obtain the excess of the conference rate to Piraeus over the nonconference, negotiated rate to the more distant Aqaba, some $101,102.03. Naturally this provoked a counterclaim by the government for the prepaid freight. The government prevailed totally before District Judge Richard Owen and Hellenic appealed. "It is understandable," Friendly observed, "that an outcome whereby the Government would receive free transportation of the cargo (except for its self-imposed burden of effecting onward shipment from Piraeus on an American-flag vessel)—something it had not sought in its counterclaim—should have led Hellenic to believe that something had gone wrong on its way to the forum."[98]

With the exception of the double counting of one item of damages, Friendly affirmed Owen on the essentially unasserted ground that the *Italia* had engaged "in a voluntary unreasonable deviation on this side of the Atlantic" (as opposed to one near the destination, which was what the government had argued, and then not particularly cogently).[99] Relegating to a footnote Hellenic's strongest argument—that it never had an opportunity at trial to take discovery on or contest that contention[100]—Friendly rejected rather casually its claim that the government never raised "this deviation issue." "[T]he record shows that the Government did raise the issue below at the pretrial conference, in its proposed conclusions of law, and in its Post-Trial Memorandum, although only in the context of an argument in support of its counterclaim for damages—recovery of prepaid freight not being then at issue. Deviation was very much a part of the Government's argument on appeal. Since the facts have been fully developed, we see no reason why we must close our eyes to the true deviation simply because on appeal the Government placed its emphasis on the wrong side of the Atlantic."[101]

Friendly granted judgment to the government on a factually laden argument that it did not argue in the district court or the court of appeals, namely, that Hellenic engaged in an improper deviation in U.S. waters. He cast the issue not, as is customary, whether the party adequately raised the issue on appeal, but in the extraordinarily charitable formulation, whether there was a "reason why we must close our eyes to the true deviation" simply because the party made the wrong contention on appeal. Friendly resurrected on his own initiative facts not appearing in the parties' briefs or appendix, but appearing only in the district court record. While Hellenic had the edge on the law, the government had the better facts, especially in view of Hellenic's repeated overreaching.

While Friendly's action in *Hellenic Lines* was another example of his willingness to reverse district court judgments on the basis of arguments not made, or made only obscurely by the party who lost below,[102] he was conflicted on the issue. An important reason he wanted to stop practicing law was, in his words, "I was getting sick of trying cases before the Civil Aeronautics Board, where it seemed to me the result bore little or no relationship to the effort that was put into [the] trial of the merits of the case."[103] But, as a judge, it was more important to him not to distort the law; maintaining the integrity of the law was his obligation. While he could penalize devious parties, he would not penalize the clients of inept lawyers. Indeed, as noted, he sometimes lent his considerable horsepower to a contestant whose legal engine was sputtering.[104] His goal as a judge was to arrive at the correct result, not reward the side with the better or more thorough advocates.

Soon after the decision, Friendly found himself in the same elevator as Judge Owen, whose judgment he had just reversed in part and otherwise affirmed on a new ground. He told Owen that he was sorry about the outcome, to which Owen replied, "Whatever else, you did the right thing." Friendly raised his eyebrows and harrumphed. Owen later explained that

Friendly "had cleared away the clouds and reached a good result, one that a district judge could not reach. It showed his humanity."[105]

Ira S. Bushey & Sons, Inc. v. United States,[106] a generally cheery vehicle, created an important legal precedent regarding the liability of an entity (the U.S. Coast Guard) for the wrongs committed by one of its employees. Friendly stated the facts:

> While the United States Coast Guard vessel Tamaroa was being overhauled in a floating drydock located in Brooklyn's Gowanus Canal, a seaman [Lane] returning from shore leave late at night, in the condition for which seaman are famed, turned some wheels on the drydock wall. He thus opened valves that controlled the flooding of the tanks on one side of the drydock. Soon the ship listed, slid off the blocks and fell against the wall. Parts of the drydock sank, and the ship partially did—fortunately without loss of life or personal injury. . . . After boarding ship at 12:11 A.M., Lane mumbled to an off-duty seaman that he had "turned some valves" and also muttered something about "valves" to another who was standing the engineering watch. Neither did anything; apparently Lane's condition was not such as to encourage proximity.[107]

District Judge Jack B. Weinstein had entered judgment in favor of the owner of the drydock against the United States, which appealed on the ground that Seaman Lane's acts were not within the scope of his employment, a requirement for recovery against Lane's employer under the doctrine of *respondeat superior*.[108] Unlike what happened in virtually all of Friendly's cases, however, here a law clerk wrote the initial draft of the opinion while the judge was away.[109] The law clerk was Bruce Ackerman, a graduate of Yale, who studied under then professor, later dean, and still later Second Circuit Judge Guido Calabresi, an early apostle of law and economics. Citing Calabresi's writings, Weinstein's opinion had ruled on the basis of law-and-economics analysis, and Ackerman's draft adhered to that approach by focusing on the best result from an economic standpoint. While Friendly did not regard himself as proficient in economics,[110] his opinion carefully considered—and rejected—a law-and-economics approach:

> The unsatisfactory quality of the allocation of resource rationale is especially striking on the facts of this case. It could well be that application of the traditional rule might induce drydock owners, prodded by their insurance companies, to install locks on their valves to avoid similar incidents in the future, while placing the burden on shipowners is much less likely to lead to accident prevention. It is true, of course, that in many cases the plaintiff will not be in a position to insure, and so expansion of liability will, at the very least, serve *respondeat superior*'s loss spreading function. But the fact that the defendant is better able to afford damages is not alone sufficient to justify legal respon-

sibility and this overarching principle must be taken into account in deciding whether to expand the reach of *respondeat superior.*[111]

Friendly refused to undermine the venerable concept of *respondeat superior* by the substitution of an economic analysis, partly because of a "deeply rooted sentiment that a business enterprise cannot justly disclaim responsibility for accidents which may fairly be said to be characteristic of its activities." His opinion acknowledged that "while Lane's return to the Tamaroa was to serve his employer, no one has suggested how he could have thought turning the wheels to be, even if—which is by no means clear—he was unaware of the consequences." After considering relevant decisions of several highly respected judges,[112] Friendly decided the case largely on grounds of human nature: "Lane's conduct was not so 'unforeseeable' as to make it unfair to charge the Government with responsibility. . . . Here it was foreseeable that crew members crossing the drydock might do damage, negligently or even intentionally, such as pushing a Bushey employee or kicking property into the water. Moreover, the proclivity of seamen to find solace for solitude by copious resort to the bottle while ashore has been noted in opinions too numerous to warrant citation. Once all this is granted, it is immaterial that Lane's precise action was not to be foreseen." In the process Friendly dismissed Second Circuit precedent without mentioning the possible need for *en banc* consideration: "Consequently, we can no longer accept our past decisions [citations omitted], since they do not accord with modern understanding as to when it is fair for an enterprise to disclaim the actions of its employees."[113]

Friendly hypothesized cases "that fall on the other side of the line." Lane's setting fire to the bar where he was drinking or running into his wife's lover and shooting him were two examples. In drawing the line, Friendly excluded "areas where the servant does not create risks different from those attendant on the activities of the community in general" and when "it would have been the most unlikely happenstance that the confrontation with the paramour occurred on a drydock rather than at the traditional spot. . . . The risk that seamen going and coming from the Tamaroa might cause damage to the drydock is enough to make it fair that the enterprise bear the loss."[114] Friendly was engaging in early sophisticated analysis of enterprise liability by focusing on "characteristic risks."[115] His conclusion cannot be considered pro-business.

Friendly's opinion received an effusive accolade from Judge Waterman: "Enthusiastically I concur. You have made new law, of course, but I am happy that you have! Indeed, after reading the opinion one would be a most unappreciative clod if he did not concur—it's magnificent!"[116] One scholar observed, "The test for vicarious liability that Friendly formulates here, and the general account of enterprise liability that it implies, instantiate a pervasive difference between the way that fairness- and efficiency-based theories conceive of enterprise liability."[117] Another academic wrote, "As early as 1968, a leading jurist had offered a rationale for vicarious liability that has subsequently been taken seriously by scholars."[118] Judge Weinstein gave his reaction: "His [Friendly's] approach to the case achieved a realistic result by diverting the law in much the way I did, although on a different ground. So I was satisfied."[119] Despite the fact that Friendly had rejected his approach, Judge Calabresi explained, "[The] irony is that Friendly got it right and Bruce [Ackerman] got it wrong. I cite the case as a great judge's response to academic theory on the basis of his own experience and intuition."[120]

An exception to the case's favorable reception came some weeks after its publication, when Friendly's old friend, Solicitor General Erwin Griswold, sent him a letter that complained about the extension of the government's liability in *Bushey*: "If Cardozo were still on the Supreme Court, I might have filed a petition [for *certiorari*]."[121] Friendly was not perturbed. "Such a wonderful mind in such a difficult personality," he told his law clerk.[122]

FRIENDLY ALSO TACKLED bread-and-butter statutory admiralty cases, where he took concepts that were showing their age and made them applicable to the current world. Under section 4(5) of the Carriage of Goods by Sea Act (COGSA),[123] enacted in 1936, unless a shipper declares a higher value for the shipped goods (and pays higher insurance), there is no liability for loss or damage "in an amount exceeding $500 per package lawful money of the United States, or in case of goods not shipped in packages, per customary freight unit." The purpose of the provision was to provide a workable standard easily ascertainable at the time of contract so the parties could allocate the risk of loss and take steps to reduce their exposure.[124] As time passed, technology changed, especially with the introduction of shipping containers in the 1960s, but the courts were still welded by statute to the concept of "package" and the diminishing $500 limit on recovery.

Writing for the court in *Leather's Best, Inc. v. S.S. Mormaclynx*, Friendly concluded that the ship's container was functionally part of the ship and not a package, but he did not decide what was a package.[125] As in many other complex cases Friendly believed that the legislature, with its extensive resources and the ability to hold hearings, was a better entity to arrive at a properly nuanced resolution, but he had no choice but to decide.[126] But then, in *Royal Typewriter Co. v. M/V Kumberland*,[127] where Friendly did not sit, Judge Oakes set forth a "functional package unit test" to determine when a shipping container should be deemed a COGSA package: when the shipper's own individual packing units are not functional, the burden of proof is on the shipper to show why the ship's container should not be treated as the package. Thus, the container was presumptively a COGSA package when the shipper's unit was not suitable for "break-bulk" shipment (shipment in separate pieces, such as a crated printing press); the shipper could avoid this result only if he could "show by other evidence that his units are themselves 'packages.'"[128] Commentators criticized Oakes's test on the ground that, contrary to the design of COGSA, he gave nearly all of the financial benefits of containerization to the economically more powerful ocean carriers, and almost none to the shipper.[129]

In 1981, in *Mitsui & Co. v. American Export Lines, Inc.*,[130] Friendly provided an alternative to the functional-economics test. A shipper sued when 1,834 gold ingots packed in five ships' containers and 1,705 rolls of floor covering shipped in thirteen containers were lost at sea after a deck of a container ship collapsed during a storm. The shipper claimed that each seventy-five-pound ingot and each roll was a package, and sought $1 7/5 million, while the carrier argued that its liability was limited to eighteen ships' containers, or $6,500, less than 1 percent of the claim. Since he viewed the containers as functionally part of the ship, Friendly found without much difficulty, first, that the containers were not the preferred unit and, second, that each roll of floor covering was a package. But the case of the ingots was more difficult. The industry spoke of "bundles" and "stacks" of ingots into which shippers supposedly gathered the ingots, but there were, in fact, neither bundles nor stacks of ingots, and, therefore, they did not constitute "packages." But, Friendly wrote, "it does not at all follow, as urged by [the carrier], that the containers become the packages. If the ingots were not shipped in packages, and we hold they were not, then, in the absence of the circumstances discussed below, the $500 limit would apply 'per customary freight unit.'"[131]

Rejecting the functional-economics test, Friendly concluded that it "simply does not take into account the important possibility that goods shipped in such containers with packaging insufficient for break-bulk shipment might be 'goods not shipped in packages.'" He concluded that the "customary freight unit" was the "bundle" referred to in the shipping documents, whether or not the ingots were shipped in bundles.[132] In a concurring opinion Oakes acknowledged the superiority of Friendly's approach.[133] Friendly took pleasure in *Mitsui* for another reason—he considered it a case study in "how to overrule another panel decision without an *en banc*."[134]

A year before Friendly died, a Second Circuit panel on which he did not sit decided *Binladen BSB Landscaping v. M.V. Nedlloyd Rotterdam*.[135]

The result was what one commentator has called the *Mitsui-Binladen* test: First, when the bill of lading lists the number of containers and describes the items inside the containers in terms that can reasonably be understood as "packages," the items inside, not the containers, will be treated as COGSA packages. Second, when the bill of lading does not clearly indicate an alternative number of packages, the container must be treated as a COGSA package if it is listed as a package on the bill of lading and if the parties have not specified that the shipment is one of "goods not shipped in packages."[136] As the twenty-first century opened every maritime judicial circuit followed the *Mitsui-Binladen* approach to COGSA.[137]

ANTITRUST WAS a relatively small part of Friendly's workload, and the mark he left on that field was faint. For the centennial of the Second Circuit in 1991 *St. John's Law Review* published an article on antitrust law in the circuit, which considered fifteen antitrust cases. None of the fifteen was a Friendly opinion,[138] although he wrote several opinions that received attention elsewhere.[139] Discussion here will be confined to a relatively inconsequential antitrust case that raised the question of whether an arguably superannuated Supreme Court holding by a legendary Justice remained the law. In *Salerno v. American League of Professional Baseball Clubs*,[140] a suit by umpires for wrongful discharge, Friendly rejected plaintiffs' request to "predict the likely overruling of the holdings in *Federal Baseball Club of Baltimore, Inc. v. National League of Professional Baseball Clubs*, 259 U.S. 200 (1922), and *Toolson v. New York Yankees, Inc.*, 346 U.S. 356 (1953), that professional baseball is not subject to the antitrust laws." He explained, "We freely acknowledge our belief that *Federal Baseball* was not one of Mr. Justice Holmes' happiest days, that the rationale of *Toolson* is extremely dubious and that, to use the Supreme Court's own adjectives, the distinction between baseball and other professional sports is 'unrealistic,' 'inconsistent' and 'illogical.' . . . While we should not fall out of our chairs with surprise at the news that *Federal Baseball* and *Toolson* have been overruled, we are not at all certain the Supreme Court is ready to give them a happy dispatch."[141]

THE ISSUE in Friendly's bankruptcy opinion *In re Gibraltor Amusements, Ltd.*[142] was whether a corporation and its wholly owned subsidiary should be counted as one or two of the three creditors necessary to place a company, the Wurlitzer Company, into involuntary bankruptcy. Judge J. Joseph Smith, writing for the court, concluded that both should be counted because each was a separate entity for income tax purposes and that the two "have scrupulously honored the separate form of the latter." Friendly dissented: "[T]he issue in each case must be resolved by reference to the policy of the applicable statutory or common law rule," a statement similar to what he said in *Powe v. Miles*, a state-action case discussed above.[143] Thus, the fact that a corporation was separate for income tax purposes had almost nothing to do with its status as a creditor in a bankruptcy proceeding. The purposes of the two rules were different.

Drawing on his college and law school roots, Friendly made expansive and persuasive use of history, legislative and otherwise, disparaging Smith's statement that the "present requirement of three petitioning creditors [was] . . . a compromise by Congress between the divergent provisions of earlier statutes, that bland statement scarcely conveys the flavor." Leading up to the passage of the Bankruptcy Act of 1898, Friendly recounted, were 200,000 business failures and acute hardship. Southern and western Populists were hostile to the concept of involuntary bankruptcy and denounced one provision as "intended to bind hand and foot the debtors of this country and place them in the vise-like grip of the greedy cormorants of the country." Friendly quoted Senator Morris Stewart of Nevada, who said that this bill "is dictated by the same spirit that hung and killed and drew and quartered women for witchery."[144] Battles were fought over just about every word, and compromises were carefully drawn.

> It is not doing justice to this history to suggest that if Congress had meant to prevent a wholly owned subsidiary from being counted as a petitioning creditor separate from its parent, it should have explicitly said so. . . . Here the purpose to require three separate creditor interests, separate in reality and not merely in legal form, is not difficult to discern. With the temper of the 55th Congress on this subject, it would have required a bold man to arise on the floor of the House of Representatives and ask that the bill be clarified to insure that a corporation with a financing subsidiary could be counted as two creditors if each unit held a claim against the debtor; it is hard to suppose the House managers would have imperiled the bill by sanctioning any such proposal and quite impossible to believe that it would have been enacted.[145]

He ended, "I cannot believe it consistent with that policy to hold that a single creditor corporation may insure its ability to initiate an involuntary bankruptcy by the simple expedient of organizing two financing subsidiaries—perhaps with independent creditors—and seeing to it that claims against each debtor are parceled out in advance of bankruptcy."[146]

LIKE HIS PRINCIPAL CONTRIBUTION to trademark law, Friendly's contribution to the field of punitive (or exemplary) damages appeared in *dicta,* in *Roginsky v. Richardson-Merrell, Inc.*[147] Sidney Roginsky sought compensatory and punitive damages for personal injuries, primarily cataracts, from a drug called MRW/29, designed to lower blood cholesterol levels, one of hundreds of similar cases filed across the country. The record revealed considerable missteps on the part of Richardson-Merrell employees. The district court sustained the jury's award of $17,500 of compensatory and $100,000 of punitive damages.

Speaking for the majority of a divided court, Friendly found the evidence of negligence sufficient to sustain compensatory damages against Richardson-Merrell under New York law but insufficient for punitive damages because of the absence of required proof of management complicity: "[A]part from negligence in policing subordinates and a somewhat stiff-necked attitude toward the FDA, is rather that [members of management] were so convinced of the value of the drug both to the public welfare and to the company's finances that they maintained a sanguine view longer than prudence warranted."[148]

While the points just discussed hardly made for an important opinion, Friendly included as *dicta* language that demonstrated foresight, namely, appreciation of historic changes that had occurred in the circumstances in which parties sought punitive damages, similar to what he did in analyzing the law of conspiracy. Traditionally, assault, battery, defamation, malicious prosecution, and trespass were typical of the torts for which punitive damages had been awarded. Recent literature, Friendly observed, discussed punitive damages in those contexts. "What strikes one is not merely that these torts are intentional but that usually there is but a single victim; a punitive recovery by him ends the matter, except for such additional liability as may be provided by the criminal law." Friendly was concerned about claims for punitive damages by hundreds of plaintiffs. Peculiarly, the defendant's brief explicitly rejected reliance on any argument against punitive damages based on multiple plaintiffs, and instead relied solely on the vagueness of the applicable standard for awarding punitive damages.[149] Thus, not only did Friendly write influential *dicta*, but he did so in a case in which the potentially benefiting party disclaimed interest in the issue.

Friendly asked whether "multiple punitive damage awards running into the hundreds may not add up to a denial of due process"[150]—a prophetic inquiry, since thirty years later a closely divided Supreme Court employed the Fourteenth Amendment's Due Process Clause to restrict punitive damages awarded by a state court in the context of a single-plaintiff wrong, over objections that the amount of punitive damages was traditionally left to the states.[151]

Friendly did not stop at identifying the problem, but he confronted the difficulties in resolving it, in line with his policy of never raising a problem without suggesting a solution. He framed his inquiry very sympathetically to business, "whether awarding punitive damages with respect to the negligent—even highly negligent—manufacture and sale of a drug governed by federal food and drug requirements . . . would not do more harm than good." He considered the role of liability policies and saw their effect either as passing along the cost to the consuming public or, if the law prohibited insurance for punitive damages, ending "the business life of a concern that has wrought much good in the past and might otherwise have continued to do so in the future, with many innocent stockholders suffering extinction of their investments for a single management sin. . . . We have the gravest difficulties in perceiving how claims for punitive damages in such a multiplicity of actions throughout the nation can be so administered as to avoid overkill." He considered the practical and immediate problem of how to frame an instruction to a jury to take account of similar pending suits: "[I]t is hard to see what the most intelligent jury would do with this, being inherently unable to know what punitive damages, if any, other juries in other states may award other plaintiffs in actions yet untried. We know of no principle whereby the first punitive award exhausts all claims for punitive damages and would thus preclude future judgments. . . . Neither does it seem either fair or practicable to limit punitive recoveries to an indeterminate number of first-comers, leaving it to some unascertained court to cry, 'Hold, enough,' in the hope that others would follow."[152]

While showing his reluctance to expand the role of federal courts in resolving questions of state law, Friendly pointed the way to a possible resolution that presaged the approach of later students of the question: "If there were any way in which all cases could be assembled before a single court, as in a limitation proceeding in admiralty, it might be possible for a jury to make one award to be held for appropriate distribution among all successful plaintiffs, although even as to this the difficulties are apparent. But we perceive no way of accomplishing that except by legislation requiring all claims in respect of drugs supervised by the FDA to be asserted in the federal courts—hardly a desirable course."[153]

Law review comments decades after *Roginsky* credited Friendly with early recognition of the explosion in awards of punitive damages in mass tort cases. Thus, one author wrote, "The appellate opinion has been cited frequently for the dicta in which Friendly warned of the danger of punitive damages 'overkill.'"[154] Another article concluded, "Despite longstanding recognition of the mass tort damages problem, attempts to find a solution have proved as challenging as Judge Friendly predicted."[155] Friendly had reconfigured the analysis of punitive damages.

CHAPTER SEVENTEEN

Intellectual Property

FRIENDLY'S INTELLECTUAL-PROPERTY DECISIONS in copyright and trademarks favored those who were creative over those who, for example, applied ingenuity to "inch as close to the plaintiff's [trade]mark as he believes he safely can,"[1] reminiscent of his extolling artists as opposed to craftsmen. He was, however, not interested in patent law and did not feel qualified to write opinions on the scientific and engineering issues raised. In a memorandum to his colleagues he wrote, "Applying the test, almost infallible, even though, in Doolingese, 'solipsistic,' that if I can understand a mechanism it must have been obvious, I penetrate the patina and conclude that the Gross insulator embodied no such invention as to be patentable."[2] In another memorandum he said, "In candor, I should finally note that my vote for affirmance is based on two policies somewhat extraneous to a strict interpretation of the patent laws. First, in these damn patent appeals perhaps our most important functions are to make sure the law was correctly stated and that the trial judge was careful. . . . Second, my sympathies are with the plaintiff."[3] Patent cases, he determined, should not even be before the circuit courts of appeals, but rather should be before a specialized appellate Patent Court, a subject he addressed in his 1972 Carpentier Lectures at Columbia University.[4] His wish for the creation of special courts became law, at least in part, but not until 1982.[5] Fittingly, in the meantime Friendly rarely wrote the first drafts of patent opinions, at least when they implicated highly technical questions.[6]

Friendly, like Learned Hand, began his career on the bench with no copyright experience. That Hand became "the chief actor" in the development of that subject[7] did not deter Friendly from disagreeing with him. As discussed in Chapter 4, on December 8, 1959, Friendly sat with Judges Hand and Lumbard on *Peter Pan Fabrics, Inc. v. Martin Weiner Corp.*,[8] a technical case involving statutory notice under the Copyright Act of 1905. Peter Pan bought a copyrighted design, known as "Byzantium," which it printed on bolts of uncolored cloth, along with proper notices of copyright on the edge of each bolt at frequent intervals. The dressmaker that converted the bolts into women's dresses, however, discarded the copyright notices. When Peter Pan brought suit against a fabricator for copying the Byzantium design on dresses, the defendant argued that Peter Pan had forfeited the copyright because its dresses were sold without statutory notices.

Writing for the majority, Hand agreed that the literal words of the statute seemed to require a victory for the defendant, but concluded that courts could disregard language "when it defeats the manifest purpose of the statute as a whole. . . . [A]t least in the case of a deliberate copyist, as in the case at bar, the absence of 'notice' is a defense that the copyist must prove, and that the burden is on him to show that 'notice' could have been embodied in the design without impairing its market value."[9] Friendly, siding with the copier in his dissent, relied on a literal and formalist reading of the statute: "Plaintiffs receive copyright protection for enabling a multitude of ladies to be caparisoned in the purple of 'Byzantium' although the copyright notices, instead of being 'affixed to each copy' of the design on the dresses, pile up in the cutting rooms." From the earliest days of the statute, he said, the notice requirement was very important and "when Congress has wished to make an exception, it has known how to do so." He explained,

> The notice requirement serves an important public purpose; the copyright proprietor is protected so long and only so long as he gives effective warning to trespassers that they are entering on forbidden ground. And if the statutory requirement of notice has not been met, it is immaterial whether a particular defendant had actual knowledge of a claim of copyright or not. . . . [I]t is not for the courts to say that something less than the statutory requirement will serve. . . . Perhaps my brothers are right in thinking that Congress wished literal compliance with § 10 to be excused under such circumstances as here; but the voice so audible to them is silent to me.[10]

Later, Friendly gave the Copyright Act a more pragmatic reading, for example, upholding a copyright notice that consisted of the owner's initials but not his full name when his initials were well known[11] (but not when they weren't).[12] When a copyright proprietor produced and sold toys in Japan without a copyright notice, for the plausible reason that toys could not be copyrighted in Japan, and then sold them with a copyright notice in the United States, Friendly sustained the copyright-infringement suit against a competitor who sold substantially identical toys.[13] He understood that the copyright proprietor had acted lawfully and diligently.

Friendly dissented in *Scherr v. Universal Match Corp.*,[14] a difficult copyright case. Steven Goodman and Stuart Scherr, who had experience in the fine arts, were assigned to prepare visual training aids while serving in the U.S. Army at Fort Dix, New Jersey. The two made a small clay model of an infantryman in full battle dress during their leisure hours. When it was brought to his attention, the deputy post commander asked them to construct a larger-than-life statue. Relieved of substantially all of their other duties for the next nine months, they devoted their duty time and much leisure time to the project. The Army bore the bulk of the direct costs of the project, some $12,367.90, and supplied additional part-time personnel. While at all times accountable to the Army, the two soldiers had complete freedom in the design. The Army placed the completed twenty-five-foot-high statue (to which the plaintiffs had affixed an inconspicuous notice of copyright) at the entrance to Fort Dix with a plaque inscribed "The Ultimate Weapon, the only indispensable instrument of war, the fighting man." When, with the consent of the Army, the Universal Match Corporation manufactured and sold matchbooks whose cover pictured the statue and its title, "The Ultimate Weapon," Goodman and Scherr filed suit for copyright infringement.[15] After the U.S. government intervened on the side of defendant Universal, the district court granted the defendants' motion for summary judgment.

A majority of the court of appeals affirmed on the ground that "the statue falls within the 'works for hire' rule of 17 U.S.C. § 26 and, therefore, any and all copyright interest [in the statue] belongs to . . . or inures to the benefit of [the government]." After noting that "authors and proprietors" are entitled to the copyright of a work of art and that an "author" is defined to include "an employer in the case of works made for hire," the majority stated, "The essential factor in determining whether an employee created his work of art within the scope of his employment as part of his employment duties is whether the employer possessed the right to direct and to supervise the manner in which the work was being performed." An employer-employee relationship existed, and the government owned the copyright; it was "strikingly obvious." "The Army's power to supervise; its exercise, though a limited one, of that power; and the overwhelming appropriation of government funds, time and facilities to the project, are all undisputed."[16]

Friendly's dissent described the usual application of the Copyright Act: when an employer tells the employee what to do, there is no difficulty finding the employer to be the author. He was the creator. At the time the relationship between the plaintiffs and the Army began, however, no one contemplated the production of copyrighted works, and there was insufficient basis "for inferring an intention to vest copyright in the Government from the circumstances under which the plaintiffs translated the model they had already created into a life-sized statue." Friendly noted that the government relied on the supposed unfairness of giving the plaintiffs the copyright when the government expended $12,367.90 of its funds. Disagreeing, Friendly stated, "[T]he unfairness is not obvious to me. The Government wanted a statue to display at Fort Dix and got it; there is nothing to suggest it ever thought about publishing copies of the work, with the consequent need for owning the copyright."[17] Friendly opted for following the policy of the Constitution and the Copyright Act and the intent of the parties.

While Friendly's pragmatic dissent was persuasive, it could have been more so. He failed to point out the majority's miscitation of cases, including the only case cited for its principal point: "The essential factor in determining whether an employee created his work of art within the scope of his employment as part of his employment duties is whether the employer possessed the right to direct and to supervise the manner in which the work was being performed. . . . *Donaldson Publishing Co. v. Bergman, Vocco & Conn, Inc.*, 375 F.2d 639 (2 Cir. 1967)."[18] But *Donaldson*, a case on which Friendly sat, said, "*an* essential element of the employer-employee relationship, the right of the employer 'to direct and supervise the manner in which the writer performs his work' . . . is lacking here."[19] The majority also miscited other cases, including one where the Second Circuit held that where the copyright resides "will always turn on the intention of the parties where the intent can be ascertained."[20] Friendly's opinion was unusual for another reason. Once again he was voting to reverse the district court on grounds that the losing party had not argued there.[21]

Polaroid Corp. v. Polarad Electronics Corp.[22] exemplifies Friendly's pedagogic approach to opinion writing, namely, discussing and virtually resolving issues unnecessary to the disposition of the case. After considering in detail an issue that "has long been vexing and does not become easier of solution with the years," he avoided deciding it "since we uphold the District Court's conclusion with respect to [another ground]." The "vexing" problem was "determining how far a valid trademark shall be protected with respect to goods other than those to which its owner has applied it," while the ground on which Friendly actually relied was "laches," an unreasonably long and prejudicial delay in asserting one's rights. He discussed both issues with equal thoroughness.

The plaintiff, the holder of eleven U.S. registrations for "Polaroid," brought suit in 1956, alleging that the defendant's use of the name "Polarad" infringed its trademark and constituted unfair competition. In its early years Polaroid became a well-known name "as applied to sheet polarizing material and products made therefrom, as well as to optical desk lamps, stereoscope viewers, etc." After World War II the plaintiff's annual sales shrank to under $2 million before exploding to $65 million in 1958 after its development of the Land camera. Polarad was organized in 1944 and its principal business was "the sale of microwave generating, receiving and measuring devices and of television studio equipment." Conceding that the parties' businesses were basically different, Polaroid nevertheless claimed some overlap and a few instances of actual confusion.[23]

Friendly expressed at least a modicum of skepticism concerning the origin of Polarad's name: "Defendant claimed it had arrived at the name Polarad by taking the first letters of the first and last names of its founder, Paul Odessey, and the first two letters of the first name of his friend and anticipated partner, Larry Jaffe, and adding the suffix 'rad,' intended to signify radio; however, Odessey admitted that at the time he had 'some knowledge' of plaintiff's use of the name Polaroid, although only as applied to glasses and polarizing filters and not to electronics."[24] Since the cases tendered by the parties as convincing authority provided little assistance, Friendly developed his own multifaceted formulation of the "vexing" problem: "Where the products are different, the prior owner's chance of success is a function of many variables: the strength of his mark, the degree of similarity between the two marks, the proximity of the products, the likelihood that the prior owner will bridge the gap, actual confusion, and the reciprocal of defendant's good faith in adopting its own mark, the quality of defendant's product, and the sophistication of the buyers."[25]

After analyzing the applicability of these factors, Friendly opined:

[W]e are thus by no means sure . . . plaintiff would not have been entitled to at least some injunctive relief if it had moved with reasonable promptness. However, we are not required to decide this since we uphold the District Court's conclusion with respect to laches. . . . Plaintiff seeks to excuse its early inactivity on the ground that defendant's sales were small. But that is the very time when the owner of a mark ought forcefully to claim protection. . . . "[I]t cannot be equitable for a well-informed merchant with knowledge of a claimed invasion of right, to wait and see how successful his competitor will be and then destroy with the aid of a court decree, much that the competitor has striven for and accomplished."[26]

Despite Friendly's holding on the ground of laches, the case has served a more important function with his *dicta*; an analysis of 693 courts of appeals cases that cited Polaroid, 92 cited it for laches, 545 for trademark infringement, and 56 for both. What is also significant is that Friendly had not intended his listing of factors to be definitive, but only illustrative. Opposed to bright lines, he was not one who ordinarily embraced definitive lists of relevant factors. Nevertheless, his list in *Polaroid* dominated subsequent opinions of the Second Circuit.[27]

Friendly, who was acutely aware of the distinction between a holding and a *dictum*,[28] persistently included *dicta* in his opinions. He told a clerk, "I don't expect to be writing decisions forever and I want to make sure I have the opportunity to say what I want to say."[29] While *dicta* are not binding on other courts, they can—when coming from a judge of Friendly's reputation—carry considerable weight. As noted, some of Friendly's most important contributions to the law were "mere" *dicta*.[30] Sometimes his *dicta* consisted of advice to the Supreme Court that a change in the law was appropriate. For example, he said, "The passing of *Ragan* would bring no tears from us."[31] Friendly's *dicta*, however, prompted a circuit judge sitting with Friendly to complain that the opinion went beyond what it was necessary for the court to decide,[32] although a district judge was grateful for his *dicta*, and said that Friendly's writing about issues when he did not have to showed kindness to lawyers and clients.[33] Friendly recognized that there may be times when it is "useful to say more than necessary because of the problems before lower courts."[34] Like other great judges, he created opportunities to develop the law.

Two other infringement cases confirm Friendly's support for persons with originality and enterprise and are examples where his vivid prose did not risk distorting the legal reasoning or rule that he articulated. In *Chandon Champagne Corp. v. San Marino Wine Corp.*,[35] the producer of the luxury Dom Perignon Champagne sued the producer of a New York low-priced sparkling wine it called Pierre Perignon. Both parties named their wine after the putative father of champagne. The district judge found for the defendant on the ground of absence of confusion or, in Friendly's parlance, "[T]he district judge thought that although the parties sold products described by the same noun, these were in fact different." On appeal Friendly affirmed, as in *Polaroid*, on the ground of laches, but took the occasion to discuss Learned Hand's opinion in a case that alleged confusion between Mumm Champagne and Mumm Rhine wine, another low-priced New York bubbly,[36] in language that itself sparkled:

On this very issue of domestic versus French champagne, with the domestic product in that case marketed under a deceptively similar label, Judge Learned Hand, taking what seems a rather personal form of judicial notice, noted that "especially as evening wears on, the label, and only a very casual glance at the label, is quite enough to assure the host and his table that he remains as free-handed and careless of cost as when he began," and that "At such stages of an entertainment nothing will be easier than for an unscrupulous restaurant keeper to substitute the domestic champagne." Even in less bibulous circumstances, one who was served the defendant's mass-produced "Pierre Perignon" with only partial disclosure of its identity by his host, or who knowingly ordered the domestic variety under mistaken assumption that it was made with the skill and taste employed at supposedly related French vineyards, would be more likely to turn thereafter on appropriate occasions to another high priced competitor rather than to Dom Perignon. Hence we would have no hesitancy in granting relief if plaintiffs had clear priority to the mark in the United States, if defendant had knowingly trampled on their rights, and if plaintiffs had moved promptly to vindicate them under 15 U.S.C. § 1114(1). But that is not this case.[37]

In *Wood & Sons v. Reese Jewelry Corp.* Friendly dissented from a holding that defendant's use of a trademark on engagement and wedding rings did not cause confusion:

> When middle-aged judges are obliged to determine the "likelihood of confusion" in the purchase of engagement and wedding rings by youthful swains not enjoying our advantage of knowing the answer in advance, I would suppose the most resolute mind must entertain some doubts. I prefer to resolve mine in favor of a plaintiff who has spent money and effort in exploiting its mark for nearly a score of years rather than of a defendant who, with the world of possible names before him, has chosen to inch as close to the plaintiff's mark as he believes he safely can, even if he has done this in a "good faith" belief that he has succeeded.[38]

Friendly favored rectitude in business dealings.

CHAPTER EIGHTEEN

Management and Labor

PRO-MANAGEMENT IN LABOR DISPUTES, Friendly's opinions tended to favor employers over workers and workers over unions and, unsurprisingly, employers over unions. In close cases, when the panel was not unanimous, Friendly sided with the employer in fourteen out of twenty-one of these cases. From his personal experience in private practice, he was conscious of what he called "business realities,"[1] and superseded any tutelage by Felix Frankfurter and Louis D. Brandeis, who were both experienced in labor law and were pro-worker and pro-union.[2] As discussed at the end of the chapter, there was one exception to Friendly's pro-management bent: he sided with workers when they sued for employment discrimination.

Before discussing labor-management relations, it is noteworthy that Friendly generally took a similarly pro-employer stance in tort actions arising in a commercial context. In actions under the Federal Employers' Liability Act,[3] covering railroad employees engaged in interstate commerce, he voted against the worker in five of the six cases in which the panel split. In maritime actions, such as under the Jones Act,[4] where the issues often related to whether the ship was "unseaworthy," Friendly voted against the worker in nine of the twelve split-panel cases.[5] Disagreeing over whether maritime statutes were de facto workmen's compensation acts, members of the panels were unusually contentious and used strong language.[6] In 1966 Friendly sought an *en banc* hearing: "I must confess I think this is a new low in our treatment of the unseaworthiness problem. We simply throw up our hands and say that the trial judge can do whatever he wants and then reverse because he may not have known he was so free to disregard our decisions."[7]

In the labor-management arena Friendly's leanings did not go unnoticed by his colleagues. Writing for the majority in *NLRB v. Golub Corp.*,[8] Friendly concluded that statements by an employer to its employees did not constitute a threat and were protected by the First Amendment, while statements by a union to employees about the effect of signing an authorization card for union representation misled them. The decision provoked a heated dissent from Judge Hays:

> It is astonishing to find that the ears of employees are so exquisitely attuned to every nuance of meaning in the employer's letters and speeches, but that when it comes to the union's representations these same employees are "ordinary working people unversed in the 'witty diversities' of labor law,'" *N.L.R.B. v. S.E. Nichols Co.*, 380 F.2d 438, 442 (2d Cir. 1967) [Friendly, J.], so dull and stupid that the union can easily pull the wool over their eyes. Employees who have not the slightest difficulty in distinguishing between a "prediction" and a "threat," are unable to read union authorization cards with even that degree of understanding which human beings ordinarily exercise. Surely enforcement of the Board's orders has not become a game of "Heads I win, tails you lose."[9]

While there is some truth to this criticism, Friendly was not so one-sided as Hays suggests, even in cases involving allegedly coercive communications by employers to employees. Friendly dissented from a holding that a union unlawfully discriminated when it favored a dues-paying member against a non-dues-paying member who had accepted a loss of seniority along with his being excused from paying dues;[10] dissented from a decision that held that the respondent union had discriminated against non-members;[11] dissented from an opinion that took a tolerant view of management's anti-union statements;[12] and wrote for a unanimous court in finding that an employer committed an unfair labor practice in failing to recognize a unanimously elected grievance committee.[13] In addition, in *NLRB v. Lorben Corp.*,[14] Friendly, dissenting, voted to uphold the National Labor Relations Board (NLRB) finding that an employer had engaged in coercive questioning of employees about their desire to have a particular union represent them, and in *NLRB v. Rollins Telecasting, Inc.*,[15] he wrote for the court in sustaining two of three NLRB findings that a corporation had made coercive statements to employees in the context of a union election.

Friendly supported management when he concluded that management was acting as management should or that the union was seeking an unfair advantage. In *NLRB v. General Electric Co.*,[16] he dissented when GE unsuccessfully appealed from the Board's finding of overall bad-faith bargaining. Following a strike in 1946 disastrous to all involved, GE adopted a new approach to collective bargaining to improve its credibility with its employees. After extensive internal deliberation, GE would announce its "fair, firm offer," which it would change only if the union presented facts it had missed. Over the union's objections GE extensively publicized its approach and offer. Aside from some minor concessions, GE held firm in subsequent negotiating sessions, and the union "capitulated completely" after a three-week strike.[17] The principal issue was GE's "take-it-or-leave-it" stance, which Judge Kaufman, writing for the majority, considered as part of the "totality of the circumstances" in deciding that GE had engaged in an unfair labor practice. GE had a "predetermined resolve not to budge from an initial position" and made no serious attempt to resolve differences and reach a common ground. Judge Waterman's concurrence was narrower: "What makes these practices unfair is GE's 'widely publicized campaign of unbending firmness,' that is, GE's communications to its employees that firmness was one of the company's independent policies." In other words, Waterman would accept GE's unyielding performance so long as it didn't announce it.[18]

Friendly's dissenting opinion argued that a finding of bad faith based on an entire course of conduct should be limited to cases where there is a "desire not to reach an agreement," such as a plan to get rid of the union, which did not exist here. He confronted Kaufman's use of the prejudicial "catchphrase" "take-it-or-leave-it" and defined it as "a resolve to adhere to a position without even listening to and considering the view of the other side." But, Friendly said, it cannot be a violation "when, after discussing the union's proposals and supporting arguments, [an employer] formulates what he considers a sufficiently attractive offer and refuses to alter it unless convinced an alteration is 'right.'" In fact, he announced, section 8(d) of the National Labor Relations Act expressly provided that the obligation to bargain "does not compel either party to agree to a proposal or require the making of a concession," and adopted a seemingly narrow (and pro-employer) interpretation of the NLRA bargaining requirements that required an employer only to listen carefully before turning down the union. Finally, rejecting the majority's argument based on GE's publicity campaign, he concluded that GE's actions were covered by section 8(c) of the Act, which protects "views, argument, or opinion."[19]

Uncharacteristically, Friendly gave little weight to process, that is, allowing both sides to feel that they were part of a system that permitted them to have an impact. GE's approach alienated workers and undercut the goal of the labor laws to provide a process in which the participants and the public would have the confidence and respect that the labor laws were designed to create.[20] In other contexts Friendly recognized process considerations: "[I]t is important that a claimant whose benefits are being terminated should not merely receive a fair hearing, but should think he received one."[21]

Friendly relied on labor market realities in *NLRB. v. Miranda Fuel Co.*,[22] where the union achieved the discharge of Michael Lopuch, an employee who was a union member, on the basis of what seems to have been a minor violation of the parties' collective-bargaining agreement. Section 8(a)(3) of the National Labor Relations Act made it an unfair labor practice for an employer "by discrimination in regard to hire or tenure of employment . . . to encourage membership in any labor organization," and section 8(a)(2) made it an unfair labor practice for a union "to cause or attempt to cause an employer to do so." Section 9 required a union to act fairly and impartially in its representative capacity. While a majority of the Board found that Lopuch's demotion was a breach of the union's duty to represent all employees fairly, the Second Circuit reversed: "An unfair labor practice has been committed only if the discrimination was deliberately designed to encourage membership in the union. . . . [H]ere the placing of Lopuch at the bottom of the seniority list, even if done through sheer whim or caprice, and even if arbitrary, unjust and 'invidious,' whatever that may mean in the context of the facts of this case, could not conceivably have been thought to encourage union membership, because the demotion affected union and nonunion men alike."[23]

Friendly filed a dissent that would have weakened union power. Unhappy with the "deliberately designed to" test just quoted, he carefully parsed the statutory language in a manner that all but read out of the statute any remnant of the requirement that the employer's purpose or motive determined whether he violates section 8(a)(3).[24]

> Congress did *not* say "to discriminate in regard to hire or tenure of employment *because* of membership in any labor organization,"—language which, indeed, would not support the result here reached by the Board. Neither did it define the unfair labor practice as being discrimination "*in order to* encourage or discourage membership in any labor organization." What Congress forbade was "to encourage or discourage membership in any labor organization" by "discrimination in regard to hire or tenure of employment." . . . If English words are to receive their ordinary meaning, I cannot see how it

could fairly be denied in such a case that the employer's yielding to unwarranted demands by a union delegate or shop steward at the instance of union members would "encourage * * * membership in any labor organization"; the non-union members would think they had better get at least that much closer to the source of power.[25]

Not mentioned in any opinion was that Lopuch was African-American, a fact noted only in the NLRB's brief.[26] No Civil Rights Act of 1964 yet existed, and if, as may have been the case, the other drivers wanted Lopuch demoted because he was black, no intent to influence union membership in the relevant sense would exist. (A year later, the NLRB made unlawful race discrimination an unfair labor practice.)[27] Whether Friendly was sympathetic to Lopuch because of his race would be speculation.

FRIENDLY WAS RECEPTIVE when employees contended they were victims of management's unlawful employment discrimination, as demonstrated by two appeals from decisions of District Judge John T. Curtin. The earlier case was under the Equal Pay Act of 1963, which, with qualifications and exceptions, equalized pay for women who did work "equal" to men. The Secretary of Labor brought suit against Corning Glass Works, whose problems started when it expanded its production by including a night shift in its factories in Corning, New York, in 1930, a time when New York law prohibited the employment of women at night. While women filled most, if not all, of the inspection jobs on the day shifts, Corning paid men filling the night inspection jobs about twice what day shift inspectors made. Over the years Corning had made efforts to integrate the workforce and improve the pay scale for the women, but it nevertheless continued to pay men more, in one case by paying extra to employees who were working as inspectors for a long time. Curtin found in favor of the women.

Affirming Curtin on the finding of discrimination,[28] Friendly concluded, "The plain fact is that the differential here at issue arose because men would not work at the lower rates paid the women day-time inspectors to perform what the men called 'female work.' This is the very condition at which the Equal Pay Act was aimed." He expressed sympathy for Corning's difficulty in changing policies that originally resulted from the New York law. "If the result here seems harsh in view of the efforts Corning has been making since 1966, the harshness is that which may be inevitable when a legislature demands a drastic change in discriminatory practices that had too long been accepted."[29] When the Third Circuit found for Corning one year later in an identical suit involving a Corning plant in

Pennsylvania, the Supreme Court reversed with an opinion that closely tracked Friendly's.[30]

In another employment-discrimination case, two retired teachers, Sarah M. Cipriano and Jeune M. Miller, sued the local board of education and the teachers' union for age discrimination. The sixty-one-year-old plaintiffs were too old to have participated in a plan created by the defendants that offered early-retirement incentives to teachers who were fifty-five to sixty. Judge Curtin granted the defendants' motion to dismiss the complaint on the basis of section 4(f)(2) of the Age Discrimination in Employment Act, which provided that it was not unlawful for an employer or labor organization to "observe the terms of a bona fide seniority system or any bona fide employee benefit plan such as a retirement, pension, or insurance plan, which is not a subterfuge to evade the purposes of the chapter." Reversing,[31] Friendly agreed that the incentive plan was a "bona fide employee benefit plan" because the employer paid employees to retire early in order to save money. Although recognizing that the plaintiffs' claim was weak, he generously remanded the case to Curtin to decide whether the plan was a "subterfuge," which would have required finding for the plaintiffs: "[I]t is rather hard to give content to the concept of 'subterfuge' when that term is applied to a plan for voluntary action, there is no claim that the option was illusory, and the complaint is made, not by employees who claim that they were tricked by the option into prematurely leaving the workforce, but rather by employees who protest at having been excluded from the option."[32]

Friendly showed respect for the rights of women in two other cases even though he did not rule in their favor. In *Ste. Marie v. Eastern R.R. Association*,[33] women plaintiffs claimed gender discrimination in hiring and promotion to technical and managerial positions. Although he reversed the judgment for plaintiffs because of errors committed by the trial judge, he explained, gratuitously, what the plaintiffs would have to show on remand in order to prevail. He suggested that presentation of evidence that it was company policy to discriminate against women would convert the few isolated examples of alleged discrimination into a company policy that might support a judgment. In the other case, *Igneri v. Cie. de Transports Oceaniques*,[34] Friendly held that a longshoreman's wife could not recover for loss of consortium when an accident paralyzed her husband's lower extremities, but observed, "Our conclusion, it should be emphasized, does not rest on the discrimination between the sexes . . . ; we would reach the same result in the rare case of the husband of a seawoman as in the common ones of the wife of the stevedore doing seaman's work."[35]

CHAPTER NINETEEN

Railroad Reorganization

MASSIVE BANKRUPTCIES of eight major railroads in the Northeast and Midwest prompted many proposed solutions and much controversy in the executive and legislative branches of the government as well as among such interested persons as railroad executives, investors, creditors, and unions, along with scholars and commentators.[1] A U.S. Senate staff report, dated December 1972, concluded that railroads in the Northeast suffered from

> (steadily) declining freight volume, particularly in traditionally rail-carried bulk commodities such as coal, steel and forest products; outdated terminals that could not efficiently handle current volume, let alone any hoped-for increased volume; service problems, including an unbelievably high incidence of damage to shipments and inability to meet delivery schedules; steadily increasing competition from the more efficient motor and water carriers; deteriorated physical plants; outdated work rules and large job protection commitments; concerns of shippers, local governments and unions that would inevitably delay abandonments of unprofitable lines; and continued losses from fulfilling obligations to provide passenger service.[2]

Another study offered a tauter description: "[T]he region by the early 1970s had become a railroad graveyard."[3]

To reorganize the freight railroads into a single system operated by a private, for-profit corporation, Congress passed the Regional Rail

Reorganization Act of 1973 (RRRA),[4] which established the U.S. Railway Association (USRA) as a new government corporation and required it to prepare a "Final System Plan" for restructuring the railroads into a "financially self-sustaining rail service system." The Plan would determine the properties to be transferred from the railroads and their price. The designated railroad lines and equipment would be conveyed to the USRA and then to a private (but government-supported) corporation, Consolidated Rail Corporation (Conrail), while the remainder would be abandoned. In return the railroads would receive securities of Conrail and up to $500 million of USRA obligations. The goal was to obtain a satisfactory system of railroads while eliminating from the system unnecessary lines and assets, including bridges, real estate, and materials.[5] A Special Court consisting of three judges was given exclusive jurisdiction to resolve legal disputes arising out of the bankruptcies of some important railroads. During the period leading up to the adoption of the Final Plan, no railroad was permitted to abandon any railroad line if an affected state or local transportation authority reasonably opposed abandonment.[6]

Taking senior status on the Second Circuit along with a reduced workload, Friendly assumed the position of Chief Judge of the Special Court, becoming largely responsible for the health of freight railroads in the northeastern United States. He loved railroads—big railroads, small railroads, even tiny spurs; to him they represented an important aspect of the development of America.[7] The work would involve him in intricate problems of administrative law as well as complex factual issues. The assignment to Friendly, who had worked extensively in private practice for bankrupt railroads during the Depression and heard appeals relating to bankrupt railroads as a judge in the late 1960s,[8] warmed his heart. Indeed his most tangible accomplishment on the bench may have been his ten-year service as Chief Judge of the Special Court. The effort was successful by just about every measure, although almost immediately the process was subjected to challenge on constitutional grounds.

As summarized by Judge John Minor Wisdom of the Fifth Circuit (who replaced Carl E. McGowan of the District of Columbia Circuit), "[C]ertain creditors of the bankrupt railroads argued that the Act violated the fifth amendment on two grounds: (1) the requirement that rail properties be conveyed to Conrail in exchange for its securities rather than for cash amounted to an unjust taking of property without adequate compensation; and (2) the requirement that rail service be maintained until adoption of the Final System Plan without compensating for the erosion of rail properties during this period was an unconstitutional taking of property (this was later termed 'compensable unconstitutional erosion' or CUE)."[9]

The briefs of the parties and others, brimming with facts and legal arguments, were competently prepared and necessarily long. Following two days of oral argument, it took the Special Court only thirty-seven days to issue a 109-page opinion.[10] Friendly composed the portion of the opinion relating to issues common to all the parties, the most important and difficult issues. His opinion rejected a decision of a three-judge court convened in Pennsylvania in the case of *Connecticut General Ins. Co. v. Blanchette*, which had held the statute unconstitutional in several respects.[11] The key issue was whether recovery under the RRRA, which Friendly demonstrated almost certainly would fail to provide sufficient funds to compensate the railroads, could be supplemented by claims filed in the U.S. Claims Court under the Tucker Act,[12] which allowed suits against the government based on contract. In other words, could relief under the Tucker Act supplement payments under the RRRA and avoid a finding that the railroads were inadequately compensated for the confiscation of their property?

Arguments based on the language and statutory scheme were roughly in balance. The legislative history slightly favored those claiming that the RRRA did not provide a Tucker Act remedy and was therefore unconstitutional. Even if statements on the floor of Congress could be considered on the meaning of legislation, a point Friendly found debatable, he composed a typically creative rejoinder: "We have been cited to no decision in which a court has resorted to statements on the floor of Congress in order to consign an ambiguous statute to destruction," carefully molding the argument to the factual context.[13]

Friendly turned to several principles of statutory construction to deal with the imprecise statute,[14] including that "when two statutes are capable of co-existence, it is the duty of the courts, absent a clearly expressed congressional intent to the contrary, to regard each as effective,"[15] and found that the Tucker Act could be employed. Quoting Frankfurter that "[p]utting the wrong question is not likely to beget right answers even in law,"[16] Friendly continued,

> Our disagreement is rooted in a belief that the *Connecticut General* court may not have framed the issue properly. . . . The *Connecticut General* court apparently viewed the availability of a Tucker Act remedy as depending on whether "Congress intended that the financial obligations of the United States be limited to the express terms of the Act [RRRA]." . . . [T]he true issue is whether there is sufficient proof that Congress intended to *prevent* such recourse. The Act being admittedly silent on the point, the issue becomes whether the scheme of the Act, supplemented by the legislative history, sufficiently evidences a Congressional intention to withdraw a remedy that would otherwise exist.[17]

Two and a half months after Friendly and his colleagues upheld the RRRA, the Supreme Court reversed *Connecticut General* in a decision entitled *Regional Rail Reorganization Act Cases*.[18] On the question of whether the Tucker Act survived the RRRA, Justice Brennan, writing for the Court, substantially adopted Friendly's opinion, starting with "The District Court made the wrong inquiry." Brennan's opinion not only quoted extensively from Friendly's opinion, but stated, "The Special Court, speaking through Judge Friendly, comprehensively canvassed both issues, and in a thorough opinion, concluded that the Rail Act does not bar any necessary resort to the Tucker Act remedy and that the remedy is adequate. Our independent examination of the issues brings us to the same conclusion, substantially for the reasons stated by Judge Friendly."[19]

The Special Court next faced an enormous problem: fixing fair compensation for assets of bankrupt railroads, which included nineteen thousand miles of railway tracks, terminals, and rolling stock, on the assumption that the RRRA had not been passed and that the sale of the railroads had proceeded privately. Friendly and Judge Wisdom, a very able judge whom Friendly admired, dealt with the statutory problems, and the capable District Judge Roszel C. Thomsen of Baltimore handled the many discovery and related disputes.[20] At least twenty-five parties and their lawyers participated in the litigation, and some parties had quite a few lawyers. Covington & Burling, which represented the Penn Central trustees, assigned thirty lawyers to the task.[21] Two other major Washington law firms, Hogan & Hartson and Wilmer, Cutler & Pickering, each supplying about twenty-five lawyers, represented the USRA along with USRA's inside counsel. Both sides relied on experts, usually leaders in their field.[22] After considering the question in some depth, the court decided to do without special masters, whose presence would have slowed progress.

Friendly imposed a merciless schedule on the lawyers and the court. In one phase of the case the lawyers asked for two years to complete discovery; Friendly gave them ninety days. He required the taking of multiple depositions simultaneously, ordered briefs to be submitted while testimony was still being taken, and set deadlines around holidays, which the lawyers interpreted as trying to make them settle.[23] Proceedings were expedited in a variety of other ways, including by having direct examination of experts and other witnesses submitted in the form of affidavits and cross-examination conducted by deposition, with the transcripts submitted to the Special Court.[24] Friendly acknowledged the burdens he imposed on the participants: "We made it known from the outset that almost nothing short of rigor mortis would be considered as a ground for an extension of time; I think we granted only one."[25]

The procedures caused Friendly to change his mind about the value of cross-examination. Previously he had valued cross-examination rather low, despite his skill as a cross-examiner and his experience observing John Harlan in the *Wendel* will case. He later revised his view in the light of his experience sitting on the Special Court, explaining in 1983, "I must say that the cross-examination, even of experts, was quite effective. I think I would now revise my position with respect to cases of this sort and say that cross-examination does have its benefits but that it need not take place in the presence of the officer who is to make the decision."[26]

For the next decade, with Friendly unquestionably in charge, the court fielded many challenges to administrative and district court interpretations and implementations of the RRRA that were necessarily long and involved, such as whether certain claims came within the jurisdiction of the Special Court[27] and whether parcels of real property were subject to compulsory conveyance in opinions.[28] One of the lawyers in the case, Louis R. Cohen, said that Friendly "was not only a judge on the case, but he pretty much created the case, the ground rules, and even some of the agreements among the parties. During one conference with counsel, Friendly took out a pen and wrote an agreement between plaintiffs and the USRA. How do you object? We signed the agreement that morning."[29]

One year later, after another round of briefs, Friendly engaged in a more extensive discussion of issues, especially of net liquidation value. Were the railroads' recoveries limited to scrap value? Could they recover the value determined by a hypothetically willing buyer and willing seller? Could they recover replacement or reproduction cost, whatever that might mean in the context of outdated and deteriorated railroads that had been made with enormous governmental and private contributions, and when no one had any thought of reproducing the railroads?[30] How likely was it that other companies, states, and localities would have acquired and run the railroads in the absence of the RRRA? Was it reasonable to assume that after the process the Northeast would be left without a railroad? Could the railroads be compensated for the extent government policies helped propel them into bankruptcy by subsidizing competitors, including trucks? In computing the value of one railroad, what assumptions should be made about the fate of other railroads, including the dominant railroad in the region, Penn Central? Nothing like this had been done before. Briefs citing hundreds of cases, articles, and books cast uncertain light on the issue of what was just compensation to the railroads. While rejecting absurd positions, Friendly allowed all reasonable scenarios to be taken into account. But that was barely the beginning of the complex analysis.[31]

The Special Court confronted the amount of recovery to be permitted for compensable unconstitutional erosion, or CUE, including administrative expenses,[32] arising out of the fact that the RRRA prohibited the railroads from abandoning lines and thereby saving money. Being forced to run unwanted lines cost the railroads money, which they sought to recover. After tracing the history of the concept and the authorities defining it, Friendly fixed the starting date for awards based on CUE. Responding to the railroads' extensive and expensive CUE claims, Friendly stated, "With deep respect for the sincerity of counsel, we believe their concentration on maximizing claims for pre-conveyance CUE has produced a certain amount of myopia as to the parlous condition of these railroads in 1973. . . . The idea that billions of dollars of liquidation proceeds of these bankrupt railroads are lurking just around the corner is unrealistic in the last degree. The prospect of having to liquidate these bankrupt estates in a region largely deprived of railroad service was scarcely enticing."[33]

After reviewing the enormous complexity of the task remaining in 1977, Friendly was very pessimistic about the future of the evaluation process. "The court is confronted in this case by a task of almost insuperable difficulty. That is to determine what action would have been taken by interests of all kinds—the [bankrupt railroads], other railroads, state and local public bodies, the United States, the ICC, labor, and shippers, in order to avoid a shutdown of the [bankrupt railroads] (including [Penn Central]) which would have entailed disaster for all."[34] Congress had grossly underestimated the scope of the problem. Four years had elapsed since the adoption of the RRRA and the process was barely under way. "[T]he problems inherent in determining value for railroad use are staggering"; without settlement the process would approach the interminable.[35]

A particularly difficult matter was the "glut" problem, namely, an excess of material on the market, about which Friendly chose to correspond with Judge Richard Posner of the Seventh Circuit, the judge and scholar he most respected. After stating, "I see now that the glut problem is more complicated than I thought; and I now think your instinct is correct," Posner set out the essence of the problem:

> An example will illustrate my present thinking. Let there be just two commuter railroads, A and B, A being in New York and B in New Jersey. If A had been scrapped but B had not, A's scrap value would have been $1 million. Likewise, if B had been scrapped but A had not, B's scrap value would have been $1 million. But if both had been scrapped, each would have had a scrap value of only $500,000, because of the glut phenomenon. But in fact we know that neither would have been scrapped, that both would have continued under public ownership; and the question is

whether the federal government must pay $500,000 or $1 million for each line. . . .

The federal government must pay whatever the states would in fact have paid for these lines; for by hypothesis, but for federal intervention, the lines would have been sold to the states. I assume that the states would have paid the scrap value of the lines, because that is what the eminent domain law would have required; so the question becomes: which scrap value would each state have paid, $500,000 or $1 million? And I think the answer is, $1 million. Each state knows that the other will in fact take over the commuter line in its state and run the railroad. Each state knows in other words that there will be no glut. In deciding what the scrap value of each line is, each state must, I would argue, take as a given that the other state will continue the line in railroad service, and must calculate the scrap value of its line on the basis of that assumption. New York, in valuing A, knows that B, in New Jersey, will continue in railroad service; and vice versa for New Jersey in valuing B. Therefore each state will have to pay $1 million for its railroad, and the federal government must pay the same for each.[36]

Considerable progress was being made, and the end of the Special Court's task was approaching in 1981. After receiving five thousand pages of argument in the railroads' opening briefs (accompanied by forty-nine maps and a thirty-two-volume supplementary appendix), along with lengthy opposing briefs by the government and reply briefs, followed by days of oral argument, the members of the Special Court commenced drafting sections of the opinion that would decide the legal issues while computing the amount of compensation due each railroad for transferring its assets to Conrail. The drafts, with the chambers of all judges contributing, repeatedly identified flaws in the parties' presentations that required the judges and clerks to work out the proper valuations. Once again, Friendly and his law clerks drafted the portions of the opinion applicable to all railroads.

As the drafting of the principal opinion reached its final stages in 1981, Friendly's law clerks, with his consent, contacted counsel for the parties to ask where certain information was located in the massive record. From these questions, the clerks surmised, the lawyers for the parties began to see where the Special Court was headed, and their desultory settlement talks intensified. All the major parties settled, first Penn Central, which received $2.1 billion, and then the other major lines.[37] The case was effectively over and the elaborate valuation opinions appeared to be stillborn. Everyone in the chambers was devastated, including Friendly. His secretary, Pat Hall, said that following the parties' announcement of the settlements she received a telephone call at her home from her despondent boss, the only occasion during the six years she worked for him that he called her there. Then Friendly got an idea. He announced to his clerks with a smile that the entire opinion would be published as part of a ratification of the settlements. They would use the publication to show that the settlements were in the best interests of all concerned, as well as to act as a guide to those few smaller railroads that had not settled.

The first of the two opinions, both *per curiam*, was issued in 1981 and dealt primarily with the railroads' property that would continue to be used for railroad purposes.[38] The court accepted that "in weighing the likelihood or unlikelihood of their proposed dispositions, the court must consider that the discontinuance of essential rail service was the most unlikely outcome of all, with the consequence that in the absence of the Rail Act some basically nonfederal solution to the problems of rail service in the Northeast would have been found." But that conclusion did not tell how much of the system would be scrapped and did not provide enlightenment on how much would be paid, which required laborious analysis. It also did not take into account such considerations as valuation methodology, rehabilitation costs, maintenance-of-way expenses, and labor-protection costs. The court's lengthy opinion produced extensive petitions for reconsideration, which required a number of revisions.

By the time the second evaluation opinion appeared in 1983,[39] additional parties had settled, leaving unresolved the claims of only two relatively minor carriers and then just one, Central Railroad of New Jersey. This second opinion, like the first, would remain as a monument commemorating the work of the Special Court. But the opinions would be monuments with few visitors. Not a single law review published a comment on the valuation decisions, and in the decades that followed, the decisions of other courts cited the two valuation opinions a grand total of nine times. Indeed, almost nothing has been written on the work of the Special Court, despite Friendly's statement: "It would be a pity if the profession were to consider the work of the Special Court to have been so special as to lie outside the mainstream of the law."[40]

The late-settling carriers received a better deal than Penn Central. Trading on the fact that everyone was exhausted, they received about four times the net liquidation value (NLV), as opposed to Penn Central's 2.7 times NLV.[41] Jersey Central, represented by Stanley Weiss, argued that it was in a unique situation because much earlier it had entered into a binding settlement agreement with New Jersey. Friendly rejected the argument but awarded the railroad over $42 million, instead of the NLV of $7 million. Weiss's reaction? "I think he thought he was generous with us under the statute. I feel I got screwed."[42]

Lawyers on all sides praised Friendly and the court. Howard Lewis, who represented the Reading Railroad, said that Friendly was a hard taskmaster, but not cruel.[43] Louis Craco, who represented the Penn Central lienholders, stated that Friendly ran the case "superbly. My side got very little in terms of winning principles, but we absolutely got the full attention of the court." Although Craco remained unconvinced that Friendly's analysis was right, he nonetheless praised Friendly in extravagant terms: "Friendly was by far the best judge I appeared before—and that's from a guy that lost. He was phenomenal."[44] John G. Harkins Jr., the lawyer for Conrail, said Friendly was totally prepared and someone who got to the heart of the issue very quickly: "I want to convey how gentle he was, how challenging it all was; he was the consummate jurist. There was no posturing. Not many people combine his personal and intellectual properties."[45]

CHAPTER TWENTY

Administrative Law

FRIENDLY WAS EXPERT in administrative law when he ascended to the bench, although he was not an architect of administrative law like Brandeis, Frankfurter, and James Landis, who helped create administrative agencies and administrative law.[1] Although he complained, with some justification, that the District of Columbia Circuit got all the good administrative-law cases,[2] the eminent authority Professor Kenneth Culp Davis wrote, "Probably no one can speak with more authority than Judge Friendly on this subject."[3] Others agreed.[4] Friendly had confidence in the independent administrative agencies and usually deferred to their decisions, both on ground of expertise and for reasons of efficiency. In *NLRB v. Miranda Fuel Co.*[5] he wrote in dissent, "I cannot share my brother Medina's qualms that sustaining the Board's ruling . . . will steer grievances of union members as to arbitrary union action away from the courts and toward the expert agency which Congress created to deal with labor matters. That would seem a rather good place for them to be." Friendly was reluctant to intervene in the internal operation of administrative agencies, finding for the FDA when a trade organization argued that the Commissioner signed an order thirteen days after taking office and could not conceivably have read the substantial record as he had certified.[6] His opinion in the case "still stands as the leading case explaining the extent to which, after *Citizens to Preserve Overton Park, Inc. v. Volpe*,[7] litigants may probe the mental processes of administrative decisionmakers."[8]

After just seven months as a judge, Friendly made a scholarly contribution to administrative law in a lecture, sponsored by the *Columbia Law Review*, which consisted of "a bill of particulars against the regulatory agencies."[9] He strongly criticized remedies others had proposed, especially splitting up the administrative agencies into three parts: policy making to be placed in the executive branch, adjudication to be transferred to an administrative court, and enforcement to be transferred to the Justice Department.[10]

Friendly returned to the subject in 1962, when he delivered the Oliver Wendell Holmes Lectures at Harvard Law School. The lectures, called "The Federal Administrative Agencies: The Need for Better Definition of Standards," considered solutions to the difficulties the agencies faced.[11] Experts, including Landis, had criticized, some harshly, administrative agencies for a variety of shortcomings, such as weak appointments and inordinate delays.[12] Friendly, however, saw the main difference between excellent and poor agency performance as whether an agency provided standards and reasoned analysis for its decisions: "A prime source of justified dissatisfaction with the type of federal administrative action which I will shortly specify is the failure to develop standards sufficiently definite to permit decisions to be fairly predictable and the reasons for them to be understood; this failure can and must be remedied. . . . My thesis is that where the initial standard is . . . general, it is imperative that steps be taken over the years to define and clarify it—to canalize the broad stream into a number of narrower ones."[13] The main problem with most agencies was "the failure to 'make law' within the broad confines of the agencies' charters," which, among other problems, led to pressure from the private sector on agency decisions.[14] "It is hardly a coincidence that the two commissions believed to have been most subject to pressure, the FCC and the CAB, are agencies which have conspicuously failed to define the standards governing their decisions," Friendly noted.[15] The Federal Communications Commission (FCC) licensed radio and television stations, and the Civil Aeronautics Board (CAB) awarded air routes.

Addressing the CAB's performance on awarding domestic air routes, Friendly observed that "a good case can be made that the inability of the CAB to develop and adhere to intelligible standards of convenience and necessity in the issuance of competitive certificates has imposed higher costs on the traveling public and serious losses on airline investors."[16] The CAB's approach, he noted, changed with its frequent personnel turnover. "Decisions that would vitally affect the economics of the domestic airline industry for a generation were taken in a tone of gay abandon more suggestive of the Lord Chancellor's 'one for thou and one for thee' than of what ought [to] be expected of a responsible regulatory agency."[17] Friendly thus placed at the feet of the CAB the bleak financial state of the airline industry at the time.[18] When Congress deregulated the airlines, he predicted that it would work out badly. When Pan American went into bankruptcy, he was crushed.[19] He blamed the CAB—"it is ironical, but characteristic of administrative agencies, that, after having destroyed Pan Am, the Board now blames the airline for its own mistakes"—but he also blamed Juan Trippe, who ran Pan American, for his rigid position on acquiring domestic routes.[20]

Friendly's Holmes lectures considered a number of other possible solutions to agencies' shortcomings. As to greater presidential involvement in setting policy, including an executive center to develop policy guidelines for the FCC, his response was terse: "Quite simply, I find it hard to think of anything worse."[21] Likewise, that the CAB engaged in egregious delays or wrote "gobblygook"[22] was not so bad as deregulation, which he believed would be disastrous for the airlines and the public. He saw "seemingly legislative paralysis," with dozens of years of inaction in important areas.[23] Reviews of his lecture were favorable, but not universally so. Landis, whose relations with Friendly had deteriorated over their battle before the CAB, called the book "a gem."[24] Less supportively, Harvard professor Louis Jaffe stated that what faced the CAB "was not a 'relatively easy problem,'" as Friendly had suggested. Friendly had not confronted the difficulty that these agencies faced polycentric problems that could not readily be resolved by the use of rational principles of general applicability.[25]

While he never changed his mind about the CAB over the years, Friendly did with respect to the National Labor Relations Board, which he had praised in his Harvard lectures.[26] He eventually came to the conclusion that its performance was abysmal, using words like "inept"[27] and "disarray"[28] in his opinions. What exasperated him most was the Board's practice of reversing, retroactively, long-held policies without prior notice in the context of litigation,[29] rather than present new positions in proposed and prospective regulations after notice and hearings.[30] Arguably, Friendly allowed his distaste for the NLRB to distort his almost universal support for allowing administrative agencies nearly total autonomy. In any event, his efforts to require the NLRB to engage in rule making were unsuccessful for the basic reason that the Supreme Court did not agree with him.

The substantive issue in *Bell Aerospace Co. v. NLRB*[31] was a union's right to organize Bell's buyers over its objection that they were managerial employees. The Board found that the buyers were not managerial employees, that they were covered by the National Labor Relations Act,[32] and that Bell had committed an unfair labor practice in refusing to bargain with their union. In the process the Board changed the standard for deciding whether an employee was managerial from what it had been since 1956, a matter that affected "tens of thousands of manufacturing, wholesale and retail units." Friendly reversed the Board on the ground that it had employed an incorrect standard in evaluating the status of the buyers.[33] Addressing the procedural question of the manner in which the Board had changed its standard—a subject not addressed in the briefs—Friendly said that, "particularly in light of the justified contrary belief the Board had engendered, it could not do this in the manner that was done here." He concluded that this was "an appropriate case in which to give effect to the Supreme Court's observation in the second *Chenery* decision,[34] largely disregarded by the Board for a quarter century," and ordered the Board to proceed by rule rather than by adjudication. "[W]hen the Board has so long been committed to a position, it should be particularly sure that it has all available information before adopting another, in a setting where nothing stands in the way of a rule-making proceeding, except the Board's congenital disinclination to follow [the] procedure."[35]

The Supreme Court by a five-to-four majority agreed with Friendly that the Board's consistent definition of managerial employees meant "that the Board 'is not now free' to read a new and more restrictive meaning into the Act." The Court, however, unanimously reversed Friendly's requirement that the Board proceed by rule rather than by adjudication. Taking a different view of precedent than had Friendly, the Court relied heavily on the second *Chenery* decision to hold that it was up to the Board whether to proceed by rule or by adjudication.[36] It quoted *Chenery*'s statement: "In performing its important functions . . . an administrative agency must be equipped to act either by general rule or by individual order. To insist upon one form of action to the exclusion of the other is to exalt form over substance." But the Court also observed that the rule was not absolute: "Although there may be situations where the Board's reliance on adjudication would amount to an abuse of discretion or a violation of the Act, nothing in the present case would justify such a conclusion," contrasting a case in which a new liability was created and fines or damages imposed.[37] Ordinarily one to allow considerable leeway to administrative agencies, Friendly's frustration with the Board's rejection of rule making may have led him to select a poor case to reject adjudication. Reaction by commentators, including the authors of the two leading treatises on administrative law, was divided on the merits of the dispute.[38] However, two law professors who had been former Friendly clerks noted, "In terms of craftsmanship Judge Friendly's opinion far surpassed that of the Supreme Court."[39]

As was his wont, Friendly was willing at least to listen to challenges to his positions, even to some of his most strongly held beliefs. In the late 1970s he served on an American Bar Association committee on regulation by administrative agencies for which Harvard professor and later Supreme Court Justice Stephen G. Breyer was a consultant and "the stage manager" of Senate hearings.[40] Breyer later observed that Friendly was open to arguments on the subject of deregulation, a position he had consistently opposed.[41] Friendly signed the committee's 1979 final report, which advocated a statute that gave the President, in circumscribed situations, the power to direct certain regulatory agencies, including independent regulatory agencies such as the FCC, "to consider or reconsider the issuance of critical regulations, within a specified period of time, and thereafter to direct such agencies to modify or reverse their decisions concerning such regulations."[42] In his individual statement in the report, Friendly acknowledged his prior "anything worse" language quoted earlier concerning the undesirability of executive branch participation, but recognized the enormous expansion of the federal bureaucracy and accepted that "[s]omeone in the Government, and in the short run that someone can only be the President, must have the power to make the agencies work together rather than push their own special concerns to the point that the country becomes ungovernable."[43]

Friendly also recognized that administrative law was entering into a new era with an altered role for the judiciary and questioned the suitability of courts to accomplish the tasks Congress imposed on them: "This petition to review so much of an order of the Department of Labor as set minimum numbers of lavatories in industrial establishments is an early illustration of the new tasks imposed on the federal courts of appeals by legislation enacted during the past decade which subjects to their review a wide variety of determinations, by agencies within the executive branch or newly created commissions, many of which are legislative in character and result from informal rulemaking."[44]

BEFORE HE ASCENDED to the bench, Friendly had had no contact with the Food and Drug Administration and he did not discuss that agency in his Holmes lectures. But starting in 1966 he was confronted with a series of hard-fought and difficult FDA cases, mostly dealing with additives and dietary supplements. Writing opinions in eleven cases over the next fifteen years, he helped mold FDA law.[45] His view of the agency was mixed, and he could be quite caustic about its performance, in one case referring to the FDA's "bumbling efforts" to withdraw approval of an application for a new drug.[46] Another time he chastised the agency, saying, "This is the second occasion within the year that we have been obliged to strike down an FDA assay into procedural brinkmanship."[47] He twice refused to allow the FDA to proceed without obtaining public input on the ground its approach was incompatible with the legislation and with public policy.[48]

On other occasions Friendly was supportive of the FDA. After a long historical and technical discussion, he placed his stamp of approval on FDA regulations expanding the definition of "adulterated," on the ground that both statutory language and legislative history supported the agency.[49] Likewise, he backed the FDA when it ruled, without holding an evidentiary hearing, that Pfizer, a leading manufacturer of pharmaceuticals, had failed to present "reasonable grounds," namely, "adequate and well-controlled investigations," to upset the FDA's decision that a long-used antibiotic was not effective. The FDA, Friendly's opinion concluded, had followed the law, and Pfizer's problem was primarily of its own making. "Its present problem arises from its apparently unexplained failure to do anything to pursue" its experiments.[50]

Toilet Goods Association v. Gardner[51] faced the question of whether a trade association could file for a declaratory judgment challenging regulations before they went into effect instead of awaiting their specific interpretation and application by the FDA. Friendly rejected traditional approaches that asked, for example, whether the regulations were "interpretive" or "substantive," whether the petitioner had "standing," or whether the issue was "ripe" for decision, arguments that occupied the overwhelming majority of the parties' briefs. Indeed, only a few sentences buried on page 47 of Toilet Goods' otherwise unhelpful brief provided the germ for a comprehensive rationale for the timing of challenges to administrative regulations, "[N]othing is gained by awaiting an enforcement proceeding consequent on failure to obtain prior listing and certification of a cosmetic. The very issue here, namely, FDA's statutory authority would be controlling there. The Court in enforcement proceedings could do no more that receive the evidence the District Court indicated it would receive at the forthcoming trial."[52] But while Toilet Goods treated the regulations as an indivisible and indistinguishable unit, Friendly disaggregated them. He concluded that it made sense to review immediately three of the four challenged regulations that involved FDA definitions of specific terms because nothing would be gained by waiting except uncertainty and confusion, a pragmatic approach. Delay was appropriate with rules that related to FDA inspections, since there were insufficient data on how inspections would proceed.[53]

Two other administrative-law opinions reflected Friendly's insistence on procedures appropriate to resolving the problem at hand. *Hanly v.*

Kleindienst[54] was an early and important opinion on environmental laws, involving the application of statutory requirements for an assessment of whether an elaborate environmental-impact statement (EIS) was required. The issue arose in connection with the construction of a new jail next door to two large cooperative apartment buildings near Chinatown and to the U.S. Courthouse where Friendly worked.[55] An earlier decision in the same case, with a panel without Friendly, ordered the General Services Administration (GSA) to prepare a more detailed assessment on whether an EIS was needed, a study seemingly required by the governing statute.[56]

On the second appeal, this time with Friendly sitting, the panel majority decided that the twenty-five-page assessment the GSA had prepared was inadequate to permit the court to decide whether to require an EIS, and ordered the GSA to provide a new assessment that contained additional data as well as the input of local residents and merchants. Dissenting, Friendly deplored the court's requiring the GSA to expend so much energy on assessing whether an EIS was required when he had no doubt that the construction of the jail warranted one: "The energies my brothers would require GSA to devote to still a third assessment to show that an impact statement is not needed would better be devoted to making one." His opinion also gave a prominent role to possible psychological and sociological effects of the facility—a role that the majority rejected—and suggested that his colleagues might be guilty of economic, if not racial, bias: "I cannot believe my brothers would entertain the same doubt concerning the relevance of psychological and sociological factors if a building like the [jail] were to be constructed at Park Avenue and East 72nd Street, assuming that zoning allowed it."[57]

The second case, *Automobile Club of New York, Inc. v. Cox*, which drew on Friendly's experiences years earlier in litigating the appropriate rate of return on the assets of the New York Telephone Company, was a legal challenge to an increase in tolls for automobiles on bridges and tunnels into Manhattan operated by the New York Port Authority (PA).[58] The principal question was not the valuation of the bridges, tunnels, and other assets, but whether the PA could include in the asset base its commuter railroad from New Jersey to Manhattan (PATH). The automobile clubs fought the inclusion of PATH, whose loss was "a staggering one of over three dollars in operating expenses for each dollar of revenue." Friendly criticized the parties for missing the issue: "The question was not whether PATH requires subsidization but whether, in the absence of Congressional action . . . the huge deficits of PATH can properly be loaded onto users of the PA bridges—three of which have almost no functional relationship and the fourth, the George Washington Bridge, only a small one."[59] His opinion showed sensitivity to the plight of the PA administrator and deference to administrative decision making:

> Still we cannot quite bring ourselves to say the action of the Administrator in approving the increased tolls was arbitrary or capricious on the record that was before him. . . . Many of the serious questions we have posed seem not to have been fully developed before the agency if they were propounded at all. The Auto Clubs chose to proceed on an all or nothing basis, resisting inclusion of anything but the four bridges. If the Administrator's choice was simply between the narrow concept urged by the Auto Clubs and the broader one he adopted, his action was not so wrong as to demand our remanding the case to him, particularly since, especially in the light of increased costs since his decision, we would leave the existing tolls in effect pending such a remand. We therefore affirm, but with the caveat that this shall not be deemed to constitute an approval or rejection of the Administrator's action or to preclude a new protest, taking into account points raised in this opinion and others.[60]

After Friendly died, the dispute returned to the Second Circuit when the PA sought to raise tolls again. Judge Oakes's majority opinion included a tribute to Friendly: "We find it easier to sustain the Port Authority's position today than the panel did ten years ago. What was a difficult leap for one of the giants of our jurisprudence has become a comfortable step for us—not because we presume to match Judge Friendly's stride, but because the situation in 1989 differs from that of the mid-1970s. There is now considerably more evidence in the record to show that PATH is related to the other river crossing facilities."[61]

CHAPTER TWENTY-ONE

Common Law and
Federal Common Law

O F THE SUPREME COURT CASES in the past century, perhaps none
has generated more interest among legal scholars than a simple suit
for negligence against a railroad by a person injured by a passing freight
train on a railroad right of way, *Erie R.R. v. Tompkins,*[1] decided in 1938
with Brandeis writing the majority opinion. Despite the fact that the issue
had not been briefed, Brandeis took the occasion to write an opinion that
overruled the 1842 decision by Justice Joseph Story in *Swift v. Tyson.* That
decision had given federal courts the power to apply their own version of
the common law, preferably in the image of Lord Mansfield, to certain
vaguely defined categories of state-created rights. Story's goal was to unify
commercial law to further economic and commercial progress hampered
by a patchwork of often inconsistent state laws.[2] Brandeis concluded that
federal courts had been acting unconstitutionally for a century.

In rough summary, *Erie* required a federal court in a case involving state
claims to apply the same state common law (along with statutes) as would
a state court sitting in the same state. *Erie* abolished the anomaly that parties engaged in a lawsuit might find different law governing their conduct
depending on whether they ended up in a federal court or a state court.
Not only was that result arguably unseemly, but it also impaired planning
by parties and made prelitigation settlement of some disputes more difficult. As Friendly noted in a speech in 1964, "If a considerable pond of ink
about *Erie* had already accumulated in 1945, this has now become a

rather large lake."[3] The flood of ink to which Friendly referred dealt with a variety of subjects, including deciding which law was "substantive" (and thus subject to *Erie*) and which "procedural," and whether the doctrine applied to questions of jurisdiction. This chapter reviews Friendly's contributions in the wake of *Erie*.

In his initial years on the bench, Friendly established himself as favoring a comprehensive view of *Erie*. Under his view, absent a contrary federal statute or rule, a federal court could not exercise jurisdiction over a party or case on state-law claims when unauthorized by applicable state law.[4] In 1964 Friendly gave an important lecture entitled "In Praise of *Erie*—and of the New Federal Common Law." He first tackled the difficult question whether the Constitution mandated *Erie*. After acknowledging that Brandeis's opinion in *Erie* had come under increasing attack, he spent the first half of his article weighing in on the necessity for a constitutional basis for *Erie*, arguing that Congress had so long acquiesced in pre-*Erie* practice that it was too late in the day to overrule *Swift v. Tyson* on the nonconstitutional ground of statutory construction.[5] Friendly said, "The constitutional argument for *Erie* is of rather stark simplicity; perhaps that is why it has not appealed to the kind of pundit who is unhappy unless he can find a problem for every solution. . . . [I]t would be . . . unreasonable to suppose that the federal courts have a law-making power which the federal legislature does not. . . . The spectacle of federal judges being able to make law without the possibility of congressional correction would not be a happy one."[6]

The nature and content of federal common law was the core of the second half of his speech. The strength of Friendly's remarks was not so much that his ideas were original (too much to expect after twenty-five years of *Erie* commentary), but rather that his explanation was clearer and more prescient than any expressed before.[7] What he called "specialized" federal common law did indeed exist in a variety of contexts where federal power prevailed: admiralty, the rights and liabilities of the government on federal instruments, many of the rights of employers and employees and their unions in industries affecting commerce, some areas of securities laws, and the rights and liabilities of interstate carriers. Many of these areas were controlled by statutes, but they obviously did not cover all contingencies.[8] *Erie* permitted the federal courts to expend their energies on much more productive efforts, which included developing federal common law that would apply in both federal and state courts:

My view is that, by banishing the spurious uniformity of *Swift v. Tyson*— what Mr. Justice Frankfurter was to call "the attractive vision of a uniform body of federal law" but a vision only—and by leaving to the states what ought to be left to them, *Erie* led to the emergence of a federal decisional law in areas of national concern that is truly uniform because, under the supremacy clause, it is binding in every forum and therefore is predictable and useful as its predecessor, more general in subject matter but limited to the federal courts, was not. The clarion yet careful pronouncement of *Erie*, "There is no federal general common law," opened the way to what, for want of a better term, we may call specialized federal common law. I doubt that we sufficiently realize how far this development has gone—let alone where it is likely to go.[9]

Friendly concluded his optimistic lecture:

> The complementary concepts—that federal courts must follow state decisions on matters of substantive law appropriately cognizable by the states whereas state courts must follow federal decisions on subjects within national legislative power where Congress has so directed or the basic scheme of the Constitution demands—seem so beautifully simple, and so simply beautiful, that we must wonder why a century and a half was needed to discover them, and must wonder even more why anyone should want to shy away once the discovery has been made.[10]

Opinions by Friendly issued soon after his article attested to the role played (or not played) by federal common law. For example, Friendly faced the question of whether state or federal law governed the rights of Iraq in a suit by the government of Iraq to recover former king Faisal II's assets in the United States: "It is fundamental to our constitutional scheme that in dealing with other nations the country must speak with a united voice. . . . The required uniformity can be secured only by recognizing . . . that all questions relating to an act of state are questions of federal law, to be determined ultimately, if need be, by the Supreme Court of the United States."[11] Friendly also decided that state law applied to activity leading up to the signing of a collective-bargaining agreement. Unlike the construction of the agreement itself, the negotiations should be governed by state law (which, in the case at hand, neither party had briefed). "We thus do not find the radiations from the policy or our national labor laws giving such clear signals in this case as to justify our holding the union to be bound by a contract which it would not be considered to have made on ordinary principles of contract law."[12]

When Friendly had to decide the content of federal common law applicable to certain commercial transactions involving the United States, he boldly accepted a brief's suggestion that he should designate the Uniform Commercial Code, a statute enacted by the states, as the federal "common law" of commerce. The superficial anomaly bothered him not at all. "When the states have gone so far in achieving the desirable goal of a uniform law governing commercial transaction, it would be a distinct disservice to insist on a different one for the segment of commerce, important but still small in relation to the total, consisting of transactions with the United States."[13] In complicated areas of the law, where there was no convenient solution like the UCC, Friendly recognized that the judiciary often lacked the resources and flexibility possessed by legislatures. Sometimes an issue that had to be decided was not one adapted to the techniques of judicial lawmaking.[14]

Scholars have continued to view Friendly's article as pivotal to the discussion of federal common law. Praising Friendly's foresight, one academic noted, "Even Friendly, however, understated [*Erie's*] significance. . . . *Erie* expanded the social and cultural power of the federal judiciary, confirming and accelerating its ascension to the position of indisputable authority on national law and the final voice on the most pressing and fundamental national controversies."[15] Another viewpoint was pessimistic regarding the vitality of federal common law, seeing a "shift away from Judge Friendly's view of federal common lawmaking."[16]

FRIENDLY CONFRONTED two cases raising the same issues that occupied Judge Benjamin Cardozo's attention forty years earlier, when he served on the New York Court of Appeals, the state's highest court. In 1923 Cardozo wrote the court's opinion in *Murray v. Cunard S.S. Co.,*[17] which considered whether Cunard could avoid liability when a passenger filed suit after the time allowed by language printed on his steamship ticket. Five years later, soon after he became Chief Judge, he wrote the court's majority opinion in *Palsgraf v. Long Island R.R.,*[18] "'[p]erhaps the most celebrated of all tort cases' and one of the best-known American common law cases of all time," which considered a railroad's liability for an arguably unforeseeable accident.[19] Discussed first is *Palsgraf's* legal sequel, *In re Kinsman Transit Co.,*[20] which presented a fact pattern that many would have thought existed only in law school examinations. Following *Kinsman* is a discussion of *Silvestri v. Italia Societa per Azioni di Navigazione,*[21] whose facts paralleled those in *Murray.* Both are examples of federal common law in the federal enclave of admiralty law. While Friendly had enormous respect for Cardozo, he was unwilling to follow uncritically the master's precepts.

In *Kinsman* ice jams on the Buffalo River broke apart on the night of January 21, 1959, when a rain and thaw followed a period of freezing weather. Propelled by the current, large chunks of ice lodged in the space between the *MacGilvray Shiras,* a ship owned by Kinsman Transit and

Continental Grain Company, and the dock of the Concrete Elevator, owned by Continental, until, at about 10:40 P.M., the *Shiras*'s stern lines parted and she drifted into the current. Careening stern first down the river, the *Shiras* struck the bow of the *Michael K. Tewksbury,* owned by another company, which had been well moored in a protected area. The collision pushed the *Tewksbury* into the river and she too drifted downstream, closely followed by the *Shiras*.[22]

Observers called the Coast Guard, which called the city fire station on the river, which in turn called the crew on the Michigan Avenue drawbridge, located three miles downstream from the Concrete Elevator. Although approximately twenty minutes had passed since the accident, and although it took just two minutes and ten seconds to raise the drawbridge to full height, the bridge was just being raised when, at 11:17 P.M., the *Tewksbury* crashed into its center. A change of shift was scheduled for 11 P.M., and it turned out that the operator on the earlier shift was in a bar when the fire station call reached the bridge, and the second shift did not arrive until shortly before a second call to the bridge—and the crash. Grounded, the *Tewksbury* stopped in the wreckage of the bridge against the stern of another ship that was moored next to the bridge. The *Shiras* plowed into the *Tewksbury*. The ships and ice substantially dammed the flow of the river, causing it to back up and flood installations on the banks as far upstream as the Concrete Elevator. In addition to property damage, two members of the bridge crew suffered injuries.[23]

Before taking up what he regarded as "the most serious issues," Friendly made several preliminary findings. First, the city was not negligent for failure to take action to prevent the buildup of ice on the river. Second, the manner of the mooring of the *Shiras* was negligent. Third, under the arcane provisions of the admiralty law, there were limitations on the extent of Kinsman's liability because the owners of the family corporation were insufficiently involved in the events to impose unlimited liability on the corporation. The president of the corporation was Henry Steinbrenner and its vice president was George Steinbrenner, later president of the New York Yankees. Friendly found that the latter's absence from the scene was not negligent because he was "without maritime studies or experience." Fourth, the *Tewksbury* and its owner Midland were not negligent in the manner in which that ship was moored.[24]

That left three major issues, the first of which was the city's failure to raise the bridge in time. Friendly recognized that under ordinary circumstances the city would prevail on its argument that it was not negligent for not promptly raising the Michigan Avenue Bridge when no ships were expected.[25] But this case was different, largely because of section 4 of the

Federal Bridge Act of 1906, applicable to a drawbridge constructed over a navigable stream: "[T]he draw shall be opened promptly by the person owning or operating such bridge upon reasonable signal for the passage of boats and other water craft."[26] A federal regulation read, "The draws of these bridges shall be opened promptly on signal for the passage of any vessel at all times during the day or night except as otherwise provided by this section."[27] No exception applied.

The second major issue was the allocation of damages between Kinsman and Continental, on the one hand, and the city, on the other hand. Under traditional tort law, Friendly explained, the last person who caused the injury was responsible for all the damages, despite the fact that the concept "grows out of the discredited notion that only the last wrongful act can be a cause—a notion as faulty in logic as it is wanting in fairness. The established principle [of sharing the payment of damages] is especially appealing in admiralty, which will divide the damages among the negligent actors or nonactors."[28] The award of damages proportionate to a party's fault eliminated the search for a sole blameworthy actor.

The third major issue was the relevance of the fact that "[t]he allegedly unexpectable character of the events [led] to much of the damage." Friendly wrote, "The very statement of the case suggests the need for considering *Palsgraf v. Long Island R.R.* . . . and the closely related problem of liability for unforeseeable consequences."[29] (Friendly noted that Learned Hand had incorporated *Palsgraf* into the law of admiralty.)[30] In *Palsgraf*, an injury to Helen Palsgraf occurred when a late-arriving passenger at the East New York station of the Long Island Railroad, fighting his way onto a crowded moving train assisted by a push by a railroad guard, dropped a newspaper-covered package onto the tracks. While nothing indicated the contents of the package, it was fireworks that exploded when they hit the ground. The force of the detonation overturned a penny weighing machine "apparently twenty-five or thirty feet [away]. Perhaps less,"[31] and it fell on Mrs. Palsgraf. She sued the Long Island Railroad for her injuries and won a jury verdict, which the Appellate Division affirmed. New York's highest court, however, reversed and dismissed the case in a four-to-three opinion, with Cardozo writing for the majority. Key for Cardozo was, in Friendly's words, "the lack of notice that the package contained a substance demanding the exercise of any care toward anyone so far away; Mrs. Palsgraf was not considered to be within the area of apparent hazard created by whatever lack of care the guard had displayed to the anonymous carrier of the unknown fireworks."[32]

Friendly compared *Kinsman* with *Palsgraf*: "We see little similarity between the *Palsgraf* case and the situation before us. . . . [A] ship insecurely moored in a fast flowing river is a known danger not only to herself but to owners of all other ships and structures down-river and the persons upon them." Foreseeable consequences included damage to the bridge and partial damming that would flood property upstream, particularly since, as Friendly noted, the length of one of the loose ships was two-and-one-half times and of the other three times the width of the channel at the bridge. Also foreseeable was that the drawbridge would not be raised "since, apart from other reasons, there was no assurance of timely warning." It may have been less foreseeable that the *Shiras* would have made it so far down the river, but the current was swift. Thus, "all the claimants here met the *Palsgraf* requirement of being persons to whom the actors owed a duty of care."[33]

Friendly's analysis favored the plaintiffs: "The weight of authority in this country rejects the limitation of damages to consequences foreseeable at the time of the negligent conduct when the consequences are 'direct,' and the damage, although other and greater than expectable, is of the same general sort that was risked."[34] His discussion of foreseeability was uncommonly pragmatic and expansive, although, he conceded, his opinion provided little guidance:

> We see no reason why an actor engaging in conduct which entails a large risk of small damage and a small risk of other and greater damage, of the same general sort, from the same forces, and to the same class of persons, should be relieved of responsibility for the latter simply because the chance of its occurrence, if viewed alone, may not have been large enough to require the exercise of care. . . . This does not mean that the careless actor will always be held for all damages for which the forces that he risked were a cause in fact. Somewhere a point will be reached when courts will agree that the link has become too tenuous—that what is claimed to be consequence is only fortuity. Thus, if the destruction of the Michigan Avenue Bridge had delayed the arrival of a doctor, with the consequent loss of a patient's life, few judges would impose liability on any of the parties here. . . . It would be pleasant if greater certainty were possible, but the very many efforts that have been made at defining the *locus* of the "uncertain and wavering line" are not very promising; what courts do in such cases makes better sense that what they, or others, say.[35]

Friendly was all but throwing up his hands at coming up with a coherent foreseeability formula and was deciding on the basis of what seemed to work and make sense. At this point he turned from consideration of the repeatedly explored law of foreseeability to an analysis that included language reflecting the budding law-and-economics movement, whose leaders included Guido Calabresi and Richard Posner.[36] "Where the line will be drawn will vary from age to age; as society has come to rely increasingly on insurance and other methods of loss-sharing, the point may lie further off than a century ago. Here it is surely more equitable that the losses from the operators' negligent failure to raise the Michigan Avenue Bridge should be ratably borne by Buffalo's taxpayers than left with the innocent victims of the flooding."[37]

An earlier memorandum that Friendly had written to his fellow judges on the panel also was attuned to the concerns of law and economics: "If there were any way in which the doctrine could be manipulated so as to correspond with probable insurance that would be fine, and in our case one may guess there to be more likelihood that the property owners were insured against flood damages than that Continental's liability insurance would be equal to the strain. But suppose Joe Doak, who was standing by the river bank, had been drowned?"[38]

Friendly entered a decree that apportioned the losses among the various responsible parties.[39] More than four decades after *Kinsman*, Judge Calabresi commented on Friendly's opinion. "I think Friendly was definitely foreseeing law and economics type analysis. He was doing it more through intuition than systematically. But . . . his judicial intuition more often got it correct than the analysis of many a law and economics scholar."[40]

The parties had provided Friendly with little help. When he saw no citation in the briefs to rules or regulations relating to the operation of the bridge, he sent his law clerk to the law library to investigate. The clerk found the Bridge Act regulation cited earlier, which played an important role in the decision.[41] Incredibly, only one of the briefs so much as cited *Palsgraf*; the City of Buffalo's brief simply quoted, without discussion or analysis, two short passages from Cardozo's opinion. The city's brief's consideration of foreseeability—also the only brief that even mentioned the issue—was limited to the question of whether the city had any expectation that ships would be on the Buffalo River that night.[42] It is startling that none of the briefs filed in *Kinsman* was as good on the principal issue as the brief for the Long Island Railroad in *Palsgraf*, argued thirty-six years earlier, without, of course, the benefit of that decision.

Despite Friendly's seeming endorsement in *Kinsman* of Cardozo's *Palsgraf* opinion, it is far from clear that he was enamored of *Palsgraf*'s usefulness in the contemporary world. His *Kinsman* opinion noted, "Since all the claimants here met the *Palsgraf* requirement . . . we are not obliged to reconsider whether that case furnishes as useful a standard for determining the boundaries of liability in admiralty for negligent conduct as was thought . . . when *Palsgraf* was still in its infancy."[43] He did not explain what he meant by his statement, which certainly suggested a measure of reservation about *Palsgraf,* until four years later, in *Ira S. Bushey & Sons, Inc. v. United States,*[44] his only other opinion that discussed *Palsgraf.*

In *Bushey,* described in Chapter 16, an inebriated seaman opened valves that flooded a dry dock, causing it serious damage, and Friendly concluded, "The risk that seamen going and coming from [their ship] might cause damage to the drydock is enough to make it fair that the enterprise bear the loss." Significantly, Friendly turned for support not to Cardozo, but to Judge William Andrews, the author of the *dissent* in *Palsgraf:* "It is not a fatal objection that the rule we lay down lacks sharp contours; in the end, as Judge Andrews said in a related context, 'it is all a question [of expediency,] * * * of fair judgment, always keeping in mind the fact that we endeavor to make a rule in each case that will be practical and in keeping with the general understanding of mankind.' *Palsgraf v. Long Island R.R. Co.,* 248 N.Y. 339, 354–355, 162 N.E. 99, 104 (1928) (dissenting opinion)."[45]

The second case in which Friendly confronted a Cardozo precedent— where the later judge had even more serious reservations—involved the extent to which a steamship company could hold a passenger to filing requirements printed on his ticket that were more restrictive than those imposed by the law. *Silvestri v. Italia Societa per Azioni di Navigazione*[46] grew out of an injury to Ciro Silvestri while a transatlantic passenger from the United States to Italy onboard the Italian line's SS *Leonardo da Vinci.* The district court granted summary judgment against Silvestri because of his failure to begin the action within one year, as required by "Article 30—Limitation of Action Against the Company," printed on his ticket.[47] Friendly's appellate opinion meticulously described the ticket, which included a "box" in the upper righthand corner in Italian and English that bore the words "Passage Contract":

> Almost all of the captions in the "box" were in capital or bold face letters, the major exception being the following statements, which appeared in the upper left hand corner of the ticket in ordinary lower-case one-eighteenth inch type: "Subject to the conditions printed on the cover of this ticket which forms part of this contract." . . . The inconspicuousness of these statements was increased by the fact that they were squeezed immediately below a caption in bold face and to the left of one in capital letters. The two "leaves" which are an integral part of the coupon retained by the passengers were headed "Terms and Conditions" in bold face. Then followed 35 numbered paragraphs in very small print. At the end were spaces for signatures, but neither Silvestri nor any steamship representative signed.[48]

Silvestri conceded that he had the ticket in his possession for at least three days before boarding the ship in New York and then while in transit to Italy; looked at it prior to embarking; and, after the injury, had consulted a lawyer in Italy, who had contacted the Italian line without obtaining a satisfactory offer of settlement. The parties' briefs were cursory—the combined number of pages in them was eighteen, including the statements of facts and descriptions of the proceeding in the trial court—and they demonstrated no particular familiarity with the law and little with the facts. Not only did the parties fail to provide substantial assistance to Friendly, but other possible sources of aid likewise failed him. While he frequently cited law review articles, treatises on the law were more uncertain quantities. In *Silvestri,* as in many other cases, treatises were of no help.[49]

At first blush the case seemed straightforward to the Second Circuit panel; after argument the judges voted unanimously to affirm summary judgment for the defendant.[50] When Friendly's opinion surfaced, however, it was written the other way—with a unanimous vote to reverse and remand for a trial. He began his legal discussion with a caustic comment: "Silvestri's alternative arguments for reversal rest on the applicability of two Supreme Court decisions, *The Majestic,* 166 U.S. 375 (1897), and *The Monrosa v. Carbon Black Export, Inc.,* 359 U.S. 180 (1959), neither of which has been cited by counsel."[51] Having chastised the lawyers, Friendly got down to work. Silvestri could prevail "only if the judge erred in ruling that the conditions were incorporated [into the passenger's contract], decision of which requires us to go back to *The Majestic,*" a case that he proceeded to discuss in prose rivaling Cardozo's in elegance:

> *The Majestic* . . . stemmed from a misadventure of the Misses Potter who, with their maid, had sailed from Liverpool to New York in 1892. Despite the improvements in transatlantic navigation since the memorable voyage exactly four centuries earlier, the estimable young ladies found on disembarking that the contents of their trunks had been badly damaged by sea water. When they libeled the Majestic, they were met, among other defenses, with a ticket provision limiting liability "for loss of or injury to or delay in delivery of luggage" to £10. The ticket contained a "box" bearing the names of the passengers, alongside which was an agreement of carriage signed by the Oceanic Steam Navigation Company. Underneath this was a "Notice to Cabin Passengers" with provisions not relevant to the issue save for a reference "See Back"; on the back, under the rubric "Notice to Passengers," like that on the front in bold type, was a statement "This contract is made subject to the following conditions," including, in fine type, the limitation of liability for luggage to which we have referred. The attention of the Misses Potter had not been called to this, nor had either of them read it.[52]

The U.S. Supreme Court unanimously allowed the sisters to recover on the ground "that the limitations 'were not included in the contract proper, in terms or by reference.'"

Two lines of authority developed in the Second Circuit. Its early decisions ruled against "incorporation" of the conditions into the agreement between the passenger and the line, which meant the passenger was not bound by them, while a later, contrary line of authority was based on Cardozo's opinion in *Murray v. Cunard S.S. Co.*[53] In *Murray,* Cardozo recited, "The plaintiff's ticket . . . is described in large type as a 'cabin passage contract ticket.' It provides, again in large type, that 'This contract ticket is issued by the company and accepted by the passenger on the following terms and conditions' . . . At the top of the ticket is printed a notice: 'The attention of passengers is specifically directed to the terms and conditions of this contract.'" Cardozo enforced a forty-day notification requirement, explaining, "This ticket, to the most casual observer, is as plainly a contract, burdened with all kinds of conditions, as if it were a bill of lading or a policy of insurance. No one who could read could glance at it without seeing that it undertook * * * to prescribe the particulars which should govern the conduct of the parties until the passengers reached the port of destination."[54]

"Despite the eminence of its authorship the *Murray* opinion did not at first have an enthusiastic reception in this court," Friendly reported.[55] Several opinions found *Murray* distinguishable and held for the passengers. But as the steamship companies created more forceful notices, the Second Circuit began to enforce the conditions in actions brought by passengers. Discussing the decisions that favored defendants, Friendly made statements like, "Examination of the record in *Baron* shows that both these legends were in solid capitals." He learned those facts by personally examining records in precedents because the facts were neither in the briefs submitted to him nor in published opinions. If he could not distinguish a precedent from what appeared in the published opinions in a case, he was prepared to rely on information that he had exhumed on his own.[56] One reason that Friendly went to such considerable lengths to distinguish cases was usually not, as he once put it, "any desire for *elegantia juris,*"[57] but because an opinion overruling past precedent would have required convening an *en banc* proceeding.

Friendly's creativity and diligence if widely followed threatened to create a problem, namely, that no one could be certain that a judge's opinion meant what it said. While engaging in a tour de force, Friendly was changing the rules of the game in a potentially disruptive way by opening the prospect that singular research could change an opinion's meaning.

A scholarly casebook on legislation made essentially the same point: "Citizens ought to be able to open up the statute books and find out what the law requires of them."[58] Indeed Friendly wrote that "where a person finds himself exempted by the words of a statute and there is no case law to the contrary, he should not have first to cogitate and then to investigate whether the legislature meant what it said."[59] The same should be true of case law, where it should not be possible to change the clear force and meaning of an opinion long after it was published. Friendly was undermining his penchant for stability.

It was still necessary to decide Silvestri's claim, and Friendly suggested a highly pragmatic standard that he gleaned from his thorough review of the decisions: "[T]he thread that runs implicitly through the cases sustaining incorporation is that the steamship line had done all it reasonably could to warn the passenger that the terms and conditions were important matters of contract affecting his legal rights."

> While we would not insist on any particular rubric, seventy years of experience under *The Majestic* doctrine should have enabled the draftsman of the ticket to produce a warning significantly more eye-catching than this. To be sure, it can be said that all this is legalism, since Silvestri should have known the Italian Line had not gone to the trouble of printing Terms and Conditions for the fun of it and would not have read them no matter what was said; and we confess some doubt how far the intensity of ticket reading correlates with the strength of the invitation to indulge in it. All this, however, could have been said with equal accuracy of the Misses Potter, yet *The Majestic* decided what it did.[60]

After noting that Silvestri had consulted a lawyer who was likely either aware of the Italian line's limitations on the time for bringing suit or had obtained a ticket, Friendly concluded, "If the company can establish that because of the lawyer's advice or otherwise Silvestri knew the ticket required him to bring suit within a year, we might have a different case. We hold only it was error to grant summary judgment for respondent. Reversed." Silvestri still faced a difficult task, but Friendly gave him a chance.[61]

Benjamin Cardozo's biographer, the Harvard Law professor Andrew L. Kaufman, said that Cardozo was often more empathetic than he was with Murray: "For some unspecified reason, Cardozo simply was not moved by his knowledge of common behavior to apply the 'method of sociology' in this case. The logic of the rules won out. Rightly or wrongly, and I think wrongly, Cardozo saw this case as he had seen the case of the woman who fell over the mechanic fixing the cash register. People had to take responsibility to look out for themselves sometimes, and Cardozo thought that this was one of these times."[62] Nevertheless, in view of *Palsgraf* and the case to which Kaufman referred, it appears that Friendly was correct in saying that Cardozo was more interested in general propositions than facts (or people).[63] Cardozo had a ready reason for deciding the case for Murray—the company had collected his ticket after he boarded, and one party to a contract ordinarily does not collect the other party's copy.

Friendly was more willing than Cardozo to accept human behavior as a fact of life and thus took a step that Cardozo was unwilling to take, namely, to accept the reality that passengers do not read all the terms in a passenger ticket. In fact, they are not really expected to read documents like passenger tickets. What would happen if renters of cars said, "One second, I want to read the contract"?[64] Also, although Friendly did not say so, this probably was a very good case for a jury of Silvestri's peers to decide. But what may have turned out to be an even more important difference between the two jurists was that Friendly and his wife took frequent cruises, while Cardozo rarely traveled.[65] Summa cum laude at Harvard College and Law School and Judge of the U.S. Court of Appeals for the Second Circuit, Friendly may not have read his passenger tickets either.

Happenstance may change the outcome of a case, and it may have with *Silvestri.* Hiring brilliant law clerks, Judge Friendly preferred them to be outspoken, and his clerk Bruce Ackerman took him at his word. Ackerman has explained that Friendly's initial reaction was to affirm on the ground that the notice provision was a contractual term. Ackerman described what happened next. "I handed him the contract and asked him to read it. That was unfair; he couldn't read shit. But he changed his mind."[66] As Ackerman (and others) well knew, Friendly had difficulty reading even ordinary-sized print.

FRIENDLY UNDERSTOOD the limited role that federal judges played in interpreting state law after *Erie,* once calling his function akin to that of Charlie McCarthy, the famous ventriloquist's dummy of his era.[67] He took very seriously all of his approximately sixty diversity-of-citizenship cases (where the parties come from different states or countries) in which he wrote opinions, although he noted one year before his death, "In my early years on the bench I did make a very real effort to determine what the court of the state would decide, often going far beyond the research of the parties. Now, whether because of the press of time or lack of interest, I rarely go beyond what the parties have said."[68]

An early Friendly opinion in a diversity-of-citizenship case was *Nolan v. Transocean Air Lines*,[69] which he described to another judge as containing "my best opening paragraph": "Our principal task, in this diversity of citizenship case, is to determine what the New York courts would think the California courts would think on an issue about which neither has thought. They have had no occasion to do so. But life, here coupled with death, casts up new problems, and the court seized of the case is obliged, as best it can, itself to blaze the trail of the foreign law that it has been directed to follow." Friendly's comment about the paragraph? "[P]eaked in my first year."[70] A few years later he extended himself in a diversity case that involved multistate liens on racehorses, *Susi v. Belle Acton Stables, Inc.*,[71] where he observed, "The horses . . . were soon to become the subject of a considerable series of security interests, of little immediate concern to them but now of much to us."

A diversity case that Friendly relished presented itself when he chose to sit as a district judge just months after he ascended to the bench. He began his opinion in *Frigaliment Importing Co. v. B.N.S. Int'l Sales Corp.*,[72] where a Swiss corporation sued under New York State law for breach of the warranty that goods sold shall correspond to their description:

> The issue is, what is chicken? Plaintiff says "chicken" means a young chicken, suitable for broiling and frying. Defendant says "chicken" means any bird of that genus that meets contract specifications on weight and quality, including what it calls "stewing chicken" and plaintiff pejoratively terms "fowl." Dictionaries give both meanings, as well as some others not relevant here. To support its [*sic*], plaintiff sends a number of volleys over the net; defendant essays to return them and adds a few serves of its own. Assuming that both parties were acting in good faith, the case nicely illustrates Holmes' remark "that the making of a contract depends not on the agreement of two minds in one intention, but on the agreement of two sets of external signs—not on the parties' having *meant* the same thing but on their having *said* the same thing." The Path of the Law, in Collected Legal Papers, p. 178. I have concluded that plaintiff has not sustained its burden of persuasion that the contract used "chicken" in the narrower sense.[73]

At issue was 125,000 pounds of "US Fresh Frozen Chicken, Grade A, Government Inspected, Eviscerated," further described only by weight—"2½–3 lbs." "Since the word 'chicken' standing alone is ambiguous, I turn first to see whether the contract itself offers any aid to its interpretation," Friendly wrote. The plaintiff contended that although cablegrams between the parties were in German, they employed the English term "chicken" because, "it was understood that 'chicken' meant young chicken whereas the German word, '*Huhn*,' included both '*Brathuhn*' (broilers) and '*Suppenhuhn*' (stewing chicken) and that defendant, whose officers were thoroughly conversant with German, should have realized this." Friendly, who knew German, did not have to resolve this linguistic issue. "Whatever force this argument might otherwise have is largely drained away by Bauer's [defendant's secretary's] testimony that he asked Stovicek [plaintiff's agent] what kind of chickens were wanted, received the answer 'any kind of chickens,' and then, in German, asked whether the cable meant '*Huhn*' and received an affirmative response."[74]

The plaintiff next contended that there was a trade usage that "chicken" meant "young chicken." But Friendly rejected the testimony of two of the plaintiff's three witnesses on the ground that in their personal dealings they referred to younger chickens as "broilers" and older ones as "fowl"; "a witness' consistent failure to rely on the alleged usage deprives his opinion testimony of much of its effect," citing as authority a 1761 decision of Lord Mansfield. A third plaintiff's witness, however, presented the usage in several published daily market reports on the poultry trade. "This would be impressive if there were nothing to the contrary. However, there was, as will now be seen."[75]

The defendant provided a wealth of contradicting evidence that a "chicken is anything except a goose, a duck, and a turkey," and that further definition is needed if what is meant is a young chicken. It cited Department of Agriculture regulations: "*Chickens*. The following are the various classes of chickens: (a) Broiler or fryer . . . (e) Hen or stewing chicken or fowl." "[T]here is force in defendant's argument that the contract made the regulations a dictionary, particularly since the reference to Government grading was already in plaintiff's initial cable to Stovicek," Friendly noted.[76] The defendant also drew blood by proving that it was impossible for it to supply young chickens at the price quoted in the contracts. "Plaintiff must have expected defendant to make some profit—certainly it could not have expected defendant deliberately to incur a loss," Friendly wrote.[77] On the basis of all the evidence Friendly concluded that the defendant believed that it could comply with the contract by delivering stewing chickens in the requisite size. "Defendant's subjective intent would not be significant if this did not coincide with an objective meaning of 'chicken.'" (By discussing the subjective intent before the objective meaning, Friendly accentuated the intricate relationship between the two in interpreting contracts.) But it did. Friendly proceeded to choose a narrow ground (one less susceptible to appellate review): "[P]laintiff has the burden of showing that 'chicken' was used in the narrower sense rather than in the broader sense, and this it has not sustained."[78]

Friendly's opinion has appeared as a principal case in Contracts casebooks[79] and has prompted analysis in law review articles whose titles attest to the sophistication required to discuss the problem intelligently. Academic interest, which has been considerable, has mainly concerned the concept of ambiguity and whether the proper way to construe a contract is to look only at objective facts as opposed to considering the party's subjective understanding.[80]

CHAPTER TWENTY-TWO

Federal Court Jurisdiction

T HE CONCEPT OF JURISDICTION—"a court's power to decide a case or issue a decree"—is not easy for a layman or even a judge to comprehend. Jurisdiction is at issue in federal litigation because a federal court has jurisdiction to decide a case only when the Constitution or an act of Congress gives it that power.[1] Virtually all cases come to the federal courts by one of two routes: diversity-of-citizenship jurisdiction or the complaint raises a federal question. In 1972 Friendly presented the Carpentier Lectures at the Columbia Law School, which he entitled "Federal Jurisdiction: A General View,"[2] where he advocated substantially eliminating diversity jurisdiction, forming a standing law-revision commission that would be an arm of Congress,[3] and many other reforms. He did not hesitate to speak out on controversial issues, in one instance opposing a large majority of lawyers who wanted to create a new national court of appeals to screen petitions for *certiorari*. He argued that such a court would be inefficient and would interfere with the autonomy of the Supreme Court, and his position prevailed.[4] Unquestionably, Friendly was a leader in the study of federal jurisdiction.[5]

Friendly wrote his only theoretical article before becoming a judge, "The Historic Basis of Diversity Jurisdiction,"[6] primarily during the summer of 1927, and he saw it published in the *Harvard Law Review* in 1928. In the article he set out to ascertain why Congress created diversity jurisdiction in the first Judiciary Act in 1789, although it did not legislate general federal-question jurisdiction until 1875. After reviewing colonial and state court decisions and other documents from around the time of the founding of the United States, he rejected the conventional wisdom, finding no evidence of actual prejudice against out-of-state parties and little apprehension that such prejudice existed. For him, the need for federal diversity jurisdiction to protect out-of-state parties was illusory in the late eighteenth century (and even more so in the twentieth): "[S]uch information as we are able to gather from the [case] reporters fails to show the existence of prejudice on the part of judges. . . . Indeed, a careful reading of the arguments of the time will show that the real fear was not of state courts so much as of state legislatures. . . . In summary, we may say that the desire to protect creditors against legislation favorable to debtors was a principal reason for the grant of diversity jurisdiction, and that as a reason it was by no means without validity."[7]

Friendly's concern over state courts had more to do with their competence than their bias; for example, many states provided for the appointment of judges by the legislature and for their removal by the legislature or the governor. "The method of appointment and tenure of the judges were not of the sort to invite confidence," he wrote.[8] He called for a reexamination of diversity jurisdiction, which diverted federal judges from their primary function, that of creating and applying federal law. Friendly's article concluded powerfully:

> The steady expansion of the jurisdiction of the federal courts, especially since Reconstruction days, has been but a reflex of the general growth of federal political power. That growth will not abate, since it is responsive to deep social and economic causes. Only one aspect of the work of the federal courts is out of the current of these nationalizing forces—the jurisdiction based on diversity of citizenship. This had its origins in fears of local hostilities, which had only a speculative existence in 1789, and are still less real today. The unifying tendencies of America here make for a recession of jurisdiction to the states, rather than an extension of federal authority. The pressure of distinctly federal legislation may call for relief of business that intrinsically belongs to the state courts. How far, if at all, the United States courts should be left with jurisdiction merely because the parties are citizens of different states is a question which calls for critical reexamination of the practical bases of diversity jurisdiction. To such a reexamination the present study may serve as an introduction.[9]

On the occasion of Friendly's twenty-fifth year on the bench in 1984, the *University of Pennsylvania Law Review* published a tribute to him composed by judges and scholars. District Judge Louis Pollak, a former law professor at Yale and a friend, entitled his twenty-four-page contribution

"In Praise of Friendly." After an introduction, he reproduced the entire paragraph just quoted, noting, "These magisterial words were written by the youthful Henry Friendly: they comprise the concluding paragraph of *The Historic Basis of Diversity Jurisdiction*, Friendly's first piece of scholarship."[10]

It appears, however, that the quoted paragraph—although not the rest of the article—was written not by Friendly, but by Professor Felix Frankfurter. On July 20, 1927, Friendly wrote to Frankfurter,

> I'm sending by registered mail the manuscript of the paper on diversity. . . . Strawbridge v. Curtiss seemed a good place to stop, since it shows how, from the very first, the scope of diversity jurisdiction depended on the Court's ideas of the policy or impolicy of a federal tribunal's taking over the work in question. I have left the paper without a conclusion—for two reasons. I don't think I've proved anything; and I know that you have rare abilities at pointing morals and adorning tales. For all I know you may have a conclusion already written, as you had to one other piece with which I don't want to invite comparisons. So won't you please adorn this one?[11]

The sentence preceding the concluding paragraph in the published article read, "What can be said is that there is little likelihood that *Strawbridge v. Curtiss* will ever be reversed by judicial decision or, assuming the power, by legislation," which is where Friendly told Frankfurter he had ended his manuscript.[12]

Friendly's antipathy to diversity jurisdiction started with Frankfurter and never stopped. As a judge, Friendly wanted to abolish diversity jurisdiction entirely except for cases involving a foreign party and in some intricate multiparty cases; he especially wanted to remove automobile accidents from the federal forum, if not from the courts entirely.[13] "It is unfortunate that the rights of the parties to the substantial sums at stake must be adjudicated by a court which can make only educated guesses on a close and serious issue of New York law."[14] "This case is another example of a federal court's being compelled by the Congressional grant of diversity jurisdiction to determine a novel and important question of state law on which state decisions do not shed even a glimmer of light."[15] Friendly looked for ways to limit federal courts to their principal function "to prevent the ships [the courts of appeals and the Supreme Court] from sinking" from an overload of work.[16] He tried, with some success, to convince Richard Posner that diversity jurisdiction should be decimated.[17] Friendly's views dominated the discussion for decades.[18]

Friendly employed a variety of methods to reduce the peripheral caseload of the federal judiciary. As noted in the discussion of *United States v.*

Archer in an earlier chapter, he opposed making essentially local crimes into federal ones, whether at the instance of Congress or the prosecutors. In a prosecution involving a small amount of narcotics, he pressed the Assistant U.S. Attorney as to whether anyone had been previously prosecuted for such a small amount of cocaine; he did not get a straight answer.[19] He wrote in an opinion in another case, "An appeal in which state officials persist in holding allegedly obscene books in defiance of applicable rulings of the Supreme Court but their distributor offers no better reason for federal injunctive relief than his preference for a federal forum does not greatly warm the cockles of the judicial heart."[20] He urged shunting claims of railway workers and seamen to administrative tribunals and creating specialized federal courts of appeals for patent cases, for tax cases, and for international trade disputes.[21] He favored reading broadly the exception to diversity jurisdiction for certain domestic-relations disputes to curtail diversity jurisdiction.[22] He also said, "Although I generally squirm to find some basis for getting around the jurisdictional amount requirement, I would not make the effort in cases of this sort where application of the jurisdictional amount relieves a federal court of a kind of business in which it ought not to engage."[23] He looked askance at retrying diversity cases: "It takes a very substantial showing to cause me to grant a new trial in a diversity case, and although the principle is more applicable when the new trial is sought by the person who invoked diversity jurisdiction, I would apply it here."[24] However, he seemed more willing to reverse than his statement suggests,[25] reversing district courts in diversity cases in 58 percent of the cases in which he wrote an opinion.[26]

IN 1875 CONGRESS GAVE the federal courts general federal-question jurisdiction in a statute that read simply, "The district courts shall have original jurisdiction of all civil actions arising under the Constitution, laws, or treaty of the United States."[27] The short sentence has led to thousands of cases and commentaries. Friendly sought to expand federal court jurisdiction when it permitted them to fulfill their proper function, namely, interpreting and applying federal law. Thus, he proposed eliminating the minimum jurisdictional amount from federal-question jurisdiction, arguing that deciding federal questions was what federal courts should do, and a small monetary claim nevertheless warranted a federal forum. The law finally was changed in 1976. He was more willing than many others to find an implied cause of action under the federal securities laws and expanded the international reach of those laws;[28] he expanded federal jurisdiction in cases "arising under" the copyright (and patent) laws;[29] and he supported giving limited partners standing when the general partner could or would not sue.[30] As will be evident from a discussion of several Friendly opinions, the subject matter is not for the casual reader.

1. *T.B. Harms Co. v. Eliscu*[31] "stands unchallenged after two decades as the leading jurisdictional discussion of the intractable problem of defining cases arising under federal law," wrote Professor David P. Currie, a former Friendly law clerk, in 1984.[32] Another professor called the decision the "most influential precedent specifically addressing when a case arises under the copyright laws,"[33] a particularly difficult jurisdictional problem. The case concerned four copyrighted songs that Vincent Youmans composed under a contract with RKO Studios, Inc. for the motion picture *Flying Down to Rio* with Fred Astaire and Ginger Rodgers. RKO hired two lyricists, one of whom was the defendant Eliscu. The principal factual dispute was whether, on June 30, 1933, Eliscu assigned his rights to an individual who in turn assigned them to the plaintiff Harms (who owned the balance of the copyrights on the songs). Harms claimed that the original assignment was lost, but that it had a conformed copy, while Eliscu denied that he ever executed an assignment. Judge Weinfeld dismissed the complaint on the ground that "a suit although charging infringement and praying for an injunction and accounting, which is in reality merely a suit to enforce a contract between an author and publisher, is not a case arising under the copyright laws so as to be within the jurisdiction of the federal courts."[34]

Friendly accepted Weinfeld's result but not his test. Weinfeld, Friendly wrote, saw the issue as whether there was infringement of a copyright, but "the jurisdictional statute does not speak in terms of infringement, and the undoubted truth that a claim for infringement 'arises under' the Copyright Act does not establish that nothing else can." Friendly created a new test based on the allegations in the complaint that borrowed salutary aspects of Weinfeld's articulation: "Mindful of the hazards of formulation in this treacherous area, we think that an action 'arises under' the Copyright Act if and only if the complaint is for a remedy expressly granted by the Act, e.g., a suit for infringement or for the statutory royalties for record reproduction or asserts a claim requiring construction of the Act." Applying the test to *Harms,* Friendly saw the issue as whether Eliscu executed an assignment of his copyright interest, and "if any aspect of the suit requires an interpretation of the Copyright Act, the complaint does not reveal it."[35]

Courts and commentators widely praised Friendly's test. Nevertheless, nearly thirty years after *Harms* a panel of the Second Circuit inexplicably announced a new test in a *dictum* in *Schoenberg v. Shapolsky Publishers, Inc.*[36] The new test was worse than the one *Harms* replaced, which led another panel, with former Friendly clerk Judge Pierre N. Leval writing the opinion, to reinstate *Harms*.[37] That Friendly wrote a sound opinion was no guarantee that another judge might not mess things up.

2. The Supreme Court held in 1966 that when certain criteria were met, a plaintiff that properly brought federal claims in a federal court could assert related state law claims against the same defendant, which it called "pendent jurisdiction."[38] Friendly expanded that principle to allow for the addition of *defendants* who were sued only under state law when plaintiffs were suing under federal law other defendants regarding the same transaction. The expansion ("pendent-party jurisdiction") reduced the number of lawsuits and provided other benefits (and some drawbacks, including increasing federal court decisions on state law). While no specific statute allowed pendent-party jurisdiction, Friendly relied on "Mr. Justice Brennan's broad language [in *United Mine Workers v. Gibbs*, 383 U.S. 715 (1966)] and common sense."[39] Unlike most cases,[40] where Friendly employed his analysis of the facts and circumstances to narrow the reach of a Supreme Court decision, here was an instance in which he fixed on an opinion's broad statement of legal principles in order to expand its reach. Friendly was a master at managing precedent. (Another example was *United States v. Beattie*,[41] where he wrote, "The significance of *Couch* for the present case is in the language of the case, not in its holding.")

More cautious than Friendly, the Supreme Court first cast doubt on pendent-party jurisdiction in 1976 and then held in 1989 in a five-to-four vote that Congress had not authorized it.[42] Justice Stevens wrote in dissent, "Today we should be guided by the wisdom of Cardozo and Friendly rather than the 'unnecessarily grudging' approach that was unanimously rebuffed in *Gibbs*."[43] One year later Congress legislatively overruled *Finley* with the passage of the Judicial Improvements Act of 1991, authorizing pendent-party jurisdiction (called "supplemental jurisdiction").[44]

3. *Eisen v. Eastman*[45] was a Friendly contribution to the analysis of the Civil Rights Act of 1866, 42 U.S.C. § 1983, which provided for a right of action against a state officer who, acting under color of state law, violated someone's constitutional rights. A landlord, Clarence Eisen, sued a New York City rent and rehabilitation director for damages, on the ground that rent control violated his civil rights by unlawfully depriving him of income. Friendly rejected Eisen's claim, endorsing Justice Stone's famous footnote 4 in *United States v. Carolene Products Co.*[46] that elevated personal rights above property rights, stating,

[T]here seems to be something essentially right [about the distinction]. . . . It has the merit of preserving not only the kind of case that was the core of congressional concern in 1871 but a good many others that Congress would probably desire to have within the statute, while at the same time excluding cases that neither the Reconstruction Congress nor later Congresses could hardly have had in mind. . . . [A contrary result] would be so destructive of proper concepts of federalism and so needlessly burdensome to the federal courts that . . . [w]e shall need much clearer directions than the Court has yet given or, we believe, will give, before we hold that plaintiffs in such cases may turn their backs and rush into a federal forum.[47]

4. Friendly produced "the first major decision by a federal appellate court exercising jurisdiction given by the Civil Rights Act of 1866 to review remand orders in civil rights removal cases" when New York prosecuted Reverend Milton Galamison and others for disturbing the peace during the 1964 New York World's Fair.[48] Defendants sought to "remove" their cases to the federal courts based on the Equal Protection Clause of the Fourteenth Amendment and section 1443(2) of the Civil Rights Act, which provides for a federal forum in cases alleging "any act under color of authority derived from any law providing for equal civil rights."

The major issue in *New York v. Galamison*[49] was the meaning of the language "any law providing for equal civil rights." Construing the language narrowly to cover only laws that affirmatively authorized the exercise of specific equal rights, Friendly returned the case to the state court. He traced the statutory language back to the Habeas Corpus Act of 1863 and concluded that the purpose of the law was to remedy state laws that singled out blacks for discriminatory treatment and to provide those state defendants with nondiscriminatory forums. Since it was undisputed that New York state courts were a nondiscriminatory forum, Galamison could not rely on the Civil Rights Act. Moreover, Friendly said, if removal were available to blacks to protect speech, then the Bill of Rights as incorporated in the Fourteenth Amendment would be laws providing for equal rights. Thus, taking a broad view of the removal statute would flood the federal courts (a practical and contemporary argument applied to a century-old provision), usurp the criminal justice systems of the states, and create serious problems of federalism. For Friendly, it was a good case to elevate values other than literalism.

Friendly chose not to resolve a number of issues, recognizing that in this difficult area a sound small step was preferable to an awkward leap. He acknowledged that he had failed to provide "a definition of 'color of authority' that will automatically determine every case," adding, "But at least we have taken the difficult road of deciding these cases as best we can, thereby giving indications that also ought to be somewhat useful for the decision of others." As in so many other important cases the parties' briefs provided almost no illumination of the issues. Indeed, neither brief provided the most persuasive argument available to his side, which was left to Friendly to supply.[50]

Friendly strongly supported civil rights in a variety of contexts. For example, he held, apparently for the first time, that a corporation could sue for racial discrimination under the Civil Rights Act.[51] But he seemed to have been less sensitive than many to the problem of biased or timid state court judges. His 1973 book *Federal Jurisdiction: A General View* stated, "In approaching the subject of private litigation under the general civil rights statute, I must own a Faustian conflict. It is hard to conceive of a task more appropriate for federal courts than to protect civil rights guaranteed by the Constitution against invasion by the states. Yet we also have state courts, whose judges, like those of the federal courts, have taken an oath to support the Constitution and were intended to play an important role in carrying it out. . . . Surely it must be more acceptable if a state statute is struck down as offending the Federal Constitution by state judges, often elected by the people, than by federal judges owing their appointment[s] to Washington."[52]

Perhaps in part because the state court judges Friendly knew best were outstanding members of New York's judiciary, he exhibited great respect for the operation of state courts.[53] But his assumption that elected state judges, including those from the South, would readily enforce the federal Civil Rights Act and other laws affecting human rights generated criticism.[54] Popularly elected state judges would be inclined to take the side of the majority against a claim by a minority, which is what the Bill of Rights and especially the Civil War Amendments and enforcing statutes were designed to limit.[55]

CHAPTER TWENTY-THREE

Other Procedural Issues

F RIENDLY REGARDED PROCEDURE as an integral part of an effective
legal system and he paid close attention to its many manifestations, as
he demonstrated in an article he wrote in 1978 entitled "The Courts and
Social Policy: Substance and Procedure."[1] After a detailed criticism of the
Supreme Court's opinions—as opposed to outcomes—in *Brown v. Board
of Education* and *Roe v. Wade,* Friendly stated, "However, the main lesson
I wish to draw from the abortion case relates to procedure—the use of
social data offered by appellants and amici curiae for the first time in the
Supreme Court itself" (rather than in the trial court). He elaborated: "If an
administrative agency, even in a rulemaking proceeding, had used similar
materials without having given the parties a fair opportunity to criticize or
controvert them at the hearing stage, reversal would have come swiftly
and inexorably."[2]

This chapter examines three of Friendly's contributions to federal judicial process in civil cases. First, problems encountered in settling representative actions, such as class actions and shareholder derivative suits, where
Friendly saw institutional problems earlier than others, much as he did
with punitive damages, discussed in an earlier chapter. Second, conflict of
laws, which requires a court to decide which jurisdiction's laws should be
applied in a multijurisdiction dispute.[3] Third, the balancing of considerations present in administering evidentiary privileges that further important public policies but interfere with the search for the truth.

One prong of Friendly's contribution to the law on the settlement of representative suits consisted of a single sentence in his 1973 book, *Federal Jurisdiction: A General View*, in which he stated that class actions produce "blackmail settlements."[4] As Friendly noted, he did not originate the juxtaposition of "blackmail" with class-action settlements, a term originally used to refer to "untriable" class actions, which defendants settled because they could not defend them or could defend them only at a prohibitive cost.[5] Friendly, however, was complaining about permitting class-action plaintiffs to aggregate their resources so as to match the considerable resources of corporate defendants—hardly blackmail.[6] He never said that class-action awards were large in relation to the merits of plaintiffs' claims; after all, the system encouraged parties to settle because they might do worse litigating, and the point of class actions was to reduce the number of trials by aggregating plaintiffs' claims. Twenty-two years after Friendly employed the term, Judge Posner elevated "blackmail settlements" to a rallying cry against certain class actions when he quoted Friendly in *In re Rhone-Poulenc.*[7] In 2005, as part of the Class Action Fairness Act,[8] Congress altered class-action procedures, including taking many class actions out of the more hospitable state courts and depositing them in the federal courts, while imposing a number of procedural restrictions on plaintiffs.

Friendly's other contribution was gradual and painstaking. Stretching over nearly twenty years, his decisions helped define procedures for effecting settlements, standards for fairness in settlements, and grounds for setting aside settlements for fraud. He emphasized transparency and equity, especially to the passive members of the class, and he was harsh on lawyers who failed to protect their clients. *Alleghany Corp. v. Kirby*[9] exercised Friendly considerably. Charging fraudulent self-dealing, shareholders in the Alleghany Corporation had earlier brought in New York state court a derivative suit against the company's officers and directors, including Allan Kirby, whom Friendly had encountered in connection with the New York Central proxy battle in 1954. Plaintiffs had claimed that the defendants had acquired from Alleghany at an unreasonably low price the stock of another corporation (IDS). After a lengthy hearing before a referee on the merits of the settlement, the defendants settled the case for $3 million. When the shareholders later learned that the directors had not produced documents that contained more specific information about the value of the IDS stock than previously disclosed and that the price of IDS had increased approximately twenty-fold, the shareholders filed suit in the federal district court against Kirby and other directors.

Judges Moore and Kaufman acknowledged the misconduct by the directors and the inadequacy of the settlement but concluded that the withheld documents were basically cumulative.[10] Central to the decision of the majority was its conclusion that the directors had no "affirmative obligation to come forward voluntarily with facts and documents" once they were sued and that the shareholders had to demonstrate that the "evidence said to have been 'nondisclosed' or concealed ... would ... 'probably have produced a different result,'" which they failed to do.[11]

Dissenting, Friendly disagreed with just about every position taken by the majority, starting with their holding that a lawsuit against a corporate director terminated his fiduciary duty to shareholders.

> I can perceive no principle that would eliminate or even lessen the fiduciary obligations of directors who wish to settle a derivative action wherein they are charged with self-dealing. At least I cannot when, as here, they remain in control of the corporation, its officers, and its files relevant to the merits of the claim and consequently to the providence of the settlement. ... I cannot agree that when judicial approval of a settlement by a fiduciary has been procured by culpable nondisclosure of evidence by a confederate, the test of materiality applicable on motions for a new trial on the ground of newly discovered evidence has any relevance.[12]

Friendly next showed why the withheld evidence, which consisted of income projections for IDS known by some of the directors, was highly valuable to plaintiffs. "The Alleghany proxy statement, which sought the approval of the exchange, gave no financial information about IDS as a company," and what little information was provided was presented obscurely; for example, none of the information was translated into per share figures.[13] Friendly continued, "How simple it would have been for Alleghany's management to ... [say] that IDS' 1949 earnings of $1,631,000 were more than $5 per share!" Challenging the majority's argument that the system worked well, he made clear that he favored exposure of directors' previous misconduct over upholding some settlements:

> The plaintiff stockholders or, more realistically, their attorneys have every incentive to accept a settlement that runs into high six figures or more regardless of how strong the claims for much larger amounts may be. ... [A] juicy bird in the hand is worth more than the vision of a much larger one in the bush, attainable only after years of effort not currently compensated and possibly a mirage. Once a settlement is agreed, the attorneys for the plaintiff and stockholders link arms with their former adversaries to defend the joint handiwork—as is vividly shown here. ... To say that "Through its representatives, it [Alleghany] elected to settle" is sheer fiction. ... [C]ourts should enforce the most exacting standards of good faith on fiduciaries desiring to settle such serious claims of self-dealing as were here alleged.[14]

Friendly, who did not like corner-cutting by devious executives, especially fiduciaries, was willing to sacrifice the abstract principle of finality for concrete justice.[15]

The shareholders of Alleghany did not give up, but their luck did not improve. The Second Circuit granted their petition for a rehearing *en banc,* but then voted four to four on the merits, leaving in place the district court's decision dismissing the complaint.[16] The shareholders were no more successful when they filed a petition for *certiorari* to the Supreme Court, which, after granting the petition and hearing oral argument, dismissed the case without explanation.[17]

Alleghany Corp. v. Kirby lasted longer than Friendly anticipated. On March 2, 1966, just days before oral argument in the Supreme Court, a column by Drew Pearson appeared on the West Coast and leveled against Friendly a misconduct charge that had its roots in his days at Cleary, Gottlieb and the bankruptcy of the New York Central Railroad: "One of the ablest U.S. Court of Appeals judges, Henry J. Friendly of New York, sat on a case now before the Supreme Court in which earlier as a lawyer he had represented one of the litigants. In the big battle over the New York Central Railroad, he represented the railroad against the late Robert Young and Allan Kirby. As a lawyer he tried to charge concealment on the part of Young and Kirby. Later, as a judge on the Second Circuit Court of Appeals, he did not step aside but wrote a strong dissent based on exactly the same charges he had previously argued as a lawyer."[18]

This item did not appear in Pearson's column the following day in New York and Washington; it had been killed. While the events leading to the item's demise are unknown, it is a safe bet that its burial was due to the fact that the item was egregiously false. Friendly had *not* represented one of the litigants in *Alleghany Corp. v. Kirby* (although he had been adverse to one of the litigants); the issues were *not* the same in the two cases; and his dissent was *not* based on the same charges he had argued as a lawyer. What made the item particularly damaging was that if the facts had been as Pearson stated them, Friendly would have violated a federal statute.[19]

The allegations did not die. Several months later Joseph B. Hyman, a former congressional aide apparently with ties to Robert Young, sent a forty-four-page complaint to members of the Senate and House Judiciary Committees. The complaint, while not repeating Pearson's falsities, made a number of related allegations, including that Friendly had examined Young in a deposition about the subject matter of *Alleghany Corp. v. Kirby.*[20] Responding to the complaint, Friendly's detailed letter argued that the allegations were false or *de minimus.* For example, he asked Young only one question about Young and Kirby's alleged misuse of corporate funds, and there was no acrimony between Young and him. Prominent in Friendly's letter was the point that neither Hyman nor anyone else had complained or sought his disqualification based on facts within their knowledge.[21]

Evidently supplied with a copy of Hyman's complaint to Congress, the *New York Times* reporter Sydney E. Zion interviewed a number of people and wrote a long story, which the *New York Times* killed. Four years later Zion published the story in *Scanlan's Monthly*, a short-lived nonmainstream magazine, of which he was coeditor. While Zion described many of the charges in Hyman's complaint, he featured Friendly's sitting on *Alleghany Corp. v. Kirby.* "In 1954 Henry J. Friendly, then a senior partner in Cleary, Gottlieb, Friendly & Hamilton, conducted an aggressive, sometimes acrimonious cross-examination of Robert R. Young on the eve of the famous proxy election for control of the New York Central Railroad. One of the issues he examined Mr. Young on was the acquisition by Mr. Young and Mr. Kirby of IDS stock from the Alleghany Corporation in 1950."[22]

Zion continued, "Leading lawyers, judges and law professors felt that [Friendly] should not have sat on the cases. They said that his decision to sit, in the context of his apparent knowledge of the issues and the people involved, was perhaps unprecedented in the federal judiciary," a rank hyperbole even if Hyman's allegations had all been true. Zion identified neither his sources nor the nature of the information that he supplied to them as the operative facts (Hyman's complaint?). The article also revealed why Kirby's lawyers, who were fully aware of Friendly's prior activity with Young and Kirby both from personal knowledge and from the *New York Times*,[23] never objected to Friendly's sitting on the case (assuming they believed they had a basis to disqualify him): "The lawyers at Donovan, Leisure would not comment, but reliable sources close to the situation said that the firm decided that, given these previous involvements [by Friendly], Judge Friendly would, if anything, 'bend over backwards' to be fair," Zion wrote.[24] In other words, Kirby and his lawyers made a tactical decision not to complain about Friendly's participation in the case on the basis of an expectation that they would reap a benefit, a conclusion that suggests that Friendly's prior relationship with Young and Kirby could not have been all that bad. Kirby warranted little sympathy for his tactical decision. The allegations finally died.

In other cases Friendly reversed district judges who had approved settlements, such as *Saylor v. Lindsley*, in which Saylor's lawyer, Abraham I. Markowitz, settled a multimillion-dollar stockholder's derivative suit for $250,000 over his client's objection.[25] Noting that Markowitz had settled the contingent-fee case quickly and was about to pocket one-third share of the recovery, Friendly's opinion stated that Markowitz's activities "impress us as designed to justify a settlement rather than as an aggressive effort to ferret out facts helpful to the prosecution of the suit. . . . There can be no blinking at the fact that the interests of the plaintiff in a stockholder's derivative suit and of his attorney are by no means congruent." Friendly proceeded to set out in some detail "what we consider plaintiff's most promising theory." His ostensible reasons were to see whether the court should waste time by remanding if a substantial recovery was hopeless and also whether settlement was improper without adversarial discovery. What followed was a sophisticated three-page discussion that was far better than anything in the plaintiffs' brief. The opinion provided the plaintiffs with ammunition to continue their suit.[26]

Another Friendly reversal was *National Super Spuds, Inc. v. New York Mercantile Exchange*,[27] where the district court approved a class-action settlement that seemed to eliminate claims that were not part of the lawsuit, without providing compensation for those claims. When a member of the plaintiff class objected, District Judge Lloyd F. MacMahon acknowledged that the settlement agreement was ambiguous, but said, in a rather bizarre statement, that the state courts could decide its scope later. Friendly reversed. "If a judgment after trial cannot extinguish claims not asserted in the class action complaint, a judgment approving a settlement in such an action ordinarily should not be able to do so either."[28] This conundrum is now called the "*Super Spuds* issue," and virtually every circuit has cited Friendly's opinion.[29]

Friendly also immersed himself in the issue of nonmonetary aspects of settling class actions. To resolve a class action the parties sometimes enter into a consent judgment or decree that imposes an injunction on one of them. Sometimes circumstances change. Thus, after individuals and an organization supporting the rights of persons with disabilities sued New York State to end overcrowding at the Willowbrook School for the Mentally Retarded, a state institution, the parties entered into a consent decree that ordered the school to send most of the residents to much smaller facilities. Years later, after the state only minimally implemented the consent decree, the plaintiffs moved to enforce the decree and New York cross-moved to relax its terms. The district court sided with the plaintiffs.

On appeal in *New York State Association for Retarded Children v. Carey*,[30] New York argued that the district court applied "an excessively rigid standard" in denying its petition to amend the decree and that it had no reasonable alternative to placing retarded children in facilities larger than the consent decree allowed. Earlier, the Supreme Court had taken a formalistic approach, looking at, for example, whether the moving party sought to expand or contract the decree.[31] While the state's brief argued that prior case law was unsatisfactory, it failed to offer a standard for amending the decree.[32] Agreeing in principle with the state and reversing the district court, Friendly created a standard that relaxed the earlier decree largely on the ground that the amendment sought by the state was "not . . . in derogation of the primary objective of the decree."[33] Years later, when the Supreme Court decided *Rufo v. Inmates of Suffolk County Jail*,[34] a case involving prison conditions, all the Justices accepted Friendly's flexible approach to amending equitable decrees, with Justice Stevens's individual opinion announcing, "Today the Court endorses the standard for modification of consent decrees articulated by Judge Friendly."[35]

CONFLICT OF LAWS is the product of living in a multisovereign world. In a suit brought in New York, one of the parties may assert that the parties lived in California or that the crucial events took place in California, so the court should apply California law. Courts and commentators have long debated what standard the forum court should employ to decide which jurisdiction's law should apply. At one time courts would apply to personal-injury actions the law where the last event creating liability occurred (*lex loci delicti*), but more recently courts have opted for less formalistic standards, such as where most of the significant events took place. Regardless, no decision may run afoul of Article IV, Section 1 of the U.S. Constitution: "Full Faith and Credit shall be given in each State to the Public Acts, Records, and Judicial Proceedings of every other State."

John S. Pearson, a New York resident who purchased his ticket and boarded a plane in New York, died in a plane crash near Nantucket, Massachusetts. The carrier, Northeast Airlines, was incorporated in Massachusetts but actively conducted business in New York, including flying many planes in and out of that state. Pearson's legal representative, his widow, a New York resident, brought suit in a federal district court in New York on the basis of diversity of citizenship. In *Pearson v. Northeast Airlines, Inc.*[36] the district judge, who applied Massachusetts law to the case, nevertheless refused Northeast's request to apply a provision of the Massachusetts General Statutes that put an upper limit of $15,000 on recovery in wrongful-death actions[37] and instructed the jury that it should award damages on the basis of economic loss, which it did in the amount of $134,000. His decision relied on *Kilberg v. Northeast Airlines, Inc.*, a suit by the estate of another passenger on the same flight, where the New York Court of Appeals, the state's highest court, concluded that the limitation would violate the strong public policy of New York and that the plaintiff should be compensated for the damages he incurred.[38]

Northeast appealed in *Pearson* on the ground that the trial court violated the Full Faith and Credit Clause by not applying Massachusetts's $15,000 maximum. A Second Circuit panel without Friendly voted two to one, with Judge Irving Kaufman dissenting, to reverse the award on the ground that the clause barred courts from awarding above $15,000 in a lawsuit "based" on the Massachusetts statute. Granting a petition for rehearing *en banc* filed by Pearson, the full court of appeals reversed the panel and reinstated the verdict. This time Kaufman wrote the majority opinion while Friendly dissented.

The majority and dissent were in agreement that, because of the extensive contacts that the events had with New York, its courts could constitutionally apply its own law to the entirety of the case. Since New York could apply its own laws to the accident, Kaufman reasoned, it could apply a mixture of Massachusetts laws and New York laws and thus apply its own measure of damages to a claim based on Massachusetts law. Citing a series of Supreme Court cases, Kaufman stated, "We construe this as recognizing that a single 'transaction' may contain within itself several distinct 'issues' legitimately made subject to the law of more than one state." He continued, "We are convinced that New York may examine each issue in the litigation—the conduct which creates liability, the parties who may bring an action, the extent of liability, the period during which the liability may be sued upon, and in appropriate cases, matters of immunity, insurance procedure, etc.—and by weighing the contacts of various states with the transaction, New York may, without interfering with the Constitution, shape its rules controlling the litigation."[39]

Dissenting, Friendly argued that it did not follow from the fact that New York courts could have applied New York law to the entire event that the Full Faith and Credit Clause permitted New York to ignore "substantial provisions of the statute which inhered in the cause of action or which named conditions on which the right to sue depend[s]." For Friendly the issue threatened the integrity of the legislative process and, indeed, of the legislature itself:

> An important reason why a forum state may not do this is that it thereby interferes with the proper freedom of action of the legislature of the sister state. The terms and conditions of a claim created by statute inevitably reflect the legislature's balancing of those considerations that favor and of those that oppose the imposition of liability. . . . The increasing scope of statutory liabilities makes it particularly vital that lawmakers of one state should know that once a transitory right has been created by them, it will receive the uniform enforcement from other states which the Full Faith and Credit Clause contemplated and that they should not be obliged to speculate that

other states may take what is liked and reject what is disliked—a prospect that might well discourage or prevent enactments otherwise deemed desirable.[40]

Professor Brainerd Currie, a renowned expert on conflict of laws on whom Kaufman's opinion relied, criticized Friendly's dissent as "largely conceptual; for how can the result in *Kilberg* be unconstitutional when the same result would be unobjectionable if rationalized on other grounds?" Observing that "the essential fault of the reasoning is that it loses sight of the fact that New York is applying New York's own wrongful-death statute, though not all of it," Currie considered Friendly's result indefensible and *Kilberg* "enlightened."[41] Student comments in law reviews were overwhelmingly unfavorable to Friendly's position.[42] Actually, it does seem fanciful that a state legislature might be offended (if that were relevant) by the rare instance in which an out-of-state court distorted its legislative product by discarding a portion of a statute its members had passed years earlier (but, according to Friendly, not if the court refused to apply any of a statute the legislature intended to apply).[43] District Judge Louis Pollak, a former professor and a friend of Friendly's, was one of the few people who supported his dissent.[44]

Friendly's other conflicts opinions were less formalistic and less controversial. One year before *Pearson*, in *Grivas v. Alianza Compania Armadora, S.A.*, an admiralty case brought by a seaman for wages and other relief, Friendly observed the traditional rule that the law of the ship's flag (Liberia) applied. But he left open the door for a more flexible approach: "We do not here decide that occasions might not arise where some law having a more meaningful relation than the law of a 'nominal foreign registration' ought not be chosen even when the choice is between two foreign laws rather than, as in the Jones Act cases, between a foreign law and our own."[45] Both before and after *Pearson* he accepted that the laws of different jurisdictions could apply to different aspects of a case.[46]

Friendly ended his writings on the subject with a tribute to Chief Justice Roger Traynor of California.[47] The single example he took to demonstrate Traynor's outstanding judicial qualities was a conflict-of-laws opinion, *Bernkrant v. Fowler*,[48] which concerned a claim based on an alleged oral agreement made in Nevada between the decedent ("one Granrud") and Nevada residents. Under that agreement the Nevada residents made partial payment of their debt to Granrud and gave him a security interest in their Nevada property to secure the remainder of the debt. In return Granrud promised that his will would forgive any portion of the debt unpaid at his death. Granrud's will, however, did not include such a provision, and the Nevada residents filed suit in California, where he had died, to have their debt expunged. Granrud's oral promise was enforceable under Nevada's statute of frauds, but not under California's. Traynor concluded that the California court should apply Nevada law regardless of the domicile of Granrud. Friendly explained:

> [S]ince California "would have no interest in applying its own statute of frauds unless Granrud remained here until his death, plaintiffs were not bound to know that California's statute might ultimately be invoked against them"— Roger must have chuckled over that one—and that "unless they could rely on their own law, they would have to look to the laws of all of the jurisdictions to which Granrud might move regardless of where he was domiciled when the contract was made"—a look that would have been not only time consuming but generally fruitless. The California statute was thus not intended to apply even if Granrud was a California resident when the contract was made, and the court could happily sustain Nevada's interest in the enforcement of a contract made in Nevada, relating to Nevada real estate, and involving at least some Nevada residents, without subordinating any legitimate interest of California's.[49]

Friendly applauded Traynor's practical and sensible solution, which was similar to the one he had implemented in *Grivas* and other cases. Friendly stood by his decision in *Pearson* to the end of his days.[50]

FRIENDLY WROTE many opinions on evidence, but only one category will be discussed, namely, nonconstitutional evidentiary privileges. While the general policy is that juries may hear all evidence that is relevant, a number of rules place limits on that principle. For example, evidence is excluded when its potential for unfair prejudice far outweighs its probative value. Also, evidence is excluded when it arises out of a highly valued confidential relationship.[51] The first two of Friendly's three significant opinions on privileges concerned the impact of an accountant's involvement on a party's otherwise valid attorney-client privilege, a previously neglected issue of considerable practical importance. In both cases he helped fashion the modern rule. His third opinion concerned a less common and pressing privilege, the spousal-testimony privilege.

For centuries Anglo-American judges and society have agreed that confidential communications between lawyer and client for the purpose of obtaining legal advice should be excluded from evidence in order to encourage parties to consult candidly with lawyers. But when people outside the relationship were present, such as a friend, there was no *confidential* communication and therefore no privilege. In time, life and business became more complex. What little law existed, including the leading treatise on evidence by Dean John Henry Wigmore, suggested that a privilege continued to exist only when the third person was performing ministerial duties, such as a secretary taking notes.[52]

In *United States v. Kovel*,[53] a law firm employed an accountant, Louis Kovel, to assist in connection with a grand jury investigation of a client for alleged income tax evasion. When the grand jury subpoenaed Kovel to ask him about conversations at which the client, his lawyer, and he were present, the client objected to Kovel's testifying. The prosecutor brought Kovel before District Judge John M. Cashin, who found the issue easy: "there is no privilege." When Kovel asked whether he might say something, Cashin said, "I am not going to listen." When Kovel persisted in refusing to answer, Cashin found him guilty of criminal contempt, sentenced him to a year in jail, ordered him committed, and denied him bail, although he was soon released.

On appeal Kovel argued that his status as an employee of a law firm automatically made all communications to him from clients privileged. Conversely, the prosecution argued that no privilege existed with respect to communications to an accountant. Friendly chastised the lawyers for "the extreme positions erroneously taken by both parties in the court below" and for making highly technical distinctions: "Laymen consulting lawyers should not be expected to anticipate niceties perceptible only to judges—and not even to all of them."[54] The briefs were worthless to Friendly, who required a more sophisticated analysis.

Friendly likened an accountant to an interpreter. "Accounting concepts are a foreign language to some lawyers in almost all cases, and to almost all lawyers in some cases."[55] The crucial issue was whether the communication was made for the purpose of obtaining legal advice from a lawyer. Friendly acknowledged that his decision drew what might seem an arbitrary line, a line that also might not be readily discernible. If the client first consults an accountant of his own choice, there is no privilege, while the result is the opposite if the client first consults a lawyer who sends him to the same accountant. "But that is the inevitable consequence of having to reconcile the absence of a privilege for accountants and the effective operation of the privilege of client and lawyer under conditions where the lawyer needs outside help."[56] The Advisory Committee on proposed Federal Rules of Evidence endorsed the decision in *Kovel* when it drafted the Federal Rule of Evidence on the attorney-client privilege in the early 1970s, although ultimately no rules were enacted on the subject of privilege and the issues were left for case-by-case development by the courts.

The question of whether the *later* involvement of an accountant destroyed what was concededly a valid attorney-client privilege also occupied Friendly. In *In re Horowitz*[57] a grand jury subpoenaed Simon Horowitz, an accountant for Alexander and Elizabeth Kasser, to produce the contents of three filing cabinets of their records. Since Horowitz regularly examined those documents while performing accounting, not legal, services, the documents he saw lost their protected status. More difficult was the status of privileged material that Horowitz had never viewed. Should confidential documents never actually seen by anyone other than a client and his lawyer lose their protected status because the client's accountant could have but did not look at them? Friendly decided that the privilege had been lost because the Kassers did not treat the materials as confidential.[58]

Friendly's opinion gratuitously considered an important question, not raised by the case and not addressed by the Supreme Court for another eight years,[59] whether, "for purposes of the privilege, low-ranking employees should be regarded as the 'client' or as third parties from whom confidential communications must be kept." Pointing out that the result may depend on the facts of the case, he warned that "special precautions to preserve strict confidentiality may prove burdensome," all *dicta*. The application of the attorney-client privilege in the context of a corporation has generated a small library of comment.

Friendly wrote his third significant privilege opinion in 1985 on the spousal-testimony privilege, which, to avoid undermining a marriage, prevents courts from compelling one spouse to testify against the other in a criminal proceeding. *United States v. Koecher*[60] raised the tantalizing question of whether the privilege should be invalidated when the couple's communications related to criminal activity—in this case spying for Czechoslovakia—in which both spouses may have been involved. Friendly rejected the analogy to the exception to the attorney-client privilege for communications made to an attorney for advancing criminal ends, saying, "The attorney-client relationship, valuable as it is, is hardly of the same social importance as that of husband and wife."[61] He also rejected the proposition that a marriage cannot be a devoted one because one or both of the partners decided to engage in criminal activity. "This is especially true with respect to political offenses, as witness some celebrated cases in this very court."[62] He did not have to mention the Rosenbergs by name.

Upholding the privilege, Friendly rested his decision on the importance of "the harmony and sanctity of the marriage relationship," and subordinated other values. He was making law without legal precedent or established principle to support him. In fact two other courts of appeals had rejected the claim of privilege in similar circumstances.[63] Friendly's solution was more consistent with the privilege's purpose, but less palatable. The Supreme Court accepted and heard argument in the case but declared the case moot and dismissed it without a decision when Mr. Koecher was exchanged for an American who had been arrested as a spy by an East European country.[64] Friendly's opinion was dated February 28, 1985, when his wife of fifty-four years was days away from death. One of his law clerks saw a draft of the opinion on a table in his bedroom.[65]

CHAPTER TWENTY-FOUR

At the End

SOPHIE'S RELATIVE LONGEVITY seemed assured; five years younger than her spouse, she was healthy, vigorous, optimistic, and a woman whose parents had lived into their nineties, while Friendly was in middling health (he had suffered a heart attack during the 1979–1980 term),[1] rather sedentary, pessimistic, and a man whose father had died at seventy-six. Certain that he would die first, Friendly prepared a detailed account of his finances and related matters so that Sophie, who had not paid attention to them, would have the full picture after he was gone.[2] He not only expected to die first; he wanted to die first.[3] Yet against all odds, Sophie died first. Around Christmas in 1984 she learned that she had incurable colon cancer, and she died on March 6, 1985. Friendly was confused and at a loss during these months, unprepared emotionally and unable to deal with his feelings. After Sophie died, his life crumbled about him and he was totally unequipped to continue. He had lost his intimate connection to life, which he could not generate internally. Unable on his own to involve himself with much of the essence of life, he despaired of ever capturing the spirit that helped illuminate it.[4]

The dreadful chasm Sophie's death created in the lives of Friendly, their children, and their grandchildren is apparent from comments made at her memorial service on March 10, 1985. Their grandson Barak Goodman observed, "Nana loved to help others. She was always trying to make the lives of her children and grandchildren better/happier and she took on multiple projects for those within her caring ambit—not just family. . . . She went back to the same spots with different [grandchildren] because she saw them through their eyes. Above all my grandmother had a capacity to love." His sister Ellen Goodman said, "Her embrace was unconditional, unhesitating, and unwavering. Like a plush towel after a warm bath, Nana wrapped herself around us taking the chill out of a first week of college or a birthday that everyone seems to have forgotten." Their father, Frank Goodman, explained her love of travel as part of her being "a tireless observer of the human scene. . . . What moved and entranced her at the Cathedral of Chartres was not its famous stained glass windows, but the wedding she delightedly chanced upon there. She was an unquenchable romantic. She devoured historical biography. She loved to read and fantasize about kings and queens, lords and ladies, great loves and great exploits."

After Sophie's death Friendly became more discouraged and even more world-weary, at times devastated and despondent. To many of those who talked to him after his wife's death he sounded terrible and depressed.[5] In contrast to his customary reticence about his emotions, he revealed his despair and overwhelming sadness to others. He seemed unashamed to let his secretary, Charlotte Kimbrough, see him crying at his desk. She had to screen calls women were placing to him, usually to extend an invitation of some sort.[6] To cheer him up former clerks and others telephoned him for lunch. Invitations for evening activities multiplied, both for dinners and cultural events. He had monthly dinners with Pierre Leval and his wife, Susana, who lived nearby, and Michael Boudin would visit from Washington to see him for Sunday evening dinners. Pat Hall Mogin would also visit from Washington; she and the judge went to museums, where he would have her describe what they were seeing.[7]

During the summer of 1985 Friendly returned to the familiar Chatham Inn on Cape Cod, which may have magnified his emotional isolation. His children and their spouses provided company for portions of the summer, and others visited him, including Paul and Pat Mogin, whose expenses he paid.[8] Friendly joked about his new status to two former clerks, Donald Board and David Seipp, who saw him there that summer; he said he had to watch out for New York City widows who had their sights on him.[9] One luncheon involved his old friend Paul Freund and a few others who drove to the Cape. They engaged in wide-ranging discussions of current events and other subjects. He told his visitors that aspects of his personal life particularly distressed him, putting his face in his hands and lamenting, "the widows, the widows, the widows."[10] The orderly life Friendly needed had evaporated.

Bothered by arthritis in addition to his more serious health problems,[11] Friendly seemed less involved with his work and permitted his clerks to do some drafting of opinions (although always keeping the statement of facts for himself).[12] He talked more to his clerks about his earlier years practicing law and the decline of Pan American World Airways, and seemed to have mellowed.[13] At the end of the last day on which he heard arguments, January 6, 1986, the panel met to discuss the cases they had heard that day and make writing assignments. There was disagreement on a commercial case. After a while Friendly uncharacteristically announced, "Why don't you guys work out an agreement on the case," and left.[14] Nevertheless, a few days later he wrote a friend, "I continue to sit fairly often, mostly because I would rather do that than do nothing."[15]

Friendly was conscious that the faculties of Justice Holmes and Learned Hand had weakened during their last years on the bench.[16] As early as 1981 he had told Edward Weinfeld, "I have indeed become concerned about slippage; I am conscious that I do not write with the same passion or verve as I did five years ago, and hope that someone will have the kindness to tell me when the time has come to quit."[17] For obvious reasons no one did. He noted, however, "I seem to have greater difficulty in making up my mind than formerly."[18] Friendly published many significant opinions during his wife's illness and the year following her death, some of which were discussed in earlier chapters. Although there was a serious physical and emotional deterioration in Friendly after Sophie's death, he was intellectually intact.[19] One of his last clerks said that Friendly seemed "at the top of his game."[20] His memory, though no longer outstanding, was excellent.

Friendly, who had virtually lost the use of his right eye a year or two earlier, feared that he would become blind or suffer a stroke and be rendered helpless, and he occasionally compared his situation with the circumstances of his father's demise.[21] Although he complained that his sight was continuing to deteriorate,[22] he said, "[I] carried on with my left, which was found to be in satisfactory condition by two eminent ophthalmologists in mid-December." His last four clerks mentioned that Friendly was very concerned with his eyesight, especially during early 1986, when his eye problems forced him to stay at home for six weeks while his two clerks visited him on alternate days, taking turns reading briefs and documents to him.[23] He complained to friends that he could not read.[24] However, some of those closest to him believed that he was not going blind, that he exaggerated his visual problems, and was talking himself into legitimizing suicide.[25]

Convinced that he would require regular assistance in his day-to-day life, he could not face being dependent and essentially alone.[26] He understood that his children would visit him now and then, but he recognized that Ellen and David, and perhaps Joan, would not be there for him as regularly as they had been for their mother. No friends could fill the void created by Sophie's death, and he could not accept having to rely on paid strangers. Many of his pleasures, including traveling and the Jewish Judges luncheons, were gone or disappearing, and, of course, there was no substitute for Sophie's attentiveness and her warm and vibrant presence. He had looked into the future and saw that it held no appeal to him. He seemed to have no fear of death, only of his future on earth. He had had enough.

Although Friendly was pessimistic and dispirited most of his life and had thoughts that he might commit suicide, there is no evidence that he had seriously contemplated suicide before his wife died, and certainly had not engaged in planning a suicide. Once she died, however, he talked about suicide frequently, even though most elderly widowed white males, who have among the highest suicide rates, usually do not disclose their suicide plans.[27] Every time he saw Joan, which was every week or two, he discussed suicide.[28] He also spoke about suicide with his son, David, and his daughter Ellen as well as with his daughter-in-law, Irene; his son-in-law Frank; his physician; his friend Judge Edward Weinfeld; his former secretary Pat Mogin; and perhaps others, but apparently with none of his current or former clerks. People with whom he shared his plans opposed suicide, and Weinfeld stopped talking to him for a time out of his hostility to the idea. Although conventional wisdom is that frequent conversations about suicide are evidence that one will not go through with the act, that would be mistaken in Friendly's case; he was not looking for advice, arguments, or sympathy, but rather was explaining his intentions.

Compared with his generally mordant character, his dinners with Pierre and Susana Leval were incongruous. Pierre described Friendly at these dinners as "cheerful" and "jolly," thoroughly enjoying himself and partaking in lively and entertaining conversation. To them Friendly's mood seemed much more positive than years earlier; it was as though he had created a special enclave for those evenings. The Levals were astonished when they learned that he had committed suicide.[29]

Friendly settled on pills. Because he was hardly conversant with what pills in what quantity were required, he studied and spoke to knowledgeable people about the subject. He wrote to the Hemlock Society in London for instructions and received manuals in reply, and enlisted members of his family in planning the event, discussing with them the timing and method. He told them that he wanted to have one of his children or a spouse present when he took the pills, but recognized that he would be placing that person in jeopardy of criminal prosecution and accepted that he would perform the act alone. Eventually, he had saved up enough pills to kill himself.[30]

In early 1986 he wrote an undated letter with no salutation, which he may have regarded as an open letter to his family, colleagues, and friends, saying, "The time has come for me to attempt to take my life rather than to be a burden to myself, my children and my friends without any compensating satisfaction." (Curiously, he said "attempt to take my life.") He could not face the agony of another operation on his remaining eye with no assurance of success. As the first anniversary of his wife's death approached, his thoughts of suicide became stronger. He had decided to leave several suicide notes and started on the note to his clerks, but then put it aside. He canceled a luncheon engagement set for a few weeks later with a former clerk (and perhaps with others), which unsettled the clerk. A few days before he died, he showed Richard Posner, who was visiting his apartment, a picture of a couple he knew, with the comment that they had committed suicide together, which, he added, was a good idea. His musings upset his listeners. When he finally made the decision to commit suicide, he called Joan to tell her of the date of his suicide, and she agreed to come up from Philadelphia the first thing the following morning. He also called Pat Mogin to say good-bye.[31]

The time Friendly selected was the evening of March 10, 1986, exactly one year after the memorial service for his wife. Uncharacteristically waiting until the last minute, perhaps because of uncertainty whether he was going to go through with the suicide, he finished the note to his clerks, which discussed the disposition of cases and other office matters in numbered paragraphs and which read matter-of-factly, like one of his vacation memos. The notes to Joan and to the housekeeper fixed on his fear of going blind. The note to his longtime housekeeper, Rosa Edmunds, assured her that she would obtain full Social Security benefits and that he was leaving her money in his will, explaining that that would provide for her future. He also mentioned that he was leaving the week's money for her and the laundress on the bureau and concluded by telling her not to enter his room, but to wait for his daughter. His note to Joan was very personal. Aside from asserting his love for her, he wrote that he should have tried harder to get close to his only son, David, but he did not write notes to him or Ellen, and assuredly not to his grandchildren. The note trailed off as he lost consciousness. Altogether, Friendly's actions leading up to his death demonstrated his limited appreciation of the emotional welfare of others.

Joan made arrangements to pick up her son Barak, a graduate student at Columbia's School of Journalism, early in the morning of March 11 on her way to her father's apartment. When Joan and Barak arrived and saw that Friendly was dead, she immediately called his doctor and the director of the funeral home, both of whom came over, and Judge Leval, who adjourned a case he was trying in order to go to the apartment. Frank Goodman followed his wife to New York to lend a hand. Friendly's clerk Thomas Curtis came to the apartment at 10 A.M., as scheduled, only to learn that the judge had died. Joan also called her father's chambers to tell the staff that the judge had died, and his clerk Thomas Dagger called Chief Judge Wilfred Feinberg, the *New York Times*, and others to inform them of the death. The police furnished to the press additional details the family would have preferred were not mentioned, including that there were three suicide notes.[32] The obituary in the *New York Times* described the death as "apparently a suicide."

In the aftermath of his death, many colleagues and friends visited the family and otherwise provided support.[33] Pat Mogin wrote Judge Weinfeld a warm note that described how highly Friendly had valued his friendship. She said that it had been very disturbing to her to hear Friendly talk of suicide, but added, "I now realize that he never wanted to be talked out of his decision, but rather to be sure that I understood his motives behind his decision."[34] In his response Weinfeld thanked her for her note, then added, "One could not dissuade him that there are others still alive who meant much to him—his children and grandchildren, particularly since Sophie and he enjoyed an unusual relationship with them."[35] Friendly could speak fondly, albeit abstractly, about his grandchildren.

The obituary in the *New York Times* included extraordinary praise from Chief Judge Feinberg ("one of the greatest Federal judges in the history of the federal bench") and Judge Posner ("the greatest federal judge of his time—in analytic power, memory, and application perhaps in any time").[36] Possibly because the *Times* had received complaints about the modest coverage of Friendly's death, its account of a later memorial session of the Second Circuit was prominently placed and much longer.[37]

Friendly left an estate of about $5.3 million, which, aside from three specific bequests, he gave to David and Joan. The will noted that Ellen was well provided for as a result of her divorce settlement with Stephen Simon, and she had generously agreed not to accept any of Friendly's estate. He left $35,000 to Pat Hall Mogin and only $2,500 to his housekeeper. The single charitable bequest, his voluminous papers, which included approximately three thousand of his case files along with extensive correspondence, went to Harvard Law School.[38]

For some unknown reason, the *Harvard Law Review* published in its June 1987 issue an obtuse and seemingly off-the-cuff commentary relating to Friendly's suicide by a young Yale professor, Paul Gewirtz, who did not know Friendly, had done no significant research on him, and wrongly pictured his entire life as totally rational and deliberative and his suicide following the death of his wife as part and parcel of that mosaic.[39] Responding to Gewirtz's article, Joan Goodman wrote him that "suicide—eventual suicide—was no stranger to his thoughts even in healthier, less unhappy days." She continued:

> My father's suicide was indeed an expression of his basic nature, but that nature was exceedingly complex and by no means confined to the "deliberate, controlling and reasoning self" best known to others. He had a darker side as well. His temperament was deeply melancholic, his outlook on the world pessimistic to the point of despair. Throughout his mature life, the world's uses seemed to him, as to Hamlet, "weary, stale, flat, and unprofitable." He struggled against this sense of futility and meaninglessness of his own life and of life generally. His achievements as a lawyer, judge, and scholar were the more remarkable because they were produced in the face of this struggle. His suicide at the age of 82 was, in part at least, a final submission to the worldweariness he had so long managed to overcome, the demons he had held at bay. . . . [A]lthough he contemplated it [suicide] with ever greater seriousness in his final months, in the event the decision was sudden, almost impetuous.[40]

CHAPTER TWENTY-FIVE

Friendly's Legacy

FRIENDLY SEEMED TO KNOW what was required to make the law better, and he influenced the law in an astonishing number of areas. His articles contained insights on the interaction of the Fifth and Sixth Amendments, the proper scope of the Fifth Amendment, the role of guilt in evaluating petitions for habeas corpus, the concept of state action, the proper scope of hearings, and the reform of both federal courts and administrative agencies, to name some of the more prominent.[1] Less obvious are Friendly's contributions contained in his judicial opinions, especially his opinions on business law, which were in part the product of his extensive experience dealing with businessmen while at Root, Clark and Cleary, Gottlieb. He understood not only the law, but the workings of the mind of businessmen, at their best and at their worst. What his one-time client Albert Einstein said, with a touch of exaggeration, was relevant to Friendly's accomplishments: "[I]ntuition is nothing but the outcome of earlier intellectual experience."[2]

Friendly's legal reforms coupled with his rigorous craftsmanship made him unique among federal appellate judges of his time. He demanded excellence from his law clerks, the litigants, district judges, his colleagues—and, most of all, himself. Whether or not the recipient would regard his criticism as constructive, Friendly pressed for quality. One measurable example is the percentage of times he wrote an opinion in support of modifying or reversing a district court compared with other judges. His opinions sought to change the district court's outcome 47.5 percent of the time. In contrast, the percentage for the entire court for the court terms 1965 through 1967 was 24.6, barely half as often.[3]

Friendly's colleague Judge Wilfred Feinberg saw another reason for Friendly's prominence: "Somehow, an unusually high percentage of the cases in which Henry wrote opinions involved interesting and important issues. This was because, like other great judges, he carried the full sweep of the law in his mind and saw issues that others might ignore."[4] Opinions that Friendly wrote in less than a day have endured for decades.[5]

Friendly had no agenda, as that term is commonly understood. He was not, for example, seeking broadly to expand or to curtail the rights of criminal defendants. While his votes in a small number of areas tended to favor one class of parties or one position, he was not doctrinaire. Rather than attach himself to one team or the other, he spent his energies leveling the playing field and tweaking the rules in the interests of legal cohesiveness and fairness. As in the *Wendel* will case, it was the intellectual exercise rather than which side or position won that most interested him. Seeing the complexities in a problem, he advocated a position that he believed resolved difficult cases intelligently. He promoted compromise and a balancing of interests while articulating concepts and standards that made the law more rational and workable.[6] He tended to shy away from seemingly simple bright-line rules. Indeed, part of his brilliance was recognizing that there were no easy answers to the problems that confronted him. Often both sides had good (or only bad) arguments.

Friendly once wrote, "Brandeis left no single testament where we can find his legal credo neatly packaged and ribboned."[7] The same can be said about Friendly, although, of course, both left material sufficient to encourage attempts at re-creation. Above all, Friendly was pragmatic as a judge, and he rationalized and expanded existing concepts; he was not attempting to construct a new theoretical framework. He was Bach or Rembrandt rather than Stravinsky or Picasso. No school of jurisprudence is associated with his name. In 1977 he acknowledged, "I fear I do not qualify as a very philosophically-minded judge."[8] He was not unfamiliar with theory, but he felt more comfortable putting his energy into more practical pursuits. He volunteered that in jurisprudential controversies "I tend to agree with whomever I have read last."[9] He read legal theorists, such as H. L. A. Hart, John Rawls, and Ronald Dworkin,[10] but he had limited reverence for the accomplishments of legal philosophers, once describing their work as "a good deal of marching up the hill and at least part of the way down again."[11] He wrote Paul Freund, "I must confess . . . that I get very little out of most of these discussions [on philosophy and jurisprudence] and sometimes wonder if the writer himself has done so."[12] His approach to the question he sometimes posed—What would a legislature have done if it had thought about the problem before the court?—was not particularly theoretical.[13] Nevertheless, he understood the nature and limited role of theories, perhaps instinctively, as Judge Calabresi described his employment of law and economics in *Ira S. Bushey & Sons, Inc. v. United States*.[14]

While largely defying labels in the interpretation of statutes,[15] Friendly was primarily a purposivist; he believed courts should read statutes in context in order to fulfill their legislative purpose. He used his enormous skills to fashion intelligent and sometimes creative readings to further the purposes of Congress and the needs of the country. He liked to refer to "the familiar warning of Judge Learned Hand that '[t]here is no surer way to misread any document than to read it literally,' as well as his oft-cited admonition that 'it is one of the surest indexes of a mature and developed jurisprudence not to make a fortress out of the dictionary.' "[16] Friendly explained, "Courts of the United States are not, like Elsa in the Lohengrin legend, forbidden to ask whence something sprang; on the contrary, they are bound to seek out the sources of a critical sentence of a statute."[17] In some 105 opinions he either rejected a literal reading of a statute or seriously considered a party's argument that a statute should not be read literally. He was obviously capable of deviating from statutory language when considerations of policy convinced him to reach a different result. He conceded that he had "refused to adhere to the letter" of the law in a 1966 tax case "where the law seem[ed] to be saying one thing and policy may point in another direction."[18] Purposivism has been the approach of the broad center of the judiciary that eschewed the rigid and often reactionary tenets of originalism and comparable attitudes on the left.[19] Friendly was a pragmatic moderate.

Friendly represented an exception to Justice Stephen G. Breyer's view of the constitutional work of a court of appeals judge in contrast to that of a Supreme Court Justice: "[T]hat work, though appellate in nature, differs from the work of a lower appellate court in an important way. Because a Justice, unlike a judge on a trial or appellate court, faces a steady diet of constitutional cases, Supreme Court work leads the Justice to develop a view of the Constitution as a whole."[20] While Friendly did not articulate an overarching constitutional theory, he knew where the constitutional chess pieces were located and had a view of what he wanted the next move to be. He respected history, including the views of the founders, hardly surprising for a student of McIlwain's.[21] On constitutional questions he tempered his textualism with interpretivism, which has been described as purposive, and focused on the value judgments embodied in the text of the

Constitution or in the overall structure of government ordained by the Constitution.[22]

Largely bound by Supreme Court precedent, Friendly usually saw his job on an "inferior" court as divining the meaning of the High Court's opinions, rather than formulating rules or even interpreting the language of the Constitution.[23] For example, in deciding an establishment-of-religion case, it made little sense to him to explore the language of the First Amendment or the framers' understanding of that Amendment—that was a task for the Supreme Court. Room for giving vent to constitutional theories was minimal at his position on the judicial ladder. To the extent that he saw historical anomalies, his law review articles, numerous in the case of the Fifth Amendment, became his platform for expressions concerning the Constitution. Articles freed him from the confines of writing about cases on which he sat.

Friendly's decisions and articles fulfilled a critical function. He pointed out that the Supreme Court lacked great Justices during almost his entire judicial career. In the criminal law, both those who supported the liberal revolution of the Warren Court and those who defended existing practices were short on intellectual leaders who could articulate their positions with reference to American and English legal traditions. No serious academics or experienced judges with constitutional grounding were writing Supreme Court opinions after Frankfurter left the Court in 1962.[24] While not necessarily wrong in result, many reform-minded High Court opinions were superficial and confusing. If there was no intellectual vacuum on the Warren Court, the scholarly breezes emanating from the liberal majority were disappointingly thin. It was in this setting that Friendly wrote his important articles. As he summarized in a letter, he was catholic in his criticisms: "Despite the clamor over the Warren Court's decisions with respect to criminal procedure, these were within the traditional area of the Court's enforcing specific provisions of the Bill or Rights. Now a supposedly more conservative Court is invalidating legislation under the general language of the due process and equal protection clauses of the Fifth and Fourteenth Amendments. The outstanding example is the abortion decisions which, with their prescription of different standards for each trimester of pregnancy, read like a statute rather than a judicial decision."[25]

Noteworthy is Friendly's sometimes cavalier attitude toward Supreme Court precedent. As noted, he sometimes construed a Supreme Court opinion to say what he wanted it to say, as he did with *Price v. Georgia*[26] in *Graham v. Smith*[27] on the issue of double jeopardy. He strained to narrow a case that stood in his way, as he did with *Santa Fe Industries, Inc. v. Green*[28] in *Goldberg v. Meridor*[29] to find a violation of federal securities law. He could rely on *dicta* to expand the reach of a case, as he did with *Holloway v. Arkansas*[30] in *Solina v. United States*[31] to find a right to counsel. He could throw a case back in the face of the Supreme Court, as he did in *Rodriguez v. McGinnis*[32] to reprimand the Court for ignoring the failure to exhaust state remedies before filing a federal petition for habeas corpus in *Wilwording v. Swenson.*[33] He simply overruled *Village of Arlington Heights v. Metropolitan Housing Dev. Corp.*,[34] where the Supreme Court stated, "As a corporation, MHDC has no racial identity and cannot be the direct target of the petitioners' [the Village et al.] alleged discrimination." Five years later, in *Hudson Valley Freedom Theater, Inc. v. Heimbach*,[35] Friendly held that Hudson Valley Freedom Theater could assert a discrimination claim: "[W]e predict that, despite the sentence in the *Arlington Heights* opinion, the Supreme Court would hold that HVFT has standing to assert claims of racial discrimination."

While there is an element of fantasy about the question, asking where Friendly would fit on today's Supreme Court is instructive. He would undoubtedly be a swing vote, supporting, with appropriate modifications to reflect his somewhat distinctive views and the passage of time, the teaching of the Legal Process School, which he respected so highly and which has more relevance today than it has had in decades, perhaps now that strides have been made in race relations and criminal justice and the threats to stability are coming from the right.[36] Friendly was cautious about expanding constitutional rights and was intent on protecting the basic rights of defendants, which he sometimes referred to as "personhood." Two cases, among others, where he probably could have changed the result were *District of Columbia v. Heller*,[37] where an emphatically originalist opinion struck down the District of Columbia's gun-control law, and *Herrera v. Collins*,[38] which denied habeas relief that was based solely on a credible claim of innocence. His votes on abortion issues would be, if unchanged, conservative, but not unsympathetic to women and the concept of choice. On most other issues he would remember his changed views on reapportionment, compulsory saluting of the flag, and the *Miranda* warning; it took a number of years before he could accept those decisions. He would be a powerful force, steadfast and occasionally creative.

As much as any twentieth-century American jurist, Friendly was in the tradition of Lord Mansfield, whose innovative thinking moved England's eighteenth-century legal doctrines closer to the demands of a commercial reformation.[39] Two centuries after Mansfield, Friendly's open, analytical, and practical mind led him to create constructive and even novel solutions to a rapidly growing economy. Friendly also embraced Brandeis's statement, "The genius of the common law lies in the process of reasoned elaboration from past precedent; unless we explain our decisions of today with all the precision and exactitude at our command, today's holdings will become but simple fiat and will provide no guidelines for tomorrow's problems."[40] Friendly referred to the "development [of] the thrust and counterthrust so often encountered in the legal as well as the political history of a country wisely addicted to the method of trial and error."[41] He preferred an incremental development and opposed extreme positions, and he was annoyed when briefs failed to examine the range of possibilities.[42] Emphasizing that subtle differences in context may require different analyses, he rejected inapplicable "analogies" proffered without regard to their purposes and functions.[43] Finally, Friendly understood his role as one judge on a multi-judge court that sat on panels. When Judge Cardamone praised him for an opinion he wrote, he replied that he didn't go as far as he wanted, adding that with a large court a judge has to chip away bit by bit. If there is another case, he said, he will do more.[44]

In nonconstitutional cases involving commerce and procedure, Friendly was a creative thinker who studied and listened. He was someone who knew the arguments and knew that sometimes there is no answer to a problem, so he would take liberties.[45] His primary goal was to clarify and rationalize the law, which would facilitate progress in the commercial arena. He was prepared to embrace precedent based on the facts of the case, the holding, or at times the *dicta*. This was not always easy or satisfying as a way of molding the law. Thus, he wrote in a letter, "I find myself increasingly in the position where I disagree not so much with the result as with the language in other Second Circuit opinions and feel obliged to make distinctions that really do not stand up."[46] He emphasized "the need for judges and administrators to decide cases on the basis of 'clear and distinct' propositions and to make their reasons for decision readily available to the persons who are affected in the case sub judice, to those who will be affected in other cases, to subordinate officials who are governed by the decisions, and to critics in the law schools and elsewhere."[47] He was apologetic when he could not fulfill that function: "We realize that, by deciding both phases of this case upon the particular facts here presented, we are not giving bankruptcy judges the guidance which they doubtlessly desire and it is our duty to provide if we properly can. But it is better to fail in this respect than to attempt to give guidance without having seen the variety of factual situations, having heard the adversarial presentations, and having the benefit of scholarly commentary which time will undoubtedly afford."[48]

Incongruities bothered Friendly and he was adept at spotting them. For example, in *George v. Douglas Aircraft Co.*, a suit brought against the company by a flight crew of a plane that crashed, Douglas moved to dismiss on the basis of the statute of limitations. While granting the motion, Friendly observed that "one could hardly support application of a different choice of law rule for airplanes than for automobiles." He also rejected an argument that "would have produced what might appear to be the anomalous result that the non-negligent manufacturer within the area of strict liability would be subject to the six year statute [of limitations] whereas the negligent manufacturer outside that area would have the benefit of the shorter three year statute."[49]

Friendly spent considerable time pondering the judicial relationship between circuit judges and district judges, including the question of how much deference to give to a ruling of a district court. Conventional wisdom is that appellate judges give a measure of deference to a trial judge's rulings on questions of fact, but not on issues of law. Friendly saw that the question was quite complicated and that the issue went beyond looking for nice-sounding definitions of fact and law. "Whether application of a legal standard to facts that are undisputed or have been found without clear error is . . . an area over which 'law' and 'fact' have battled for a century. Perhaps clarity of thought would be promoted by recognizing that it is not exactly one or the other. Jural concepts are not limited to binary systems. . . . Once this is understood, appellate courts can formulate such standards of review, subject, of course, to governing legislation, as comport with good sense and institutional allocations of power."[50]

Friendly also shed light on the concept that in certain circumstances appellate courts reverse trial courts only for "an abuse of discretion," concluding that when enough information is acquired, a trial judge's right to exercise discretion may give way to a rule of law.[51] In 1982 Friendly wrote an article about discretion in which he concluded that there were "a half dozen definitions of 'abuse of discretion' ranging from ones that would require the appellate court to come close to finding that the trial court had taken leave of its senses to others which differ from the definition of error by only the slightest nuance, with numerous variations between the extremes." He concluded by quoting Chief Justice John Marshall, that "discretionary choices are not left to a court's 'inclination, but to its judgment; and its judgment is to be guided by sound legal principles,'" a less helpful conclusion than he had hoped to provide.[52]

Friendly did not seem to care about style, decidedly not in his personal life, but also less than many judges in his opinions. Arguably, his lack of stylistic flair may have added to his greatness as a writer of clear opinions, but it also limited the range of his reputation. His prose sometimes bordered on the conversational, with references to the closeness of the case and similar observations.[53] The circuit judge and Yale professor Guido

Calabresi stated that Friendly never let himself be taken in by style or epigrams, such as "The Constitution is not a suicide pact" or "danger invites rescue." Friendly's priority was clarity, which was exactly right, Calabresi noted.[54] Friendly "opposed the tendency of lawyers and judges to use shibboleths rather than understand the principles behind the words they use," another judge stated.[55] What Friendly said about Brandeis—"Brandeis' style lacks the magic of those supreme composers of judicial literature, Holmes and Learned Hand"[56]—likewise applied to himself, although perhaps with less force.[57] Also, where Friendly made an elegant turn of phrase or wrote a provocative sentence, it almost always appeared in the statement of facts, so as not to create confusion in the law. His sometime colleague John Minor Wisdom summarized, "The striking feature that distinguishes his opinions is their measured reasoning, with a minimum of rhetorical flourishes."[58]

WHEN FRIENDLY'S REPUTATION is discussed, the discussion must be confined to his reputation among judges, professors, and the bar. To the general public he is all but unknown.[59] Some judges and scholars said he was an equal of Oliver Wendell Holmes Jr., Louis Brandeis, Benjamin Cardozo, and Learned Hand. It is also worthwhile pointing out that some have said that he may have exceeded the person whom many consider the best lower court judge ever, Learned Hand. Justice Scalia has said, "I think Friendly was better than Learned Hand. Hand's prose could be dense and difficult to follow; Friendly's was always clear and lucid."[60] Judge Posner considered Friendly smarter and a better lawyer than Hand, but lacking Hand's flair both personally and in his writing.[61]

Hand was flamboyant and quotable, and he had a more memorable name and the face of a judge from Central Casting. He served almost twice as long on the bench as Friendly, from 1909 to 1961, which covered two world wars, a depression, and periods of government repression. He was on the bench when the courts first directed their attention to many important issues, including the scope of freedom of speech. It also must be kept in mind that Hand was not a widely known public figure until May 1944, when he spoke at a gathering of 150,000 newly naturalized citizens in Central Park and led the assemblage in the Pledge of Allegiance on "I Am an American Day." Another one and a half million heard the proceedings over loudspeakers.[62] He returned a year later for a similar and similarly attended event. Friendly was far less conspicuous.

A statistical presentation compares Friendly with five of his contemporaries (as well as Learned Hand) on circuit courts on the number of Supreme Court opinions that mentioned them by name and the number of times law review articles have mentioned them by name, as of August 1,

2011. Specifying the name of the author of a lower-court opinion is a sign of respect. Chief Justice Roberts has said that Friendly is one of the few names you can cite that make people pause.[63] Justice O'Connor spoke about her practice: "When we are looking for a Court of Appeals decision for use as authority, we look first for opinions of Henry Friendly."[64] Friendly would have seen the citation of his opinions accompanied by his name as something special, since he noted, "I doubt whether many of the Justices even read our opinions, at least on constitutional issues."[65]

Table 1 lists the number of opinions in which Justices cited Friendly and six other respected circuit judges: Learned Hand, who served many more years than Friendly, and five contemporaries of Friendly—J. Edward Lumbard and Irving R. Kaufman of the Second Circuit; Carl E. McGowan of the District of Columbia Circuit; Clement F. Haynsworth Jr. of the Fourth Circuit; and John Minor Wisdom of the Fifth Circuit. The gap between Friendly and his contemporaries is remarkable.

One other fact deserves mention: every Supreme Court Justice who served at least five years since 1966 mentioned Friendly by name in an opinion, a remarkable nineteen. Justices of all persuasions respected him.

Table 2 states the number of times law review articles and shorter publications cited each of the judges at least five times. This number, while somewhat arbitrary, tends to identify articles that engaged in serious discussions of the opinions or the scholarly articles by the particular judge.

Formal tributes to Judge Friendly began in 1984, two years before he died, when the *University of Pennsylvania Law Review* published articles by six writers in celebration of his twenty-five years on the bench.[66] Judge Michael Boudin, Professor David P. Currie, Professor Frank Goodman, Judge Carl E. McGowan, Judge Louis Pollak, and Judge John Minor Wisdom were the contributors. Boudin and Currie were former clerks. Three months after Friendly's death the *Harvard Law Review* published a tribute, with another prestigious array of writers: Professor Bruce A. Ackerman, Judge Wilfred Feinberg, Professor Paul Freund, Dean Erwin N. Griswold,

Table 1.   Number of opinions in which Justices mention judges by name

Learned Hand	362
Friendly	281
Wisdom	41
Lumbard	36
McGowan	23
Kaufman	20
Haynsworth	10

Table 2. Number of law review articles mentioning judges at least five times

Learned Hand	1,386
Friendly	955
Wisdom	211
Kaufman	139
Haynsworth	58
McGowan	43
Lumbard	37

Note: Judge Posner did a study of law review mentions employing different criteria, in which Hand surpassed Friendly by a count of 679 to 551. Richard A. Posner, *Cardozo: A Study in Reputation* (1990), Table 3, at 77.

Professor Louis Loss, Judge Richard A. Posner, and Professor Todd Ra-koff.[67] Ackerman and Rakoff were former clerks. There have been many individual articles on his accomplishments.

Courts and bar associations also recognized the loss resulting from Friendly's death. The Second Circuit, as it normally did when a member of the court died, held a memorial service for Friendly. But his was different. Because the Second Circuit's courtroom was not large enough, the memorial was held for the first time in the Great Hall of the Association of the Bar of the City of New York, on June 9, 1986. The Chief Justice of the United States Warren Burger and Justice Thurgood Marshall (a former colleague and the Supreme Court's circuit Justice for the Second Circuit) attended, along with the judges of the Second Circuit. The flight of rhetoric soared much higher than for the great majority of judges, with talks by both Justices, Chief Judge Wilfred Feinberg, and others who were not judges.[68] The Judicial Panel on Multidistrict Litigation also commemorated Friendly's contribution to the law and legal profession, with a statement by Judge Pollak that was typical of the tributes lavished on Friendly:

> I think it's a fair estimate that there is no other judge of our time who has exercised such an extraordinary influence over the entire range of judicial activity in the federal court, no other judge of such influence, saving, of course, the Justices of our highest Court. But Henry Friendly, in a judicial career beginning in 1959 and lasting for 27 extraordinary years, gave shape to our jurisprudence in a way that, in this century, no judge of a court below the Supreme Court has done, with the exception—and I would say "exception" only on a level of parity, not anything higher—of Learned Hand in the Federal Courts and Benjamin Cardozo in the state courts. . . . Through the many articles and the book length studies of the federal jurisdiction and the opinions,

one after another after another, that have given frame to our common enterprise, it is the achievement of a giant.[69]

Upon reading Pollak's comment, Justice Lewis F. Powell Jr. wrote him, "I fully share your view of Henry Friendly. His intellect can be ranked with that of Paul Freund—the most brilliant members of our profession I have ever known personally."[70]

Among the many extravagant, but warranted, compliments paid to Friendly were made by Chief Justice Burger ("I can't possibly identify any judicial colleague more highly qualified to have come to the Supreme Court of the United States than Henry Friendly");[71] Justice Frankfurter ("the best judge now writing opinions on the American scene");[72] Judge Posner ("the greatest judge of his time");[73] Judge Wisdom ("Within my lifetime, except for the giants (Holmes, Brandeis, and Cardozo) and possibly Learned Hand, no federal appellate judge has commanded more respect for his opinions and his writings than Henry Friendly");[74] and Dean Erwin Griswold ("the ablest lawyer of my generation").[75] Many, including Justices John Paul Stevens and Antonin Scalia, have coupled Friendly with Hand as the two greatest lower-court federal judges who never sat on the Supreme Court.[76]

Many honors befell Friendly, such as the Presidential Medal of Freedom, the nation's highest civilian award, given by President Gerald Ford in 1977; the first annual Fordham-Stein Award in 1976 for outstanding scholarship and the advancement of justice; the Learned Hand Medal for Excellence in Federal Jurisprudence in 1972; and the Thomas Jefferson Memorial Award in 1978. Friendly also received honorary degrees from Harvard University, Columbia University, and New York University, among many others. In 1993 Harvard Law School established a Henry J. Friendly professorship, funded by a close friend of the judge's.

Friendly's bible was *The Federal Courts and the Federal System*, first published in 1953 by Professors Henry M. Hart Jr. and Herbert Wechsler.[77] Each of the work's six editions has been dedicated to a pillar of the law; the first was to Frankfurter and the second to Hart. The editors dedicated the third edition (1988) to Friendly, the only nonacademic to be so honored, with the inscription "Man for all seasons in the law; master of this subject."[78]

Other tributes were intimate and unpublicized, such as one by Second Circuit Judge Ellsworth Van Graafeiland, who was appointed in 1974. During his last full term on the bench, 2003–2004, he showed his clerk one of his prized possessions, a note from Friendly written seventeen years earlier. Friendly had circulated a proposed majority opinion to the members of his panel, to which Van Graafeiland circulated his dissent. Friendly's note said that the dissent had changed his mind.[79]

Friendly's most public tribute occurred at the televised confirmation hearings of John G. Roberts Jr. to become Chief Justice of the United States, where Roberts testified, "Judge Friendly . . . had such a total commitment to excellence in his craft, at every stage of the process. Just a total devotion to the rule of law and the confidence that if you just worked hard enough at it, you'd come up with the right answers. And it was his devotion to the rule of law that he took most pleasure in. . . . [H]e wasn't adhering to a political ideology, he was adhering to the rule of law. . . . [T]o this day, lawyers will say, when they get into an area of the law and they pick up one of his opinions, that you can look at it and it's like having a guide to the whole area of the law."[80]

Perhaps Friendly's greatest legacy was his fifty-one clerks who served during twenty-seven terms of court. Their immediate impact was in the large number who became clerks for Justices of the Supreme Court—twenty-one. This number would have been even larger had the Justices required, as they do now, that applicants first serve a year as a clerk to a lower-court judge, since some third-year students went directly to the Supreme Court who might otherwise have clerked for Friendly on the way.

Seven of his clerks became federal judges: the Chief Justice of the United States, five circuit judges, and one Bankruptcy Court judge. Like Friendly with Brandeis, judges who clerked for Friendly have applied what they saw in their mentor. For example, despite the burgeoning workload imposed on circuit judges, they try to write as many first drafts of opinions as time permits. They also listen to their clerks' suggestions and go back and forth with them as a way to make their opinions as sound as possible.[81] While it is unlikely that Friendly significantly affected the views of his strong-minded clerks, he had a major impact on their work habits and attitude toward judging. Chief Justice Roberts has been the most prominent of the select group. When nominated for Chief Justice by President George W. Bush, some of his fellow clerks assisted in his confirmation.[82] In an emotional moment at a clerks' reunion in May 2010, Circuit Judge Pierre Leval presented to Chief Justice Roberts the judicial robe worn by Judge Friendly in honor of his achieving the highest judicial position in the United States. In accepting the honor, Roberts said that he would wear that robe at the Court on special occasions.[83]

Nineteen of the judge's clerks became professors of law at Harvard, Yale, Chicago, Stanford, Berkeley, and elsewhere. Collectively, they have written hundreds of books and articles covering huge swaths of the law and taught tens of thousands of future lawyers. Other clerks went into private practice, most with leading firms in New York, Boston, Washington, and Seattle, but also in London and Paris.[84] Because of their achievements, Friendly would have been even more proud of his clerks today.

After their clerkships ended, Friendly valued their company. When he received the Medal of Freedom, he told Michael Boudin that he preferred being with former clerks to receiving honors.[85] After his death, former clerks, working with the American Law Institute, created in his honor a medal with his profile etched into it. A change had to be made during its preparation; the medal showed Friendly with a smile, and Pierre Leval asked the sculptor to alter it—people did not see Friendly smiling that often.[86] It would have pleased Friendly that the first Friendly medal was awarded to his friend Edward Weinfeld at his bedside one day before he died.

The tribute that Friendly probably would have most appreciated was one bestowed by his colleagues on the Second Circuit. He also would have appreciated the care that went into its preparation. Since 1966 only one statue stood in the court's courtroom, representing the severe, slightly scowling visage of the legendary Learned Hand. When the judges of the Second Circuit added Friendly's bust in 1989, the primary impetus came from Judge Jon O. Newman, who concluded that he was as deserving of the honor as Hand.[87]

When Newman approached the other judges, he saved Irving Kaufman until last. "I knew my man," explained Newman. After securing the support of the rest of his colleagues for the project, he went to Kaufman's chambers to tell him of his plan. Kaufman was not enthusiastic. "I don't know" was his slow response. Newman explained that all the other judges on the circuit had agreed. "At that point Irving knew he had no choice and he agreed. But he added, 'Oh, and then we can add Hays and Moore.' I saw where Irving was going, so I said, of course, we would only include judges that are dead. Well, now I had everyone on board."[88] (When asked about the events, another circuit judge said about the project, "I'll put it this way. At least one other judge expressed interest in having his likeness added to those of Hand and Friendly in the Second Circuit's courtroom.")[89]

Newman became the unofficial chairman of the unofficial committee. With advice from Judge Amalya Kearse and others, they selected a distinguished sculptor, Eliot Goldfinger, to create the bust. ("Some name for a sculptor," Newman said.) Newman and Kearse went to see Goldfinger, but he said that he did not like to sculpt from pictures and wanted to work from life. Newman and Kearse explained the difficulty and proposed that they bring Goldfinger pictures, that he work from them, and that if anyone was not satisfied, they would simply walk away from the project. Goldfinger agreed. The judges had trouble finding photographs of Friendly; he was not a person who craved the limelight or the flashbulb. They eventually found a dozen or so of him at different ages.

When Goldfinger asked the two judges if they wanted to see the work in progress, they readily agreed. When the work was almost complete, however, they felt that something was not quite right. They asked an artist friend of Goldfinger, who was in his studio at the time, how old she thought the subject was. She answered that he was in his early sixties. Since neither of the judges knew him at that stage of his life, they decided they needed to bring in someone who did. They chose Judge Pierre N. Leval, Friendly's clerk in 1963–1964, who with his wife, Susana, visited the studio and made suggestions. With the help of Leval, who walked about Goldfinger's studio for hours mimicking his former boss for the benefit of the sculptor, Goldfinger completed the sculpture. The remaining question was where to put the statue. The clerk of the court suggested that it stand on the opposite side of the courtroom facing the bust of Hand. Newman disagreed, saying, "We don't need him to look at the spectators, we need him to keep an eye on the judges."[90]

Judges on other courts will have to use their imaginations.

Friendly's Clerks

Friendly's clerks, together with their law schools, Supreme Court clerkship (if any), and their most relevant professional position.

1959 Milton J. Grossman
Harvard Law School
Miller, Balis & O'Neil, Washington, D.C.

1960 David P. Currie (deceased)
Harvard Law School
Justice Felix Frankfurter
Professor, University of Chicago Law School

1961 Peter B. Edelman
Harvard Law School
Justice Arthur Goldberg
Professor, Georgetown Law Center

1962 Stephen R. Barnett (deceased)
Harvard Law School
Justice William Brennan
Professor, University of California at Berkeley

1963 Pierre N. Leval
Harvard Law School
Judge, U.S. Court of Appeals for the Second Circuit

1964 Michael Boudin
Harvard Law School
Justice John Marshall Harlan
Judge, U.S. Court of Appeals for the First Circuit

1965 Stephen A. Grant
Columbia Law School
Sullivan & Cromwell, New York City

1966 Robert M. Berger
University of Chicago Law School
Meyer, Brown & Platt, Chicago

Richard B. Glickman
Harvard Law School
Pillsbury Madison, San Francisco

1967 Bruce Ackerman
Yale Law School
Justice John Marshall Harlan
Professor, Yale Law School

Richard A. Daynard
Harvard Law School
Professor, Northeastern University School of Law

1968 William T. Lake
Stanford Law School
Justice John Marshall Harlan
WilmerHale, Washington, D.C.

William F. Pederson Jr.
Harvard Law School
Perkins & Coie, Washington, D.C.

1969 Marvin L. Gray Jr.
Harvard Law School

Justice John Marshall Harlan
Davis Wright, Seattle

A. Raymond Randolph Jr.
University of Pennsylvania Law School
Judge, U.S. Court of Appeals for the District of Columbia Circuit

1970　Walter Hellerstein
Harvard Law School
Professor, University of Georgia Law School

Neil J. King
Harvard Law School
WilmerHale, Washington, D.C.

1971　Henry S. Bryans
University of Pennsylvania Law School
Drinker, Biddle & Reath, Philadelphia

Martin Glenn
Rutgers Law School
Judge, U.S. Bankruptcy Court, New York City

Stuart C. Stock
Harvard Law School
Justice Thurgood Marshall
Covington & Burling, Washington, D.C.

1972　Frederick T. Davis
Columbia Law School
Justice Potter Stewart
Sherman & Sterling, Paris

Ira M. Feinberg
Harvard Law School
Justice Thurgood Marshall
Hogan & Hartson, New York City

Lawrence P. Pedowitz
Harvard Law School
Justice William J. Brennan
Wachtell, Lipton, Rosen & Katz, New York City

1973   William C. Bryson
        University of Texas Law School
        Justice Thurgood Marshall
        Judge, U.S. Court of Appeals for the Federal Circuit

        David L. Engel
        Harvard Law School
        Bingham, Dana & Gould, Boston

1974   Gregory K. Palm
        Harvard Law School
        Justice Lewis Powell
        Executive Vice President, Goldman, Sachs & Co., New York City

        James R. Smoot
        Yale Law School
        Professor, University of Memphis Law School

1975   Phillip C. Bobbitt
        Yale Law School
        Professor, Columbia Law School

        Todd D. Rakoff
        Harvard Law School
        Professor, Harvard Law School

1976   Ruth Glushien Woodward
        Yale Law School
        Justice Harry A. Blackman
        Professor, John Hopkins School of Advanced International
            Studies, Washington, D.C.

        Theodore N. Mirvis
        Harvard Law School
        Wachtell, Lipton, Rosen & Katz, New York City

1977   Merrick B. Garland
        Harvard Law School
        Justice William J. Brennan
        Judge, U.S. Court of Appeals for the District of Columbia Circuit

Robert Weiner
Yale Law School
Justice Thurgood Marshall
Arnold & Porter, Washington, D.C.

1978 Mary I. Coombs
University of Michigan Law School
Professor, University of Miami Law School

Warren R. Stern
Harvard Law School
Wachtell, Lipton, Rosen & Katz, New York City

1979 John G. Roberts Jr.
Harvard Law School
Justice William Rehnquist
Chief Justice, U.S. Supreme Court

Reinier Kraakman
Yale Law School
Professor, Harvard Law School

1980 Paul Mogin
Harvard Law School
Justice Thurgood Marshall
Williams & Connelly, Washington, D.C.

A. Richard Feldman
University of Pennsylvania Law School
Bazelon, Less & Feldman, Philadelphia

Mark Wolinsky
University of Chicago Law School
Wachtell, Lipton, Rosen & Katz, New York City

1981 Gary Born
University of Pennsylvania Law School
Justice William Rehnquist
WilmerHale, London

Louis Kaplow
Harvard Law School
Professor, Harvard Law School

1982   Jonathon R. Macey
Yale Law School
Professor, Yale Law School

Michael P. Madow
Columbia Law School
Professor, Brooklyn Law School

David J. Seipp
Harvard Law School
Professor, Boston University Law School

1983   Donald P. Board
Harvard Law School
Kirkpatrick & Lockhart, Boston

Michael Lazerwitz
University of Chicago Law School
Chief Justice Warren E. Burger
Cleary, Gottlieb, Washington, D.C.

1984   Larry Kramer
University of Chicago Law School
Justice William J. Brennan
Dean, Stanford Law School

Raymond B. Ludwiszewski
Harvard Law School
Gibson, Dunn & Crutcher, Washington, D.C.

1985   Thomas A. Curtis
Columbia Law School
Counsel, Deutsche Bank, New York City

Thomas G. Dagger
University of Chicago Law School
General Counsel, Philbro Animal Health Corp., Ridgefield Park, N.J.

Friendly's Published Nonjudicial Writings

Books

The Federal Administrative Agencies: The Need for a Better Definition of Standards (Harvard University Press, 1962)

Benchmarks (University of Chicago Press, 1967)

The Dartmouth College Case and the Public-Private Penumbra (published as a bound Supplement to *Texas Quarterly*, Vol. 12, No. 2, 1971)

Federal Jurisdiction: A General View (Columbia University Press, 1973)

Published Articles and Book Reviews

"The Historic Basis of Diversity Jurisdiction," 41 *Harvard Law Review* 483 (1928)

Book Review: I. L. Sharfman, *Interstate Commerce Commission,* Vols. 1 & 2, 45 *Harvard Law Review* 941 (1932)

"Some Comments on the Corporate Reorganization Act," 48 *Harvard Law Review* 39 (1934)

Book Review, I. L. Sharfman, *Interstate Commerce Commission,* Part 3, Volume A, 49 *Harvard Law Review* 163 (1935)

"Amendment of the Railroad Reorganization Act," 36 *Columbia Law Review* 27 (1936)

Book Review: Alfred Lief, *Brandeis: A Personal History of an American Ideal,* 85 *University of Pennsylvania Law Review* 330 (1937)

Book Review: Luther D. Swanstrom, *Chapter Ten: Corporate Reorganization under the Federal Statute,* 52 *Harvard Law Review* 540 (1939)

Book Review: Henry G. Hotchkiss, *A Treatise on Aviation Law,* 52 *Harvard Law Review* 860 (1939)

Book Review: Jean Van Houtte, *La Responsibilite Civile dans les Transports Aeriens Interieurs et Internationaux,* 54 *Harvard Law Review* 169 (1940)

"Relative Treatment of Securities in Railroad Reorganizations under Section 77," 7 *Law & Contemporary Problems* 420 (1940) (with Lyman M. Tondel Jr.)

Book Review: Oliver James Lissitzyn, *International Air Transport and National Policy,* 56 *Harvard Law Review* 565 (1943)

Book Review: Alpheus Thomas Mason, *Brandeis: A Free Man's Life,* 56 *Yale Law Journal* 423 (1947)

"Mr. Justice Brandeis: The Quest for Reason," 108 *University of Pennsylvania Law Review* 985 (1960)

"A Look at the Federal Administrative Agencies," 60 *Columbia Law Review* 429 (1960)

"Reactions of a Lawyer Newly Become a Judge," 71 *Yale Law Journal* 195 (1961) (reprinted in *Benchmarks* 1)

Book Review: Karl N. Llewellyn, *Common Law Tradition: Deciding Appeals,* 109 *University of Pennsylvania Law Review* 1040 (1961)

Book Review: Lord Radcliff, *The Law,* 14 *Journal of Legal Education* 275 (1961)

"Judge Learned Hand: An Expression from the Second Circuit," 29 *Brooklyn Law Review* 2 (1962) (reprinted in *Benchmarks* 309)

"The Federal Administrative Agencies: The Need for Better Definition of Standards," 75 *Harvard Law Review* 863, 1055, 1265 (1962)

"The Gap in Lawmaking—Judges Who Can't and Legislatures Who Won't," 63 *Columbia Law Review* 787 (1963) (reprinted in *Benchmarks* 41)

Book Review: Mark de Wolfe Howe, *Justice Oliver Wendell Holmes—The Proving Years, 1870–1882, New York Times Book Review,* Aug. 11, 1963 (reprinted in *Benchmarks* 285)

Book Review: DeForest Billyou, *Air Law,* 77 *Harvard Law Review* 582 (1964)

"Mr. Justice Frankfurter and the Reading of Statutes," in Wallace Mendelson, *Felix Frankfurter, the Judge* (1964) (reprinted in *Benchmarks* 196)

"In Praise of Erie—and the New Federal Common Law," 39 *New York University Law Review* 383 (1964) (reprinted in *Benchmarks* 155)

"The Bill of Rights as a Code of Criminal Procedure," 53 *California Law Review* 929 (1965) (reprinted in *Benchmarks* 235)

"On Entering the Path of the Law," 13 *University of Chicago Law School Record* 17 (1965) (reprinted in *Benchmarks* 22)

"Satisfaction, Yes—Complacency, No!" 51 *A.B.A. Journal* 715 (1965)

"Mr. Justice Frankfurter," 51 *Virginia Law Review* 547 (1965) (reprinted in *Benchmarks* 318)

Book Review, *The Courts, the Public and the Law Explosion* (Harry W. Jones, ed., 1965), 11 *New York Law Forum* 348 (1965)

Book Review: Arnold H. Bennett, *The Commission and the Common Law: A Study in Administrative Interpretation,* 16 *Syracuse Law Review* 707 (1965)

Book Review: Harry Kalver Jr. and Hans Zeisel, *The American Jury,* 33 *University of Chicago Law Review* 884 (1966)

"The Idea of a Metropolitan University Law School," 19 *Case Western Reserve Law Review* 7 (1967)

"The Fifth Amendment Tomorrow: The Case for Constitutional Change," 37 *University of Cincinnati Law Review* 671 (1968)

"'Limited Office' of the *Chenery* Decision," 21 *Administrative Law Review* 1 (1968)

Remarks published in Arthur E. Sutherland, *The Path of the Law from 1967,* at 85 (1968)

Book Review: *The Unpublished Opinions of Mr. Justice Brandeis* (Alexander Bickel, ed.) (1967), 106 *University of Pennsylvania Law Review* 766 (1968)

Book Review: Lon L. Fuller, *Anatomy of the Law* (1968), 7 *Duquesne Law Review* 332 (1969)

"A Federal Court of Administrative Appeals?" 74 *Case & Comment* 23 (1969)

"*Chenery* Revisited: Reflections on Reversal and Remand of Administrative Order," 1969 *Duke Law Journal* 199 (1969)

"The Dartmouth College Case and the Public-Private Penumbra," 12 *Texas Quarterly,* No. 2 (Supp.) (1969)

"Time and Tide in the Supreme Court," 2 *Connecticut Law Review* 213 (1969)

"Is Innocence Irrelevant? Collateral Attack on Criminal Judgments," 38 *University of Chicago Law Review* 142 (1970)

"Mr. Justice Harlan, as Seen by a Friend and Judge of an Inferior Court," 85 *Harvard Law Review* 382 (1971)

"Judicial Control of Discretionary Administrative Action," 23 *Journal of Legal Education* 63 (1971)

Book Review: Marvin Schick, *Learned Hand's Court,* 86 *Political Science Quarterly* 470 (1971)

"In Memoriam: Honorable John Marshall Harlan," 92A *Sup. Ct.* 13 (1972)

Resolution of the faculty in honor of Judge Paul H. Hays, 72 *Columbia Law Review* 441 (1972)

Foreword to Bernard Schwartz and H. W. R. Wade, *Legal Control of Government: Administrative Law in Britain and the United States* (1972)

"The Law of the Circuit and All That," 46 *St. John's Law Review* 406 (1972)

Book Review: *History of the Supreme Court of the United States* (Paul A. Freund, ed., 1971), 87 *Political Science Quarterly* 439 (1972)

"Erwin N. Griswold—Some Fond Recollections," 86 *Harvard Law Review* 1365 (1973)

Book Review: Leonard W. Levy, *Judgments: Essays on American Constitutional History,* 73 *Columbia Law Review* 179 (1973)

"Empirical Approaches to Judicial Behavior: Of Voting Blocs and Cabbages and Kings," 42 *University of Cincinnati Law Review* 589 (1973)

"Conflict on the U.S. Courts of Appeal, 1965–1971: A Quantitative Analysis," 42 *University of Cincinnati Law Review* 635 (1973)

Preface to Note, "The United States Courts of Appeals 1972–73 Term—Criminal Law and Procedure," 62 *Georgetown Law Journal* 401 (1973)

"Averting the Flood by Lessening the Flow," 59 *Cornell Law Review* 571 (1974)

"New Trends in Administrative Law," 61 *Maryland Bar Journal* 9 (1974)

"Some Kind of Hearing," 123 *University of Pennsylvania Law Review* 1267 (1975)

"Edward Weinfeld, The Ideal Judge," 50 *New York University Law Review* 977 (1975)

"Grenville Clark: Legal Preceptor," in *Memoirs of a Man: Grenville Clark* 88 (collected by Mary Clark Dimond; Norman Cousins and J. Garry Clifford, eds., 1975)

Book Review: Bernard Schwartz, *Administrative Law,* 51 *New York University Law Review* 896 (1976)

Book Review: Kenneth Culp Davis, *Police Discretion,* 44 *University of Chicago Law Review* 255 (1976)

"The Federal Courts," *N.Y.U. Bicentennial Conference of American Law* 197 (1976)

"Federalism: A Foreword," 86 *Yale Law Journal* 1018 (1977)

"The Courts and Social Policy: Substance and Procedure," 33 *University of Miami Law Review* 21 (1978) (reprinted in David M. O'Brien, ed., *Judges on Judging; View from the Bench,* 1997)

"In Praise of Herbert Wechsler," 78 *Columbia Law Review* 974 (1978)

Book Review: Kenneth Culp Davis, *Administrative Law Treatise,* 8 *Hofstra Law Review* 471 (1980)

Book Review: Lord Devlin, *The Judge,* 79 *Michigan Law Review* 634 (1981)

"Indiscretion about Discretion," 31 *Emory Law Journal* 747 (1982)

"The Public-Private Penumbra—Fourteen Years Later," 130 *University of Pennsylvania Law Review* 1289 (1982)

"In Memoriam—Roger John Traynor, Ablest Judge of His Generation," 71 *California Law Review* 1039 (1983)

"From a Fellow Worker on the Railroads," 60 *Tulane Law Review* 244 (1985)

Miscellaneous

American Bar Assoc., Section of Corporations, Banking and Business Law, Conference on Codification of the Federal Securities Laws. 22 *Business Lawyer* 793, 900 (1967)

"Some Equal Protection Problems of the 1970's," published as a booklet by New York University School of Law (1970)

"The Constitution," Equal Justice Under Law, U.S. Department of Justice, Bicentennial Lecture Series, Vol. 1 at 1, Jan. 29, 1976

"Marching into the Third Century; A Portrait and Prediction about How Our Federal Courts Will Operate Tomorrow" (1976)

"Improving the Governance of a Corporation," *ALI-ABA Course Materials Journal*, vol. 3, no. 3 (1978)

Notes

Abbreviations

COH—The Center for Oral History, Washington, D.C. On July 4 and 5, 1974, David Epstein, an attorney, and Ellen Robinson Epstein, the director of the Center, conducted lengthy interviews of Friendly that occupied nine cassette tapes, most on both sides. Friendly's children arranged for the interviews. The citations are to a transcript of those interviews prepared by the Epsteins. The author has the tape recordings as well as the transcripts, a comparison of which shows that there were errors. When the transcript inaccurately reflects what is on the tape, an accurate transcription has been used, but the references remain to the transcript. For example, a statement by Friendly, "This is my first day in the Courts," was in fact "This is my first day in Torts." COH, Pt. 5, Side 1, at 5.

CUAP—Columbia University Oral History Research Office, Aviation Project, interview July 1960 (transcript).

FJPOH—Federation of Jewish Philanthropies, American Jewish Archives, Hebrew Union College, Cincinnati, Ohio, interview Jan. 12, 1984 (transcript).

FTD—On Nov. 14, 1981, one of Friendly's former law clerks, Frederick T. Davis, interviewed and tape-recorded Friendly, producing more than one hundred pages of transcript. None of this lengthy interview has been previously published, or even edited. The author thanks Davis for providing him with this pristine source. A transcript of the cassette tapes had been prepared that at places states that words were inaudible and erroneously transcribes what Friendly said. Davis was able to locate approximately half of the original tapes, and the author corrected and completed those portions of the transcript. The portions of transcript without a corresponding tape recording have been used with caution, and some obvious errors have been corrected.

HLS-HJF—Harvard Law School Library's collection of Friendly's papers; in the case of other Harvard collections, the last name of the collection follows "HLS."

HLS-HP/MS—On May 11, 1970, Professor Herbert Packer interviewed Friendly for a history of the U.S. Court of Appeals for the Second Circuit between 1910 and 1972, a history that was never completed. The transcript of the interview is at the Harvard Law School Library in the Michael Smith and Herbert Packer Research Materials on the U.S. Court of Appeals for the Second Circuit 1910–1972. References in the same format are to other material in that collection.

JFGC—Joan Friendly Goodman Collection, Philadelphia, Pa.

LOC—Library of Congress, Manuscript Division.

PAWA—History of Pan American World Airways, transcript of interview June 8, 1973, by John C. Leslie. HLS-HJF, Box 230, Folder 6; PAA-U. Miami, 50.06.02 at 27–28 (Pan American Airways collection at the University of Miami, Florida).

On Interviews and Quotations

"Author interview" signifies that the interview was conducted in person; telephone interviews are indicated as "author telephone interview."

Quotations have been reproduced accurately with the following qualifications:
Parallel citations are routinely omitted.
Some interior quotation marks are omitted for clarity.
Internal footnotes are omitted.
Deletions of only citations to cases or to other authorities are not indicated.
Ellipses by the author of this book are marked with periods; ellipses in the original document are marked with asterisks.
Paragraphing within indented quotations has not been uniformly followed.

Foreword

1. Richard A. Posner, "Judicial Biography," 70 *New York University Law Review* 502 (1995).
2. Michael Holroyd, "Literary and Historical Biography," in *New Directions in Biography* (Anthony M. Friedson, ed., 1981), 12, 18.
3. Richard A. Posner, *Cardozo: A Study in Reputation* (1990), viii, 150.
4. The first two have been published as "Judge Henry Friendly and the Mirror of Constitutional Law," 82 *New York University Law Review* 975 (2007), and "Judge Henry Friendly and the Craft of Judging," 159 *University of Pennsylvania Law Review* 1 (2010). A third lecture is in the works.

Introduction

1. Harvard Law School discontinued numerical grades in 1969.
2. Mark Tushnet, "Following the Rules Laid Down: A Critique of Interpretivism and Neutral Principles," 96 *Harvard Law Review* (1983), 781, 807.
3. Author interview of Larry Kramer, Apr. 16, 2007.

1. Early Years

1. Natalie Brooks Friendly, *The Friendly Family: The Descendants of the Freundlichs of Bavaria* (1998), 3. The book traces the first known Freundlich back to 1730.
2. Ibid., 27, 68–69; COH, Tape 1, Side 1, pp. 7–8.
3. In the mid-nineteenth century many German Jews came from Bavaria and many migrated toward smaller cities. Stephen Birmingham, *Our Crowd* (1967), 23, 58–61, 173.
4. N. B. Friendly, *Friendly Family*, 70–73.
5. COH, Tape 1, Side 1, pp. 1–2.
6. Henry J Friendly Baby Book, HLS-HJF, Box 236.
7. Author interview of Joan Friendly Goodman, May 19, 2007; author interview of Ellen Friendly Simon, May 14, 2008.
8. COH, Tape 1, Side 1, p. 5, Side 2, p. 10.
9. COH, Tape 1, Side 1, pp. 3, 5.
10. COH, Tape 2, p. 6.
11. COH, Tape 1, Side 1, p. 6.
12. Author telephone interview of Morris Lasker, June 12, 2007.
13. COH, Tape 1, Side 2, pp. 2, 11–13.
14. COH, Tape 1, Side 1, p. 4.
15. Ibid., 3–4.
16. Ibid., 9, 11–12.
17. Ibid., 6–7, 13.
18. Ibid., 12–13.
19. Ibid., 9–10, 14–15.
20. Ibid., 10–11, 13.
21. COH, Tape 2, p. 7.
22. COH, Tape 1, Side 1, p. 4, Side 2, pp. 7–9; Friendly's *Baby Book*, HLS-HJF, Box 236; FTD, Tape 1, p. 7; author interview of Irene Baer Friendly (widow of Friendly's son, David), May 27, 2007.
23. COH, Tape 1, Side 2, pp. 20, 23; COH, Tape 7, Side 2, p. 2. When one of Friendly's grandsons gave him a Sony Walkman as a present, he watched with wonder as his grandfather was unable to operate it. Author interview of Daniel Simon, May 28, 2007. A granddaughter said, "When he opened a doorknob, that was something." Author interview of Ellen Goodman, May 27, 2007.
24. Author interview of Joan Goodman, May 19, 2007; author interview of Ellen Simon, Feb. 5, 2006; COH, Tape 8, Side 1, p. 5.

25. COH, Tape 8, Side 1, p. 5.

26. Friendly letter to Leah Friendly, May 13, 1916, HLS-HJF, Box 304, Folder 1.

27. COH, Tape 1, Side 2, pp. 3, 8. The transcript of Friendly's high school grades on file in the Harvard University Archives shows that his highest grades (100) were in algebra and plane geometry.

28. COH, Tape 4, Side 1, p. 6.

29. COH, Tape 1, Side 2, pp. 7–8; Fred Kaplan, *The Singular Mark Twain* (2003), 230, 243–245, 311, 393–394; Justin Kaplan, *Mr. Clemens and Mark Twain* (1966), 88–93, 112–113, 178–181, 196–198.

30. Friendly's Baby Book, HLS-HJF, Box 236.

31. COH, Tape 1, Side 2, pp. 18–19, Tape 2, pp. 3–4; Elmira Free Academy yearbook, *The Signum*, 1919, HLS-HJF, Box 236.

32. COH, Tape 2, pp. 7–8, 14–15.

33. COH, Tape 1, Side 2, pp. 6–7.

34. COH, Tape 2, pp. 3, 8.

35. COH, Tape 1, Side 2, pp. 13–14; draft of talk given by Friendly in Elmira in 1970, HLS-HJF, Box 202, Folder 8.

36. COH, Tape 3, Side 1, pp. 1–2. After his freshman year Friendly lived in one of the private dormitories for two years and in the Harvard Yard for his senior year, as was the practice. COH, Tape 3, Side 2, p. 8.

37. COH, Tape 2, p. 3.

38. Official transcript of Henry J. Friendly '23, Harvard University Archives; COH, Tape 3, Side 2, p. 4; author interview of Albert H. Gordon, May 17, 2008.

39. Author interview of Albert H. Gordon, May 17, 2008. Later, Gordon and Friendly served together as overseers of Harvard College.

40. COH, Tape 3, Side 1, pp. 7–8, Side 2, p. 7.

41. Author interview of Gordon, May 17, 2008; COH, Tape 3, Side 1, p. 7.

42. COH, Tape 3, Side 1, 3–4, Side 2, p. 8; Harvard College Archives, Henry J. Friendly folder.

43. COH, Tape 3, Side 2, pp. 5, 8–9, Tape 6, Side 2, p. 1.

44. FTD, Tape 1, pp. 8–10; COH, Tape 3, Side 2, pp. 2–4; Friendly letter to Paul H. Buck, Aug. 15, 1974, HLS-HJF, Box 220, Folder 7.

45. Harvard University Library, HU 89.165.862.

46. Friendly letter to John G. Buchanan, July 17, 1968, HLS-HJF, Box 217, Folder 5.

47. Henry Friendly, "Risorgimento," 37.

48. Henry Friendly, "Palmerston," 33, 130–135.

49. Henry Friendly, "Columbus," 1, cover page. Friendly's other three papers were "The Political Theories of Marsiglio of Padua," a fourteenth-century church reformer; "The Savonarola of 'Romola,'" the only historical novel by George Eliot, which focused on the last decade of the fifteenth century; and "Who Was Responsible for the Sack of Rome, in May 1527?"

50. Friendly, "Rome," 5.

51. There were occasional exceptions: "The story in 'Romola' begins with an interview between Camilla Rucellai and the heroine, in which the former announces

that she has received a direct revelation from God, ordering her to have Bernardo thrown from a window, and that Savonarola has not dared to dispute the genuine character of the inspiration" (Friendly, "Savonarola," 3).

52. Friendly, "Columbus," 4, 6.

53. Friendly letter to John G. Buchanan, July 17, 1968, HLS-HJF, Box 217, Folder 5; COH, Tape 3, Side 1, pp. 8–9, Side 2, p. 3.

54. Harvard University Library, HU 89.165.872. With a punch of irony, Friendly later called it "an absolutely thrilling subject." COH, Tape 3, Side 2, p. 1.

55. Friendly, "Church and State," 50.

56. Ibid., 19, 45–47.

57. Ibid., 51–52.

58. FTD, Tape 1, p. 15; author telephone interview of Frank Goodman, Sept. 29, 2009.

59. Charles McIlwain letter to Friendly, Sept. 7, 1923, JFGC.

60. Friendly letter to Joan Friendly (undated), JFGC.

61. Friendly letter to Paul H. Buck, Aug. 15, 1974, HLS-HJF, Box 220, Folder 7.

62. COH, Tape 3, Side 2, p. 9, Tape 4, Side 1, p. 3.

63. There are many accounts of this matter, e.g., Jerome Karabel, *The Chosen* (2005), 77–109.

64. Ibid., 6; FTD, Tape 1, p. 12.

65. Karabel, *Chosen*, 90; Harry Barnard, *The Forging of an American Jew: The Life and Times of Judge Julian Mack* (1974), 293; Michael E. Parish, *Felix Frankfurter and His Times* (1982), 155–156.

66. COH, Tape 3, Side 1, p. 6; Barnard, *Forging American Jew*, 299.

67. *Harvard Graduates' Magazine*, quoted in Seymour Martin Lipset and David Riesman, *Education and Politics at Harvard* (1975), 147–148.

68. COH, Tape 3, Side 1, pp. 5–6. In another interview he said he was "seriously considering" whether he would return to Harvard if the plan went through. FJPOH, p. 3.

69. COH, Tape 3, Side 1, p. 6; FTD Tape 1, pp. 12–13; see Henry Aaron Yeomans, *Abbott Lawrence Lowell* (1948), 209–213. Friendly wrote along similar lines to Justice Byron R. White, Sept. 17, 1976, HLS-HJF, Box 230, Folder 4.

70. Friendly letter to the editor, *Harvard Alumni Bulletin*, Mar. 11, 1967, p. 2.

71. Author interview of Frank Gilbert and Daniel Rezneck, May 31, 2007. Gilbert, grandson of Brandeis, and Rezneck, a former research assistant to Freund, attended a luncheon with Freund and Friendly on Cape Cod during the summer of 1985.

72. Friendly letter to his mother, Oct. 10, 1919, HLS-HJF, Box 234, Folder 1. Six letters he wrote in law school are extant in Friendly's files at the Harvard Law School.

73. HLS-HJF, Box 234, Folder 1, May 13, 1922.

74. HLS-HJF, Box 234, Folder 1, Oct. 10, 1924; May 7, 1925; Oct. 11, 1925; May 8, 1926; May 5, 1927.

75. Leah Friendly letter to Friendly, Sept. 16, 1919, JFGC.

76. COH, Tape 3, Side 1, p. 9, Tape 6, Side 2, p. 2; FTD Tape 1, p. 11; HLS-HP/MS, Box 14, Folder 26, pp. 22–23. For Friendly the issue was a close one. He

wrote Paul H. Buck, a history professor at Harvard, "Despite F. Frankfurter's urging that I should at least try the law school for a year, I might very well have gone back to study with McIlwain except for the fact that I would have had to spend a good deal of time improving my Latin . . . and . . . acquiring some competence in mediaeval French and paleography." Friendly letter to Buck, Aug. 15, 1974, HLS-HJF, Box 219, Folder 3.

77. COH, Tape 4, Side 1, pp. 8–10; FTD, Tape 1, pp. 16–19; Friendly letter to Prof. Austin W. Scott, Sept. 25, 1974, HLS-Scott, Box 35, Folder 5.

78. COH, Tape 4, Side 2, p. 1, Side 1, pp. 4, 10–11. For many years, when he traveled he carried a dime with him so he could telephone his mother: "I knew she was very nervous, and so, instead of waiting until I got home, I'd call her from the airport." COH, Tape 9, Side 1, pp. 3–4.

79. COH, Tape 5, Side 1, p. 1; John Bartlow Martin, *Adlai E. Stevenson of Illinois* (1976), 67. Stevenson, who was one year ahead of Friendly at Harvard Law School, flunked out after his second year (73).

80. COH, Tape 5, Side 1, pp. 5–6. The author thanks Prof. David J. Seipp, a former Friendly clerk, for his help regarding the case.

81. COH, Tape 5, Side 1, p. 6.

82. Henry Friendly, "On Entering the Path of the Law," in Friendly, *Benchmarks* (1967), 25–26; see Oliver Wendell Holmes, "The Path of the Law," in *The Mind and Faith of Justice Holmes* (Max Lerner, ed., 1954), 87 (advising young lawyers "to follow the existing body of dogma into its highest generalizations by the help of jurisprudence").

83. COH, Tape 4, Side 2, pp. 2–4, 8.

84. Friendly, *Benchmarks*, 202.

85. Calvert Magruder letter to Friendly, June 13, 1925, JFGC.

86. Friendly letter to Calvert Magruder, June 16, 1925, HLS-Magruder.

87. David Riesman, "Some Observations on Law and Psychology," 19 *University of Chicago Law Review* (1951), 30, 39.

88. Friendly letter to mother, Mar. 10, 1926, HLS-HJF, Box 234, Folder 1.

89. Paul Sayer, *The Life of Roscoe Pound* (1948), 214, 238; COH, Tape 4, Side 2, pp. 5–7.

90. COH, Tape 5, Side 1, p. 3.

91. Ibid., 3–4.

92. FTD, Tape 2, p. 9.

93. COH, Tape 4, Side 2, p. 7, Tape 5, Side 1, p. 1.

94. Friendly letter to parents, Oct. 5, 1926, HLS-HJF, Box 234, Folder 1.

95. Friendly letter to Frankfurter, Aug. 6, 1927, HLS-Frankfurter Papers, Part 3, Reel 34; see COH, Tape 3, Side 2, pp. 10–11, Tape 4, Side 1, pp. 1–2.

96. COH, Tape 4, Side 1, pp. 4, 10, Tape 4, Side 2, p. 9. Frankfurter was going to visit England in 1928–1929, so he wanted Friendly to clerk then for Brandeis.

97. Friendly letter to parents, Oct. 5, 1926, Myer Friendly letter to Friendly, Oct. 7, 1926, HLS-HJF, Box 234, Folder 1; Friendly letter to Donald Robinson, Mar. 26, 1984, HLS-HJF, Box 98, Folder 14.

98. Brandeis letter to Frankfurter, Oct. 28, 1926; *"Half Brother, Half Son": The Letters of Louis D. Brandeis to Felix Frankfurter* (Melvin I. Urofsky and David W. Levy, eds., 1991), 256; COH, Tape 4, Side 2, pp. 8–9.

99. Michael Boudin, "Judge Henry Friendly and the Mirror of Constitutional Law," 82 *New York University Law Review* (2007), 975, 977; Frankfurter letter to Judge Philip Halpern, Aug. 15, 1955, HLS-HJF, Box 192, Folder 1. Before Friendly the highest average since Brandeis belonged to Landis, who also clerked for Brandeis. Donald A. Ritchie, *James M. Landis* (1980), 18.

100. COH, Tape 4, Side 2, p. 6.

101. Friendly letter to Joan Friendly (undated, but probably Sept. 1954), JFGC.

102. Friendly letter to Frankfurter, July 8, 1927, LOC, Frankfurter Collection, Part 3, Reel 34.

103. Friendly letter to Cloyd Laporte, Mar. 16, 1972, HLS-HJF, Box 231, Folder 1; Notes for Talk at Harvard Law Review Dinner, Apr. 7, 1978, HLS-HJF, Box 92, Folder 8.

104. Paul Freund, "In Memoriam: Henry J. Friendly," 99 *Harvard Law Review* (1986), 1715, 1716–1717.

105. 37 *Harvard Law Review* (1928), 483; COH, Tape 5, Side 1, p. 4. In his first footnote Friendly wrote, "The writer desires to acknowledge his very great indebtedness to Prof. Felix Frankfurter of the Harvard Law School, both for suggesting the subject of this paper and for constant help in its preparation" (483 n.*). It seems, however, that it was Brandeis who suggested the topic to Frankfurter for Friendly. Apparently by agreement between Brandeis and Frankfurter, the latter behaved as though it was entirely his. *Half Brother, Half Son*, 327–328. When asked about the fact that Brandeis had proposed the article, Friendly responded, "It's news to me." *New York Times*, Feb. 14, 1982, p. 58.

106. *Christian Science Monitor*, Sept. 12, 1927, p. 1.

107. COH, Tape 5, Side 1, pp. 7–8.

108. *In re* Howard, 210 F. Supp. 301 (W.D. Pa. 1962); see Arthur E. Sutherland, *The Law at Harvard* (1967), 198 n.44. Harvard Law School ceased giving numerical grades in 1969. Office of the Registrar, Harvard Law School, email to author, July 15, 2009.

109. Alpheus Thomas Mason, *Brandeis, a Free Man's Life* (1946), 612; Melvin I. Urofsky, *Louis D. Brandeis* (2009), 473–474; Lochner v. New York, 198 U.S. 45 (1905).

110. Friendly letter to Lewis Paper, Harvard-Paper, Box 1, Folder 3; FTD Tape 2, pp. 4–6; COH, Tape 5, Side 1, p. 8.

111. FTD, Tape 2, p. 7; Friendly letter to parents, Oct. 5, 1927, HLS-HJF, Box 234, Folder 1.

112. For example, in Untermyer v. Anderson, 276 U.S. 440 (1928), Brandeis dissented from the invalidation of a ten-day retroactivity in the imposition of a gift tax. Friendly had found fifteen instances where the Court had sustained retroactive taxes. Friendly, *Benchmarks*, 299–300.

113. COH, Tape 5, Side 2, p. 5.

114. Lochner v. New York, 198 U.S. 45 (1905).

115. Friendly letter to Frankfurter (undated), HLS-Frankfurter Papers, Part 3, Reel 25; COH, Tape 5, Side 1, p. 5. Brandeis also had a wealth of information about railroads. Melvin I. Urofsky, *Louis D. Brandeis* (2009), 277–299; Thomas K. McCraw, *Prophets of Regulation* (1986), 91–94.

116. Frankfurter letter to Attorney General Herbert Brownell, Jan. 14, 1957, HLS-HJF, Box 174, Folder 4.

117. Author interview of Warren Stern, Nov. 20, 2006.

118. COH, Tape 5, Side 2, pp. 4–5. The case was Louisville Gas & Electric Co. v. Coleman, 277 U.S. 32, 42 (1928) (Brandeis, J., dissenting). Friendly letter to Erwin Griswold, Oct. 8, 1968, HLS-Griswold, Box 182, Folder 19; *accord,* Friendly, *Benchmarks,* 301.

119. 277 U.S. 438, 471 (1928) (Brandeis, J., dissenting).

120. See Lewis J. Paper, *Brandeis* (1983), 311–312; COH, Tape 5, Side 2, p. 2; Friendly letter to Attorney General Elliot Richardson, July 11, 1973, HLS-HJF, Box 67, Folder 18.

121. 116 U.S. 616 (1886).

122. 277 U.S. at 478.

123. Katz v. United States, 389 U.S. 347 (1967).

124. COH, Tape 5, Side 2, pp. 2–3.

125. See Daniel A. Rezneck, "Paul Freund Remembered," 62 *American Scholar* (1993), 277, 280; COH, Tape 5, Side 2, pp. 2–3. Friendly contributed to the resolution of a case involving a claim that a state tax violated the Commerce Clause. The Court was unanimous, but Friendly concluded that the Court was wrong and convinced Brandeis to change his mind, and the two wrote a dissenting opinion the other way. FTD, Tape 2, pp. 7–8.

126. Friendly letter to Louis Paper, Dec. 29, 1980, HLS-HJF, Box 219, Folder 5.

127. Todd C. Peppers, "Isaiah and His Young Disciples: Justice Brandeis and His Law Clerks," 34 *Journal of Supreme Court History* (2009), 75, 85–86.

128. Friendly letter to Eliot Janeway, Oct. 7, 1984, HLS-HJF, Box 220, Folder 6; FJPOH, p. 6. Friendly was directing his comment to Brandeis's pre-judicial years.

129. COH, Tape 5, Side 1, pp. 10–11, Side 2, p. 1.

130. COH, Tape 5, Side 1, p. 10. Nevertheless, Friendly criticized Brandeis for taking him only once to see Holmes, and then very briefly. COH, Tape 5, Side 1, p. 10.

131. Friendly letter to Michael Boudin, Dec. 6, 1983, HLS-HJF, Box 218, Folder 3.

132. COH, Tape 5, Side 2, pp. 5–6.

133. COH, Tape 5, Side 1, pp. 9–10.

134. Louis Paper notes of interview of Friendly, New York City, Dec. 27, 1980, HLS-Paper, Box 1, Folder 3; COH, Tape 5, Side 1, pp. 9–10. The author thanks Paper for permitting him to quote from his notes.

135. Interview of Gilbert, May 31, 2007; see Peppers, "Isaiah," 86–87.

136. 13 *Cleargolaw News* (1959), 7; undated notes by Friendly for a speech in honor of Judge David Peck, HLS-HJF, Box 227, Folder 16.

137. Friendly letter to James Landis, Apr. 7, 1928, LOC, Landis Papers, Box 5; see author interview of Michael Boudin, Mar. 7, 2007; *The Yale Biographical Dictionary of American Law* (2009) (entry by Stephen Barnett), 208.

138. Milton S. Gould, *The Witness Who Spoke to God and Other Tales from the Courthouse* (1979), x–xii; see Michael E. Parrish, *Felix Frankfurter and His Times: The Reform Years* (1982), 157–158; Nochem S. Winnet, *Vignettes of a Lucky Life* (1989), 24–25; Joseph M. Proskauer, *A Segment of My Times* (1950), 30; Louis Loss, *Anecdotes of a Securities Lawyer* (1995), 28; Jerome E. Carlin, *Lawyers' Ethics; A Survey of the New York City Bar* (1966), 17–40.

139. Gerald T. Dunne, *Grenville Clark, Public Citizen* (1986), 49; Martin Mayer, *Emory Buckner: A Biography* (1968), 141–143.

140. Friendly apparently never considered going with a "Jewish firm."

141. Nancy Lisagor and Frank Lipsius, *A Law unto Itself: The Untold Story of the Firm of Sullivan & Cromwell* (1989). The biography of the firm states that Jaretzky Sr. "had been a poor Jewish boy who went to Harvard," where he met George Sullivan, the founder's son (59).

142. Author interview of Stephen A. Grant, July 27, 2007; author telephone interview of Grant, Feb. 17, 2011. Peck started with the firm in 1930. Lisagor and Lipsius, *Law unto Itself,* 226–227. In his oral history with Frederick Davis, Friendly said, "I, at Frank Downey's urging, did allow myself to be interviewed by Sullivan & Cromwell, but I thought the atmosphere was a bit frosty." Davis asked, "Meaning towards you personally?" Friendly answered, "Well, toward Jews, in spite of the fact that they had a great many Jewish partners from an earlier age and these were fellows who I don't think ever denied they were Jews, [they] certainly didn't look at it very hard." FTD, Tape 2, pp. 13–14. Friendly insisted to at least one clerk that he accept an offer for a clerkship the same day. Author interview of Donald Board, Mar. 14, 2007.

2. Private Practice

1. Henry Friendly, "Grenville Clark: Legal Preceptor," in Norman Cousins and J. Garry Gifford, eds., *Memoirs of a Man: Grenville Clark* (1975), 88–89; COH, Tape 6, Side 1, pp. 1–2. Many of the cases litigated the rates railroads could charge their customers, e.g., 9 *The Bull* (Dec. 8, 1928), No. 49, p. 5; 10 *The Bull* (Apr. 27, 1929), No. 17, p. 1, (May 25, 1929), No. 21, p. 5, (Aug. 10, 1929), No. 32, p. 2, (Oct. 15, 1929), No. 43, p. 7. *The Bull* was the internal house organ of Root, Clark that kept lawyers abreast of recent legal developments in which the firm was involved. Except where otherwise noted, Friendly wrote the items cited.

2. Friendly letter to Dr. Edmunds Grey Dimond, June 30, 1983, HLS-HJF, Box 220, Folder 5.

3. CUAP, 1–2.

4. FTD, Tape 2, p. 20; Paul Hoffman, *Lions in the Street* (1973), 62.

5. Author interview of Pierre N. Leval, Oct. 17, 2006; COH, Tape 6, Side 1, p. 7. Many years later Friendly was able to tell Trippe, "I'm going to leave around

quarter of seven, unless there is some real emergency. There can't be an emergency *every* night." COH, Tape 6, Side 1, p. 7.

6. Although Lindbergh was anti-Semitic, he and Friendly got along well. Author interview of Judge Richard A. Posner, Aug. 22, 2007.

7. CUAP, 3; 10 *The Bull* (Aug. 31, 1929), No. 35, p. 8; HLS-HJF-Col. 2–3; Marylin Bender and Selig Altschul, *The Chosen Instrument* (1982), 178–181, 195–196, 337; Matthew Josephson, *Empire of the Air* (1943), 27–79.

8. COH, Tape 6, Side 2, p. 8; Measuring Worth, www.measuringworth.com/uscompare/ (CPI).

9. COH, Tape 6, Side 2, pp. 9–10, Tape 7, Side 1, pp. 1–4. Justice Stern was first in his class at the University of Pennsylvania and then at the University of Pennsylvania Law School. *New York Times*, Apr. 15, 1959, p. 47. Only one letter has been located between Horace Stern and Friendly, dated Dec. 12, 1961, in which Stern provided a long quotation from a letter from Thomas Jefferson to Samuel Kercheval dated July 12, 1816, that argued for mandatory consideration of constitutional amendments by every generation on the basis that current generations were not inferior to prior ones.

10. Friendly letter to mother (undated), HLS-HJF, Box 234, Folder 1, his last letter to his mother in the Harvard Law School Friendly Collection. Friendly's daughter Joan Goodman agreed with the description of her mother but described the comparison of her mother with Friendly's mother as "weak." Joan Goodman email to author, May 27, 2009.

11. Author interview of Joan Goodman, May 19, 2007.

12. Ibid.

13. *"Half Brother, Half Son," The Letters of Louis D. Brandeis to Felix Frankfurter* (Melvin I. Urofsky and David W. Levy, eds., 1991), 457. The law school's efforts included Frankfurter's writing to Friendly on Apr. 30, 1931; Magruder's writing to him on Apr. 30, 1931; and Morgan's telegraphing him on May 2, 1931, all in JFGC; Friendly letter to Frankfurter, May 7, 1931, LOC, Frankfurter Collection, Part 3, Reel 34.

14. Friendly letter to Landis, May 7, 1931, LOC, Landis Collection, Box 5.

15. *"Half Brother, Half Son,"* 475, 477; Friendly letter to Frankfurter, Feb. 16, 1932; Frankfurter letter to Friendly, Feb. 17, 1932, LOC, Frankfurter Collection, Part 3, Reel 34.

16. COH, Tape 8, Side 2, p. 3; *"Half Brother, Half Son,"* 475, 531; Friendly letter to Prof. Austin W. Scott, Sept. 25, 1974, HLS-Scott, Box 35, Folder 5.

17. For example, ever since Wendel was a girl, she had a series of poodles all named Tobey, who had the run of a $2 million yard and all of whom she buried individually in waterproof vaults in the garden of the mansion or on other Wendel estates. Arthur Garfield Hays, *City Lawyer* (1942), 292–293.

18. Henry Friendly, "Mr. Justice Harlan, as Seen by a Friend and Judge of an Inferior Court," 85 *Harvard Law Review* (1971), 382–383. With his health slipping, Buckner turned the day-to-day operation of the case over to Harlan and Friendly.

19. *In re* Wendel's Estate, 262 N.Y.S. 41, 43 (Sur. Ct. 1933).

20. Mervin Rosenman, *Forgery, Perjury, and an Enormous Fortune* (1984), which had the benefit of interviews with Friendly, provides a comprehensive account

of the *Wendel* litigation; see Hays, *City Lawyer*, 289–336. The Rosenmans and the Friendlys were friends. Author telephone interview of Audrey Rosenman, May 2, 2007.

21. FTD, Tape 3, p. 19.

22. FTD, Tape 3, pp. 21–23; see 13 *The Bull* (Aug. 27, 1932), No. 34, p. 1 (C. C. MacLean Jr.). Harlan had set up his Scotland headquarters in St. Andrews, a famous golf venue.

23. FTD, Tape 3, p. 21.

24. Hays, *City Lawyer*, 318, 325. The Surrogate said, "All this may be a monstrous hoax or it may be absolutely true" (319).

25. FTD, Tape 3, p. 21.

26. *In re* Wendel's Estate, 262 N.Y.S. 41, 46, 53–56 (Sur. 1933); Rosenman, *Forgery*, 136–149 (citing documents in the files of Root, Clark).

27. 14 *The Bull* (Jan. 7, 1933), 6, (Apr. 1, 1933), 115; John M. Harlan, *The Evolution of a Judicial Philosophy: Selected Opinions and Papers of John M. Harlan* (David L. Shapiro, ed., 1970), xxi; *In re* Wendel's Estate, 267 N.Y.S. 33 (Sur. Ct. 1933).

28. Friendly noted that in his book Hays "took credit for the investigation of the Morris claim, which, in fact, John Harlan and I had performed." Friendly letter to Sir Arthur Goodhart, May 29, 1967, HLS-HJF, Box 217, Folder 5.

29. Rosenman, *Forgery*, back cover, quoting Friendly.

30. Upon his death, Friendly's personal papers contained a copy of the forged certificate of marriage that Morris introduced to prove his claim. HLS-HJF, Box 236; see Henry Friendly, "Harlan," 85 *Harvard Law Review* (1970), 384.

31. FTD, Tape 3, p. 23.

32. The formal name of the committee was the Emergency Committee of Life Insurance Companies and Savings Banks.

33. 12 *The Bull* (Oct. 24, 1931), No. 43, pp. 1, 12, (June 20, 1931), No. 25, p. 2, (July 25, 1932), No. 30, p. 1, (Sept. 26, 1931), No. 39, pp. 1, 8.

34. *In re* Paramount Publix Corp., 85 F.2d 83 (2d Cir. 1936); *In re* Adolf Gobel, Inc., 80 F.2d 849 (2d Cir. 1936). Friendly also did legal work for several clients in an assortment of other commercial matters. E.g., *In re* Ashner's Estate, 246 N.Y.S. 129 (App. Div. 1930) (suit against executrix of estate alleging embezzlement); Monro-King and Gemmels Realty Corp. v. 9 Avenue-31 Street Corp., 253 N.Y.S. 401 (App. Div. 1931) (commercial landlord-tenant dispute in context of first landlord's bankruptcy); Sears, Roebuck & Co. v. 9 Ave.-31 St. Corp., 9 N.E.2d 20 (N.Y. 1937) (commercial lease dispute).

35. 288 U.S. 517 (1933). Friendly saw Brandeis only a few times after his clerkship. There also does not seem to have been much correspondence between the two. The five-volume collection of Brandeis's letters contains only two to Friendly. 5 *Letters of Louis Dembitz Brandeis* (Melvin I. Urofsky and David W. Levy, eds., 1978) (letters dated Sept. 1, 1928, Apr. 1, 1937), 350, 588. One other letter from Brandeis to Friendly has been found.

36. FTD, Tape 4, pp. 6–7; see Lewis J. Paper, *Brandeis* (1983), 335. Brandeis was aware of the messy, corrupt legislative process from his many battles with the Massachusetts legislature and its committees. Melvin I. Urofsky, *Louis D.*

Brandeis (2009), 141–150, 175–176, 192–197. Despite his growing sophistication there remained a naïveté or impracticality about Friendly. For example, after he became a judge he wondered why a repairman preferred to be paid in cash. Author interview of Pat Hall Mogin, Dec. 9, 2006.

37. Josephson, *Empire*, 134–137; PAWA, 9. It was not until 1936 or 1937 that national governments became directly involved on a regular basis.
38. PAWA, 27–28; COH, Tape 6, Side 1, pp. 6–7; Josephson, *Empire*, 134–137.
39. 48 *Harvard Law Review* (1934), 39.
40. 36 *Columbia Law Review* (1936), 27. He also wrote an article with a colleague: Henry Friendly and Lyman M. Tondel Jr., "Relative Treatment of Securities in Railroad Reorganization under Section 77," 7 *Law and Contemporary Problems* (1940), 420.
41. FTD, Tape 2, pp. 15–17; COH, Tape 7, Side 1, p. 6. Page went on to have a distinguished career in law and industry. D. Bret Carlson, *Debevoise & Plimpton* (1971), 60.
42. Carlson, *Debevoise & Plimpton*, 62–63.
43. FTD, Tape 2, pp. 16–17.
44. Many firms actively discouraged associates from bringing in new clients. Edwin O. Smigel, *The Wall Street Lawyer* (1969), 234.
45. Natalie Brooks Friendly, *The Friendly Family* (1998), 113; author interview of Irene Baer Friendly (widow of David Friendly), May 25, 2008; Measuring Worth, www.measuringworth.com/uscompare/.
46. COH, Tape 7, Side 2, pp. 1, 5–6.
47. HLS-HJF, Box 226, Folder 6.
48. Friendly letter to Brainard Currie, Aug. 13, 1963, HLS-HJF, Box 212, Folder 2; see FTD, Tape 4, p. 5.
49. Brandeis letter to Friendly, Apr. 1, 1937, *Letters of Louis Dembitz Brandeis* (Melvin I. Urofsky and David W. Levy, eds., 1978), 588–589; Friendly letter to Melvin I. Urofsky and David W. Levy, June 14, 1967, HLS-HJF, Box 217, Folder 5; FTD, Tape 4, pp. 7–9; Henry Friendly, "Time and Tide in the Supreme Court," 2 *Connecticut Law Review* (1969), 213–214.
50. 28 *Cleargolaw News* (Apr. 18, 1986), 177 (Robert C. Bonard).
51. Friendly letter to Howard C. Westwood, June 14, 1963, HLS-HJF, Box 212, Folder 3.
52. Frederick A. Ballard, "Federal Regulation of Aviation," 60 *Harvard Law Review* (1947), 1235, 1251–1252. Trippe apparently was the origin of a story that Friendly drafted the Civil Aeronautics Act. Bender and Altschul, *Chosen Instrument*, 271.
53. Author interview of Jerome Hyman, Feb. 22, 2006.
54. 2 C.A.B. 334 (1940).
55. Sanford B. Kauffman, *Pan American Pioneer* (1995), 70–73.
56. Transcript of oral argument by Friendly before examiner C. Edward Leisure, Jan. 22, 1940, PAA-U. Miami; Neil G. Melone, "Controlled Competition: Three Years of the Civil Aeronautics Act," 12 *Journal of Air Law and Commerce* (1941), 318, 339 n.121; Josephson, *Empire*, 134–147.
57. American Export Lines, Inc., 2 C.A.B. 16, 32–33 (1940).

58. Pan American Airways Co. v. CAB, 121 F.2d 810, 814 (2d Cir. 1941).

59. Had it done so, he would have faced an uphill fight in trying to convince the Court that the CAB had abused its discretion in allowing AEA to compete with Pan American. Melone, *Controlled Competition*, 341–342.

60. Even though section 408 of the Civil Aeronautics Act prohibited a steamship company from owning an airline, the CAB had granted American Export Lines the right to own AEA.

61. The domestic carrier TWA complained that it was unfair for both American Airlines and Pan American to have international routes while it had none. Charles J. Kelly Jr., *The Sky's the Limit* (1963), 159; 23 *The Bull* (Aug. 8, 1942), 302.

62. Deborah W. Ray, *Pan American Airways and the Trans-African Air Base Program of World War II* (1973), 80 (doctoral thesis).

63. Bender and Altschul, *Chosen Instrument*, 331–335, 338, 566; Robert Daley, *An American Saga* (1980), 310–312; Henry L. Stimson, *Diaries*, Nov. 2, 1940; FTD, Tape 3, p. 9.

64. CUAP, 13–14; *accord*, COH, Tape 7, Side 2, pp. 5–6; Ray, *Pan American*, i–v; Daley, *American Saga*, 302–304.

65. Henry Friendly, "Grenville Clark: Legal Preceptor," in *Memoirs of a Man: Grenville Clark* (1975), 91.

66. Stimson, *Diaries*, July 25, 1940, Oct. 30, 1940.

67. CUAP, 14. Duggan was later revealed to have been a Soviet spy. John Earl Hayes and Harvey Klehr, *Verona: Decoding Soviet Espionage in America* (2000), 201–204.

68. Bender and Altschul, *Chosen Instrument*, 334, 338.

69. CUAP, 15–16; Bender and Altschul, *Chosen Instrument*, 333, 362–364. Pan American also required legal assistance on matters not directly related to the war, including route issues. 25 *The Bull* (May 27, 1944), 268 (unsigned).

70. Ray, *Pan American*, 243.

71. Bender and Altschul, *Chosen Instrument*, 13.

72. Northeast Airlines, Inc., *et al.*, North Atlantic Route Case, 6 C.A.B. 319 (1945); Bender and Altschul, *Chosen Instrument*, 400–406.

73. Bender and Altschul, *Chosen Instrument*, 406.

74. FTD, Tape 4, p. 1.

75. See Exceptions of New York Telephone Company and Request for Oral Argument on the Proposed Report of the Commission, July 16, 1943, ¶ 32(11); Transcript of Record in Supreme Court, 107. New York Telephone Co. v. United States, 56 F. Supp. 932 (S.D.N.Y. 1944).

76. FTD, Tape 4, pp. 1–2. To sustain his victory Friendly tried to rewrite the hearing record to limit New York Telephone's claim to property not retired from service. Brief for Appellee New York Telephone Company, 2 ("the Government completely misstates appellee's position").

77. Wells v. United States, 318 U.S. 257 (1943) (per *curiam*). Unlike Brandeis, Friendly apparently did not engage in much interesting pro bono legal work.

78. 318 U.S. at 261; FTD, Tape 4, p. 4.

79. The account that follows is taken primarily from descriptions by Leo Gottlieb and others in the firm's internal newsletter, 28 *Cleargolaw News* (Apr. 18,

1986), No. 5, 30 (Oct. 7, 1988), No. 12, and Leo Gottlieb, *Cleary, Gottlieb, Steen & Hamilton: The First 30 Years* (1983). Two other books played smaller roles: one, a memorial to Hugh B. Cox, *The Perfect Advocate* (1976), to which many of his friends and former colleagues contributed; the other, *Leo Gottlieb, June 21, 1986, Liber Amicorum* (James W. Johnson, ed., 1986), a collection of tributes, published in connection with Gottlieb's ninetieth birthday.

80. COH, Tape 8, Side 2, p. 6; Gottlieb, *Cleary Gottlieb,* 53–55. Friendly told a number of his law clerks that anti-Semitism was involved in his leaving Root, Clark. E.g., author interview of Frederick T. Davis, Mar. 20, 2007.

81. Hoffman, *Lions,* 61–63 ("At the end of World War II, there was no finer array of legal talent in New York than the aggregation known as 'the Root Clark firm.' . . . The exact cause of the breach remains shrouded in secrecy.").

82. COH, Tape 8, Side 2, p. 6; see 28 *Cleargolaw News* (Apr. 18, 1986), 157 (Leo Gottlieb).

83. 26 *The Bull* (Oct. 20, 1945), 585; Hoffman, *Lions,* 63–65; Smigel, *Wall Street Lawyers,* 258. When Harlan left Root, Ballantine, Harlan, Bushby & Palmer (as the firm was renamed in 1946) in 1954 to become a judge in the U.S. Court of Appeals for the Second Circuit and Chase Bank absorbed one of its major clients, Bank of Manhattan, the situation became dire. The firm's solution was to enlist the New York Governor and twice presidential candidate Thomas E. Dewey. The reconstituted firm thrived under the name Dewey, Ballantine, Bushby, Palmer & Wood.

84. George W. Ball, 25th Anniversary Issue, 13 *Cleargolaw News* (Jan. 1971), No. 1.

85. Unless otherwise stated, this account is based on numerous in-person and telephone interviews and exchanges of emails with Friendly's daughters, Joan Friendly Goodman and Ellen Friendly Simon, with the former providing most of the information.

86. Friendly letter to Sophie, Sept. 4, 1967, JFGC.

87. Ibid.

88. Friendly letter to Joan Goodman, Aug. 28 (year omitted but in the early 1980s), JFGC.

89. Author interview of grandson Daniel Simon, May 28, 2007.

90. Andrew Solomon, *The Noonday Demon; An Atlas of Depression* (2001), 15–16. For some psychiatrists the fact that symptoms are unwarranted or disproportionately enduring or severe is an essential part of the diagnosis, and a diagnosis of depression should not include "normal sadness." These psychiatrists consider the symptom-driven approach of the *Diagnostic and Statistical Manual of Mental Disorders* overinclusive. Allan V. Horwitz and Jerome C. Wakefield, *The Loss of Sadness* (2007).

91. Author telephone interview of Joan Goodman, Feb. 3, 2010.

92. COH, Tape 7, Side 2, p. 7.

93. See American Psychiatric Association, *Diagnostic Criteria from DSM-IV-TR* (2000), 168–179. The author acknowledges the assistance of Ira Dosovitz, M.D., a clinical professor of psychiatry at George Washington University and a practicing psychiatrist.

94. Joan Goodman email to author, July 15, 2009.

95. Author interview of Irene Friendly, May 26, 2007.

96. Author interview of Mogin, Dec. 9, 2006; author interview of Irene Friendly, Oct. 5, 2008.

97. Author interview of Ellen Simon, May 27, 2007; author interview of grand-daughter Ellen Goodman, May 26, 2007.

98. FTD, Tape 3, pp. 14–15; interview of Joan Goodman, May 19, 2007; author interview of grandson Daniel Simon, May 28, 2007.

99. Author interview of Frank Goodman, Oct. 22, 2006.

100. COH, Tape 8, Side 1, p. 1.

101. "The making of something out of nothing is the special province of the creative mind." Aaron Copeland, *Music and Imagination* (1952), 42.

102. Henry Friendly, "Memorandum for Judge Moore," Feb. 21, 1961, HLS-HJF, Box 226, Folder 5.

103. When interviewed in 1973, Friendly did not recall getting into heated discussions with his daughter. COH, Tape 7, Side 2, p. 4.

104. Friendly letter to Joan Friendly, Dec. 20, 1955. A friend of Joan's when she was at Radcliffe wrote Friendly a note that remarked on how wonderful it was to see someone with such respect and affection for his daughter. Author telephone interview of Herbert Hershfang, Nov. 14, 2010.

105. Joan Goodman email to author, July 22, 2009.

106. Author interview of Joan Goodman, Oct. 22, 2006.

107. Author interview of Robert M. Berger, Oct. 24, 2006.

108. Friendly letter to President, Central Synagogue, Apr. 3, 1985, HLS-HJF, Box 221, Folder 2.

109. FJPOH, 14. Friendly also was a member of the building committee of the 92nd Street YMHA in Manhattan, an important cultural institution. HLS-HJF, Box 197, Folder 6.

110. COH, Tape 8, Side 1, pp. 1–2.

111. FJPOH, 33, 37.

112. COH, Tape 8, Side 1, pp. 8–9.

113. 28 *Cleargolaw News* (Apr. 18, 1986), 157 (Leo Gottlieb) (Friendly agreed to devote three-quarters of his time to Pan American).

114. Erwin Griswold, "In Memoriam: Henry J. Friendly," 99 *Harvard Law Review* (1986), 1721.

115. United States v. New York Telephone Co., 326 U.S. 638 (1946).

116. FTD, Tape 4, p. 3.

117. See New York Telephone Co. v. Public Service Comm'n, 142 N.Y.S.2d 68 (App. Div. 1955), *aff'd*, 132 N.E.2d 847 (N.Y. 1956).

118. Automobile Club of New York, Inc. v. Cox, 592 F.2d 658 (2d Cir. 1979), discussed in Chapter 20.

119. Additional Service to Latin America, 6 C.A.B. 857 (1946). At about the same time Friendly suffered a partial loss in W. R. Grace & Co. v. CAB, 154 F.2d 271 (2d Cir. 1946).

120. The CAB was also strangling Pan American's prospects in the Pacific. Northwest Airlines, Inc., Pacific Route Case, 7 C.A.B. 209 (1946); see Bender and Altschul, *Chosen Instrument,* 408–409.

121. COH, Tape 9, Side 1, p. 1; *New York Times*, Mar. 22, 1949, p. 50; Bender and Altschul, *Chosen Instrument*, 438–445. As amended, the agreement called for a cash payment of $17.45 million. *North Atlantic Route Transfer Case*, 11 C.A.B. 676, 677 (1950).

122. Tr. 3527–3567 (June 20, 1949).

123. Tr. 2174–2195 (June 6, 1949).

124. Tr. 2201–2213 (June 6, 1949).

125. Tr. 1610 (May 27, 1949).

126. Tr. 3804 (June 23, 1949).

127. Tr. 2953, 2997 (June 14, 1949).

128. COH, Tape 8, Side 2, p. 9.

129. COH, Tape 9, Side 1, p. 1. In 1963 Landis pleaded guilty to failure to file five years of federal income tax returns and was sentenced to thirty days in jail. Donald A. Ritchie, *James M. Landis* (1980), 189, 199.

130. Ritchie, *Landis*, 160–169; see Bender and Altschul, *Chosen Instrument*, 440 (nominal fee).

131. Tr. 3122–3125 (June 15, 1949). Later Friendly added the annual reports of United Fruit Company and Monsanto Chemical Company (3152 (June 15, 1949)).

132. SEC Rule 10(14)(A)(III).

133. Tr. 3125, 3150 (June 15, 1949).

134. TWA Motion for Stay of CAB Order, July 12, 1950, C.A.B. Dkt. No. 3589. The decision also awarded TWA routes to London and Frankfurt, which it had not sought in the proceeding.

135. North Atlantic Route Transfer Case, 11 C.A.B. 676 (1950); Brief in Support of Petitioner's [TWA] Motion for a Stay and Other Interlocutory Relief, July 12, 1950 (2d Cir.); author interview of Roswell Perkins, Dec. 19, 2007; Bender and Altschul, *Chosen Instrument*, 439–444.

136. Memorandum of Pan American Airways, Inc. in Opposition to Stay and Other Interlocutory Relief, 10, in Pan American Airways Co. v. CAB, 121 F.2d 810 (2d Cir. 1941); Chicago and Southern Air Lines, Inc. v. Waterman S.S. Corp., 333 U.S. 103 (1948).

137. Trans World Airlines, Inc. v. CAB, 184 F.2d 66 (2d Cir. 1950).

138. *New York Times*, July 23, 1948, p. 35.

139. FTD, Tape 3, pp. 13–14.

140. PAWA, 32–33, HLS-HJF, Box 230, Folder 6; Daley, *American Saga*, 373.

141. 11 C.A.B. 852 (1950); Jerome E. Hyman email to author, May 25, 2007.

142. In March 1949 the firm became the first American firm to open a Paris office. Gottlieb, *Cleary, Gottlieb*, 63–67.

143. Tribute by Leo Gottlieb for Hugh Cox in *The Perfect Advocate*, 31–32.

144. Gottlieb, *Cleary, Gottlieb*, 99–100.

145. For background the author has drawn heavily on Joseph Borkin, *Robert R. Young: The Populist of Wall Street* (1969), 94–226. However, the book says almost nothing about the lawyers.

146. *New York Times*, Apr. 1, 1954, p. 49, May 12, 1954, pp. 47, 49, May 21, 1954, p. 31.

147. *New York Times*, May 25, 1954.

148. Borkin, *Robert Young*, 221–225. Young committed suicide in January 1958. Friendly successfully represented Sherman Fairchild in another major proxy fight. 28 *Cleargolaw News* (Apr. 18, 1986), 160 (Leo Gottlieb).

149. American Overseas Airlines, Inc. v. CAB, 254 F.2d 744 (D.C. Cir. 1958) (Pan American could recover losses due to strikes when carrying mail); Pan American World Airways, Inc. v. CAB, 256 F.2d 711 (D.C. Cir. 1958) (losing CAB rate determination); Pan American World Airways, Inc. v. CAB, 261 F.2d 754 (D.C. Cir. 1958) (barring other airlines from carrying transatlantic mail).

150. New York Telephone Co. v. Public Service Comm'n, 132 N.E.2d 847 (N.Y. 1956), *aff'g* 142 N.Y.S.2d 68 (App. Div. 1955).

151. Equity Corp. v. Brickley, 237 F.2d 839 (1st Cir. 1956). Other appeals Friendly argued included Gamewell Co. v. Public Serv. Comm'n, 188 N.Y.S. 107 (App. Div. 1959); Tenney v. Rosenthal, 160 N.E.2d 463 (N.Y. 1959).

152. Author interview of Prof. Norman Dorsen, Oct. 18, 2006. (Prof. Dorsen and the author are brothers.) Friendly's brief was excellent, too. For example, it cited four of the five cases on which Magruder's opinion relied, compared to one by his adversary.

153. Author interview of Joan Goodman, May 19, 2007; author interview of Jerome Hyman, July 31, 2007.

154. COH, Tape 9, Side 1, pp. 2–3.

155. Ibid., p. 3.

156. Ibid.

157. Author telephone interview of George DeSipio, Aug. 3, 2006.

158. Pierre N. Leval, "In Memoriam, Henry J. Friendly, Extraordinary Session of Second Circuit," 805 F.2d at xcvii. The quip has been attributed to Samuel Johnson by *The Wordsworth Dictionary of Quotations* (3d ed., 1998), 190.

159. Author interview of Hyman, July 31, 2007.

160. Lyman M. Tondel Jr., "Henry J. Friendly: Practicing Lawyer 1928–1959," 1978 *N.Y.U. Annual Survey of American Law* (1978), xxvi; *accord*, 28 *Cleargolaw News* (Apr. 18, 1986), 187 (Jerome E. Hyman).

161. HLS-HP/MS, May 21, 1968, Box 14, Folder 39, p. 9.

162. Richard W. Hulbert email to author, May 23, 2007.

163. Edward Wooley email to author, Sept. 15, 2006.

3. Nomination and Confirmation

1. COH, Tape 8, Side 2, p. 4.

2. FTD, Tape 4, pp. 11–12. Friendly said in 1962, "[I]nstead of the decision of a case being based upon the findings of fact and determination of policy disclosed in the agency opinion, the findings and determinations are based on the decision." William E. Fruhan Jr., *The Fight for Competitive Advantage* (1972), 160.

3. Author interview of Philip Bobbitt, July 3, 2007.

4. Author telephone interview of Abraham Sofaer, Aug. 21, 2009.

5. Author interview of Philip Bobbitt, Sept. 16, 2010.

6. J. Woodford Howard Jr., *Courts of Appeals in the Federal Judicial System* (1981), 130.

7. United States v. New York Telephone Co., 326 U.S. 638 (1946); Pan American Airways Co. v. C.A.B., 121 F.2d 810, 814 (2d Cir. 1941).

8. *New York Times*, Apr. 1, 1954; May 12, 1954; May 21, 1954; May 25, 1954.

9. Gerald Gunther, *Learned Hand* (1994), 647–652; Bruce Allen Murphy, *The Brandeis/Frankfurter Connection* (1982), 326–338. Years later Friendly told Professor Murphy, "I was not aware of the efforts made by Mr. Justice Frankfurter on my behalf in 1954 and 1957 and would have discouraged them had I known about them. I was aware of the efforts that he made in 1959, although I made no request for them and did not know exactly what he was doing." Murphy, *Brandeis/Frankfurter*, 331–332. Friendly seemed careful in using the word "exactly."

10. FTD, Tape 4, pp. 12–13.

11. HLS-HJF, Box 192, Folder 3.

12. COH, Tape 7, Side 1, p. 6.

13. Gunther, *Learned Hand*, 649.

14. Ibid., 650–651; HLS-HJF, Box 192, Folder 3 (containing correspondence relating to the vacancy).

15. Lawrence E. Walsh, *A Gift of Insecurity; A Lawyer's Life* (2003), 174.

16. Friendly letter to George W. Ball (undated), HLS-HJF, Box 192, Folder 3.

17. *New York Times*, Jan. 16, 1959, p. 25; *New York Times*, Feb. 8, 1959, p. 76; Jim Bishop, *New York Journal American*, Mar. 24, 1959.

18. Ronald Dworkin letter to author, Dec. 13, 2007.

19. HLS-HJF, Box 192, Folder 3.

20. Friendly letter to Harlan, Jan. 15, 1959, Seeley G. Mudd Ms. Library, Princeton University, JMH files, Box 537; *see New York Times*, Feb. 8, 1959, p. 76.

21. Murphy, *Connection*, 335; FTD, Tape 4, p. 13. Friendly and Wyzanski were in the same dining club at Harvard.

22. During Nelson Rockefeller's campaign for governor of New York, Friendly arranged a reconciliation between him and Harold Pearlman, the president of the New York Central Railroad. On May 5, 1959, Friendly sent a $100 check to the New York Republican Club, HLS-HJF, Box, 192, Folder 1. Earlier he had made contributions similar in size to the Republicans Senator Javits, Governor Rockefeller, and Mayor John Lindsay. HLS-HJF, Box 192, Folder 7; FTD, Tape 4, pp. 15–16.

23. Author interview of Milton Grossman, Apr. 10, 2006.

24. Author interview of Pat Hall Mogin, Dec. 9, 2006; author interview of Warren Stern, Nov. 20, 2006.

25. Friendly told Harlan, "Javits has been promoting this." Friendly letter to Harlan, Feb. 17, 1959, Seeley G. Mudd Ms. Library, Princeton University, JMH files, Box 537.

26. Hand letter to President, Jan. 22, 1959, HLS-HJF, Box 235; *New York Times*, Feb. 17, 1959, p. 34. Friendly's papers include letters in support of his nomination, e.g., a letter from Charles Percy of Elmira to Senators Javits and Keating, Feb. 17, 1959, that Friendly solicited. Friendly letter to Percy, Feb. 25, 1959, HLS-HJF, Box 192, Folder 3.

27. Friendly related the events to his former clerk Frederick T. Davis in an unrecorded portion of an oral history given to Davis on Nov. 14, 1981. Frederick Davis memorandum, Nov. 24, 1981, copy in possession of author.

28. Walsh, *Gift of Insecurity*, 174–175.

29. Friendly letter to Hand, Mar. 11, 1959, HLS-Hand, Box 88, Folder 19.

30. *New York Times*, Mar. 11, 1959, p. 34; *Washington Post*, Mar. 13, 1959, p. A18.

31. Senator Everett Dirksen, a Republican and the minority leader, withheld his approval because Senators Javits and Keating had not been asked for their approval. Sheldon Goldman, *Picking Federal Judges* (1997), 133.

32. HLS-HJF, Box 192, Folder 2.

33. *New York Times*, May 16, 1959, p. 60; *New York Times*, May 18, 1959, p. 21.

34. *New York Times*, May 16, 1959, p. 22.

35. Friendly letter to Benjamin Goodman, June 1, 1959, HLS-HJF, Box 192, Folder 2.

36. Friendly letter to Samuel R. Rosenthal, June 1, 1959, HLS-HJF, Box 192, Folder 2.

37. George W. Ball memorandum for Friendly, June 5, 1959, HLS-HJF, Box 192, Folder 2.

38. Friendly memorandum for Ball, June 6, 1959, HLS-HJF, Box 192, Folder 2.

39. *Washington Post*, June 9, 1959, p. 14.

40. Davis Mem., Nov. 24, 1981; Davis email to author, Nov. 14, 2006. Friendly had told other former clerks the story. E.g., author interview of Michael Boudin, June 16, 2010. Gunther, *Learned Hand*, 651–652, states only that to assist Friendly, on Aug. 19, 1959, Hand wrote a letter to Frankfurter, who "showed it . . . to Senate Majority Leader Lyndon Johnson." Frankfurter reported back to Hand by letter, "Your letter done it! Senator Lyndon Johnson just phoned me that he has 'seen the gentleman,' one Dodd of Connecticut, and 'all will be O.K.'" Frankfurter's letter to Hand speaks of a meeting between Johnson and Dodd and a telephone call from Johnson, rather than the opposite. The two versions can be reconciled if Johnson and Dodd met after the barbershop telephone conversation and Johnson then telephoned Frankfurter.

4. Getting Started

1. Henry Friendly, "In Praise of Herbert Wechsler," 78 *Columbia Law Review* (1978), 974. *Wigmore on Evidence* is dry and demanding reading, to say the least.

2. Friendly letter to Gunther, Aug. 19, 1975, HLS-HJF, Box 230, Folder 3. Other books on the shelf were *The Spirit of Liberty* by Learned Hand, *The Common Law* by Holmes, *The Federalist Papers,* and *Fowler's Modern English Usage.* Author interview of Monty Gray, Nov. 2, 2007; Gray email to author, Nov. 12, 2007.

3. Friendly letter to Harvard President Nathan Pusey, Mar. 23, 1971, HLS-HJF, Box 227, Folder 2.

4. Morton J. Horowitz, *The Transformation of American Law 1870–1960* (1977), 254. It would be more accurate to say the late 1950s and early 1960s. Author interview of Norman Dorsen, Feb. 16, 2011.

5. J. D. Hyman, "Constitutional Jurisprudence and the Teaching of Constitutional Law," 28 *Stanford Law Review* (1976), 1271, 1286 n.70.

6. It was not until 1994, after both Hart and Sacks had died, that the book finally appeared in printed form, edited by Professors William N. Eskridge Jr. and Philip P. Frickey. The editors reproduced the book as Hart and Sacks left it but added an important eighty-five-page "Historical and Critical Introduction." Henry M. Hart Jr. and Albert M. Sacks, *The Legal Process* (William N. Eskridge Jr. and Philip P. Frickey, eds., 1994), li.

7. "Law is the material of jurisprudence, jurisprudence is the rationalization of law." Charles Howard McIlwain, *Constitutionalism: Ancient and Modern* (1940, 2007), 54.

8. Hart and Sacks, *Legal Process*, 1118–1126, 1142–1144, 1187–1197, 1236–1243.

9. *Accord,* Stephen Breyer, *Active Liberty* (2005), 85 ("judges should pay primary attention to a statute's purpose in difficult cases of interpretation in which language is not clear").

10. Norman Dorsen, "John Marshall Harlan, Civil Liberties, and the Warren Court," 36 *New York Law School Law Review* (1991), 81, 106.

11. 347 U.S. 483 (1954).

12. Even before the publication of the temporary edition, signs of change had begun to appear, such as Brown v. Board of Education in 1954, which discarded established precedent largely on the basis of sociological concepts, although its status as a harbinger of future jurisprudence was not appreciated by many scholars.

13. *Hart and Sacks, Legal Process,* 1313–1336.

14. Roberson v. Rochester Folding Box Co., 64 N.E. 442 (N.Y. 1902); Hart and Sacks, *Legal Process,* 450–457.

15. Norman Dorsen, "In Memoriam—Albert H. Sacks," 105 *Harvard Law Review* 11 (1991). A number of Justices frequently followed the teaching of the Legal Process School: John Marshall Harlan, Louis F. Powell Jr., and Sandra Day O'Connor. Harlan, considered a conservative Justice during his service on the Court, had many law clerks who had studied under Hart and Sacks and professors teaching *The Legal Process* at other law schools. Author telephone interview of Norman Dorsen, Jan. 22, 2011. Harlan's opinion in Moragne v. States Marine Lines, Inc., 398 U.S. 375 (1970), which relied on *The Legal Process*, is the sole principal case in the discussion of the legal-process era in William N. Eskridge Jr. et al., *Cases and Materials on Legislation* (2007), 601.

16. Alexander M. Bickel, *The Least Dangerous Branch* (1962); Alexander M. Bickel, *The Supreme Court and the Idea of Progress* (1970).

17. Herbert Wechsler, "Toward Neutral Principles of Constitutional Law," 73 *Harvard Law Review* (1959), 1.

18. Author interview of Philip Bobbitt, July 3, 2007.

19. Friendly knew that Brandeis had maintained a commonplace book. Henry Friendly, *Benchmarks* (1967), 293.

20. Jerome Frank, *Courts on Trial* (1949), 116.

21. Note from Judge Marvin Frankel to Friendly, dated Mar. 14, 1967, quoting Thurman Arnold quoting Thomas Reed Powell in an article in 40 *Yale Law Journal*.
22. Roscoe Pound, *Introduction to the Philosophy of Law* (1922), vii.
23. Charles McIlwain, *The American Revolution* (1923), 64.
24. Frederic Maitland, *Bracton's Note Book*, Vol. I (1887), 104.
25. Cabell v. Markham, 148 F.2d 737, 739 (2d Cir. 1945) (L. Hand, J.).
26. Pope v. Atlantic Coast Line R.R., 345 U.S. 379, 390 (1953) (Frankfurter, J.).
27. Ho Ah Kow v. Nunan, 12 Fed. Cas. 6546, at 255 (C.C.D. Cal. 1879).
28. Friendly, *Benchmarks*, 7.
29. Friendly letter to Frankfurter, Sept. 10, 1959. LOC, Frankfurter Collection, Part 3, Reel 34.
30. Jeffrey Cole, "An Interview with Judge Randolph," 25 *Litigation* (1999), 16, 17.
31. 276 F.2d 525 (2d Cir. 1960).
32. 49 U.S.C. § 45. Brandeis had written an opinion on the Expediting Act while Friendly was his clerk. Swift & Co. v. United States, 276 U.S. 311, 322–323 (1928).
33. Frankfurter letter to Friendly, Feb. 12, 1960; Friendly letter to Frankfurter, Feb. 17, 1960, LOC, Frankfurter Collection, Part 3, Reel 34.
34. In over a dozen cases Friendly discussed the court's jurisdiction when the parties had not raised the issue, dismissing at least seven of them. E.g., Danlon Industries, Inc. v. Forte, 402 F.2d 935 (2d Cir. 1968).
35. Author interview of Monty Gray, Nov. 2, 2007.
36. 190 F. Supp. 116 (S.D.N.Y. 1960).
37. 274 F.2d 487 (2d Cir. 1960).
38. 274 F.2d 899 (2d Cir. 1960).
39. 275 F.2d 745 (2d Cir. 1960).
40. Henry Friendly, "Some Equal Protection Problems of the 1970's" (1970), 5, HLS-HJF, Box 204, Folder 7.
41. Case Note, 74 *Harvard Law Review* (1961), 788, 790, commenting on Fifth Ave. Coach Lines v. Commissioner of Internal Revenue, 281 F.2d 556, 563 (2d Cir. 1960) (Friendly, J., dissenting); Case Note, 74 *Harvard Law Review* (1960), 414. commenting on Cargill, Inc. v. Commodity Credit Corp., 275 F.2d 745 (2d Cir. 1960); Case Note, 74 *Harvard Law Review* (1960), 1662, commenting on Jaftex Corp. v. Randolph Mills, Inc., 282 F.2d 788 (2d Cir. 1960); Case Note, 73 *Harvard Law Review* (1960), 1616, commenting on United States v. Maybury, 274 F.2d 899 (2d Cir. 1960). An article by recent Harvard Law School graduates published the next year, however, endorsed Friendly's position in *Maybury*. Daniel K. Mayers and Fletcher L. Yarbrough, "*Bix Vexari*: New Trials and Successive Prosecutions," 74 *Harvard Law Review* (1960), 1–3, 27–28, 41–43.
42. 276 F.2d 280 (2d Cir. 1960) (conflict-of-laws question involving statute of limitations in diversity-of-citizenship case), *vacated,* 365 U.S. 293 (1961).
43. Case Note, 74 *Harvard Law Review* (1961), 606, 609.
44. Case Note, 73 *Harvard Law Review* (1961), 1613, 1616.

45. Friendly Voting Mem., Dec. 31, 1959, HLS-HJF, Box 2, File 35.

46. Friendly Mem., July 7, 1960, HLS-HJF, Box 3, Folder 15, in NLRB v. Adhesive Products, 281 F.2d 89, 92 (2d Cir. 1960) (Friendly, J., dissenting).

47. Judges Edward Weinfeld and Richard A. Posner have mentioned Friendly's modesty and lack of vanity. Weinfeld, "A Tribute to Henry J. Friendly," 1978 *N.Y.U. Annual Survey of American Law* (1978), xx; Posner "In Memoriam: Henry J. Friendly," 99 *Harvard Law Review* (1986), 1724–1725.

48. Hand letter to Frankfurter, Mar. 26, 1960, quoted in Gerald Gunther, *Learned Hand* (1994), 652.

5. Judge Friendly

1. Author interview of Pat Hall Mogin (secretary), Dec. 9, 2006; author interview of Frederick T. Davis, Mar. 20, 2007; author interview of Theodore R. Mirvis, Nov. 21, 2006.

2. E.g., author interview of Sydney Schwartz (secretary), Jan. 30, 2007. Friendly said that good shoes were important and worth spending money on. Author interview of Michael Lazerwitz, Nov. 28, 2006.

3. Friendly composed articles the same way he wrote opinions. Author interview of Peter Edelman, Nov. 28, 2006; author interview of Neil King, Nov. 15, 2007.

4. Henry Friendly, "A Look at the Federal Administrative Agencies," *Benchmarks* (1967), 65.

5. Henry Friendly, "The Federal Administrative Agencies: The Need for Better Definition of Standards," 75 *Harvard Law Review* 863, 1055, 1263 (1962), reprinted as a book of the same title in 1962 and in condensed form in *Benchmarks*, 86, 108.

6. Henry Friendly, "Reflections of a Lawyer-Newly-Become-Judge," *Benchmarks*, 1.

7. Henry Friendly, "Mr. Justice Brandeis: The Quest for Reason," *Benchmarks*, 291.

8. Henry Friendly, "Judge Learned Hand: An Expression from the Second Circuit" (1962), *Benchmarks*, 308.

9. Henry Friendly, book review of *The Common Law Tradition: Deciding Appeals,* by Karl N. Llewellyn (1960), 109 *University of Pennsylvania Law Review* (1961), 1040, *Benchmarks,* 34.

10. Pierre N. Leval, "Henry J. Friendly: In Memory of a Great Man," 52 *Brooklyn Law Review* (1986), 571, 572.

11. Author interview of Larry Kramer, Apr. 16, 2007; *accord,* Richard A. Posner, *Cardozo, A Study in Reputation* (1990), 133. Professor Herbert Wechsler wrote, "Only the genius that Henry Friendly was could produce scholarly material of this quality and volume while carrying for much of the period a full judicial assignment." 805 F.2d at xcviii, c.

12. Author interview of Akhil Reed Amar, Apr. 21, 2008.

13. Author interview of Judge Posner, Aug. 22, 2007; *accord,* e.g., Warren Burger, "Tribute," 1978 *N.Y.U. Annual Survey of American Law,* xi; Carl McGowan, "The Judge's Judge," 133 *University of Pennsylvania Law Review* (1984), 34, 38.

14. Friendly letter to Joan Goodman, July 4, 1967, JFGC.

15. Author interview of Thomas Curtis, June 20, 2007.
16. Author interview of Lazerwitz, Nov. 28, 2006.
17. Author interview of Warren Stern, Nov. 20, 2006.
18. Author interview of David Seipp, May 17, 2010.
19. Author interview of Monty Gray, Nov. 2, 2007. Friendly would permit his clerks to divide the cases as they saw fit.
20. Author interview of Renier H. Kraakman, Dec. 12, 2006.
21. Author interview of Lazerwitz, Nov. 28, 2006.
22. Friendly letter to Birg E. Sergent, May 11, 1972, HLS-HJF, Box 231, Folder 1; Wilfred Feinberg, "Unique Customs and Practices of the Second Circuit," 14 *Hofstra Law Review* (1986), 297, 299. More than two thousand voting memoranda are part of the Friendly Collection at Harvard Law School.
23. Voting Mem., Jan. 3, 1967, HLS-HJF, Box 32, Folder 27. Each judge on a panel prepared and sent to his colleagues a voting memorandum shortly after argument. In subsequent notes in this chapter, "Voting Mem." will be further abbreviated "VM."
24. Friendly VM, Feb. 9, 1967, HLS-HJF, Box 33, Folder 25.
25. E.g., Friendly VM, Jan. 23, 1961, HLS-HJF, Box 8, Folder 31.
26. Friendly VM, Nov. 7, 1961, HLS-HJF, Box 11, Folder 33.
27. Friendly VM, Sept. 15, 1970, HLS-HJF, Box 53, Folder 18.
28. Friendly VM, June 8, 1967, HLS-HJF, Box 35, Folder 2.
29. Friendly VM, Dec. 11, 1978, HLS-HJF, Box 91, Folder 12.
30. Friendly VM, Jan. 23, 1961, HLS-HJF, Box 9, Folder 5.
31. Friendly VM, June 9, 1961, HLS-HJF, Box 7, Folder 2.
32. Friendly VM, Apr. 9, 1970, HLS-HJF, Box 47, Folder 19.
33. Friendly VM, Apr. 19, 1961, HLS-HJF, Box 7, Folder 20.
34. Friendly VM, Aug. 8, 1963, HLS-HJF, Box 20, Folder 15; Friendly VM, Dec. 11, 1962, HLS-HJF, Box 17, Folder 27.
35. Friendly VM, Apr. 19, 1961, HLS-HJF, Box 7, Folder 26.
36. Friendly VM, Nov. 16, 1982, HLS-HJF, Box 127, Folder 26, in United States v. Ivic, 700 F.2d 51 (2d Cir. 1983). Friendly made similar comments in letters to academics. See Friendly letter to Charles Corbin, Jan. 26, 1962, HLS-HJF, Box 213, Folder 4 ("The ignorance displayed by the Trial Judge and by counsel on both sides was truly awesome").
37. Friendly VM, Feb. 27, 1967, HLS-HJF, Box 32, Folder 8.
38. Friendly VM, Dec. 21, 1964, HLS-HJF, Box 26, Folder 7.
39. But see Friendly VM, July 17, 1961, HLS-HJF, Box 6, Folder 22 (criticizing U.S. Attorney).
40. Friendly VM, Oct. 21, 1975, HLS-HJF, Box 52, Folder 7.
41. Friendly VM, Jan. 17, 1962, HLS-HJF, Box 13, Folder 11 (parenthetical in original). The law firms were, respectively, Nizer, Benjamin, Krim & Ballon and Rosenman Colin Kaye Petchek & Freund. Friendly enjoyed ribbing the purported cream of the bar.
42. Friendly VM, Oct. 31, 1977, HLS-HJF, Box 86, Folder 3.
43. Avis Rent A Car System, Inc. v. Hertz Corp., 782 F.2d 381, 384 (2d Cir. 1986); author telephone interview of Stephen Stein, Aug. 18, 2008.

44. Author telephone interview of Judge Ralph K. Winter, June 19, 2006.
45. Author interview of Judge Peter K. Leisure, Apr. 11, 2007.
46. Friendly letter to Judge Marvin E. Frankel, Dec. 21, 1977, HLS-HJF, Box 230, Folder 3.
47. The panel majorities befuddled Friendly in a pair of tax cases in which he dissented. Both cases involved taxpayers who had litigated the underlying state-law issue in the state courts. In Estate of Borax v. Commissioner of Internal Revenue, 349 F.2d 666, 676 (2d Cir. 1965) (Friendly, J., dissenting), the majority refused to bind a party who had fully litigated the key issue in state court because the Commissioner of Internal Revenue was not a party to the case (he was not prejudiced), while in Commissioner of Internal Revenue v. Estate of Bosch, 363 F.2d 1009, 1015 (2d Cir. 1966) (Friendly, J., dissenting), *rev'd*, 387 U.S. 456 (1967), the majority gave binding effect against the Commissioner to a collusive state lawsuit (filed after the Commissioner commenced tax proceedings against the taxpayer), where all of the parties sought the same result.
48. Friendly Mem., Jan. 24, 1963, HLS-HJF, Box 18, Folder 17, in United States v. Evans, 312 F.2d 556 (2d Cir. 1963).
49. Todd Rakoff, "In Memoriam: Henry J. Friendly," 99 *Harvard Law Review* 1726 (1986).
50. Author interview of Raymond B. Ludwiszewski, July 24, 2007; author interview of Richard A. Daynard, Dec. 14, 2006.
51. Author interview of Frank Tuerkheimer, Apr. 16, 2009, who represented the government in the case.
52. Author interview of Mary Coombs, Jan. 30, 2007; author interview of Todd Rakoff, Nov. 13, 2006; author interview of Jerome Hyman, Feb. 22, 2006.
53. Author interview of Davis, March 20, 2007.
54. Author interview of Rakoff, Nov. 13, 2006. Friendly's voting memorandum said, "From looking at the contraption itself—an almost forbidden practice according to defendants. . . . Although in the light of hindsight the invention seems to be simplicity itself, no one else had come near it and a walk up Lexington Avenue last Saturday afternoon demonstrated to me the wide acceptance it has received." Friendly VM, Apr. 12, 1976, HLS-HJF, Box 49, Folder 14.
55. Author interview of Stern, Nov. 20, 2006.
56. Author interview of Merrick Garland, Nov. 16, 2006.
57. Aguayo v. Richardson, 473 F.2d 1090, 1097 (2d Cir. 1973) (referring to Adele M. Blong); see, e.g., SEC v. Talley Industries, Inc., 399 F.2d 396, 402 (2d Cir. 1968) (referring to Donovan, Leisure's "conspicuously able brief").
58. William C. Conner, *Informal Memoir* (undated), 143, provided by Judge Conner to author; author interview of Kraakman, Dec. 12, 2006; author interview of Lazerwitz, Nov. 28, 2006; HLS-HJF, Box 86, Folder 3.
59. Friendly VM, Mar. 22, 1961, HLS-HJF, Box 8, Folder 13.
60. Friendly VM, Nov. 20, 1967, HLS-HJF, Box 38, Folder 31.
61. Friendly VM, Nov. 8, 1971, HLS-HJF, Box 59, Folder 26.
62. Friendly VM, Aug. 30, 1972, HLS-HJF, Box 61, Folder 5.
63. Friendly VM, Mar. 8, 1972, HLS-HJF, Box 61, Folder 7.

64. Friendly VM, Nov. 8, 1972, HLS-HJF, Box 67, Folder 16.
65. Friendly Mem., Jan. 24, 1977, HLS-HJF, Box 182, Folder 5.
66. Friendly VM, Jan. 19, 1971, HLS-HJF, Box 8, Folder 34.
67. Friendly Preliminary VM, Dec. 10, 1964, HLS-HJF, Box 25, Folder 3.
68. Friendly VM, June 2, 1970, HLS-HJF, Box 46, Folder 1.
69. Friendly VM, Sept. 22, 1975, HLS-HJF, Box 51, Folder 13.
70. Friendly VM, Nov. 12, 1974, HLS-HJF, Box 77, Folder 8.
71. Friendly VM, Apr. 14, 1961, HLS-HJF, Box 8, Folder 3.
72. Author interview of John G. Roberts Jr., Nov. 29, 2007; author interview of Kraakman, Dec. 12, 2006; author interview of Bruce Ackerman, Aug. 6, 2007.
73. Author interview of Michael Madow, Feb. 23, 2007; author interview of Lazerwitz, Nov. 28, 2006.
74. E.g., Friendly VM, Mar. 18, 1964, HLS-HJF, Box 22, Folder 15, in Pauling v. News Syndicate Co., 335 F.2d 659 (2d Cir. 1964).
75. Author interview of Judge Jon O. Newman, Mar. 29, 2006. Exceptions include Friendly VM, Nov. 8, 1961, HLS-HJF, Box 12, Folder 12, in Van Carpals v. SS American Harvester; Friendly Mem., June 18, 1962, HLS-HJF, Box 15, Folder 4, in S. D. Hicks & Co. v. J. T. Baker Chem. Co., 307 F.2d 750 (2d Cir. 1962) (Hays, J.).
76. E.g., United States v. Maybury, 274 F.2d 899 (2d Cir. 1960).
77. Author interview of Judge Newman, Mar. 9, 2008; author interview of Judge Winter, Nov. 20, 2006. (Friendly's moral authority kept the voting memos going.)
78. 274 F.2d 899 (2d Cir. 1960).
79. 304 F.2d 125 (2d Cir. 1962).
80. 378 F.2d 832 (2d Cir. 1967).
81. Friendly Mem., Jan. 16, 1967, HLS-HJF, Box 73, Folder 21.
82. 283 F.2d 916 (2d Cir. 1960).
83. Friendly Mem., May 6, 1974, HLS-HJF, Box 21, Folder 5; *accord*, Friendly Mem., July 5, 1984, Box 117, Folder 17; Friendly Mem., May 7, 1964, HLS-HJF, Box 21, Folder 5; author interview of Ludwiszewski, July 24, 2007.
84. In Scherr v. Universal Match Corp., 417 F.2d 497 (2d Cir. 1969), Friendly drafted a four-page memorandum to Judge Waterman that said, "I agree with the thrust of the opinion. . . . However, I do have a few reservations about the discussion." Friendly Mem., Aug. 11, 1969, HLS-HJF, Box 41, Folder 9. Friendly did not send the memorandum, but instead wrote a dissenting opinion.
85. Author interview of Donald Board, Mar. 14, 2007. Other judges did it, too. Tinsley E. Yarbrough, *Harry A. Blackmun* (2008), 85–106.
86. Howard J. Woodford Jr., *Courts of Appeals in the Federal Judicial System* (1981), 130 (ellipses in original).
87. Friendly, *Benchmarks,* 307 (referring to "Brandeis' profound belief in the need for facts").
88. United States v. Taylor, 464 F.2d 240, 245 (2d Cir. 1972) (Friendly, J.); see Lawrence B. Pedowitz, "Judge Friendly: A Clerk's Perspective," 1978 *N.Y.U. Annual Survey of American Law* (1979), xxix; "Manual for Law Clerks" (undated), HLS-HJF, Box 147, Folder 1.

89. Benjamin N. Cardozo, "Law and Literature," in *Selected Writings* (1947), 339, 341; see Richard A. Posner, *Cardozo, A Study in Reputation* (1990), 43 (Cardozo "makes things up").

90. Friendly, *Benchmarks*, 278.

91. It is likely that Friendly was influenced by his examination of the facts while writing an opinion in Pearlstein v. Scudder & German, 429 F.2d 1136, 1145 (2d Cir. 1970) (Friendly, J., dissenting); his opinion was far stronger for the plaintiff than was his voting memorandum.

92. *In Memoriam, Henry J. Friendly, Extraordinary Session of Second Circuit* (Remarks of Judge Pierre N. Leval), 805 F.2d at XCVII. For a cogent discussion by a former law clerk of Friendly's skill in writing opinions, read Michael Boudin, "Judge Henry Friendly and the Craft of Judging," 159 *University of Pennsylvania Law Review* (2010), 1.

93. Author interview of Judge Weinstein, Aug. 23, 2006.

94. Author interview of Chief Justice Roberts, Nov. 29, 2007; A. Raymond Randolph, "Administrative Law and the Legacy of Henry J. Friendly," 74 *New York University Law Review* (1999), 1, 3; author telephone interview of Judge Feinberg, Nov. 15, 2006 ("The speed with which he turned out opinions amazed me, with a quality that was unbelievable"). Because Friendly did not date the drafts he sent to the other judges, it is impossible to determine when he completed them. Cf. Seth Stern and Stephen Wermiel, *Justice Brennan: Liberal Champion* (2010), 283 ("[Justice] Douglas dashed off his first draft by hand on a yellow pad within ten days").

95. Author interview of Pierre N. Leval, Dec. 6, 2006.

96. See, e.g., discussions of Cortright v. Resor, 447 F.2d 245 (2d Cir. 1971), in Chapter 9, and *In re* Biaggi, 478 F.2d 489 (2d Cir. 1973), in Chapter 14.

97. See generally John T. Noonan Jr., *Persons & Masks of the Law* (1976).

98. 336 F.2d 306 (2d Cir. 1964).

99. 293 F.2d 373, 375 (2d Cir. 1961).

100. The author was sitting at government's counsel table.

101. Author interview of Milton Grossman, Apr. 10, 2006.

102. Author interview of Mary Coombs, Jan. 30, 2007; author interview of Robert Weiner, Nov. 9, 2006.

103. Author interview of Judge Leval, Dec. 6, 2006.

104. Friendly complained to Congress about the shortage of secretarial help. Friendly letter to Sen. Joseph Tydings, Apr. 10, 1969, HLS-HJF, Box 151, Folder 16; *accord*, Friendly letter to Judge Theodore Levin, July 19, 1967, HLS-HJF, Box 217, Folder 3; author interview of Richard Glickman, Apr. 17, 2007.

105. On Friendly's production, see Margaret V. Sachs, "Judge Friendly and the Law of Securities Regulation: The Creation of a Judicial Reputation," 50 *Southern Methodist Law Review* (1997), 777, 812, Table 5. Another study of three terms of court produced a slightly lower gap, namely, 12 percent. Howard, *Courts of Appeals*, 236.

106. Author interview of William Lake, Nov. 29, 2006.

107. Author interview of Martin Glenn, Feb. 21, 2007; author interview of Walter Hellerstein, June 21, 2007.

108. Author interview of Joan Goodman, May 19, 2007.
109. Friendly letter to Judge Harry T. Edwards, July 9, 1984, HLS-HJF, Box 220 Folder 7. Friendly's letter showed his concern about the problem of "arguments [that] were simply wild. . . . It does not really seem that one could say, 'The arguments in this case have been so wide of the mark that we simply chose between them. However, no one should regard this opinion as representing our view of the law.' "
110. New York State Assoc. for Retarded Children, Inc. v. Carey, 706 F.2d 956 (2d Cir. 1983).
111. Friendly letter to Judge Hufstedler, Mar. 14, 1975, HLS-HJF, Box 219, Folder 3.
112. Author interview of Board, Mar. 14, 2007.
113. Author interview of Pat Mogin. Dec. 9, 2006. More than two dozen handwritten drafts rest in the Friendly Collection at Harvard Law School. Because at times Friendly would have bubble inserts in the margin, and some bubbles would have bubbles, clerks gave him a two-by-three-foot pad, which he used on occasion and filled up the pages. Author interview of William Pederson, Nov. 17, 2006.
114. Author interview of Stern, Nov. 20, 2006; interview of Mirvis, Nov. 21, 2006.
115. E.g., Cianci v. New Times Publishing Co., 639 F.2d 54, 64 (2d Cir. 1980) ("The sort of idea which can never be false was illustrated by, , , ."). Friendly also omitted commas and rarely employed the hyphen in multiword terms used as adjectives before a noun, e.g., "white collar worker."
116. Author interview of Stephen Barnett, Apr. 17, 2007.
117. Engel email to author, Apr. 19, 2011.
118. Schilling v. A/S D/S Dannebrog, 320 F.2d 628, 629 (2d Cir. 1963) (district judge); Escott v. Bachris Construction Corp., 340 F.2d 731, 735 (2d Cir. 1965) (Friendly, J., concurring) (fellow judges); Seas Shipping Co. v. Commissioner of Internal Revenue, 371 F.2d 528 (2d Cir. 1967) (Friendly, J., concurring) (both).
119. McMillan v. Board of Education, 430 F.2d 1145, 1148–1149 (2d Cir. 1970) ("There is indeed some difficulty in conceiving. . . . But the Supreme Court evidently does not regard the point as even meriting discussion.").
120. Seas Shipping Co. v. Commissioner of Internal Revenue, 371 F.2d 528 (2d Cir. 1967).
121. 569 F.2d 705 (2d Cir. 1977).
122. HLS-HJF, Box 83, Folder 10.
123. Waterman Mem., Dec. 16, 1977, HLS-HJF, Box 83, Folder 10.
124. Friendly Mem., Dec. 19, 1977, HLS-HJF, Box 83, Folder 10.
125. E.g., Sanford Levinson, "The Rhetoric of Judicial Opinions," in *Law's Stories* (Peter Brooks and Paul Gewirtz, eds., 1996), 187.
126. United States v. Briggs, 457 F.2d 908, 910 (2d Cir. 1972).
127. United States v. Comissiong, 429 F.2d 834, 836–837 (2d Cir. 1970); see Friendly VM, July 17, 1961, HLS-HJF, Box 6, Folder 22.
128. Gras v. Steven, 415 F. Supp. 1148 (S.D.N.Y. 1976).
129. United States v. Reed, 517 F.2d 953, 963 (2d Cir. 1975); see Cheng Yih-Chun v. FRB, 442 F.2d 460, 463 (2d Cir. 1971).

130. E.g., Colonial Realty Corp. v. Bache & Co., 358 F.2d 178, 182 (2d Cir. 1966).

131. Gambling v. Commissioner of Internal Revenue, 682 F.2d 296, 301 (2d Cir. 1982) (Friendly, J., concurring).

132. 336 F.2d 376, 393 (2d Cir. 1964).

133. 378 F.2d 832, 842 n.17 (2d Cir. 1967).

134. *Accord,* NLRB v. Kelly Bros. Nurseries, Inc., 341 F.2d 433, 437 (2d Cir. 1965) (Friendly, J.) ("we shall hold it to that concession, without implying whether it was a necessary one").

135. 442 F.2d 216 (2d Cir. 1971), *rev'g* 309 F. Supp. 271 (S.D.N.Y. 1970).

136. 395 U.S. 653 (1969).

137. 442 F.2d at 221. Brief for Plaintiff-Appellee, 47; William C. Conner, *Informal Memoir* (undated), 119–121, provided by Judge Conner to author; Roger M. Milgrim, "*Sears* to *Lear* to *Painton:* Of Whales and Other Matters," 46 *New York University Law Review* (1971), 17, 23–24, n.31.

138. 442 F.2d at 232. The runner-up was Friendly's comment in LaReau v. Manson, 651 F.2d 96, 111 (2d Cir. 1981) (Friendly, J., concurring and dissenting), in which he referred to "the inflexible [position] by the district judge, which reminds me of the old saw, 'If the ship is leaking, sink it.'"

139. Friendly would sometimes remove caustic comments about judges before his opinions were published. Author interview of Barnett, Apr. 17, 2007; author interview of Richard Feldman, Feb. 13, 2007.

140. Friendly letter to Adams, Nov. 20, 1970, HLS-HJF, Box 56, Folder 23, in connection with United States v. Vaughan, 443 F.2d 92 (2d Cir. 1971).

141. Author interview of Glenn, Feb. 21, 2007.

142. See Judge Waterman letter to Friendly, Jan 20, 1967, HLS-HJF, Box 153, Folder 2.

143. Judge J. Edward Lumbard, Comments on Unveiling the Bust of Friendly, Mar. 27, 1989, p. 12, United States Courthouse, New York, N.Y.

144. See Friendly VM, Nov. 24, 1967, HLS-HJF, Box 33, Folder 14 ("Since you are away today and I shall be on Monday and Tuesday, I am giving you my thoughts in writing rather than orally as I would have preferred").

145. Author interview of Mirvis, Nov. 21, 2006.

146. Clark note to Friendly, June 14, 1972, HLS-HJF, Box 62, Folder 17.

147. Oakes Mem., June 13, 1972, in Goodwin v. Oswold, 462 F.2d 1237 (2d Cir. 1972), personal files of Judge Oakes. Friendly, who was furious with Oakes for having expanded prisoners' rights, had written him a blistering memorandum.

148. Author interview of Glenn, Feb. 21, 2007.

149. Author interview of Stern, Nov. 20, 2006.

150. Friendly letter to Prof. Michael W. McConnell, June 5, 1978, HLS-HJF, Box 230, Folder 3; Silver Chrysler Plymouth, Inc. v. Chrysler Motors Corp., 496 F.2d 800 (2d Cir. 1974) (*en banc*) (Moore, J.) (appealability of order disqualifying counsel).

151. Friendly VM, June 9, 1970, HLS-HJF, Box 47, Folder 8, in United States v. Lamia, 429 F.2d 373 (2d Cir. 1970).

152. Dadourian Export Corp. v. United States, 291 F.2d 178, 187 and n.4 (2d Cir. 1961) (Friendly, J., dissenting). *Frigaliment* is discussed in Chapter 21.

153. Friendly, like Brandeis, said that he could do a year's work in eleven months, but not twelve. Author interview of James Smoot, Apr. 18, 2008; Melvin I. Urofsky, *Louis D. Brandeis* (2009), 34.

154. Author interview of Glenn, Feb. 21, 2007; author interview of Mirvis, Nov. 21, 2006.

155. E.g., Friendly Mem., July 21, 1961, HLS-HJF, Box 6, Folder 22, in United States v. Annunziato, 293 F.2d 272 (2d Cir. 1961).

156. HLS-HJF, Box 219, Folder 6.

157. Author interview of Justice Stevens, June 30, 2008; see Jerome Frank, *Law and the Modern Mind* (1936), 103 ("you will study these opinions in vain to discover anything remotely resembling a statement of the actual judging process").

158. "A dictum consists essentially of a comment on how the court would decide some other, different case, and has no effect on its decision of the case before it." Pierre N. Leval, "Judging under the Constitution: Dicta about Dicta," 81 *New York University Law Review* (2006), 1249, 1257.

159. See ibid., 1255.

160. Richard A. Posner, *How Judges Think* (2008), 319–320; see, e.g., David McGowan, "Judicial Writing and the Ethics of Judicial Office," 14 *Georgetown Journal of Legal Ethics* (2001), 509, 555–567.

161. Posner, *Judges*, 162 (speaking generally).

162. Author interviews of Frank Goodman, Oct. 22, 2006, May, 19, 2007.

163. Author interview of Glenn, Feb. 21, 2007.

164. Author interview of Mark Wolinsky, Nov. 20, 2006.

165. Author interview of Glickman, Apr. 17, 2007; see Bruce Ackerman, "In Memoriam," 99 *Harvard Law Review* (1986), 1709 ("Henry Friendly did his own work"); Jeffrey Cole, "An Interview with Judge Randolph," 25 *Litigation* (1999), 16, 17 ("He did all his own research").

166. Author interview of A. Raymond Randolph, Feb. 12, 2007.

167. ITT v. Vencap, Ltd., 519 F.2d 1001, 1011 n.17 (2d Cir. 1975). Robert Vesco was a prominent defendant in a number of major stock-fraud cases.

168. Eugene R. Anderson letter to Friendly, Oct. 16, 1975, HLS-HJF, Box 78, Folder 2.

169. Friendly letter to Anderson, Oct. 20, 1975, HLS-HJF, Box 78, Folder 2.

170. Dolan responded by attacking Friendly for not apologizing. Dolan letter to Friendly, July 27, 1962, HLS-HJF, Box 14, Folder 11. In another case Friendly apologized to a lawyer for saying that he conceded a point when he had not, and changed his opinion accordingly. Catholic Med. Center of Brooklyn v. NLRB, 589 F.2d 1166 (2d Cir. 1978), HLS-HJF, Box 91, Folder 12.

171. Author interview of William J. Bryson, Nov. 2, 2006; author interview of Pat Mogin, Dec. 9, 2006. The Friendly chambers "General Office Procedure" states that "from time to time [Friendly] will ask one of the clerks to purchase

the brand." HLS-HJF, Box 159, Folder 1. Some clerks said they shopped for Friendly, others said they did not.

172. Some former clerks were hesitant about telephoning Friendly when they were in town. E.g., author interview of David Currie, Oct. 24, 2006.

173. Henry Friendly, "Edward Weinfeld, The Ideal Judge," 50 *New York University Law Review* (1975), 977; Edward Weinfeld, 1978 *N.Y.U. Annual Survey of American Law,* xxiii; Edward Weinfeld, "In Memoriam," Henry J. Friendly, Extraordinary Session of Second Circuit, 805 F.2d at xcii–xcv; Friendly letter to Erwin Griswold, July 3, 1985, HLS-Griswold Papers, Box 122, Folder 4; author interview of Judge Harold Baer, Apr. 11, 2007 (regularity of lunches).

174. Author interview of Leval, Mar. 22, 2011.

175. HLS-HJF, Box 98, Folders 1–19.

176. E.g., Friendly letter to Prof. Kenneth F. Ripple, Dec. 15, 1981, HLS-HJF, Box 207, Folder 3. Friendly once wrote about a student piece, "Ordinarily I do not find time to respond to such requests [for comment]. However, your comment seems to me so incomplete, to put it mildly, that I am making an exception." Friendly letter to *Journal of International Law and Politics*, Sept. 30, 1983, HLS-HJF, Box 220, Folder 6.

177. E.g., Friendly letter to Prof. Frank H. Easterbrook, Feb. 8, 1983, HLS-HJF, Box 220, Folder 4; author interview of Stern, Nov. 20, 2006.

178. Friendly letter to George Ball, Oct. 18, 1961, HLS-HJF, Box 213, Folder 6.

179. Friendly letter to Sen. Robert F. Kennedy et al., May 26, 1967, HLS-HJF, Box 215, Folder 2.

180. Friendly letter to Mayor Wagner, Nov. 29, 1965, HLS-HJF, Box 217, Folder 3.

181. Friendly letter to the editor, *New York Times*, May 12, 1967.

182. Friendly letter to President Ford, Sept. 3, 1974, HLS-HJF, Box 227, Folder 14.

183. Author interview of Stuart Stock, Dec. 1, 2006.

184. A clerk who served during the year Friendly became Chief Judge said that Friendly's attitude was "the last things I need are administrative tasks." Author interview of Neil King, Nov. 15, 2007; *accord,* author telephone interview of former Circuit Executive Stephen Flanders, Oct. 2, 2006; see HLS-HJF, Box 150 (files relating to administrative issues).

185. HLS-HJF, Box 208, Folders 1–4.

186. Friendly letter to Administrative Office of the United States Courts, Oct. 8, 1964, HLS-HJF, Box 184, Folder 4.

6. Law Clerks

1. HLS-HJF, Box 147, Folders 1, 2.

2. Author interview of Louis Kaplow, Nov. 14, 2006. Michael Madow raised the issue of politics at his interview, volunteering that he was far to the left of Friendly. Friendly said that he knew that and added, "I think I can handle it."

He hired Madow. Author interview of Michael Madow, Feb. 23, 2007. Earlier, Friendly had asked a former clerk, "Why in the name of heaven are law clerks always so plaintiff-minded?" Friendly letter to David Currie, Sept. 25, 1963, HLS-HJF, Box 211, Folder 15.

3. Henry Friendly, book review of *Administrative Law Treatise* by Kenneth Culp Davis, 8 *Hofstra Law Review* (1980), 471, 482.

4. Author telephone interview of applicant David B. Jaffe, Jan. 6, 2010. Edward Levi had been president of the University of Chicago and Attorney General of the United States. Jaffe later clerked for Justice Rehnquist with the former Friendly clerk Gary Born.

5. Two of the fifty-one clerks had serious reservations about their clerkships, for reasons discussed below.

6. Author interview of Robert M. Berger, Oct. 24, 2006, who found the limited personal contact with Friendly disappointing and the clerkship unsatisfactory.

7. Author interview of William J. Bryson, Nov. 2, 2006.

8. Author interview of William Lake, Nov. 29, 2006. A district judge wrote, "Watching Henry Friendly on the bench is the legal equivalent of going surfing with the Beach Boys." Thomas Croake, quoted in *National Law Journal*, Sept. 27, 1982, p. 11.

9. Author interview of Larry Kramer, Apr. 16, 2007.

10. Bruce Ackerman, "In Memoriam," 99 *Harvard Law Review* (1986), 1709, 1711 (ellipses in original).

11. David Currie email to author, Oct. 2, 2006.

12. Pierre N. Leval, *Extraordinary Session of the Court of Appeals for the Second Circuit*, June 9, 1986, 805 F.2d at xcviii.

13. Friendly clerks who became judges are Chief Justice John G. Roberts Jr., Circuit Judges Michael Boudin (First Circuit), Pierre N. Leval (Second Circuit), A. Raymond Randolph (D.C. Circuit), Merrick Garland (D.C. Circuit), and William C. Bryson (Federal Circuit), and Bankruptcy Judge Martin Glenn (S.D.N.Y.).

14. Author interview of Philip Bobbitt, July 3, 2007.

15. HLS-HJF, Box 147, Folder 1. There also was a manual titled "General Office Procedure," HLS-HJF, Box 159, Folder 1.

16. HLS-HJF, Box 207, Folder 9 (emphasis in original). The manual is close to what Brandeis told his law clerks: "My instructions regarding his work were to look with suspicion on every statement of fact until it was proved from the record of the case, and on every statement of law until I had exhausted the authorities." Dean Acheson, *Morning and Noon* 47 (1965). Friendly added to the manual such statements as "Because of the speed at which the judge works. . . ." Author interview of William Pederson, Nov. 17, 2006; *accord,* author interview of Stephen Barnett, Apr. 17, 2007.

17. Author interview of David Currie, Oct. 24, 2006.

18. Author interview of Michael Boudin, Oct. 16, 2006. Friendly's division of labor, as well as his relationship to his clerks, was almost identical as during his clerkship with Brandeis. Louis Paper notes of interview of Friendly, New

York City, Dec. 27, 1980, HLS-Paper, Box 1, Folder 3. Courtesy of Lewis J. Paper.

19. Author interview of Kaplow, Nov. 14, 2006.

20. Author interview of Michael Lazerwitz, Nov. 28, 2006. Friendly did not care about neatness in these memoranda. Author interview of Richard Glickman, Apr. 17, 2007.

21. Leval, "In Memoriam," 805 F.2d at xcvii; author interview of Pierre N. Leval, Dec. 6, 2006; author interview of Stuart Stock, Dec. 1, 2006.

22. Friendly Mem., Jan. 11, 1960, HLS-HJF, Box 4, Folder 4, in Bromberg v. Moul, 275 F.2d 574 (2d Cir. 1960); see author interview of Stephen Grant, July 27, 2007.

23. Friendly Voting Mem, June 19, 1964, HLS-HJF, Box 23, Folder 11 (referring to Leval), in United States v. Borelli, 336 F.2d 376 (2d Cir. 1974).

24. Rubin v. Manufacturers Hanover Trust Co., 661 F.2d 979 (2d Cir. 1981) (Kearse, J.); Friendly Mem., Mar. 30, 1981, attaching Wolinsky's undated memorandum, HLS-HJF, Box 101, Folder 10. When a clerk learned that a new treatise had not been delivered to stores, she arranged to visit the publisher's warehouse, where she found the reference at 4:30 A.M. Author interview of Ruth Wedgwood, Mar. 1, 2007.

25. Author interview of Monty Gray, Nov. 2, 2007; author interview of John G. Roberts Jr., Nov. 29, 2007.

26. Ackerman, "In Memoriam," 1711. Other clerks praised the collegial nature of this part of the work. E.g., author telephone interview of Gary Born, June 23, 2010.

27. Lawrence B. Pedowitz, "Judge Friendly: A Clerk's Perspective," 1978 *N.Y.U. Annual Survey of American Law* (1979), xviii, xix.

28. Author interview of Leval, Dec. 6, 2006; Friendly letter to David Currie, Dec. 31, 1959 ("I am sure that we will have a good deal of fun together and that you will be a tremendous help next year"), HLS-HJF, Box 147, Folder 2.

29. Author interview of Glickman, Apr. 17, 2007.

30. Leval, "In Memoriam," 805 F.2d at xcvii (1986); author interview of Todd Rakoff, Nov. 13, 2006; author interview of Jonathan Macey, Apr. 21, 2008.

31. Author interview of Robert Weiner, Nov. 9, 2006.

32. Author interview of Lawrence Pedowitz, Apr. 4, 2007; author interview of Grant, July 27, 2007. Grant explained that for Friendly it was not personal; at times it was even affectionate.

33. Author interview of Wedgwood, Mar. 1, 2007; author interview of Lake, Nov. 29, 2006.

34. Leval, "In Memoriam," 805 F.2d at xcvii.

35. Author interview of Peter Edelman, Nov. 28, 2006.

36. Mayer v. Oil Field Systems Corp., 721 F.2d 59, 66 (2d Cir. 1983).

37. Author interview of Bryson, Nov. 2, 2006.

38. Author interview of David Seipp, May 17, 2010.

39. Author interview of Kramer, Apr. 16, 2007.

40. Ibid.

41. Author interview of Boudin, Oct. 16, 2006; A. Raymond Randolph, "Administrative Law and the Legacy of Henry J. Friendly," 74 *New York University Law Review* (1999), 1, 3.

42. When he left the clerkship, Robert Berger gave his successor a large box of Maalox. Author interview of Bruce Ackerman, Aug. 6, 2007.

43. Author interview of Roberts, Nov. 20, 2006. Friendly's reputation for intimidation captured Yale professor Akhil Reed Amar, who repeatedly pressed his Yale colleague, Jonathan Macey, a former Friendly clerk, to admit that working for Friendly was intimidating and traumatic. Macey insisted that he had not been intimidated by Friendly. The day after one such exchange Macey approached Amar and told him that he had had nightmares the previous night about his clerkship and realized that he had been repressing his feelings about Friendly. Amar accepted and has continued to repeat Macey's confession. When told of Amar's repetition of the story, Macey replied, "I was just pulling his leg. Akhil is so confident that everyone who worked for Friendly was traumatized." Author interviews of Macey, Apr. 21, 2008; author interview of Akhil Reed Amar, Apr. 21, 2008.

44. Author interview of Grant, July 27, 2007; author interview of Theodore R. Mirvis, Nov. 21, 2006.

45. Author interview of Roberts, Nov. 20, 2006. When Friendly was hospitalized he would listen to tapes of oral arguments and do other judicial work. Author interview of Reinier H. Kraakman, Dec. 12, 2006.

46. Author interview of Ackerman, Aug. 6, 2007 (waited until Friendly left before he departed); author interview of David Currie, Oct. 24, 2006 (left when Friendly left); author interview of Boudin, Dec. 11, 2006 (long hours).

47. Author interview of Gregory Palm, Apr. 10, 2007; author interview of James Smoot, Apr. 18, 2008. Several clerks pulled all-nighters. E.g., author interview of Kramer, Apr. 16, 2007.

48. Smoot recalled the figure as a nearly unbelievable eighty hours a week. Smoot email to author, Mar. 7, 2010.

49. Author interview of Boudin, Dec. 11, 2006; author interview of Ira Feinberg, Nov. 20, 2006; author interview of Glickman, Apr. 17, 2007.

50. Author interview of Richard A. Daynard, Dec. 14, 2006.

51. Author interview of Glickman, Apr. 17, 2007; author interview of Leval, Nov. 6, 2006.

52. Author interview of Walter Hellerstein, June 21, 2007; author interview of Boudin, Dec. 11, 2006. The clerks were not necessarily talking about their personal experience.

53. Law clerk's memorandum to Friendly (undated), HLS-HJF, Box 65, Folder 1. Other clerks said that they never saw him angry or impolite. E.g., author interview of Glickman, Apr. 17, 2007.

54. Author interview of Boudin, Dec. 11, 2006; author telephone interview of Thomas Dagger, May 5, 2011.

55. Author interview of Mirvis, Nov. 21, 2006.

56. Author interview of Boudin, Dec. 11, 2006.

57. Author interview of Sydney Schwartz (secretary), Jan. 30, 2007.

58. Ibid.; author interview of Mary Coombs, Jan. 30, 2007 ("I felt that this was petty or silly and I was not very good at hiding how I felt").

59. Author interview of Pederson, Nov. 17, 2006. When he started his clerkship, one clerk couldn't remember whether he was supposed to leave the rubber bands on or take them off, at least until he saw Friendly struggling with them. The clerk knew he was in trouble. Author interview of Raymond B. Ludwis-zewski, July 24, 2007.

60. Author interview of A. Raymond Randolph, Feb. 12, 2007.

61. Author interview of Kraakman, Dec. 12, 2006.

62. Author interview of Madow, Feb. 23, 2007.

63. Author interview of Pedowitz, Nov. 20, 2006; author interview of Donald Board, Mar. 14, 2007.

64. Author interview of Mirvis, Nov. 13, 2006.

65. Author telephone interview of Judge Conner, Apr. 22, 2007.

66. Author interview of Pat Mogin (secretary), Dec. 9, 2006.

67. Author interview of Pederson, Nov. 17, 2006.

68. Author interview of Ludwiszewski, July 24, 2007.

69. Author interview of Glickman, Apr. 17, 2007; author telephone interview of Glickman, Mar. 5, 2010.

70. Author interview of Mirvis, Nov. 13, 2006.

71. Author interview of Board, Mar. 14, 2007.

72. Author interview of Madow, Feb. 23, 2007.

73. Friendly letter to Joan Goodman, Dec. 19, 1962 (comparing two clerks "from a sheer intellectual standpoint").

74. Friendly letter to Solicitor General Wade H. McCree, Apr. 12, 1978, HLS-HJF, Box 209, Folder 11; author interview of Pedowitz, Nov. 20, 2006.

75. Friendly letter to William H. Webster, Mar. 26, 1984, HLS-HJF, Box 232, Folder 2.

76. The identifications are based largely on interviews and are therefore subject to omissions.

77. Author interview of Glickman, Apr. 17, 2007; author interview of Daynard, Dec. 14, 2006. Daynard, who was hired at the last minute because Friendly had fired a clerk at the start of the court term, was in the top 10 percent of his class, but not in the top 5 percent or higher, as were his other clerks. When Daynard performed successfully as a clerk, Friendly concluded that there must be something wrong in the grading system. Author interview of Daynard, Dec. 14, 2006.

78. Convinced that Friendly was serious, the former clerk asked not to be identified.

79. Author interview of Smoot, Apr. 18, 2008.

80. Author interview of Harry Bryans, Feb. 12, 2007; author interview of Frank Goodman, July 20, 2009. Friendly fired a clerk who had set up a business in the chambers selling radical posters that his girlfriend shipped him from Paris. Author interview of Lake, Nov. 29, 2006.

81. Author interview of Pat Mogin, Dec. 9, 2006.

82. Author interview of Louis Cohen, Feb. 11, 2008.

83. Author interview of Lazerwitz, Nov. 28, 2006, one clerk who welcomed the task.

84. Author telephone interview of Judge Cardamone, May 14, 2007.

85. Joan Goodman email to author, July 22, 2009; see author interview of Roberts, Nov. 20, 2006 ("he had a curmudgeon attitude; I saw it as an act").

86. Weinfeld letter to Friendly, Dec. 13, 1984. Weinfeld Collection, N.Y.U. Law Library, Box 10; *accord,* Judge Edward Weinfeld, *In Memoriam, Henry J. Friendly, Extraordinary Session of Second Circuit,* 805 F.2d at xciv; Jack Weinstein, "Every Day Is a Good Day for a Judge to Lay Down His Life for Justice," 32 *Fordham Urban Law Journal* (2004), 131, 155 n.109 (Learned Hand).

87. Author interview of Bobbitt, Sept. 16, 2010; author interview of Edelman, Nov. 28, 2006.

88. Author interview of Board, Mar. 14, 2007. Friendly assisted other former clerks in this manner, in one case providing a clerk with the book *Turn Left at the Pub* by George W. Oakes. Author telephone interview of Randolph, Dec. 9, 2009.

89. Richard Posner email to author, Oct. 1, 2010.

90. Author interview of Pedowitz, Nov. 20, 2006.

91. Author interview of Edelman, Nov. 28, 2006.

92. Friendly invited Bobbitt to see Tom Stoppard's play *Travesties.* The clerk "was roaring throughout the play," while Friendly sat silently. Afterward Friendly asked Bobbitt if he liked it, and he replied he did. Friendly said, "I thought so." Author interview of Bobbitt, July 3, 2007.

93. Author interview of Palm, Apr. 10, 2007.

94. Author interview of Rakoff, Nov. 13, 2006.

95. Friendly sometimes wrote rave recommendations, e.g., a letter about clerk William I. Lake used words like "remarkable," "uncanny," and "priceless." Friendly letter to Harlan, Oct. 21, 1968, Seeley G. Mudd Manuscript Library, Princeton University, JMH files, Box 537.

96. Author interview of Smoot, Apr. 18, 2008; see HLS-HJF, Box 227, Folder 22. Professor Yale Kamisar of Michigan Law School, who telephoned judges about their former clerks in connection with deciding whom to have teach at his law school, said Friendly was extremely negative when he disliked a clerk. Author telephone interview of Yale Kamisar, Dec. 12, 2010; see author interview of Boudin, Dec. 11, 2006.

97. HLS-HJF, Box 193, Folder 3.

98. Author interview of Boudin, Dec. 11, 2006; author interview of Leval, Dec. 6, 2006.

99. Author interview of Feinberg, Nov. 20, 2006; author interview of Mirvis, Nov. 13, 2006; author interview of Paul Mogin, Nov. 28, 2006.

100. Author interview of Boudin, Dec. 11, 2006.

101. HLS-HJF, Box 221, Folder 6; see author interview of Currie, Oct. 24, 2006.

102. Author interview of Pederson, Nov. 17, 2006.

103. Author interview of Kramer, Apr. 16, 2007.

104. Ibid.

105. Author interview of Leval, May 13, 2010.

106. Author interview of Bobbitt, Sept. 16, 2010.

107. See, e.g., "I would much sooner have lobbying in the hands of lawyers of this quality [Cutler] than in the hands of professional lobbyists whose approach to a legislative question is too often in the liberal distribution of cases of whiskey." Friendly letter to Stephen Barnett, July 5, 1977, HLS-HJF, Box 209, Folder 8.

108. Author interview of Bobbitt, Sept. 16, 2010.

109. Undated nine-page double-spaced document entitled "General Office Procedure," HLS-HJF, Box 159, Folder 1.

110. Author interview of Schwartz, Jan. 30, 2007.

111. Author telephone interview of Charlotte A. Kimbrough, June 6, 2009.

112. Author interview of Schwartz, Jan 30, 2007; author interview of Pat Mogin, Dec. 9, 2006.

113. Author interview of Kimbrough, June 6, 2009.

114. Author interview of Pat Mogin, Dec. 9, 2006. Friendly would glance at the sports page in the morning, but that was about it. He did not attend or watch games. Joan Goodman email to author, Sept. 5, 2007.

115. Author interview of Board, Mar. 14, 2007.

116. Ibid. Friendly went to other clerks' ceremonies, for example, the wedding of Richard Glickman and to the "Jewish Christening" of the son of Peter Edelman and his wife, Marian Wright Edelman. Author interview of Glickman, Apr. 17, 2007; author interview of Edelman, Nov. 28, 2006.

7. Judges and Justices

1. The Senior Judges were Learned Hand, Thomas W. Swan, Harrie Brigham Chase, Harold R. Medina, and Carroll Hincks.

2. J. Woodford Howard Jr., *Courts of Appeals in the Federal Judicial System* (1981), 222. Friendly said that he missed the older judges, including Clark, and acknowledged rather mildly, "I don't think we've had people of the same quality since." HLS-HP/MS, Box 14, Folder 26, p. 6.

3. Jeffrey B. Morris, *Federal Justice in the Second Circuit* (1987), 174.

4. Consisting of Brooklyn, Queens, Staten Island, and Long Island.

5. Morris, *Federal Justice*, 175.

6. Unlike in the Supreme Court, where the issues are clearly identified with higher stakes, collegial deliberation by a panel in a court of appeals could be productive. See Richard A. Posner, *How Judges Think* (2008), 301–304 (deliberation of little value in Supreme Court).

7. Medina was best known for having presided over the trial of the leaders of the Communist Party in Dennis v. United States, 341 U.S. 494 (1951), *aff'g* 183 F.2d 201 (2d Cir. 1950) (L. Hand, J.). Friendly told a clerk that Medina was incapable of letting counsel tell the judges what they knew. Author interview of James Smoot, Apr. 18, 2008.

8. Marvin Schick, *Learned Hand's Court* (1971), 32; Prof. Stephen Burbank letter to Friendly (undated), HLS-HJF, Box 220, Folder 4 ("It will not come as a

surprise to you that, as a result of my research in the Clark papers, I came thoroughly to dislike the man"); author interview of Milton Grossman, Apr. 10, 2006 (Clark was irascible).

9. Frankfurter letter to Friendly, Sept. 14, 1959, JFGC.

10. Author interview of Stephen Barnett, Apr. 17, 2007. Friendly was also opposed to the Federal Rules of Evidence: "[M]y basic position is that it is now undesirable to have a Federal Code of Evidence in any form." Testimony of Friendly on Proposed Rules of Evidence, Subcommittee on Reform of the Federal Criminal Laws, Committee of the Judiciary, House of Representatives, 93d Cong., 1st Session (1973), 258; *accord*, Friendly letter to Chief Justice Warren Burger, Nov. 17, 1970, John Marshall Harlan Papers, MC071, Box 537, Seeley G. Mudd Manuscript Library, Princeton University.

11. Author interview of Judge Posner, Aug. 22, 2007.

12. Author telephone interview of Prof. Barbara Black, Sept. 15, 2008; author telephone interview of Prof. Harvey Goldschmid, Mar. 27, 2008.

13. 347 U.S. 483 (1954).

14. Morris, *Federal Justice*, 175–179.

15. Friendly letter to Frankfurter, Jan. 9, 1962, Frankfurter Papers, LOC, Part 3, Reel 34, quoted in Mark Tushnet, "Thurgood Marshall and the Brethren," 80 *Georgetown Law Journal* (1992), 2109, 2114; author interview of Joan Goodman, May 19, 2007,

16. Juan Williams, *Thurgood Marshall* (1998), 304–305. When Friendly recommended a clerk to Justice Marshall, the latter said, "If you're good enough for Friendly, you're good enough for me." Author interview of Ira Feinberg, Nov. 20, 2006.

17. Morris, *Federal Justice*, 181–182. Johnson also appointed Robert P. Anderson from Connecticut.

18. The four were Oakes, William H. Mulligan, Walter R. Mansfield, and William Timbers.

19. Morris, *Federal Justice*, 179–180.

20. Author telephone interview of Judge Thomas Meskill, Mar. 16, 2006.

21. Author interview of Judge Newman, Mar. 29, 2006.

22. Author interview of David Seipp, May 17, 2010; author interview of Donald Board, Mar. 14, 2007. Friendly sent Kearse a note complimenting her on one of her first opinions. Author interview of Paul Mogin, Nov. 28, 2006.

23. Friendly letters to Richard Posner, Oct. 14, 1982, Oct. 25, 1985, HLS-HJF, Box 221, Folder 7.

24. Morris, *Federal Justice*, 172.

25. Wilfred Feinberg, "In Memoriam: Henry J. Friendly," 99 *Harvard Law Review* (1986), 1713–1715.

26. Author telephone interview of Judge Cardamone, May 14, 2007.

27. Author interview of Meskill, Mar. 16, 2006.

28. Author interview of Newman, Mar. 29, 2006.

29. Author telephone interview of Newman, June 30, 2009.

30. *Glimpses of Walter Mansfield* (1995), 160 (comment of Thomas P. Olson).

31. Friendly's eightieth birthday party scrapbook, HLS-HJF, Box 235; LOC, Irving R. Kaufman Collection, Container 78.

32. Author interview of Mark Wolinsky, Nov. 20, 2006; author interview of Richard Feldman, Feb. 13, 2007; see Philip P. Frickey, "Wisdom on *Weber*," 74 *Tulane Law Review* (2000), 1169, 1171.

33. Friendly letter to Posner, Sept. 19, 1984, HLS-HJF, Box 221, Folder 7. On his desk Friendly kept an outbox dedicated to items for Posner. Author interview of Board, Mar. 14, 2007. See generally William Domnarski, "The Correspondence of Henry Friendly and Richard A. Posner 1982–86," 51 *American Journal of Legal History* (2011), 359.

34. Friendly letters to Posner, Oct. 14, 1982, Sept. 19, 1984, HLS-HJF, Box 221, Folder 7; Friendly letter to A. Richard Feldman, Mar. 6, 1984, HLS-HJF, Box 221, Folder 6; author interview of Frank Goodman, Oct. 22, 2006. When Senator Howard Metzenbaum (D. Ohio) blocked Easterbrook's confirmation in 1984, Friendly wrote to Posner, "I am sorry to hear the bad news about Easterbrook's confirmation. This adds to my 'little list' on Senator Metzenbaum. I distrust multi-million dollar liberals, whether their names are Kennedy or Metzenbaum." Friendly letter to Posner, Oct. 11, 1984, HLS-HJF, Box 221, Folder 7.

35. Author interview of Newman, Mar. 29, 2006. Friendly was disturbed enough to describe the event to two individuals, one soon after it occurred and the other years later; both requested anonymity. Justice Ginsburg did not respond to a request for comment.

36. Edward Weinfeld, "A Tribute to Henry J. Friendly," 1978 *N.Y.U. Annual Survey of American Law*, xxiii.

37. Friendly letter to Weinfeld, Apr. 20, 1979, Weinfeld Collection, N.Y.U. Law Library, Box 10. See generally William E. Nelson, *In Pursuit of Right and Justice; Edward Weinfeld as Lawyer and Judge* (2004).

38. Author interview of Board, Mar. 14, 2007.

39. E.g., Friendly letter to Weinfeld, July 1, 1983, Weinfeld Collection, N.Y.U. Law Library, Box 10.

40. Author telephone interview of Prof. William Nelson, Feb. 20, 2007.

41. Author interview of Peter Edelman, Nov. 28, 2006.

42. Author interview of Walter Hellerstein, June 21, 2007.

43. Howard, *Courts of Appeals*, 48. Weinfeld was tied for the lowest nonaffirmance rate in the Second Circuit. The average nonaffirmance rate of district judges during the three years was 23.4 percent, more than double Weinfeld's.

44. Friendly Voting Mem., Mar. 28, 1979, HLS-HJF, Box 97, Folder 12. In subsequent notes in this chapter, "Voting Mem." will be further abbreviated "VM."

45. Friendly VM, June 5, 1967, HLS-HJF, Box 35, Folder 33; Friendly Letter to Council of Foreign Relations, Apr. 12, 1985, HLS-HJF, Box 227, Folder 5.

46. Author interview of Michael Boudin, May 9, 2007. Friendly said that in Besseyev v. Commissioner of Internal Revenue, 379 F.2d 252 (2d Cir. 1967), Gurfein gave the best oral argument he had heard in his first seven years on the bench. Author telephone interview of Richard Glickman, Mar. 5, 2010.

47. Author interview of Michael Boudin, Nov. 12, 2006.
48. Friendly letter to Sofaer, Apr. 22, 1964, HLS-HJF, Box 211, Folder 14; see HLS-HJF, Box 175, Folder 49 (calling Sofaer's student note "magnificent").
49. Friendly VM, Sept. 29, 1969, HLS-HJF, Box 46, Folder 8.
50. Friendly VM, Sept. 24, 1961, HLS-HJF, Box 175, Folder 49.
51. Friendly VM, June 26, 1966, HLS-HJF, Box 35, Folder 3.
52. Friendly letter to Sifton, June 26, 1984 ("The Circuit is fortunate to have a District Judge who possesses such thoroughness, learning and good judgment"), HLS-HJF, Box 222, Folder 1.
53. Author interview of Martin Glenn, Feb. 21, 2007. Friendly made the statement in connection with the United States v. Weinstein, 452 F.2d 704, 705 (2d Cir. 1971), a decision in which he praised Weinstein as a "conscientious and ingenious judge [whose] praiseworthy effort has presented us with problems of no little complexity."
54. Friendly letter to Weinstein, Sept. 21, 1979, HLS-HJF, Box 98, Folder 7. The case was United States v. Rubin, 609 F.2d 51, 66 (2d Cir. 1979) (Friendly, J., concurring), *aff'd,* 449 U.S. 424 (1981) (when a statement the witness made prior to the trial that is consistent with his trial testimony can be used as affirmative evidence of the statement's truth). Weinstein had written to Friendly, "I have read with great interest and admiration your concurring opinion in United States v. Rubin. . . . While I regret that my treatise is somewhat equivocal on the point, I expect to be rewriting these sections during the coming year and I will take much the position you espoused." Weinstein letter to Friendly, Sept. 18, 1979, HLS-HJF, Box 98, Folder 7. When a law clerk proposed a fuller explanation of a pivotal ruling, Friendly replied, "Henry Hart will understand it." Michael Boudin, "Judge Henry Friendly and the Craft of Judging," 159 *University of Pennsylvania Law Review* (2010), 1, 10.
55. Friendly and Weinfeld evidently discussed Kaufman's foibles. Found among Weinfeld's papers relating to Friendly was a page from the July 8–15, 1978, edition of *The Nation,* a magazine of the left, an editorial that unmercifully attacked Irving Kaufman's handling of the *Rosenberg* treason case, including alleging that he "secretly was in communication with the FBI, seeking to expedite the time of execution and immunize his judicial conduct from appellate review." Weinfeld Collection, N.Y.U. Law Library, Box 10.
56. Friendly letter to Joan Goodman, July 4, 1967.
57. Author telephone interview of Craig Whitney, Dec. 17, 2007. Tolchin added that Kaufman's opinions frequently were newsworthy. Author interview of Tolchin, Dec. 17, 2007.
58. Author interview of Mark Wolinsky, Nov. 20, 2006.
59. Author interview of Charles Stillman, former Kaufman clerk-bailiff, May 22, 2008; see author interview of Wolinsky, Nov. 20, 2006.
60. Author interview of Seipp, May 17, 2010.
61. Friendly, who complained about the cost of taxis, obtained reimbursement for many taxi rides home as "official travel within circuit." His tips to the service employees in the apartment house in which he lived were "embarrassingly small." Author interview of Pat Hall Mogin, Dec. 9, 2006; *accord,* author

interview of Sydney Schwartz, Jan. 30, 2007 ("he was cheap about his personal needs").

62. After Frederick Davis saw one such instance when he was clerking, Friendly told him that that was the third time that year that it had happened. Author interview of Davis, Mar. 20, 2007.

63. Author interview of Seipp, May 17, 2010; author interview of Board, Mar. 14, 2007.

64. Henry Friendly, *Benchmarks* (1967), 309.

65. Friendly letter to Michael Boudin, July 2, 1984, HLS-HJF, Box 221, Folder 4.

66. Friendly letter to Posner, Oct. 25, 1985, HLS-HJF, Box 221, Folder 7; see Friendly letter to Posner, Mar. 14, 1983, HLS-HJF, Box 221, Folder 7 ("I think one can find many, many examples of error in Holmes' opinions").

67. Author interview of William Lake, Nov. 29, 2006.

68. Friendly letter to R. Chris Edley, May 4, 1972, HLS-HJF, Box 231, Folder 1. Black and Harlan were the last Supreme Court Justices regarded as great in a poll of two hundred law professors taken in 1998 by Prof. Michael Cominsky. Henry J. Abraham, *Justices and Presidents* (1999), 372. Friendly, who told a friend that Harlan had done better on the Supreme Court than he expected, tended to provide a more generous opinion of people in writing than in person. Richard Posner email to author, Oct. 1, 2010.

69. Friendly letter to Freund, Sept. 7, 1977, HLS-Freund, Box 17, Folder 4. Friendly on occasion joined with clerks and others who awarded particularly incompetent and indefensible High Court opinions with the sobriquet "Shermie," named after Justice Sherman Minton. Friendly letter to A. Raymond Randolph, June 28, 1977, HLS-HJF, Box 210, Folder 27.

70. Friendly letter to Posner, Oct. 25, 1985, HLS-HJF, Box 221, Folder 7. Friendly was ahead of most observers in detecting Brennan's pivotal role. Author interview of Larry Kramer, Apr. 16, 2007; see generally Seth Stern and Stephen Wermiel, *Justice Brennan: Liberal Champion* (2010), 195–324.

71. Henry Friendly, "Reactions of a Lawyer—Newly Become a Judge," 71 *Yale Law Journal* (1961), 218, 235–36. When the article was reprinted in 1967 as part of *Benchmarks* (p. 1), the quoted sentence, along with other criticisms of recent judicial performance, was omitted.

72. Author interview of Posner, Aug. 22, 2007. Friendly respected Lewis F. Powell Jr., although he and Powell were never close, and, for reasons that are not clear, it took him four years before he recommended a clerk to Powell, who hired the clerk. Author interview of Lawrence Pedowitz, Apr. 4, 2007; author interview of Gregory Palm, Apr. 10, 2007. Friendly was very negative on Justice Arthur Goldberg. Friendly letter to Paul Freund, Oct. 26, 1965, HLS-Freund, Box 17, Folder 13; Friendly letter to Erwin Griswold, Feb. 8, 1971, HLS-Griswold, Box 122, Folder 4; author interview of Feldman, Feb. 13, 2007.

73. E.g., "I think your point that legislative history is all too easy a refuge for the judge who is lazy or who is seeking justification for a predetermined result is indeed a sound one. I am doubtless prejudiced, but I thought the Chief Justice's

opinion in Foti v. I.N.S., 375 U.S. 217, 223, a particularly outrageous example." Friendly letter to Prof. William R. Bishkin, Feb. 8, 1964, HLS-HJF, Box 215, Folder 3. The Court reversed Foti v. INS, 308 F.2d 779 (2d Cir. 1962) (Friendly, J.). See Friendly letter to Prof. Napoleon Williams Jr., July 7, 1978, HLS-HJF, Box 230, Folder 3.

74. Author interview of Michael Madow, Feb. 23, 2007; author interview of Raymond B. Ludwiszewski, July 24, 2007.

75. Henry Friendly, "In Memoriam—Roger John Traynor, Ablest Judge of His Generation," 71 *California Law Review* (1983), 1039. Seeing the article, Judge Posner wrote Friendly, "One thing I am sure of, though; as you and Traynor are of the same generation, your statement that he was the ablest judge of his generation is incorrect." HLS-HJF, Box 227, Folder 1.

76. While on the bench, Traynor published forty-four articles or tributes in law reviews or anthologies along with one book, *The Riddle of Harmless Error.* After retiring in 1970 at the age of seventy, he published eighteen additional items in law reviews. Roger J. Traynor, *The Traynor Reader: Nous Verrons* (1987).

77. Holmes published *The Common Law* in 1881, the year before his appointment to the Massachusetts Supreme Judicial Court. Afterward, aside from letters, he wrote a number of articles, most of them published in the *Harvard Law Review.* See Oliver Wendell Holmes Jr., *The Essential Holmes* (Richard A. Posner, ed., 1992), 117, 160, 180, 185, 296. Friendly particularly admired the writing styles of Holmes and Jackson. Friendly letter to Posner, Oct. 25, 1985, HLS-HJF, Box 221, Folder 7.

78. Ben Field, *Activism in the Pursuit of the Public Interest* (2003), 121 (Traynor "was an activist judge in that he departed from precedent in his conception of the public interest"); J. Edward Johnson, "Roger J. Traynor," in *History of the Supreme Court Justices of California,* vol. 2, 1900–1950 (1966), 182–196.

79. Friendly, *Benchmarks,* 311–312.

80. Ibid., 311.

81. Henry Friendly, book review of *The Unpublished Opinions of Mr. Justice Brandeis,* by Alexander M. Bickel, 106 *University of Pennsylvania Law Review* (1958), 766, 767.

82. Friendly letter to Prof. Louis Jaffe, Dec. 4, 1960, HLS-HJF, Box 194, Folder 1.

83. Friendly, *Benchmarks,* 313.

84. Henry Friendly, book review of *Justice Oliver Wendell Holmes—The Proving Years, 1870–1882,* by Mark de Wolfe Howe, *New York Times Book Review Section,* Aug. 11, 1963, *Benchmarks,* 285.

85. Friendly letter to Frankfurter, Aug. 14, 1963, HLS-HJF, Box 188, Folder 13. Twenty years later Friendly commented that the works of Holmes and Cardozo had far less relevance, largely because of the prevalence of statutes. Notes for lecture, "Statutorification of Federal Law," probably late 1981, HLS-HJF, Box 225, Folder 10.

86. Friendly, *Benchmarks,* 315.

87. Ibid., 316.

88. Henry Friendly, book review of *Learned Hand's Court* by Irving Schick, 86 *Political Science Quarterly* (1971), 470, 476; HLS-HP/MS, Box 14, Folder 26, p. 29.

89. Richard A. Posner, *Law and Literature* (2d ed., 1998), 375–376; author interview of Posner, Aug. 22, 2007.

90. Henry M. Hart Jr. and Herbert Wechsler, *The Federal Courts and the Federal System* (1953), 192.

91. 328 U.S. 549 (1946).

92. 369 U.S. 186 (1962).

93. Friendly letter to Frankfurter, Apr. 3, 1962, HLS-HJF, Box 213, Folder 3.

94. *The Path of the Law from 1967* (Arthur E. Sutherland, ed., 1968), 86.

95. Minersville School District v. Gobitis, 310 U.S. 586 (1940).

96. West Virginia Board of Education v. Barnette, 319 U.S. 624 (1943).

97. Norman Dorsen letter to author, Apr. 25, 2007. Friendly was prepared to concede in other contexts that his initial reaction was wrong. He never accepted the reasoning and specificity of Miranda v. Arizona, 384 U.S. 436 (1966), but he admitted that the case did not prove to be the hindrance to police and prosecutors that he had anticipated. Friendly letter to Prof. Yale Kamisar, July 21, 1975, HLS-HJF, Box 230, Folder 5.

98. Wechsler, director of the American Law Institute (1963–84), had argued New York Times Co. v. Sullivan in the Supreme Court and was the author of many influential books and articles.

99. Friendly letter to Gerald T. Dunne, Mar. 23, 1983, HLS-HJF, Box 222, Folder 6. Black turned down all honorary degrees after 1955. Roger K. Newman, *Hugo Black* (1994), 572.

100. Gerald Gunther, *Learned Hand* (1994), 183–189; see Friendly letter to Hand, Mar. 11, 1959 (comparing Hand with Dionysus rather than Zeus), HLS-Hand, Box 88, Folder 19.

8. Away from the Courthouse

1. Author interview of Irene Friendly, May 27, 2007; author interview of Joan Goodman, Oct. 22, 2006.

2. Friendly letter to Louis Lusky, Sept. 6, 1977, HLS-HJF, Box 230, Folder 3; author interview of Goodman, July 18, 2007.

3. Author interview of Michael Boudin, Apr. 7, 2006.

4. Author interview of Irene Friendly, Feb. 8, 2008.

5. Author interview of Pat Hall Mogin, Dec. 9, 2006; *accord,* author interview of Philip Bobbitt, July 3, 2007. Boudin saw the relationship as avuncular and did not accept Mogin's characterization. Boudin resembled Friendly in many ways, including his right-of-center politics, brilliance, disciplined work habits, conscientiousness, extensive knowledge of a broad range of subjects, generally restrained personality, dry wit, and even traces of Old World formality. They talked about intellectual matters, not about Friendly's family and personal matters. Author interview of Michael Boudin, Dec. 11, 2006.

6. Author interview of Stephen Simon, Oct. 28, 2010; see Friendly Memorandum for Judge Moore, Feb. 21, 1961, HLS-HJF, Box 226, Folder 5.

7. Author interview of Simon, Oct. 28, 2010; Joan Goodman email to author, Nov. 29, 2010.

8. Author interview of Simon, Oct. 28, 2010; author interview of Irene Friendly, Oct. 5, 2008; Ellen Simon email to author, Oct. 16, 2010.

9. E.g., Friendly letter to Joan Goodman, May 3, 1961, HLS-HJF, Box 213, Folder 3 (four-page single-spaced letter Friendly sent during the Cuban missile crisis).

10. Author interview of Richard Posner, Aug. 22, 2007.

11. Friendly letter to Joan Goodman, Dec. 20, 1979, JFGC.

12. Friendly letter to Bobbitt, Mar. 5, 1985, HLS-HJF, Box 221, Folder 2.

13. Author interview of Daniel Reznek, July 4, 2010.

14. Author interview of Frank Goodman, July 18, 2007; author interview of grandson David Simon, May 28, 2007.

15. Author interview of Joan Goodman, July 18, 2006; HLS-HJF, Box 224, Folders 1–17, 19; Box 225, Folder 15–19; Box 226, Folders 1–3.

16. Author interview of Pat Mogin, Dec. 9, 2006.

17. The author spoke to ten of the eleven Friendly grandchildren at a family reunion in May 2007.

18. Author interviews of grandchildren Deborah Friendly, Ellen Goodman, Barak Goodman, and Adam Simon, May 27, 2007; author interview of Irene Friendly, May 26, 2008; Friendly letter to Judge Scovel Richardson, Apr. 18, 1979 (in support of David Simon), HLS-HJF, Box 219, Folder 4.

19. Author interview of grandson Daniel Simon, May 28, 2007.

20. Friendly letter to Ellen Goodman, Oct. 15, 1985. Copy in possession of author.

21. Author interview of Doris Wechsler, Jan. 29, 2008; author interview of Joan Goodman, July 18, 2007. The Wechslers and the Friendlys went out to dinner and to the theater together.

22. Author telephone interview of Alice Henkin, Mar. 26, 2010.

23. Author interview of Judge Sofaer, Apr. 16, 2007; author telephone interview of Alice Henkin, Mar. 26, 2010; author telephone interview of Judge Conner, Apr. 22, 2007.

24. Remarks on the Unveiling of a Portrait of Judge Reuben Oppenheimer (undated), HLS-HJF, Box 206, Folder 3.

25. Natalie Brooks Friendly, *The Friendly Family* (1998) 131, 163.

26. Friendly letter to Solicitor General Archibald Cox, May 19, 1964, HLS-HJF, Box 22, Folder 14. Friendly wrote the letter in response to an objection to his sitting on a case involving CBS.

27. Friendly would read the 250-page volume in one evening. Author interview of Stuart Stock, Dec. 1, 2006; Friendly letter to Posner, Aug. 27, 1982, HLS-HJF, Box 221, Folder 7.

28. 87 *Political Science Quarterly* (1972), 439.

29. Author telephone interview of Kathleen (Kit) Wisdom, July 7, 2008; *accord,* Pat Mogin letter to Joan Goodman, Mar. 21, 1986; author interview of Joan Weiss (first cousin of Sophie Friendly), June 7, 2007.

30. Author interview of Irene Friendly, Aug. 30, 2009.

31. Friendly letter to H. L. A. Hart, Oct. 30, 1964, HLS-HJF, Box 211, Folder 13; Friendly letter to Justice Byron R. White, Sept. 17, 1976, HLS-HJF, Box 230, Folder 3.

32. HLS-HJF, Box 217, Folder 2. Clerks noted Friendly's broad intellectual curiosity. E.g., author interview of Jonathan Macey, Apr. 21, 2008.

33. Author interview of Posner, Aug. 22, 2007.

34. Author interview of Donald Board, Mar. 14, 2007.

35. While a judge he served on the boards of the National Society for the Prevention of Blindness and the Tebil Foundation, private foundations headed by his friend William K. Jacobs Jr. HLS-HJF, Box 228, Folder 3. Lawrence Wien letter to Friendly, June 22, 1960; Friendly letter to Wien, June 24, 1960, HLS-HJF, Box 195, Folder 1.

36. COH, Tape 8, Side 1, pp. 7–9; Friendly letter to Melvin C. Steen, Apr. 2, 1975, HLS-HJF, Box 222, Folder 1.

37. HLS-HJF, Box 226, Folder 14. For example, on February 9, 1959, Friendly contributed $10,000 out of a goal of $35,000 to the University of Pennsylvania Law School to name a dining commons after his father-in-law, Chief Justice Horace Stern. HLS-HJF, Box 87, Folder 5. A few months earlier he created an $800 tuition scholarship at Harvard Law School. HLS-HJS, Box 192, Folder 4. He gave $1,000 to the United Jewish Appeal in 1983. HLS-HJF, Box 220, Folder 7.

38. Kristen David Adams, "Blaming the Mirror: The Restatement and Common Law," 40 *Indiana Law Review* (2007), 205; Herbert F. Goodrich, "Judge Learned Hand and the Work of the American Law Institute," 60 *Harvard Law Review* (1947), 345.

39. John Minor Wisdom, "Views of a Friendly Observer," 133 *University of Pennsylvania Law Review* (1984), 63–64.

40. Author interview of Geoffrey Hazard, Apr. 14, 2007.

41. Author telephone interview of Yale Kamisar, Dec. 12, 2010.

42. Rosewell Perkins, "The President's Letter," *ALI Reporter*, Vol. 8, No. 3 (April 1986).

43. Author interview of Monty Gray, Nov. 2, 2007.

44. HLS-HJF, Box 195, Folders 1, 7; Box 211, Folders 8, 9. Friendly served, for example, on visiting committees to the university's history department and the Harvard University Press, sometimes as chairman, and as chairman of the Special Overseers Committee on Restructuring the University. HLS-HJS, Box 195, Folders 1–3; Box 196, Folder 4; Box 197, Folders 1–4, 8. He also was on visiting committees to the University of Chicago and Case Western Law Schools. HLS-HJF, Box 216, Folder 10; Box 222, Folder 12; author interview of former Harvard President Derek C. Bok, Apr. 23, 2009.

45. Friendly letter to Pusey, Feb. 17, 1964, HLS-HJF, Box 196, Folder 2. Friendly acted boldly in other Harvard activities. He wrote Michael Boudin, "Thanks for sending me the copy of President Bok's speech. He is quite right that I turned the practices of the Visiting Committee on their head." Friendly letter to Boudin, June 18, 1979, HLS-HJF, Box 219, Folder 4.

46. Friendly previously had read Aristotle, Santayana, Ludwig Wittgenstein, and Alfred North Whitehead. Henry Friendly, *Commonplace Book*, JFGC.

47. HLS-HJF, Box 195, Folders, 3, 6–12; Box 196, Folders 1–3; Box 196, Folders 4–8; Box 197, Folders 1–4, 8; Box 198, Folders 2, 15; Box 211, Folders 8, 9; Box 215, Folders 5, 6.

48. E.g., Friendly letter to Judge Paul Reardon, Nov. 1, 1963, HLS-HJF, Box 196, Folder 2.

49. Author telephone interview of Judge Morris Lasker, June 12, 2007; author interview of Joan Goodman, Oct. 22, 2006.

50. Author telephone interview of Poindexter, Mar. 19, 2010; author interview of Louis Kaplow, Nov. 14, 2006.

51. COH, Tape 8, Side 2, p. 1.

52. *New York Times*, Sept. 19, 1969, pp. 1, 28.

53. Joan Goodman email to author, June 20, 2009.

54. Author interview of Pat Mogin, Dec. 9, 2006.

55. Author interview of Millard Midonick, July 31, 2007; author interview of Louis Pollak, Nov. 19, 2007; author telephone interview of Michael Stern, Aug. 14, 2006; author telephone interview of Ernst Rubenstein, Mar. 18, 2008; HLS-HJF, Box 159, Folder 1.

56. Friendly wrote the foreword to Bernard Schwartz and H. W. R. Wade, *Legal Control of Government: Administrative Law in Britain and the United States* (1972), xv–xvi.

57. Friendly eightieth birthday party scrapbook, HLS-HJF, Box 235.

58. "Itinerary—Summer 1970," HLS-HJF, Box 226, Folder 1.

59. "I think we have covered every country in Europe this side of the Iron Curtain, some of them pretty thoroughly." Friendly Mem. for Judge Moore, Feb. 21, 1961, HLS-HJF, Box 226, Folder 5.

60. HLS-HJF, Box 205, Folder 2.

61. Friendly letter to Joan Goodman, Mar. 4, 1977.

62. HLS-HJF, Box 97, Folder 11.

63. Friendly letter to Richard Moore, Sept. 13, 1966, HLS-HJF, Box 97, Folder 1.

64. Author interview of Joan Goodman, July 18, 2007.

65. HLS-HJF, Box 224, Folders 18, 20.

66. Friendly undated memorandum for clerks and secretary, marked "rec'd 3/13/70." Courtesy of Judge Randolph.

67. Dennis Hutchinson, *The Man Who Was Once Wizzer White* (1998), 314–315. Forty-five years later Sorenson had no recollection of the list or of any consideration of Friendly. Author telephone interview of Sorenson, June 26, 2008. Newspapers gave Friendly some coverage as a candidate. *Washington Post*, Mar. 30, 1962, p. 1.

68. Bruce Allen Murphy, *Fortas* (1988), 175–181; Henry J. Abraham, *Justices, Presidents, and Senators* (1999), 214–215.

69. Nixon White House Tape, Oct. 19, 1971, Conversation 596-3, Nixon Project, Archives 2, College Park, Md.

70. FTD, Tape 4, pp. 34–35; *Baltimore Sun*, May 16, 1969; *Time*, Nov. 29, 1968.

71. *New York Times*, May 23, 1969, p. 26.

72. Friendly letter to Wyzanski, Jan. 31, 1983, HLS-HJF, Box 220, Folder 4. Friendly specifically cited "speaking at bar association meetings, maintaining contacts with Congress, and being a big wheel in Washington social life."

73. FTD, Tape 4, p. 35; Friendly letter to Wyzanski, Jan. 31, 1983, HLS-HJF, Box 220, Folder 4. Sophie Friendly was strongly against moving from New York City for any reason. Joan Goodman email to author, July 1, 2009.

74. 37 *University of Cincinnati Law Review* (1968), 671.

75. Friendly letter to Annenberg, Nov. 25, 1968, HLS-HJF, Box 225, Folder 9. Friendly's proposal received coverage, including a column in the *New York Times*, Nov. 10, 1968, p. 73.

76. *New York Daily News*, Aug. 13, 1969, p. 20; see, e.g., *New York Times*, May 23, 1969, pp. 1, 26 (Friendly mentioned "in speculation"); *New York Times*, Nov. 29, 1969 (Friendly one of eight persons mentioned).

77. John W. Dean, *The Rehnquist Choice* (2001), 15; Richard Kleindienst, *Justice; The Memoirs of an Attorney General* (1985), 116.

78. John P. Frank, *Clement Haynsworth, the Senate, and the Supreme Court* (1991), 75.

79. Dean, *Rehnquist Choice*, xiii–xiv, lists the thirty-six candidates considered; *accord*, author interview of Dean, Apr. 1, 2010.

80. Friendly letter to Wyzanski, Jan. 31, 1983, HLS-HJF, Box 220, Folder 4; author interview of Robert Weiner, Nov. 9, 2006. When asked about his non-appointment to the Supreme Court, Friendly said that because he and Justice John Harlan had been law partners, he did not expect to be appointed, a curious response, especially since the two had not been law partners for fifteen years. Author interview of Raymond Ludwiszewski, July 24, 2007.

81. Dean, *Rehnquist Choice*, 116.

82. Ibid., 14–15, 52, 153; see Natalie Brooks Friendly, *The Friendly Family* (1998), 184 ("Many people felt he was not appointed because of President Nixon's anti-Semitism").

9. First Amendment

1. Only one question of six, involving a prosecution under a New York statute that made it a crime for any citizen of New York to assist in obtaining an annulment of a New York marriage by a foreign "ecclesiastical organization," included Bill of Rights issues.

2. FTD, Tape 4, p. 47.

3. Robert H. Bork, *The Tempting of America* (1989), 143–145, 154–155 ("All that counts is how the words used in the Constitution would have been used at the time").

4. "Congress shall make no law respecting an establishment of religion, or prohibiting the free exercise thereof; or abridging the freedom of speech, or of the press; or the right of the people peaceably to assemble, and to petition the Government for a redress of grievances."

5. Henry Friendly, "Time and Tide in the Supreme Court," 2 *Connecticut Law Review* (1969), 213.

6. Ibid., 216–217. He also opposed "emasculat[ing] the Court's appellate jurisdiction as was seriously contemplated by Congress in 1968" and Congress's passing statutes "flouting" the Court's constitutional decisions.

7. Cf. Norman Dorsen and Joel Gora, "The Burger Court and the Freedom of Speech," in *The Burger Court* (Vincent Blasi, ed., 1983), 28–45 (free-speech opinions of Burger Court favored property interests). Another example is administrative agencies, a subject discussed in Chapter 20.

8. 299 F. Supp. 117 (S.D.N.Y. 1969), *aff'd*, 401 U.S. 154 (1971).

9. Konigsberg v. State Board of California, 353 U.S. 252 (1957).

10. Author interviews of Prof. Norman Dorsen, Oct. 18, 2006, Nov. 17, 2010, who argued the case on behalf of the bar applicants in the Supreme Court.

11. Shortly after the lawsuit was filed, New York deleted from its questionnaire a number of especially invasive questions, including to provide "any favorable or unfavorable incidents in your life . . . not called for by the questions contained in this questionnaire or disclosed in your answers thereto." 299 F. Supp. at 137–139 (Motley, J., dissenting).

12. Ibid., 131–132; *accord*, 133 ("Counsel for the character committees emphasized at oral argument that 'these State Courts are not stiff-necked about this thing' ").

13. Ibid., 146.

14. 401 U.S. 154, 157 (1971) (Stewart, J.).

15. Ibid., 174, 185.

16. 447 F.2d 245 (2d Cir. 1971). Judge Hays joined Friendly's opinion; Judge Oakes dissented.

17. App. 307a; 447 F.2d at 246–249. Some other members of the band were transferred to bases elsewhere in the United States or to Vietnam or Korea.

18. 10 U.S.C. § 938.

19. 447 F.2d at 249–250.

20. Cortright v. Resor, 325 F. Supp. 797 (E.D.N.Y. 1971).

21. Ibid., 806.

22. 447 F.2d at 252. Weinstein considered Cortright's fiancée quite independent and more extreme on the war than Cortright. Author interview of Judge Weinstein, Aug. 23, 2006.

23. 447 F.2d at 252 (emphasis added). A dictionary in wide use at the time gives a definition of "sanction" as "solemn or ceremonious ratification; confirmation; approbation." Merriam-Webster, *Webster's New Collegiate Dictionary* 748 (1961). The word seems to require an affirmative manifestation of approval.

24. 447 F.2d at 252 and n.7.

25. 345 U.S. 83 (1953).

26. 447 F.2d at 254, quoting 345 U.S. at 94. Friendly quoted Chief Justice Earl Warren: "So far as the relationship of the military to its own personnel is concerned, the basic attitude of the Court has been that the latter's jurisdiction is most limited." Earl Warren, "The Bill of Rights and the Military," 37 *New York University Law Review* (1962), 181, 186.

27. 447 F.2d at 252, quoting Thomas I. Emerson, "Toward a General Theory of the First Amendment," 72 *Yale Law Journal* (1963), 877, 936.

28. 447 F.2d at 253.
29. Ibid., 254–255.
30. Ibid., 255–256 (Oakes, J., dissenting).
31. Case Note, 26 *Rutgers Law Review* (1973), 290, 317–318.
32. App. 195a–197a (testimony of David Cortright); *accord*, App. 302a–305a, 309a (testimony of Monica Emily Cortright); author telephone interview of Cortright, Aug. 29, 2006.
33. App. 370a–372a (emphasis added), an admission that the Army lacked evidence.
34. Ibid.
35. App. 199a (testimony of David Cortright). While Flores's statement could not bind the Army, see Schweiker v. Hansen, 450 U.S. 785 (1981) (low-level government employee can not bind the United States), *rev'g* Hansen v. Harris, 619 F.2d 942, 949 (2d Cir. 1980) (Friendly, J., dissenting), government counsel raised no objection to the testimony. App. 197a–199a.
36. Interview of Weinstein, Aug. 23, 2006; App. 299a; see Brief for Appellees, 7. Gen. Higgins's deposition, which was introduced into evidence at the trial, did not cover Cortright's transfer.
37. Friendly Mem., Aug. 16, 1971, from Garmisch, Germany, HLS-HJF, Box 58, File 8.
38. Chemical Transporter Inc. v. Reading Co., 426 F.2d 436, 439 (2d Cir. 1970) (Friendly, J., dissenting) ("I fear this is another case like [M. P. Howlett, Inc. v. Tug Michael Moran, 425 F.2d 619, 624 (2d Cir. 1970) (Friendly, J., dissenting)], where appellate judges are whetting their appetite for dealing with facts rather than leaving these to the district judge who saw and heard the witnesses"); Friendly Voting Mem., Apr. 15, 1960, HLS-HJF, Box 2, Folder 2 ("This is the kind of case that makes one want to give rousing cheers for the clearly erroneous rule"), in Tide-Water Pipe Co. v. The Crest, 278 F.2d 489 (2d Cir. 1960).
39. Weinstein considers Friendly to have been "a scrupulous judge who wanted to keep the First Amendment on track," adding that Friendly did not want to assist Cortright and his fiancée, but also wanted to make sure that his opinion had little value as a precedent limiting freedom of speech, which could account for his taking uncharacteristic liberties with the facts on appellate review. Author interview of Weinstein, Aug. 23, 2006.
40. Brief for Appellants, 25.
41. The government's brief identified only one finding as clearly erroneous: "The court below observed that Cortright's transfer had some financial impact and implicitly held that the $10,000 [jurisdictional] requirements [*sic*] was satisfied (App. 520a). This finding is clearly erroneous." Brief for Appellant, 25. It is also arguable that this was not a finding of fact.
42. Friendly Voting Mem., Dec. 3, 1985, HLS-HJF, Box 127, Folder 22, in Mitsui & Co. (USA) v. Hudson Tank Terminals Corp., 790 F.2d 226 (2d Cir. 1986).
43. Cortright completed his tour of duty in Fort Bliss, Texas, where he did pretty much as he wanted; his superiors were afraid of him. Author telephone interview of David Cortright, Aug. 29, 2006.

44. 376 U.S. 254 (1964).
45. Pauling v. News Syndicate Co., 335 F.2d 659, 671 (2d Cir. 1964).
46. The newspaper, which had not raised the *Sullivan* argument in its brief, did not seek leave to file a supplemental brief on the constitutional status of public figures.
47. 388 U.S. 130 (1967).
48. Buckley v. New York Post Corp., 373 F.2d 175, 182–183 (2d Cir. 1967).
49. 465 U.S. 783 (1984).
50. 373 F.2d at 182. Friendly's statement reflects not only Legal Realism but the later, and more extreme, Critical Legal Studies.
51. 639 F.2d 54 (2d Cir. 1980).
52. Cianci v. New Times Publishing Co., 486 F. Supp. 368, 372–374 (S.D.N.Y. 1979).
53. Recording of oral argument in Cianci v. New Times Pub. Co., Dkt. 80–7030, U.S. Archives. Without exaggeration Friendly called the briefs and arguments "wretched." Friendly Mem., May 30, 1980. Cianci (who did not attend the oral argument) thought he was well represented in the case. Author telephone interview of Cianci, Feb. 21, 2011.
54. Plaintiff's brief argued only a narrower point, namely, that nothing in the article indicated that the statements were the publication's opinion. Brief for Appellant, 2, 34.
55. 639 F.2d at 61–62.
56. Ibid., 64. Cianci settled the case with the defunct magazine for $8,500 plus a letter of apology. Mike Stanton, The *Prince of Providence: The True Story of Buddy Cianci, America's Most Notorious Mayor, Some Wiseguys and the Fed* (2003), 121. Friendly also cited Humpty Dumpty in New York State Comm'n on Cable Television v. FCC, 571 F.2d 95, 100 (2d Cir 1978) (Friendly, J, dissenting). Since the Supreme Court has quoted Lewis Carroll only twice—TVA v. Hill, 437 U.S. 153, 173 n.18 (1978); Zschernig v. Miller, 389 U.S. 429, 435 n.6 (1968)—Friendly relied on that linguistic authority as many times as did the Supreme Court in the history of the Republic.
57. Stanton, *Prince of Providence*. Cianci is now a radio talk show host and has published a book, Vincent Cianci Jr., *Politics and Pasta* (2011).
58. 497 U.S. 1 (1990) (Rehnquist, J.).
59. Ibid., 19.
60. 404 F.2d 196 (2d Cir. 1968).
61. 19 U.S.C. § 1305.
62. These were criteria announced by the Supreme Court in A Book Named "John Cleland's Memoirs of a Woman of Pleasure" v. Attorney General of Massachusetts, 383 U.S. 413 (1966). Hays's description of the movie seems more accurate than Lumbard's.
63. 404 F.2d at 202–204.
64. 354 U.S. 476, 489 (1957).
65. 404 F.2d at 200.
66. Ibid., 200–201. Neither party's brief referred to a nexus between the redeeming material and the remainder of the movie.

67. Citing Ginzburg v. New York, 390 U.S. 629 (1968).
68. 404 F.2d at 202.
69. Friendly Voting Mem., July 24, 1968, HLS-HJF, Box 38, Folder 32.
70. Friendly letter to Prof. Louis Henkin, Apr. 15, 1963, HLS-HJF, Box 95, Folder 12.
71. For example, the same people, including G. Gordon Liddy and E. Howard Hunt, who burglarized the psychiatrist of Daniel Ellsberg, who had leaked the documents, also burglarized the offices of the Democratic National Committee in the Watergate office complex in Washington, D.C.
72. Excellent accounts of the *Pentagon Papers Case* are David Rudenstine, *The Day the Presses Stopped* (1996), and Floyd Abrams, *Speaking Freely* (2005), 1–61.
73. Author telephone interview of Michael Hess, Nov. 7, 2007. The government had refused to tell Seymour and Hess which documents threatened national security on the ground that the information was classified. Rudenstine, *Presses Stopped,* 116.
74. United States v. New York Times Co., 328 F. Supp. 324, 330 (S.D.N.Y. 1971); James L. Oakes, "Judge Gurfein and the Pentagon Papers," 2 *Cardozo Law Review* (1980), 5; Rudenstine, *Presses Stopped*, 177–181.
75. The district judge was Gerhard A. Gesell, an experienced judge who in the late 1930s had worked with Friendly on Pan American matters at Root, Clark.
76. 18 U.S.C. § 793(e). Since the Espionage Act was a criminal statute, the government was arguing that it contained the basis for an implied civil action for an injunction against the press.
77. 283 U.S. 697 (1931).
78. Ibid., 716.
79. Author interview of Judge Wilfred Feinberg, June 30, 2010; Judge Guido Calabresi email to author, Feb. 3, 2010. Friendly preferred to write the term "in banc."
80. Transcript, 4–24 (June 22, 1971).
81. Ibid., 21.
82. See United States v. A Motion Picture Entitled "I Am Curious-Yellow," 404 F.2d 196 (2d Cir. 1968); see Ruby v. American Airlines, Inc., 329 F.2d 11, 22–25 (2d Cir. 1964) (Friendly, J., dissenting) (de novo review required when factual finding is infused with legal issue), *vacated sub nom.*, O'Connell v. Manning, 381 U.S. 277 (1965).
83. Bickel was an apostle of judicial restraint. E.g., Alexander M. Bickel, *The Supreme Court and the Idea of Progress* (1970), 175 ("For all these reasons, [the judicial process] is, in a vast, complex, changeable society, a most unsuitable instrument for the formulation of policy"). Friendly wrote Bickel, "I have just finished [the book] and am consumed by admiration." Friendly letter to Bickel, Mar. 11, 1970, Bickel Papers, Yale University Library, Box 3, Folder 58. As explained by Second Circuit Judge Guido Calabresi, then a friend and colleague of Bickel's on Yale's Law School faculty, Friendly did not want Bickel to represent the *New York Times* in the Supreme Court because of his concern that his doing so would doom his chances for appointment to that Court, and

he wanted Bickel to become a Justice. Bickel informed Calabresi that people in the Nixon administration told him that if he turned down the case, he would get on the Supreme Court. But Bickel decided that it would not be consistent with his principles to refuse to take the case for that reason. Author interview of Calabresi, Mar. 21, 2008. Bickel, who died prematurely in 1974, was the same age as William Rehnquist.

84. Transcript, 38–39, June 22, 1971. Embezzlement is the crime when the initial receipt was lawful, as Daniel Ellsberg's receipt of the Pentagon Papers may have been. Bickel appears to have been basing his argument on the formal record of the case, which apparently included nothing about the *Times'* source for the Pentagon Papers. Ignoring the historical facts, however, was a difficult position to sustain in a case of such prominence.

85. Author interview of Hess, Aug. 23, 2006; author interview of Anthony Lewis, Nov. 11, 2007.

86. Abrams, *Speaking Freely*, 32–33; Abrams emails to author, May 13, 2009, Mar. 12, 2010; Transcript, 47, 70.

87. Transcript, 40–41.

88. The court gave the ACLU five minutes to argue on behalf of the *New York Times*. Ibid., 73–77.

89. Ibid., 23.

90. Ibid., 44–45. That, however, was exactly what happened for over a day. Since the Pentagon Papers stopped with the inauguration of President Nixon, he was inclined to let the *Times* trash his Democratic predecessors, although Seymour did not know that at the time. Rudenstine, *Presses Stopped*, 71–76.

91. Transcript, 45–46.

92. Author interview of Walter Hellerstein, June 21, 2007; author telephone interview of Hellerstein, Mar. 11, 2011.

93. The author expresses his gratitude to Judge Feinberg.

94. Judge Kaufman Mem., June 23, 1971.

95. Mansfield Mem, June 23, 1971. Smith employed similar language, and Lumbard agreed by implication.

96. Judge Feinberg letter to author, July 12, 2010.

97. United States v. New York Times Co., 444 F.2d 544 (2d Cir. 1971) (*en banc*) (*per curiam*). Friendly, Lumbard, Smith, Hays, and Mansfield signed the order; Kaufman, Feinberg, and Oakes noted their dissent.

98. Rudenstine, *Presses Stopped*, 237–238.

99. HLS-HJF, Box 56, Folder 14.

100. For example, it left blanks for a citation and a quotation.

101. Friendly spent a page and a half discussing the history and operation of the government's declassification procedure.

102. After his wife died in March 1985, Friendly's grandson, Barak Goodman, who was studying journalism as a graduate student at Columbia University, visited him weekly. On one visit he asked his grandfather about a comment made by the columnist Anthony Lewis in the *New York Times* that Friendly had voted the "wrong" way in the *Pentagon Papers* case. Friendly replied that he felt that he had no choice but to vote that way. The *Times* was obviously right, he

indicated, but it was up to the Supreme Court to make that decision. Author interview of Barak Goodman, May 26, 2007.

103. Interviews of Hellerstein, June 21, 2007, Mar. 11, 2011, whose handwritten editing appears on the document. Hellerstein's initial description preceded the author's locating the document.

104. Feinberg letters to author, Apr. 12, 2011, Apr. 15, 2011.

105. Another casual statement follows Friendly's reference to the government's classification system: "The briefs do not inform us how far back this goes; some of us can testify from personal experience that it antedates World War II."

106. Friendly also expressed concern about reading the secret material contained in the parties' appendixes. Interviews of Hellerstein, June 21, 2007, Mar. 11, 2011.

107. Friendly wrote "Espionate [*sic*] Act" in one place and quoted Gesell as stating that "'even a momentous [should be moment's] delay' in publication would have serious consequences."

108. Interviews of Hellerstein, June 21, 2007, Mar. 11, 2011. Canon 17 of the ABA Canons of Judicial Ethics, promulgated in 1924 and not replaced until August 1972 (1973 in the federal courts), on its face did not apply to Friendly, but did to Harlan: a judge "shall not permit private interviews or communications designed to influence his judicial actions, where interests to be affected thereby are not represented before him." The subsequent Canon 3.A(4) of the ABA Model Code of Judicial Conduct (adopted by the ABA in 1972 and by the Judicial Conference of the United States in 1973), reads more broadly: "A judge should . . . neither initiate nor consider *ex parte* or other communications concerning a pending or impending proceeding."

109. New York Times Co. v. United States, 403 U.S. 713 (1971).

110. Ibid., 752–753, 755–756.

111. Author telephone interview of Monty Gray, Mar. 17, 2011 (the Harlan clerk assigned to the case); author telephone interview of Thomas G. Krattenmaker, Mar. 21, 2011 (other Harlan clerk). Gray had clerked for Friendly the preceding year.

112. John Marshall Harlan Papers, MC071, Boxes 440, 537, Seeley G. Mudd Manuscript Library, Princeton University.

113. 370 U.S. 421 (1962).

114. The "Regents' Prayer" was a prayer created by the Board of Regents of the State of New York.

115. Stein v. Oshinsky, 348 F.2d 999, 1001–1002 (2d Cir. 1965), *rev'g* 224 F. Supp. 757 (E.D.N.Y. 1963).

116. 484 F.2d 1348 (2d Cir. 1973) (*per curiam*).

117. Friendly Voting Mem., Sept. 13, 1973, HLS-HJF, Box 70, Folder 5.

118. 484 F.2d at 1350. The case is not on Friendly's list of *per curiam* opinions he authored.

119. 739 F.2d 48 (2d Cir. 1984), *aff'd,* 473 U.S. 402 (1985).

120. Ibid., 49–50.

121. Ibid., 64.
122. Author interview of Frank Goodman, Sept. 29, 2009. Board, Friendly's law clerk at the time, described him as "hyper-concerned with the separation of church and state." Author interview of Donald Board, Mar. 14, 2007.
123. 421 U.S. 349, 369 (1975).
124. Friendly letter to Posner, Oct. 11, 1984, HLS-HJF, Box 98, Folder 19; see Friendly letter, July 16, 1985, to Donald Board, HLS-HJF, Box 221, Folder 6. One scholar called Friendly's opinion "masterful." Norman Redlich, "Separation of Church and State," in *The Burger Years* (Herman Schwartz, ed., 1987), 87.
125. 473 U.S. 402, 406 (1985). During the post-argument conference, several Justices praised Friendly's opinion. Bernard Schwartz, *The Ascent of Pragmatism* (1990), 199.
126. School District of Grand Rapids v. Ball, 473 U.S. 373 (1985).
127. *Aguilar*, 473 U.S. at 420–421 (Rehnquist, J., dissenting).
128. Agostini v. Felton, 521 U.S. 209 (1997).
129. Ibid., 234, 237.

10. Fifth Amendment

1. Henry Friendly, "The Bill of Rights as a Code of Criminal Procedure," *Benchmarks* (1967), 235.
2. 377 U.S. 201 (1964).
3. 378 U.S. 478 (1964).
4. 384 U.S. 436 (1966).
5. Friendly, *Benchmarks*, 236–237, 242–243.
6. Ibid., 271–274.
7. E.g., ibid., 245–246, 247, 251–253.
8. Henry Friendly, "Time and Tide in the Supreme Court," 2 *Connecticut Law Review* (1969), 213, 216.
9. Friendly, *Benchmarks,* 237
10. Friendly letter to Bickel, Mar. 11, 1970, Yale-Bickel, Box 3, Folder 58. He also wrote, "The Court disserves its great role as vindicator of the Bill of Rights when it constructs from plainly inadequate data a generalization refuted by the common experience of mankind." Friendly, *Benchmarks*, 273.
11. Yale Kamisar, "A Look Back on a Half-Century of Teaching, Writing and Speaking about Criminal Law and Criminal Procedure," 2 *Ohio State Journal of Criminal Law* (2004), 69, 87.
12. LOC, Frankfurter Collection, Part 3, Reel 34.
13. Ibid.
14. Friendly, *Benchmarks*, 263; Friendly letter to Prof. Arnold N. Enker, Dec. 22, 1964, HLS-HJF, Box 211, Folder 14.
15. The lecture was after *Massiah* and *Escobedo* but before *Miranda*.
16. Friendly applied this reasoning to vote for affirming a conviction for espionage, United States v. Drummond, 354 F.2d 132, 155 (2d Cir. 1965) (*en banc*)

(Friendly, J. concurring), where federal agents refused to allow the suspect to telephone his wife and lawyer in the course of a three-hour interrogation. He relied on the "interests of society."

17. Friendly, *Benchmarks*, 254–255. Friendly supported the requirement of assigned counsel, mandated by Gideon v. Wainright, 372 U.S. 335 (1963), on the basis of the Fifth Amendment's Due Process Clause, not the Sixth Amendment's right to counsel. *Benchmarks,* 253–254.

18. Friendly, *Benchmarks*, 258–259.

19. Friendly letter to Sofaer, Jan. 19, 1966, HLS-HJF, Box 219, Folder 1; see Friendly, *Benchmarks*, 251–259. More than a decade later Friendly stated, "I must say I am getting a little sick of the term 'public interest' lawyers. These lawyers do not represent the public but rather their clients or, more often, themselves. I do not see why it is necessarily in the public interest to give the broadest possible interpretation to a provision of the Social Security Act or, for that matter, to the Fourth Amendment. Still less do I understand why all-out opposition to nuclear energy is in the public interest; many well informed people think just the contrary. When the lights go out in 1999 I do not think opponents of nuclear energy will be very popular." Friendly letter to Judge James Oakes, Sept. 23, 1977, HLS-HJF, Box 230, Folder 3.

20. Henry Friendly, "A Postscript on Miranda," *Benchmarks*, 273.

21. Friendly letter to Prof. Alexander Bickel, June 6, 1966, HLS-HJF, Box 217, Folder 3. Enforcing that distinction could prove difficult.

22. The latter concept dates to colonial times. See Leonard W. Levy, *Origins of the Bill of Rights* (1999), 200–201.

23. Friendly letter to Prof. Paul Bator, May 23, 1966, HLS-HJF, Box 215, Folder 2.

24. Schmerber v. California, 384 U.S. 757 (1966); Breithaupt v. Abram, 352 U.S. 432 (1957); Friendly, *Benchmarks*, 276.

25. Friendly, "A Postscript on Miranda," *Benchmarks*, 266.

26. Yale Kamisar, "On the 'Fruits' of Miranda Violations, Coerced Confessions, and Compelled Testimony," 93 *Michigan Law Review* (1995), 929, 977–980.

27. Friendly, *Benchmarks*, 281–282.

28. Ibid., 280, quoted by Justice O'Connor in New York v. Quarles, 467 U.S. 649, 671 (1984) (O'Connor, J., concurring in part and dissenting in part).

29. Friendly, *Benchmarks*, 277; see Akhil Reed Amar, *The Constitution and Criminal Procedure* (1997), 63–65.

30. Kamisar, "On the Fruits," 977–980.

31. Kamisar, "A Look Back," 87.

32. See Friendly, *Benchmarks*, 282.

33. For Kamisar, a *Miranda* violation produced a coerced confession and was not a technical violation, as Friendly seemed to contend. Author telephone interview of Kamisar, Dec. 2, 2010; Kamisar email to author, Dec. 6, 2010. In any event, *Miranda* had to be a constitutional ruling.

34. The address, the 1968 Robert S. Marx Lectures at the University of Cincinnati Law School, was published as Henry Friendly, "The Fifth Amendment Tomorrow: The Case for Constitutional Change," 37 *University of Cincinnati Law Review* (1968), 671, 712, 721–722. Friendly's proposed version of the Fifth

Amendment dealt with the issues specifically. The proposal generated some media comment, including an editorial in the conservative *New York Daily News*, which, while sympathizing with Friendly's goals, characterized his amendment as "windy." *New York Daily News*, Nov. 18, 1968.

35. Friendly, "Fifth Amendment," 671–672. Friendly collected many comments antagonistic to a broad reading of the Self-incrimination Clause (672–674).

36. Ibid., 680–681. Friendly also maintained that "the privilege against self-incrimination is a subject for rational discussion and a fair balancing of state and individual interests and not a fetish requiring blind and unthinking worship and extension to the furthest possible bounds." Friendly notes for speech (1969), HLS-HJF, Box 225, Folder 11.

37. Friendly, "Fifth Amendment," 689.

38. 116 U.S. 616, 631–632 (1886).

39. Friendly, "Fifth Amendment," 702.

40. Ibid., 683–695, 702, 722.

41. Ibid., 703. Friendly briefly discussed requiring production but barring the government from using the act of production as evidence: "The prosecution wants the chattels, typically documents; it will find its own way for authenticating them" (702).

42. Ibid., 696–697.

43. E.g., *New York Times*, Dec. 8, 1968 (article by Sidney Zion); see Friendly letter to Annenberg, Nov. 25, 1968, HLS-HJF, Box 225, Folder 9.

44. United States v. Beattie, 522 F.2d 267, 270–271, 276 (2d Cir. 1976), *vacated*, 425 U.S. 967 (1976).

45. Brief for the United States, 24.

46. 425 U.S. 391, 397 (1976).

47. Ibid., 411, 413 and n.12. The Supreme Court relied on three Friendly opinions, referring to him by name each time: *Beattie*; *In re* Horowitz, 482 F.2d 72, 75–80 (2d Cir. 1973); and United States v. Bennett, 409 F.2d 888, 897 (2d Cir. 1969).

48. 425 U.S. 967 (1976).

49. 467 U.S. 649 (1984).

50. Ibid., 668 and n.3, 671, 673 (O'Connor, J., concurring). O'Connor cited Friendly, "The Bill of Rights as a Code of Criminal Procedure" and "A Postscript on Miranda," *Benchmarks*, 235, 260, 266, 279–282.

51. 470 U.S. 298 (1985) (O'Connor, J.); see United States v. Patane, 542 U.S. 630 (2004).

52. 711 F.2d 1187 (2d Cir. 1983).

53. Ibid., 1197 (Friendly, J. dissenting).

54. Ibid., 1194–1199.

55. 397 U.S. 254, 262 (1970).

56. Ibid., 262, 267–271. Welfare was once treated as a privilege. Bernard Schwartz, *Administrative Law* (1994), 412–418.

57. 123 *University of Pennsylvania Law Review* (1975), 1267.

58. 397 U.S. at 269 ("In almost every setting where important decisions turn on questions of fact, due process requires an opportunity to confront and

cross-examine adverse witnesses," citing, *inter alia,* an Interstate Commerce Commission case).

59. Friendly, "Hearing," 1268.
60. E.g., Wolff v. McDonnell, 418 U.S. 539, 557–558 (1974) (Stewart, J.) (employing the term "some kind of hearing").
61. Friendly, "Hearing," 1295–1296.
62. Friendly letter to Kenneth Culp Davis, Oct. 14, 1975, HLS-HJF, Box 204, Folder 10.
63. Friendly, "Hearing," 1269 and n.10. This point continued to concern Friendly. Henry Friendly, foreword to Bernard Schwartz and H. W. R. Wade, *Legal Control of Government: Administrative Law in Britain and the United States* (1972), xvii–xviii; Statement of Friendly before Committee on Governmental Affairs, U.S. Senate, May 16, 1979, HLS-HJF, Box 159, Folder 1.
64. Friendly sent a copy of the lecture to Justice Powell. Powell letter to Friendly, Aug. 14, 1975, HLS-HJF, Box 204, Folder 10.
65. See Mathews v. Eldridge, 424 U.S. 319, 343, 348 (1976) (Powell, J., crediting Friendly).
66. Davis letter to Friendly, Sept. 20, 1977, HLS-HJF, Box 83, Folder 14.
67. Kerner v. Flemming, 283 F.2d 916 (2d Cir. 1960).
68. Ibid., 918–919.
69. Friendly Voting Mem., Oct. 14, 1960, HLS-HJF, Box 10, Folder 6.
70. 283 F.2d at 921–922. Other circuits promptly adopted Friendly's test: Butler v. Flemming, 288 F.2d 591 (5th Cir. 1961); Hall v. Flemming, 289 F.2d 290 (6th Cir. 1961); Graham v. Ribocoff, 295 F.2d 391 (9th Cir. 1961).
71. Friendly letter to Jaffe, Dec. 9, 1960, HLS-HJF, Box 10, Folder 6.
72. Friendly letter to Beryl Levi, Jan. 25, 1962, HLS-HJF, Box 95, Folder 20. Friendly wrote in another Social Security case, "The attitude of the Department of HEW in these disability cases beats me; if any private employer were half as tough, he would be hounded out of town as a Simon Legree." Friendly Voting Mem., May 18, 1964, HLS-HJF, Box 9, Folder 4, in Ber v. Celebrezze, 332 F.2d 293 (2d Cir. 1964).
73. Friendly letter to Martha K. Selig, Nov. 21, 1960, HLS-HJF, Box 10, Folder 6.
74. Friendly letter to Judge John R. Brown, Apr. 14, 1961, HLS-HJF, Box 10, Folder 6. Friendly wrote Louis Jaffe that "getting Kerner into a sheltered workshop . . . will do him a lot more good than the pension." Friendly letter to Jaffe, Dec. 9, 1960, HLS-HJF, Box 10, Folder 6.
75. Author telephone interview of Harold Tompkins, Feb. 8, 2007. Tompkins went on to serve as a justice on the New York State Supreme Court and saw Friendly on social occasions.
76. 340 F.2d 736, 738 (2d Cir. 1965).
77. Friendly later noted about administrative records, "Generally the size of the record varies inversely with its usefulness." Friendly, foreword to *Legal Control*, vii.
78. Friendly satisfied himself that "the letter of our remand order" did not preclude the SSA from adding to the evidence on Kerner's condition. 340 F.2d at 738–739.

79. Author telephone interview of Tompkins, Feb. 8, 2007. *Kerner* led Congress to change the law adversely for disability claimants by making the availability of a job irrelevant. Social Security Amendments of 1967, Pub. L. No. 90–248, § 158(d)(2)(A), 81 Stat. 868, codified at 42 U.S.C. § 423(d)(2)(A). Friendly letter to Judge Weinstein, Mar. 23, 1984, HLS-HJF, Box 221, Folder 5.

80. Author telephone interview of Tompkins, Feb. 8, 2007; author telephone interview of Carl Golden (attorney for government on second appeal), June 1, 2007. There is no evidence of a notification by Friendly to counsel or to his judicial colleagues about his prior efforts to help Kerner.

81. See Jeffrey M. Shaman et al., *Judicial Conduct and Ethics* (1990), 149; Richard E. Flamm, *Judicial Disqualification* (2007), 373–377.

82. 515 F.2d 57, 58 (2d Cir. 1975). Five years earlier Friendly had said that he accepted the decision sustaining the maximum family allowance "because the legislature had good reasons for the ceiling, including one that nobody dared even to mention—a desire to decrease the spread of the population bomb." Henry Friendly, "Some Equal Protection Problems of the 1970's" (1970), 11, published in booklet form by N.Y.U. Law School, HLS-HJF, Box 204, Folder 7.

83. 515 F.2d at 65–66.

84. *Dunn v. United States*, 284 U.S. 390 (1932).

85. 274 F.2d 899 (2d Cir. 1960).

86. Marvin Schick, *Learned Hand's Court* (1971), 137–138.

87. United States v. Maybury, Appellant's Appendix, A31–A32.

88. Ibid., Brief for Appellant, 10–11.

89. 274 F.2d at 908.

90. Ibid., 902; author interview of Justice Antonin Scalia, June 26, 2010.

91. 274 F.2d at 905. Res judicata is related to double jeopardy, which applies only to criminal cases. Res judicata can be summarized as mandating that once a claim has been litigated and decided, the determination forever binds the parties. See *Black's Law Dictionary* (9th ed., 2009), 1425. Friendly's second sentence seems inconsistent with his position that the law can be different in jury and nonjury criminal cases.

92. United States v. Ball, 163 U.S. 662, 671 (1896); see Burks v. United States, 437 U.S. 1, 16 (1978) (decided subsequent to *Maybury*) ("we necessarily afford absolute finality to a jury's verdict of acquittal").

93. The law at the time the Bill of Rights was adopted seemed to contradict Friendly's position. Leonard W. Levy, *Origins of the Bill of Rights* (1999), 206–208 ("a person acquitted at trial could never be tried a second time," paraphrasing Roger Sherman of Connecticut in congressional debate on the Bill of Rights).

94. See Palko v. Connecticut, 302 U.S. 319 (1937); Zapico v. Bucyrus-Erie Co., 579 F.2d 714, 725 (2d Cir. 1978) (Friendly, J.).

95. *Ball*, 163 U.S. at 671.

96. 602 F.2d 1078, 1082 (2d Cir. 1979).

97. 398 U.S. 323 (1970).

98. 348 F.2d 844 (2d Cir. 1965) (Marshall, J.).

99. 602 F.2d at 1082 (emphasis added). Friendly held for the prisoner on a narrow ground.

100. Friendly, *Benchmarks*, 158.
101. United States v. Cioffi, 487 F.2d 492 (2d Cir. 1973).
102. United States v. Jenkins, 490 F.2d 868 (2d Cir. 1973). Lumbard dissented.
103. United States v. Kramer, 289 F.2d 909 (2d Cir. 1961).
104. 404 F.2d 836, 845 (2d Cir. 1968) (*en banc*).
105. Ibid., 846–847. Disagreeing with a decision of the First Circuit, Friendly also stated that events occurring between the first and second trials could legitimately influence the second judge's sentence; that was a risk that the defendant took in seeking to reverse the first conviction and obtain a retrial (842, 845–846).

11. Other Bill of Rights Amendments

1. 367 U.S. 643 (1961).
2. Henry Friendly, *Benchmarks* (1967), 262.
3. United States v. Dunnings, 425 F.2d 836, 840 (2d Cir. 1969); see Friendly, *Benchmarks*, 260–262.
4. 468 U.S. 897 (1984); see Hudson v. Michigan, 547 U.S. 586 (2006).
5. *In re* Schwartz, 457 F.2d 895, 898–890 (2d Cir. 1972). Schwartz claimed that the government must demonstrate probable cause for any compelled production of her handwriting, while the government argued that the Fourth Amendment was inapplicable to all evidence sought by the grand jury except for an overbroad subpoena.
6. 409 F.2d 888, 896–897 (2d Cir. 1969).
7. Friendly letter to Taylor, Apr. 7, 1969, HLS-HJF, Box 41, Folder 19.
8. The complaint relied on 42 U.S.C. § 1983 and did not mention the Fourth Amendment. The author is indebted to Stephen A. Grant, who represented Bivens, for providing him with his file in the case.
9. 276 F. Supp. 12 (E.D.N.Y. 1967).
10. Bell v. Hood, 327 U.S. 678, 684 (1946), a landmark case decided twenty-five years earlier, expressly left open the issue of whether a citizen could sue directly under the Constitution.
11. Order, July 12, 1968; author interview of Stephen Grant, July 27, 2007. Friendly once assigned another attorney in a case for less lofty motives. When Cravath Swain and Moore raised its starting salary for incoming lawyers to $15,000 in the mid-1960s, Friendly was so angry that he assigned Thomas Barr, a Cravath senior partner, to represent a gangster. Author interview of Richard Draynard, Dec. 14, 2006.
12. Bivens v. Six Unknown Named Agents of the Fed. Bur. of Narcotics, 409 F.2d 718 (2d Cir. 1969).
13. Friendly letter to Grant, Apr. 5, 1969. When Grant asked Friendly whether he thought there would be any impropriety in his advising him in regard to the brief, Friendly told him, "[T]here would not be on the understanding that if the case were remanded, I would not sit." Friendly recounted the conversation to Judge Timbers years later. Friendly Mem., Apr. 30, 1975, HLS-HJF, Box 76, Folder 20.

14. 403 U.S. 388 (1971). In the 1988 edition of Hart and Wechsler, *The Federal Courts and the Federal System* (3d ed., 1988), *Bivens* was the third most cited case, an indication of its importance. The first two were Erie R.R. v. Tompkins, 304 U.S. 64 (1938), and Younger v. Harris, 401 U.S. 37 (1971), which denied federal courts the right to enjoin state criminal proceeding, except in exceptional circumstances.

15. 403 U.S. at 430 (Black, J., dissenting). While arguing against the creation of cause of action in the post-argument conference, Burger agreed that it was a good first step toward abolishing the exclusionary rule because it gave subjects of an unlawful police search a vehicle to vindicate their rights. Bernard Schwartz, *The Ascent of Pragmatism* (1990), 358–359.

16. Gregoire v. Biddle, 177 F.2d 579 (2d Cir. 1949).

17. COH, Tape 5, Side 2, p. 2; Friendly letter to Attorney General Elliot Richardson, July 11, 1973, HLS-HJF, Box 67, Folder 18.

18. Author interview of Grant, July 27, 2007. Randolph had a different view of the settlement, namely, that there were serious discrepancies in Bivens's account and that he may have made up the whole thing. Author interview of Randolph, Feb. 12, 2007.

19. Dale v. Bartels, 732 F.2d 778, 785 (2d Cir. 1984). Arguably, Bivens provided support for the government in the Pentagon Papers case.

20. Richard H. Fallon et al., *Hart and Wechsler's The Federal Courts and the Federal System* (6th ed., 2009), 738–740.

21. Correctional Services Corp. v. Malesko, 534 U.S. 61 (2001); see Marsha S. Berzon, "Securing Fragile Foundations: Affirmative Constitutional Adjudication in Federal Courts," 84 *New York University Law Review* (2009), 681, 699–700 ("*Bivens* today appears to be hanging by a thread").

22. 372 U.S. 335 (1963); Friendly, *Benchmarks*, 254.

23. 709 F.2d 160 (2d Cir. 1983).

24. 432 F.2d 324, 327 (2d Cir. 1970) (Friendly, J., dissenting). The last quoted sentence reflects Friendly's preference for relying on nonconstitutional grounds.

25. United States v. Fiore 443 F.2d 112 (2d Cir. 1971). When a witness testified at the trial, that was different; Friendly allowed grand jury testimony to be used as affirmative evidence. United States v. De Sisto, 329 F.2d 929 (2d Cir. 1964).

26. Henry Friendly, "'The Law of the Circuit' and All That," 46 *St. John's Law Review* (1972), 406, 411 (Rule 801(d)(1), Federal Rules of Evidence, while generally requiring prior statements to be under oath in order to be admitted as affirmative evidence, "dangerously and wrongly [would] allow such use of any prior utterance by a witness [of a prior identification of a person made after perceiving the person], even an oral one which he denies having made").

27. In 2004 the Supreme Court held in Crawford v. Washington, 541 U.S. 36 (2004) (Scalia, J.), that grand jury testimony of a witness was not admissible to prove facts unless the witness testifies at the trial.

28. Friendly's seven opinions on the right to trial by jury involved the question of the construction of a statute or of the Federal Rules of Civil Procedure as well as of the Seventh Amendment. E.g., Fitzgerald v. United States Lines Co., 306 F.2d 461 (2d Cir. 1962) (*en banc*) (constitutional issue), *rev'd*, 374 U.S. 16

(1963); United States v. J. B. Williams, Inc., 498 F.2d 414 (2d Cir. 1974) (constitutional and statutory issues); Damsky v. Zavatt, 289 F.2d 46 (2d Cir. 1961) (resolving whether an issue was of constitutional or statutory construction).

29. 275 F.2d 745 (2d Cir. 1960).

30. Ibid., 748–749.

31. Bruce A. Ackerman, *Reconstructing American Law* (1984), 66–67.

32. Giuseppe v. Walling, 144 F.2d 608, 624 (1944) (L. Hand, J., concurring), *aff'd sub nom.*, Gemsco, Inc. v. Walling, 224 U.S. 344 (1945). Friendly began a response to a brief with "plaintiff . . . argues with impeccable literalness." Graziano v. Pennell, 371 F.2d 761, 762–763 (2d Cir. 1967).

33. 708 F.2d 80, 86 (2d Cir. 1983).

34. Case Note, 74 *Harvard Law Review* (1960), 414, 415.

35. Friendly Mem., Jan. 17, 1969, HLS-HJF, Box 41, Folder 24, in United States v. Dancis, 406 F.2d 729 (2d Cir. 1969).

36. Friendly, *Benchmarks*, 319–320.

37. 481 F.2d 1028 (2d Cir. 1973).

38. For example, neither brief considered the specific constitutional source of Johnson's claim and other important issues.

39. The Supreme Court confirmed Friendly's view in Ingraham v. Wright, 430 U.S. 651, 671 n.40 (1977).

40. 481 F.2d at 1032. The text of the Eighth Amendment does not appear to require Friendly's conclusion. The language could be applied to a detainee who was disciplined following a hearing for violating a rule of the institution in which he was confined. Another part of the Eighth Amendment applies to detainees ("Excessive bail shall not be required").

41. 342 U.S. 165 (1952).

42. 481 F.2d at 1033. Friendly expressed concern one year earlier about the administrators of prisons (as well as the constitutional balance of federalism) in a case in which a panel majority, relying on the Fourteenth Amendment, ordered the prison to allow nine hundred prisoners to receive unopened a seven-page single-spaced letter from the Legal Aid Society that encouraged the inmates to establish a prisoners' "union." Goodwin v. Oswald, 462 F.2d 1237, 1248 (2d Cir. 1972) (Friendly, J., dissenting).

43. Whitley v. Albers, 475 U.S. 312, 320–321 (1986) (O'Connor, J.) (quoting Friendly on relevance of good faith); Hudson v. McMillan, 503 U.S. 1, 7 (1992) (O'Connor, J.) ("This Court derived the *Whitley* test from one articulated by Judge Friendly in *Johnson v. Glick, supra*").

44. United States v. Roy, 734 F.2d 108, 111 (2d Cir. 1984) (Meskill, J.) (Friendly, J., concurring in the result).

45. Ibid., 113. The government's able brief did not describe Roy as a trespasser on society.

46. 183 F.2d 201 (2d Cir. 1950), *aff'd*, 341 U.S. 494 (1951). Neither brief discussed the framers or whether the deprivation of the franchise was a punishment.

47. Green v. Board of Elections, 380 F.2d 445, 449–450 (2d Cir. 1967).

48. Friendly relied on John Locke's "social contract" theory to exclude felons from voting. Ibid., 451.

49. Henry Friendly, "The Courts and Social Policy: Substance and Procedure," 33 *University of Miami Law Review* (1978), 21, 27–28, reprinted in *Judges on Judging; View from the Bench* (David M. O'Brien, ed., 1997) ("Social Policy").
50. 410 U.S. 113 (1973).
51. A. Raymond Randolph, "Before *Roe v. Wade:* Judge Friendly's Draft Abortion Opinion," 29 *Harvard Journal of Public Policy* (2006), 1035; HLS-HJF, Box 163, Folder 8.
52. Author interview of Randolph, Feb. 12, 2007.
53. Friendly letter to Prof. Louis Lusky, Sept. 6, 1977, HLS-HJF, Box 231, Folder 1.
54. Ibid. The draft contained just two footnotes.
55. 381 U.S. 479 (1965).
56. Friendly read the galley proofs of David W. Louisell and John T. Noonan Jr., "Constitutional Balance," in *The Morality of Abortion* (John T. Noonan, ed., 1970), 220, which discusses, *inter alia,* a right to privacy, equal protection based on economic status, and the unique burden imposed on women. "As a result of reading the galley proofs of Noonan's book, I have pretty much crystallized my thinking about the abortion case." Friendly Mem. for Randolph, "rec'd 3/13/70." The 1970 book was the product of a conference at the Harvard Divinity School, which the Kennedy family sponsored in the hope of defusing the abortion issue before Robert Kennedy ran for President. Judge Noonan email to author, July 2, 2009.
57. Randolph, "Before *Roe v. Wade*," 1057, 1059–1061.
58. Friendly called the experience "soul wrenching." Henry Friendly, "Some Equal Protection Problems of the 1970's," (1970), 14, published in booklet form by N.Y.U. Law School, HLS-HJF, Box 204, Folder 7.
59. Randolph, "Before *Roe v. Wade*," 1058–1059.
60. Ibid., 1059–1060.
61. Friendly, "Social Policy," 34–35.
62. Ibid., 33, 35–36. Later, he said, "The Constitution provides no general guarantee of privacy." Friendly, "Notes for Talk at Harvard Law Review Dinner," April 7, 1978. HLS-HJF, Box 203, Folder 2.
63. Friendly, "Social Policy," 33, 36; see Helen Garfield, "Privacy, Abortion, and Judicial Review; Haunted by the Ghost of *Lochner*," 61 *Washington Law Review* (1986), 293, 342 n.305.
64. Friendly, "Social Policy," 35–36.
65. Ibid., 35. Friendly struggled over the issue. Later, in a memorandum relating to Population Services International v. Wilson, 398 F. Supp. 321 (S.D.N.Y. 1975), *aff'd sub nom.*, Carey v. Population Services Int'l, 431 U.S. 678 (1977), where the panel struck down portions of a New York statute that restricted the dissemination of nonprescription contraceptive devices, Friendly said, "I've rarely had a case where I had such difficulty in seeing my way." Friendly Mem., Mar. 17, 1975, HLS-HJF, Box 162, Folder 7.
66. Author interview of Frederick T. Davis, Mar. 20, 2007. It was years before anyone argued that the Equal Protection Clause gave women rights because only women can suffer the major physical consequence of pregnancy. Ruth

Bader Ginsburg, "Some Thoughts on Autonomy and Equality in Relation to *Roe v. Wade*," 63 *North Carolina Law Review* (1985), 375; Laurence H. Tribe, *Constitutional Choices* (1985), 243–245.

67. HLS-HJF, Box 205, Folder 1.

12. Other Constitutional Provisions

1. 109 U.S. 3 (1883).
2. Trustees of Dartmouth College v. Woodward, 17 U.S. 518 (1819) (Marshall, C.J.).
3. Gerald Gunther letter to Friendly, Nov. 14, 1968, HLS-HJF, Box 225, Folder 4.
4. Michael Boudin, "Judge Henry Friendly and the Mirror of Constitutional Law," 82 *New York University Law Review* (2007), 975, 995.
5. Vol. 12, No. 2 (1969).
6. Henry Friendly, *The Dartmouth College Case and the Public-Private Penumbra* (1971), 7.
7. Ibid., 11–12.
8. Ibid., 12.
9. Ibid., 18.
10. Engaging in a balancing test "is one of the defining characteristics of the pragmatic, instrumental, 'realist' style of judging." Richard A. Posner, *The Problems of Jurisprudence* (1990), 408.
11. Friendly, *Penumbra,* 21. Friendly's analysis was subtly different from most others. Gerald Gunther cited Friendly's "emphasis on the degree of state involvement as one of the factors going to the constitutionality of the action. I think the question of the centrality of the state's involvement is best faced in that context" rather than "as a separate threshold issue," an approach that provided a more flexible and rational development. Gunther letter to Friendly, Nov. 14, 1968, HLS-HJF, Box 225, Folder 4.
12. Friendly, *Penumbra,* 22–23, quoting LeRoy Fibre Co. v. Chicago, Milwaukee & St. Paul Ry., 232 U.S. 340, 354 (1914) (Holmes, J.).
13. Friendly, *Penumbra,* 17, 23. Friendly cited prior statements of his point (38 n.5).
14. Ibid., 26.
15. Ibid., 29–31.
16. Boudin, "Judge Henry Friendly," 990.
17. 407 F.2d 73 (2d Cir. 1968); Friendly, *Penumbra,* 24–29.
18. 407 F.2d at 74–76 and n.3.
19. 294 F. Supp. 1269 (W.D.N.Y. 1968).
20. 407 F.2d at 81.
21. Ibid., 81–82. This statement included a possible negative pregnant that was incorrect, namely, that if the CC students did not regard their college as an arm of the state, there would be no state action. While the rejection of the negative pregnant did not appear in the published opinion, it appeared in Friendly's voting memorandum: "Here there is no reason to think the liberal arts students so regarded the dean of students; indeed, the CC students very likely didn't either

and the reason for holding there was state action in their cases is that *in fact* the dean *was* exercising power over them delegated by the state." Friendly Voting Mem., Nov. 8, 1968, HLS-HJF, Box 40, Folder 43.

22. 407 F.2d at 80.

23. Ibid., 82.

24. Ibid.

25. Ibid., 83. None of the briefs argued that the two groups of students were distinct, possibly because the same attorney represented all of them, while the defendant wanted to win the entire case.

26. 407 F.2d at 81.

27. 42 U.S.C. § 1983.

28. 407 F.2d at 85. Friendly wrote significant state action opinions in other contexts: Langevin v. Chenango Court, Inc., 447 F.2d 296 (2d Cir. 1971) (no state action when government did not itself increase rents in a public-housing project, but simply allowed landlord to institute an increase); United States v. Solomon, 509 F.2d 863 (2d Cir. 1975) (no state action when the New York Stock Exchange, acting independently of the SEC, conducted an internal investigation).

29. Friendly, *Penumbra*, 39 n. 107.

30. 429 F.2d 1126, 1126 (2d Cir. 1970) (Friendly, J., concurring).

31. Richard A. Posner email to author, May 7, 2011.

32. 496 F.2d 623, 625 (2d Cir. 1974). One foundation was concededly public and is excluded from the discussion.

33. Ibid., 634. Jackson's chaotic *pro se* brief provided virtually no enlightenment.

34. Ibid., 636–637.

35. Ibid., 637. Friendly *rejected* a similar argument by a party in a tax case: "Garfinckel stresses the emphasis placed by these opinions on the 'shell' character of the corporation and on the complete or nearly complete discontinuity in stock ownership. But this was simply the normal practice of a court's deciding an easier case on a satisfying basis that was readily available rather than unnecessarily wrestling with a more difficult one." Julius Garfinckel & Co. v. Commissioner of Internal Revenue, 335 F.2d 744, 749 (2d Cir. 1964).

36. 496 F.2d at 638–640, quoting Powe v. Miles, 407 F.2d at 81. Friendly favored individualized decisions based on all the facts. While he opposed racism in universities, he objected to the view of the majority that denial of a tax exemption was required by statute in the case of Bob Jones University v. United States, 461 U.S. 574 (1983). He wrote to Judge Posner, "I think that Rehnquist was absolutely right in his dissent in the *Bob Jones* case and am appalled that he did not attract the vote of a single colleague, although it seemed to me that Powell quite obviously agreed with him." Friendly letter to Posner, June 28, 1983, HLS-HJF, Box 221, Folder 7.

37. 496 F.2d at 641; 420 U.S. 927 (1975).

38. Jackson v. Statler Foundation, 1975 WL 690 (W.D.N.Y. July 18, 1975); author interview of Judge Curtin, Oct. 12, 2006.

39. Henry Friendly, "The Public-Private Penumbra—Fourteen Years Later," 130 *University of Pennsylvania Law Review* (1982), 1289, 1290–1291. Scholars

are still struggling with the concept. E.g., Erwin Chemerinsky, "Rethinking State Action," 80 *Northwestern Law Review* (1985), 503; William R. Huhn, "The State Action Doctrine and the Principle of Democratic Choice," 34 *Hofstra Law Review* (2006), 1379; cf. Richard Feynman, "Superfluidity and Superconductivity," 29 *Review of Modern Physics* 205 (1957), quoted in James Gleick, *Genius* (1992), 303 ("We have no excuse that there are not enough experiments, it has nothing to do with experiments. Our situation is unlike the field, say, of mesons, where we say that there aren't enough clues for even a human mind to figure out what is the pattern. . . . The only reason that we cannot do this problem of superconductivity is that we haven't got enough imagination").

40. 347 U.S. 483 (1954).

41. Henry Friendly, "The Courts and Social Policy: Substance and Procedure," 33 *University of Miami Law Review* (1978), 21, 29, 30–32, reprinted in *Judges on Judging; View from the Bench* (David M. O'Brien, ed., 1997). Friendly, who offered alternative formulations, was not alone in criticizing the *Brown* opinion. E.g., Edmund Cahn, "Jurisprudence," 30 *New York University Law Review* (1955), 150.

42. 163 U.S. 537 (1896).

43. 347 U.S. 497 (1954).

44. 438 U.S. 265 (1978).

45. Friendly letter to Benjamin Goodman, June 10, 1977, HLS-HJF, Box 226, Folder 11.

46. Friendly letter to Erwin Griswold, Sept. 20, 1979, HLS-Griswold, Box 122, Folder 4 ("his opinion is hard to defend on strictly logical grounds, but I think it saved the country from what might have been a catastrophe").

47. 438 U.S. at 316–319.

48. Friendly letter to Justice Powell, July 1, 1978, quoted in John C. Jeffries Jr., *Justice Lewis F. Powell, Jr.* (1994), 498.

49. 392 U.S. 1 (1968).

50. 464 F.2d 667 (2d Cir. 1972).

51. Ibid., 675 (Friendly, J., concurring) (emphasis in original).

52. Friendly Voting Mem., June 6, 1972, HLS-HJF, Box 62, Folder 9.

53. In Aguayo v. Richardson, 473 F.2d 1090, 1109–1110 (2d Cir. 1973), a state inaugurated a controlled experiment that required recipients of public assistance in specified geographical areas of the state to accept employment. Rejecting an equal-protection claim, Friendly quoted Justice Brandeis about the importance of allowing states to conduct experiments. New State Ice Co. v. Liebman, 285 U.S. 262, 311 (1932) (Brandeis, J., dissenting).

54. 435 F.2d 1248 (2d Cir. 1970), *vacated*, 404 U.S. 807 (1971).

55. Phillip Kurland, "The Privileges or Immunities Clause: 'Its Hour Come Around at Last?,' " 1972 *Washington University Law Quarterly* 405, 415–418. In Ramey v. Rockefeller, 348 F.2d 780 (2d Cir. 1972), Friendly rejected the argument that a state could deny college students living in college housing the right to vote without analyzing separately the claim of each student.

56. The Fourteenth Amendment, Section 1, reads, "No State shall make or enforce any law which shall abridge the privileges or immunities of citizens of the United States." See Kathleen M. Sullivan and Gerald Gunther, *Constitutional Law* (16th ed., 2007), 347–354.

57. 364 F.2d 161 (2d Cir. 1966), *rev'd*, 364 F.2d 168 (2d Cir. 1966) (*en banc*).

58. Ibid., 171. Friendly chose this definition over the traditional one: "A strong opinion [is] one in which by the employment of pure legal reasoning one arrived inescapably at a conclusion which no layman could possibly have foreseen." Karl N. Llewellyn, *The Common Law Tradition: Deciding Appeals* (1960), 39 n. 31.

59. Author telephone interview of Richard Gyory, counsel for Spanos, Nov. 13, 2009.

60. Lumbard dissented on the basis of his original opinion; Smith switched positions.

61. 364 F.2d at 168.

62. Brief for Appellant, 8.

63. 364 F.2d at 168–169; see Brief for Appellee, 9.

64. 364 F.2d at 169–170.

65. Case Note, 55 *Georgetown Law Journal* (1966), 371, 375.

66. Henry Friendly, book review of *The Unpublished Opinions of Mr. Justice Brandeis,* by Alexander Bickel, 106 *University of Pennsylvania Law Review* (1958), 766, 768.

67. 304 U.S. 64 (1938). The case is discussed in Chapter 17.

68. Henry Friendly, *Benchmarks* (1967), 172 n. 71.

69. After it lost, Skouras could not ask for rehearing because the constitutional ground was an alternative holding and Skouras had no basis for upsetting the nonconstitutional ground for the court's decision. In other words, even if Skouras demonstrated that Friendly had decided the constitutional issue incorrectly, they would still lose the case, so they could not seek a rehearing or apply for *certiorari.*

70. For example, the bar association's brief considered the *Slaughter-House* cases and Alaska Packers Assoc. v. Industrial Accident Comm'n of California, 294 U.S. 532, 547 (1935). None of the cases Friendly cited involved the Privileges and Immunities Clause. The case Friendly discussed most, Sperry v. Florida, 373 U.S. 379 (1963), implicated Article VI's Supremacy Clause.

71. E.g., Selover, Bates & Co. v. Walsh, 226 U.S. 112, 126 (1912).

72. See United States v. Sobell, 314 F.2d 314, 323 (2d Cir. 1963) (Friendly, J.), discussed in Chapter 13; see Note, "Constitutional Limits on State Power to Regulate Out-of-State Attorneys," 52 *Cornell Law Quarterly* (1967), 1020, 1023; Note, "Retaining Out-of-State Counsel: The Evolution of a Federal Right," 67 *Columbia Law Review* (1967), 731, 743 (lawyer should be treated like the physician in Griswold v. Connecticut, 381 U.S. 479 (1965) and have standing to raise the constitutional issue).

73. 18 U.S.C. § 1584; see also 18 U.S.C. § 1581. The Thirteenth Amendment reads, "Neither slavery nor involuntary servitude, except as a punishment for

crime whereof the party shall have been duly convicted, shall exist within the United States."

74. United States v. Shackney, 333 F.2d 475, 480 (2d Cir. 1964).

75. Author telephone interview of Ira B. Grudberg, Shackney's attorney, May 12, 2009. Friendly admired creativity in advocacy and Shackney's brief was creative.

76. 333 F.2d at 480.

77. United States v. Mussry, 726 F.2d 1448, 1453 (9th Cir. 1984).

78. 487 U.S. 931 (1988); see Joyce E. McConnell, "Beyond Metaphor: Battered Women, Involuntary Servitude and the Thirteenth Amendment," 4 *Yale Journal of Law and Feminism* (1992), 207.

79. 487 U.S. at 950.

13. Habeas Corpus

1. Article I, Section 9, Clause 2, of the Constitution reads, "The Privilege of the Writ of Habeas Corpus shall not be suspended, unless when in Cases of Rebellion or Invasion the public Safety may require it." Statutes defined the scope of the right. 28 U.S.C. §§ 2254–2255.

2. Paul Bator, "Finality in Criminal Law and Federal Habeas Corpus for State Prisoners," 76 *Harvard Law Review* (1963), 441, 499.

3. Charles Alan Wright, *The Law of the Federal Courts* (1976), 246.

4. 344 U.S. 443 (1953).

5. Bator, "Finality," 500.

6. 372 U.S. 391 (1963).

7. Henry Friendly, "Is Innocence Irrelevant? Collateral Attack on Criminal Judgments," 38 *University of Chicago Law Review* (1970), 142, 143–144.

8. J. Woodford Howard Jr., *Courts of Appeals in the Federal Judicial System* (1981), 12.

9. Bator, "Finality," 441, 501–507.

10. Friendly letter to Bator, Jan. 28, 1963, HLS-HJF, Box 212, Folder 5.

11. 306 F.2d 417 (2d Cir. 1962). LaNear was ably represented by a Legal Aid attorney, Leon Polsky.

12. 28 U.S.C. § 2254(b)(1) (subparagraphing omitted).

13. 306 F.2d at 420–421. Friendly made a persuasive argument for the defendant that did not appear in any brief. "That the violation of due process in such cases is by New York, not by the foreign state, is neatly demonstrated by the decisions permitting a prisoner to show that a Canadian conviction used as a basis for a multiple offender sentence was obtained by methods that would offend the Fourteenth Amendment if the judgment had been rendered by a state court" (420–421). Since Canada has no Fourteenth Amendment, its courts could not deprive the offender of any constitutional rights, so it was the sentencing by the American court that had violated the defendant's constitutional rights.

14. 228 F.2d 188 (2d Cir. 1955).

15. *LaNear*, 306 F.2d at 421–422.

16. Pierre N. Leval, "Judging under the Constitution: Dicta about Dicta," 81 *New York University Law Review* (2006), 1249, 1257.

17. United States *ex rel.* LaNear v. LaVallee, 306 F.2d 417, 421 (2d Cir. 1962); Commissioner of Internal Revenue v. Ferrer, 304 F.2d 125, 134 (2d Cir. 1962); see Hudson Valley Freedom Theater, Inc. v. Heimbach, 671 F.2d 702, 705–706 (2d Cir. 1982).

18. 348 F.2d 823 (5th Cir. 1965) (Friendly, J., concurring).

19. Friendly letter to Tuttle, May 28, 1965, HLS-HJF, Box 27, Folder 41. The week Friendly sat on the Fifth Circuit was the only time he sat on any appellate court other than the Second Circuit.

20. United States *ex rel.* Ross v. McMann, 409 F.2d 1016, 1021 (2d Cir. 1969) (*en banc*) (Friendly, J., dissenting), *vacated and remanded sub nom.*, McCann v. Richardson, 397 U.S. 759 (1970).

21. 409 F.2d at 1042 (Friendly, J., dissenting) (describing majority opinion as a "cumulation of resounding adjectives").

22. "I should hardly have thought it necessary, but for my brothers' dissent, even to mention the judicial precept that the ultimate guilt or innocence of the defendants has no bearing on the issues before us." Ibid., 1025 (Kaufman, J., concurring). Friendly also pointed out the difficulty of deciding when a coerced confession should invalidate a guilty plea.

23. 397 U.S. 759 (1970).

24. Friendly Voting Mem., Oct. 12, 1971, HLS-HJF, Unprocessed Box 59, Folder "Rodriguez v. McGinnis." In a subsequent thirteen-page memorandum in the same case to the members of the court sitting *en banc* Friendly provided an analysis of the relationship between remedies available under habeas corpus and under 42 U.S.C. § 1983, the Civil Rights Act, that could have been a law review article: habeas corpus should be applicable to many cases that did not involve the immediate release of the prisoner, such as objections to prison conditions. "[T]he conditions under which a prisoner is held affect the legality or illegality of his present custody. . . . In my view, prisoner complaints under § 1983 would henceforth be limited to claims for damages; all others would be treated as applications for habeas under § 2254." Friendly Mem., Nov. 15, 1971, HLS-HJF, Unprocessed Box 59, Folder "Rodriguez v. McGinnis." Friendly's recommendation would have extended to more cases the requirement that prisoners exhaust their state remedies.

25. 404 U.S. 249, 251 (1971) (*per curiam*) ("State prisoners are not held to any stricter standard of exhaustion than other civil rights plaintiffs"). Chief Justice Burger was the sole dissenter.

26. Rodriguez v. McGinnis, 456 F.2d 79, 81 (2d Cir. 1972) (*en banc*) (Friendly, J., concurring) (one of eight opinions), *rev'd sub nom.*, Preiser v. Rodriguez, 411 U.S. 475 (1973).

27. Brief for Petitioners, 10–12.

28. Friendly, "Innocence," 142.

29. A strong proponent of habeas corpus relief agrees that meritorious petitions were few. Jeffrey B. Morris, *Leadership on the Bench: The Craft and Activism of Jack Weinstein* (2011), 293–294.

30. 372 U.S. 391, 405 (1963); Friendly, "Innocence," 170–172.
31. Friendly letter to H. W. R. Wade, Dec. 4, 1969, HLS-HJF, Box 204, Folder 10; see Lee Kovarsky, "Death Ineligibility and Habeas Corpus," 95 *Cornell Law Review* (2010), 329, 334 ("Professor Bator and Judge Friendly produced landmark scholarship that, although inconsistent in many ways, shaped the conservative position on habeas for the next forty years").
32. 394 U.S. 217, 235–236, 242 (1969) (Black, J. dissenting).
33. Friendly, "Innocence," 142–143.
34. Ibid., 155. Friendly was including the tendency to treat such trial errors as admitting hearsay as the denial of the right of confrontation.
35. Mark Tushnet email to author, Jan. 22, 2011.
36. Friendly, "Innocence," 160; see Kuhlmann v. Wilson, 477 U.S. 436, 454 and n.17 (1986) (Powell, J., concurring). The precise showing needed to satisfy the innocence requirement has provoked considerable debate. Brandon L. Garrett, "Claiming Innocence," 92 *Minnesota Law Review* (2008), 1629.
37. 384 U.S. 436 (1966).
38. Friendly, "Innocence," 164–172. While serving as Chief Judge of the Second Circuit Friendly worked with Senator Sam J. Ervin Jr. to draft a statute to revise habeas corpus procedure. Friendly letter to Ervin, June 2, 1972, HLS-HJF, Box 208, Folder 4. In contrast, when William Rehnquist, then Assistant Attorney General for the Office of Legal Counsel under President Nixon, sent Friendly a proposed bill on habeas corpus, Friendly replied, "Opposed to collateral attack as I am, I think this is too restrictive." Friendly letter to Rehnquist, Mar. 11, 1971, HLS-HJF, Box 207, Folder 5. A dozen years later Friendly made a similar comment about a proposal by John G. Roberts Jr., then a Justice Department official. Friendly letter to Roberts, Apr. 2, 1981, HLS-HJF, Box 220, Folder 2; see Henry Friendly, "Averting the Flood by Lessening the Flow," 59 *Cornell Law Review* (1974), 634, 636–637.
39. Friendly, "Innocence," 150; Herrera v. Collins, 506 U.S. 390, 399 (1993); Mark Tushnet email to author, Jan 22, 2011 ("there's no historical evidence whatever that innocence was ever thought relevant to the habeas inquiry"); see District Attorney's Office v. Osborne, 129 S.Ct. 2308 (2009).
40. United States v. Miller, 411 F.2d 825, 832 (2d Cir. 1969); United States *ex rel.* Cannon v. Montanye, 486 F.2d 263, 268 (2d Cir. 1973) (Friendly, J., dissenting in part); United States v. Frattini, 501 F.2d 1234, 1238 (2d Cir. 1974) (Friendly, J., concurring and dissenting). In preparation for the article Friendly searched unsuccessfully for statistics on the number of petitioners who alleged they were innocent. Daniel L. Breen, *Henry J. Friendly and the Pragmatic Tradition in American Law* (2002), 202–205 (doctoral thesis).
41. Author interview of William J. Bryson, Nov. 28, 2006.
42. Friendly did not mention two problems. First, it is difficult to ascertain guilt or innocence from a dry record. Second, requiring a showing of probable innocence would cause many more petitioners to argue their guilt, thereby offsetting some of the time saved by limiting relief to those who might be innocent.
43. United States *ex rel.* Owen v. McMann, 435 F.2d 813 (2d Cir. 1970); but see Wright v. United States, 732 F.2d 1048, 1056 (2d Cir. 1984) (Friendly, J.)

(alternative holding) (holding defendant to strict standard of review on habeas corpus when prosecution withheld information during direct appeal). In 1989 the Supreme Court, in Teague v. Lane, 489 U.S. 288 (1989), rejected Friendly's fourth ground for granting habeas corpus relief by holding that habeas corpus petitioners could not obtain the benefit of a new rule.

44. Friendly, "Innocence," 152–153; Teague v. Lane, 489 U.S. at 300; see Note, "Rewriting the Great Writ: Standards of Review for Habeas Corpus under the New 28 U.S.C. § 2254," 110 *Harvard Law Review* (1997), 1868, 1870.

45. United States v. Marshall, 458 F.2d 446 (2d Cir. 1972).

46. Coleman took the bar examination twice and failed both times. He later pleaded guilty to practicing law without a license.

47. Solina v. United States, 709 F.2d 160, 161 (2d Cir. 1983).

48. Friendly's research went far beyond the briefs.

49. 709 F.2d at 165. Solina had four prior convictions for theft or on dangerous-weapons charges. Furthermore, he had attempted to escape while awaiting trial and had tried to disrupt the trial on several occasions (164 nn.3, 4).

50. Ibid., 164. It could be argued that Coleman had more to fear from a dismal performance.

51. Ibid., 169. After reversal of his conviction, Solina, who had served twelve years in prison, pleaded guilty and was sentenced to five years' probation on condition that he obtain psychiatric treatment. United States v. Solina, 70 Cr. 771, E.D.N.Y., Aug. 24, 1987. He violated his probation and returned to prison.

52. 435 U.S. 475 (1978).

53. Ibid., 488, 490–491.

54. Ibid., 489. The internal quotation came from Chapman v. California, 386 U.S. 18, 23 (1967), where a prosecutor commented on the defendant's failure to testify.

55. 388 U.S. 293 (1967), *aff'g* 355 F.2d 731, 739 (2d Cir. 1966) (*en banc*) (Friendly, J., dissenting).

56. 355 F.2d at 743–744. *Stovall* was one of Friendly's favorite opinions. Author telephone interview of Frank Goodman, Sept. 8, 2009.

57. Michael Boudin, "Judge Henry Friendly and the Craft of Judging," 159 *University of Pennsylvania Law Review* (2010), 1, 9. Because the panel's decision, No. 29208 (2d Cir. Mar. 31, 1965), was vacated and superseded by the *en banc* decision, it is not reported.

58. 388 U.S. 218 (1967).

59. 388 U.S. 263 (1967).

60. 388 U.S. 293 (1967).

61. 672 F.2d 266, 271 (2d Cir. 1982).

62. 428 U.S. 465, 480 n.13 (1976) (Powell, J.).

63. 394 U.S. 217 (1969).

64. 477 U.S. 436, 454 (1986) (Powell, J.).

65. 506 U.S. 390, 404 (1993).

66. Roger Berkowitz, "Error-Centricity, Habeas Corpus, and the Rule of Law as the Law of Rulings," 64 *Louisiana Law Review* (2004), 477, 501; *accord,* Irene Merker Rosenberg and Yale Rosenberg, "Guilt: Henry Friendly Meets

the Maharal of Prague," 90 *Michigan Law Review* (1991), 604, 605. In 1991 one academic wrote, "The philosophical background of the new habeas is found in two extremely influential law review articles" by Bator and Friendly. Kathleen Patchel, "The New Habeas," 42 *Hastings Law Journal* (1991), 941, 943.

67. Joseph L. Hoffman and William J. Stuntz, "Habeas after the Revolution," 1993 *Supreme Court Review* (1993), 65; Pub. L. No. 104–132, 110 Stat. 1214 (1996).
68. Note, "Rewriting the Great Writ," 110 *Harvard Law Review*, 1877.
69. United States v. Sobell, 314 F.2d 314 (2d Cir. 1963).
70. 353 U.S. 391 (1957).
71. Friendly Voting Mem., Dec. 7, 1962, HLS-HJF, Box 18, Folder 2.
72. 314 F.2d at 318–322.
73. Ibid., 323.

14. Nonconstitutional Criminal Procedure

1. 308 F.2d 125 (2d Cir. 1962) (Friendly, J., dissenting), *vacated*, 375 U.S. 29 (1963) (*per curiam*).
2. 308 F.2d at 130 (Friendly, J., dissenting).
3. Undated, handwritten note by Friendly in file, HLS-HJF, Box 133, Folder 5, in United States v. Palumbo, 401 F.2d 270 (2d Cir. 1968).
4. Henry Friendly, "'The Law of the Circuit' and All That," 46 *St. John's Law Review* (1972), 406, 411.
5. Friendly Voting Mem., Oct. 10, 1975, HLS-HJF, Box 48, Folder 26, in Brathwaite v. Manson, 527 F.2d 363 (2d Cir. 1975) (Friendly, J.), *rev'd,* 432 U.S. 98 (1977). Unlike the cache from an illegal search and seizure, suggestive identification was unreliable, and Friendly praised the Supreme Court for "laying down specific safeguards with respect to suggestive identification." Chief Justice Burger told his colleagues at the Supreme Court conference on the case, "Henry has carried this torch for years." Bernard Schwartz, *The Ascent of Pragmatism* (1990), 323.
6. Friendly Mem., Oct. 14, 1960, HLS-HLS, Box 11, Folder 11.
7. 391 U.S. 123 (1968).
8. 365 F.2d 206 (2d Cir. 1966).
9. 289 F.2d 909 (2d Cir. 1961).
10. List of Friendly's notable cases, HLS-HJF, Box 226, Folder 7.
11. Friendly Voting Mem., Mar. 11, 1976, HLS-HJF, Box 52, Folder 5, in United States v. Swiderski, 539 F.2d 854 (2d Cir. 1976).
12. Henry Friendly, *Federal Jurisdiction: A General View* (1973), 36–37; Friendly letter to Chief Justice Warren Burger, Nov. 5, 1976, HLS-HJF, Box 206, Folder 4.
13. Friendly letter to Erwin Griswold, July 18, 1962, HLS-HJF, Box 213, Folder 3.
14. Author interview of Edward I. Koch, Apr. 10, 2007.
15. *New York Times*, Apr. 18, 1973, p. 1.
16. *New York Times*, Apr. 23, 1973, p. 1; *New York Times*, April 24, 1973, p. 1.

17. *New York Times*, Apr. 25, 1973, p. 1. Friendly told his clerk, Frederick T. Davis, to attend the argument before Palmieri because he was on the panel the following week and was likely to hear any appeal. Author interview of Davis, Mar. 20, 2007.

18. *New York Times*, May 1, 1973, p. 1, 34.

19. Earl of Shaftesbury's Trial, 8 How. St. Tr. (33 Chars. 2) 759 (1681).

20. United States v. Socony-Vacuum Oil Co., 310 U.S. 150, 234 (1940).

21. United States v. Howard, 569 F.2d 1331 (5th Cir. 1978); United States v. Stone, 633 F.2d 1272 (9th Cir. 1980).

22. Friendly's clerk Davis obtained tickets to Broadway shows for Jameson. Davis email to author, Nov. 14, 2006. Jameson brought his wife, secretary, and law clerk with him to New York City. Author telephone interview of Richard McCann (clerk to Jameson), May 16, 2007.

23. Author interview of Davis, Mar. 20, 2007. Friendly was outraged by Biaggi's deception. Author interview of Ira Feinberg, Nov. 11, 2006.

24. 478 F.2d 489, 490 (2d Cir. 1973).

25. The Supreme Court has stated that the rule of secrecy is "indispensable." United States v. Johnson, 319 U.S. 503, 513 (1943); *accord*, Pittsburgh Plate Glass Co. v. United States, 360 U.S. 395, 399 (1959); see, e.g., Richard M. Calkins, "Grand Jury Secrecy," 63 *Michigan Law Review* (1965), 455, 456.

26. 478 F.2d at 491–492 and n 4. Friendly took his version from the dissenting opinion of Justice Brennan in Pittsburgh Plate Glass Co. v. United States, 360 U.S. 395, 405 (1959).

27. 478 F.2d at 493. Thirty-three years later Biaggi's lawyer, former U.S. Attorney Arthur H. Christy, was still chastising himself for having filed the motion that asked for the release of unredacted grand jury minutes. Author telephone interview of Christy, Sept. 6, 2006.

28. Ben Field, *Activism in Pursuit of the Public Interest: The Jurisprudence of Chief Justice Roger J. Traynor* (2003), 9.

29. 478 F.2d at 493.

30. Case Note, 2 *Fordham Urban Law Journal* (1973), 151.

31. 478 F.2d at 493–494.

32. *New York Times*, May 5, 1973, p. 20.

33. 255 F.2d 118, 119 (2d Cir. 1958).

34. Doe v. Rosenberry "went on the ground that disclosure of grand jury minutes to the Grievance Committee of the Bar of the City of New York for investigation whether disciplinary proceedings should be instituted before the Appellate Division of the New York Supreme Court was preliminary to a judicial proceeding." *Biaggi*, 478 F.2d at 492 n.7.

35. 452 F.2d 704 (2d Cir. 1971).

36. Ibid., 714–715. Friendly applied the rules even though he seemed convinced of the justice of Weinstein's action. Other uncited cases supported Hays. *In re* Grand Jury Proceedings, 309 F.2d 440, 443 (3d Cir. 1962); United States v. Scott Paper Co., 254 F. Supp. 759, 763 (W.D. Mich. 1966).

37. Biaggi, 478 F.2d at 494.

38. Biaggi Affidavit, Apr. 26, 1973; *accord*, Biaggi Affidavit, May 1, 1973.

39. 478 F.2d at 494. Disturbed by the leak, Friendly directed Seymour to conduct an investigation. On July 10, 1973, Seymour issued a detailed report that exonerated those who investigated Biaggi. HLS-HJF, Box 64, Folder 12. Friendly rejected the government's request that the report be sealed. Friendly Mem., July 6, 1973, HLS-HJF, Box 64, Folder 12.

40. Twenty-five years later the Second Circuit endorsed Friendly's approach in *In re* Craig, 131 F.3d 99 (2d Cir. 1997) (Calabresi, J.). *Craig* routinized *Biaggi* by providing a list of specific criteria for releasing grand jury minutes outside the authority of Rule 6(e). Recently, historians relied on *Biaggi* and *Craig* in seeking to obtain a copy of the transcript of Richard Nixon's Watergate grand jury testimony. *In re* Kutler, D.D.C., 10-MC-00547, Sept. 13, 2010.

41. *New York Times*, Nov. 6, 1987; *New York Times*, Nov. 19, 1988.

42. Author interview of Koch, Apr. 10, 2007; Koch email to author, Apr. 26, 2011.

43. 350 U.S. 359 (1956).

44. 363 F.2d 996, 1000 (2d Cir. 1966) (Friendly, J. dissenting).

45. Largely as a result of Friendly's criticism, the practice generally ceased by 1968. United States v. Arcuri, 405 F.2d 691, 693 n.4 (2d Cir. 1968) (Friendly, J.).

46. E.g., United States v. Umans, 368 F.2d 725 (2d Cir. 1966); United States v. Arcuri, 405 F.2d 691 (citing lack of prejudice to the defendant, including the overwhelming evidence of his guilt).

47. Author telephone interview of Judge Thomas Meskill, Mar. 16, 2006. Friendly wrote to his colleagues, "I think we should reverse this case. It is time to teach a lesson to the smart little boys in the D.A.'s office, and we aren't going to do that by a slap on the wrist." Friendly Voting Mem., Jan. 28, 1963, HLS-HJF, Box 18, Folder 18, in United States v. Glaze, 313 F.2d 757 (2d Cir. 1963).

48. 471 F.2d 1132 (2d Cir. 1972).

49. Ibid., 1137, quoting *Payton*. Later, Friendly indicated that the requirement was not constitutionally mandated, but rather the exercise of the court's supervisory powers over lower federal courts and grand juries. United States v. Catino, 403 F.2d 491, 496–497 (2d Cir. 1968).

50. United States v. Schlesinger, 598 F.2d 722 (2d Cir. 1979); United States v. Brito, 907 F.2d 393 (2d Cir. 1990); Marvin E. Frankel and Gary P. Naftalis, *The Grand Jury* (1975, 1977), 48; Sarah Sun Beale et al., 2 *Grand Jury Law and Practice* (2d ed. 2004), § 9:6 at 9–26 to 9–28.

51. Bergman v. Lefkowitz, 569 F.2d 705, 707–708 and n.3 (2d Cir. 1977).

52. Oral argument of Alan Dershowitz in Bergman v. Lefkowitz, Dkt. 77–2133, U.S. Archives.

53. 569 F.2d at 710 and n.9.

54. Ibid., 712.

55. Ibid., 712 and n.12. The footnote said that the word should be "thank."

56. Ibid., 714.

57. Ibid., 714–716. The state had argued that Melia would have regarded any stronger statement by Hynes as hypocritical, with the result that it would have been counterproductive. It is not known whether Friendly was tempted to paraphrase what he had said in United States *ex rel.* Stovall v. Denno, 355 F.2d

731, 743–744 (2d Cir. 1966) (*en banc*) (Friendly, J., dissenting), *aff'd*, 388 U.S. 293 (1967), discussed in Chapter 13: "[I]f the state officials were motivated by such solicitude, the natural course would have been to ask [Bergman] whether he wanted [such a statement]."

58. Friendly Mem., Jan. 26, 1978, HLS-HJF, Box 83, Folder 10.

59. Alan M. Dershowitz, *The Best Defense* (1982), 150 (emphasis supplied by Dershowitz).

60. Author interview of Alan Dershowitz, Apr. 7, 2008. Friendly's decision similarly agitated Nathan Lewin, Dershowitz's predecessor as Bergman's attorney: "Bergman got screwed." Author telephone interview of Lewin, Aug. 29, 2006.

61. While the statement of facts in Hynes's brief mentioned Gustave Newman's "thank you," the brief's argument section made no mention of it; the writers of the brief did not appreciate its significance. Brief for Appellee, 19, 24–29.

62. United States v. Arroyo-Angulo, 580 F.2d 1137, 1150 (2d Cir. 1978) (Friendly, J., concurring).

63. United States v. Ciambrone, 601 F.2d 616, 627 (2d Cir. 1978) (Friendly, J., dissenting); *accord*, Friendly Voting Mem., Apr. 19, 1961, HLS-HJF, Box 7, Folder 20 (criticizing prosecutor and judge for "playing blind man's buff . . . on this stupid defense lawyer"); see United States v. Certain Property in Manhattan, 306 F.2d 439, 453 (2d Cir. 1962); Kyle v. United States, 297 F.2d 507, 513–515 (2d Cir. 1961).

64. 486 F.2d 670 (2d Cir. 1973). Friendly may have acquired his distaste for government instigation of crimes from Casey v. United States, 276 U.S. 413 (1928), where Brandeis dissented from an affirmance when the government arranged to have morphine sold to inmates in a federal prison. See 486 F.2d at 675, n.3 ("Mr. Justice Butler . . . thought the 'dirty business' issue was not properly before the Court. 277 U.S. at 486"). See Friendly Voting Mem., Oct. 14, 1960, HLS-HJF, Box 11, Folder 11, referring to "the dirty business of entrapment," in United States v. Smith, 283 F.2d 760 (2d Cir. 1960).

65. 486 F.2d at 673.

66. Friendly recounted, "The plan threatened to miscarry when a grand juror asked whether the existence of the Nevada pistol license had been verified, but Archer stepped into the breach by falsely asserting that it had." Ibid., 674.

67. Ibid., 672. Friendly asked his law clerk, "[W]hat are they doing creating a crime?" Author interview of William Bryson, Nov. 28, 2006.

68. 486 F.2d at 674–675, quoting 277 U.S. 438, 485 (1928) (Brandeis, J., dissenting); see Lewis J. Paper, *Brandeis* (1983), 307–314.

69. 486 F.2d at 676–677. When, during oral argument, the Assistant U.S. Attorney commenced his defense of the government's undercover operation, Friendly swung his swivel chair so that his back was to him, where he remained for about ten minutes. Author telephone interview of former Assistant U.S. Attorney Kenneth R. Feinberg, July 16, 2006, who attended the argument. While Friendly was directing his anger at the prosecutors who proceeded with the case, he had enormous respect for government agents, especially undercover agents, who put their lives on the line. Author interview of Theodore Mirvis, Nov. 21, 2006.

70. See Case Note, 20 *New York Law Forum* (1974), 177, 183–185. Friendly strongly opposed converting essentially local crimes into federal crimes. Henry Friendly, *Federal Jurisdiction: A General View* (1973), 56–62; Henry Friendly, "Federalism: A Foreword," 86 *Yale Law Journal* (1977), 1019, 1026–1027.

71. The government relied on Wasserberger's unsuccessful attempts to reach Bario at the Sahara Hotel in Las Vegas as one instance of interstate telephone calls. Friendly rejected use of those calls on two grounds. First, they resulted from "a plant of misinformation," since Bario knew he could not be reached in Las Vegas. Second, the calls "could not have been any actual use of a facility in interstate commerce which would in fact promote, etc., any unlawful activity. . . . We refuse to construe the 'intent' language of § 1952 so broadly as to include a call to an innocent telephone operator who had not the faintest idea what was afoot." 486 F.2d at 682.

72. In United States v. Bottone, 365 F.2d 389 (2d Cir. 1966) (Friendly, J.), defendants, who copied valuable documents on their own photocopying machines using their own paper and then made off with the copies, were convicted under 18 U.S.C. § 2314, for transporting stolen goods in interstate commerce. Friendly found that no stolen "goods" were transported, but nevertheless affirmed the conviction, stating, "[D]efendants could not have doubted the criminal nature of their conduct, and the sole issue is whether they subjected themselves to punishment by the United States as well as by a state." That statement, of course, would apply to United States v. Archer and other cases.

73. The government's petition for rehearing informed the court that the Queens District Attorney's Office allegedly had violated the Travel Act earlier. Friendly Mem., Aug. 30, 1973, HLS-HJF, Box 67, Folder 18.

74. 486 F.2d at 684.

75. Archer v. Commissioner of Corrections, 646 F.2d 44, 46–47 (2d Cir. 1981).

76. United States v. Miller, 411 F.2d 825, 833 (2d Cir. 1969) (Moore, J., concurring).

77. United States v. Miller, 381 F.2d 529 (2d Cir. 1967) (Friendly, J.).

78. Author interview of Judge Newman, Mar. 29, 2006; Newman email to author, Feb. 28, 2010; author telephone interview of Stephen Duke (now professor at Yale Law School), Jan. 29, 2007; 411 F.2d at 827–829. Newman, understandably concerned about being wrongly suspected of concealing the hypnotism, wrote the panel a letter saying that he was not aware of the hypnotism when Caron testified. Newman letter to Friendly, Jan. 24, 1969, HLS-HJF, Box 42, Folder 7.

79. 411 F.2d at 830, 832 n.10.

80. Ibid., 830 n.10. Hypnosis did not change Caron's testimony; he had previously given the identical testimony three times. Newman email to author, Feb. 28, 2010.

81. 411 F.2d at 832 n.15. While the state courts have a variety of rules to deal with the testimony of hypnotized witnesses, People v. Hughes, 453 N.E.2d 484 (N.Y. 1983), the federal courts have approved of a totality-of-the-circumstances approach similar to United States v. Miller. Borawick v. Shay, 68 F.3d 597 (2d

Cir. 1995). Once again, Friendly opted for a complex solution and not a bright line.

82. Friendly, who was intrigued by hypnosis, agonized over making the decision. Author interview of William Lake, Nov. 29, 2006.

83. Friendly noted "that the appeal was rather unusual these days in that Miller claims he was innocent of the crime charged." 411 F.2d at 827. Friendly also may have been influenced by the fact that Miller had already served five years in prison. Newman email to author, Apr. 6, 2011.

84. Author interview of Newman, Mar. 29, 2006.

85. David L. Faigman et al., *Science in the Law: Social and Behavioral Science Issues* (2002), 460–462.

15. Specific Crimes

1. 487 F.2d 492, 499 (2d Cir. 1973).

2. Smith v. United States, 508 U.S. 223, 241 (1993) (Scalia, J., dissenting). Because he was not made aware of Friendly's opinion in *Cioffi*, Justice Scalia, another student of words and meanings, did not cite *Cioffi*. Author interview of Scalia, Aug. 26, 2006; see Antonin Scalia, *A Matter of Interpretation* (1997), 23–24 (textualist approach supports Smith, not the government).

3. 18 U.S.C. §§ 1961, 1962.

4. 700 F.2d 51 (2d Cir. 1983). Friendly wrote, "The argument that RICO is inapplicable to a case where there is no charge of economically motivated activity was not advanced in any intelligible form in the district court. The brief (pp. 14–16) and reply brief (pp. 5–7) for Ivic and Sovulj in this court could be charitably read as making the point." A reading of the briefs shows that Friendly's statement was correct only if "charitably" is equated with "gift." Friendly also explained that he was obliged to consider the argument whether or not defendants had raised it, 700 F.2d at 59 n.5, so it is not clear why he stretched to find that defendants objected.

5. Author interview of Robert M. Morgenthau, Oct. 16, 2006.

6. 328 F.2d 854 (2d Cir. 1964).

7. Ibid., 856.

8. Ibid., 861.

9. Ibid., 863.

10. 425 F.2d 796 (2d Cir. 1969).

11. Ibid., 798–799. Friendly commented gratuitously on the wisdom of a lawful sentence, mostly to note that he considered sentences too lenient in white-collar criminal cases. E.g., United States v. Jacobs, 475 F.2d 270, 274 (2d Cir. 1973); United States v. Leonard, 524 F.2d 1076, 1081 (2d Cir. 1975); cf. Manley v. United States, 432 F.2d 1241, 1247 (2d Cir. 1970) (*en banc*) (Friendly, J., concurring) (revocation of parole for theft of single car "exceedingly harsh result").

12. Author interview of Paul R. Grand, May 22, 2008; author telephone interview of Judge Charles T. Sifton, Jan. 16, 2007. Both interviewees were Assistant U.S. Attorneys who attended the argument.

13. The footnote read in its entirety, "The amount receivable from Valley Commercial Corp. (an affiliated company of which Harold Roth is an officer, director and stockholder) bears interest at 12% a year. Such amount, less the balance of the notes payable to that company, is secured by the assignment to the Company of Valley's equity in certain marketable securities. As of February 15, 1963, the amount of such equity at current market quotations exceeded the net amount receivable." 425 F.2d at 800.

14. Author interview of Morgenthau, Oct. 16, 2007.

15. 425 F.2d at 810.

16. Ibid., 805; author interview of Morgenthau, Oct. 16, 2007.

17. 425 F.2d at 806.

18. In an older English case involving the sale of goods by auction, the seller employed a "puffer" to bid up the price. Lord Mansfield found the practice improper: "The practice is a fraud upon the sale, and upon the public. I cannot listen to the argument that it is common practice." Bexwell v. Christie, 1 Cowp. 395, discussed in Edmund Heward, *Lord Mansfield* (1998), 102–103.

19. 425 F.2d at 813.

20. Ted J. Fiflis, "Current Problems of Accountants' Responsibilities to Third Parties," 28 *Vanderbilt Law Review* (1973), 31.

21. Friendly letter to Fiflis, June 19, 1973, HLS-HJF, Box 230, Folder 6.

22. 336 F.2d 376, 380 (2d Cir. 1964). Interestingly, Friendly did not include *Borelli* in a list of his most noteworthy opinions, numbering eighteen, which he sent to a circuit judge in response to his request. Friendly letter to Judge Ruggero J. Aldisert, June 22, 1983, HLS-HJF, Box 226, Folder 7.

23. 336 F.2d at 380.

24. Ibid., 380–382.

25. Ibid., 382–383.

26. Author interview of Leval, Dec. 16, 2006.

27. 336 F.2d at 384.

28. Pierre N. Leval, "Henry J. Friendly; In Memory of a Great Man," 52 *Brooklyn Law Review* (1986), 571, 574–575.

29. 336 F.2d at 388–390.

30. Ibid., 382–387. On the appeal the focus of the defendants was on the evidence and not the instructions.

31. After the argument Friendly, on his way to the judges' private dining room, saw Peter Fleming, who argued for the government, having lunch. He leaned over and whispered, "Good argument." Author telephone interview of Fleming, Mar. 28, 2007; author interview of Paul R. Grand, May 22, 2008.

32. Friendly authored other significant opinions that advanced the law of conspiracy. E.g., United States v. Annunziato, 293 F.2d 373 (2d Cir. 1961) (statement of past circumstances was in furtherance of conspiracy when used to bring coconspirator up to date); United States v. Stanchich, 550 F.2d 1294 (2d Cir. 1977) (conspiracy count not needed to admit statements of coconspirators).

33. Two weeks after President Kennedy ordered the invasion of the Bay of Pigs in Cuba in 1961, Friendly wrote a four-page single-spaced letter to his daughter Joan about the serious threat that Fidel Castro held for the United States, end-

ing, "So I deeply regret, not that the first attempt was made, but that the President did not do whatever was necessary to make it succeed; and I hope the lesson he will draw is not to listen to the do-gooders and breast-beaters, but, the next time, to act with whatever force is required to achieve that goal. I am sure the American People will support him." Friendly letter to Joan Goodman, May 3, 1961, HLS-HJF, Box 213, Folder 3. The passage must be read in the context of the entire letter, which was about the military and political threat of a Russian-dominated Latin-American neighbor during the cold war.

34. Author interview of Ellen Simon, May 14, 2008.
35. Author interview of Irene Friendly, Mar. 22, 2008.
36. J. Woodford Howard Jr., *Courts of Appeals in the Federal Judicial System* (1981), 194.
37. Friendly Voting Mem., Sept. 19, 1968, HLS-HJF, Box 42, Folder 11, in United States v. Purvis, 403 F.2d 555 (2d Cir. 1968).
38. 426 F.2d 691 (2d Cir. 1970) (Friendly, J.), *aff'd*, 402 U.S. 479 (1971).
39. A. Raymond Randolph, "Administrative Law and the Legacy of Henry J. Friendly," 74 *New York University Law Review* (1999), 1, 5. Randolph's article related that he should have paid more attention to what Friendly had said in *Benchmarks*, that "the decider should cerebrate rather than emote about what he is deciding."
40. Ibid., 5–6.
41. Author interview of Randolph, Feb. 12, 2007.
42. 402 U.S. 479 (1971).
43. McGee v. United States, 462 F.2d 243 (2d Cir. 1972).
44. Ibid., 247 (Timbers, J., dissenting).
45. United States v. McGee, 344 F. Supp. 442, 443 (S.D.N.Y. 1972).
46. Ibid., 443–445 (parenthetical in original).
47. Ibid., 445; see Jeffrey B. Morris, *Federal Justice in the Second Circuit* (1987), 131–135.
48. 344 F. Supp. at 445.
49. Friendly letter to Randolph, May 18, 1972 (provided by Randolph to the author).
50. Friendly letter to Randolph, June 1, 1972 (same).
51. Author telephone interview of Francis McGee, Apr. 3, 2007. McGee has spent the years after the case engaging in humanitarian work.
52. 325 F.2d 409 (2d Cir. 1963), *aff'd sub nom.*, United States v. Seeger, 380 U.S. 163 (1965).
53. 50 U.S.C. § 456(j).
54. 325 F.2d at 411.
55. Ibid., 414, citing, *inter alia*, Toraso v. Watkins, 367 U.S. 488, 495 (1961) (Maryland notary-public oath case).
56. Ibid., 412–413.
57. 325 F.2d at 415–416 and nn. 5 and 6, quoting from four of Tillich's books.
58. Brief for Jakobson, 16–18.
59. Friendly had asked his clerk to write a detailed memorandum on Tillich's theology. Author telephone interview of Pierre Leval, Mar. 11, 2009.

60. Author telephone interview of Arno Jakobson, Mar. 11, 2010; Jakobson email to author, Mar. 15, 2010.

61. 325 F.2d at 417.

62. United States v. Seeger, 380 U.S. 163, 180 (1965).

63. Author interview of Judge Jon Newman, Mar. 29, 2006; see Juan Williams, *Thurgood Marshall* (1998), 304–305 (Friendly was "a politically conservative judge").

64. Sheldon Goldman, "Conflict in the U.S. Courts of Appeals, 1965–1971: A Quantitative Analysis," 42 *University of Cincinnati Law Review* (1973), 635, 647–650; but see Michael Boudin, "Judge Henry Friendly and the Mirror of Constitutional Law," 82 *New York University Law Review* (2007), 975, 993 ("his generally moderate views appear conservative . . . against the backdrop [of] the most liberal federal judiciary in American history)."

65. Author interview of Stuart Stock, Dec. 1, 2006.

66. E.g., author interview of Alan M. Dershowitz, Apr. 7, 2008.

67. Author telephone interview of Phyllis Skloot Bamberger, July 21, 22, 2008.

68. Author interview of Eleanor Jackson Piel, Nov. 21, 2006.

69. See Richard A. Posner, *How Judges Think* (2008), 24.

70. The total percentage of nonaffirmances, including per curiams and dismissals from the bench, was 3.2 percent. J. Woodward Howard Jr., *Courts of Appeals in the Federal System* (1981), 48.

71. E.g., Dickerson v. Fogg, 692 F.2d 238, 248 (2d Cir. 1982) (Friendly, J., dissenting) (voting to uphold an out-of-court identification over objection that it was unduly suggestive); United States v. Fisher, 702 F.2d 372, 379 (2d Cir. 1983) (Friendly, J., dissenting) (voting to uphold search and seizure over objection that description in search warrant was too general).

72. Friendly tended to dissent more than his colleagues (*Howard, Courts of Appeals*, 194), possibly because the most and least able judges stretch the zone of reasonableness. Posner, *How Judges Think*, 86–87.

16. Business Law

1. Henry Friendly, *Benchmarks* (1967), 296.

2. See United States v. Wegematic Corp., 360 F.2d 674, 675 (2d Cir. 1966) (Friendly, J.).

3. Pat Mogin email to author, May 27, 2009; author interview of Philip Bobbitt, July 3, 2007; author interview of Ruth Wedgwood, Feb. 28, 2007.

4. E.g., SEC v. Geon Industries, Inc., 531 F.2d 39 (2d Cir. 1976).

5. 445 F.2d 1337 (2d Cir. 1971); see Note, "Fiduciary Requirements and the Succession Fee upon the Change of Mutual Fund Advisors," 85 *Harvard Law Review* (1972), 655 (praising *Rosenfeld*).

6. Frank Goodman, "Judge Friendly's Contribution to Securities Law and Criminal Procedure: 'Moderation Is All,'" 133 *University of Pennsylvania Law Review* (1984), 10, 12.

7. 425 F.2d 796 (2d Cir. 1969), discussed in Chapter 15.

8. 445 F.2d at 1342, 1345. The parties' briefs were excellent. See Donavan v. Bierwith, 680 F.2d 263 (2d Cir. 1982) (Friendly, J.) (defining obligation of trustees of corporate pension plan who were also officers of the corporation); *In re* Beck Ind., Inc., 605 F.2d 624, 636 (2d Cir. 1979) (Friendly, J.) ("Courts do not take kindly to arguments by fiduciaries who have breached their obligations that, if they had not done this, everything would have been the same").

9. *New York Times*, Sept. 12, 1971, p. 3.

10. Section 10 of the Securities Exchange Act of 1934, 15 U.S.C. § 78j. The SEC adopted an implementing regulation, Rule 10b-5, § 240.10b-5.

11. E.g., Cort v. Ash, 422 U.S. 66 (1975).

12. 442 U.S. 560 (1979).

13. 444 U.S. 11 (1979).

14. See Goodman, "Judge Friendly's Contribution," 13–14.

15. Fogel v. Chestnutt, 533 F.2d 731 (2d Cir. 1975); Goldberg v. Meridor, 567 F.2d 209 (2d Cir. 1977); Leist v. Simplot, 638 F.2d 283 (2d Cir. 1980), *aff'd sub nom.*, Merrill, Lynch, Pierce, Fenner & Smith v. Curran, 456 U.S. 353 (1982); Sam Wong & Son, Inc. v. New York Mercantile Exch., 735 F.2d 653 (2d Cir. 1984). Friendly refused to imply a civil cause of action from a stock exchange rule in Colonial Realty Corp. v. Bache & Co., 358 F.2d 178 (2d Cir. 1966).

16. Author interview of Roberts, Nov. 29, 2007.

17. Edward A. Purcell Jr., *Brandeis and the Progressive Constitution* (2000), 290.

18. 567 F.2d 209 (2d Cir. 1977).

19. 430 U.S. 462, 476 (1977); 15 U.S.C. § 78j; 17 C.F.R. § 240.10b-5.

20. Judge Meskill dissented on the ground that there was no *material* deception. Ibid., 222.

21. Notes for lecture entitled "Re: Santa Fe v. Green," dated Apr. 14, 1978, HLS-HJF, Box 205, Folder 1.

22. 567 F.2d at 221.

23. 401 F.2d 833 (2d Cir. 1968) (*en banc*).

24. Ibid., 866–867.

25. 407 F.2d 453 (2d Cir. 1968) (*en banc*).

26. Credit & Financial Corp. v. Warner & Swasey Co., 638 F.2d 563 (2d Cir. 1981), was another suit based on an allegedly false and fraudulent press release in which Friendly reversed in favor of plaintiff.

27. 478 F.2d 1281 (2d Cir. 1973).

28. See Emanuel Becker, letter to panel, Feb. 21, 1973, HLS-HJF, Box 65, Folder 1.

29. Louis Loss, "In Memoriam: Henry J. Friendly," 99 *Harvard Law Review* (1986), 1722, 1723. Louis Loss and Joel Seligman, *Securities Regulation* (3d ed., 2000), 2105–2107, contains a block quotation of four pages from the opinion as well as other references to the case. Friendly's list of some of his noteworthy opinions in 1983 described *Gerstle* as "the best of my securities law opinions." HLS-HJF, Box 226, Folder 7.

30. Bersch v. Drexel Firestone, Inc., 519 F.2d 974, 985 (2d Cir. 1975).

31. Schoenbaum v. Firstbrook, 405 F.2d 200, 206, 208–209 (2d Cir. 1968), *mod. on other grounds en banc*, 405 F.2d 215 (2d Cir. 1968).

32. 468 F.2d 1326, 1337 (2d Cir. 1972). When the case first reached the Second Circuit, the parties had not even briefed or argued whether the district court had jurisdiction over the subject matter. The panel instructed the parties to furnish briefs on the issue (1330).

33. 519 F.2d 974 (2d Cir. 1975).

34. 519 F.2d 1001 (2d Cir. 1975).

35. *Leasco*, 519 F.2d at 989. The last words became the title of a law review article by Frank Goodman quoted above. In *Vencap* Friendly rejected plaintiff's reliance on an obscure statute, 28 U.S.C. § 1350, with the comment, "This old but little used section is a kind of legal Lohengrin; although it has been with us since the first Judiciary Act, no one seems to know whence it came." 519 F.2d at 1015.

36. *Bersch*, 519 F.2d at 993–994. Friendly applied this criterion to *Vencap*, where the plundering was plotted in Vencap's New York lawyers' office: "We do not think Congress intended to allow the United States to be used as a base for manufacturing fraudulent security devises for export, even when these are peddled only to foreigners." *Vencap*, 519 F.2d at 1017; see, e.g., Note, "Transnational Securities Fraud Jurisdiction under Section 10(b): The Case for a Flexible and Expansive Approach," 47 *Washington and Lee Law Review* (1990), 637, 649.

37. E.g., Andreas F. Lowenfeld, *International Litigation and Arbitration* (2d ed., 2002), 60–69, 86–91

38. 130 Sup. Ct. 2869 (2010). *Morrison* corrected the misapprehension of Friendly and others that the issue involved jurisdiction rather than the coverage of the statutes.

39. Ibid., 2888–2890.

40. Born email to author, July 11, 2010. Born wrote the first casebook devoted to international civil litigation. Gary B. Born, *International Civil Litigation in United States Courts* (1989).

41. 411 F.2d 1046, 1049 (2d Cir. 1969).

42. Gruss v. Curtis Publishing Co., 534 F.2d 1396, 1403 (2d Cir. 1976). Friendly presumably took the name from the 1958 musical *Auntie Mame*, which recounted the adventures of the ebullient eponymous character.

43. 429 F.2d 1136 (2d Cir. 1970).

44. Securities Exchange Act of 1934, § 7(c), 15 U.S.C. § 78(g)(c); Regulation T of the Federal Reserve System, 12 C.F.R. § 220.4(c)(2).

45. 429 F.2d at 1137–1139, 1145–1146.

46. Ibid., 1141.

47. Ibid., 1145, 1149 (Friendly, J., dissenting). Neither defendant's brief nor Friendly's voting memorandum contained the opinion's passion. Friendly had indicated his vote for Pearlstein on one transaction and for the defendants on the other, noting, "I have found it more than ordinarily difficult to come to a conclusion about this case. One's sympathies are certainly with the defendants but unhappily that is not enough." Friendly Voting Mem., Nov. 11, 1969, HLS-HJF, Box 45, Folder 23.

48. 429 F.2d at 1148. Neither party's briefs discussed the purpose of the statute or cited Lord Mansfield's decision in connection with Pearlstein's claim for restitution.

49. 429 F.2d at 1145. This was a case where Friendly relied on events subsequent to the passage of a statute to assist in its interpretation.

50. 438 F.2d 1167, 1173 (2d Cir. 1971).

51. Ibid., 1176 (Friendly, J., dissenting from the denial of reconsideration *en banc*).

52. Ibid., 1172 (panel majority opinion).

53. 576 F.2d 465, 470 (2d Cir. 1978).

54. 901 F.2d 624, 628 (7th Cir. 1990).

55. Mitu Gulati et al., "Fraud by Hindsight," 98 *Northwestern Law Review* (2004), 773. Friendly also sided with an honest corporation in Abrams v. Occidental Petroleum Corp., 450 F.2d 157 (2d Cir. 1971). Reversing the district court, he decided that a corporation that had lost out in a battle with another company in a hostile stock tender offer could share in the profits, along with other shareholders. Writing to Judge Posner, Friendly said, "I submitted the opinion [in *Abrams*] to the panel that had decided the *Wolf* case and found to my amazement that they were completely satisfied, although I believe the opinions are basically irreconcilable." Friendly letter to Posner, Dec. 30, 1983, HLS-HJF, Box 221, Folder 7.

56. Friendly letter to Eisenberg, June 2, 1982, HLS-HJF, Box 220, Folder 2. Friendly favored having "a 'clear majority' of the board [of directors] be independent of management" and placing "a strict limit on the number of directorships that may be held." Henry Friendly, "Improving the Governance of a Corporation," *ALI-ABA Course Materials J.* (Vol. 3, Dec. 1978), 6–8. He opposed federal legislation to accomplish his goals, preferring rule making by the SEC (7).

57. When Friendly advised Eisenberg that he had to leave an ALI meeting early, Eisenberg retorted, "We are losing a division." Author interview of Eisenberg, Oct. 18, 2007. Others similarly praised Friendly. Author interview of Prof. Geoffrey Hazard, Apr. 17, 2007; author telephone interview of Prof. John Coffee, Mar. 25, 2008; author telephone interview of Prof. Harvey Goldschmid, Mar. 27, 2008.

58. Author interview of Hazard, Apr. 17, 2007. Friendly helped draft the new *Third Restatement of Foreign Relations Law* (1981), which included a new section 416 that applies to securities not registered on a U.S. market. Prof. Andreas Lowenfeld of New York University Law School noted that some of the participants in the drafting process took the position that if it was good enough for Friendly, it was good enough for them. Author interview of Lowenfeld, Feb. 22, 2007.

59. Loss, "In Memoriam," 1723; see Margaret V. Sachs, "Judge Friendly and the Law of Securities Regulation: The Creation of a Judicial Reputation," 50 *Southern Methodist Law Review* (1977), 777, 780. Nineteen of Friendly's securities opinions have appeared in law school casebooks (781).

60. Friendly letter to Bok, Mar. 16, 1979, HLS-HJF, Box 219, Folder 4. Friendly went on to apply the same analysis to the university community. He was precise in using the word "simply"; expectations of shareholders or the government apparently could legitimately influence a corporation's or university's decision. Author interview of David Nissen, Ph.D., July 18, 2010.

61. Henry Friendly, *Federal Jurisdiction: A General View* (1973), 161–171; Henry Friendly, "Averting the Flood by Lessening the Flow," 59 *Cornell Law Review* (1974), 634, 644; author interview of Robert Weiner, Nov. 9, 2006.

62. Friendly told a law clerk that neither he nor, he suspected, any of his judicial colleagues who did not have a prior tax background could master tax law because of its complexity and enormous volume. Author interview of David Engel, Apr. 8, 2008.

63. And also influential. Jacob Mertens Jr., *Mertens' The Law of Federal Income Taxation* (2008), cites thirty-three of Friendly's tax opinions. See, e.g., Fawick Corp. v. Commissioner of Internal Revenue, 342 F.2d 823, 826 (6th Cir. 1965) ("The opinion of Judge Friendly in Julius Garfinckel & Co. v. Commissioner of Internal Revenue, 335 F.2d 744 (CA2 1964), ably gathers and finds without validity the various arguments which have been advanced to ameliorate the *Libson* rule. We will not attempt to extend or improve on his learned discussion").

64. Estate of Carter v. Commissioner of Internal Revenue, 453 F.2d 61, 69 (2d Cir. 1971); see Paddock v. United States, 280 F.2d 563, 567 (2d Cir. 1960) (Friendly, J.); author interview of Harry Bryans, Feb. 12, 2007.

65. Author interviews of Judge Leval, Oct. 17, 2006, and Dec. 6, 2006.

66. Modern textualists go beyond the words of the provision in question and include, for example, the context in which the provision appears. Justice Scalia has stated that "the good textualist is not a literalist." Antonin Scalia, *A Matter of Interpretation* (1997), 24; *accord*, e.g., John F. Manning, "Textualism and Legislative Intent," 91 *Virginia Law Review* (2005), 419, 434 ("modern textualists are not literalists"); see generally John F. Manning, "The Absurdity Doctrine," 116 *Harvard Law Review* (2003), 2387, 2454–2476.

67. Author interview of Leval, Feb. 5, 2009.

68. 500 F.2d 1041, 1058–1059 (2d Cir. 1974) (Friendly, J., dissenting).

69. 289 F.2d 69 (2d Cir. 1961), *rev'd sub nom.*, Hanover Bank v. Commissioner of Internal Revenue, 369 U.S. 672 (1962).

70. 382 F.2d 499 (2d Cir. 1967), *rev'd*, 391 U.S. 83 (1968).

71. 382 F.2d at 510–512 (Friendly, J., dissenting).

72. The Supreme Court concluded that to comply with the percentage requirements of § 355(a)(1)(D) the distribution need not take the form of a single distribution or occur in a single tax year, but if not, a binding commitment must exist to complete the multistep transaction (*Gordon*, 391 U.S. at 96), a qualification that Friendly had mentioned. 382 F.2d at 511.

73. 304 F.2d 125, 126 (2d Cir. 1962). Friendly referred to *Ferrer* as "Supposedly my best tax opinion." HLS-HJF, Box 226, Folder 7.

74. 304 F.2d at 126.

75. Friendly Mem., May 2, 1962, HLS-HJF, Box 14, Folder 16.

76. E.g., Lattera v. Commissioner of Internal Revenue, 437 F.3d 399, 408–409 (3d Cir. 2006).

77. E.g., Sanford M. Guerin et al., *Problems and Materials in Federal Income Taxation* (7th ed., 2008), 514–516, 519–520. One academic commented on Friendly's opinion, "On a statutory basis and the wake of prior cases, the logic of Judge Friendly's opinion appears beyond reproach." Jay A. Soled, "The Sale of Donors Eggs: A Case Study of Why Congress Must Modify the Capital Asset Definition," 32 *University of California at Davis Law Review* (1999), 919, 952.

78. 762 F.2d 264 (2d Cir. 1985).

79. § 7701(a)(26) (2000) defined the term "trade or business" as including "the performance of the functions of a public office." Friendly noted that Congress added the language to the Code because of doubts as to whether Senators were engaged in a "trade or business" so as to permit deduction of extra staff and telephone expenses. 762 F.2d at 265.

80. I.R.C. § 162(a) (2000) makes deductible "ordinary and necessary expenses paid or incurred . . . in carrying on any trade or business."

81. 762 F.2d at 268 (emphasis in original), citing, e.g., Edward C. Lee, T.C. Memo, 1981–16 (1981), *aff'd on other grounds*, 729 F.2d 1424 (9th Cir. 1984) (disallowing deduction for helicopter training expenses by airline pilot).

82. 762 F.2d at 268–270.

83. Friendly was annoyed at Rockefeller for claiming the deduction and may have included the gap issue in order to forestall the possibility that the Supreme Court would grant *certiorari* on the "same trade or business" issue. Author interview of Raymond B. Ludwiszewski, July 24, 2007.

84. 438 F.2d 905 (2d Cir. 1971).

85. § 162(a)(2); 438 F.2d at 912.

86. John A. Lynch Jr., "Travel Expense Deduction under I.R.C. § 162(a)(2)—What Part of 'Home' Don't You Understand?" 57 *Baylor Law Review* (2005), 705, 769, 772.

87. E.g., Lau Ow Bew v. United States, 133 U.S. 47, 49 (1892). For modern textualists the absurdity doctrine is "problematic because it permits judges to alter clear statutory language based on vaguely defined social values." Manning, "Absurdity Doctrine," 2392; *accord*, Melvin A. Eisenberg, "Strict Textualism," 29 *Loyola Law Review* (1955), 13, 28–29.

88. 143 U.S. 457 (1892).

89. 310 U.S. 534, 543 (1940).

90. Later, the Tax Court refused to permit "absurd" results. E.g., Phillips Petroleum Co. v. Commissioner of Internal Revenue, 101 T.C. 43, 107 (1991); see Ilse Barkan, "New Challenges to the Use of the Plain Meaning Rule to Construe the I.R.C. and Regs," 69 *Tax Notes* (1995), 1403.

91. Bongiovanni v. Commissioner of Internal Revenue, 470 F.2d 921, 924 (2d Cir. 1972) (Hays, J.). Only ten tax opinions in the U.S. courts of appeals and the Tax Court relied on the "absurdity" doctrine in the seven-year period January 1, 2000, through December 31, 2006. David F. Shores, "Textualism and Intentionalism in Tax Litigation," 61 *Tax Law* (2007), 53.

92. 312 F.2d 65, 66 (2d Cir. 1962).
93. I.R.C. § 337(C)(2).
94. 312 F.2d at 68. Friendly took a similar approach in Burde v. Commissioner, 352 F.2d 995, 1003 (2d Cir. 1965) (Friendly, J., "concurring in the result").
95. Statler Trust v. Commissioner of Internal Revenue, 361 F.2d 128, 131 (2d Cir. 1966). Peculiarly, Friendly cited only a Fifth Circuit case that can be distinguished. Read v. United States, 320 F.2d 550 (5th Cir. 1963).
96. 512 F.2d 1196, 1199 (2d Cir. 1975).
97. Ibid., 1201. Friendly's statement of the facts was more detailed than the parties', something he did on a number of occasions. He never explained what criteria he used to decide whether and to what extent he could selectively present facts from the record in addition to those that a party thought made its argument and to which the opposing party had not been alerted.
98. Ibid., 1204–1205.
99. Ibid., 1205. The government's brief on appeal said on the issue of deviation in the United States only that "[t]he ITALIA loaded cargo at four ports in the Gulf during the period of May 5 to May 13, 1967. Instead of sailing directly to Aqaba, she thereupon sailed to Norfolk to load additional cargo, and subsequently to Brooklyn to load further cargo. . . . At both ports, the cargoes loaded were owned by private shippers." Brief for the United States, 5. The quoted passage was part of the statement of facts and did not appear in the brief's argument section.
100. Reply Brief for Appellant, 12–14 (section entitled "Issues Not Raised and Relief Not Sought").
101. 512 F.2d at 1206 n.15.
102. See, e.g., Kakavas v. Flota Brasileira, S.A., 789 F.2d 112, 113 (2d Cir. 1986) (Friendly, J.) ("[plaintiff's] counsel sufficiently, albeit clumsily, brought this point to the judge's attention"); United States v. Ivic, 700 F.2d 51, 59 n.5 (2d Cir. 1983).
103. FTD, Tape 4, pp. 11–12.
104. E.g., Ste. Marie v. Eastern R.R. Assoc., 650 F.2d 395 (2d Cir. 1981); Saylor v. Lindsley, 456 F.2d 896 (2d Cir. 1972).
105. Author telephone interview of Owen, Feb. 16, 2007. Another district judge said, "Friendly was such a learned judge that being taken to task by him was somewhat of an honor. You felt that if he was trying to teach you something, perhaps he thought . . . that you were worthy of the instruction." Jack B. Weinstein letter to the author, June 3, 2009.
106. 398 F.2d 167 (2d Cir. 1968).
107. Ibid., 168, 169–170.
108. The liability of an employer for the acts of its employee acting within the scope of his authority.
109. Author interview of Ackerman, Aug. 6, 2007.
110. Author interview of Joan Goodman, May 19, 2007. Friendly thought economics was important for a judge and he attended a seminar in economics for judges in the late 1970s. The main lecturer, Prof. Armen Alchian, remarked that Friendly was the best "student" he had in the program. Author telephone

interview of Alchian, Aug. 7, 2007; *accord*, Prof. Henry G. Manne email to author, Aug. 13, 2007; author telephone interview of Judge Richard Dean Rogers, Aug. 28, 2007.

111. 398 F.2d at 170–171.

112. Justice Wiley Rutledge and Judges Cardozo and Traynor. Ibid., 171.

113. Ibid., 171–172.

114. 398 F.2d at 172.

115. For a discussion of *Bushey*'s place in the context of law and economics and enterprise liability, see Gregory C. Keating, "The Idea of Fairness in the Law of Enterprise Liability," 95 *Michigan Law Review* (1997), 1266.

116. Waterman Mem., June 11, 1968, HLS-HJF, Box 36, Folder 19.

117. Keating, "Idea of Fairness," 1281.

118. Steven P. Crowley, "Vicarious Liability in Tort: On the Sources and Limits of Employee Reasonableness," 69 *Southern California Law Review* (1996), 1705, 1749.

119. Author interview of Judge Weinstein, Oct. 11, 2007.

120. Author interview of Judge Calabresi, Aug. 6, 2007; see Posner email to author, Sept. 3, 2007 ("I sense that Judge Friendly was, unsurprisingly, uncomfortable with the economics approach, which, in effect, he rejected in that opinion").

121. Griswold letter to Friendly, Sept. 13, 1968, HLS-Griswold Collection, Box 182, Folder 19.

122. Author interview of William Lake, Nov. 29, 2006.

123. 46 U.S.C. § 1304(5).

124. Standard Electrica, S.A. v. Hamburg Sudamerkacanische Dampfschiffahrts-Gesellschaft, 375 F.2d 943, 945 (2d Cir. 1967).

125. 451 F.2d 800, 815–816 (2d Cir. 1971). The plaintiff had argued that the container was not a package because a "package . . . requires some packaging preparation for transportation. . . . A container is merely a receptacle in which cargo is carried." Brief for [Leather's Best], 12–13.

126. "The problem demands a solution better than the courts can afford, preferably on an international scale." 451 F.2d at 814.

127. 483 F.2d 645 (2d Cir. 1973).

128. Ibid., 649.

129. See generally Craig Still, "Thinking Outside the Box—The Application of COGSA's $500 per Package Limitation to Shipping Containers," 24 *Houston Journal of International Law* (2001), 81.

130. 636 F.2d 807 (2d Cir. 1981).

131. Ibid., 822. Mitsui's excellent brief made this argument.

132. Ibid., 818–819, 821–823.

133. Ibid., 825 (Oakes, J., concurring). Friendly changed a standard that favored the more economically powerful ocean carriers to one more supportive of the shippers.

134. Friendly list of notable opinions, June 22, 1983, HLS-HJF, Box 226, Folder 7.

135. 759 F.2d 1006 (2d Cir. 1985).

136. Still, "Thinking Outside the Box," 121.

137. Ibid., 135.

138. Edward D. Cavanagh, "Antitrust in the Second Circuit," 65 *St. John's Law Review* (1991), 795.
139. A leading antitrust treatise, Phillip Areeda, *Antitrust Law* (1978–), cites Friendly's antitrust opinions twenty-two times.
140. 429 F.2d 1003 (2d Cir. 1970).
141. Ibid., 1005. The Supreme Court reproduced this language in Flood v. Kuhn, 407 U.S. 258, 268 n.9 (1972), while adhering to its old rule. Henry M. Hart Jr. and Albert M. Sacks, *The Legal Process* (William N. Eskridge Jr. and Philip P. Frickey, eds., 1994), 1333–1335, employs the applicability of antitrust law to professional baseball as an exemplary case of the Supreme Court's misapplying the doctrine of *stare decisis*.
142. 291 F.2d 22, 24 (2d Cir. 1961). This bankruptcy led to an important criminal case in which Friendly wrote an opinion affirming the convictions of Justice James Vincent Keogh of the New York Supreme Court (the trial court of general jurisdiction) and Elliott Kahaner, Chief Assistant, and later Acting U.S. Attorney for the Eastern District of New York. United States v. Kahaner, 317 F.2d 459 (2d Cir. 1963).
143. 407 F.2d 73 (2d Cir. 1968).
144. 291 F.2d at 27 and n.3 (Friendly, J., dissenting), quoting from a statement by Congressman Henry of Texas, 31 *Cong. Rec.* 1803.
145. 291 F.2d at 27–29. Friendly's opinion was an example of legal realism, which tends to show that he could be flexible in selecting which jurisprudential school to follow.
146. Ibid., 29; see Friendly, *Benchmarks*, 214 (praising Justice Frankfurter's similar use of history in opinions). Only one sentence in Gibraltor's brief came even within sight of the issue: "This creditor was a wholly financed, directed, and captive offspring of the Wurlitzer Company with practically the same officers and directors." Brief for Appellant, 8. But that stated no more than the obvious. Friendly wrote other significant bankruptcy opinions. E.g., *In re B.D. International Discount Corp.*, 701 F.2d 1071 (2d Cir. 1983) (leading to statutory addition, 11 U.S.C. § 303(h)(1), regarding standard for involuntary bankruptcy); United States v. Whiting Pools, 674 F.2d 144 (2d Cir. 1982), *aff'd*, 462 U.S. 198 (1983).
147. 378 F.2d 832 (2d Cir. 1967).
148. Ibid., 849, 850 ("Here again it is all too easy to be misled by hindsight").
149. Plaintiff's brief had addressed the problem of multiple recoveries, but defendant's reply brief said that discussion was irrelevant. "Defendant's claim of lack of due process is not based upon multiple recoveries or the excessiveness of this particular verdict. This is a claim that the standards for recovery are unconstitutionally vague and that the standards to determine the amount of damages are non-existent." Reply Brief for Defendant-Appellant, 30.
150. 378 F.2d at 838–841.
151. BMW of North America, Inc. v. Gore, 517 U.S. 559 (1996); see State Farm Mutual Auto Insurance Co. v. Campbell, 538 U.S. 408 (2003).
152. 378 F.2d at 839–840.

153. Ibid., 839 n.11. Nine years later Friendly repeated his concerns in Morrissey v. National Maritime Union of America, 544 F.2d 19, 34 (2d Cir. 1976). In 2005 Congress passed the Class Action Fairness Act, which dealt with similar problems in the context of class actions. Pub. L. 109–2 (2005), 119 Stat. 4, codified in scattered sections in 28 U.S.C.

154. Richard A. Seltzer, "Punitive Damages in Mass Tort Litigation: Addressing the Problems of Fairness, Efficiency and Control," 52 *Fordham Law Review* (1983), 37, 53.

155. Laura J. Hines, "Obstacles to Determining Punitive Damages in Class Actions," 36 *Wake Forest Law Review* (2001), 889, 897.

17. Intellectual Property

1. Wood & Sons v. Reese Jewelry Corp., 278 F.2d 157, 160 (2d Cir. 1960) (Friendly, J., dissenting); *accord*, Friendly Voting Mem., Oct. 10, 1971, HLS-HJF, Box 59, Bolder 25, in King Research, Inc. v. Shulton, Inc., 454 F.2d 66 (2d Cir. 1972).

2. Friendly Voting Mem., Jan. 23, 1963, HLS-HJF, Box 8, Folder 12, in Gross v. JDF Mfg. Co., 314 F.2d 196 (2d Cir. 1963). Friendly made a similar statement in his Voting Mem., Jan. 25, 1967 ("My golden rule is that any invention I can understand is unpatentable leads speedily to affirmance here"), HLS-HJF, Box 33, Folder 9, in Kerr v. State Farm Life Insurance Co., 373 F.2d 62 (2d Cir. 1967).

3. Friendly Voting Mem., Apr. 12, 1976, HLS-HJF, Box 49, Folder 14, in Maclaren v. B-I-W Group, Inc., 535 F.2d 1367 (2d Cir. 1976) (Mansfield, J.).

4. Henry Friendly, *Federal Jurisdiction: A General View* (1973), 154–161.

5. 28 U.S.C. § 1295, 96 Stat. 37 (1982).

6. E.g., author interview of Walter Hellerstein, June 21, 2007. Friendly enjoyed engaging in the research for and writing the opinion in International Latex Corp. v. Warner Bros. Co., 276 F.2d 557 (2d Cir. 1960), a relatively simple and buoyant patent case involving latex girdles. Author interview of Milton Grossman, Apr. 10, 2006.

7. Benjamin Kaplan, *An Unhurried View of Copyright* (1967), 41.

8. 274 F.2d 487 (2d Cir. 1960) (Friendly, J., dissenting).

9. Ibid., 489–490. Hand cited Holy Trinity Church v. United States, 143 U.S. 457 (1892), but not United States v. American Trucking Assocs., 310 U.S. 534 (1940), as authority for the first sentence. Hand took advantage of the absurdity doctrine, too.

10. 274 F.2d at 490–491.

11. Herbert Rosenthal Jewelry Corp. v. Grossbardt, 436 F.2d 315 (2d Cir. 1970).

12. Puddu v. Buonamici Statuary, Inc., 450 F.2d 401 (2d Cir. 1971).

13. Hasbro Bradley, Inc. v. Sparkle Toys, Inc., 780 F.2d 189 (2d Cir. 1985).

14. 417 F.2d 497 (2d Cir. 1969) (Friendly, J., dissenting).

15. The suit against Universal was a test case. Other companies were using the "Ultimate Weapon" statue for commercial purposes, on kerchiefs, pillowcases, pads of paper, and many other products. According to Scherr, if they

won they could have "earned millions." Because they had no money, Scherr and Goodman had trouble getting a lawyer and hired a lawyer who would take the case on a contingent-fee basis. Author telephone interview of Stuart Scherr, Mar. 21, 2011.

16. 417 F.2d at 501. The Army was responsible for one change. "At one point the officer in charge of the project, noting what he deemed a similarity between Goodman's face and that on the statue, ordered the latter to be changed, which was done." Scherr v. Universal Match Corp., 297 F. Supp. 107, 109 (S.D.N.Y. 1967), *aff'd*, 417 F.2d 497 (2d Cir. 1968). Goodman had been using a photograph of himself for a model. Interview of Scherr, Mar. 21, 2011.

17. 417 F.2d at 502–503. For several months after argument on March 24, 1969, Friendly had been set to vote for Universal Match Corporation: "I would view the work as done in the normal course of military service." Friendly Mem., Aug. 11, 1969, HLS-HJF, Box 41, Folder 9 (marked "not sent").

18. 417 F.2d at 500. In *Donaldson*, Hays wrote the opinion, which Lumbard and Friendly joined.

19. 375 F.2d at 643 (emphasis added).

20. Brattleboro Publishing Co. v. Winmill Publishing Corp., 369 F.2d 565, 568 (2d Cir. 1966) (Kaufman, J.).

21. Friendly also placed his mark on copyright law in Rohauer v. Killiam Shows, Inc., 551 F.2d 484 (2d Cir. 1977), relating to renewals of copyrights on derivative works. One student work said that the opinion "created an exception" to the Copyright Act. Note, "*Rohauer v. Killiam Shows, Inc.* and the Derivative Work Exception to the Termination Right: Inequitable Anomalies under Copyright Law," 52 *Southern California Law Review* (1979), 635–637.

22. 287 F.2d 492 (2d Cir. 1961).

23. Ibid., 493–494.

24. Ibid., 494.

25. Ibid., 495. Friendly made another contribution in the classification of trademarks: "In the context of word marks, courts have applied the now-classic test originally formulated by Judge Friendly, in which word marks that are 'arbitrary' ('Camel' cigarettes), 'fanciful' ('Kodak' film) or 'suggestive' ('Tide' laundry detergent) are held to be inherently distinctive." Wal-Mart Stores, Inc. v. Samara Bros., 529 U.S. 205, 210–211 (2000) (Scalia, J.). Friendly wrote other significant opinions: Ives Laboratories, Inc. v. Darby Drug Co., 601 F.2d 631 (2d Cir. 1979) (trademark protection for nonfunctional color of drug); Abercrombie & Fitch Co. v. Hunting World, Inc., 537 F.2d 4 (2d Cir. 1976) (discussing trademark "Safari" in the context of "generic," "suggestive," or "merely descriptive" terms).

26. 287 F.2d at 496, 498. During the ten years of Polaroid's inactivity, Polarad's sales rose from $12,000 to $6 million.

27. Author interview of Judge Newman, Mar. 29, 2006. A commentator wrote in 2001, "The long, divisive struggle to work out a new consumer confusion test ended by the early 1960s in favor of those who supported broad protection. In *Polaroid,* Judge Friendly used *dicta* to propose his famous eight-factor formula for infringement analysis." Gerald N. Magliocca, "One and Inseparable:

Dilution and Infringement in Trademark Law," 85 *Minnesota Law Review* (2001), 949, 1005.

28. In more than one hundred instances Friendly identified assertions in other opinions of his as *dicta*.

29. Author interview of Warren Stern, Nov. 20, 2006.

30. See, e.g., Pauling v. News Syndicate Co., 335 F.2d 659 (2d Cir. 1964); *In re Horowitz*, 482 F.2d 72 (2d Cir. 1973); Moviecolor Ltd. v. Eastman Kodak Co., 288 F.2d 80 (2d Cir. 1961); Damsky v. Zavatt, 289 F.2d 46 (2d Cir. 1961) (whether Congress could constitutionally provide for an action *in personam* to enforce a tax lien without a jury trial).

31. Graziano v. Pennell, 371 F.2d 761, 763 (2d Cir. 1967); see, e.g., Salerno v. American League of Professional Baseball Clubs, 429 F.2d 1003 (2d Cir. 1970) (antitrust).

32. Kaufman v. Edelstein, 539 F.2d 811, 822–823 (2d Cir. 1976) (Gurfein, J., concurring).

33. Author interview of Judge Leonard Sand, Feb. 22, 2007.

34. J. Woodford Howard Jr., *Courts of Appeals in the Federal Judicial System* (1981), 130.

35. 335 F.2d 531 (2d Cir. 1964).

36. G. H. Mumm Champagne v. Eastern Wine Corp., 142 F.2d 499 (2d Cir. 1944).

37. 335 F.2d at 534, quoting 142 F.2d at 501.

38. 278 F.2d 157, 160 (2d Cir. 1960) (Friendly, J., dissenting).

18. Management and Labor

1. NLRB v. Bausch & Lomb, Inc., 526 F.2d 817, 828 (2d Cir. 1975) (Friendly, J., concurring and dissenting); *accord*, Prudential Insurance Co. of America v. NLRB, 412 F.2d 77, 86 (Friendly, J., dissenting).

2. E.g., Sanford H. Kadish, "Labor and the Law," *Felix Frankfurter, the Judge* (Wallace Mendelson, ed., 1964), 154–155, 185–186, 202–205.

3. 56 U.S.C. §§ 51–60.

4. 46 U.S.C. § 688; see Longshoremen's and Harbor Workers' Act, Ch. 509, 44 Stat. 1424–1446, *formerly*, 33 U.S.C. §§ 901–950, amended by the Longshoremen's and Harbor Workers Compensation Act Amendment, 86 Stat. 1251 (1972).

5. A Ninth Circuit judge criticized Friendly's efforts to restrict recovery by long-shoremen: "We reject what we regard as the ill-advised attempts as exemplified in ... *Forkin* [v. Furness Withy & Co., 323 F.2d 638 (2d Cir. 1963) (Friendly, J.)] ... to attach unwarranted exceptions to the rules heretofore applied by the Supreme Court in this field." Huff v. Matson Navigation Co., 338 F.2d 205 (9th Cir. 1964).

6. Author interview of Judge Jon O. Newman, Mar. 29, 2006; author telephone interview of Judge Ralph K. Winter, June 19, 2006; e.g., Skibinski v. Waterman S.S. Co., 360 F.2d 539, 544 (2d Cir. 1966) (Friendly, J., dissenting); see James C. Stokes, "Henry J. Friendly—Opinions in Admiralty and Maritime Law, 1959–1974," 7 *Journal of Maritime Law and Commerce* (1975), 275, 282–290 (citing "Judge Friendly's belief in a limited, reasonable application of the absolute

duty of seaworthiness" regarding seamen and a narrower application relating to longshoremen). Congress reformed the area when it passed the 1972 amendments to the Harbor Workers' Compensation Act, 33 U.S.C. § 901 *et seq.*

7. Friendly letter to Kaufman (bcc to Lumbard), July 21, 1966, HLS-HJF, Box 217, Folder 2.

8. 388 F.2d 921 (2d Cir. 1967).

9. Ibid., 929–930 (Hays, J., dissenting).

10. NLRB v. Local 50, American Bakery Workers, 339 F.2d 324, 329 (2d Cir. 1964) (Friendly, J., dissenting).

11. Local 138, International Union of Operating Engineers v. NLRB, 321 F.2d 130, 138 (2d Cir. 1963) (Friendly, J., concurring in part, dissenting in part).

12. Bon-R Reproductions, Inc. v. NLRB, 309 F.2d 898, 907–909 (2d Cir. 1962) (Friendly, J., concurring in part and dissenting in part).

13. NLRB v. Lundy Mfg. Corp., 316 F.2d 921 (2d Cir. 1963) (Friendly, J.).

14. 345 F.2d 346, 349 (2d Cir. 1965) (Friendly, J., dissenting).

15. 404 F.2d 80 (2d Cir. 1974).

16. 418 F.2d 736 (2d Cir. 1969).

17. Ibid., 740–746.

18. Waterman nevertheless wrote, "I fully concur with my brother Kaufman." Ibid., 763.

19. Ibid., 768–771 (Friendly, J., concurring and dissenting).

20. The NLRA requires giving employees' representatives meaningful joint participation in the "shared process" of negotiation. General Electric Co., 150 N.L.R.B. 192, 194 (1964).

21. Henry Friendly, "New Trends in Administrative Law," 6 *Maryland Bar Journal* (1974), 9, 12; *accord*, Hanly v. Kleindienst, 471 F.2d 823, 839 (2d Cir. 1972) (Friendly, J.) ("such a policy has the added benefits of allowing opponents to blow off steam and giving them the sense that their objections have been considered").

22. 326 F.2d 172 (2d Cir. 1963) (Medina, J.). Filing briefs as *amici curiae* were the American Civil Liberties Union, the AFL-CIO, the NAACP, and the United Automobile Workers of America, all supporting the NLRB and, by extension, employee Lopuch.

23. Ibid., 176, 180.

24. See Case Note, 18 *Vanderbilt Law Review* (1964), 262, 271, 274.

25. 326 F.2d at 181, 183 (Friendly, J., dissenting). The NAACP's brief stated constructively, "When the bargaining agent can use the employer's power to give effect to its arbitrary decisions, union membership will be encouraged." Brief for NAACP as Amicus Curiae, 7.

26. Brief for NLRB, 11.

27. Longshoremen, Local 1367, 148 N.L.R.B. 897 (1964), *enforced,* 368 F.2d 1010 (5th Cir. 1966).

28. Hodgson v. Corning Glass Works, 474 F.2d 226 (2d Cir. 1973). Friendly narrowed the scope of Judge Curtin's injunction on the ground that there was a limited violation of the Equal Pay Act and Corning had made sincere efforts to

bring itself into compliance. The parties' briefs did not analyze separately Corning's allegedly discriminatory acts, which Friendly's opinion did.

29. Ibid., 233, 235–236.

30. Corning Glass Works v. Brennan, 417 U.S. 188, 198 (1974) (Marshall, J.).

31. Cipriano v. Board of Education of the School District of North Tonowanda, 785 F.2d 51 (2d Cir. 1986).

32. Ibid., 58. Victory eluded Cipriano and Miller. On remand Curtin first creatively found in their favor, 700 F. Supp. 1199 (W.D.N.Y. 1988), but finally was forced to find against them on the basis of a pair of new Supreme Court decisions. 772 F. Supp. 1346 (W.D.N.Y. 1991); author interview of Judge Curtin, Oct. 12, 2006.

33. 650 F.2d 395 (2d Cir. 1981).

34. 323 F.2d 257, 268 (2d Cir. 1963).

35. Friendly wrote other employment-discrimination opinions favoring plaintiffs, e.g., Vulcan Society of N.Y.C. Fire Dept. v. Civil Service Comm'n, 490 F.2d 387 (2d Cir. 1973).

19. Railroad Reorganization

1. E.g., Ari Hoogenboom and Olive Hoogenboom, *A History of the ICC: From Panacea to Palliative* (1976), 179–182; George W. Hilton, *The Northeast Railroad Problem* (1975).

2. Quoted in *In re* Valuation Proceeding under Reg. Rail Reorg. Act, 531 F. Supp. 1191, 1215 (R.R.R. Ct. 1981) (*per curiam*) (parenthetical in original).

3. *Ohio History, Scholarly Journal of Ohio Historical Society* (1998), Vol. 101, p. 15.

4. 45 U.S.C. §§ 101 *ff.* Meanwhile, under a different process, the government was creating Amtrak to deal with passenger rail service.

5. John Minor Wisdom, "Views of a Friendly Observer," 133 *University of Pennsylvania Law Review* (1984), 63; author interview of John G. Harkins Jr. (attorney for Conrail), Dec. 19, 2007.

6. Regional Rail Reorganization Act Cases, 419 U.S. 102, 116–117 (1974).

7. Author interview of Ruth Wedgwood, Mar. 1, 2007.

8. E.g., New York, New Haven, & Hartford R.R. v. United States, 305 F. Supp. 1049 (S.D.N.Y. 1969) (Friendly, J.), *vacated sub nom.*, New Haven Inclusion Cases, 399 U.S. 392 (1970).

9. Wisdom, "Views," 69. Wisdom replaced original court member Judge Carl McGowan of the District of Columbia Circuit.

10. *In re* Penn Central Transp. Co., 384 F. Supp. 895 (R.R.R. Ct. 1974). Individual judges on the Special Court wrote a portion of the opinion and joined in the portions written by the other judges. Former Friendly clerks William Lake and Stuart C. Stock, who each argued a portion of the case for the side he represented, feared an onslaught by their former boss. Friendly, however, asked them no questions, but smiled as Wisdom quizzed each of the two closely. Author interview of Stock, Dec. 1, 2006.

11. 383 F. Supp. 510 (E.D. Pa. 1974), *rev'd sub nom.*, Railroad Reorganization Cases, 419 U.S. 102 (1974).

12. 28 U.S.C. § 1491.

13. 384 F. Supp. at 939–943. Friendly was suspicious of congressional reports and had previously expressed concern over committee reports being "manufactured" to create legislative history. Henry Friendly, *Benchmarks* (1967), 216 n.114; Notes for Talk, "Statutorification of Federal Law," late 1981 or early 1982, HLS-HJF, Box 227, Folder 23.

14. "I am not sure whether the lack of clarity was due to haste or a desire to pass the buck, or to both." Friendly letter to Prof. Guido Calabresi, June 14, 1982, HLS-HJF, Box 220, Folder 2.

15. 384 F. Supp. at 943–948.

16. Vanston Bondholders Protective Comm'n v. Green, 329 U.S. 156, 170 (1946), quoted in Friendly's *Commonplace Book*. The same entry also quoted Lord Frederic Maitland: "If we can ask the right question we shall have done something for a good end."

17. 384 F. Supp. at 939. Louis Craco, a prominent lawyer in the case, said it was the best judicial opinion he had ever seen. Author interview of Louis Craco (attorney for Penn Central lienholders), Mar. 18, 2008.

18. 419 U.S. 102 (1974).

19. Ibid., 121.

20. Nevertheless, and unfairly to Wisdom, the saying emerged that Wisdom was friendly, but Friendly had the wisdom. Author interview of Warren Stern, Nov. 20, 2006.

21. Author interview of Edwin Zimmerman (attorney for Penn Central), Jan. 22, 2008.

22. E.g., author interview of Robert Kapp (attorney for USRA), Jan. 25, 2008. One expert called the RRRA the "Consultants Compensation Act." Author interview of Lewis M. Schneider, Nov. 8, 2010.

23. Author interview of Howard H. Lewis (attorney for Reading Railroad), Jan. 28, 2008.

24. Henry Friendly, "From a Fellow Worker on the Railroads," 60 *Tulane Law Review* (1985), 249–250.

25. Ibid., 244, 254; see author interview of William Lake, Nov. 29, 2006.

26. Friendly letter to Jerry W. Ryan, Apr. 4, 1983, HLS-HJF, Box 220, Folder 5.

27. E.g., Consolidated Rail Corp. v. Pittsburgh & Lake Erie R.R., 459 F. Supp. 1013 (R.R.R. Ct. 1978); Consolidated Rail Corp. v. Delaware & Hudson Ry., 543 F. Supp. 1079 (R.R.R. Ct. 1982).

28. E.g., Norwich & Worcester R.R. v. United States, 408 F. Supp. 1398 (R.R.R. Ct. 1976); Penn Central Corp. v. United States Ry. Assoc., 475 F. Supp. 165 (R.R.R. Ct. 1979).

29. Author interview of Louis Cohen (attorney for USRA), Feb. 11, 2008.

30. Friendly indicated that any attempt to rely on reproduction costs would have to overcome some very high hurdles. 445 F. Supp. at 1036–1037.

31. *In re* Valuation Proceeding under Reg. Rail Reorg. Act, 445 F. Supp. 994 (R.R.R. Ct. 1977) (fifty-two-page opinion). Friendly had previously written opinions on

just compensation, e.g., United States v. Certain Property in Manhattan, 306 F.2d 439 (2d Cir. 1962).

32. *In re* Valuation Proceeding under Reg. Rail Reorg. Act, 439 F. Supp. 1351 (R.R.R. Ct. 1977).

33. Ibid., 1387.

34. 531 F. Supp. at 1214.

35. 445 F. Supp. at 1044–1047.

36. Posner letter to Friendly, June 8, 1982, HLS-HJF, Box 183, Folder 3.

37. Howard C. Westwood, *Covington and Burling, 1919–84* (1986), 241.

38. *In re* Valuation Proceeding under Reg. Rail Reorg. Act, 531 F. Supp. 1191, 1210–1214 (R.R.R. Ct. 1981) *(per curiam)* (201 pages).

39. *In re* Valuation Proceeding under Reg. Rail Reorg. Act, 571 F. Supp. 1269 (R.R.R. Ct. 1983) *(per curiam)* (seventy-two pages) (dealing with evaluation of assets not directly involved in future railroad operations of Conrail, mostly real estate).

40. Friendly, "From a Fellow Worker," 244, 250.

41. Author interview of Lewis, Jan. 28, 2008.

42. Author interview of Weiss (attorney for Jersey Central), Jan. 24, 2008. Weiss felt his client was entitled to at least twice as much. See Friendly, "From a Fellow Worker," 254 ("the figure, $42,509,299, at which we arrived after pages of discussion, fell between the amounts contended for by the two sides and seemingly did not provoke outcries from either").

43. Author interview of Lewis, Jan. 28, 2008.

44. Author interview of Craco, Mar. 18, 2008.

45. Author interview of Harkins, Dec. 19, 2007.

20. Administrative Law

1. Thomas K. McGraw, *Prophets of Regulation* (1984).

2. While he ordinarily welcomed complex cases, Friendly criticized one plaintiff for having brought his case to the Second Circuit rather than to the District of Columbia Circuit, which had previous connections to the case. Lead Industry Assoc. v. OSHA, 610 F.2d 70, 79 (2d Cir. 1979).

3. Kenneth Culp Davis, 1 *Administrative Law Treatise* (2d ed., 1978), § 1:1, at 2.

4. Mary Ann Glendon, *A Nation under Lawyers* (1994), 133 ("Federal Judges like Learned Hand, Augustus A. Hand, and later Henry Friendly did for regulatory law what Cardozo had done for private law"); *accord*, Richard A. Posner, "The Rise and Fall of Administrative Law," 72 *Chicago-Kent Law Review* (1997), 953, 954–955 (for many decades the "dominant voices in administrative law" in the judiciary were Frankfurter and Friendly).

5. 326 F.2d 172, 186 n.7 (2d Cir. 1963).

6. National Nutritional Foods Assoc. v. FDA, 491 F.2d 1141 (2d Cir. 1974).

7. 401 U.S. 402, 420 (1971).

8. A. Raymond Randolph, "Administrative Law and the Legacy of Henry J. Friendly," 74 *New York University Law Review* (1999), 8. Still, Friendly rejected the idea that agencies were immune from judicial review for allegedly

arbitrary actions. Cappadora v. Celebrezze, 356 F.2d 1 (2d Cir. 1966). Friendly supported oversight by Congress. Statement of Friendly before Subcommittee on Separation of Powers of the Committee of the Judiciary, U.S. Senate, May 23, 1968, HLS-HJF, Box 153, Folder 8.

9. Henry Friendly, "A Look at the Federal Administrative Agencies," 60 *Columbia Law Review* (1960), 429, reprinted in Henry Friendly, *Benchmarks* (1967), 65. Friendly also criticized agency appointments and administrative delay. *Benchmarks*, 68–71, 78–81.

10. Ibid., 78–85.

11. The lectures appear at 75 *Harvard Law Review* (1962), 863, 1055, 1263, and were published as a book, Henry Friendly, *The Federal Administrative Agencies: The Need for Better Definition of Standards* (1962). Subsequent notes are cited to the book.

12. E.g., James M. Landis, "Report on Regulatory Agencies to the President-elect," U.S. Senate, Committee on Judiciary, 86th Cong., 2d Sess. (Dec. 1960).

13. Friendly, *Better Definition*, 5–6, 14.

14. Ibid., viii.

15. Ibid., 22–23. Friendly had good company in criticizing these agencies. E.g., Landis, "Report on Regulatory Agencies," 41, 53. Friendly cited Landis's effort liberally.

16. Friendly, *Better Definition*, 74.

17. Ibid., 97, quoting *Iolanthe* (W. S. Gilbert).

18. Ronald A. Giannella, book review of Friendly, *The Federal Administrative Agencies*, 8 *Villanova Law Review* (1963), 629, 630.

19. Author interview of Frank Goodman, July 20, 2009. Friendly followed the fortunes of the airline as well as of New York Telephone Company. E.g., Friendly letter to C. W. Phelan, Mar. 27, 1962, HLS-HJF, Box 213, Folder 4.

20. Friendly, Remarks, in Hugh B. Cox, *The Perfect Advocate* (1976), 28; FTD, Tape 3, pp. 13–14.

21. Friendly, *Better Definition*, 152–153.

22. Ibid., 97.

23. Ibid., 165.

24. James M. Landis, book review of Friendly, *Better Definition*, 30 *University of Chicago Law Review* (1963), 597.

25. Louis L. Jaffe, book review of Friendly, *Better Definition*, 76 *Harvard Law Review* (1963), 858, 859, 862; see Louis J. Hector, book review of Friendly, *Benchmarks*, 81 *Harvard Law Review* (1968), 1590, 1596–1597 (Friendly should consider "whether an insistence on general substantive standards for broad economic decisions might not create the same sort of straight jacket the Judge has feared recent Supreme Court decisions may have created in the field of criminal procedure"); Carl McFarland, book review of Friendly, *Better Definition*, 37 *New York University Law Review* (1962), 1171, 1173–1174 (mixed review).

26. Friendly, *Better Definition*, 36–52.

27. Trico Products Corp. v. NLRB, 489 F.2d 347, 348 (2d Cir. 1973).

28. Long Island College Hospital v. NLRB, 566 F.2d 833, 844 (2d Cir. 1977).

29. E.g., NLRB v. A.P.W. Products Co., 316 F.2d 899, 906 (2d Cir. 1963).

30. In 1967 Friendly explained his dissatisfaction with the NLRB in a previously unpublished chapter in *Benchmarks*, 135, "Watchman, What of the Night?"

31. 475 F.2d 485 (2d Cir. 1973) (Friendly, J.), *aff'd in part, rev'd in part*, 416 U.S. 267 (1974).

32. 29 U.S.C. §§ 151 *ff.*

33. 475 F.2d at 495–497.

34. SEC v. Chenery Corp., 332 U.S. 194 (1947) ("*Chenery II*"). The Court had earlier decided SEC v. Chenery Corp., 318 U.S. 80 (1943) ("*Chenery I*"); see Friendly letter to Prof. Louis Jaffe, Nov. 12, 1962, HLS-HJF, Box 212, Folder 9.

35. 475 F.2d at 497. Friendly had previously admonished the Board to proceed by rule making. H. & F. Binch Co. v. NLRB, 456 F.2d 357, 365 (2d Cir. 1972); NLRB v. Majestic Weaving Co., 355 F.2d 854, 860–861 (2d Cir. 1966). He did not discuss whether the courts or the administrative agencies were more expert on whether rules or adjudication was the superior approach.

36. NLRB v. Bell Aerospace Co., 416 U.S. 267 (1974). Friendly had written two articles on *Chenery*: Henry Friendly, "'Limited Office' of the *Chenery* Decision," 21 *Administrative Law Review* (1968), 1, 3; Henry Friendly, "*Chenery* Revisited: Reflections on Reversal and Remand of Administrative Orders," 1969 *Duke Law Journal*, 199.

37. 267 U.S. at 293–295. Friendly's opinion had considered that point: "To be sure, the change in policy here in question did not expose an employer to new and unexpected liability." 475 F.2d at 497.

38. Compare Kenneth Culp Davis and Richard J. Pierce Jr., *Administrative Law Treatise* (3d ed., 1994), 268 ("The law remains as Justice Murphy described in [*Chenery*], and his reasons probably cannot be answered satisfactorily") with Bernard Schwartz, *Administrative Law* (3d ed., 1991), 218 ("The Supreme Court reversal in *Bell Aerospace* is unfortunate," providing reasons similar to Friendly's).

39. Randolph, "Administrative Law," 12; Todd Rakoff, "In Memoriam: Henry J. Friendly," 99 *Harvard Law Review* (1986), 1725, 1727.

40. McCraw, *Prophets*, 91–94.

41. Author interview of Justice Breyer, Apr. 8, 2008. Prof. Yale Kamisar remarked on Friendly's open-mindedness in connection with the ALI's drafting a pre-arraignment code. Author telephone interview of Kamisar, Dec. 2, 2010.

42. ABA, Commission on Law and Economy, *Federal Regulation: Roads to Reform* (1979), 2. The recommendation limited the nature, scope, and duration of presidential interventions.

43. Ibid., 163–164. For a succinct summary of the deregulation of airlines, see McCraw, *Prophets*, 259–294.

44. Associated Industries of New York State, Inc. v. Department of Labor, 487 F.2d 342, 344–345 (2d Cir. 1973). This is one of Friendly's long sentences. See Henry Friendly, "Marching into the Third Century," 16 *Judges Journal* (1977), 6, 51.

45. The leading casebook in the field currently has three Friendly opinions as principal cases. Peter Barton Hutt and Lewis A. Grossman, *Food and Drug Law: Cases and Materials* (3d ed., 2007).

46. Sterling Drug, Inc. v. Weinberger, 509 F.2d 1236, 1237 (2d Cir. 1975).

47. Becton, Dickinson & Co. v. FDA, 589 F.2d 1175, 1182 (2d Cir. 1978).

48. Ibid.; National Nutritional Foods Assoc. v. Califano, 603 F.2d 327 (2d Cir. 1979).

49. National Assoc. of Pharmaceutical Manufacturers v. FDA, 637 F.2d 877 (2d Cir. 1981).
    387 U.S. 136 (1967).

50. Pfizer, Inc. v. Richardson, 434 F.2d 536, 541 (2d Cir. 1970). Involved was the drug tetracycline, manufactured in combination with other drugs.

51. 360 F.2d 677 (2d Cir. 1966), *aff'd,* 387 U.S. 158, 167 (1967).

52. Appellee's Brief, 47.

53. 360 F.2d at 685–687. One year later the Supreme Court in *Abbott Laboratories v. Gardner,* 387 U.S. 136 (1967) (see Randolph, "Administrative Law," 9), adopted Friendly's approach nearly word-for-word when it resolved the question of pre-enforcement reviewability of agency regulations. Harvard professors Stephen G. Breyer and Richard B. Stewart commented, "Before *Abbott Laboratories* the courts typically reviewed the lawfulness of an agency's rule, not when it was promulgated, but when it was enforced. After *Abbott Laboratories* reviewing practice changed radically." Stephen G. Breyer and Richard B. Stewart, *Administrative Law and Regulatory Policy* (2d ed., 1985), 1136.

54. 471 F.2d 823 (2d Cir. 1972). *Hanly* has appeared in environmental law casebooks, e.g., Peter S. Menell and Richard B. Stewart, *Environmental Law and Policy* (1994), 910; William Murray Tabb and Linda A. Malone, *Environmental Law: Cases and Materials* (1997), 243.

55. See Comment, 5 *Rutgers-Camden Law Journal* (1974), 380.

56. Hanly v. Mitchell, 460 F.2d 640 (2d Cir. 1972); section 102(2)(C) of the National Environmental Policy Act of 1969 required an EIS for the construction of all federal projects "significantly affecting the quality of the human environment."

57. 471 F.2d at 833, 839–840. Friendly likewise rejected the majority's view that an EIS was required when environmental impact would be minimal.

58. 592 F.2d 658 (2d Cir. 1979).

59. Ibid., 668, 672.

60. Ibid., 673. This was yet another case in which Friendly faulted a lawyer's performance. "[T]he Auto Clubs made a miserable presentation both before the Administrator and here." Friendly Voting Mem., Jan. 4, 1979.

61. Automobile Club of New York, Inc. v. Port Authority, 887 F.2d 417, 423 (2d Cir. 1989).

21. Common Law and Federal Common Law

1. 304 U.S. 64 (1938). "Probably no single decision in the whole of Anglo-American legal history ever overturned so many prior decisions at a single stroke as Erie R.R. v. Tompkins, 304 U.S. 64 (1938). Overnight, whole treatises were rendered obsolete." Henry M. Hart Jr. and Albert M. Sacks, *The*

Legal Process (William N. Eskridge Jr. and Philip P. Frickey, eds., 1994), 1338–1339; see Akhil Reed Amar, book review of *Hart and Wechsler's The Federal Courts and the Federal System,* by Paul M. Bator et al. (3d ed., 1988), 102 *Harvard Law Review* (1989), 688, 695. *Erie* was the most frequently cited case in the first three editions of *Hart and Wechsler.*

2. 41 U.S. 1, 19 (1842) ("The law respecting negotiable instruments may be truly declared in the language of Cicero, adopted by Lord Mansfield in Luke v. Lyde, 2 Burr. R. 883, 887, to be in a great measure, not the law of a single country only, but of the commercial world"). Federal commercial law, by encouraging commerce, tended to favor business over the consumer. See Edward A. Purcell Jr., *Brandeis and the Progressive Constitution* (2000), 64–67; Morton J. Horwitz, *The Transformation of American Law, 1780–1860* (1992), 249.

3. Horowitz, *Transformation,* 155. Henry Friendly, "In Praise of *Erie*—and of the New Federal Common Law," 39 *New York University Law Review* (1964), 383, reprinted in Henry Friendly, *Benchmarks* (1967), 155, 179. *Erie* all but removed one argument for diversity jurisdiction, because federal courts could rarely influence state law. Purcell, *Brandeis,* 248–251.

4. Jaftex Corp. v. Randolph Mills, Inc., 282 F.2d 508 (2d Cir. 1960) (Friendly, J., dissenting); Arrowsmith v. United Press International, 320 F.2d 219 (2d Cir. 1963) (*en banc*) (Friendly, J.).

5. The Federal Judiciary Act of Sept. 24, 1789, 28 U.S.C. § 725, read, "The laws of the several States, except where the Constitution, treaties, or statutes of the United States otherwise require or provide, shall be regarded as rules of decision in trials at common law, in the courts of the United States, in cases where they apply." Swift v. Tyson had construed the "laws of the several States" to apply only to statutes, a position Friendly considered quite reasonable. Friendly letter to David Currie, Mar. 18, 1964, HLS-HJF, Box 211, Folder 15.

6. Friendly, *Benchmarks,* 167–168. Friendly cited statements by both Hamilton and Madison in *The Federalist* Nos. 33 and 44. Judge Louis Pollak summed it up: "Friendly canvassed the major (and minor) criticisms of *Erie* and left them pulverized." Louis Pollak, "In Praise of Friendly," 133 *University of Pennsylvania Law Review* (1984), 39, 50.

7. All editions of *Hart and Wechsler* that followed Friendly's speech have published a lengthy quotation on this point, which included the passage just quoted. E.g., Richard H. Fallon Jr. et al., *Hart and Wechsler's The Federal Courts and the Federal System* (5th ed., 2003), 693; see Daniel J. Meltzer, "State Court Forfeiture of Federal Rights," 99 *Harvard Law Review* (1985), 1128, 1167–1176.

8. "[T]he achievements of these two great judges [Learned Hand and Friendly] have been principally in crafting common law, and most impressively, a common law of statutes." Philip Bobbitt, *Constitutional Fate: Theory of the Constitution* (1982), 53; *accord,* author interview of Merrick Garland, Nov. 16, 2006 (regarding Friendly).

9. Friendly, *Benchmarks,* 178. The first sentence of this quotation and the following quotation are examples of long Friendly sentences.

10. Ibid., 195.

11. Republic of Iraq v. First National City Bank, 353 F.2d 47, 50–51 (2d Cir. 1965); see Edward M. Morgan, "Act of Blindness, State of Insight," 13 *Boston University International Law Journal* (1995), 1, 24–28.

12. Genesco, Inc. v. Joint Counsel 13, United Shoe Workers, 341 F.2d 482, 489 (2d Cir. 1965).

13. United States v. Wegematic Corp., 360 F.2d 674, 676 (2d Cir. 1966). Friendly believed that Congress could, if so inclined, enact the Uniform Commercial Code, although, he observed, that would allow every action based on the UCC to be brought in a federal court.

14. Friendly, *Benchmarks*, 13, discussing McWeeney v. New York, New Haven & Hartford R.R., 282 F.2d 34 (2d Cir. 1960) (*en banc*), where the issue was whether a jury should be instructed on the taxability or nontaxability of awards under the Federal Employers' Liability Act, 45 U.S.C. §§ 51-60. See Jay Tidmarsh and Brian J. Murray, "A Theory of Federal Common Law," 100 *Northwestern Law Review* (2006), 585, 587 ("Following the analysis of Paul Mishkin and Henry Friendly, the Supreme Court has held that courts are not required to exercise their federal common lawmaking power in all cases").

15. Purcell, *Brandeis*, 290; Larry Kramer, "The Lawmaking Power of the Federal Courts," 12 *Pace Law Review* (1992), 263–264.

16. Philip J. Weiser, "Federal Common Law, Cooperative Federalism, and the Enforcement of the Telecom Act," 76 *New York University Law Review* (2001), 1692, 1704; *accord*, Richard B. Stewart and Cass B. Sunstein, "Public Programs and Private Rights," 95 *Harvard Law Review* (1982), 1193, 1223 ("The 'mid-century type of federal common law' celebrated by Friendly seems rapidly headed for oblivion," referring to interstate unfair competition, implied causes of action, and the interpretation and enforcement of certain labor-management agreements).

17. 139 N.E. 226 (N.Y. 1923).

18. 162 N.E. 99 (N.Y. 1928).

19. Andrew L. Kaufman, *Cardozo* (1998), 287, quoting William Prosser, "*Palsgraf* Revisited," 52 *Michigan Law Review* (1953), 1. For a discussion of why the case is so famous, see Richard A. Posner, *Cardozo: A Study in Reputation* (1990), 41–47; John T. Noonan Jr., *Persons and Masks of the Law* (1976), 111.

20. 338 F.2d 708 (2d Cir. 1964).

21. 388 F.2d 11 (2d Cir. 1968).

22. 338 F.2d at 712.

23. Ibid., 712–713.

24. Ibid., 713–717.

25. Ibid., 717.

26. 33 U.S.C. §§ 494, 499.

27. 33 C.F.R. § 203.707.

28. 338 F.2d at 719.

29. Ibid., 721.

30. Sinram v. Pennsylvania R.R., 61 F.2d 767, 770 (2d Cir. 1932).

31. *Palsgraf*, 162 N.E. at 105 (Andrews, J., dissenting). Judge Posner called Cardozo's statement of facts "both elliptical and slanted." Posner, *Cardozo*, 38–40.

32. 338 F.2d at 721. Friendly employed a footnote to observe, "There was exceedingly little evidence of negligence of any sort. . . . How much ink would have been saved over the years if the Court of Appeals had reversed Mrs. Palsgraf's judgment on the basis that there was no evidence of negligence at all!" (721, n.5).

33. Ibid., 721–722.

34. Friendly noted that English law imposed liability when the injury was caused somewhat differently than could be expected, providing the damages were "direct." Ibid., 723–724. No brief mentioned English law.

35. Ibid., 725.

36. E.g., Guido Calabresi, "The Decision for Accidents: An Approach to Non-Fault Allocation of Costs," 78 *Harvard Law Review* (1965), 713, 725–734; Guido Calabresi, *The Costs of Accidents* (1970); Richard A. Posner, *Economic Analysis of the Law* (1972, 1973).

37. 338 F.2d at 725–726.

38. Friendly Mem., Apr. 13, 1964, HLS-HJF, Box 21, Folder 19.

39. Judge Moore dissented from the portion of Friendly's opinion that awarded damages for harm caused by the flooding of the upstream properties. 338 F.2d at 727.

40. Calabresi email to author, Sept. 18, 2008.

41. Author interview of Pierre N. Leval, Oct. 17, 2006.

42. Brief for the City of Buffalo, 5–12.

43. 338 F.2d at 722.

44. 398 F.2d 167, 172 (2d Cir. 1968).

45. Ibid. (ellipses and parenthetical in original); see Noonan, *Persons and Masks*, 112 ("William S. Andrews, who wrote an opinion in the case no less eloquent than Cardozo's, saw negligence as a breach of duty of a man to observe care toward 'his fellows,' not toward specific persons he should have seen as endangered by what he did"). Friendly chose to accept Cardozo's more cumbersome approach that included the arguably superfluous concept of "duty" to specific individuals. Andrews's dissent focused on proximate cause. Friendly noted that Cardozo "did not reach the issue of 'proximate cause' for which the case is often cited." 338 F.2d at 722–723 and n.8.

46. 388 F.2d 11 (2d Cir. 1968).

47. The first sentence of Article 30 read, "No action or proceeding against the Company for death or injury of any kind to the passenger shall be instituted, unless written notice is given to the Company or its duly authorized Agent within six months from the day when the death or injury occurred and the action or suit arising therefrom is commenced within one year from the date when the death or injury occurred." 388 F.2d at 12.

48. Ibid., 14. Reproducing the Italian version of the last sentence, Friendly's opinion pointed out that the English version was different from the Italian because the latter indicated "cover and leaves" while the English referred just to "cover." Friendly rejected any argument that Silvestri was misled; Silvestri's deposition showed he understood both Italian and English (18 and n.6). So did Friendly.

49. *Williston on Contracts* said, "[T]o be valid, a limitation [on a passenger ticket] must be fair and reasonable and not contrary to the dictates of public policy." There followed a listing of some of the types of limitations, with footnotes citing representative cases, including *Murray*, but no indication of their facts or outcome. 10 *Williston on Contracts* § 1098 (3d ed. 1967),186–187 and nn.7–9. Another leading treatise said, "[A passenger] can not hold the insurer or carrier to a promise other than that contained in the document because the latter has made no other promise; and he can not have the contract set aside for mistake, because he has made no mistake," citing, *inter alia*, *Murray*, but without discussing the case. 3 *Corbin on Contracts* (1960), § 607, pp. 661–662 and n.17.

50. HLS-HJF, Box 37, Folder 30.

51. 388 F.2d at 13; see, e.g., Conte v. Flota Mercante del Estado, 277 F.2d 664, 671 (2d Cir. 1960) ("None of these authorities was called to the District Court's attention or, for that matter, to ours").

52. 388 F.2d at 13–14.

53. 139 N.E. 226 (N.Y. 1923).

54. Ibid., 227–228 (asterisks in original to show original deletion).

55. 388 F.2d at 15.

56. Ibid., 15–16 and n.4, referring to Baron v. Compagnie Generale Transatlantique, 108 F.2d 21 (2d Cir. 1939). When he effectively overruled Wm. H. Muller & Co. v. Swedish American Line, Ltd., 224 F.2d 806 (2d Cir. 1955), in Indussa Corp. v. S.S. Ranborg, 377 F.2d 200, 203 (2d Cir. 1967) (*en banc*), Friendly observed, "Examination of the *Muller* briefs shows that counsel had not called the court's attention to Knott v. Botany Mills, 179 U.S. 69 (1900)." In United States *ex rel.* LaNear v. La Valle, 306 F.2d 417, 421–422 (2d Cir. 1962), Friendly disposed of a precedent by referring to the "meager *pro se* brief filed by the [petitioner] [that] did not contend that such exhaustion was not required." In Weight Watchers of Philadelphia, Inc. v. Weight Watchers International, Inc., 455 F.2d 770, 774 (2d Cir. 1972), Friendly wrote that "examination of the briefs confirms [that] the issue of appellate jurisdiction was not raised." In Escott v. Barchris Construction Corp., 340 F.2d 731, 735 (2d Cir. 1965) (Friendly, J. concurring), the judge avoided an arguable precedent in part because "the [court's] statement was initially framed without the benefit of argument from counsel," adding, "While the question was raised on rehearing, the court's attention at that time undoubtedly centered on the quite different problems." Friendly sometimes had his clerks read briefs submitted in precedents to see if the parties there had made or fully briefed an argument. Author interview of Paul Mogin, Nov. 28, 2006.

57. United States v. Maybury, 274 F.2d 899, 905 (2d Cir. 1960).

58. William N. Eskridge Jr. et al., *Cases and Materials on Legislation: Statutes and the Creation of Public Policy* (4th ed., 2007), 751.

59. Lehman v. Dow Jones & Co., 783 F.2d 285, 294 (2d Cir. 1986).

60. 388 F.2d at 17–18.

61. Ibid., 18. Friendly did not explain why the Italian line should have had to prove actual notice on the part of Silvestri.

62. Andrew L. Kaufman, *Cardozo* (1998), 358. The reference was to Greene v. Sibley, Lindsay & Curr Co., 177 N.E. 416 (N.Y. 1931), where Cardozo had denied relief to a woman who walked before she looked.

63. Noonan, *Persons and Masks*, 144. "I suppose that my implicit criticism of Cardozo in *P&M* was that he focused solely on the principle he sought to establish." Judge Noonan email to author, May 18, 2010.

64. Author interview of Prof. Melvin A. Eisenberg, Oct. 18, 2007.

65. Kaufman, *Cardozo*, 147–149, 472–473. Kaufman did note that Cardozo had been on an ocean liner, although he did not say how many times (357–358). The implication was that it was a small number, perhaps one.

66. Author interview of Bruce Ackerman, Aug. 6, 2007.

67. Friendly Mem., Nov. 8, 1962, HLS-HJF, Box 13, Folder 11, in Essex Universal Corp. v. Yates, 305 F.2d 572, 580 (2d Cir. 1962) (Friendly, J., concurring).

68. Friendly letter to Michael Boudin, Feb. 7, 1985, HLS-HJF, Box 221, Folder 4. Significant Friendly state-law cases not discussed elsewhere in this volume include Jaftex Corp. v. Randolph Mills, Inc., 282 F.2d 508, 516 (2d Cir. 1960) (Friendly, J., concurring) (choosing between state rule and federal rule on the issue of joinder of parties in diversity case); Feldman v. Allegheny Airlines, Inc., 524 F.2d 384, 390 (2d Cir. 1975) (Friendly, J., concurring) (propriety of allowing for inflation in monetary award for wrongful death); Bloor v. Falstaff Brewing Corp., 601 F.2d 609 (2d Cir. 1979) (computation of damages for breach of contract that provided for exercise of a party's best efforts), discussed in Victor Goldberg, "In Search of Best Efforts: Reinterpreting *Bloor v. Falstaff*," 44 *St. Louis University Law Journal* (2000), 1465; see Jeanneret v. Vichey, 693 F.2d 259 (2d Cir. 1982) (analyzing the law on licensing the export of works of art from Italy).

69. 276 F.2d 280, 281 (2d Cir. 1960), *vacated and remanded*, 365 U.S. 293 (1961), *adhered to*, 290 F.2d 904 (2d Cir. 1961).

70. HLS-HJF, Box 226, Folder 7.

71. 360 F.2d 704, 706 (2d Cir. 1966).

72. 190 F. Supp. 116 (S.D.N.Y. 1960).

73. Ibid., 117. Friendly was more surefooted in his use of metaphors in music and mathematics than in sports. The plaintiff was suing under N.Y. Personal Prop. Law, ch. 41, § 95. The case was featured in the eightieth birthday party his colleagues gave for him. LOC, Kaufman Papers, Box 78 (lyrics of skits).

74. 190 F. Supp. at 118.

75. Ibid., 119.

76. Ibid., 120, quoting 7 C.F.R. §§ 70.300–70.371.

77. Ibid., 120. Relying on price to determine the meaning of a contract runs contrary to most contract thinking but is sometimes reasonable. Author interview of Todd Rakoff, Nov. 13, 2006.

78. 190 F. Supp. at 121. Months later, in Dadourian Export Corp. v. United States, 291 F.2d 178, 187 and n.4 (2d Cir. 1961) (Friendly, J., dissenting), Friendly expressed some doubts about his reasoning in *Frigaliment*, namely, that it "might better have been placed on that ground [no meeting of the minds],

with the loss still left on the plaintiff because of defendant's not unjustifiable change of position."

79. E.g., E. Allan Farnsworth and William F. Young, *Cases and Materials on Contracts* (5th ed., 1995), 585; Edward J. Murphy and Richard E. Speidel, *Studies in Contract Law* (4th ed., 1991), 789.

80. Donald H. J. Hermann, "Phenomenology, Structuralism, Hermeneutics, and Legal Study: Applications of Contemporary Continental Thought to Legal Phenomena," 36 *Miami Law Review* (1982), 379, 407 ("Friendly's belief in the term's [chicken] ambiguity resulted from the extrinsic evidence of conflicting meanings rather than from the word itself"); Claire Dalton, "An Essay in the Deconstruction of Contract Doctrine," 94 *Yale Law Journal* (1985), 997, 1059 (Friendly "shift[s] from an intent-based model to a responsibility model: The defendant is liable because of what he should have known rather than what he knew, even though the language of intent is artificially preserved"); Madeline Plasencia, "Who's Afraid of Humpty Dumpty: Deconstructionist References in Judicial Opinions," 21 *Seattle Law Review* (1997), 215, 240–241 ("Friendly pretended to follow an objective theory of contracts, but engaged in a wide-ranging review of the relevant community's meaning of chicken in order to decide the meaning of the word 'chicken' "); Richard L. Barnes, "Rediscovering Subjectivity in Contracts: Adhesion and Unconscionability," 66 *Louisiana Law Review* (2005), 123, 137 ("Because the importer failed to show the significance of his subjective meaning, the seller's subjective meaning was significant, but only because it coincided with the objective meaning of 'chicken' ").

22. Federal Court Jurisdiction

1. *Black's Law Dictionary* (9th ed., 2009), 927; Turner v. Enrille, 4 U.S. 7 (1799); Henry Friendly, "The Historic Basis of Diversity Jurisdiction," 41 *Harvard Law Review* (1928), 483, 504–508. Henry M. Hart Jr. and Herbert Wechsler, *The Federal Courts and the Federal System* (1953), devoted almost five hundred pages to the subject matter of this chapter.

2. Henry Friendly, *Federal Jurisdiction: A General View* (1973), was an expansion of the lectures; see Henry Friendly, "Averting the Flood by Lessening the Flow," 59 *Cornell Law Review* (1974), 634.

3. One was formed. Ruth Bader Ginsburg and Peter W. Huber, "The Intercircuit Committee," 100 *Harvard Law Review* (1987), 1417, 1430–1431. Friendly's proposal remains the subject of scholarly comment. Kristen David Adams, "The American Law Institute: Justice Cardozo's Ministry of Justice?" 32 *Southern Illinois Law Journal* (2007), 173, 180–187.

4. *Federal Jurisdiction*, 49–54; *New York Times*, Nov. 14, 1973, p. 27; *New York Times*, Jan. 27, 1975, p. 56; see James L. Oakes, book review of *Federal Jurisdiction*, 53 *Boston University Law Review* (1973), 1160 (Friendly "struck the first solid blow at the proposal and served almost overnight to solidify, if not to create, a considerable dissatisfaction with the concept advanced by the prestigious Study Group on the Caseload of the Supreme Court").

5. Friendly has been cited as "the classic example" of the federal judiciary's making a careful analysis of the jurisdiction and operation of the federal courts. Martin H. Redish, book review of *The Federal Courts: Crisis and Reform*, by Richard A. Posner, 85 *Columbia Law Review* (1985), 1378; *accord*, Thomas J. Maroney, "'Averting the Flood': Henry J. Friendly and the Jurisdiction of the Federal Courts—Part I," 27 *Syracuse Law Review* (1976), 1071, 1072 (referring to "Friendly's preeminence among those displaying scholarly or practical concern with [federal court jurisdiction]").

6. 41 *Harvard Law Review* (1928), 483.

7. Ibid., 493, 495, 496–497.

8. Ibid., 497.

9. Ibid., 510.

10. Louis H. Pollak, "In Praise of Friendly," 133 *University of Pennsylvania Law Review* (1984), 39, 40.

11. Friendly letter to Frankfurter, July 20, 1927, LOC, Frankfurter Papers, Part 3, Reel 34, Frame 490. In Strawbridge v. Curtiss, 7 U.S. 767 (1805), Chief Justice John Marshall held that a suit brought by citizens of Massachusetts against defendants who were citizens of Massachusetts and a citizen of Vermont did not satisfy the requirements for diversity jurisdiction; complete diversity was required.

12. 41 *Harvard Law Review*, 510.

13. *Federal Jurisdiction*, 133–138, 149. Friendly favored no-fault legislation and maintained a file on the subject (133–134); HLS-HJF, Box 190, Folder 11.

14. Modave v. Long Island Jewish Medical Center, 501 F.2d 1065, 1067 (2d Cir. 1974).

15. Feldman v. Allegheny Airlines, Inc., 524 F.2d 384, 390 (2d Cir. 1975) (Friendly, J., concurring).

16. *Federal Jurisdiction*, 198. Decisions by courts of appeals rose from 3,765 in 1960 to 33,360 in 1985, while the number of judges rose only from 68 to 168. Ashlyn K. Kuersten and Donald R. Songer, *Decisions on the U.S. Courts of Appeals* (2001), 28, 30.

17. Friendly wrote Posner, "You can't be really serious in thinking . . . that retention of the heavy burden of diversity jurisdiction is needed to qualify federal judges to decide state law issues that arise in federal question cases." Posner said that for a variety of reasons he was interested in state law, including that he had taught common-law subjects and served on a court that was not dominated by a single state with a distinctive tradition (i.e., New York), so that federal judges could make a contribution to state law. Posner letters to Friendly, Jan. 3, 1983, Jan. 13, 1983, and May 31, 1983, Friendly letters to Posner, Jan. 18, 1983, and May 31, 1983, HLS-HJF, Box 221, Folder 7. The letters were long and dense, sometimes running to five single-spaced pages.

18. Robert L. Jones, who wrote "Finishing a Friendly Argument: The Jury and the Historical Origins of Diversity Jurisdiction," 82 *New York University Law Review* (2007), 997, which contended that the more sophisticated panels of jurors in federal courts made federal courts more sympathetic to creditors and more understanding of commercial litigants, credits Friendly for being the first

to see that it was not about impartiality. Author telephone interview of Jones, Apr. 1, 2008; see Richard H. Fallon Jr. et al., *Hart and Wechsler's The Federal Courts and the Federal System* (6th ed., 2009), 1356–1358.

19. Author interview of Michael Lazerwitz, Nov. 28, 2006.

20. Potwora v. Dillon, 386 F.2d 74 (2d Cir. 1967).

21. *Federal Jurisdiction*, 153–171, 173–196.

22. Ibid., 56–62; Henry Friendly, "Federalism: A Foreword," 86 *Yale Law Journal* (1977), 1019, 1026–1027; Friendly letter to Posner, Dec. 27, 1982; Posner letter to Friendly, Jan. 3, 1983, HLS-HJF, Box 221, Folder 7.

23. Friendly Mem., Apr. 9, 1975, HLS-HJF, Box 77, Folder 2, in Economic Opportunity Comm'n of Nassau County, Inc. v. Weinberger, 524 F.2d 393, 404 (2d Cir. 1975) (Friendly, J., concurring) (dispute between two state agencies over right to administer federal program).

24. Friendly Voting Mem., Jan. 15, 1973, HLS-HJF, Box 145, Folder 7, in Begley v. Ford Motor Co., 476 F.2d 1276 (2d Cir. 1973).

25. In San Antonio v. Timpko, 368 F.2d 983 (2d Cir. 1966), Friendly reversed and remanded for a retrial an automobile accident diversity case even when there was no objection.

26. Any case that was not affirmed is counted as a reversal. He reversed in thirty-two of fifty-eight diversity cases in which he wrote an opinion.

27. Specific federal court jurisdictional statutes cover copyright, admiralty, bankruptcy, patents, federal antitrust, federal tax, and certain civil rights claims, among others. E.g., 28 U.S.C. § 1332.

28. Morrison v. National Australia Bank, 130 S.Ct. 2869 (2010).

29. T.B. Harms Co. v. Eliscu, 339 F.2d 823 (2d Cir. 1964).

30. Klebanow v. New York Produce Exchange, 344 F.2d 294 (2d Cir. 1965); cf. Crimpers Promotions, Inc. v. Home Box Office, 724 F.2d 290 (2d Cir. 1983) (Friendly, J.) (granting standing under Clayton Antitrust Act). Friendly also dissented from a panel decision that permitted the parties to grant to an *arbitrator* rather than a federal court the power to decide whether a claim had been discharged in bankruptcy, "perhaps the most important objective of an individual bankruptcy." Fallick v. Kehr, 369 F.2d 899, 905–906 (2d Cir. 1966) (Friendly, J., dissenting).

31. 339 F.2d 823 (2d Cir. 1964).

32. David P. Currie, "On Blazing Trails: Judge Friendly and Federal Jurisdiction," 133 *University of Pennsylvania Law Review* (1984), 5, 7.

33. Amy B. Cohen, "'Arising Under' Jurisdiction and the Copyright Laws," 44 *Hastings Law Journal* (1993), 337, 360.

34. 226 F. Supp. 337 (S.D.N.Y. 1964).

35. *T.B. Harms*, 339 F.2d at 827. Friendly considered and rejected another test, namely, whether copyright constituted the "essence" of the dispute, or whether, instead, the copyright issues were "incidental to" the contract dispute. Bassett v. Mashantucket Pequot Tribe, 204 F.3d 343, 347–348 (2d Cir. 2000) (Leval, J.). That test, Friendly observed, created two difficulties. First, if the case was dismissed, the plaintiff, who had possibly valid copyright claims, had no forum

in which to pursue them. Second, the test often required a full trial to determine whether the copyright was or was not the essence of the dispute.

36. 971 F.2d 926, 932–933 (2d Cir. 1992).

37. *Bassett*, 204 F.3d at 352–355.

38. United Mine Workers of America v. Gibbs, 383 U.S. 715 (1966); see Paul M. Bator et al., *Hart and Wechsler's The Federal Courts and the Federal System* (2d ed., 1973), 921–926.

39. Friendly's first opinion on the subject was Astor-Honor, Inc. v. Grosset & Dunlap, Inc., 441 F.2d 627 (2d Cir. 1971) (parties briefed issue); see Leather's Best, Inc. v. S.S. Mormaclynx, 451 F.2d 800, 809 (2d Cir. 1971) (parties missed jurisdictional issue).

40. E.g., Graham v. Smith 602 F.2d 1078 (2d Cir. 1979) (double jeopardy), discussed above; Goldberg v. Meridor, 567 F.2d 209 (2d Cir. 1977) (discussed above).

41. 522 F.2d 267, 269 (2d Cir. 1976), *vacated*, 425 U.S. 967 (1976).

42. Aldinger v. Howard, 427 U.S. 1 (1976); Finley v. United States, 490 U.S. 545, 548, 556 (1989).

43. 490 U.S. 580.

44. Codified in 28 U.S.C. § 1367; see generally Fallon et al., *Hart and Wechsler's The Federal Courts and the Federal System* (6th ed. 2009), 831–836.

45. 421 F.2d 560 (2d Cir. 1969). Friendly's voting memorandum was nine pages long, while his colleagues' memoranda were one page each. HLS-HJF, Box 44, Folder 4.

46. 304 U.S. 144, 152 n.4 (1938).

47. 421 F.2d at 565–566, 568–569; see Henry Friendly, *Benchmarks* (1967), 303–304. The next edition of *Hart and Wechsler's The Federal Courts and the Federal System* (2d ed., 1973), 958–960, quoted verbatim four pages of Friendly's opinion in *Eisen*. Friendly wrote Posner, "The amount of time federal courts are spending in Section 1983 cases which have absolutely nothing to do with the purpose of the framers is frightening." Friendly letter to Posner, Dec. 30, 1983, HLS-HJF, Box 221, Folder 7. But see Gerald Gunther, *Constitutional Law* (12th ed., 1991), 464 ("In fact, a fundamental interdependence exists between the personal right to liberty and the personal right to property").

48. Anthony G. Amsterdam, "Criminal Prosecutions Affecting Federally Guaranteed Civil Rights: Removal and Habeas Corpus Jurisdiction to Abort State Court Trial," 113 *University of Pennsylvania Law Review* (1965), 793, 864.

49. 342 F.2d 255, 272 (2d Cir. 1965). Judge Thurgood Marshall dissented vigorously. In a pair of cases the following year, Georgia v. Rachel, 384 U.S. 780 (1966) and City of Greenwood v. Peacock, 384 U.S. 808, 822 (1966), the Supreme Court took a position similar to Friendly's, with the opinion in the latter case quoting from Friendly's opinion.

50. 342 F.2d at 272. The brief for the District Attorney of Queens County did not discuss the meaning of the language "any law providing for equal civil rights," which was the most important issue in the case and the one on which he prevailed. About Galamison's brief, Friendly later said, "[T]he would be removers

for some strange reason made success for themselves impossible by choosing the wrong section of the Removal Act. However, we really treated the whole problem on its merits." Friendly letter to Michael Boudin, Feb. 7, 1985, HLS-HJF, Box 221, Folder 4.

51. Hudson Valley Freedom Theater, Inc. v. Heimbach, 671 F.2d 702 (2d Cir. 1982); *New York Times*, Feb. 3, 1982, p. B2.

52. *Federal Jurisdiction*, 90.

53. Friendly's experience with state courts contrasted sharply with Thurgood Marshall's, which may partially account for their different approaches in New York v. Galamison. Friendly was a proponent of federalism in economic matters, taking a position similar to Brandeis's and citing his dissents. See Swift & Co. v. Wickham, 364 F.2d 241 (2d Cir. 1966); Chrysler Corp. v. Tofany, 419 F.2d 499 (2d Cir. 1969).

54. Oakes, book review of *Federal Jurisdiction*, 1165–1166; Clement F. Haynsworth Jr., book review of *Federal Jurisdiction*, 87 *Harvard Law Review* (1974), 1082, 1086; Monroney, " 'Averting the Flood,' " 1071, 1034; Sandra Day O'Connor, *Majesty of the Law* (2003), 253–254, 275 (the implementation of Brown v. Board of Education unlikely if overseen by elected judges).

55. See Ronald Dworkin, *Law's Empire* (1986), 369–379.

23. Other Procedural Issues

1. 33 *University of Miami Law Review* (1978), 21.

2. Ibid., 36, 37. Friendly emphasized that he was not advocating inflexible rules of procedure, only that fair notice and an opportunity to controvert the evidence should be provided. His position was reminiscent of his article "Some Kind of Hearing," 123 *University of Pennsylvania Law Review* (1975), 1267.

3. While this issue is considered substantive for some purposes, it is not a rule that defines out-of-court conduct.

4. Henry Friendly, *Federal Jurisdiction: A General View* (1973), 120.

5. Milton Handler, "The Shift from Substance to Procedural Innovations in Antitrust Suits—The Twenty-Third Annual Antitrust Review," 71 *Columbia Law Review* (1971), 1, 9.

6. Charles Silver, " 'We're Scared to Death': Class Certification and Blackmail," 78 *New York University Law Review* (2003), 1357.

7. 51 F.3d 1293 (7th Cir. 1995); see Allan Kanner and Tibor Nagy, "Exploding the Blackmail Myth: A New Perspective on Class Action Settlements," 57 *Baylor Law Review* (2005), 681, 693–694; Silver, " 'We're Scared to Death,' " 1373–1375.

8. Pub. L. 109–2 (2005), 119 Stat. 4, codified in scattered sections in 28 U.S.C.

9. 218 F. Supp. 164 (S.D.N.Y. 1963), *aff'd*, 333 F.2d 327 (2d Cir. 1964), *aff'd by equally divided court en banc*, 340 F.2d 311 (2d Cir. 1965), *cert. dismissed sub. nom.*, Holt v. Alleghany Corp., 384 U.S. 28 (1966).

10. 333 F.2d at 336, 338.

11. Ibid., 333, 334.

12. Ibid., 338, 343 (Friendly, J., dissenting). Friendly relied on his dissent in Wolf v. Barkes, 348 F.2d 994, 997 (2d Cir. 1965), which argued that the pendency of a stockholder's derivative action challenging arrangements between a corporation and its officers did not deprive the corporation and its officers of the power to make an out-of-court settlement in the derivative suit without either notice to stockholders or court approval. He was consistent in stating that the obligations and powers of corporate officers are not abolished by a lawsuit against them.

13. 333 F.2d at 344–346.

14. Ibid., 347.

15. The two law reviews that published comments on the case divided between the majority and dissent. Case Note, 6 *Boston College Industrial and Commercial Law Review* (1965), 320 (dissent); Case Note, 33 *Fordham Law Review* (1964), 97 (majority).

16. 340 F.2d 311 (2d Cir. 1965). In all, the parties filed 494 pages of briefs in the Second Circuit. Friendly wrote two memoranda totaling fourteen pages urging a rehearing *en banc*. Friendly Mems., Sept. 25, 1964, Oct. 19, 1965, HLS-HJF, Box 24, Folder 9. The opinions of the panel have no precedential status. Baker v. Pataki, 85 F.3d 919, 921 and n.2 (2d Cir. 1996) (*en banc*).

17. *Cert. granted,* 381 U.S. 933 (1965), *cert. dismissed as improvidently granted sub nom.,* Holt v. Alleghany Corp., 384 U.S. 28 (1966).

18. *Los Angeles Times,* Mar. 2, 1966, Part 2, p. 6. The remainder of the item consisted of Pearson's praising his own public spiritedness in publishing his attack on Friendly.

19. 28 U.S.C. § 455 reads, "Any justice or judge of the United States shall disqualify himself in any case in which he has a substantial interest, has been counsel, is or has been a material witness, or is so related or connected with any party or his attorney as to render it improper, in his opinion, for him to sit on the trial, appeal, or other proceeding therein."

20. HLS-HJF, Box 234.

21. Friendly letter to Representative John Conyers Jr., Aug. 28, 1969, HLS-HJF, Box 234, Folder 4.

22. Sidney E. Zion, "Interest Conflict Laid to Jurist," *Scanlan's Magazine* (May 1970), 11–12, 16. Zion, who was controversial at times (for example, though a liberal, he outed Daniel Ellsberg as the person who had leaked the Pentagon Papers to the *New York Times*), claimed that not only the *Times* but the *Wall Street Journal* and *Time* magazine killed the story (10). Friendly's files included a copy of Zion's article, HLS-HJF, Box 233, Folder 7. Other Zion allegations against Friendly appear insubstantial to the author.

23. *New York Times,* Apr. 1, 1954, p. 49; *New York Times,* May 12, 1954, pp. 47, 49.

24. Zion, "Interest Conflict," 14.

25. 456 F.2d 896 (2d Cir. 1972) (reversing approval of settlement). Earlier, the Second Circuit had reversed a grant of summary judgment to defendants. 391 F.2d 965 (2d Cir. 1968).

26. 456 F.2d at 899–901. After prolonged delays, a different district judge dismissed the suit *sua sponte* for the plaintiff's failure to prosecute it, but in the process somehow reinstated the $250,000 settlement. Friendly again reversed on a variety of grounds, including lack of notice to plaintiff and placing too much responsibility for the delay on plaintiff. Saylor v. Bastedo, 623 F.2d 230 (2d Cir. 1980). The parties ultimately agreed to a settlement of $1 million. Author telephone interview of Avrom Fischer, a lawyer in the case, Feb. 4, 2010. When claims were weak, Friendly accepted low settlements of class actions or derivative suits. Newman v. Stein, 464 F.2d 689, 698 (2d Cir. 1972); Weinberger v. Kendrick, 698 F.2d 61, 73–74 (2d Cir. 1982).

27. 660 F.2d 9 (2d Cir. 1981). This was a rare case where another circuit judge, namely, Amalya Kearse, persuaded Friendly to change his mind between his voting memorandum and final opinion. Kearse Voting Mem., Mar. 12, 1981, HLS-HJF, Box 100, Folder 17. She also made significant contributions to Friendly's opinion. Kearse Mems., Apr. 27, 1981, May 6, 1981, HLS-HJF, Box 100, Folder 17.

28. 660 F.2d at 18.

29. E.g., Newby v. Enron Corp., 394 F.3d 296, 305 (5th Cir. 2004); Epstein v. MCA, Inc., 50 F.3d 644, 663–664 (9th Cir. 1995); Grimes v. Vitalink Communications Corp., 17 F.3d 1553, 1564 (3d Cir. 1994).

30. 706 F.2d 956 (2d Cir. 1983).

31. United States v. United Shoe Machinery Corp., 391 U.S. 244 (1968); United States v. Swift & Co., 286 U.S. 106 (1932).

32. Brief for Defendants-Appellants, 6–13.

33. While some law review articles were critical of Friendly's opinion, courts widely followed it. E.g., Duran v. Elrod, 760 F.2d 756, 760 (7th Cir. 1985) (Posner, J.).

34. 502 U.S. 367 (1992).

35. Ibid., 399 (Steven, J., dissenting on other grounds).

36. 309 F.2d 553 (2d Cir. 1962) (*en banc*).

37. Mass. Gen. Laws Ann. Ch. 229, § 2 (Supp. 1961).

38. 172 N.E.2d 526 (N.Y. 1961).

39. 309 F.2d at 560–561. Six judges formed the majority; three dissented.

40. Ibid., 565–566. Friendly strengthened Northeast Airlines' claim by pointing out that the New York courts transformed the nature of the Massachusetts statute from one that was punitive to one that was compensatory. Perhaps a stronger argument for Northeast was the unwelcome specter of a court's picking and choosing snippets of law from different jurisdictions, possibly with no criteria other than to help a party. Judge Stephen F. Williams email to author, Apr. 19, 2011.

41. Brainerd Currie, *Selected Essays on the Conflict of Laws* (1963), 741 and n.150.

42. *Pearson* was the subject of nineteen student law review comments. Of the fifteen student comments that took a position, a remarkable fourteen, including the *Harvard Law Review*, supported Kaufman and only one Friendly.

43. Professor Alexander Bickel noted in another context, "Congress is an institution of government. It has no rights; it has functions, and it may have duties." Alexander M. Bickel, *The Least Dangerous Branch* (1962), 173–174. Friendly seemingly was affording rights to a legislature, or at least the product of a legislature.

44. Louis Pollak, "In Praise of Friendly," 133 *University of Pennsylvania Law Review* (1984), 39, 61 ("Most federal judges do not relish skewering an unwise but clearly authoritative state court rule except in those rare instances, of which the dissent by Friendly, J., in *Pearson* is a notable example, in which the unwisdom of the state court rule is deemed so egregious as to be unconstitutional"). Friendly thanked Pollak: "I was particularly pleased that you agree with my dissent in the *Pearson* case, which has not had many admirers." Friendly letter to Pollak, Feb. 15, 1985. Courtesy of Judge Pollak.

45. 276 F.2d 822, 825 (2d Cir. 1960).

46. Sack v. Low, 478 F.2d 360 (2d Cir. 1973); George v. Douglas Aircraft Co., 332 F.2d 73, 78 (2d Cir. 1964); Moviecolor Ltd. v. Eastman Kodak Co., 288 F.2d 80 (2d Cir. 1961) (*dicta*) (in damage suit under § 4 of the Clayton Act, which had no federal statute of limitations, Friendly applied New York's six-year statute of limitations, but also the federal tolling doctrine, an approach that appears inconsistent with the later-decided *Pearson*).

47. Henry Friendly, "In Memoriam—Roger John Traynor, the Ablest Judge of His Generation," 71 *California Law Review* (1983), 1039. Friendly wrote, "I have inserted the words 'of his generation' in order to avoid the need for comparison with Judge Learned Hand, who had preceded him on the bench by thirty years but continued to sit until 1961" (1039 n. 1).

48. 360 P.2d 906 (Cal. 1961).

49. Friendly, "In Memoriam," 1041–1042. The paragraph consists of Friendly's long sentences.

50. Friendly letter to Judge Louis Pollak, Feb. 15, 1985.

51. See, e.g., Christopher B. Mueller and Laird C. Kirkpatrick, *Evidence* (3d ed., 2003), § 5.1.

52. 8 *Wigmore on Evidence* (McNaughton Revision, 1961), §§ 2301, 2311. The only federal case cited was Himmelfarb v. United States, 175 F.2d 924, 939 (9th Cir. 1949) (no privilege because the accountant's "presence was not indispensable in the sense that the presence of an attorney's secretary may be. It was a convenience," citing a prior edition of *Wigmore on Evidence* as its only support).

53. 296 F.2d 918 (2d Cir. 1961).

54. Ibid., 919, 922.

55. Brandeis, among others, described accounting (or bookkeeping) as the universal language of business. Thomas K. McCraw, *Profits of Regulation* (1984), 85.

56. 296 F.2d at 922–923.

57. 482 F.2d 72 (2d Cir. 1973).

58. Ibid., 81–82. In this case the government made the argument on which Friendly relied.

59. Upjohn Co. v. United States, 449 U.S. 383 (1981) (privilege encompasses communications from lower-ranking employees acting within the scope of their employment).

60. 755 F.2d 1022 (2d Cir. 1985), *vacated*, 475 U.S. 133 (1986).

61. 755 F.2d at 1027, citing Griswold v. Connecticut, 391 U.S. 479, 486 (1965).

62. 755 F.2d at 1026.

63. Ibid., 1028, quoting United States v. Trammel, 445 U.S. 40, 44 (1980). The parties' briefs did not discuss policy questions, only case precedents. The government's argument consisted of just one clause of a sentence and provided no analysis: "Koecher's use of his wife even as an unwitting courier of stolen state secrets would bar invocation of the marital privilege. [Citations omitted.]" Brief for the United States, 15. The issue is still unresolved. Stephen A. Saltzburg et al., 2 *Federal Rules of Evidence Manual* (9th ed., 2006), 501.02[8].

64. 475 U.S. 133 (1986).

65. Author interview of Larry Kramer, Apr. 16, 2007.

24. At the End

1. Author interview of Pat Hall Mogin, Dec. 9, 2006.

2. Ibid.; author interview of Richard Posner, Aug. 22, 2007.

3. Friendly told his clerk that during the 1983–1984 term. Donald Board email to author, Mar. 15, 2007.

4. Author interview of Ira Dosovitz, M.D., Nov. 16, 2010.

5. Author interview of Abraham Sofaer, Apr. 16, 2007; author interview of Larry Kramer, Apr. 16, 2007; author interview of Peter Edelman, Nov. 28, 2006.

6. Author telephone interview of Charlotte Kimbrough, June 6, 2009.

7. Author interview of Mogin, Dec. 9, 2006.

8. Ibid.

9. Donald Board email to author, Mar. 15, 2007.

10. Author interview of Frank Gilbert and Daniel Rezneck, May 31, 2007. Gilbert, a grandson of Brandeis, and Rezneck, a former research assistant to Freund, attended the luncheon.

11. Friendly letter to Michael Boudin, May 22, 1985, HLS-HJF, Box 221, Folder 4.

12. Author interview of Posner, Aug. 22, 2007.

13. Author interview of Larry Kramer, Apr. 16, 2007.

14. Author telephone interview of Judge Ralph Winters, June 19, 2006; see Friendly letter to Posner, Apr. 29, 1985, HLS-HJF, Box 221, Folder 7.

15. Friendly letter to Kenneth Culp Davis, Jan. 17, 1986, HLS-HJF, Box 227, Folder 8.

16. See United States v. Carbone, 378 F.2d 420, 422 (2d Cir. 1967) (Friendly, J.) ("The escape from the dilemma lies in owning that in this, his last opinion, written in his ninety-first year, the Justice [Holmes] was mistaken in identifying the two situations").

17. Friendly letter to Weinfeld, Feb. 2, 1981, Weinfeld Collection, N.Y.U. Law Library, Box 10.
18. Friendly letter to Posner, Apr. 29, 1985, HLS-HJF, Box 221, Folder 7.
19. Author interview of Posner, Aug. 22, 2007.
20. Author interview of Thomas Dagger, July 26, 2007; author interview of Thomas Curtis, June 20, 2007.
21. Author interviews of Joan Goodman, Oct. 22, 2006, July 18, 2007; author interview of Irene Friendly, May 27, 2007.
22. Friendly undated letter with no salutation. The letter ended, "I had intended to write individual letters to some, but the effort proved too great."
23. Author interview of Dagger, June 20, 2007.
24. Author interview of Posner, Aug. 22, 2007.
25. Author interviews of Goodman, Oct. 22, 2006, and July 18, 2007.
26. Author interview of Mogin, Dec. 9, 2006; author interview of Dosovitz, Nov. 16, 2010.
27. Andrew Solomon, *The Noonday Demon: An Atlas of Depression* (2001), 258–259.
28. Author interview of Joan Goodman, Oct. 22, 2006.
29. Author interview of Pierre Leval, June 30, 2010.
30. Author interview of Mogin, Dec. 9, 2006. Knowledge of the size of a fatal dose indicates the potential suicide is serious, although making public statements about suicide suggests that one is not serious. Seymour Perlin and Chester W. Schmidt Jr., "Psychiatry," in *A Handbook for the Study of Suicide* (Seymour Perlin, ed., 1975), 151–152.
31. Author interview of Mogin, Dec. 9, 2006.
32. Author interviews of Goodman, Oct. 22, 2006, July 18, 2007; author interview of Friendly's grandson Barak Goodman, May 27, 2007; author interview of Dagger, June 20, 2007; author interview of Curtis, June 20, 2007.
33. Author telephone interview of Judge William C. Conner, Apr. 22, 2007.
34. Mogin letter to Weinfeld, Mar. 21, 1986, N.Y.U. Archives, Weinfeld Collection, Box 10.
35. Weinfeld letter to Mogin, Mar. 24, 1986, N.Y.U. Archives, Weinfeld Collection, Box 10.
36. Richard A. Posner, "In Memoriam: Henry J. Friendly," 99 *Harvard Law Review* (1986), 1724.
37. *New York Times*, June 10, 1986; see "In Memoriam, Honorable Henry J. Friendly," 805 F.2d at LXXX (June 9, 1986); author interview of a federal judge who requested anonymity.
38. Friendly's will, dated July 17, 1985, was probated in New York County's Surrogate Court, 31 Chambers St., New York City.
39. Paul Gewirtz, "A Lawyer's Death," 100 *Harvard Law Review* (1987), 2053. Gewirtz interviewed two Friendly clerks for his article. Author interview of Paul Gewirtz, Oct. 4, 2008.
40. Goodman letter to Gewirtz, July 24, 1986. Gewirtz did not respond. Author interview of Joan Friendly, Oct. 22, 2006.

25. Friendly's Legacy

1. For a complete list of Friendly's books and articles, see Appendix B.
2. Walter Isaacson, *Einstein* (2007), 113.
3. J. Woodford Howard Jr., *Courts of Appeals in the Federal System* (1981), 48 (figures for court).
4. Wilfred Feinberg, "In Memoriam: Henry J. Friendly," 99 *Harvard Law Review* (1986), 1709, 1714.
5. Not part of this volume are other judicial contributions, including a "family resemblance" test to define "security" under federal securities laws, Exchange National Bank v. Touche Ross & Co., 544 F.2d 1126, 1137–1138 (2d Cir. 1976); Zeller v. Bogue Electric. Mfg. Corp., 476 F.2d 795, 799–800 (2d Cir. 1973), which the Supreme Court adopted in Reeves v. Ernst & Young, 494 U.S. 56, 63–67 (1990); the procedure for extradition, United States v. Doherty, 786 F.2d 491 (2d Cir. 1986); *In re* Mackin, 668 F.2d 122 (2d Cir. 1981); the procedure for deportation, Wong Wing Hang v. INS, 360 F.2d 715 (2d Cir. 1966); Foti v. INS, 308 F.2d 779 (2d Cir. 1962) (*en banc*), *rev'd*, 375 U.S. 217 (1963); statutory construction in naturalization and denaturalization proceedings, Cannon v. United States, 288 F.2d 269, 271 (2d Cir. 1961) (Friendly, J., dissenting); Simons v. United States, 452 F.2d 1110 (2d Cir. 1971); and intervention by environmental organization in environmental suits, United States v. Hooker Chemicals & Plastics Corp., 749 F.2d 968 (2d Cir. 1984).
6. Examples previously discussed are Johnson v. Glick, 481 F.2d 1028 (2d Cir. 1973) (factors relevant to whether an assault of a detainee by a prison guard violated 42 U.S.C. § 1983); Polaroid Corp. v. Polarad Electronics Corp., 287 F.2d 492 (2d Cir. 1961) (trademark infringement on different products).
7. Henry Friendly, *Benchmarks* (1967), 295.
8. Friendly letter to Dr. John Umana, Apr. 7, 1977, HLS-HJF, Box 230, Folder 4.
9. Henry Friendly, "The Courts and Social Policies: Substance and Procedure," 33 *University of Miami Law Review* (1978), 21, 24 n.14.
10. Ibid., 24 n.14, 27 n.30. In a letter to Justice Byron White, Friendly criticized a talk by Dworkin given at the Second Circuit Judicial Conference in 1976: "Although I now have a better idea of what [Dworkin] means by treatment as equals, the doctrine seems to me a potentially dangerous one. I do not know who except Professor Dworkin is to determine what constitutes justification for departure from equal treatment on the basis that a particular statute or administrative action treats people as equals." Friendly letter to White, Sept. 17, 1976, HLS-HJF, Box 230, Folder 3.
11. Friendly letter to Prof. Charles Fried, Apr. 6, 1964, HLS-HJF, Box 211, Folder 14.
12. Friendly letter to Freund, Sept. 7, 1977, HLS-Freund, Box 17, Folder 4.
13. See Ronald Dworkin, *A Matter of Principle* (1985), 15, 21–23; Ronald Dworkin, *Taking Rights Seriously* (1977), 108–110.
14. 398 F.2d 167 (2d Cir. 1968).
15. A doctoral thesis was devoted to Friendly as a pragmatist, and a long article written by the same person described him as a prudentialist. Daniel L. Breen,

Henry J. Friendly and the Pragmatic Tradition in American Law (2002), 202–204 (doctoral thesis); Daniel L. Breen, "Avoiding 'Wild Blue Yonders': The Prudentialism of Henry J. Friendly and John Roberts," 52 *South Dakota Law Review* (2007), 73.

16. Avis Rent A Car System, Inc. v. Hertz Corp., 782 F.2d 381, 385 (2d Cir. 1986). A strongly purposive opinion was Abrams v. Occidental Petroleum Corp, 450 F.2d 157 (2d Cir. 1971), where Friendly held that certain conduct did not fall within the statute because the conduct did not lend itself to "speculative abuse."

17. Federal Maritime Comm'n v. DeSmedt, 366 F.2d 464, 470 (2d Cir. 1966).

18. Friendly letter to Prof. Bernard Wolfman, Feb. 20, 1967, HLS-HJF, Box 218, Folder 3, referring to Statler Trust v. Commissioner of Internal Revenue, 361 F.2d 128 (2d Cir. 1966), where Friendly voted in favor of a trust that was required to make substantial charitable contributions. In Escott v. Barchris Construction Corp., 340 F.2d 731, 736 (2d Cir. 1965) (Friendly, J., concurring), the language pointed one way, although there was no legislative history or other evidence that Congress intended that result. Friendly wrote, "Still the words are what they are, and I see no sufficient reason for refusing to follow them when they lead to no untoward results." Nevertheless, he qualified his conclusion, "But one ought not press too far," and confined his opinion to a small class of similar cases.

19. Stephen G. Breyer, *Making Our Democracy Work: A Practical Judge's View* (2010), 94–98.

20. Stephen G. Breyer, *Active Liberty* (2005), 8.

21. Friendly letter to Arthur Schlesinger Jr., Jan. 11, 1973, HLS-HJF, Box 230, Folder 5.

22. Thomas C. Grey, "Do We Have an Unwritten Constitution?" 27 *Stanford Law Review* (1975), 703, 706 n.9.

23. U.S. Constitution, Art. 3, § 1; see, e.g., United States v. Cone, 354 F.2d 119, 130 (2d Cir. 1965) (Friendly, J., concurring).

24. Friendly referred to the Warren Court's "lack of analysis and restraint [that] has created a jerry-built structure." Friendly letter to Bickel, Mar. 11, 1970, Yale-Bickel, Box 3, Folder 58.

25. Friendly letter to Mary Clark Dimond, Nov. 7, 1974, HLS-HJF, Box 226, Folder 11. A Justice until 1975, William O. Douglas had been a former Yale professor grounded in securities law and was disinclined to write thorough opinions.

26. 398 U.S. 323 (1970).

27. 602 F.2d 1078 (2d Cir. 1979).

28. 430 U.S. 462 (1977).

29. 567 F.2d 209 (1977).

30. 435 U.S. 475 (1978).

31. 709 F.2d 160 (2d Cir. 1983).

32. 456 F.2d 79, 81 (2d Cir. 1972) (*en banc*) (Friendly, J., concurring).

33. 404 U.S. 249 (1971) (*per curiam*).

34. 429 U.S. 252, 263 (1977).

35. 671 F.2d 702, 707 (2d Cir. 1982).

36. See William N. Eskridge et al., *Cases and Materials on Legislation* (2007), 628–629 (discussion of "new" legal-process theory based on "positivism, pragmatism, principles").

37. 128 S.Ct. 2783 (2008); Prof. Mark Tushnet email to author, Jan. 22, 2011.

38. 506 U.S. 390 (1993). Friendly's position on the unconstitutionality of convicting a demonstrably innocent person is not an originalist position. Tushnet email, Jan. 22, 2011.

39. The author thanks Justice Breyer for this insight. Mansfield had limited influence in Britain compared to the United States. As described by Grant Gilmore, *The Ages of American Law* (1977), 24, Mansfield's "radical approach to the problem of judicial law-making was in course of being scrapped in favor of a quasi-Blackstonian approach which emphasized adherence to precedent." Gilmore also points out that Mansfield was more influential in the United States, with scholars like Justice Story's adopting and praising Mansfield's "idea that judges are supposed to make law" (24).

40. United States v. Drummond, 354 F.2d 132, 143 (2d Cir. 1965).

41. Friendly, *Benchmarks*, 195.

42. United States v. Kovel, 296 F.2d 918 (2d Cir. 1961); United States v. Doe, 457 F.2d 895 (2d Cir. 1972) (witness's rights in grand jury).

43. *In re* Gibralter Amusements, Ltd. 291 F.2d 22 (2d Cir. 1961) (test for independent corporation not relevant in determining meaning of separate "creditor"); Powe v. Miles 407 F.2d 73 (2d Cir. 1968) (immunity for tort claims irrelevant for determining meaning of "state action"); see NLRB v. Kelly Bros. Nurseries, Inc., 341 F.2d 433, 437–438 (2d Cir. 1965) (phrase "employee employed in agriculture" has different meaning in National Labor Relations Act than in Fair Labor Standards Act).

44. Author telephone interview of Judge Cardamone, May 14, 2007.

45. Author interview of Michael Boudin, Dec. 11, 2006.

46. Friendly letter to Richard Posner, Dec. 30, 1983, HLS-HJF, Box 221, Folder 7.

47. Friendly, *Benchmarks*, vii.

48. *In re* B.D. International Discount Corp., 701 F.2d 1071, 1077 (2d Cir. 1983).

49. 332 F.2d 73, 75, 77 (2d Cir. 1964).

50. *In re* Hygrade Envelope Corp., 336 F.2d 584, 588 (2d Cir. 1966).

51. Noonan v. Cunard Steamship Co., 375 F.2d 69 (2d Cir. 1967) (reversing Judge Weinfeld, who had purported to exercise discretion). Friendly created the ground on which he reversed Weinfeld; Cunard had not made the argument.

52. Henry Friendly, "Indiscretion about Discretion," 31 *Emory Law Journal* (1982), 747, 763, 784.

53. See William D. Popkin, *Statutes in Court* (1999), 218 (unusual to show doubt in published opinion).

54. Author interview of Judge Calabresi, Apr. 6, 2007; *accord*, Pierre N. Leval, "Judicial Opinions as Literature," in *Law's Stories* (Peter Brooks and Paul Gewirtz, eds., 1996), 206.

55. Author telephone interview of Leval, May 9, 2006. "Pursuit of literary techniques is more likely to undermine than to reinforce the success of the opinion in meeting its judicial obligation." Leval, "Judicial Opinions," 207.

56. Friendly, *Benchmarks,* 294.
57. E.g., Leval, "Judicial Opinions," 209 ("Not a quotable judge. Not a maker of aphorisms"). Friendly confined his florid language to the statement of facts.
58. John Minor Wisdom, "Views of a Friendly Observer," 133 *Pennsylvania Law Review* (1984), 64.
59. The Bayside Federal Savings and Loan Association of Bayside, New York, tried to register the name "Judge Friendly," which annoyed Friendly. The Patent and Trademark Office turned down the application. HLS-HJF, Box 217, Folder 4.
60. Author interview of Justice Scalia, Apr. 8, 2006. While Friendly's sentences were sometimes long, they rarely confused the reader.
61. Author interview of Richard Posner, Aug. 22, 2007; see, e.g., Akhil Reed Amar, "*Heller, HLR,* and Holistic Legal Reasoning," 122 *Harvard Law Review* (2008), 145, 181 (Friendly is "quite possibly the greatest twentieth century jurist never to sit on the Supreme Court").
62. Gerald Gunther, *Learned Hand* (1994), 547–552.
63. Author interview of Roberts, Nov. 29, 2007.
64. Author interview of Justice O'Connor, Apr. 13, 2006.
65. Henry Friendly, "The 'Law of the Circuit' and All That," 46 *St. John's Law Review* (1972), 406, 407.
66. 133 *University of Pennsylvania Law Review* (1984), 1
67. 99 *Harvard Law Review* (1986), 1709.
68. Irving Kaufman looked like he was "going to explode" out of frustration at not being one of the speakers. Author interview of Prof. Stephen Burbank, Apr. 12, 2010.
69. Before the Judicial Panel on Multidistrict Litigation, *In Memoriam, The Honorable Henry J. Friendly, U.S. Circuit Judge, Second Circuit,* San Francisco, Mar. 27, 1986.
70. Powell letter to Pollak, May 21, 1986. Copy provided by Judge Pollak.
71. Warren Burger, "In Memoriam," 805 F.2d at LXXXVI, June 9, 1986.
72. Frankfurter letter to Friendly, Aug. 16, 1963, LOC, Frankfurter Papers, Part 3, Reel 35.
73. *Yale Biographical Dictionary of American Law* (Roger K. Newman, ed., 2009), 209.
74. John Minor Wisdom, "Views of a Friendly Observer," 133 *University of Pennsylvania Law Review* (1984), 63.
75. Erwin N. Griswold, "In Memoriam," 99 *Harvard Law Review* (1986), 1720; see, e.g., Howard, *Courts of Appeals,* 231 ("Of them all, Henry J. Friendly came closest to universal recognition as the most respected federal circuit judge."); Judge Pierre N. Leval, "In Memory of a Great Man," 52 *Brooklyn Law Review* (1986), 571–572; A. Raymond Randolph, "Administrative Law and the Legacy of Henry J. Friendly," 74 *New York University Law Review* (1999), 1, 3.
76. Author interview of Justice Stevens, June 30, 2008; author interview of Justice Scalia, Apr. 18, 2006.
77. The sixth (2009) edition of *Hart and Wechsler* cites five articles by Friendly.

78. Quoting Herbert Wechsler, 805 F.2d at xcviii ("Of no one else in our time can it be said, I think with quite the same objective basis, that he was a 'man for all seasons' in the law").

79. Author telephone interview of Michael J. Harwin, Sept. 24, 2008.

80. "Confirmation Hearings on the Nomination of John G. Roberts, Jr., to be Chief Justice of the United States, Sen. Comm. on the Judiciary," 109th Cong., 1st Sess. (2005), 202. Roberts's comments about Friendly were far more laudatory than what he said about Justice Rehnquist, for whom he clerked next.

81. E.g., author interview of Judge William Bryson, Nov. 28, 2006; author interview of Judge Merrick Garland, Nov. 16, 2006.

82. At least one, Peter Edelman, opposed Roberts's appointment on the basis of his conservative philosophy. Author interview of Edelman, May 1, 2010.

83. Interview of Leval, June 30, 2010; author telephone interview of Ruth Wedgwood, June 23, 2010, who called the ceremony a "lapidary event."

84. Several clerks, including Gary Born, moved to private practice after spending some years in academia and are not included in the total. The work of some former clerks was highly conceptual. E.g., Philip Bobbitt, *Constitutional Fate* (1982); Bruce Ackerman, *Social Justice in the Liberal State* (1980); Larry T. Kramer, *The People Themselves: Popular Constitutionalism and Judicial Review* (2004).

85. Author interview of Boudin, Dec. 11, 2006.

86. Author interview of Boudin, Apr. 12, 2010.

87. Friendly had played an important role in the creation and installation of the bust of Learned Hand in 1965. HLS-HJF, Box 96, Folder 5.

88. Author interview of Judge Newman, Mar. 29, 2006.

89. Author interview of Cardamone, May 14, 2007.

90. Author interview of Newman, Mar. 29, 2006; author telephone interview of Eliot Goldfinger, Mar. 6, 2008; interview of Leval, Oct. 1, 2008; Kearse letter to author, May 21, 2010.

Acknowledgments

I wish to acknowledge the permission of *Pace Law Review* for the republication of my article, "Judges Henry J. Friendly and Benjamin Cardozo: A Tale of Two Precedents, " 31 *Pace Law Review* (2011), 599, in a somewhat different form in Chapter 21.

Obviously, this book could not have been written and published without the assistance of many, many people, and I want to express my gratitude. There are some individuals and organizations that I want to single out for special thanks for their enormous support.

The family of Judge Henry J. Friendly—Joan Friendly Goodman and Ellen Friendly Simon, the judge's daughters; Irene Baer Friendly, the widow of David Friendly, who died in 1993; and Frank Goodman, the husband of Joan—offered patient and tireless assistance and unstintingly gave of their time and thoughts. Stephen Simon, Ellen's former husband, graciously provided an interview.

The law firm of Wallace, King, Domike & Reiskin, LLP (especially Rick Wallace and Tony King), supplied me with an office and other essential support when, starting in early 2006, I devoted all my time to this biography. In August 2011, Wallace King merged into Sedgwick, LLP, which has continued to provide me with undiminished support.

Harvard University, Langdell Library, Special Collections (David Warrington, Lesley Schoenfeld, Edwin Moloy, and Margaret Peachey) provided me with all the help one could ask for in reviewing the Friendly Collection along with other document collections.

The National Archives and Records Administration Northeast Region Archives (Gregory J. Plunges, archivist, and Richard Gelbke, Chris Gushman, Scott Jobson, Carol Savo, Joan Young, and Joseph Majid Jr.) supplied invaluable information.

All of the fifty-one former law clerks of Judge Friendly generously gave me the benefit of their time, recollections, and thoughts.

While I do not have the space to list the many scores of other people who assisted my effort by providing me with their recollections, I want to assure them that they are appreciated. Many of them are identified in the endnotes to this volume.

Many people were generous of their time in agreeing to read and comment on my earlier drafts. First, I want to thank those who read the entire volume: Justice Stephen G. Breyer, John W. Dean, Professor Norman Dorsen, Dr. Ira Dosovitz, Marc Fleischaker, Professor Andrew L. Kaufman, Judge Pierre N. Leval, Judge Richard A. Posner, Justice Antonin Scalia, and David Warrington. Many others provided important assistance by reading portions of earlier drafts, including Judge Guido Calabresi, Professor Melvin Eisenberg, Professor Frank Goodman, Joan Friendly Goodman, Eugene Granoff, Judge James Halpern, Louis Lowenfels, Judge Louis H. Pollak, and Judge James R. Zazzali.

I was lucky to have excellent student researchers from George Washington University Law School, who helped me enormously: Douglas T. Hoffman (J.D. GWU '07), Emily Crandall Harlan (J.D. GWU '08), Terry Schoone-Jongen (J.D. GWU '10), and Christopher Healey (GWU '11).

In addition to the above, a number of law firms provided me with documents and other assistance (beyond the assistance of Friendly's former clerks):

Cleary, Gottlieb, Steen & Hamilton
Dewey & LeBoeuf
Hogan & Hartson
Paul, Weiss, Rifkind, Wharton & Garrison
Sullivan & Cromwell

Many other people and entities provided important assistance in obtaining relevant documents:

American Law Institute
Association of the Bar of the City of New York
Columbia University Oral History Project (Air History Project)
Federation of Jewish Philanthropies, Oral History Project
George Washington University Law School
Stephen A. Grant
Historical Society of Pennsylvania
Jacob Rader Marcus Center of the American Jewish Archives
Kiev Collection, Gellman Library, George Washington University
Renier Kraakman
Library of Congress Manuscript Division
Massachusetts Historical Society
National Archives II, College Park, Maryland
New York University Law School

Lewis J. Paper
A. Raymond Randolph
Richard M. Nixon Archives
Richard M. Nixon Presidential Library
Seeley G. Mudd Manuscript Library, Princeton, New Jersey
David J. Seipp
Steele Memorial Library, Elmira, New York
Stony Brook University, Frank Melville, Jr., Memorial Library, Special
    Collections
U.S. Court of Appeals for the Second Circuit
University of Miami, Richter Library, Special Collections, Pan Am documents
Yale Law School

Last in chronological order, but of immense importance and value to me and this volume, have been the many people at Harvard University Press, including Mike Aronson and Kathi Drummy. I also want to thank Christine Dahlin and Judith Hoover for their help in editing the manuscript.

I apologize if I inadvertently omitted anyone.

Index

Abortion, 190–193, 349, 431n56
Abrams, Floyd, 155
Abruzzo, Matthew T., Jr., 177
Absurdity doctrine, 260–261
Accountants, 236–240, 335–338
Ackerman, Bruce, 105, 109–110, 266, 314, 354
Administrative law, 294–301. *See also individual federal agencies and cases*
Admiralty law, 261–268, 305–310
African-Americans, 9, 231–233, 282–283
Age Discrimination in Employment Act, 284
Alfred University, 198–200
Alleghany Corp. v. Kirby, 327–330
Amar, Akhil Reed, 86, 403n43
American Airlines, Inc., 87
American Bar Association, 132, 256
American Civil Liberties Union, 155, 245
American Export Airlines, Inc., 46–47
American Law Institute (ALI), 131–132, 256–257
American Overseas Airways, 47, 61
American Psychiatric Association, 53
American Telephone & Telegraph Company, 51
Andrews, William, 310
Annenberg, Walter, 127, 137

Anti-Semitism, 9, 32–33
Antitrust law, 268
Arnold, Richard, 118
Association of the Bar of the City of New York, 206
Attorney-client privilege, 335–338

Baker v. Carr, 125
Ball, George W., 51, 67, 76, 101
Bankruptcy law, 268–269
Barnett, Stephen, 94–95
Baseball, 8, 9
Bates College, 13
Bator, Paul, 311
Bavaria, Germany, 5
Bell Aerospace Co. v. NLRB, 296–297
Bell Telephone system, 49
Benchmarks, 86
Bergman v. Lefkowitz, 95, 227–231
Biaggi, In re, 222–226
Bickel, Alexander, 152–155, 165, 207, 420–421n83
"Bill of Rights as a Code of Criminal Procedure, The," 166
Bivens v. Six Unknown Named Agents, 183–185
Black, Hugo, 42–43, 121, 214–215
"Blackmail settlements," 327

Blackmun, Harry, 137
Blumenfeld, M. Joseph, 119
Board, Donald, 91, 340
Bobbitt, Philip, 104, 111, 112
Bok, Derek, 257
"Book Review: Marvin Schick's *Learned Hand's Court*," 124
Bork, Robert, 118
Born, Gary, 254
Boudin, Michael, 109, 111–112, 340, 354, 357
Bowdoin Prize, 15, 17, 109
Brandeis, Alice Goldmark, 31
Brandeis, Louis: Friendly clerkship with, 26, 27–31, 232; Friendly evaluation of, 28–29, 30, 121–124, 207, 249, 350–351, 353; Friendly post-clerk relationship with, 37–38, 42, 45
Braniff, Thomas F., 62–63
Brennan, William, 121, 288
Breyer, Stephen G., 118, 298, 348
Bridges, Styles, 74, 75
Brown v. Allen, 210–211
Brown v. Board of Education, 122, 203, 326
Brownell, Herbert, 25, 71
Bryson, William, 109, 110
Buckley v. New York Post Corp., 145–147
Buckner, Emory, 25, 32, 43, 50
Bull, The, 41, 42, 51
Burbank, Stephen, 101
Burger, Warren, 122, 136, 355, 356
Burlingham, C. C., 25
Bush, George W., 357
Bushby, Wilkie, 50

Calabresi, Guido, 266, 308–309, 348, 352–353
Cambridge University, 21
Cape Cod, Mass., 44, 340
Cardamone, Richard J., 116, 351
Cardozo, Benjamin, 116, 240, 305–314, 353
Cargill, Inc. v. CCC, 83, 186–187
Carriage of Goods by Sea Act (COGSA), 266–268
Carswell, Harold, 137
Cashin, John M., 256
Cavers, David, 103
Chase, Harrie Bingham, 73, 114
Chasins v. Smith, Barney & Co., 256
Chicago, Ill., 8, 20
"Chosen Instrument," 46, 49, 66

Cianci v. New Times Pub. Co., 147–149
Civil Aeronautics Act of 1938, 45–46
Civil Aeronautics Board (CAB), 46–47, 61–66, 295–296
Civil Rights Acts, 183, 194–195, 213, 323–325
Clark, Charles E., 45, 114–115, 177
Clark, Grenville, 32, 34, 43, 45, 67
Clark, Tom, 97
Class actions, 327–332
Cleary, George, 51
Cleary, Gottlieb, Friendly & Cox (or other names), 50–52, 60–70
Cocke, E. O., 62–63
Cohen, Louis R., 289
Commissioner of Internal Revenue v. Ferrer, 286, 290
Compensable unconstitutional erosion (CUE), 286–290
Conflict of laws, 332–335
Confrontation Clause, 186
Conner, William F., 119, 130
Conrail, 285–293
Conscientious objectors, 242–247
Consent decrees, 331–332
Conspiracy, 240–241
Cook, Ray, 68–69
Coolidge, Archibald Carey, 14
Cooper, John, 48
Copyright law, 273–275
Corbin, Arthur, 101
Corcoran, Thomas, 23, 25
Cortright v. Resor, 141–145
"Court Packing Plan," 45
"Courts and Social Policy, The: Substance and Procedure," 326
Covington & Burling, 288
Cox, Archibald, 134
Cox, Hugh, 51, 66–67
Craco, Louis, 293
Cruel and unusual punishment, 187–190
Currie, Brainerd, 101, 334
Currie, David, 104, 109, 129, 322, 354
Curtin, John T., 198–203, 283–284
Curtis, Thomas, 344
Cutler, Lloyd, 112

Dagger, Thomas, 344
Dartmouth College Case and the Public-Private Penumbra, The, 195–203
Davis, Frederick, 109, 223
Davis, Kenneth Culp, 101, 173–174, 294
Dawson, Archie O., 75

Daynard, Richard, 109
Deregulation, 111
Dershowitz, Alan M., 229–231
Dewey, Ballantine, 384n83
Dicta (or *dictum*), 98–99, 212, 217, 269–271, 337
Diversity-of-citizenship jurisdiction, 314–321
Dodd, Thomas, 66–67
Dolan, Harry T., 100
Double Jeopardy Clause, 177–180
Duggan, Lawrence, 48
Duke, Steven, 234
Duniway, Ben C., 101
Dworkin, Ronald, 74, 131

Eastabrook, Bob, 76
Easterbrook, Frank, 101, 118, 408n34
Edelman, Peter, 111, 119
Edwards, Harry T., 101
Ehrensweig, Albert A., 101
Eighth Amendment, 187–190
Einstein, Albert, 68, 346
Eisen v. Eastman, 323–324
Eisenberg, Melvin, 257
Eisenhower, Dwight D., 72–73
Eliot, Charles W., 18
Ellsberg, Daniel, 151
Elmira, N.Y., 6–12, 24–25
Elmira Free Academy, 10–11, 12–13
Employment discrimination, 283–284
Engel, David, 95
Environmental law, 299–300
Equal Pay Act of 1963, 283–284
Erie R.R. v. Tompkins, 207, 302–305
Espionage Act, 152, 158
Estate of Rockefeller v. Commissioner of Internal Revenue, 259–260
Evidentiary privileges, 335–338
Exclusionary rule. *See* Fourth Amendment
Extraterritorial jurisdiction, 253–254

Federal Administrative Agencies: The Need for Better Definition of Standards, The, 295–296
Federal common law, 302–314
Federal Communications Commission (FCC), 49, 295
Federal Courts and the Federal System, The, 78, 356
Federal Employee Liability Act (FELA), 279
Federal Jurisdiction: A General View, 318, 325, 327

Federal Rules of Civil Procedure, 115
Federal Rules of Criminal Procedure, 223–225
Federal Rules of Evidence, 186, 336, 407n10
Federation of Jewish Philanthropies, 131
Feinberg, Wilfred, 116, 134, 156, 159, 243
Felton v. Secretary, Dept. of Education, 162–163
Fifth Amendment: double jeopardy, 177–180; Friendly's proposed amendment of, 169–171; relation to Sixth Amendment, 169–171; right to hearing, 172–177; self-incrimination, 165–172
"Fifth Amendment Tomorrow, The," 169–171
First Amendment: establishment of religion, 161–163; freedom of the press, 151–161; freedom of speech, 139–161; libel and slander, 145–149; pornography, 149–151
Flynn, Elizabeth, 109, 112
Foley, James, 39–40
Food and Drug Administration (FDA), 298–299
Ford, Gerald, 101
Fortas, Abe, 137
Fourteenth Amendment: due process clause, 161, 194; equal protection clause, 195–203; privileges and immunities, 205–208; reverse discrimination, 203–204; state action, 195–203
Fourth Amendment, 181–185, 204
Frank, Jerome, 73, 114
Frankel, Marvin, 100, 119, 130, 134, 228–229
Frankfurter, Felix: as Harvard Law School professor, 20, 23, 25–26, 37–38, 279, 320; as Supreme Court Justice, 82, 115, 122–125, 287, 356
Freund, Max, 134
Freund, Paul, 130–136, 347, 354
Freundlich family, 5
Fried, Charles, 101
Friendly, Alfred, 130
Friendly, David (son), 127–128, 342, 343, 344; as child, 44, 53, 57
Friendly, Ellen. *See* Simon, Ellen
Friendly, Fred W., 130
Friendly, Henry J.: appointment to Second Circuit, 71–72; bar associations, 60; Brandeis and, 27–31; commonplace book, 80–81; correspondence with mother, 19–20; death of, 339–345;

Friendly, Henry J. *(continued)*
  district court sittings, 315–317; Elmira
  Free Academy, 10–11, 12–13; eye
  problems, 10, 12, 73, 341–342; finances,
  36, 51–52, 344; Harvard College, 12–18;
  Harvard Law School, 21–27; Harvard
  Law School offers, 31, 38; honors, 133,
  354–359; Jewish refugees, 44–59; job
  hunting, 31–32, 38; lack of physical
  coordination, 9; moods, 19, 44, 52,
  349–354; nomination and confirmation
  as Circuit Judge, 71–77; private practice,
  34–70; religion and, 9, 24, 32, 59, 161;
  Shaw Travelling Fellowship, 20–21;
  Supreme Court appearances, 49–50,
  60; Supreme Court prospects, 136–138;
  vacations and traveling, 44, 55–56,
  135–136; votes in criminal cases,
  247–248; will of, 344
Friendly, Irene (daughter-in-law), 127–128,
  131, 342
Friendly, Joan. *See* Goodman, Joan
Friendly, Leah (mother), 6–7, 19–20, 44
Friendly, Myer (father), 5–8, 44
Friendly, Samson (uncle), 5, 8
Friendly, Sophie (wife): background, 36–37;
  death of, 339–340; grandchildren of,
  129–130; marriage to Friendly, 36–37,
  44, 52, 55–56
*Frigaliment Importing Co. v. B.N.S. Int'l
  Sales Corp.*, 98, 315–317
Fuld, Stanley, 134
Full Faith and Credit Clause, 332–335

Garibaldi, Giuseppe, 15
Garland, Merrick, 109
Gelhorn, Walter, 101
Gender discrimination, 284
General Services Administration (GSA), 102
Gewirtz, Paul, 344–345
Gilmore, Grant, 80, 101
Ginsburg, Ruth Bader, 118
Goldberg v. Kelly, 172–174, 176
Goldberg v. Meridor, 251–252
Goldfinger, Elliot, 358–359
Goldmark, Karl, 31
Goodman, Barak, 339–340, 343–344,
  421–422n102
Goodman, Ellen, 340
Goodman, Frank, 127–129, 162–163
Goodman, Joan, 15, 52–59, 94, 127–129,
  342–345
Goodman, Lisa, 52

Gordon, Albert, 14
Gottlieb, Leo, 32, 50–51, 100
Gould, Milton, 32
Grand jury, 222–227
Grant, Stephen, 32–33, 183–185
Griswold, Erwin, 25, 266, 354, 356
Griswold v. Connecticut, 190–191
Grossman, Milton, 75
Gunther, Gerald, 70, 78, 101
Gurfein, Murray I., 112, 119, 151–153,
  157–159

Habeas corpus, 210–220, 437n24
Hall, Pat. *See* Mogin, Pat Hall
Hall v. Lefkowitz, 190–191
Hamilton, Fowler, 51
Hand, Augustus, 25, 114
Hand, Learned: Friendly's early contact
  with, 25; Friendly's nomination and,
  73–77, 84; Friendly's opinion of,
  121–124, 353; Friendly's relationship
  with, 82, 100; Friendly's reliance on, 80,
  348; judicial activity, 83, 114, 177–179,
  354–355, 359
Handler, Milton, 134
Harkins, John G., Jr., 293
Harlan, John Marshall: Friendly's opinion
  of, 41, 121; Justice, 73, 85, 137, 140,
  160–161, 390n14; Root, Clark, 34,
  38–41, 50, 289
Harmless error, 81
Harmonie Club, 134
Hart, Henry M., Jr., 78, 79, 101, 125
Hart, H. L. A., 347
Harvard College, 12–18
Harvard Law Review, 24–25, 43, 71, 83–84
Harvard Law School, 21–27, 31, 133
Harvard University, 132–134
Haskins, Charles Homer, 14
Haynsworth, Clement F., Jr., 137, 354–355
Hays, Arthur Garfield, 39–40
Hays, Paul R., 115, 149, 280
Hazard, Geoffrey, 132
Hegarty, William E., 150–151
Heimerdinger, Mattie and Max, 8, 20
Hellenic Lines, Ltd. v. United States, 261–264
Hellerstein, Walter, 159–160
Hemlock Society, 342
Henkin, Lewis, 101, 130
Hincks, Carroll C., 73
"Historic Basis of Diversity Jurisdiction,
  The," 27, 318–320
Hogan & Hartson, 288

Holmes, Oliver Wendell, Jr., 30, 121–124, 341, 353

Horowitz, In re, 337

Hudson, Manley O., 21–22

Hufstedler, Shirley M., 101

Hughes, Howard, 61–65, 68–69

Hulbert, Richard W., 70

Humpty Dumpty, 149, 167, 419n56

Hynes, Charles J., 227–230

Hypnosis, 233–235

I.D.S. & Wife v. W.D.S., 21–22

Implied causes of action, 183–185, 251

"In Memoriam—Roger Traynor, the Ablest Judge of His Generation," 334–335

"In Praise of *Erie*—and of the New Federal Common Law," 303–304

Interstate Commerce Commission (ICC), 31–32, 42, 82

Involuntary servitude, 208–209

Ira S. Bushey & Sons, Inc. v. United States, 264–266, 310, 348

"Is Innocence Irrelevant? Collateral Attack on Criminal Judgments," 213, 218

Ives, Irving, 73

Jackson, Robert, 73, 122, 126

Jackson v. Statler Foundation, 201–203

Jaffe, Louis, 130, 296

Jameson, William J., 223–226, 244

Jaretsky, Alfred, Sr., 32–33

Javits, Jacob, 74–76, 101

Jefferson, Thomas, 158

Jennings, Richard W., 101

"Jewish Judges Club," 134

Johnson, Lyndon Baines, 73, 77

Johnson v. Glick, 188–189

Jones Act, 279

Jurisdiction, federal court, 82–83, 318–325. See also "Historic Basis of Diversity Jurisdiction, The"

Jury trial, 186–187

Kamisar, Yale, 132, 165, 168–169

Katzenbach, Nicholas, 136

Kaufman, Andrew L., 313

Kaufman, Irving R.: ambition of, 73–75, 358; conduct as a circuit judge, 102, 115, 213, 333, 354–355, 409n55; conduct as district judge, 219; Friendly's relationship with, 120–121

Kearse, Amalya, 116, 358

Kennedy, Anthony, 140

Kennedy, John F., 446–447n33

Kennedy, Robert F., 101, 119

Kennedy, William F., 63

Kerner v. Flemming, 174–176

Kimbrough, Charlotte, 112–113, 340

Kinsman Transit Co. v. City of Buffalo, 305–310

Kirby, Allan P., 67–68, 72, 329–330

Koch, Edward I., 226

Kramer, Larry, 86

Krim, Arthur, 134

Kurland, Phillip, 201

Labor law, 279–284

Landis, James, 23, 25, 38, 64–65, 72

Langdell, Christopher Columbus, 22

Langston, Livy, 10

Lasker, Morris, 7, 119, 182

Lefkowitz, Louis, 134

Legal Process School, the, 78–80, 350, 390n15

Leval, Pierre N.: as judge, 119, 323, 357, 359; as law clerk, 106, 109–110; social relationship with Friendly, 112, 340, 342, 344

Leval, Susana, 112, 119, 340, 342

Levi, Edward, 103, 136

Lewin, Nathan, 229

Lewis, Anthony, 101

Lewis, Howard, 292

Libel and slander, 145–140

Lindbergh, Charles, 35

Loss, Lewis, 130, 355

Lowell, A. Lawrence, 13, 18–19

Lumbard, J. Edward: Friendly's sitting with, 149–150, 156, 177–79, 206; other activities, 73, 83, 114–115, 354–355

Lybrand, Ross Bros. & Montgomery, 237

Macey, Jonathan, 403n43

Mack, Julian, 20, 25

MacMahon, Lloyd, 331

Magruder, Calvert, 23–24, 68

Maguire, John, 101

Maitland, Frederic, 21

Mandeville, Hubert, 12

Mansfield, Lord (William Murray), 239, 350

Mansfield, Walter, 116, 153–156, 238

Marshall, John, 158, 352

Marshall, Thurgood, 115–116, 355

McGowan, Carl E., 117, 286, 354–355

McIlwain, Charles, 14, 16–17, 20, 139, 348

McNamara, Robert, 151
McReynolds, James, 31
Medina, Harold, 115
Melia, Aloysius J., 228–231
Merchants Club, 100, 134
Merck, Frederick, 15, 101
Meskill, Thomas, 116
Metzner, Charles, 119
Meyers, Allan Murray, 134
Midonick, Millard, 134
Miranda v. Arizona, 164, 167–172, 215
Mishler, Jacob, 119
Mitchell, John N., 137–138
Mitsui & Co. v. American Export Lines, Inc., 267–268
Mogin, Pat Hall, 112, 291, 340, 342, 343
Mogin, Paul, 112, 340
Moore, Leonard P., 73–74, 114–115
Morgenthau, Robert M., 236–237
Morris, Thomas Patrick, 39–40
Morrison, Samuel Elliot, 15
Murmane, George, 50
Murphy, Thomas F., 243–245
Murray, William. *See* Mansfield, Lord
Murray v. Cunard S.S. Co., 305, 310–314

Nader, Ralph, 111
National Labor Relations Act, 280–283
National Labor Relations Board, 279–283, 296–297. *See also individual cases*
Nelson, William, 118
Newman, Bernard, 134
Newman, Gustave, 229, 231
Newman, Jon O., 116, 234, 358–359
New York Central Railroad, 67–68
New York Civil Liberties Union, 243
New York Daily News, 137, 145
New York Port Authority, 300–301
New York Post, 146
New York State Assoc. for Retarded Children v. Carey, 331–332
New York Telephone Company, 49, 51
New York Times, 67, 75, 101, 148, 151–161, 222–226
New York Times v. Sullivan, 145–149
New York Times v. United States (*Pentagon Papers* case), 151–161
New York v. Galamison, 324–325
Nixon, Richard M., 116, 136–138, 151
NLRB v. General Electric Co., 281–282
NLRB v. Miranda Fuel Co., 282–283, 294
Nonprofit organizations, 194–203
Noonan, John T., 431n56

North Atlantic Transfer Case, 61–66
Numerus clausus at Harvard, 18–19

Oakes, James L., 97, 116, 156, 143–145, 301
O'Connor, Sandra Day, 140, 163
Olmstead v. United States, 29–30, 192, 232–233
Oppenheimer, Martin, 130
Originalism, 139, 189
Oxford University, 221

Page, Robert, 41
Palm, Gregory, 107, 111
Palmerston, Lord, 15–16
Palmieri, Edmund, 223
Palsgraf v. Long Island R.R., 305–310
Pan American (World) Airways: and CAB, 46–47, 48–49, 61–66; early years, 34, 42–43; and World War II and thereafter, 47, 61–66, 68–69
Paper, Lewis J., 30
Patent law, 272
Pearlstein v. Scudder & German, 254–256
Pearson, Drew, 329
Pearson v. Northeast Airlines, Inc., 332–335
Peck, David W., 33, 74, 238
Pendent-party jurisdiction, 323
Penn Central Railroad, 289–293
"Pentagon Papers," 151–161
Peter Pan Fabrics, Inc. v. Martin Weiner Corp., 83–84, 273
Piel, Eleanor Jackson, 89
Plea bargains, 277–231
Poindexter, Michael, 133
Polaroid Corp. v. Polarad Electronics Corp., 275–277
Pollack, Milton, 134
Pollak, Louis, 319–320, 355
Pornography, 149–150
Posner, Richard A.: evaluation of Friendly, 86, 344, 355, 356; as a judge, 308, 327; relationship with Friendly, 101, 117, 290–291
Powe v. Miles, 198–200, 432–433n21
Powell, Lewis F., Jr., 127, 140, 163, 204, 356
Prisoners' rights, 187–190
Privacy, right to, 190–193
Privileges and Immunities Clause, 205–208
Prosecutorial excess, 231–233
Punitive damages, 269–271

Radcliffe College, 17, 57–58
Railroads, 41–42, 285–293

Rakoff, Todd, 111, 355
Randolph, A. Raymond, 108, 109, 184, 243–245
Rawls, John, 347
Reconstruction Finance Corp. (RFC), 38
Regional Rail Reorganization Act of 1973 (RRRA), 285–293
Rehnquist, William H., 137, 140
Respondeat superior, 264–265
Reston, James, 136
Reverse discrimination, 203–204
Riesman, David, 24
Rifkind, Simon, 134
Right to counsel. *See* Sixth Amendment
Right to privacy, 190–191
Roberts, John M., Jr., 107, 109, 140, 357
Roe v. Wade, 190–193, 326
Rogers, William P., 75, 77
Roginsky v. Richardson Merrell, Inc., 96, 269–271
Roosevelt, Franklin Delano, 45, 47–48
Root, Clark, Buckner, Howland & Ballantine, 31–50
Root, Elihu, Jr., 32, 44, 49, 67
Rosenberg, Julius and Ethel, 219–220
Rosenfeld v. Black, 250–251
Rosenwald, Julius, 51

Sacco and Vanzetti, 26
Sacks, Albert M., 79–80
Scalia, Antonin, 103, 140, 353, 356
Scanlan's Monthly, 330
Scherr v. Universal Match Corp., 274–275
Schick, Marvin, 124
Schwartz, Sydney, 112
Securities and Exchange Commission (SEC), 252–253
Securities law, 236–240, 250–257, 482n5
SEC v. Chenery Corp., 297
SEC v. Texas Gulf Sulfur Corp., 252–253
Segal, Bernard, 137
Seipp, David, 109, 340
Selective Service law, 242–247
Self-incrimination, 165–172
Settling cases, 327–332
Seventh Amendment, 186–187
Seymour, Whitney North, Jr., 152–156
Sifton, Charles T., 119
Silberman, Samuel, 134
Silvestri v. Italia Societa per Azioni di Navagazione, 305, 310–314
Simon, Daniel, 130

Simon, Ellen, 15, 53–55, 57, 127–128, 342–344
Simon, Stephen, 127–128
Seventh Amendment, 186–187
Sixth Amendment, 165–168, 185–186, 215–217
Smith, J. Joseph, 115, 156, 201, 206, 243
Smoot, James, 107
Social Security Administration (SSA), 174–177
Sofaer, Abraham D., 119, 130
Solina v. United States, 215–216
"Some Kind of Hearing," 173, 191–193
Sorenson, Theodore, 136
Spanos v. Skouras Theatres Corp., 205–208
State action (Fourteenth Amendment), 194–203
Steefel, Ernst, 55, 134
Steen, Melvin, 113
Steinbrenner, George, 306
Stern, Henrietta Pfaelzer, 36–37
Stern, Horace, 36, 55
Stern, Mike, 134
Stern, Sophie. *See* Friendly, Sophie
Stern, Warren, 113
Stevens, John Paul, 98–99, 323, 356
Stewart, Charles E., 99
Stimson, Henry L., 48
Stone, Harlan Fiske, 122, 126
Stone, Marshall, 14
Stovall v. Denno, 217–218
Suicide, 340–345
Sullivan & Cromwell, 32–33, 379n142
Supreme Court. *See individual justices and cases*
Swan, Thomas W., 73, 114
Swift v. Tyson, 301–303

Tax exemptions, 201–203, 433n36
Tax law, 257–261
T. B. Harms Co. v. Eliscu, 322–323
Thirteenth Amendment, 208–209
Thomas, Clarence, 140
Thomson, Roszel C., 288
Tillich, Paul, 246–247
Timbers, William, 244–245
Toilet Goods Association v. Gardner, 299
Tolchin, Martin, 120
Tompkins, Harold, 175–176
Tondel, Lyman M., Jr., 69–70, 100
Trademark law, 275–278, 458n25
Transworld Airlines, 61–65
Travel Act, 232–233

Traynor, Roger, 122–126, 334–335
Trippe, Juan, 35–36, 48, 61–66, 68–69.
    See also Pan American (World) Airways
Truman, Harry F., 48, 49, 61, 65–66
Tucker Act, 287–288
Turner, Frederick Jackson, 14
Twain, Mark, 10

Uniform Commercial Code, 304–305
Unions. *See* Labor law
United States ex rel. LaNear v. LaVallee,
    211–212
*United States v. American Trucking
    Associations*, 260–261
United States v. Archer, 231–233
United States v. Beattie, 171
United States v. Borelli, 95–96
United States v. Jakobson, 245–247
United States v. Koecher, 337–338
United States v. Kovel, 336
United States v. Maybury, 83, 177–179
United States v. McGee, 243–245
*United States v. Motion Picture Entitled
    "I Am Curious Yellow,"* 149
United States v. New York Times, 151–161,
    421–422n102
United States v. Simon, 237–240, 250
United States v. Sobell, 219–220
Untermeyer, Samuel, 39–40
U.S. Post Office, 34–36, 42–43
U.S. Supreme Court. *See individual justices
    and cases*

Van Devanter, Willis, 31
Van Graffeiland, Ellsworth, 356
Vietnam War, 140–151, 242
Voting memoranda, 87–91. *See also
    individual cases*

Wagner, Robert F., Jr., 191
Walsh, Lawrence E., 75
Warburg, Felix, 59

Warren, Earl (or Warren Court), 80,
    121–122, 136, 165–166, 190, 210–11,
    248, 349
Washington Post, 75–77, 152
Waterman, Sterry R., 114–115
Wechsler, Herbert, 78–80, 101, 130
Wedgwood, Ruth, 109
Weinfeld, Edward: Friendly's death and,
    341, 342; Friendly's efforts to promote to
    Second Circuit, 119; Friendly's friendship
    with, 100, 110, 118, 137; Friendly's
    review of, 119, 322
Weinstein, Jack: activity as a judge,
    141–145, 225, 264–265; activity relating
    to Friendly, 92, 101, 119–120, 134, 266,
    409n54
Weiss, Stanley, 292
Wells, Selvie Winfield, 50
Wendel, Ella Virginia von Echtzel, 38–41
Wendel, John G., 38–41
West Publishing Co., 98
"What is chicken?" See *Frigaliment
    Importing Co. v. B.N.S. Int'l Sales Corp.*
White, Byron R., 137
Whitney, Craig, 120
Wigmore, John Henry, 78
William the Conqueror, 11
Wilmer, Cutler & Pickering, 288
Winter, Ralph, 116
Wisdom, John Minor, 117, 131, 286, 288,
    354–355, 356
Wisdom, Kathleen (Kit), 131
Wolinsky, Mark, 105
Wright, Charles Alan, 101
Wyzanski, Charles, 74, 101, 137

Yale College, 35, 68
Yale Law Journal, 25, 45, 71
Young, Robert R., 67–68, 72

Zion, Sydney E., 330
Zionism, 20, 30–31